THE DIMWIT'S DICTIONARY

SECOND EDITION

THE DIMWIT'S DICTIONARY

SECOND EDITION

More Than 5,000 Overused Words and Phrases and Alternatives to Them

Marion Street Press, Inc.

Cover design by Michael Cox

ISBN 1-933338-11-3
Printed in U.S.A.
Printing 10 9 8 7 6 5 4 3 2 1

Marion Street Press, Inc.
PO Box 2249
Oak Park, IL 60304
Toll-Free 866-443-7987
www.marionstreetpress.com

A Note on the Second Edition

Aside from new entries and commentary, throughout this second edition you will find quotations from classic and contemporary authors of fiction. These quotations, however well written they or their surrounding words may be, are marred, adulterated by dimwitticisms.

Each dimwitticism is a failure to write clearly and compellingly, an admission that the author could not manage an original thought or a better turn of phrase, or could not be bothered to think of one.

Dimwitticisms, as these examples make startlingly clear, yield only facile writing, only false sentiment.

About the Author

Robert Hartwell Fiske is the editor and publisher of The Vocabula Review (www.vocabula.com), a monthly online journal about the English language.

Other Books by Robert Hartwell Fiske

The Dictionary of Concise Writing (Marion Street Press, second edition, 2006)

The Dictionary of Disagreeable English Deluxe Edition (Writer's Digest Books, 2006)

101 Wordy Phrases (Vocabula Books, 2005)

101 Foolish Phrases (Vocabula Books, 2005)

101 Elegant Paragraphs (Vocabula Books, 2005)

Vocabula Bound: Outbursts, Insights, Explanations, and Oddities (editor) (Marion Street Press, 2004)

Apologia

The Dimwit's Dictionary will annoy some people and amuse others. People who feel as though I am referring to them in some of the commentary in this book may be annoyed by what I write; those who feel as though I am referring to others may be amused by it. This is an annoying, amusing book.

If the tone of my commentary is sometimes acerbic, it's because tempered persuasion is effete, and considered argument tiresome. Few of us are able to learn well by pedantic or rote methods. But if I disturb or annoy a person, is he not more likely to remember what bothered him; is he not more likely to retain what was said; is he not more likely to learn? This pedagogy may strike some as unworkable, and perhaps its efficacy is suspect, but we surely know that other methods of tutelage are largely unsuccessful.

Robert Hartwell Fiske
editor@vocabula.com

Contents

To Laura
Virtual officemate (VOM); purveyor of recipes and reason; and my good, lovely friend

The great enemy of clear language is insincerity. When there is a gap between one's real and one's declared aims, one turns as it were instinctively to long words and exhausted idioms, like a cuttlefish squirting out ink.

George Orwell, "Politics and the English Language"

Thoughts, that breathe, and words, that burn.

Thomas Gray, The Progress of Poesy

For I have neither wit, nor words, nor worth,
Action, nor utterance, nor the power of speech,
To stir men's blood

William Shakespeare, Julius Caesar, act 3, scene 2

Watch your thoughts; they become words.
Watch your words; they become actions.
Watch your actions; they become habits.
Watch your habits; they become character.
Watch your character; it becomes destiny.

Anonymous

Never do I ever want to hear another word. There isn't one I haven't heard.

Alan Jay Lerner and Frederick Loewe, My Fair Lady

Foreword

When Robert Hartwell Fiske confronts Saint Peter, I hope he remembers to tell the man that he is the founding editor of *The Vocabula Review,* the online magazine devoted to contemporary language, its delights and its disasters. Saint Peter will immediately understand that Mr. Fiske has been on the side of the angels and therefore been doing the Lord's work. My worry is that, in reply, Saint Peter will commit one or another of the solecisms, illogicalities, or barbarisms that Mr. Fiske spends his days excoriating and that he will feel the need to correct him, causing him to lose his place on the other side of the gates.

Meanwhile, on this side of the gates, to hew to this theological metaphor a bit longer, Robert Hartwell Fiske has been doing a hell of a job.

Mr. Fiske has signed on, evidently for life, for that best of all losing causes, the battle to keep language clear, fresh, free from the pollution of empty jargon, idiotic euphemism, self-serving imprecision, comic redundancy, nonsense generally. He has many famous comrades from among the dead in this battle: Jonathan Swift, H. L. Mencken, George Orwell, H. W. Fowler, Sir Ernest Gowers, and others. And, as I am sure he has discovered, many unknown, still living allies in unexpected places who get quite properly worked up over politicians, advertisers, social scientists, so-called educators, and others attempting to swindle the rest of us through nicely calculated verbal fog.

You are what you eat, the old food faddists used to say. As I read him, Robert Hartwell Fiske is saying that we are, or soon become, what we say and write. Use language slovenly, dully, dopily and we soon ourselves become sloppy, dull, dopey. In *The Dimwit's Dictionary,* he explains his reigning idea in the first paragraph of his first chapter, when he announces that "Dimwitticisms are worn-out words and phrases; they are expressions that dull our reason and dim our insight, formulas that we rely on when we are too lazy to express what we think or even to discover how we feel. The more we use them, the more we conform — in thought and feeling — to everyone else who uses them." We know soon enough what makes them "dim"; the witticism comes into play because most people who adopt such overworked words as "scenario" or such cumbersome academic locutions as "in terms of" think they are being clever, if not highly sophisticated.

Language mavens come in various intensities of aggression. Some come as recent graduates of the Gestapo school of language correction; one has only to read them to feel the leather glove sting across one's cheeks, the word *schweinhund* ringing in one's ears. Some come on as school masters, simply unable to understand why anyone would wish to split an infinitive or end a sentence with a preposition. Some come on as pussycats passing along to us their amazement at the wild and wayward curiosities of language, but always attempting to avoid seeming either formidable or forbidding.

My own favorite among the great language mavens is H. W. Fowler, whose tone I should describe as superior commonsensical. Here, for example, is the great man on those damnable split infinitives: "The English-speaking world may be divided into (1) those who neither know nor care what a split infinitive is; (2) those who do not know but care very much; (3) those who know and condemn; (4) those who know and approve; and (5) those who know and distinguish." Such is Fowler's elevated superiority. Here is his commonsense: "We maintain, however, that a real split infinitive, though not desirable in itself, is preferable to either of two things, to real ambiguity and to patent artificiality." In other words, the Fowler line is, split away before writing anything stupid. But then he adds: "We will split infinitives sooner than be ambiguous or artificial; more than that, we will freely admit that sufficient recasting will get rid of any split infinitives without involving either of those faults, and yet reserve to ourselves the right of deciding in each case whether recasting is worthwhile." Superior, as I say, with a saving commonsense.

Robert Hartwell Fiske's desire — it informs his tone — is to bring us to our senses, to make us understand that "our knowledge of the world expands as our familiarity with words increases" and contracts when we fall back on the categories of ineptitude he has designated the Moribund Metaphor, the Overworked Word, the Plebeian Sentiment, all of which may be said — he, in fact, does say — "blunt our understanding and quash our creativity. They actually shield us from our thoughts and feelings, from any profound sense of ourselves." He is, *au fond*, a reformer who wants us to be the fully developed men and women we "were meant to be."

But Mr. Fiske's reforming impulse doesn't get in the way of his scorning clichés and trite sentiments. His lists of Overworked Words and of Torpid Terms — "off-putting," "operative," "prioritize," "pursuant to," qualify for the latter category — are there because they "keep us dumb and dispassionate. They elicit the least from us." He also suggests words that he thinks worthy of being revitalized — lovely words such as "bedizen," "bootless," "quondam" — while what he calls Withered Words ought, in the phrase of Paul Valery, the great French critic, to be turned over to the "numismaticians of language" to be put "away in their Cabinets, with many another verbal coin that has passed from circulation."

Robert Hartwell Fiske is a verbal trainer, the linguistic equivalent of the personal trainer one sees in gyms and health clubs. He wants us to trim the fat off our mental life; to knock off those Ineffectual Phrases, Inescapable Pairs, Infantile Phrases, and Wretched Redundancies. He has the relentlessness but none of the dogmatism of the drill sergeant.

Reformer, verbal trainer, drill sergeant, in the end Robert Hartwell Fiske is a fisher of souls, a catcher in the wry, a man who, through looking carefully at language, understands its potency and loathes its power, when misused, for making life more dreary than it ought to be. After noting the spread of flat and predictable language in the contemporary world, he exclaims: "No wonder so many of us feel barren or inconsolable: There are few words that inspire us, few words that move us, few words that thrill or overwhelm us. Persuasion has lost much of its sway, conviction, much of its claim."

Mr. Fiske is, in short, a fanatic, an extremist who apparently believes that clear language is our only hope for clear thought, that dull language deadens the mind and dampens the imagination, that a felicitous phrase is good news, that a strong prose style is a gift to be cultivated and cherished, that nothing, no, nothing in the world exceeds language in its significance to the human enterprise. As it happens, I believe in all this, too, which makes it an honor to salute a fellow fanatic and wish him and his book the great good fortune both deserve.

JOSEPH EPSTEIN

Joseph Epstein, former editor of *The American Scholar*, teaches writing and literature at Northwestern University and is the author of many books, including *Narcissus Leaves the Pool* and *Snobbery: The American Version.*

Part 1

On Dimwitticisms

Chapter 1

Expressions That Dull Our Reason and Dim Our Insight

Whereas a witticism is a clever remark or phrase — indeed, the height of expression — a "dimwitticism" is the converse; it is a commonplace remark or phrase. Dimwitticisms are worn-out words and phrases; they are expressions that dull our reason and dim our insight, formulas that we rely on when we are too lazy to express what we think or even to discover how we feel. The more we use them, the more we conform — in thought and feeling — to everyone else who uses them.

The Dimwit's Dictionary is a compilation of thousands of dimwitticisms (clichés, colloquialisms, idioms, and the like) that people speak and write excessively.*

The Dimwit's Dictionary categorizes dimwitticisms by the following types:†

Foreign phrases
Grammatical gimmicks
Ineffectual phrases
Inescapable pairs
Infantile phrases

---

* Many of the entries in this book are followed by synonyms that may be used in place of the worn-out word or phrase; others are followed by commentary; and still others by both. But even the mere inclusion of an entry — one unaccompanied by synonyms or commentary — damns it as a dimwitticism.

All dimwitticisms can be defined, but not all can be translated into one- or two-word synonyms. When this is so, the best solution may be to rewrite the sentence entirely.

† Dimwitticisms, quite obviously, could be categorized by more than one of these fourteen types. Many wretched redundancies are also torpid terms, many moribund metaphors also infantile phrases, but I have sought to identify them by their principal type.

Moribund metaphors
Overworked words
Plebeian sentiments
Popular prescriptions
Quack equations
Suspect superlatives
Torpid terms
Withered words
Wretched redundancies

Foreign phrases

Expressions such as *ad infinitum, ad nauseam, c'est la vie, crème de la crème, fait accompli, in loco parentis, je ne sais quoi, joie de vivre, mea culpa, mirabile dictu, modus vivendi, ne plus ultra, non compos mentis, par excellence, persona non grata, quid pro quo, raison d'être, sine qua non, très, verboten,* and *vive la différence,* though perfectly good foreign words and phrases, are, when used by English-speaking people, simply wearisome.

Grammatical gimmicks

Quite simply, *and everything* is a babbler's way of describing what he was unable to. This phrase and so many others like it — *and everything like that; and stuff (things); and (or) stuff (things) like that; and this and that; anyway; I mean; (and that) kind of stuff (thing); or something or other; or whatever; this, that, and the other (thing); you had to be there* — are grammatical gimmicks that we use to make up for the misfashioned words that precede them.

These are devices that we resort to whenever we are unable to adequately explain our thoughts or feelings. Grammatical gimmicks attest to just how dull and dimwitted we have become.

Ineffectual phrases

Ineffectual phrases are the expressions people use to delay or obstruct, to bewilder or make weary. The intent of those who use ineffectual phrases is to make it appear as though their sentences are more substantial than they actually are, but not one sentence is made more meaningful by their inclusion: *(please) be advised that; I'll tell you (something); it has come to (my) attention; it is important to realize (that); it is interesting to note (that); make no mistake (about it); (to) take this opportunity (to); the fact of the matter is; the fact remains; the thing about it is; what happened (is).*

How a person speaks often reveals how he thinks. And how he thinks determines how he behaves. A person who speaks ineffectually may think ineffectually, and a person who thinks ineffectually may behave ineffectually — perhaps badly.

Ineffectual phrases add only to our being ineffectual people.

Inescapable pairs

In an inescapable pair, the first word means much the same as the second or so often accompanies the second that any distinction between them is, in effect, forfeited.

Only occasionally, that is, do we see the word *allied* without the word *closely; asset* without *valuable; baby* without *beautiful; balance* without *delicate; distinction* without *dubious; error* without *egregious; tied* without *inextricably; missed* without *sorely; poverty* without *abject; principle* without *basic.*

And only occasionally do we see the word *aid* without the word *abet; alive* without *well; effective* without *efficient; hope* without *pray; hue* without *cry; pure* without *simple.*

When two words are treated as though they were one — the plight of every inescapable pair — our keenness is compromised, our discernment endangered.

No longer does every word tell; the words themselves have become witless.

Infantile phrases

Any thought or feeling in which these expressions are found is likely to be made instantly laughable: *absolutely, positively; all of the above; because (that's why); because why?; (as) compared to what?; going on (19); I'll bet you any amount of money; in no way, shape, or form; intestinal fortitude; it takes one to know one; me, myself, and I; mission accomplished; mutual admiration society; never (not) in a million years; real, live; really and truly; (you) started it; (I) take it back; the feeling's mutual; the (L)-word; (my) whole, entire life; with a capital (A); without further ado; (62) years young; (a) zillion(s) (of).*

Also included among these phrases that strike all but the dimwitted as derisory are notorious advertising slogans (*inquiring minds want to know; where's the beef*), song and film titles (*a funny thing happened to me on the way to; I can't get no satisfaction*), and alliterative or rhymed phrases (*a bevy of beauties; chrome dome*).

Other infantile phrases are more disturbing, for they reveal an adolescent, unformed reasoning. Explanations like *in the wrong place at the wrong time, it just happened, it's a free country,* and *everything's (it's all) relative* are as farcical as they are possibly fallacious.

Moribund metaphors*

Metaphors, like similes, should have the briefest of lives. Their vitality depends on their evanescence.

Yet must we ever endure the dimwitted *(it's) a jungle (out there), an emotional roller coaster, a stroll (walk) in the park, (like) being run over (getting hit) by a (Mack) truck, (as) cool as a cucumber, everything but the kitchen sink, (as) hungry as a horse, leak like a sieve, light at the end of the tunnel, out to lunch, over the hill, pass like ships in the night, (as) phony as a three-dollar bill, (a) piece of cake, rule the roost, window of opportunity, (every parent's) worst nightmare,* and countless other metaphors that characterize people as dull, everyday speakers and writers, indeed, as platitudinarians? Nothing new do they tell us. Nothing more do they show us.

Moreover, if it weren't for our plethora of metaphors, especially, sports images — *above par, a new ballgame, batting a thousand, do (make) an end run around, down for the count, hit a home run, off base, pull no punches, stand on the sidelines, step up to the plate, took the ball and ran with it* — and war images — *a call to arms, an uphill battle, battle lines are drawn, draw fire, earn his stripes, first line of defense, in the trenches, on the firing line, take by storm* — men and, even, women would be far less able to articulate their thoughts. We would speak and write more haltingly than we already do; our thoughts and feelings more misshapen than they already are.

Moribund metaphors interfere with our understanding not only when we use them singly but also, and especially, when we use them simultaneously, that is, when we use them together, metaphor on metaphor. Frequently incongruous, these metaphors disfigure any sentence in which they are found.

■ Putting yourself under pressure to churn out work for the *cream of the crop* at the beginning of your writing career may *put the brakes on* your creativity.

■ They want to get *all their ducks in a row* and make sure they're all *singing from the same hymn sheet.*

■ And by last Christmas, for any defense contractor, the dwindling Soviet threat had evolved from *meal ticket* into *writing on the wall.*

■ Our restaurant *cost* me and my wife *an arm and a leg,* but we didn't build it without planning and we certainly wouldn't let it *go down the drain.*

■ Right now, USAir's problem is trying to determine whether this is *a soft*

*Rather than have a separate section on "insipid similes," I include them here. Since a metaphor can be thought of as a condensed simile (which often uses the word *as* or *like*) and a simile usually can be converted into a metaphor, this does not strike me as taking too much license.

landing for the economy or a recession, and *the jury is still out.*

■ For 20 years she was *a rising star* in the business, but by last year her success had *gone to the dogs.*

■ In the face of mounting pressure to gut or eliminate the IRS, it continues to *shoot itself in the foot* by *biting the hands that feed them.*

■ Looking at those things, *it didn't take a rocket scientist* to see there was *something rotten in Denmark.*

■ Thanks to Clinton, Lewinsky, & Co., I'm *off the hook* and it's *on the table.*

■ We expect them to *cast their net* as far and wide as possible because any *stone that's not unturned* will be questioned.

We rely on metaphors not because we feel they make our speech and writing more vivid and inviting but because we fail to learn how to express ourselves otherwise; we know not the words.

In truth, the more of these metaphors that we use, the less effective is our speech and writing. Neither interesting nor persuasive, their expression fatigues us where we thought it would inform us, annoys us where we believed it would amuse us, and benumbs us where we hoped it would inspire us.

Overworked words

The broader your knowledge of words, the greater your ability to express yourself precisely and persuasively. So many speakers and writers, however, rely on certain words — overworked words like *action, actively, amazing, appreciate, approach, attitude, awesome, basically, crisis, definitely, devastate, effect, excellence, great, impact, implement, incredible, interesting, lasting, major, meaningful, mindset, natural, nice, ongoing, parameter, pretty, really, scenario, significant, situation, strange, thing, unbelievable, very, weird.*

Words, when overworked, diminish the meaning of all that they are used to describe. Our remarks and questions both are enfeebled by these tired terms. Nothing that we express with these overworked words has the force or effectiveness of less habitually spoken, less repeatedly written words.

Moreover, since a person understands little more than what the words he is knowledgeable of convey — a word means *only* so much — to rely on so few words reveals just how limited a person's understanding of himself, and those about him, is.

Our knowledge of the world increases as our familiarity with words does.

Plebeian sentiments

Plebeian sentiments reflect the views and values of the least thoughtful among us: *be nice; (I) gave (him) the best years of (my) life; (it) gives (me) something to do; (these things) happen to other people, not to (me); I (just) don't think about it; I just work here; I'm bored (he's boring); (it) keeps (me) busy; (it's) something to look forward to; there are no words to describe (express); you think too much; what can you do; why me?*

What's more, these expressions, base as they are, blunt our understanding and quash our creativity. They actually shield us from our thoughts and feelings, from any profound sense of ourselves.

People who use these expressions have not become who they were meant to be.

Popular prescriptions

Powerless to repeat an author's epigram, unfit to recite a poet's verse, more than many of us are utterly able to echo a society's slogans and clichés: *absence makes the heart grow fonder; actions speak louder than words; a picture is worth a thousand words; beauty is in the eye of the beholder; better late than never; do as I say, not as I do; forgive and forget; hope for the best but expect the worst; it takes two; keep (your) nose to the grindstone; live and learn; misery loves company; money isn't everything; neither a borrower nor a lender be; take it one day (step) at a time; the best things in life are free; the meek shall inherit the earth; the sooner the better; time flies when you're having fun; two wrongs don't make a right; what goes around, comes around; you can't be all things to all people; you can't have everything.*

Popular prescriptions are the platitudes and proverbs by which people live their lives. It is these dicta that determine who we are and how we act; they define our intellectual and moral makeup.

Dull-witted speakers and writers depend on prescriptions like these to guide them through life. For this poor populace, life is, we may surmise, laid out. From the popular or proper course, there is scant deviation; a stray thought is, for them, a gray thought.

Popular prescriptions endure not for their sincerity but for their simplicity. We embrace them because they make all they profess to explain and all they profess to prescribe seem plain and uncomplicated.

Inexorably, we become as simple as they — we people, we platitudes.

Quack equations

This is the sort of simplicity much favored by mountebanks and pretenders, by businesspeople and politicians: *a deal is a deal; a politician is a politician; a promise is a promise; a rule is a rule; bald is beautiful; bigger is better; enough is enough; ethics is ethics; fair is fair; God is love; it is what it is; less is more; more is better; perception is reality; (what's) right is right; seeing is believing; talk is cheap; the law is the law is the law; what happened happened; what's done is done.* Quack equations too readily explain behavior that the undiscerning may otherwise find inexplicable and justify attitudes otherwise unjustifiable. No remedies for shoddy reasoning, no restoratives for suspect thinking, these palliatives soothe only our simple-mindedness.

Equally distressing is that there is no end to these quack equations: *alcohol is alcohol; he is who he is; math is math; money is money is money; people are people; plastic is plastic; prejudice is prejudice; their reasoning is their reasoning; the past is the past; wrong is wrong.* Forever being fabricated and continually being merchandized, shoddy thinking is far more easily dispensed than sound thinking.

Suspect superlatives

In dimwitted usage, superlatives are suspect. That which seems most laudable is often least, that which seems topmost, bottommost, that which seems best, worst: *an amazing person; (I'm) a perfectionist; area of expertise; celebrity; class; gentleman; great; personal friend; pursuit of excellence; the best and (the) brightest; the rich and famous.*

Torpid terms

Torpid terms are vapid words and phrases that we use in place of vital ones: *a majority of; a moving experience; a number of; a step (forward) in the right direction; cautiously optimistic; (take) corrective action; degree; effectuate; extent; (a) factor; incumbent upon; indicate; input; leaves a little (a lot; much; something) to be desired; move forward; negative feelings; off-putting; operative; prioritize; proactive; pursuant to; remedy the situation; represent(s); send a message; shocked (surprised) and saddened (dismayed); significant other; subsequent to; utilize; weight in proportion (proportionate) to height.*

Formulas as flat as these keep us dumb and dispassionate. They elicit the least from us.

With these unsound formulas, little can be communicated and still less can be accomplished. Torpid terms interfere with our understanding and with our taking action; they thwart our thinking and frustrate our feeling.

Withered words

There are many rare and wonderful words that we would do well to become familiar with — words that would revitalize us for our revitalizing them — words like *bedizen; bootless; caliginous; compleat; cotquean; hebdomadal; helpmeet; logorrhea; quondam; wont.*

Withered words, however — words like *albeit; amidst; amongst;*

behoove; betwixt; ergo; forsooth; perchance; said; sans; save; thence; unbeknownst; verily; whence; wherein; whereon; wherewith; whilst — are archaic and deserve only to be forgotten. People who use them say little that is memorable.

Wretched redundancies*

Reckless writers and slipshod speakers use many words where few would do: *advance planning; at this time; consensus of opinion; dead body; due to the fact that; first and foremost; free gift; just recently; in advance of; in and of itself; in spite of the fact that; in terms of; make a determination; on a ... basis; on the part of; past experience; period of time; (the) reason (why) is because; refer back; the single best (most); until such time as.* Yet for all the words, their expression is but impoverished; more words do not necessarily signify more meaning.

Life is measured by its meaning, and a good deal of that meaning is inherent in the words we use. If so many of our words are superfluous — and thus do not signify — so much of our life is, ineluctably, meaningless.

In the end, we are no more superfluous than are the words we use.

In themselves, dimwitticisms are as innocuous as any other single word or phrase might be, but within sentences, among thoughts struggling to be expressed and ideas seeking to be understood, dimwitticisms ravage the writer's efforts as much as they do the reader's, the speaker's as much as the listener's.

Dimwitticisms give rise to ineloquence, and it is precisely this that marks so much of our speech and writing. Whatever the occasion, whether celebratory or funereal, quotidian or uncommon, people speak and write the same dimwitted words and phrases. No wonder so many of us feel barren or inconsolable: there are few words that inspire us, few words that move us, few words that thrill or overwhelm us. Persuasion has lost much of its sway, conviction, much of its claim.

Consider these further examples of dimwitted usage.

1. From a dialogue between a television correspondent and a school superintendent:

> So you feel like you were *left holding the bag*?
> Yes, it's fair to say we were *left out in the cold.*

*For a more complete listing of redundancies, see my *Dictionary of Concise Writing* (also published by Marion Street Press).

Left holding the bag and *left out in the cold* are both moribund metaphors.
2. From the spoken words of a high school "genius":

> It was *like her worst nightmare or something.*

Like is an infantile phrase, *her worst nightmare* is a moribund metaphor, and *or something* is a grammatical gimmick.

3. From the words of a computer scientist:

> The encryption technology used today is the same as that used twenty years ago by military establishments *and that type of stuff.*

And that type of stuff is a grammatical gimmick.

4. From a business consultant's economic forecast:

> *Basically,* it's a *pretty nice* forecast.

Basically, pretty, and *nice* are all overworked words.

5. From a political lobbyist's analysis:

> If we could *level the playing field,* it would be better than having them *stick out like a sore thumb.*

Level the playing field and *stick out like a sore thumb* are both moribund metaphors.

6. From the author of a college textbook:

> In the beginning, and certainly before democratic forms of government *arrived on the scene,* tribal chieftains used their armies to maintain order.

Arrive on the scene is an infantile phrase.

7. From a news program's report on the death of a woman:

> The company released a statement saying she was an outstanding employee and her colleagues are *shocked and saddened* by her death.

Shocked and saddened is a torpid term.

8. From an article by a health-care professional:

> *It is interesting to note* the impressive array of distinguished mental health professionals who have assumed a derogatory stance on prevention.

It is interesting to note is an ineffectual phrase.

9. From a meteorologist's weather forecast:

> *Averagewise,* around November 10, we see the first snowflakes of the season fall.

Averagewise is a grammatical gimmick.

10. From a police report on the death of a vagrant:

> This could have happened to anyone; he happened to be *in the wrong place at the wrong time.*

In the wrong place at the wrong time is an infantile phrase.

11. From a man speaking before a congressional committee:

> *There are no words to describe* how *devastating* this experience has been.

There are no words to describe is a plebeian sentiment, and *devastating* is an overworked word.

12. From a questionnaire soliciting opinions about a business service:

> *Thank you in advance* for your time and assistance; your answers can *make a difference.*

Thank you in advance is a plebeian sentiment, and *make a difference* is a suspect superlative.

13. From the CEO of a multimillion-dollar company:

> A mensch is a man *with a capital M.*

With a capital M is an infantile phrase.

14. From an elementary school principal's letter to parents:

> *Please be advised that* Mr. Kline will no longer be your child's fifth-grade teacher as of Monday, November 22.

Please be advised that is an ineffectual phrase.

15. From an interview with a local government official:

> *The fact of the matter is* these are tolls that should have been removed long ago.

The fact of the matter is is an ineffectual phrase.

16. From a newspaper article:

> But few couples even bother to discuss the *"F" word* — finances — before they *tie the knot*.

The *"F" word* is an infantile phrase, and *tie the knot* is a moribund metaphor.

17. From a U.S. government official:

> We will *take corrective action to the extent that* we can; we're not going to be *caught asleep at the switch*.

Both *take corrective action* and *to the extent that* are torpid terms, and *caught asleep at the switch* is a moribund metaphor.

18. From a television news correspondent:

> *At the end of the day, the bottom line is,* no matter how powerful Karl Rove is, defending their guy here does mean protecting the president, *period*.

At the end of the day and *the bottom line* are moribund metaphors, and *period* is an infantile phrase.

19. From a high school counselor's letter of recommendation:

> If he continues to get support in college, with his *incredible* effort to overcome his difficulties, he can *definitely* succeed.

Both *incredible* and *definitely* are overworked words.
20. From a letter written by a lawyer:

> The $325 is *an ounce of prevention* that will alleviate you having to *play* expensive *catch up later on down the road.*

An ounce of prevention is a moribund metaphor, *play catch up* is a moribund metaphor, and *later on down the road* is a wretched redundancy.

People who rely on dimwitticisms like these appear to express themselves more fluently and articulately than those few who do not. But this is a sham articulateness, for without the use of phrases like left holding the bag, left out in the cold, her worst nightmare, and that type of stuff, basically, level the playing field, stick out like a sore thumb, arrive on the scene, shocked and saddened, it is interesting to note, in the wrong place at the wrong time, with a capital M, a breath of fresh air, incredible, and definitely, most people would stammer helplessly.

As unsettling and dissatisfying as it can be to read a sentence in which a single dimwitticism occurs, more than one in a sentence heightens our perturbation. Moreover, to *mix* dimwitticisms, as in some of the preceding examples, compounds our distress. To mix metaphors, as in example 5 (and even example 1), has long been frowned upon by grammarians and careful users of the language. But equally disheartening is it to mix one of these categories with another. Joining a plebeian sentiment with an overworked word, as in example 11, or with a suspect superlative, as in example 12, makes a sentence, let us say, less convincing. Joining an infantile phrase with a moribund metaphor, as in example 18, surely makes a sentence less clever. What's more, to join not two but three or more categories, as in example 2, makes a sentence altogether comical and inconsiderable. No less than mixed metaphors are these combinations worthy of our derision.

Dimwitticisms are ubiquitous, and we cannot easily escape them. Few of us can express a thought without them. We learn them unknowingly; insidiously do they become part of our wording unless we recognize what they are and withstand their onslaught. Genuine articulateness is writing and speech that scarcely makes use of dimwitticisms, and it is achieved only with much effort.

Certainly, it is the least effective speakers and writers who use the most dimwitticisms. A person's ability to express himself well is inversely proportional to the number of dimwitticisms he uses.

A person who expresses himself with genuineness instead of in jargon, with feeling instead of in formulas is capable as few have been, as few are, and as few will be; this is a person to heed.

CHAPTER 2

Writing That Demands to Be Read Aloud, Speech That Calls to Be Captured in Print

The Dimwit's Dictionary would be incomplete without a brief discussion of what it means to express oneself well and *wittily*.

Though some dictionaries divide usage into standard English and nonstandard English — and others into standard, nonstandard, and substandard — today, our understanding of the English language would be best served if we were to recognize more exacting labels.

Let us then consider the adoption of four categories of usage.

Egregious English
Uneducated English
Everyday English
Elegant English

This scheme is largely an attempt to give recognition to speech and writing that is beyond standard, or everyday, English — to elegant English. Without such a listing, people may not understand that they *can* speak and write elegantly. Certainly, as the superfluity of dimwitticisms makes plain, elegant English is English rarely heard, English seldom seen.

Here, first, are some examples of egregious English, uneducated English, and everyday English.

Egregious English

About egregious English there is little to say — other than it is a lifeless, indeed, death-inducing, dialect that ought not to be said. Here, though, are a few examples.

■ He knew they *was* out there for 10 to 15 minutes before he *done* anything.

■ I *seen* things out there in the world that I never thought I would see.

■ My mom is the one that *brung* me up.

■ Don't you have family members that you could *of went* to?

■ Men have treated me *terrible*.

■ I took everything *literate*.

■ She wasn't being abused about *nothing*.

■ We don't go to parties *no* more; we don't go *no* where.

■ That *don't* matter, I'm still there with you, *ain't* I?

■ I shouldn't have *did* it.

■ I shot *me* a burglar.

■ Let's start over here with the two of *yous*.

■ I *gots* a lot of thinking to do.

Uneducated English

Abuses of language abound, especially among those who speak and write uneducated English.

Whereas people who aspire to write and speak the language well still maintain standards of speech and observe distinctions between words, the uneducated, like some juggernaut, massacre and obliterate. They slay nearly all that they say.

afeard (*ascared*). ■ He says he's *afeard* of being alone in the dark. USE *afraid* or *scared.*
alls. ■ *Alls* I can say is he was a good cop. USE *All.* ■ *Alls* you hear them talk about is their baby. USE *All.* ■ *Alls* I wanted to say is that I forgive him. USE *All.*

anyways. ■ *Anyways,* I have to go now. USE *Anyway* or DELETE. ■ You shouldn't be sleeping around when you're married *anyways.* USE *anyway* or DELETE.

anywheres. ■ He hasn't got *anywheres* to go. USE *anywhere.*

a (long) ways. ■ I think magazines can go *a long ways* to effecting that. USE *a long way.* ■ Is it *a long ways*? USE *a long way.*

being as. ■ *Being as* he's such a great dad, I thought he wouldn't mind. USE *Because, Considering (that), In that,* or *Since.*

being as how. ■ That's not so bad, *being as how* we didn't even know we would be on the ballot. USE *because, considering (that), in that,* or *since.*

being that. ■ *Being that* we seem to be getting along so well, I thought we might go to dinner. USE *Because, Considering (that), In that,* or *Since.*

better had. ■ You *better had* do as your father says. USE *had better, ought to,* or *should.*

complected. ■ I'm 5′2″, 110 lbs., and very *light-complected.* USE *light-complexioned.*

could of. ■ I *could of* if I wanted to. USE *could have.*

don't let's (*let's don't*). ■ *Don't let's* get upset about it. USE *Let's not.*

drownded. ■ Two men *drownded* when their boat capsized. USE *drowned.*

drug. ■ He *drug* up the past and complained about the argument we had that time. USE *dragged.* ■ What I've done is *drug* all the chapters into one folder. USE *drag.*

good. ■ He did *good* last night. USE *well.* ■ He helps me to do *good* in school. USE *well.*

had(n't) ought. ■ I *had ought* to go. USE *ought* or *should.* ■ You *hadn't ought* tell him what she said. USE *ought not to* or *should not.*

heighth. ■ She's over 6 feet in *heighth.* USE *height.* ■ I am the same size as you in *heighth.* USE *height.*

hisself. ■ I heard it from Walter *hisself.* USE *himself.* ■ I was afraid he was going to hurt *hisself.* USE *himself.*

in regards to. ■ The system has failed me *in regards to* disciplining my kids. USE *in regard to.* ■ *In regards to* your question, the most important thing is that we don't have a father figure in our lives. USE *Concerning.*

irregardless (of). ■ Remember to treat all patients with respect and compassion *irregardless of* their health status. USE *despite, irrespective of, no matter what, regardless of,* or *whatever.*

irregardless of the fact that. ■ *Irregardless of the fact that* she was raised by someone else, she is still our daughter. USE *Although, Even though,* or *Though.*

leastways. ■ There's no sense of accomplishment, *leastways* not for me. USE *at least.*

leave us. ■ *Leave us* go now before it starts to pour. USE *Let us.*

like. ■ It's *like* déjà vu all over again. DELETE *like.* ■ And she's *like,* "*Like,* he wasn't *like* anyone I've, *like,* ever met." DELETE *like.* ■ And I'm *like* I just couldn't believe it. DELETE *like.*

may of. ■ I *may of* met him once before. USE *may have.*

might of. ■ It *might of* been me; I *might of* been sitting in the back seat. USE *might have; might have.*

more -(i)er. ■ You're probably *more busier* than I am. USE *busier* or *more busy.* ■ I've gotten a lot *more braver.* USE *braver* or *more brave.* ■ At Christmas time, people are a little *more friendlier.* USE *friendlier* or *more friendly.*

most -(i)est. ■ We want to take this opportunity to humbly express to you our *most sincerest* appreciation for the many expressions of sympathy you have shown us. USE *most sincere* or *sincerest.* ■ The panel consisted of some of the town's *most lustiest* women. USE *most lusty* or *lustiest.*

muchly. ■ Thank you *muchly.* USE *very much.*

not hardly. ■ Is she plump? *Not hardly.* USE *Hardly.* ■ I *couldn't hardly* breathe because he had broken my ribs. USE *could hardly.*

not scarcely. ■ I *can't scarcely* hear you. USE *can scarcely.*

nowheres. ■ He was *nowheres* near their house. USE *nowhere.*

seeing as. ■ *Seeing as* you're a woman, does the audience respond to you differently? USE *Because, Considering (that), In that,* or *Since.*

seeing as how. ■ Quite possibly it is my fault *seeing as how* I did not respond the way I thought I would. USE *because, considering (that), in that,* or *since.*

seeing that. ■ *Seeing that* this isn't a programming book, you should have little trouble. USE *Because, Considering (that), In that,* or *Since.*

(my)self. ■ How about *yourself?* USE *you.* ■ She told my sister and *myself* that she was pregnant by him. USE *me.* ■ Richard and *myself* are going to lunch. USE *I.* ■ Very large people like *yourselves* can eat tiny amounts of food and not lose an ounce. USE *you.* ■ Let's hope someone comes along, like *myself,* to take his place. USE *me.* ■ We feel Mr. Roedler's comments do an injustice to collectors like *ourselves* who currently pay $1,500 to $2,000 for radios of this type. USE *us.*

should of. ■ I *should of* known. USE *should have.*

somewheres. ■ I left it *somewheres.* USE *somewhere.*

that there (*those there*). ■ *That there* man was the one who hit her. DELETE *there.* ■ *That* way *there,* I can get my degree a few months sooner. DELETE *there.*

theirself (*theirselves*). ■ Irish people I know don't think of *theirselves* as Irish. USE *themselves.*

this here (*these here*). ■ *This* is my little brother *here.* DELETE *here.* ■ *These* shirts *here* are lighter than those. DELETE *here.*

thusly. ■ *Thusly,* I feel he was irresponsible and I feel I should tell him.

USE *Thus.* ■ Because this was described as school shootings and *thusly* presented as gender neutral, the gendered nature of the killing and shooting was ignored. USE *thus.*

went and. ■ We *went and* called 911. DELETE *went and.* ■ He *went and* left me. DELETE *went and.*

what all. ■ She can't seem to find anyone who understands *what all* she has been through. DELETE *all.* ■ I don't know *what all* the deal was with her, but she rejected me. DELETE *all.*

where at. ■ Nobody knows *where* the $100 is *at.* DELETE *at.* ■ I know *where* she is *at.* DELETE *at.* ■ I know *where* he works *at.* DELETE *at.*

with regards to. ■ Customers are looking for standard-based applications *with regards to* networking. USE *with regard to.* ■ *With regards to* the paper you gave out recently, I don't want to read about what you have against your opponent but what you are going to do for the city. USE *With regard to.*

would have. ■ What I am sure of is if we *would have* never confronted them, these white kids would have never given in to us. USE *had.* ■ If I *would have* been Paula, I would not have started a sexual harassment lawsuit. USE *had.* ■ I wish none of this *would have* ever happened. USE *had.*

would of. ■ I asked myself what I *would of, could of,* and *should of* done. USE *would have, could have,* and *should have.*

Indeed, much uneducated English is everyday English. The language pullulates with people who hover between the uneducated and the everyday.

Everyday English

Though there are many gauges of it, everyday English is certainly marked, as well as marred, by an ignorance of the meanings of words and the distinctions between words.

Everyday speakers and writers are apt to confuse the meaning of one word for that of another. Half-conscious of the words they use and the meanings of them, these people speak and write words as if they scarcely mattered.

Everyday speakers and writers often confuse the first of the following expressions (no more than a few of the many hundreds that are confused) with the second:

amount is confused with *number.* ■ Buy a qualifying *amount* of books and save 10% on all your subsequent purchases of non-discounted books. USE *number.* ■ All these methods will get you a minuscule *amount* of terrorists and a maximum *amount* of drug dealers instead. USE *number.*

breech is confused with *broach.* ■ I really respect that kind of honesty, and have *breeched* the subject at times to encourage fellow pioneers to bring some integrity to the table in such matters. USE *broached.* ■ When discussing changes in the current severance package, *breech* the topic within the context of changes of other benefit plans. USE *broach.* ■ Since we've *breeched* the subject, I have to say the Associated Press poll shows John Kerry doing better with women by 1 percentage point than Al Gore did with women. USE *broached.*

collaborate is confused with *corroborate.* ■ As our feedback reflects, we applaud some comments that *collaborate* our views on the proposals for further enhancement of relay services across the nation. USE *corroborate.* ■ At this point, we really only have Daniel's word and to back it up, it would be necessary to find Aerojet employees or White Sands people who could *collaborate* his statement. USE *corroborate.*

flaunt is confused with *flout.* ■ Why is Ted Kennedy a "pseudo-Catholic" — he claims to be a Catholic but *flaunts* the rules of the church he belongs to. USE *flouts.* ■ Companies regularly *flaunt* the laws, collecting and disseminating personal information. USE *flout.* ■ North Korea continues to *flaunt* international law by speeding ahead with their nuclear program with no consequences whatsoever. USE *flout.*

irrelevant is confused with *irreverent.* ■ It was full of *irrelevant* fun almost to the point of Marx Brothers-style of antics, with a small dose of the horrors of war thrown in. USE *irreverent.* ■ His *irrelevant* style of humour is both witty and makes us think of how we see ourselves. USE *irreverent.*

it's is confused with *its.* ■ By now, even the most out of touch among you must realize that the government of the United States is at war against *it's* own people. USE *its.* ■ Freemasonry requires that *it's* members confess a belief in a supreme being. USE *its.*

medias is confused with *media.* ■ When suicide bombers attack schools, bus stations, marketplaces, or other highly populated civilian areas, the biased liberal *medias* of the world all turn a blind eye. USE *media.* ■ Her art covers many aspects and *medias,* but today she is most widely noted for her sport action figures, portraits and pet portraits, but also does seascapes, landscapes, or still life should a client request them. USE *media.* ■ I want extra batteries for the remotes, an extra bulb for the projector, two backup copies of the presentation (naturally, in two different *medias*). USE *media.*

meretricious is confused with *meritorious.* ■ I informed her that that was a *meretricious* plan except for the fact that it involves lying. USE *meritorious.* ■ They serve the public interest by reminding readers not to believe a message simply because it is widely distributed, and carries the *meretricious* authority of the published word. USE *meritorious.*

palatable is confused with *palpable.* ■ If only we could only capture that *palatable* feeling in a bottle so that it can touch us on a more regular basis, it would do so much good. USE *palpable.* ■ About six months later I remember thinking that we were headed for a full-fledged recession, there was an almost *palatable* uneasiness in the air. USE *palpable.*

proscribe is confused with *prescribe.* ■ We are on record to abide by the 1949 Geneva Conventions and their relevant sections that *proscribe* the rules of war. USE *prescribe.* ■ They often *proscribe* rules of behavior which we must follow to attain rewards or avoid punishment in this or the after world. USE *prescribe.*

respectively is confused with *respectfully.* ■ Graduates of St. Clare School will act *respectively* towards self and others. USE *respectfully.* ■ Behave *respectively* to adults and each other. USE *respectfully.*

straight-laced is confused with *strait-laced.* ■ He's as healthy and *straight-laced* a guy as you'll meet, and in today's society, that is amazing. USE *strait-laced.* ■ Anyone who's worked in advertising knows it's not exactly a *straight-laced* environment. USE *strait-laced.*

vociferous is confused with *voracious.* ■ No, he wasn't a *vociferous* reader or running a recycling business. USE *voracious.* ■ At the age of 18 she opened her own studio and began to teach; a *vociferous* reader, she read everything she could about dance and took master classes from all the recognized leaders. USE *voracious.*

where is confused with *that.* ■ I saw on TV *where* he was awarded a prize. USE *that.* ■ I read *where* your neighbor was sentenced for soliciting sex.

Use *that.* ■ It is wonderful, although I can see *where* they might have thought it went on too long. Use *that.*

who is confused with *whom.* ■ You all know exactly *who* I am talking about — which is odd considering that we don't have princes. Use *whom.* ■ This is a man *who* even Republican cohorts sometimes find disturbing, for the way he uses almost anything to his advantage. Use *whom.*

Soon, it is clear, we will be a society unable to distinguish one word from another, sense from nonsense, truth from falsehood, good from evil. We will soon utter only mono- and disyllabic words, be entertained only by what pleases our peers, and adore whatever is easy or effortless. Unfamiliar wording and original phrasing will soon sound incoherent or cacophonic to us, while well-known inanities like *have a nice day, what goes around comes around,* and *hope for the best but expect the worst* will serve as our mantra, our maxim, our motto.

Elegant English

We all know far too well how to write everyday English, but few of us apparently know how to write elegant English — English that is expressed with music as well as meaning, style as well as substance. The point of this category is to show that the language can, indeed, be spoken or written with grace and polish — qualities that much contemporary English is bereft of and could benefit from.

So prevalent is everyday English that the person who speaks correctly and uses words deliberately is often thought less well of than the person who speaks solecistically and uses slang unreservedly. Today, fluency is in disfavor. Neither everyday nor even uneducated English seems to offend people quite as much as does elegant English. People neither fume nor flinch when they hear sentences like those illustrated earlier; but let them listen to someone who speaks, or read someone who writes, elegantly, and they may be instantly repelled. Doubtless, well-turned phrases and orotund tones suggest to them a soul unslain.

Even so, it is not classism but clarity, not snobbery but sensibility that users of elegant English prize and wish to promote. Nothing so patently accessible as usage could ever be justly called invidious. As long as we recognize the categories of usage available to us, we can decide whether to speak and write the language well or badly. And we might more readily decide that elegant English is indeed vital were it more widely spoken by our public figures and more often written in our better books. Countless occasions where elegant English might have been used — indeed, ought to have been used — by a president or politician, a luminary or other notable, have passed with uninspired, if not bumbling, speech or writing.

Further, elegant English needs to be reliably compiled in a new type of dictionary — one that does indeed pay more attention to the phrases and rhetorical figures we use or might use, one that can accommodate the category of elegant English. Such a dictionary would be as new as it is old, for it would also need to note and, more than that, endorse the distinctions between words. It would even prescribe distinctions between words where, perhaps, there have been none.

Here are some examples of elegant English.

The grammatically correct *It is I* is elegant, and the grammatically incorrect *It is me* is not. ■ *It was her* who spoke to me that way. USE *It was she.* ■ He knew it was *her,* but she didn't know it was *him.* USE *she; he.*

The ubiquitous *like* is everyday, whereas *as, as if,* and *as though* are elegant. ■ He felt *like* he had been cheated by the system. USE *as though.* ■ *Like* I was saying, he didn't know what the circumstances were. USE *As.*

Elegant is *graduated from* or *was graduated from;* everyday is *graduated.* ■ Even before *graduating* college, Hughes had published two books of poetry. USE *graduating from* or *he was graduated from.* ■ I *graduated* one of the finest medical schools in the country. USE *graduated from* or *was graduated from.*

How come is everyday English, and *how has it come about that* or *how is it that* is elegant. ■ *How come* everyone else is wrong and you are right? USE *How is it that.*
Me neither, that makes two of us, and *you're not the only one* are everyday; *neither do I, no more do I,* and *nor do I* elegant. ■ I no longer trust her. *You're not the only one.* USE *Neither do I, Nor do I,* or *No more do I.* ■ I myself know nothing about the subject. *Me neither.* USE *Neither do I, Nor do I,* or *No more do I.*

Likewise or *likewise, I'm sure* in the following examples is everyday, even uneducated; the alternatives are not. ■ I'm so happy to have met you. *Likewise, I'm sure.* USE *And I, to have met you,* or *And I, you.* ■ I enjoy meeting intelligent people. *Likewise.* USE *As I do.*

A lot, very, and *very much* are hopelessly everyday expressions; *enormously, hugely, immensely, mightily, monstrously,* and *prodigiously* are not. ■ We are *very* proud of her. USE *enormously.*

All right, O.K., and *whatever* are everyday, but *(just) as you like, (just) as you please,* and *very well* are elegant. ■ I think I'll stay here for the night. *O.K.*

USE *Just as you please.* ■ I'm supposed to say that, not you. *Whatever.* USE *Very well.*

Phrases like *aren't I? aren't you?* and *wasn't I?* are everyday, but *am I not? are you not?* and *was I not?* are elegant. ■ *Aren't I* going with you next week? USE *Am I not.* ■ He was right, *wasn't he?* USE *was he not.*

Everyday are words like *awful, bad, horrible,* and *terrible.* Elegant are words like *abominable, dreadful, frightful, ghastly, hideous, insufferable, intolerable, monstrous, unspeakable,* and *unutterable.* ■ What a *terrible* place this city of yours is. USE *monstrous.* ■ This peach pie looks *horrible.* USE *frightful.*

The fact that is everyday, and the largely forgotten *that* elegant. ■ *The fact that* they declared bankruptcy means little to me if not to you. USE *That.* ■ Yes, *the fact that* she behaved like an imbecile did influence any interest we might have had in befriending her. USE *that.*

Similarly, *in order that* and *so that* are everyday; *that* is elegant. ■ We spoke to her sternly *in order that* she might learn from her mistakes. USE *that.* ■ *In order that* we might profit from our experience, he had us write an essay on what we learned from it. USE *That.*

Words like *absolutely, definitely,* and *totally* are everyday; *itself* is elegant. ■ She is *definitely lovely.* USE *loveliness itself.* ■ Throughout the whole affair, he was *absolutely kind.* USE *kindness itself.*

Extremely, so, terribly, and *very* are everyday; *in the extreme* and *too* are not. ■ It's *very* lovely. USE *too.* ■ I found his book *extremely confusing.* USE *confusing in the extreme.*

I don't believe so, I don't think so, and *no (I don't)* are everyday; *I think not* is elegant. ■ Would you like to walk along with us? Thanks, but *I don't think so.* USE *I think not.* ■ Do you have any other questions for our guest? *No.* USE *I think not.*

Phrases such as *am I to* are elegant, but *shall I* or *will I* is everyday. ■ What *will I* do with her? USE *am I to.*

Everyday are *(that's) correct, (most) definitely, I agree, (you're) right, sure;* elegant are *exactly so, just so, precisely so, quite right, quite so,* and *yes.* ■ August is hardly the time to visit Paris. *That's right.* USE *Quite right.* ■ She is the wisest person I know. *Most definitely.* USE *Exactly so.*

Expressions like *that's correct, you're right,* and *yes, she has* are everyday. Expressions like *I am* and *she has* are elegant. ■ Is it really your birthday today? *That's right.* USE *It is.* ■ Are we there already? *Yes.* USE *We are.*

A phrase such as *do you have* is everyday next to the elegant *have you.* ■ *Do I have* time to take a shower? USE *Have I.* ■ *Do you have* anything to drink? USE *Have you.*

An understood *you* is decidedly everyday; the plainly stated *do* is not. ■ We had a little adventure last night. Oh, *tell* me all about it. USE *do tell.* ■ *Leave* me alone. USE *Do leave.*

Although the first three categories of usage, egregious, uneducated, and everyday English, comprise rudimentary structures — a single word, sometimes two or three words — elegant English, a more developed style, generally requires at least a few, and often many, words, as these further examples illustrate.

1. Those who profess to favor freedom, and yet deprecate agitation, are men who want crops without plowing up the ground. They want rain without thunder and lightning. They want the ocean without the awful roar of its waters.

FREDERICK DOUGLASS, Speech

2. I confess I love littleness almost in all things. A little convenient estate, a little cheerful house, a little company, and a very little feast; and, if I were to fall in love again (which is a great passion, and therefore, I hope, I have done with it), it would be, I think, with prettiness, rather than with majestical beauty.

ABRAHAM COWLEY, *Of Greatness*

3. Take away but the pomps of death, the disguises and solemn bugbears, the tinsel, and the actings by candle-light, and proper and fantastic ceremonies, the ministrels and the noise-makers, the women and the weepers, the swoonings and the shriekings, the nurses and the physicians, the dark room and the ministers, the kindred and the watchers; and then to die is easy, ready, and quitted from its troublesome circumstances.

JEREMY TAYLOR, *The Rule and Exercises of Holy Dying*

4. Let me wither and wear out mine age in a discomfortable, in an unwholesome, in a penurious prison, and so pay my debts with my bones, and recompense the wastefulness of my youth, with the beggary of mine age; Let me wither in a spittle under sharp, and foul, and infa-

mous diseases, and so recompense the wantonness of my youth, with that loathsomeness in mine age.

JOHN DONNE, *Let Me Wither*

5. A poor relation — is the most irrelevant thing in nature, — a piece of impertinent correspondency, — an odious approximation, — a haunting conscience, — a preposterous shadow, lengthening in the noontide of your prosperity, — an unwelcome remembrancer, — a perpetually recurring mortification, — a drain on your purse, — a more intolerable dun upon your pride, — a drawback upon success, — a rebuke to your rising, — a stain in your blood, — a blot on your scutcheon, — a rent in your garment, — a death's head at your banquet, — Agathocles' pot, — a Mordecai in your gate, — a Lazarus at your door, — a lion in your path, — a frog in your chamber, — a fly in your ointment, — a mote in your eye, — a triumph to your enemy, an apology to your friends, — the one thing not needful, — the hail in harvest, — the ounce of sour in a pound of sweet.

CHARLES LAMB, *Poor Relations*

6. Somewhere, I knew not where — somehow, I knew not how — by some beings, I knew not whom — a battle, a strife, an agony, was conducting, — was evolving like a great drama, or piece of music; with which my sympathy was the more insupportable from my confusion as to its place, its cause, its nature, and its possible issue. I, as is usual in dreams (where, of necessity, we make ourselves central to every movement), had the power, and yet had not the power, to decide it. I had the power, if I could raise myself, to will it; and yet again had not the power, for the weight of twenty Atlantics was upon me, or the oppression of inexpiable guilt. "Deeper than ever plummet sounded," I lay inactive. Then, like a chorus, the passion deepened. Some greater interest was at stake; some mightier cause than ever yet the sword had pleaded, or trumpet had proclaimed. Then came sudden alarms; hurryings to and fro; trepidations of innumerable fugitives. I knew not whether from the good cause or the bad; darkness and lights; tempest and human faces; and at last, with the sense that all was lost, female forms, and the features that were worth all the world to me, and but a moment allowed — and clasped hands, and heart-breaking partings, and then — everlasting farewells! and, with a sigh, such as the caves of hell sighed when the incestuous mother uttered the abhorred name of death, the sound was reverberated — everlasting farewells! and again, and yet again reverberated — everlasting farewells!

THOMAS DE QUINCEY, *Confessions of an Opium Eater*

7. Great is all townsmen's dread of the Beduw, as if they were the demons of this wild waste earth, ever ready to assail the Haj passengers; and there is no Beduwy durst chop logic in the dark with these often ferocious shooters, that might answer him with lead and who are heard, from time to time, firing backward into the desert all night.

CHARLES M. DOUGHTY, *Travels in Arabia Deserta*

8. Listen! for if you are not totally callous, if your consciences are not seared, I will speak daggers to your souls, and awake you to all the horrors of guilty recollection. I will follow you with whips and stings through every maze of your unexampled turpitude, and plant thorns under the rose of ministerial approbation.

EDMUND BURKE, Speech

9. As to my old opinions, I am heartily sick of them. I have reason, for they have deceived me sadly. I was taught to think, and I was willing to believe, that genius was not a bawd, that virtue was not a mask, that liberty was not a name, that love had its seat in the human heart. Now I would care little if these words were struck out of the dictionary, or if I had never heard them. They are become to my ears a mockery and a dream. Instead of patriots and friends of freedom, I see nothing but the tyrant and the slave, the people linked with kings to rivet on the chains of despotism and superstition. I see folly join with knavery, and together make up public spirit and public opinions. I see the insolent Tory, the blind Reformer, the coward Whig! If mankind had wished for what is right, they might have had it long ago.

WILLIAM HAZLITT, *On the Pleasure of Hating*

10. Poor Cromwell, — great Cromwell! The inarticulate Prophet; Prophet who could not speak. Rude, confused, struggling to utter himself, with his savage depth, with his wild sincerity; and he looked so strange, among the elegant Euphemisms, dainty little Falklands, didactic Chillingworths, diplomatic Clarendons! Consider him. An outer hull of chaotic confusion, visions of the Devil, nervous dreams, almost semi-madness; and yet such a clear determinate man's-energy working in the heart of that. A kind of chaotic man. The ray as of pure starlight and fire, working in such an element of boundless hypochondria, unformed black of darkness! And yet withal this hypochondria, what was it but the very greatness of the man? The depth and tenderness of his wild affections: the quantity of sympathy he had with things, — the quantity of insight he would yet get into the heart of things, the mastery he would yet get over things: this was his hypochondria. The man's misery, as man's misery always does, came of his greatness. Samuel Johnson too is that kind of man. Sorrow-stricken, half-distracted; the wide element of mournful

black enveloping him, — wide as the world. It is the character of a prophetic man; a man with his whole soul seeing, and struggling to see.

THOMAS CARLYLE, *Heroes and Hero Worship*

11. The character of the Italian statesman seems, at first sight, a collection of contradictions, a phantom as monstrous as the portress of hell in Milton, half divinity, half snake, majestic and beautiful above, grovelling and poisonous below. We see a man whose thoughts and words have no connection with each other, who never hesitates at an oath when he wishes to seduce, who never wants a pretext when he is inclined to betray. His cruelties spring, not from the heat of blood, or the insanity of uncontrolled power, but from deep and cool meditation. His passions, like well-trained troops, are impetuous by rule, and in their most headstrong fury never forget the discipline to which they have been accustomed. His whole soul is occupied with vast and complicated schemes of ambition, yet his aspect and language exhibit nothing but philosophical moderation. Hatred and revenge eat into his heart; yet every look is a cordial smile, every gesture a familiar caress. He never excites the suspicion of his adversaries by petty provocations. His purpose is disclosed, only when it is accomplished. His face is unruffled, his speech is courteous, till vigilance is laid asleep, till a vital point is exposed, till a sure aim is taken; and then he strikes for the first and last time. Military courage, the boast of the sottish German, of the frivolous and prating Frenchman, of the romantic and arrogant Spaniard, he neither possesses nor values. He shuns danger, not because he is insensible to shame, but because, in the society in which he lives, timidity has ceased to be shameful. To do an injury openly is, in his estimation, as wicked as to do it secretly, and far less profitable. With him the most honorable means are those which are the surest, the speediest, and the darkest. He cannot comprehend how a man should scruple to deceive those whom he does not scruple to destroy. He would think it madness to declare open hostilities against rivals whom he might stab in a friendly embrace, or poison in a consecrated wafer.

THOMAS BABINGTON MACAULAY, *Machiavelli*

12. Animated by this important object, I shall disdain to cull my phrases or polish my style; — I aim at being useful, and sincerity will render me unaffected; for, wishing rather to persuade by the force of my arguments, than dazzle by the elegance of my language, I shall not waste my time in rounding periods, nor in fabricating the turgid bombast of artificial feelings, which, coming from the head, never reach the heart. — I shall be employed about things, not words! — and, anxious to render my sex more respectable members of society, I shall try to avoid that flowery diction which has slided from essays into novels, and from novels into famil-

iar letters and conversation.

These pretty nothings — these caricatures of the real beauty of sensibility, dropping glibly from the tongue, vitiate the taste, and create a kind of sickly delicacy that turns away from simple unadorned truth; and a deluge of false sentiments and overstretched feelings, stifling the natural emotions of the heart, render the domestic pleasures insipid, that ought to sweeten the exercise of those severe duties, which educate a rational and immortal being for a nobler field of action.

MARY WOLLSTONECRAFT, *A Vindication of the Rights of Woman*

Elegant English, as these examples show, is exhilarating; it stirs our thoughts and feelings as ably as dimwitted English blurs them.

The Dimwit's Dictionary will aid us in our quest for elegant, for *wittier,* speech and writing. The goal is to promote understanding and rouse people to action. The goal is to express ourselves as never before — in writing that demands to be read aloud, in speech that calls to be captured in print.

THE DIMWIT'S DICTIONARY

SECOND EDITION

abandon all hope, ye who enter here An infantile phrase (see page 20).

(the) ABCs of A moribund metaphor (see page 21). *basics; basis; elements; essentials; foundation; fundamentals; principles; rudiments.* ■ The program will discuss the *ABCs of* eating right. REPLACE WITH *fundamentals.*

abject poverty An inescapable pair (see page 20).

abortive attempt (effort) An inescapable pair (see page 20). *breakdown; failure; malfunction.*

above and beyond the call of duty A moribund metaphor (see page 21).

above par A moribund metaphor (see page 21). *excellent; exceptional; first-class; first-rate; outstanding; remarkable; superior; superlative.*

absence makes the heart grow fonder A popular prescription (see page 23).

absence of A torpid term (see page 24). SEE ALSO *lack of; less than (enthusiastic).*

absolutely An overworked word (see page 22). *altogether; categorically; completely; entirely; fully; perfectly; positively; quite; roundly; thoroughly; totally; unconditionally; unreservedly; utterly; wholly.* SEE ALSO *definitely; most assuredly; most (very) definitely.*

absolutely, positively An infantile phrase (see page 20). ■ A programmer must *absolutely, positively* keep a finger on the format's pulse. DELETE *absolutely, positively.* ■ On a wide range of topics, he is the go-to guy — when you *absolutely, positively* have to know what happened. DELETE *absolutely, positively.*

Here's a variation that the writer may have prided himself on: ■ But what you *positively, absolutely* do not want is to get hurt in a stupid exhibition game. DELETE *positively, absolutely.*

absurd An overworked word (see page 22). *comical; extravagant; farcical; foolhardy; foolish; idiotic; illogical; imbecilic; impractical; inane; incongruous; irrational; laughable; ludicrous; moronic; nonsensical; preposterous; ridiculous; senseless; silly; unreasonable.*

accentuate the positive An infantile phrase (see page 20). *be confident; be encouraged; be heartened; be hopeful; be optimistic; be positive; be rosy; be sanguine.*

(an) accident waiting to happen A moribund metaphor (see page 21). ■ Any network that does not have a standardized backup procedure in place is *an accident waiting to happen.* ■ The fire at the InterRoyal mill was a tragic *accident waiting to happen.*

An accident waiting to happen twists seriousness into silliness. The significance of what we say, the danger, perhaps, in what we do, we seldom see when we think with such frivolous phrases. Our understanding may be distorted, our responses dulled.

accidents will happen A popular prescription (see page 23).

according to Hoyle An infantile phrase (see page 20). *accurately; by the rules; conventionally; correctly; customarily; properly; regularly; rightly; traditionally.*

ace in the hole A moribund metaphor (see page 21).

Achilles' heel (tendon) A moribund metaphor (see page 21). *defect; deficiency; disadvantage; failing; fault; flaw; foible; fragility; frailness; frailty; handicap; imperfection; liability; limitation; shortcoming; susceptibility; susceptibleness; vulnerability; vulnerableness; weakness.* ■ If the Bruins had an *Achilles' heel* last season, it was that they were a tad oversized. REPLACE WITH *weakness.*

acid test A moribund metaphor (see page 21). *assay; crucible; ordeal; proof; test; trial.*

across the board A moribund metaphor (see page 21). *(for) all; all over; (for) everyone; everyplace; everywhere; throughout (the land); universally.* ■ There is increased consumer confidence — not just here but *across the board.* REPLACE WITH *everywhere.*

> The war was over, things looked robust across the board, and Big Don was living the charmed life at the age of thirty-three. — Kevin Brennan, *Parts Unknown*

action plan A torpid term (see page 24). *action; course; direction; intention; method; move; plan; policy; procedure; route; scheme; strategy.* ■ The UN is expected to produce a global *action plan* aimed at reducing demand and improving treatment, rehabilitation, and interdiction. REPLACE WITH *strategy.*

actions speak louder than words A popular prescription (see page 23).

active An overworked word (see page 22). Only thoughtless speakers and writers, apes and jackanapes, use the adjective *active* to modify a noun. In doing so, they emasculate the meaning of these words. So common is the adjectival *active,* we might easily wonder if anything is possible or achievable, serious or sincere that does not have this word preceding it. ■ Please believe me when I tell you that the only thing that stands between you and a better, more responsive government is your *active participation* in the process. DELETE *active.* ■ Nor did the president demonstrate *active interest* in the issue. DELETE *active.* ■ Some practitioners think that *active movement* might be the key to a cure. DELETE *active.* ■ An *active search* is on for the shooter. DELETE *active.* SEE ALSO *actively.*

actively An overworked word (see page 22). The popular use of *actively* suggests that any verb not affixed to it is feckless.

We cannot simply *consider* an idea lest we be accused of not thinking; we cannot simply *engage* in a pursuit lest we be accused of not trying; we cannot simply *participate* in a conversation lest we be accused of not speaking. ■ Another possibility is *actively being considered* by the administration: the use of force. DELETE *actively.* ■ The core group of ASC founders worried that the membership was restricted too narrowly to policing, so they *actively encouraged* others to participate. DELETE *actively.* ■ I have no intention of mailing a second letter to anyone who does not *actively show* an interest in becoming part of my collectors club. DELETE *actively*. ■ Police are *actively searching* for the killer, *actively looking* in all areas, and *actively examining* all the evidence. DELETE *actively*. ■ Not only do many people not enjoy speaking in public, they *actively dislike* and even fear it. DELETE *actively*. ■ Seek them out *actively*. DELETE *actively*. ■ Right now we're not *actively aware* of what her true motivation was. DELETE *actively*. ■ Reporters get mired in routine like everyone and need, from time to time, to *actively work* on expanding the number of places they go and the variety of people with whom they talk. DELETE *actively*.

Here is an example of just how absurd our fixation on *actively* has become: ■ Among the new features of WSF2 R3.3 that he is *actively looking forward to* is the statistical information that can be provided through SMF records. DELETE *actively*. SEE ALSO *active*.

acutely aware An inescapable pair (see page 20). ■ Fans have become *acutely aware* that player strikes and lockouts are battles over who gets the biggest piece of what the fan provides.

adamantly oppose An inescapable pair (see page 20).

add fuel to the fire A moribund metaphor (see page 21). *activate; aggravate; agitate; animate; arouse; awaken; encourage; enkindle; enliven; exacerbate; excite; feed; foment; heighten; ignite; impassion; incite; increase; inflame; intensify; invigorate; make worse; nourish; prod; provoke; rejuvenate; revitalize; revive; rouse; shake up; stimulate; stir up; vitalize; worsen.*

add insult to injury A moribund metaphor (see page 21). *aggravate; arouse; enkindle; enliven; exacerbate; excite; feed; foment; heighten; ignite; impassion; incite; increase; inflame; intensify; invigorate; make worse; nourish; prod; provoke; rouse; shake up; stimulate; stir up; what's worse; worsen.*

ad infinitum A foreign phrase (see page 19). *ceaselessly; endlessly; evermore; forever; forevermore; to infinity; without limit.*

ad nauseam A foreign phrase (see page 19).

advance planning A wretched redundancy (see page 25). *planning*. ■ This project will require a lot of *advance planning*. DELETE *advance*.

advance warning A wretched redundancy (see page 25). *warning*. ■ Although the bank's 17,000 employees have known for more than a month that the ax was about to fall, the *advance warning* did little to blunt the effect. DELETE *advance*. SEE ALSO *forewarn; warn in advance*.

advice is cheap A quack equation (see page 23).

afraid (frightened; scared) of (his) own shadow A moribund metaphor (see page 21). *afraid; alarmed; apprehensive; cowardly; craven; diffident; fainthearted; fearful; frightened; pavid; pusillanimous; recreant; scared; terror-striken; timid; timorous; tremulous.*

after (once; when) all is said and done A wretched redundancy (see page 25). *all in all; all told; altogether; eventually; finally; in all; in the end; on the whole; overall; ultimately.* ■ *After all is said and done,* it truly was an exceptional decade. REPLACE WITH *On the whole.* ■ *When all is said and done,* we humans are a curious species. REPLACE WITH *All told.*

> Inside the sack was a spool of twine, a sugar cane knife to sever the umbilical cord, and a garden spade to bury the creature once all was said and done. — Kathy Hepinstall, *The House of Gentle Men*

after the fact A torpid term (see page 24). *afterward; later.* ■ We don't have a choice, *after the fact.* REPLACE WITH *afterward.*

age before beauty A popular prescription (see page 23).

(the) agony and the ecstasy A moribund metaphor (see page 21).

agree to disagree An infantile phrase (see page 20).

ahead of the game A moribund metaphor (see page 21). *advantageous; auspicious; blessed; charmed; enchanted; favored; felicitous; flourishing; fortuitous; fortunate; golden; happy; in luck; lucky; propitious; prosperous; successful; thriving.*

ahead of (his) time A moribund metaphor (see page 21). *advanced; ground-breaking; innovative; inventive; new; original; pioneering; progressive; radical; revolutionary; unconventional.*

aid and abet An inescapable pair (see page 20). *abet; aid; assist; encourage; help; support.* ■ One of the best-known detectives comes from literature in the person of Sherlock Holmes, a private investigator *aided and abetted* by his friend Dr. Watson. REPLACE WITH *assisted.*

> The two women were simply aiding and abetting each other to disband the Seraglio. — Penelope Fitzgerald, *Human Voices*

airtight alibi An inescapable pair (see page 20).

à la A foreign phrase (see page 19) (see page 19). *according to; in the manner of; like.* ■ I don't want to put myself in a bad position and get beat *à la* this man. REPLACE WITH *like.* ■ The media may be engaged in a witch hunt *a la* the late U.S. Senator Joe McCarthy and perhaps should cut back on their coverage. REPLACE WITH *in the manner of.*

alas A withered word (see page 24). *regrettably; sadly; sorrowfully; unfortunately; unhappily.* ■ *Alas,* the program checks only the first two directory entries. REPLACE WITH *Unfortunately.*

alas and alack An infantile phrase (see page 20). *regrettably; sadly; sorrowfully; unfortunately; unhappily.*

albatross around (my) neck A moribund metaphor (see page 21). *affliction;*

burden; charge; cross; difficulty; encumbrance; hardship; hindrance; impediment; load; obstacle; obstruction; onus; oppression; ordeal; problem; trial; trouble; weight. ■ Then came that unspeakable song, "Begin the Beguine," which is still *an albatross around my neck.* REPLACE WITH *a burden.*

albeit A withered word (see page 24). *although; even if; even though; though.* Like other withered words, *albeit* strikes some people as more exquisite sounding — and therefore, apparently, more intellectual sounding — than any of its synonyms. But this is perceived by only the deaf and the dimwitted. ■ *Albeit* somewhat dated, a study performed eight years ago is attracting attention once again. REPLACE WITH *Although.*

alive and kicking A moribund metaphor (see page 21). *alive; blooming; doing well; energetic; existent; existing; extant; fit; flourishing; growing; hale; hardy; healthful; healthy; hearty; live; lively; living; prospering; robust; sound; still exists; strong; surviving; thriving; vigorous; vital; well; well-off.* One of the consequences of endlessly saying and hearing and writing and reading formulaic phrases is that, eventually, people *do* become weary of them.

But instead of expressing themselves differently — more eloquently or more inventively, perhaps — people will simply substitute one word in these selfsame formulas for another.

Thus, along with *alive and kicking,* there is, for instance, *alive and well* (SEE) and even *alive and thriving*; along with *a thing of the past,* there is *a phenomenon of the past*; along with *business as usual,* there is *politics as usual* (SEE) and *life as usual;* along with *mover and shaker,* there is *mover and shaper;* along with *neck of the woods,* there is the noisome *portion of the earth;* along with *needs and wants,* there is *needs and desires;* along with *in no way,* there is *in no way, shape, or form* and the preposterous *in no way, shape, form, or fashion;* along with *remedy the situation,* there is *rectify the situation;* along with *out the window,* there is *out the door;* and along with *nothing could be further from the truth,* there is, incomprehensibly, *nothing could be further from the actual facts.*

Would that it ended here, but there are also far too many people who begin with a hackneyed phrase and then transmogrify it into an ever-so-silly, garish one.

Thus, *between a rock and a hard place* (SEE) becomes: ■ In the past decade, newspaper publishers have been squeezed *between the Net and a hard place.* ■ The Al Queda fighters are *between an anvil and a hammer.*

A needle in a haystack (SEE) becomes: ■ Her friend wrote back and said this was impossible, like looking for *a needle on the bottom of the ocean.*

From bad to worse (SEE) becomes: ■ Moscow now has about 90 days to try to keep a *bad situation from collapsing into something infinitely worse.*

Doesn't have a snowball's chance in hell (SEE) becomes: ■ There is nobody on Russia's political horizon who embraces Mr. Yeltsin's westernized brand of economic policy and *has a Siberian snowball's chance of winning a presidential election.*

An accident waiting to happen (SEE) becomes: ■ The holidays are *a cornucopia of awkward moments waiting to happen.* ■ Expectations are resentments *waiting to happen.*

Not with a bang but with a whimper

(SEE) becomes: ■ This week *started out with a bang and ended with a whimper* for bank stocks. ■ Hurricane Bonnie hit New England *with a whimper, not a bang.* ■ After *beginning my career there with a bang, I cannot end with a whimper.* ■ It could *end with a whimper or a wallop.*

Walk softly and carry a big stick (SEE) becomes: ■ The guiding principle in foreign policy of this administration seems to be *speak loudly and carry a twig.*

Snatch victory from the jaws of defeat (SEE) becomes: ■ In the end, Republicans will simply *snatch defeat from the jaws of victory* if they successfully oust a president they loathe but lose their majorities in both houses of Congress as a result.

Light at the end of the tunnel (SEE) becomes: ■ Is it possible that we're actually seeing a *light at the end of* Star Trek*'s TV continuum*?

Not worth the paper it's written (printed) on (SEE) becomes: ■ Consumers can put their trust in a few of these Web site seals, but in many cases they *aren't worth the pixels that they're painted with.*

Going to hell in a hand basket (SEE) becomes: ■ The good news, culturally speaking, is that if we're *going to Hell in a Saks shopping bag,* at least we are going there slowly.

People propagate these monstrosities. Equally distressing is that, in doing so, they think they *are* being clever and inventive. Among pedestrian people, this is what it means to be thoughtful, this is what it means to be creative.

Is it any wonder that speech is so often soporific, writing so often wearisome?

alive and well An infantile phrase (see page 20). *alive; blooming; doing well; energetic; existent; existing; extant; fit; flourishing; growing; hale; hardy; healthful; healthy; hearty; live; lively; living; prospering; robust; sound; still exists; strong; surviving; thriving; vigorous; vital; well; well-off.* ■ Scholarship and readership are *alive and well* and will outlast the publishing binge of the commercial houses. REPLACE WITH *flourishing.* ■ The work ethic of American workers is unquestionably *alive and well.* REPLACE WITH *sound.*

all and sundry A wretched redundancy (see page 25). *all; everybody; everyone; everything.* SEE ALSO *various and sundry.*

> From morning till night you saw her sitting on a low chair in the kitchen, surrounded by a Chinese cook and two or three native girls, giving her orders, chatting sociably with all and sundry, and tasting the savoury messes she devised. — W. Somerset Maugham, *The Moon and Sixpence*

all dressed up and no place to go An infantile phrase (see page 20).

all ears A moribund metaphor (see page 21). *attentive; heedful; listening; paying attention; paying heed.*

(as) all get-out A moribund metaphor (see page 21). *acutely; awfully; consumedly; exceedingly; extraordinarily; extremely; greatly; hugely; immensely; intensely; mightily; prodigiously; severely; terribly; very.* ■ He was *funny as all get-out.* REPLACE WITH *extremely funny.*

all hell broke loose A moribund metaphor (see page 21).

all mouth A moribund metaphor (see page 21). *boastful; vainglorious.*

all of the above An infantile phrase (see page 20). ■ Are you just looking for a companion or are you looking for a sexual partner? *All of the above.* SEE ALSO *none of the above.*

all over the lot (map) A moribund metaphor (see page 21). *diffuse; dispersed; disseminated; scattered; strewn; unfocused.*

all roads lead to Rome A moribund metaphor (see page 21).

all rolled into one A moribund metaphor (see page 21). *admixture; amalgam; blend; combination; mix; mixture.*

all's fair in love and war A popular prescription (see page 23).

all's well that ends well A popular prescription (see page 23).

all systems (are) go A moribund metaphor (see page 21).

all that glitters isn't gold A popular prescription (see page 23).

(and) all that jazz A grammatical gimmick (see page 19) (see page 19). ■ He tells me what to do *and all that jazz.* DELETE *and all that jazz.*

all the world's a stage A moribund metaphor (see page 21).

all things considered A wretched redundancy (see page 25). *all in all; all told; altogether; in all; on the whole; overall.*

all (good) things must end A popular prescription (see page 23).

all thumbs A moribund metaphor (see page 21). *ambisinister; awkward; blundering; bumbling; bungling; clumsy; gawky; gauche; ham-handed; heavy-handed; inapt; inept; lubberly; lumbering; maladroit; uncoordinated; uncouth; ungainly; ungraceful; unhandy; unskillful; unwieldy.*

all-time record A wretched redundancy (see page 25). *record.* ■ If anyone spent time skiing here this past winter, they'd be happy to find the boycott has resulted in an *all-time record* number of skiers. DELETE *all-time.* SEE ALSO *record-breaking; record-high.*

all to the good A moribund metaphor (see page 21). *adequate; advantageous; beneficial; satisfactory; sufficient.*

(from) all walks of life A moribund metaphor (see page 21).

all wet A moribund metaphor (see page 21). *amiss; astray; deceived; deluded; erring; erroneous; fallacious; false; faulty; inaccurate; incorrect; in error; misguided; misinformed; mislead; mistaken; not correct; not right; wrong.* ■ Whoever told you that alcohol is less of a problem than drugs is *all wet.* REPLACE WITH *mistaken.*

all wool and a yard wide A moribund metaphor (see page 21). *actual; authentic; earnest; genuine; heartfelt; honest; legitimate; pure; real; sincere; sterling; true; unadulterated; unalloyed; veritable.*

all work and no play makes Jack a dull boy A popular prescription (see page 23).

(the) almighty dollar A moribund metaphor (see page 21).

along the lines of A wretched redundancy (see page 25). *akin to; close to; like; resembling; similar to; such as.* ■ It's generally safe to ask people in the field if they've ever heard of anything *along the lines of* your idea. REPLACE WITH *similar to*.

> It turned out that Agent Samson was something along the lines of a circuit-court speech therapist. — David Sedaris, *Me Talk Pretty One Day*

(the) alpha and omega of A moribund metaphor (see page 21).

amazing An overworked word (see page 22). *astonishing; astounding; extraordinary; marvelous; outstanding; remarkable; spectacular; startling; stunning; wonderful; wondrous.*

(an) amazing person A suspect superlative (see page 24). *An amazing person* is so only in the eyes of another who, we can be confident, is not.

(as) American as apple pie An insipid simile. *all-American; decent; good; honorable; moral; proper; pure; right; straight; upright; virtuous; wholesome.*

(the) American dream A suspect superlative (see page 24). ■ *The American dream* has become a nightmare.

amidst A withered word (see page 24). *amid; among.* ■ *Amidst* all of life's distractions, what is it that keeps us going? REPLACE WITH *Amid*.

(9:00) a.m. ... (in the) morning A wretched redundancy (see page 25). *(9:00) a.m.; (in the) morning.* ■ Monday's events can be defined to occur from *8 a.m.* Monday *morning* to *8 a.m.* Tuesday *morning*. DELETE *morning*. ■ This *morning* at 9:35 *a.m.* a violent clash took place between prisoners. DELETE *a.m.*.

amongst A withered word (see page 24). *among. Amongst*, among the potentially bright, is preferable to *among*, but only because their potential has yet to be realized. ■ If there is a lack of confidence *amongst* those concerned, the strictly political element will be more obvious. REPLACE WITH *among*. ■ Someday, perhaps, you'll be able to find it *amongst* the software programs at the store, next to SimCity: the ultimate Language Architect simulator game. REPLACE WITH *among*. ■ I'm sorry to say that after passing this *amongst* some colleagues, we've agreed that it is not thorough enough to be a reference book. REPLACE WITH *among*.

a (absolute) must An infantile phrase (see page 20). *compulsory; critical; essential; imperative; important; indispensable; mandatory; necessary; needed; obligatory; required; requisite; vital.* ■ Prior experience writing user and technical documentation in the computer field is *a must*. REPLACE WITH *necessary*. ■ It is not *an absolute must* to read this part in order to use the second half of the book. REPLACE WITH *essential*. SEE ALSO *(a) must have; (a) must see; a (definite) plus.*

analyze to death A moribund metaphor (see page 21). *analyze; anatomize; dissect; examine; inspect; investigate; scrutinize; study.* SEE ALSO *to death.*

(that's) ancient history A moribund metaphor (see page 21). *aged; ancient; antediluvian; antique; archaic; elderly; history; hoary; old; past; prehistoric; seasoned; superannuated.*

> He knew that it had something to do with the scandal, but that was ancient history. — Frederick Buechner, *The Storm*

and all A grammatical gimmick (see page 19) (see page 19). — We're going to look at all these nice buildings *and all.* DELETE *and all.* SEE ALSO *and all like that; and everything (else); and everything like that; and stuff (things); and (or) stuff (things) like that.*

and all like that A grammatical gimmick (see page 19). ■ We went to different agencies for help *and all like that.* DELETE *and all like that.* ■ He caught me off guard by asking for my name and address *and all like that.* DELETE *and all like that.* SEE ALSO *and all; and everything (else); and everything like that; and stuff (things); and (or) stuff (things) like that.*

and etc. (et cetera) A wretched redundancy (see page 25). *and so forth; and so on; and the like; etc.* ■ We bought the generic-brand products *and et cetera.* REPLACE WITH *and the like.*

and everything (else) A grammatical gimmick (see page 19). ■ We're responsible for this baby *and everything else.* DELETE *and everything else.* ■ You guys fight *and everything,* but she really does love you. DELETE *and everything.* SEE ALSO *and all; and all like that; and everything like that; and stuff (things); and (or) stuff (things) like that.*

and everything like that A grammatical gimmick (see page 19). ■ They adopted that way of speaking *and everything like that.* DELETE *and everything like that.* ■ Don't you feel cheap and used *and everything like that?* DELETE *and everything like that.* SEE ALSO *and all; and all like that; and everything (else); and stuff (things); and (or) stuff (things) like that.*

and/or A wretched redundancy (see page 25). *and; or.* ■ Implant dentistry can be an effective alternative to dentures *and/or* missing teeth. REPLACE WITH *or.* ■ But computers may make both more attractive than the alternatives adopted by those who have abandoned wives *and/or* children by failing to meet their financial obligations. REPLACE WITH *and.*

and so on, and so forth A grammatical gimmick (see page 19). *and so forth; and so on; and the like; etc.* ■ I'm more interested in films about human relationships *and so on, and so forth.* DELETE *and so on, and so forth.* SEE ALSO *blah, blah, blah; et cetera, et cetera.*

and stuff (things) A grammatical gimmick (see page 19). ■ His legs had black bruises on them *and stuff.* DELETE *and stuff.* ■ The customers are really nice people; they're friends *and stuff.* DELETE *and stuff.* ■ They wanted him to go for a bike ride *and things.* DELETE *and things.* ■ We got invited to a lot of Hollywood parties *and things.* DELETE *and things.* SEE ALSO *and all; and all like that; and everything (else); and everything like that; and (or) stuff (things) like that.*

and (or) stuff (things) like that A grammatical gimmick (see page 19). ■ I love women — the way they look *and stuff like that.* DELETE *and stuff like that.* ■ People shouldn't shoot others over money *or things like that.* ■ I was upset because my mother went through two divorces *and stuff like that.* DELETE *and stuff like that.* ■ As a big man, they look at you as big and healthy *and things like that.* DELETE *and things like that.* SEE ALSO *and all; and all like that; and everything (else); and everything like that; and stuff (things); and (or) stuff (things) like that.*

and that kind of stuff (thing) A grammatical gimmick (see page 19). ■ He's a changed man; he's learned to read and write *and that kind of thing.* DELETE *and that kind of thing.* ■ I was working on getting the house settled *and that kind of stuff.* DELETE *and that kind of stuff.* SEE ALSO *(and that) sort of stuff (thing); (and that) type of stuff (thing).*

and that sort of stuff (thing) A grammatical gimmick (see page 19). ■ I enjoy walking in the park *and that sort of thing.* DELETE *and that sort of thing.* SEE ALSO *(and that) kind of stuff (thing); (and that) type of stuff (thing).*

and that type of stuff (thing) A grammatical gimmick (see page 19). ■ I like interesting conversation and interacting *and that type of thing.* DELETE *and that type of thing.* SEE ALSO *(and that) kind of stuff (thing); (and that) sort of stuff (thing).*

and this and that A grammatical gimmick (see page 19). ■ He told me how much he cared for me *and this and that.* DELETE *and this and that.* SEE ALSO *and this, that, and the other (thing).*

and this, that, and the other (thing) A grammatical gimmick (see page 19). ■ She would say to me, you've got the best of both worlds, you're special, you're loved, *and this, that, and the other thing.* DELETE *and this, that, and the other thing.* SEE ALSO *and this and that.*

an embarrassment of riches A moribund metaphor (see page 21). ■ It's a city with *an embarrassment of riches.*

anent A withered word (see page 24). *about; concerning.*

angel of mercy A suspect superlative (see page 24). *liberator; redeemer; rescuer; savior.*

anon A withered word (see page 24). 1. *at another time; later.* 2. *shortly; soon.* 3. *at once; immediately.*

another day, another dollar A popular prescription (see page 23).

ants in (his) pants A moribund metaphor (see page 21). *aflame; agitated; animated; anxious; eager; ebullient; effervescent; enthusiastic; excitable; excited; fervent; fervid; fidgety; frantic; frenzied; impassioned; impatient; jittery; jumpy; lively; nervous; restive; restless; skittish; spirited.*

a ... number (of) A torpid term (see page 24). ■ You can use the computer to discover students who are making *a large number of* mistakes. REPLACE WITH *many.* ■ *A good number* of troops have arrived in Moscow. REPLACE WITH *Hundreds.* ■ *An overwhelming number of* the participatory lenders have now joined the major banks in supporting our plan. REPLACE WITH *Almost all.* ■

They are dependent upon the teacher's pension, which is fully given at the age of 62 after *a large number of teaching years*. REPLACE WITH *years of teaching*. SEE ALSO *a (the) ... majority (of); a sufficient number (of)*.

any and all A wretched redundancy (see page 25). *all; any.* ■ *Any and all* accidental needle sticks must be reported to the physician at once. REPLACE WITH *All*. ■ We welcome *any and all* comments and suggestions regarding this project. REPLACE WITH *any*.

anyhow A grammatical gimmick (see page 19). ■ *Anyhow*, we got the divorce in 1992. DELETE *Anyhow*. SEE ALSO *anyway*.

any port in a storm A moribund metaphor (see page 21).

anything and everything A wretched redundancy (see page 25). *anything; everything.* ■ A deadbeat is generally defined as a person dedicated to getting *anything and everything* possible for nothing. REPLACE WITH *anything* or *everything*.

anything (everything) is possible A popular prescription (see page 23).

any (every) (reason) under the sun A moribund metaphor (see page 21). *any; anything; every; everything.* ■ Americans sue each other for almost *every reason under the sun*. REPLACE WITH *every reason*. ■ Our catering staff has designed a menu and planned a party for almost *every reason under the sun*. REPLACE WITH *every reason*. ■ Capricorns have the ability to write about *any subject under the sun*. REPLACE WITH *anything*.

> Maybe from the old habit of doing everything as one man; maybe when you have lived for four years in a world ordered completely by men's doings, even when it is danger and fighting, you don't want to quit that world: maybe the danger and the fighting are the reasons, because men have been pacifists for every reason under the sun except to avoid danger and fighting. — William Faulkner, *The Unvanquished*

anyway A grammatical gimmick (see page 19). ■ But *anyway*, I'll talk to you later in the week. DELETE *anyway*. ■ So *anyway*, I just wanted to verify that with you. DELETE *anyway*. SEE ALSO *anyhow*.

appearances can be deceiving A popular prescription (see page 23).

(first) appear (arrive; come) on the horizon (scene) An infantile phrase (see page 20). *appear; arise; become available; begin; be introduced; come forth; develop; emerge; occur; originate; present itself; rise; spring; start; surface; turn up.* ■ TTAPS first *appeared on the scene* in 1983 with a paper in *Science* on the global atmospheric consequences of nuclear war. REPLACE WITH *emerged*. ■ It is at the time of William the Conqueror and the Norman conquest of England that the office of shire reeve first *appears on the scene*. REPLACE WITH *appears*. ■ Clearly, oil used in the internal combustion engine presented such a change when it *came on the scene* in the early part of the twentieth century. REPLACE WITH *became available*. ■ The Component Object Model (COM) has caused more confusion since its inception than any other programming technology that has ever *appeared on the horizon.* REPLACE WITH *been introduced.*

(an) apple a day keeps the doctor away A popular prescription (see page 23).

(the) apple doesn't fall far from the tree A popular prescription (see page 23).

(the) apple of (my) eye A moribund metaphor (see page 21). *hero; idol; star.*

apple polisher A moribund metaphor (see page 21). *apparatchik; bootlicker; fawner; flatterer; flunky; follower; lackey; minion; stooge; sycophant; toady; yes-man.*

(like comparing) apples and oranges A moribund metaphor (see page 21). *different; discordant; discrepant; dissimilar; dissonant; divergent; incommensurable; incommensurate; incomparable; incompatible; incongruent; incongruous; inconsistent; inconsonant; inharmonious; unlike.*

(I) appreciate (it) An overworked word (see page 22). 1. *grateful for; thankful for; thank you.* 2. *admire; cherish; esteem; prize; relish; treasure; value; welcome.* ■ We *appreciate* your help. REPLACE WITH *are grateful for.* ■ We *appreciate you* being here. REPLACE WITH *thank you for.* ■ I *appreciate* every letter that I have received. REPLACE WITH *treasure.* SEE ALSO *common courtesy.*

(take) appropriate (corrective) action A torpid term (see page 24). This ponderous phrase will stem one person's drive while it saps another's desire. From such a phrase, only dull-minded deeds and uninspired acts may result, which is quite likely all that the user of it, bureaucrat he routinely is, either wishes for or can imagine. ■ If there's enough public pressure, they may rethink their defensiveness and begin to *take corrective action.* REPLACE WITH *behave differently.* ■ The bus driver was not exercising caution in this instance, and *corrective action has been taken.* REPLACE WITH *he was fired.* ■ By the time someone decides to *take corrective action*, the customer may be in too deep. REPLACE WITH *act.* ■ The district will *take appropriate action* to ensure such occurrences do not continue. REPLACE WITH *do what it must.*

April showers bring May flowers A popular prescription (see page 23).

area of expertise A suspect superlative (see page 24). *area; business; calling; craft; field; forte; job; line; métier; occupation; profession; specialty; strength; trade; vocation.*

(we) aren't going to take it anymore A popular prescription (see page 23).

(cost an) arm and a leg A moribund metaphor (see page 21). 1. *a big (brobdingnagian; colossal; enormous; gargantuan; giant; gigantic; grand; great; huge; immense; large; massive; monstrous; prodigious; tremendous; vast) amount; a great deal; a lot.* 2. *costly; dear; expensive; high-priced; precious; priceless; valuable.*

armed and dangerous An inescapable pair (see page 20).

armed (themselves) to the teeth A moribund metaphor (see page 21).

(an) army of A moribund metaphor (see page 21). SEE ALSO *a barrage of.*

paround about A wretched redundancy (see page 25). *about; around.* ■ Let's meet *around about* noon. REPLACE WITH *about* or *around.*

(work) around the clock A moribund metaphor (see page 21). *always; ceaselessly; constantly; continually; continuously; endlessly; eternally; everlastingly; evermore; forever; forevermore; frequently; interminably; nonstop; permanently; perpetually; persistently; recurrently; regularly; repeatedly; unceasingly; unremittingly.*

(just; right) around the corner A moribund metaphor (see page 21). *approaching; at hand; close; close by; coming; forthcoming; imminent; impending; near; nearby; nearing; pending; vicinal.* ■ Deregulation of the utility industry was *just around the corner*, and several other companies were prepared to enter the market. REPLACE WITH *at hand.*

arrow in the heart A moribund metaphor (see page 21). *injury; wound.*

(another) arrow in the quiver A moribund metaphor (see page 21). *device; gambit; maneuver; means; plan; ploy; ruse; scheme; stratagem; strategy; tactic; tool; trick.*

art is long, and life is short A popular prescription (see page 23).

as a man sows so shall he reap A popular prescription (see page 23).

as a matter of fact A wretched redundancy (see page 25). *actually; indeed; in fact; in faith; in reality; in truth; truly.* ■ *As a matter of fact,* children get disappointed when they grow up to find the adult's prescription didn't match the real world. REPLACE WITH *In truth.*

as a result of A wretched redundancy (see page 25). *after; because of; by; due to; following; for; from; in; out of; owing to; through; with.* ■ *As a result of* this letter, ten of us did not attend the wedding. REPLACE WITH *Because of.*

as defined in (the dictionary) An infantile phrase (see page 20). This is a device that only abecedarian writers would ever use; even so, it should always be *x'*d. ■ *As defined in the dictionary,* "Health is the absence of disease." ■ Creationism, *as defined in Webster's New Universal Dictionary,* is the doctrine that matter and all things were created, substantially as they now exist, by an omnipotent creator, and not gradually evolved or developed. SEE ALSO *(the) dictionary defines.*

as far as ... (goes; is concerned) A wretched redundancy (see page 25). *about; as for; as to; concerning; for; in; of; on; over; regarding; respecting; to; toward; with.* ■ *As far as* improvements *go*, you'd have a battle. REPLACE WITH *As for.* ■ *As far as* those bargains *are concerned,* attempts to place measures on the table would be regressive and an illegal act. REPLACE WITH *Concerning.* SEE ALSO *where ... is concerned.*

as far as the eye can see An insipid simile. *all around; all over; all through; broadly; everyplace; everywhere; extensively; panoramically; panoptically; throughout; ubiquitously; universally; widely.*

> The room was enormous, like something in a nightmare, one could hardly see from one end of it to the other, and as far as the eye could see was dotted with tables which were all full. — Barbara Pym, *Excellent Women*

ashes to ashes (dust to dust) A moribund metaphor (see page 21).

(like) asking for the moon An insipid simile.

ask me no questions and I'll tell you no lies A popular prescription (see page 23).

asleep at the switch (wheel) A moribund metaphor (see page 21). 1. *forgetful; careless; heedless; inattentive; lethean; neglectful; negligent; oblivious; remiss; slack; thoughtless; unmindful; unthinking.* 2. *asleep; daydreaming.*

(as) (wholesome) as mom and apple pie An insipid simile. *decent; ethical; exemplary; good; honest; honorable; just; moral; pure; righteous; straight; upright; virtuous; wholesome.*

as (you) sow, so shall (you) reap A popular prescription (see page 23).

as the crow flies A moribund metaphor (see page 21). *by air; directly; lineally; linearly; straight.*

(as) (vain) as the day is long An insipid simile. *acutely; awfully; consumedly; enormously; exceedingly; extraordinarily; extremely; greatly; hugely; immensely; intensely; mightily; prodigiously; severely; terribly; very.* ■ She's *as neurotic as the day is long.* REPLACE WITH *prodigiously neurotic.* ■ Celeste is *as bright as the day is long.* REPLACE WITH *enormously bright.*

as the saying goes (is) An infantile phrase (see page 20). This phrase reminds us of our ordinariness. *As the saying goes (is)* announces our having spoken, and thought, words that countless others have spoken and thought. What thoughts are we missing, what images are unavailable to us because we use the same damn words and phrases again and again? Let us strive for better than banality.

as to A torpid term (see page 24). *about; for; from; in; of, on; to; with.* Except when used to begin a sentence, *as to* is if not solecistic then certainly sloppy for a more precise *about* or *of, for* or *with, from* or *to, on* or *in.* This phrase, midsentence, identifies a philistine, a person who, though he writes, doesn't much care to. ■ One hint *as to* his possibly altered standing comes from the latest version of the *Encyclopaedia Britannica,* which, although Roget was an editor of the seventh edition and a contributor of more than 300,000 words to it, gives him somewhat short shrift today, with an entry of a mere twenty lines. REPLACE WITH *of.* ■ Suddenly expectations and preconceptions *as to* how things should be done and what steps could be taken disappear, often leaving the displaced family members feeling confused, resentful and, perhaps most importantly, alone. REPLACE WITH *of.* ■ For example, testing of a graphics library will require a very different approach *as to* that of a calendar manager. REPLACE WITH *from.* ■ Depending on the night, the meal and the energy of the evening, I also made distinctions *as to* the drink best suited to the occasion. REPLACE WITH *in.*

As to the phrase *as to whether* (A wretched redundancy (see page 25)), delete *as to.* ■ If your browser is not secure, or there is any question *as to whether* or not it is, please download Netscape Navigator, Microsoft Internet Explorer, or an equivalent browser. DELETE *as to.* ■ Yet there has been some question *as to* whether their hearts can take it. DELETE *as to.*

(even) as we speak An infantile phrase (see page 20). *at present; currently; (just; right) now; presently.* Whenever someone says *as we speak*, we should hear *as we misspeak,* for the person who uses this sad phrase instead of, say, *now* or even *at this moment*, speaks unhappily. ■ The team is having a pep rally on campus *as we speak.* REPLACE WITH *now.* ■ Are your forces, *even as we speak*, looking for him in a military way? REPLACE WITH *currently.*

Most often, though, *as we speak,* as well as its synonyms, should be unspoken. ■ But how can we not be afraid with weapons of mass destruction looming over our lives *even as we speak.* DELETE *even as we speak.* ■ The Reno police are holding a news conference right now *as we speak.* DELETE *as we speak.* ■ The hostage situation is still unfolding now *as we speak.* DELETE *as we speak.*

as you make your bed, so you must lie on it A popular prescription (see page 23).

at a crossroad A moribund metaphor (see page 21).

at a fast (good) clip A moribund metaphor (see page 21). *apace; briskly; expeditiously; fast; hastily; hurriedly; posthaste; quickly; rapidly; speedily; swiftly; wingedly.*

at a loss A moribund metaphor (see page 21). *baffled; befuddled; bewildered; confounded; confused; disconcerted; flummoxed; mixed up; muddled; nonplused; perplexed; puzzled.*

at a loss for what to say (words) A moribund metaphor (see page 21). *dumb; mute; quiet; reserved; restrained; reticent; silent; speechless; still; taciturn; tongue-tied; uncommunicative; voiceless; withdrawn; wordless.*

> Gen, in his genius for languages, was often at a loss for what to say when left with only his own words. — Ann Patchett, *Bel Canto*

at a low ebb A moribund metaphor (see page 21).

(hold) at arm's distance (length) A moribund metaphor (see page 21).

> She had always felt that he wanted to keep her at arm's length, and she thought that by showing sympathy she might make him like her more. — Luanne Rice, *Stone Heart*

at a snail's pace A moribund metaphor (see page 21). *deliberately; gradually; laggardly; languidly; lazily; leisurely; slothfully; slowly; sluggishly; snail-paced; unhurriedly.* ■ We have been working day after day with him, but he is improving *at a snail's pace.* REPLACE WITH *unhurriedly.*

at (my) beck and call A moribund metaphor (see page 21). *accepting; accommodating; acquiescent; complacent; complaisant; compliant; cowed; deferential; docile; dutiful; obedient; passive; prostrate; resigned; submissive; subservient; tolerant; tractable; yielding.*

at death's door A moribund metaphor (see page 21). *decaying; declining; deteriorating; disintegrating; dying; ebbing; expiring; fading; failing; near death; sinking; waning.*

at each other's throats A moribund metaphor (see page 21). *arguing; battling; bickering; brawling; clashing; disagreeing; fighting; quarreling; squabbling; wrangling.*

at (my) fingertips A moribund metaphor (see page 21). 1. *recall; recollect; remember; think of.* 2. *accessible; at hand; close; close by; handy; near; nearby; neighboring; vicinal.*

at loggerheads A moribund metaphor (see page 21). *arguing; battling; bickering; brawling; clashing; disagreeing; disputing; fighting; quarreling; squabbling; wrangling.*

at loose ends A moribund metaphor (see page 21). 1. *confused; disorganized; drifting; faltering; in between; irresolute; loose; shaky; swaying; tottering; uncertain; undecided; unfixed; unresolved; unsettled; unsteady; unsure; vacillating; wavering; wobbly.* 2. *bored; idle; inactive; unemployed; unoccupied.*

at (in) one fell swoop A moribund metaphor (see page 21).

> "I was talking," he said through his teeth, and his arm flew in one fell swoop. — Kate Manning, *White Girl*

(all) at sea A moribund metaphor (see page 21). *baffled; befuddled; bewildered; confounded; confused; disconcerted; flummoxed; lost; mixed up; muddled; nonplused; perplexed; puzzled.*

at sixes and sevens A moribund metaphor (see page 21). 1. *baffled; bewildered; confused; flummoxed; muddled; perplexed; uncertain.* 2. *disarranged; disorganized; entangled; jumbled; in disarray; in disorder; tangled.*

at that time A wretched redundancy (see page 25). This phrase and several others like it, including *at that juncture in life, at that moment in our national life, at that point in time, at that stage in the history of my life, at that time in our history*, mean no more than *then.* ■ I wasn't happy with what I was doing *at that juncture in life.* REPLACE WITH *then.* ■ DFSMS did not include any cost input parameters *at that point in time.* REPLACE WITH *then.* SEE ALSO *at this time.*

at the breaking point A moribund metaphor (see page 21).

at the crack of dawn A moribund metaphor (see page 21). *very early.*

(stand) at the crossroads of history A moribund metaphor (see page 21).

at the drop of a hat A moribund metaphor (see page 21). *at once; directly; fast; forthwith; hurriedly; immediately; instantly; momentarily; promptly; quickly; rapidly; right away; speedily; straightaway; summarily; swiftly; without delay.* ■ You can get additional information to reporters *at the drop of a hat* if you make up a press kit in advance. REPLACE WITH *speedily.*

> She also said there was a community of radicals who considered her a heroine and would help her at the drop of a hat. — Danzy Senna, *Caucasia*

at the eleventh hour A moribund metaphor (see page 21). *belatedly; late.*

at the end of (my) rope (tether) A moribund metaphor (see page 21). *dejected; despairing; desperate; despondent; disconsolate; distressed; forlorn; frantic; frenetic; frenzied; hopeless; in despair; woebegone; woeful; wretched.*

at the end of the day A moribund metaphor (see page 21). 1. *eventually; finally; in the end; in time; ultimately.* 2. *all in all; all told; altogether; in all; on the whole; overall.*

The popular phrase was once the equally silly *in the final* (or *last*) *analysis.* More sensible phrases include *eventually, finally, in the end, in time, ultimately* (or, perhaps, *all in all, all told, overall*), but people, unsure of who they are, imitate one another; people today say *at the end of the day.* If we were less inclined to say what others say (and do what others do), the world might be a wholly different place. Reason might even prevail.

In most instances, *at the end of the day* is unnecessary and can, without forfeiting any meaning, be deleted from a sentence. ■ We simply have to acknowledge the fact that the better side won *at the end of the day.* DELETE *at the end of the day.* ■ He wants each library, old or new, to be a place people want to come to, think is enjoyable, get a lot out of and have fun at, because *at the end of the day,* it'll just make their lives better. DELETE *at the end of the day.* ■ Like every other relationship you have personally or professionally you don't always agree on things, but *at the end of the day* he was the manager so even if I didn't like something what could I do about it? DELETE *at the end of the day.* ■ That is a step in the right direction; I just do hope that the alliance will work *at the end of the day.* DELETE *at the end of the day.*

at the helm A moribund metaphor (see page 21). *in charge; in control.*

at the top of (his) game A moribund metaphor (see page 21).

at the top of (my) lungs A moribund metaphor (see page 21). *blaringly; boisterously; boomingly; deafeningly; earsplittingly; loudly; noisily; obstreperously; resoundingly; roaringly; stentorianly; thunderingly; thunderously; tumultuously; vociferously.*

at (behind) the wheel A moribund metaphor (see page 21). *in charge; in control.*

at this time A wretched redundancy (see page 25). This phrase and several others like it, including *at the present* *time, at this juncture in life, at this moment in our national life, at this point in time, at this point in time right now, at this stage in the history of my life, at this time in our history,* mean no more than *at present, now, today,* or *yet.* ■ We don't see any significant breakthroughs *at this juncture.* REPLACE WITH *now.* ■ What can she do to help you *at this stage of the game?* REPLACE WITH *now.* ■ *At this point in time,* the conditions for an agreement have not been met. REPLACE WITH *The conditions for an agreement have not yet been met.* SEE ALSO *at that time.*

attitude An overworked word (see page 22). For example: *attitude problem; holier-than-thou attitude; patronizing attitude; superior attitude; wait-and-see attitude.*

attributable to the fact that A wretched redundancy (see page 25). *because; considering; for; in that; since.* ■ This is *attributable to the fact that* people at Pan Am have done such a good job. REPLACE WITH *because.* SEE ALSO *due to the fact that; owing to the fact that.*

at (his) wit's end A moribund metaphor (see page 21). *baffled; befuddled; bewildered; confounded; confused; disconcerted; flummoxed; mixed up; muddled; nonplused; perplexed; puzzled.*

audible (inaudible) to the ear A wretched redundancy (see page 25). *audible (inaudible).* SEE ALSO *visible (invisible) to the eye.*

au naturel A foreign phrase (see page 19). *bare; disrobed; naked; nude; stripped; unclothed; uncovered; undressed.*

(an) avalanche of A moribund metaphor (see page 21). ■ His antics on the court spawned *an avalanche of* imitators. SEE ALSO *a barrage of.*

(your) average Joe A moribund metaphor (see page 21). *average; common; commonplace; conventional; customary; everyday; familiar; mediocre; middling; normal; ordinary; quotidian; regular; standard; typical; unexceptional; unremarkable; usual.*

avid reader A suspect superlative (see page 24). An *avid reader* suggests someone who reads little more than mysteries, gothic novels, and self-help books.

These are people whose avidity is more for how many books they read than it is for any meaning in books — people, that is, who prefer counting to reading. ■ I am an *avid reader* and my advanced education includes writing courses and an intensive two-year writing course.

avoid (it) like the plague An insipid simile. 1. *abhor; abominate; detest; hate; loathe.* 2. *avoid; dodge; elude; eschew; evade; recoil from; shirk; shrink from; shun; spurn.* ■ Your clients will probably either love Los Angeles or *avoid it like the plague.* REPLACE WITH *loathe it.*

> The clientele were mostly businessmen in three-piece suits laughing boisterously and blowing cigarette smoke in each other's faces, or talking earnestly and confidently to well-dressed young women who were more probably their secretaries than their wives. In short, it was the kind of establishment that Robyn would normally have avoided like the plague. — David Lodge, *Nice Work*

awesome An overworked word (see page 22). Like *awful* and *terrific*, the word *awesome* has been made ridiculous by those who are bent on using it solely in its most popular sense.

Awesome means *awe-inspiring, majestic*, or *terrifying*, but of late, it most often merely means *fantastic* or *terrific* or *great*, worn words all. SEE ALSO *awful; terrific*.

awful An overworked word (see page 22). *Awful* means *awe-inspiring* or *terrifying*, but of late, it means no more than *very bad* or *unpleasant*. SEE ALSO *awesome; terrific*.

(the) ax fell A moribund metaphor (see page 21).

ax (axe) to grind A moribund metaphor (see page 21). *animosity; bitterness; enmity; grievance; grudge; hostility; indignation; ill will; offense; rancor; resentment; spite; umbrage*.

B

babe in the woods A moribund metaphor (see page 21). *amateur; apprentice; beginner; greenhorn; neophyte; newcomer; novice; novitiate; tyro*. ■ He's a *babe in the woods* compared to Clinton and the Democrats. REPLACE WITH *neophyte*.

back (up) against the wall A moribund metaphor (see page 21). 1. *catch; corner; enmesh; ensnare; entangle; entrap; net; snare; trap*. 2. *at risk; endangered; imperiled; in danger; in jeopardy; threatened*. ■ People will do amazing things when *their backs are against the wall*. REPLACE WITH *they're endangered*.

(meanwhile) back at the ranch A moribund metaphor (see page 21).

back in the saddle (again) A moribund metaphor (see page 21).

> Maybe the convertible was not an attempt to get a concert pianist back in the saddle — back, as it were, on the horse that had thrown him — but an invitation to the mindless, happy, noisy, unambitious life that till then had been denied him. — Christopher Miller, *Sudden Noises from Inanimate Objects: A Novel in Liner Notes*

back into a corner A moribund metaphor (see page 21). *catch; corner; enmesh; ensnare; entangle; entrap; net; snare; trap*.

(get) back on (his) feet A moribund metaphor (see page 21). *ameliorate; amend; come round; convalesce; gain strength; get better; heal; improve; look up; meliorate; mend; rally; recover; recuperate; refresh; regain strength; renew; revive; strengthen*. ■ Even the construction industry is starting to *get back on its feet*. REPLACE WITH *recover*.

back on track A moribund metaphor (see page 21).

back to basics A torpid term (see page 24). ■ Banks and savings and loans are getting *back to basics* and concentrating on home mortgages.

back to square one A moribund metaphor (see page 21).

(go) back to the drawing board A moribund metaphor (see page 21). ■ Beware of protracted and angry discussions; they are usually a sign that there is not enough support for the idea, and you should go *back to the drawing board.*

back to the salt mines A moribund metaphor (see page 21).

back to the wall A moribund metaphor (see page 21). 1. *at risk; endangered; hard-pressed; imperiled; in a bind; in a fix; in a jam; in a predicament; in a quandary; in danger; in difficulty; in jeopardy; in peril; in trouble; jeopardized.* 2. *at bay; caught; cornered; enmeshed; ensnared; entangled; entrapped; netted; snared; trapped.*

bad apple A moribund metaphor (see page 21). *brute; degenerate; fiend; knave; lout; rake; rascal; rogue; ruffian; scamp; scoundrel; villain.*

bad blood (between them) A moribund metaphor (see page 21). *abhorrence; anger; animosity; antipathy; aversion; detestation; enmity; hate; hatred; hostility; ill will; loathing; malice; malignity; rancor; repugnance; revulsion; venom; virulence.*

bad egg A moribund metaphor (see page 21). *brute; degenerate; fiend; knave; lout; rake; rascal; rogue; ruffian; scamp; scoundrel; villain.*

badge of courage (honor) A moribund metaphor (see page 21).

(a) bad penny A moribund metaphor (see page 21). *bastard; blackguard; cad; charlatan; cheat; cheater; fake; fraud; impostor; knave; mountebank; phony; pretender; quack; rascal; rogue; scoundrel; swindler; undesirable; villain; wretch.*

(a) bad penny always turns up A popular prescription (see page 23).

bag and baggage An inescapable pair (see page 20). 1. *accouterments; baggage; bags; belongings; cases; effects; encumbrances; equipment; gear; impedimenta; luggage; portmanteaus; possessions; property; sacks; satchels; stuff; suitcases; supplies; things.* 2. *altogether; completely; entirely; fully; roundly; thoroughly; totally; utterly; wholly.*

bag of bones A moribund metaphor (see page 21). *asthenic; attenuated; bony; cachectic; emaciated; gaunt; lank; lanky; lean; narrow; rail-thin; scraggy; scrawny; skeletal; skinny; slender; slight; slim; spare; spindly; svelte; sylphid; thin; trim; wispy.*

bag (bagful) of tricks A moribund metaphor (see page 21). *accouterment; equipage; equipment; gear; paraphernalia; resources; supplies; things; tools.*

baker's dozen A moribund metaphor (see page 21). *thirteen.*

(as) bald as a baby's backside An insipid simile. *alopecic; bald; baldheaded; baldpated; glabrous; hairless; depilated; pilgarlic; smooth; tonsured.*

(as) bald as a billiard ball An insipid simile. *alopecic; bald; baldheaded; bald-*

pated; glabrous; hairless; depilated; pilgarlic; smooth; tonsured.

bald is beautiful A quack equation (see page 23).

ball of fire A moribund metaphor (see page 21). *active; animated; ardent; dynamic; emotional; energetic; impassioned; intense; lively; passionate; spirited; sprightly; vigorous; vital; vivacious.*

ballpark figure A moribund metaphor (see page 21). *appraisal; assessment; estimate; estimation; guess; idea; impression; opinion; sense.* ■ Can you give me a *ballpark figure* of how much you made last year? REPLACE WITH *idea.*

(the) ball's in (your) court A moribund metaphor (see page 21). ■ I think, nationally, *the ball is* definitely *in our court* now.

bang for (your) buck An infantile phrase (see page 20). *quality; value; worth.*

banging (my) head against the wall A moribund metaphor (see page 21).

baptism of fire A moribund metaphor (see page 21).

bare-bones (budget) A moribund metaphor (see page 21).

bare essentials (necessities) An inescapable pair (see page 20).

barefaced (bold-faced) lie An inescapable pair (see page 20).

bargaining chip A moribund metaphor (see page 21).

bark at the moon A moribund metaphor (see page 21).

(her) bark is worse than (her) bite A moribund metaphor (see page 21).

bark up the wrong tree A moribund metaphor (see page 21). *amiss; astray; deceived; deluded; erring; erroneous; fallacious; false; faulty; inaccurate; incorrect; in error; misguided; misinformed; mislead; mistaken; not correct; not right; wrong.*

> Ray had neither encouraged nor discouraged her over Minkie — he hadn't seemed at all interested in the party — although he said something about her barking up the wrong tree with John Lenier. — Tessa Hadley, *Everything Will Be All Right*

(a) barking dog never bites A popular prescription (see page 23).

(a) barrage of A moribund metaphor (see page 21). If our language seems languid, it's partly because our metaphors are moribund.

This, *a barrage of,* is one of a certain kind of moribund metaphor that is especially irksome to come upon; *a bastion of, a chorus of, a cloud of, a deluge of, a firestorm of, a flood of, a flurry of, a hailstorm of, a mountain of, an army of, an avalanche of, an explosion of, an ocean of, an orgy of, a rising tide of, a sea of, a small army of, a spate of, a storm of, a symphony of, a torrent of, a world of* are all shabby, unimaginative expressions.

These are the least evocative, the least metaphorical, of metaphors. ■ He says *the barrage of marketing* has made teens tougher to teach.

barrel of laughs A moribund metaphor (see page 21). *hilarious; hysterical; side-splitting; uproarious.*

basically An overworked word (see page 22). People often use *basically* thinking it lends an intellectual air to the meaning of their words. *Basically*, in truth, only steals the sense from whatever words accompany it, for it proclaims their uncertainty and inexactitude as loudly as it does the speaker's or writer's pomposity.

Of course, there are also people, with few pretensions, who use *basically* either because they do not know what they say or because they do not know what to say. ■ *Basically*, the program is designed to operate with the same skills used when doing the exercise with a pencil and paper. ■ If the man wants custody, he must prove the woman to be *basically* unfit. ■ The rest of the day will be *basically* partly cloudy. ■ What *basically* began as an experiment to determine whether a family-type YMCA would survive quickly evolved into a challenge to serve a very enthusiastic community. ■ *Basically*, the next step is adding the molasses.

basic (and) fundamental A wretched redundancy (see page 25). *basal; basic; elementary; essential; fundamental; primary; rudimentary.*

basic principle An inescapable pair (see page 20). Seldom do we find *principle* without the word *basic* preceding it. A principle, however, is a basic truth or assumption. ■ Whether or not you are aware of it, there are *basic principles* of human interaction. DELETE *basic*. ■ The *basic principle* of laser protection is the same as for any direct fire weapon. DELETE *basic*.

basis in fact (reality) A wretched redundancy (see page 25). *basis; fact; reality; truth; veracity.* ■ The June 2 editorial that describes the final, wheezy stages of the movement to eliminate cigarettes has no *basis in fact*. REPLACE WITH *basis*. ■ To see whether such beliefs have any *basis in fact*, five different brands of fruit cocktail were chosen. REPLACE WITH *veracity*.

(a) bastion of A moribund metaphor (see page 21). SEE ALSO *a barrage of.*

bathed in tears A moribund metaphor (see page 21).

(like) a bat out of hell An insipid simile. *abruptly; apace; at once; briskly; directly; expeditiously; fast; forthwith; hastily; hurriedly; immediately; instantaneously; instantly; posthaste; promptly; quickly; rapidly; rashly; right away; speedily; straightaway; suddenly; swiftly; wingedly.*

> The word saved me, as words always have, and I could stir again, and stir I did, charging up the eastern loop of the trail back like a bat out of hell. — Jincy Willett, *Winner of the National Book Award: A Novel of Fame, Honor, and Really Bad Weather*

(has) bats in (his) belfry A moribund metaphor (see page 21). *batty; cracked; crazy; daft; demented; deranged; fey; foolish; goofy; insane; lunatic; mad; maniacal; neurotic; nuts; nutty; psychotic; raving; silly; squirrelly; touched; unbalanced; unhinged; unsound; wacky; zany.*

batten down the hatches A moribund metaphor (see page 21).

batting a thousand A moribund metaphor (see page 21).

> I was batting a thousand on predicting human behavior. Maybe *I* should become a psychologist. — Jane Mendle, *Kissing in Technicolor*

(good) batting average A moribund metaphor (see page 21).

battle lines are drawn A moribund metaphor (see page 21).

(a) beacon (ray) of hope A moribund metaphor (see page 21). *anticipation; expectancy; expectation; hope; hopefulness; optimism; possibility; promise; prospect; sanguinity.*

(please) be advised that An ineffectual phrase (see page 19) (see page 19). This phrase is designed to make the reader pay attention to whatever follows it. The effect it has on anyone with sensibility, however, is quite the opposite: *(please) be advised that* stupefies the attentive reader thereby ensuring that whatever follows it is hardly attended to and, even, roundly ridiculed. ■ *Please be advised that* some of the ads in this category may require a fee for services or processing. DELETE *Please be advised that.* ■ *Please be advised that* the valuation below is proposed and not final. DELETE *Please be advised that.* ■ *Please be advised that* this office has been retained by North American Mortgage Company to conduct real estate closing for the above-referenced property. DELETE *Please be advised that.* ■ *Please be advised that* it takes seven to ten days to process any request for medical records information. DELETE *Please be advised that.* ■ *Please be advised that* the Norfolk County Mosquito Control Project is now accepting applications for the position of Assistant Superintendent. DELETE *Please be advised that.* ■ *Please be advised that* I will be on vacation from June 26 to July 10. DELETE *Please be advised that.* SEE ALSO *(please) be informed that; this is to inform you that.*

be-all and end-all A moribund metaphor (see page 21). *acme; ideal; perfection; quintessence; ultimate.*

(catch a) bear by the tail A moribund metaphor (see page 21).

beat about (around) the bush A moribund metaphor (see page 21). *avoid; be equivocal; be evasive; dissemble; dodge; doubletalk; equivocate; evade; fence; hedge; palter; prevaricate; quibble; shuffle; sidestep; stall; tergiversate; waffle.*

beat a path to (your door) A moribund metaphor (see page 21). *dash; hasten; hurry; hustle; make haste; race; run; rush; scamper; scurry; sprint.*

beat a (hasty) retreat A moribund metaphor (see page 21). *abscond; clear out; decamp; depart; desert; disappear; escape; exit; flee; fly; go; go away; leave; move on; part; pull out; quit; retire; retreat; run away; take flight; take off; vacate; vanish; withdraw.*

beat (his) brains out A moribund metaphor (see page 21). 1. *assail; assault; attack; batter; beat; cudgel; flagellate; flog; hit; lambaste; lash; lick; mangle; pound; pummel; strike; thrash; trounce.* 2. *annihilate; assassinate; butcher; destroy; exterminate; kill; massacre; murder; slaughter; slay.* 3. *beat; conquer; crush; defeat;*

outdo; overcome; overpower; overwhelm; prevail; quell; rout; succeed; triumph; trounce; vanquish; win. 4. *attempt; drudge; endeavor; essay; exert; grind; grub; labor; moil; slave; strain; strive; struggle; sweat; toil; travail; try; work.*

beat (them) hands down A moribund metaphor (see page 21). *beat; conquer; crush; defeat; outdo; overcome; overpower; overwhelm; prevail; quell; rout; succeed; triumph; trounce; vanquish; win.*

(like) beating (flogging) a dead horse An insipid simile. *barren; bootless; effete; feckless; feeble; fruitless; futile; impotent; inadequate; inconsequential; inconsiderable; ineffective; ineffectual; infertile; insignificant; inutile; meaningless; meritless; nugatory; null; of no value; pointless; powerless; profitless; purposeless; redundant; sterile; superfluous; trifling; trivial; unavailing; unimportant; unnecessary; unproductive; unprofitable; unserviceable; unworthy; useless; vain; valueless; weak; worthless.*

beat (smashed) into (to) a pulp A moribund metaphor (see page 21). 1. *assail; assault; attack; batter; beat; cudgel; flagellate; flog; hit; lambaste; lash; lick; mangle; pound; pummel; strike; thrash; trounce.* 2. *beat; conquer; crush; defeat; outdo; overcome; overpower; overwhelm; prevail; quell; rout; succeed; triumph; trounce; vanquish; win.* 3. *crush; flatten; macerate; mash; pound; pulp; pulverize; squash.*

> He knew that the baby was going to hit first, and he would see it, would know it for a whole fraction of a second before he was smashed into a pulp himself. — Katherine Dunn, *Geek Love*

beat (it) into the ground A moribund metaphor (see page 21). *debilitate; deplete; drain; empty; enervate; exhaust; fatigue; overdo; overwork; sap; tire; wear out; weary.*

beat the bushes A moribund metaphor (see page 21). *hunt; look for; quest; ransack; rummage; scour; search; seek.*

beat the (living) daylights out of A moribund metaphor (see page 21). 1. *assail; assault; attack; batter; beat; cudgel; flagellate; flog; hit; lambaste; lash; lick; mangle; pound; pummel; strike; thrash; trounce.* 2. *beat; conquer; crush; defeat; outdo; overcome; overpower; overwhelm; prevail; quell; rout; succeed; triumph; trounce; vanquish; win.* 3. *castigate; chastise; discipline; penalize; punish.*

beat the drum A moribund metaphor (see page 21). *advertise; announce; broadcast; cry out; declaim; disseminate; exclaim; proclaim; promulgate; publicize; publish; shout; trumpet; yell.*

beat the stuffing out of A moribund metaphor (see page 21). 1. *assail; assault; attack; batter; beat; cudgel; flagellate; flog; hit; lambaste; lash; lick; mangle; pound; pummel; strike; thrash; trounce.* 2. *beat; conquer; crush; defeat; outdo; overcome; overpower; overwhelm; prevail; quell; rout; succeed; triumph; trounce; vanquish; win.*

beat to death A moribund metaphor (see page 21). 1. *annihilate; assassinate; butcher; destroy; exterminate; kill; massacre; murder; slaughter; slay.* 2. *debilitate; deplete; drain; empty; enervate; exhaust; fatigue; overdo; overwork; sap; tire; wear out; weary.* SEE ALSO *to death.*

beat (him) to the punch A moribund metaphor (see page 21).

beat up on (each other) A moribund metaphor (see page 21). *assail; assault; attack; batter; beat; cudgel; flagellate; flog; hit; lambaste; lash; lick; mangle; pound; pummel; strike; thrash; trounce.*

beauteous A withered word (see page 24). *beautiful.* ■ Saturday should be a *beauteous* day. REPLACE WITH *beautiful.*

beautiful baby An inescapable pair (see page 20).

beauty and the beast A moribund metaphor (see page 21).

beauty is in the eye of the beholder A popular prescription (see page 23).

because (that's why) An infantile phrase (see page 20). ■ Why did you hit him? *Because.* SEE ALSO *it just happened.*

because of the fact that A wretched redundancy (see page 25). *because; considering; for; given; in that; since.* ■ I married him only *because of the fact that* his family has money. REPLACE WITH *because.* ■ Many people told me I had to break off my relationship with her *because of the fact that* I was being unfair to her. REPLACE WITH *because.* SEE ALSO *by virtue of the fact that; considering the fact that; given the fact that; in consideration of the fact that; in view of the fact that; on account of the fact that.*

because why? An infantile phrase (see page 20). ■ They were afraid of him, too. *Because why?* DELETE *Because.*

(no) bed of roses A moribund metaphor (see page 21). *agreeable; ambrosial; beguiling; celestial; charming; delectable; delicious; delightful; divine; enchanting; engaging; enjoyable; fun; heavenly; glorious; gratifying; inviting; joyful; joyous; luscious; pleasant; pleasing; pleasurable.*

(a) beehive of activity A moribund metaphor (see page 21). *active; astir; bustling; busy; buzzing; energetic; humming; hopping; hustling; lively; vigorous.*

(a) bee in (her) bonnet A moribund metaphor (see page 21). 1. *caprice; crotchet; fancy; humor; impulse; maggot; notion; quirk; urge; vagary; whim.* 2. *craze; enthusiasm; fixation; infatuation; mania; obsession; passion; preoccupation.*

> Poor Nelson. He has this bee in his bonnet — doing something for this girl nobody knows. — John Updike, *Rabbit Remembered*

(she's) been around the block (and back) A moribund metaphor (see page 21). 1. *adult; aged; aging; elderly; full-grown; hoary; hoary-headed; mature; old; worn.* 2. *able; adept; apt; capable; competent; deft; dexterous; experienced; expert; practiced; proficient; seasoned; skilled; skillful; veteran.*

before (you) can say (Jack Robinson) A moribund metaphor (see page 21). *abruptly; apace; at once; briskly; directly; expeditiously; fast; forthwith; hastily; hurriedly; immediately; instantaneously; instantly; posthaste; promptly; quickly; rapidly; rashly; right away; speedily; straightaway; suddenly; swiftly; unexpectedly; wingedly.*

beg, borrow, or steal A moribund metaphor (see page 21).

beggars can't be choosers A popular prescription (see page 23).

begin (start) a new chapter (in my life) A moribund metaphor (see page 21).

behind closed doors A moribund metaphor (see page 21). *clandestinely; confidentially; covertly; furtively; mysteriously; in private; in secret; privately; quietly; secludedly; secretly; slyly; stealthily; surreptitiously; undercover.*

behind every successful man stands a woman A popular prescription (see page 23).

behind the eight ball A moribund metaphor (see page 21). *at risk; endangered; hard-pressed; imperiled; in a bind; in a fix; in a jam; in a predicament; in a quandary; in danger; in difficulty; in jeopardy; in peril; in trouble; jeopardized.*

(work) behind the scenes A moribund metaphor (see page 21). *clandestinely; confidentially; covertly; furtively; mysteriously; in private; in secret; privately; quietly; secludedly; secretly; slyly; stealthily; surreptitiously; undercover.*

behind the times A moribund metaphor (see page 21). *antediluvian; antiquated; archaic; dead; obsolescent; obsolete; old; old-fashioned; outdated; outmoded; out of date; out of fashion; passé; superannuated.*

(I'll) be honest with you A plebeian sentiment (see page 23).

behoove A withered word (see page 24). 1. *be advantageous for; benefit; be worthwhile to.* 2. *be necessary for; be proper for.*

(please) be informed that An ineffectual phrase (see page 19) (see page 19). ■ *Please be informed that* your wife has retained my office in the matter of her petition for a divorce. DELETE *Please be informed that.* ■ If you are running a version of Almanac earlier than 3.0, *please be informed that* the format of the desktop data files has been changed. DELETE *please be informed that.* SEE ALSO *(please) be advised that; this is to inform you that.*

(like) being run over (getting hit) by a (Mack) truck An insipid simile. *atomized; crushed; dashed; demolished; depleted; depressed; destroyed; devastated; distraught; distressed; exhausted; obliterated; overcome; overpowered; overwhelmed; prostrate; ravaged; ruined; shattered; undone; upset.* ■ I feel *like I've been run over by a Mac truck.* REPLACE WITH *obliterated.*

bells and whistles A moribund metaphor (see page 21). *adornments; attributes; characteristics; decorations; embellishments; features; flourishes; frills; highlights; innovations; novelties; ornaments; properties; qualities; specialties; traits.* ■ They sport few of the *bells and whistles* found in programs like Netscape and Mosaic. REPLACE WITH *features.*

bell the cat A moribund metaphor (see page 21).

> It was time to bell the cat, or at least inquire about its alibi. — Joan Hess, *The Murder at the Mimosa Inn*

below par A moribund metaphor (see page 21). *inferior; poor; second-class; second-rate; shoddy; subordinate; substandard.*

(hit) below the belt A moribund metaphor (see page 21). *dishonorable; foul; inequit-able; unconscientious; underhanded; unethical; unfair; unjust; unprincipled; unscrupulous; unsportsmanlike.*

below (under) the radar (of) (screen) A moribund metaphor (see page 21). 1. *disregarded; hidden; ignored; imperceptible; indiscernible; invisible; overlooked; undetectable; undetected; unheard of; unknown; unnoticeable; unnoticed; unobserved; unperceived; unrevealed; unseen.* 2. *discreet; inconspicuous; self-effacing; unassuming; understated; unobtrusive.* ■ The underreported remain *below the radars of* most news organizations. REPLACE WITH *imperceptible to.* ■ We don't need to be *under the radar* anymore, we need to be out there. REPLACE WITH *unobtrusive.*

belt-tightening (measures) A moribund metaphor (see page 21).

bend (my) ear A moribund metaphor (see page 21).

bend over backward(s) A moribund metaphor (see page 21). *aim; attempt; endeavor; essay; exert; labor; moil; strain; strive; struggle; toil; try hard; undertake; work at.* ■ If anything, he will have to *bend over backward* to not appear to be showing favoritism. REPLACE WITH *struggle.*

be nice A plebeian sentiment (see page 23). "*Be nice,*" we often are admonished. There can be no complaint with being agreeable when agreeability is warranted, but to soporiferously accept niceness as a virtue, untarnished and true, is utterly benighted.

To be capable of expressing anger and indignation is thwarted by our society's placing a premium on politeness.

Let us not, of course, be rude gratuitously, nor seek to be singular for its own sake, nor foolish or fantastic for the quick cachet. Do, however, let us become more concerned with giving fuller expression to ourselves.

We do possibly irreparable harm to ourselves when we, to avoid unpleasantness, fail to show another how we truly feel. Unknown to ourselves and unknowable to others we homunculi are, for anonymity is won when anger is lost. SEE ALSO *if you can't say something nice, don't say anything; I'm sorry.*

bent out of shape A moribund metaphor (see page 21). 1. *agitated; anxious; aroused; displeased; disquieted; excited; flustered; perturbed; troubled; upset; worried.* 2. *acerbated; angered; annoyed; bothered; disturbed; exasperated; galled; irked; irritated; miffed; nettled; provoked; rankled; riled; roiled; upset; vexed.*

(the) best and (the) brightest A suspect superlative (see page 24). *best; brightest; choice; choicest; elite; excellent; finest; first-class; first-rate; foremost; greatest; highest; matchless; nonpareil; optimal; optimum; outstanding; paramount; peerless; preeminent; premium; prominent; select; superior; superlative; top; unequaled; unexcelled; unmatched; unrivaled; unsurpassed.* ■ He decried the "cult of efficiency" into which have fallen so many of *the best and brightest* of the conservative young. REPLACE WITH *the brightest.* ■ Bandied about were the names of several of *the best and brightest* of the next generation. REPLACE WITH *the elite.*

(the) best defense is a good offense A popular prescription (see page 23).

(the) best (that) money can buy A suspect superlative (see page 24).

(in) (the) best of all (possible) worlds A suspect superlative (see page 24). *best; choice; elite; excellent; finest; first-class; first-rate; foremost; greatest; highest; ideal; matchless; nonpareil; optimal; optimum; outstanding; paramount; peerless; preeminent; premium; prominent; select; superior; superlative; supreme; top; unequaled; unexcelled; unmatched; unrivaled; unsurpassed.* ■ *In the best of all possible worlds,* test procedures for which neither type of error is possible could be developed. REPLACE WITH *ideally.*

best of the bunch (lot) A suspect superlative (see page 24). *best; brightest; choice; choicest; elite; excellent; finest; first-class; first-rate; foremost; greatest; highest; matchless; nonpareil; optimal; optimum; outstanding; paramount; peerless; preeminent; premium; prominent; select; superior; superlative; top; unequaled; unexcelled; unmatched; unrivaled; unsurpassed.*

best-selling author A suspect superlative (see page 24). *Best-selling authors,* of course, are often responsible for the worst written books. SEE ALSO *a good read; a (must) read.*

(the) best (greatest) thing since sliced bread A moribund metaphor (see page 21).

(the) best things in life are free A popular prescription (see page 23).

(she's) (the) best thing that ever happened to (me) A plebeian sentiment (see page 23).

bet (your) bottom dollar (life) A moribund metaphor (see page 21). ■ I would have *bet my bottom dollar* that this would not have happened.

(my) better half An infantile phrase (see page 20). *consort; helpmate; helpmeet; husband; mate; spouse; wife.*

better late than never A popular prescription (see page 23).

better safe than sorry A popular prescription (see page 23).

(it's) better than nothing A popular prescription (see page 23).

bet the farm (ranch) (on) A moribund metaphor (see page 21).

between a rock and a hard place A moribund metaphor (see page 21). *at risk; endangered; hard-pressed; imperiled; in a bind; in a dilemma; in a fix; in a jam; in a predicament; in a quandary; in danger; in difficulty; in jeopardy; in peril; in trouble; jeopardized.* ■ When you need to regenerate a degraded stripe set with parity, you will be faced with a *rock and a hard place* dilemma. DELETE *rock and a hard place.*

> But now my father's advice and my sister's counsel war in my head. Between a rock and a hard place, I must find a middle ground. — Donna Hill, *An Ordinary Woman*

between Scylla and Charybdis A moribund metaphor (see page 21). *at risk; endangered; hard-pressed; imperiled; in a bind; in a dilemma; in a fix; in a jam; in a predicament; in a quandary; in danger; in difficulty; in jeopardy; in peril; in trouble; jeopardized.*

between the devil and the deep blue sea A moribund metaphor (see page 21). *at risk; endangered; hard-pressed; imperiled; in a bind; in a dilemma; in a fix; in a jam; in a predicament; in a quandary; in danger; in difficulty; in jeopardy; in peril; in trouble; jeopardized.*

between you and me (and the four walls) A moribund metaphor (see page 21). *classified; confidential; personal; private; privy; restricted; secret.*

betwixt A withered word (see page 24). *between.*

betwixt and between An inescapable pair (see page 20). *divided; drifting; faltering; in between; irresolute; loose; shaky; swaying; torn; tottering; uncertain; undecided; unfixed; unresolved; unsettled; unsteady; unsure; vacillating; wavering; wobbly.*

(a) bevy of beauties An infantile phrase (see page 20).

beware of Greeks bearing gifts A popular prescription (see page 23).

beyond (without) a shadow of a doubt A moribund metaphor (see page 21). *absolutely; conclusively; decidedly; definitely; incontrovertibly; indisputably; indubitably; irrefragably; irrefutably; positively; unconditionally; uncontestably; undeniably; undoubtedly; unequivocally; unmistakably; unquestionably.*

beyond the pale A moribund metaphor (see page 21). *improper; inappropriate; unacceptable; unreasonable; unseemly; unsuitable; unthinkable.*

beyond (my) wildest dreams A moribund metaphor (see page 21). *astonishing; astounding; beyond belief; beyond comprehension; breathtaking; extraordinary; fabulous; fantastic; implausible; imponderable; inconceivable; incredible; marvelous; miraculous; outlandish; overwhelming; prodigious; sensational; spectacular; unbelievable; unimaginable; unthinkable; wonderful.*

> I was incredulous because this was so far beyond my wildest hopes. — Chris Stewart, *Driving Over Lemons*

(as) big as a house An insipid simile. *big; brobdingnagian; colossal; enormous; gargantuan; giant; gigantic; grand; great; huge; immense; large; massive; monstrous; prodigious; tremendous; vast.*

(as) big as life An insipid simile.

big cheese A moribund metaphor (see page 21).

1. *administrator; boss; brass; chief; commander; director; executive; foreman; head; headman; leader; manager; master; (high) muckamuck; officer; official; overseer; president; principal; superintendent;*

supervisor. 2. *aristocrat; dignitary; eminence; lord; luminary; magnate; mogul; notable; patrician; personage; ruler; sovereign; worthy.*

big deal An infantile phrase (see page 20). *appreciable; central; climacteric; consequential; considerable; critical; crucial; essential; grave; major; material; important; meaningful; momentous; pivotal; pregnant; principal; serious; significant; substantial; vital; weighty.*

big fish in a small pond A moribund metaphor (see page 21).

bigger is better A quack equation (see page 23).

bigger isn't necessarily better A popular prescription (see page 23).

(the) bigger the better A quack equation (see page 23).

(the) bigger they are, the harder they fall A popular prescription (see page 23).

big gun A moribund metaphor (see page 21). 1. *administrator; boss; brass; chief; commander; director; executive; foreman; head; headman; leader; manager; master; (high) muckamuck; officer; official; overseer; president; principal; superintendent; supervisor.* 2. *aristocrat; dignitary; eminence; lord; luminary; magnate; mogul; notable; patrician; personage; ruler; sovereign; worthy.*

(the) big picture A moribund metaphor (see page 21). ■ Let's not make decisions without looking at *the big picture.*

big shot A moribund metaphor (see page 21). 1. *administrator; boss; brass; chief; commander; director; executive; foreman; head; headman; leader; manager; master; (high) muckamuck; officer; official; overseer; president; principal; superintendent; supervisor.* 2. *aristocrat; dignitary; eminence; lord; luminary; magnate; mogul; notable; patrician; personage; ruler; sovereign; worthy.*

big-ticket (item) A moribund metaphor (see page 21). 1. *costly; expensive; high-priced.* 2. *all-important; central; chief; imperative; important; key; main; significant; vital.* ■ We can market these *big-ticket* items, which have a large profit margin. REPLACE WITH *expensive.*

> In the many months it had taken me to retrieve the box from the closet, I discovered that I had forgiven her for a number of things, although for none of the big-ticket items — like having existed at all, for instance, and then having lived so long. — Anne Lamott, *Plan B: Further Thoughts on Faith*

(like a) big weight has been lifted from (my) shoulders An insipid simile. 1. *allay; alleviate; assuage; lighten; mitigate; relieve; soothe.* 2. *deliver; disburden; disencumber; disentangle; emancipate; extricate; free; liberate; manumit; release; relieve; save; set free; unburden; unchain; unencumber; unfetter; unshackle.*

big wheel A moribund metaphor (see page 21). 1. *administrator; boss; brass; chief; commander; director; executive; foreman; head; headman; leader; manager; master; (high) muckamuck; officer; official; overseer; president; principal; superintendent; supervisor.* 2. *aristocrat;*

dignitary; eminence; lord; luminary; magnate; mogul; notable; patrician; personage; ruler; sovereign; worthy.

(a) bird in the hand (is worth two in the bush) A popular prescription (see page 23).

bird's-eye view A moribund metaphor (see page 21). *outline; overview; profile; review; sketch; summary; survey.*

birds of a feather (flock together) A moribund metaphor (see page 21). *akin; alike; commensurate; comparable; consonant; duplicate; equal; equivalent; identical; indistinguishable; interchangeable; like; same; similar; undifferentiated.* ■ Politically, they are *birds of a feather.* REPLACE WITH *indistinguishable.*

bite (his) head (nose) off A moribund metaphor (see page 21). *admonish; animadvert; berate; castigate; censure; chasten; chastise; chide; condemn; criticize; denounce; denunciate; discipline; excoriate; fulminate against; imprecate; impugn; inveigh against; objurgate; punish; rebuke; remonstrate; reprehend; reprimand; reproach; reprobate; reprove; revile; scold; swear at; upbraid; vituperate.*

bite off more than (he) can chew A moribund metaphor (see page 21). 1. *overcommit; overpledge. 2. arrogant; brazen; cocksure; overconfident.* ■ Even in private circles, there is concern that the government has *bitten off more than it can chew.*

> The truth was that Joe was a talented but careless performer, liable to bite off more than he could chew. — Michael Chabon, *The Amazing Adventures of Kavalier & Clay*

bite the bullet A moribund metaphor (see page 21). *bear; endure; put up with; stand; suffer; tolerate.*

bite the dust A moribund metaphor (see page 21). 1. *decease; depart; die; expire; extinguish; pass away; pass on; perish; terminate.* 2. *be beaten; be conquered; be crushed; be defeated; be outdone; be overcome; be overpowered; be overwhelmed; be quelled; be routed; be trounced; be vanquished.* 3. *cease; close; complete; conclude; derail; desist; discontinue; end; finish; halt; quit; settle; stop; terminate.* 4. *be unsuccessful; bomb; break down; collapse; fail; fall short; falter; fizzle; flop; fold; founder; mess up; miscarry; not succeed; stumble; topple.*

(they) bite the hand that feeds (them) A moribund metaphor (see page 21). *unappreciative; ungrateful; unthankful.*

bite your tongue A moribund metaphor (see page 21).

bits and pieces An inescapable pair (see page 20). *bits; chunks; components; crumbs; elements; factors; fragments; ingredients; modicums; morsels; nuggets; parts; particles; pieces; scraps; segments; shreds; snips; snippets; specks.* ■ All the *bits and pieces* that make up the whole must be carefully and objectively examined. REPLACE WITH *elements.*

> The ancestors of the place hovered over the bits and pieces of their finished lives. — Annie Proulx, *That Old Ace in the Hole*

bitter acrimony An inescapable pair (see page 20).

(a) bitter (tough) pill to swallow A moribund metaphor (see page 21).

(as) black as coal An insipid simile. *black; blackish; caliginous; dark; ebony; ecchymotic; fuliginous; inky; jet; nigrescent; nigritudinous; raven; sable; swarthy; tenebrific; tenebrous.*

(as) black as night An insipid simile. *black; blackish; caliginous; dark; ebony; ecchymotic; fuliginous; inky; jet; nigrescent; nigritudinous; raven; sable; swarthy; tenebrific; tenebrous.*

> After that speech he glared at me in silence, then flung down the spear he had snatched up in his sudden rage and stalked out of the house and into the wood, but before long he was back again seated in his old place, brooding on my words with a face as black as night. — W. H. Hudson, *Green Mansions*

(as) black as pitch An insipid simile. *black; blackish; caliginous; dark; ebony; ecchymotic; fuliginous; inky; jet; nigrescent; nigritudinous; raven; sable; swarthy; tenebrific; tenebrous.*

(as) black as the ace of spades An insipid simile. *black; blackish; caliginous; dark; ebony; ecchymotic; fuliginous; inky; jet; nigrescent; nigritudinous; raven; sable; swarthy; tenebrific; tenebrous.*

black sheep (of the family) A moribund metaphor (see page 21). *curiosity; deviant; eccentric; extremist; iconoclast; individual; individualist; maverick; misfit; nonconformist; oddball; oddity; renegade; undesirable.*

> Nate had been labeled the black sheep of the family years ago. — Robin Jones Gunn, *Gardenias for Breakfast*

blah, blah, blah A grammatical gimmick (see page 19). ■ He told me, I want you to come out here; I miss you; *blah, blah, blah.* DELETE *blah, blah, blah.* SEE ALSO *and so on, and so forth; et cetera, et cetera.*

blast from the past An infantile phrase (see page 20).

blatant lie An inescapable pair (see page 20).

blessed event An infantile phrase (see page 20). 1. *baby; infant; newborn.* 2. *birth; childbearing; childbirth; parturition.*

blessed with (has) the gift of gab An infantile phrase (see page 20). *babbling; blathering; chatty; facile; fluent; garrulous; glib; jabbering; logorrheic; long-winded; loquacious; prolix; talkative; verbose; voluble; windy.*

(a) blessing in disguise A moribund metaphor (see page 21).

(as) blind as a bat An insipid simile. 1. *blind; eyeless; purblind; sightless; unseeing; unsighted; visionless.* 2. *addleheaded; bovine; cretinous; decerebrate; dense; dull; dull-witted; fatuous; fat-witted; half-witted; harebrained; hebetudinous; idiotic; ignorant; imbecilic; incogitant; insensate; mindless; moronic; muddled; nescient; obtuse; phlegmatic; slow; slow-witted; sluggish; thick; torpid; undiscerning; unintelligent; vacuous; witless.*

blind faith An inescapable pair (see page 20).

(the) blind leading the blind A moribund metaphor (see page 21).

(a) blip on the (radar) screen A moribund metaphor (see page 21). *frivolous; inappreciable; immaterial; inconsequential; inconsiderable; insignificant; meager; meaningless; minor; negligible; next to nothing; nugatory; paltry; petty; scant; scanty; scarcely anything; slight; trifling; trivial; unimportant; unsubstantial; worthless.*

As laughable as it is moribund, *a blip on the (radar) screen* belies the writing ability of whoever uses it. ■ War and peace abroad was *barely a blip on the screen* compared with gun control at home. REPLACE WITH *inconsiderable.*

blondes have more fun An infantile phrase (see page 20).

bloodcurdling scream (yell) An inescapable pair (see page 20).

blood is thicker than water A popular prescription (see page 23).

blood, sweat, and tears A moribund metaphor (see page 21). *assiduity; diligence; discipline; drudgery; effort; endeavor; exertion; grind; hard work; industry; labor; moil; persistence; slavery; strain; struggle; sweat; toil; travail; work.* ■ However unautobiographical or fictional a book is, it still comes out by *blood, sweat, and tears.* REPLACE WITH *toil.*

(the) bloom is off the rose A moribund metaphor (see page 21).

blow a fuse A moribund metaphor (see page 21). *bellow; bluster; clamor; explode; fulminate; fume; holler; howl; rage; rant; rave; roar; scream; shout; storm; thunder; vociferate; yell.*

blow a gasket A moribund metaphor (see page 21). *bellow; bluster; clamor; explode; fulminate; fume; holler; howl; rage; rant; rave; roar; scream; shout; storm; thunder; vociferate; yell.*

blow away A moribund metaphor (see page 21). 1. *annihilate; assassinate; butcher; destroy; exterminate; kill; massacre; murder; slaughter; slay.* 2. *amaze; astonish; astound; awe; dazzle; dumbfound; flabbergast; overpower; overwhelm; shock; startle; stun; stupefy; surprise.*

blow by blow A moribund metaphor (see page 21).

blow (his) cover A moribund metaphor (see page 21). *ascertain; discover; expose; find out; learn.*

blow (run) hot and cold A moribund metaphor (see page 21). 1. *ambivalent; divided; indecisive; irresolute; torn; uncertain; uncommitted; undecided; unsure.* 2. *capricious; changeable; erratic; fickle; fitful; flighty; fluctuating; haphazard; inconsistent; inconstant; intermittent; irregular; mercurial; occasional; random; sometime; spasmodic; sporadic; unpredictable; unsettled; unstable; unsteady; vacillating; volatile; wavering; wayward.*

blow (my) mind A moribund metaphor (see page 21). *amaze; astonish; astound; awe; dazzle; dumbfound; flabbergast; overpower; overwhelm; shock; startle; stun; stupefy; surprise.*

> And Elizabeth said one thing at the very end that really blew Rosie's mind, about how when she first got sober, she felt as if the mosaic she had been assembling out of life's little shards got dumped to the ground, and there was no way to put it back together. — Anne Lamott, *Crooked Little Heart*

blow off steam A moribund metaphor (see page 21). 1. *bellow; bluster; clamor; complain; explode; fulminate; fume; holler; howl; object; protest; rage; rant; rave; roar; scream; shout; storm; thunder; vociferate; yell.* 2. *be merry; carouse; carry on; celebrate; debauch; disport; frolic; party; play; revel; riot; roister; rollick; romp; skylark.*

blow on the cue ball A moribund metaphor (see page 21).

blow (things) out of proportion A moribund metaphor (see page 21). *elaborate; embellish; embroider; enhance; enlarge; exaggerate; hyperbolize; inflate; magnify; overdo; overreact; overstress; overstate; strain; stretch.* ■ It was not the sort of event that has now been exaggerated and *blown out of proportion.* DELETE *and blown out of proportion.*

blow (them) out of the water A moribund metaphor (see page 21). 1. *annihilate; assassinate; butcher; destroy; exterminate; kill; massacre; murder; slaughter; slay.* 2. *beat; conquer; crush; defeat; outdo; overcome; overpower; overwhelm; prevail; quell; rout; succeed; triumph; trounce; vanquish; win.* 3. *amaze; astonish; astound; awe; dazzle; dumbfound; flabbergast; overpower; overwhelm; shock; startle; stun; stupefy; surprise.*

blow (your) own horn A moribund metaphor (see page 21). *acclaim; applaud; bluster; boast; brag; celebrate; cheer; commend; compliment; congratulate; crow; extol; flatter; gloat; hail; honor; laud; praise; puff; salute; self-congratulate; strut; swagger.*

blow smoke A moribund metaphor (see page 21). *adumbrate; becloud; befog; camouflage; cloak; cloud; conceal; cover; disguise; dissemble; enshroud; harbor; hide; keep secret; mask; obfuscate; obscure; overshadow; screen; shroud; suppress; veil; withhold.*

blow (his) stack A moribund metaphor (see page 21). *bellow; bluster; clamor; explode; fulminate; fume; holler; howl; rage; rant; rave; roar; scream; shout; storm; thunder; vociferate; yell.*

blow the whistle (on) A moribund metaphor (see page 21). 1. *bare; betray; disclose; divulge; expose; give away; reveal; show; tell; uncover; unveil.* 2. *betray; deliver up; inform on; report; turn in.* ■ Fear of reprisal arises when people consider whether or not to *blow the whistle on* someone who violates ethical standards. REPLACE WITH *report.* ■ He *blew the whistle on* company corruption. REPLACE WITH *exposed.*

blow to bits A moribund metaphor (see page 21). *annihilate; assassinate; butcher; demolish; destroy; devastate; eradicate; exterminate; kill; massacre; murder; oblit-*

erate; pulverize; rack; ravage; raze; ruin; shatter; slaughter; slay; smash; undo; wrack; wreck.

blow (my) top A moribund metaphor (see page 21). *bellow; bluster; clamor; explode; fulminate; fume; holler; howl; rage; rant; rave; roar; scream; shout; storm; thunder; vociferate; yell.*

blow to smithereens A moribund metaphor (see page 21). *annihilate; assassinate; butcher; demolish; destroy; devastate; eradicate; exterminate; kill; massacre; murder; obliterate; pulverize; rack; ravage; raze; ruin; shatter; slaughter; slay; smash; undo; wrack; wreck.*

(until) (I'm) blue in the face A moribund metaphor (see page 21). 1. *angry; annoyed; enraged; exasperated; furious; incensed; infuriated; irate; irked; irritated; mad; raging; wrathful.* 2. *beat; bushed; debilitated; depleted; exhausted; fatigued; fed up; spent; tired; wearied; weary; worn out.*

blue-ribbon commission (committee; panel) A suspect superlative (see page 24).

boggle (my) mind An infantile phrase (see page 20). *baffle; befuddle; bemuse; bewilder; confound; confuse; disconcert; flummox; muddle; mystify; nonplus; perplex; puzzle.*

> They had been friends forever, sitting in this room for longer than Amy had been alive, although it boggled Amy's mind to think that. — Elizabeth Strout, *Amy and Isabelle*

(as) bold as brass An insipid simile. *audacious; bold; brash; brass; brassy; brazen; cheeky; forward; impertinent; impudent; insolent; outrageous; saucy; shameless; unabashed.*

a bolt from (out of) the blue A moribund metaphor (see page 21). *bombshell; shock; surprise; thunderbolt; thunderclap.*

bone of contention A moribund metaphor (see page 21).

bone to pick A moribund metaphor (see page 21). *animosity; bitterness; enmity; grievance; grudge; hostility; indignation; ill will; offense; rancor; resentment; spite; umbrage.*

(cite) book, chapter, and verse A moribund metaphor (see page 21). *explain; expound; lecture.* ■ She will *give me chapter and verse* about the merits of XYZ Chemical and why it should be a glorious investment. REPLACE WITH *lecture me.*

book of woes A moribund metaphor (see page 21).

bore the pants off (me) A moribund metaphor (see page 21). *annoy; bore; discourage; disgust; exasperate; exhaust; fatigue; irk; irritate; sicken; tire; wear out; weary.*

bore to death (extinction) A moribund metaphor (see page 21). *annoy; bore; discourage; disgust; exasperate; exhaust; fatigue; irk; irritate; sicken; tire; wear out; weary.* SEE ALSO *to death.*

bore to tears A moribund metaphor (see page 21). *annoy; bore; discourage; disgust; exasperate; exhaust; fatigue; irk; irritate; sicken; tire; wear out; weary.*

born to the purple A moribund metaphor (see page 21).

born under a lucky star A moribund metaphor (see page 21). *advantageous; auspicious; blessed; charmed; enchanted; favored; felicitous; flourishing; fortuitous; fortunate; golden; happy; in luck; lucky; propitious; prosperous; successful; thriving.*

born with a silver spoon in (his) mouth A moribund metaphor (see page 21). *advantageous; auspicious; blessed; charmed; enchanted; favored; felicitous; flourishing; fortuitous; fortunate; golden; happy; in luck; lucky; propitious; prosperous; successful; thriving.*

bottle up (inside) A moribund metaphor (see page 21). *block; check; contain; control; curb; hide; hold back; repress; restrain; smother; stem; stifle; suppress.*

> I became more guilty and more frightened, and kept all this bottled up inside me, and naturally, inescapably, one night, when this woman had finished preaching, everything came roaring, screaming, crying out, and I fell to the ground before the altar. — James Baldwin, *The Fire Next Time*

(the) bottom fell out A moribund metaphor (see page 21). *break down; break up; collapse; crash; crumple; disintegrate; end; fail; fall apart; fold; stop.* ■ He elected to stop financing condominium projects nearly two years before *the bottom fell out* of that business.

bottomless pit A moribund metaphor (see page 21). *abyss; hades; hell; inferno; netherworld; perdition.*

(the) bottom line A moribund metaphor (see page 21). This is a bottomlessly ordinary term. People bewitched by words that have a trace of technicality to them are inclined to use it. In striving to sound technical, they manage to sound only typical. 1. *conclusion; consequence; culmination; decision; denouement; effect; end; outcome; result; upshot.* 2. *crux; essence; key; keynote; main point; salient point.* ■ The *bottom line* is that America can compete if the politicians are kept out of the picture. REPLACE WITH *upshot.* ■ The *bottom line* is that both kinds of water are generally safe. REPLACE WITH *conclusion.* ■ The *bottom line* is you get what you pay for. REPLACE WITH *main point.* ■ The *bottom line* for parents: choose gifts carefully. REPLACE WITH *keynote.* SEE ALSO *feedback; input; interface; output; parameters.*

bottom of the barrel A moribund metaphor (see page 21). 1. *alluvium; debris; deposit; detritus; dregs; grounds; lees; precipitate; remains; residue; residuum; sediment; settlings; silt; wash.* 2. *close; completion; conclusion; end; ending; finale; finish; termination.* 3. *bums; deadbeats; derelicts; duds; failures; flobs; hobos; losers; pariahs; rabble; renegades; riffraff; scum; tramps; vagabonds; vagrants; washouts.*

bottom of the heap A moribund metaphor (see page 21). *bottom; depths; nadir; pits; rock bottom.*

You slip around the truth once, and then again, and one more time, and there you are, feeling, for a moment, that it was sudden, your arrival at the bottom of the heap. — Jane Hamilton, *A Map of the World*

bound and determined An inescapable pair (see page 20). *bent on; determined; resolute; resolved.*

While I'm not vain enough to buy a new winter coat — I will not spend hundreds of dollars on a piece of clothing I am bound and determined not to need a month from now — I am sufficiently self-conscious to leave the coat open, counting on a thick scarf to keep out the bitter damp. — Ayelet Waldman, *Love and Other Impossible Pursuits*

bow and scrape A moribund metaphor (see page 21). *bootlick; bow; crawl; cringe; crouch; fawn; grovel; kowtow; slaver; stoop; toady; truckle.*

bowled over A moribund metaphor (see page 21). *amazed; astonished; astounded; flabbergasted; shocked; staggered; stunned; surprised.*

(like a) bowl of cherries An insipid simile. *agreeable; ambrosial; beguiling; celestial; charming; delectable; delicious; delightful; divine; enchanting; engaging; enjoyable; fun; heavenly; glorious; gratifying; inviting; joyful; joyous; luscious; pleasant; pleasing; pleasurable.*

brain drain An infantile phrase (see page 20).

brand new An inescapable pair (see page 20). ■ Did you forget he got himself a *brand new* car to drive around in? DELETE *brand.*

(the) bread always falls on the buttered side A moribund metaphor (see page 21).

bread and butter A moribund metaphor (see page 21). 1. *food; keep; livelihood; living; subsistence; support; sustenance.* 2. *basis; center; core; essence; foundation; heart; hub; mainstay; nucleus; root; soul; spirit.* ■ Interfaces are the *bread and butter* of component technology. REPLACE WITH *core.*

breadth and depth An inescapable pair (see page 20). *ambit; area; breadth; compass; degree; extent; field; magnitude; range; reach; scope; sphere; sweep.*

break (his) back A moribund metaphor (see page 21). *attempt; drudge; endeavor; essay; exert; grind; grub; labor; moil; slave; strain; strive; struggle; sweat; toil; travail; try; work.*

break down (the) barriers A moribund metaphor (see page 21).

break (my) neck A moribund metaphor (see page 21). *attempt; drudge; endeavor; essay; exert; grind; grub; labor; moil; slave; strain; strive; struggle; sweat; toil; travail; try; work.*

break out of the mold A moribund metaphor (see page 21).

(it) breaks (my) heart A moribund metaphor (see page 21). *desolate; disappoint; discourage; dishearten; dispirit; distress; sadden.*

break the bank A moribund metaphor (see page 21). *bankrupt; deplete; drain; exhaust; impoverish; pauperize; ruin.*

break the ice A moribund metaphor (see page 21).

breathe (new) life into A moribund metaphor (see page 21). *animate; arouse; enliven; exhilarate; inspire; inspirit; invigorate; revivify; spur; stimulate; vitalize; vivify.* ■ The Citizens for Limited Taxation petition would block school reform at the very time it is needed most to *breathe life into* our public schools. REPLACE WITH *invigorate.*

breathless anticipation An inescapable pair (see page 20).

(a welcome) breath of fresh air A moribund metaphor (see page 21). *animating; arousing; bracing; enlivening; exciting; exhilarating; inspiring; inspiriting; invigorating; provoking; refreshing; rousing; stimulating; vivifying.*

Of what it purports to describe, *a (welcome) breath of fresh air* offers the opposite. If intelligent or heartfelt sentences are invigorating, this dimwitticism should make us gasp as though we've been throttled by foul-smelling thoughtlessness. ■ A toy industry analyst called the news *a breath of fresh air.* REPLACE WITH *exciting.* ■ Ordinarily, I find Friedman *a welcome breath of fresh air* — he has little patience for fools and plagiarists. REPLACE WITH *refreshing.*

(a) breed apart (unto itself) A moribund metaphor (see page 21). *aberrant; abnormal; anomalistic; anomalous; atypical; bizarre; curious; deviant; different; distinct; distinctive; eccentric; exceptional; extraordinary; fantastic; foreign; grotesque; idiosyncratic; independent; individual; individualistic; irregular; novel; odd; offbeat; original; peculiar; puzzling; quaint; queer; rare; remarkable; separate; singular; uncommon; unconventional; unexampled; unique; unnatural; unorthodox; unparalleled; unprecedented; unusual; weird.*

(it's) a breeze A moribund metaphor (see page 21). *apparent; basic; clear; clear-cut; conspicuous; distinct; easily done; easy; effortless; elementary; evident; explicit; facile; limpid; lucid; manifest; obvious; patent; pellucid; plain; simple; simplicity itself; straightforward; translucent; transparent; unambiguous; uncomplex; uncomplicated; understandable; unequivocal; unmistakable.*

bright and early An inescapable pair (see page 20).

(as) bright as a (new) button An insipid simile. 1. *beaming; bright; brilliant; burnished; dazzling; effulgent; gleaming; glistening; glittering; glossy; incandescent; luminous; lustrous; radiant; resplendent; shiny; sparkling.* 2. *able; adroit; alert; apt; astute; bright; brilliant; capable; clever; competent; discerning; enlightened; insightful; intelligent; judicious; keen; knowledgeable; learned; logical; luminous; perceptive; perspicacious; quick; quick-witted; rational; reasonable; sagacious; sage; sapient; sensible; sharp; shrewd; smart; sound; understanding; wise.*

(as) bright as a new penny An insipid simile. 1. *beaming; bright; brilliant; burnished; dazzling; effulgent; gleaming; glistening; glittering; glossy; incandescent; luminous; lustrous; radiant; resplendent; shiny; sparkling.* 2. *able; adroit; alert; apt;*

astute; bright; brilliant; capable; clever; competent; discerning; enlightened; insightful; intelligent; judicious; keen; knowledgeable; learned; logical; luminous; perceptive; perspicacious; quick; quick-witted; rational; reasonable; sagacious; sage; sapient; sensible; sharp; shrewd; smart; sound; understanding; wise.

(as) bright as a new pin An insipid simile. 1. *beaming; bright; brilliant; burnished; dazzling; effulgent; gleaming; glistening; glittering; glossy; incandescent; luminous; lustrous; radiant; resplendent; shiny; sparkling.* 2. *able; adroit; alert; apt; astute; bright; brilliant; capable; clever; competent; discerning; enlightened; insightful; intelligent; judicious; keen; knowledgeable; learned; logical; luminous; perceptive; perspicacious; quick; quick-witted; rational; reasonable; sagacious; sage; sapient; sensible; sharp; shrewd; smart; sound; understanding; wise.*

(she) brightens up a room A moribund metaphor (see page 21). *is beaming; is brilliant; is dazzling; is gleaming; is glowing; is incandescent; is luminescent; is luminous; is radiant; is resplendent; is shimmering; is sunny.* ■ When she walks into a room, she *brightens up the room.* REPLACE WITH *is incandescent.*

bright-eyed and bushy tailed A moribund metaphor (see page 21). *active; adroit; alert; alive; animated; dynamic; eager; energetic; frisky; hearty; lively; nimble; peppy; perky; quick; ready; spirited; sprightly; spry; vibrant; vigorous; vivacious.*

bring (take) (her) down a notch (peg) A moribund metaphor (see page 21). *abase; chasten; debase; decrease; deflate; degrade; demean; depreciate; depress; diminish; disgrace; dishonor; embarrass; humble; humiliate; lower; mortify; puncture; shame.*

bring (her) down from (her) high horse A moribund metaphor (see page 21). *abase; chasten; debase; decrease; deflate; degrade; demean; depreciate; depress; diminish; disgrace; dishonor; embarrass; humble; humiliate; lower; mortify; puncture; shame.*

bring down the house A moribund metaphor (see page 21). *acclaim; applaud; bellow; cheer; clamor; holler; howl; roar; scream; shout; vociferate; yell.*

bring home the bacon A moribund metaphor (see page 21). *earn a living; earn money; prosper; succeed.*

bring to a close (a halt; an end; a stop) A wretched redundancy (see page 25). *cease; close; complete; conclude; derail; discontinue; end; finish; halt; settle; stop; terminate.* ■ We are pleased to be able to *bring* this longstanding litigation *to a close.* REPLACE WITH *conclude.* ■ You might be contributing to *bringing* the nation's longest peacetime economic expansion *to a grinding halt.* REPLACE WITH *halting.* SEE ALSO *come to a close (a halt; an end; a stop); grind to a halt.*

bring to a head A moribund metaphor (see page 21). *cap; climax; conclude; consummate; crest; crown; culminate; peak.*

bring (come) to closure A torpid term (see page 24). 1. *cease; close; complete; conclude; discontinue; end; finish; halt; stop.* 2. *conclude; decide; determine; establish; resolve; settle.*

bring (them) to (their) knees A moribund metaphor (see page 21). *beat; conquer; cow; cripple; crush; defeat; disable; dispirit; enervate; enfeeble; humble; incapacitate; lame; make helpless; neutralize; oppress; overcome; overpower; overrun; overthrow; overwhelm; repress; subdue; subjugate; suppress; vanquish.* ■ A network of computers was *brought to its knees* by something out of our control that seemed to live in and even infect the system. REPLACE WITH *vanquished.*

bring to the table A moribund metaphor (see page 21). *advance; bring up; broach; contribute; give; introduce; offer; present; proffer; propose; provide; raise; submit; suggest; tender.* ■ As a company that knows education, we thought we had something to *bring to the table.* REPLACE WITH *offer.*

brought it home to (me) A moribund metaphor (see page 21).

(as) brown as a berry An insipid simile. *beige; bronze; bronzed; brown; burnished; chestnut; copper; coppery; ecru; fawn; mahogany; ocherous; russet; sienna; sun-tanned; tan; tanned; tawny.*

(win) brownie points A moribund metaphor (see page 21).

brutally honest An inescapable pair (see page 20).

brute force An inescapable pair (see page 20).

bucket of bolts A moribund metaphor (see page 21).

(won't) budge an inch A moribund metaphor (see page 21). 1. *be influenced; be persuaded; be swayed; be won over.* 2. *budge; move; nudge; shift.*

build a better mousetrap (and the world will beat a path to your door) A popular prescription (see page 23).

build bridges A moribund metaphor (see page 21).

build bridges where there are walls A moribund metaphor (see page 21).

build castles in Spain (the air) A moribund metaphor (see page 21). *brood; daydream; dream; fantasize; imagine; meditate; muse; reflect.*

building blocks of A moribund metaphor (see page 21).

(like a) bull in a china closet (shop) An insipid simile. *awkward; blundering; bumbling; bungling; clumsy; gawky; gauche; ham-handed; heavy-handed; inapt; inept; lubberly; lumbering; maladroit; uncoordinated; uncouth; ungainly; ungraceful; unhandy; unskillful; unwieldy.*

bump in the road A moribund metaphor (see page 21). *bar; barrier; block; blockage; check; deterrent; difficulty; encumbrance; handicap; hindrance; hurdle; impediment; interference; obstacle; obstruction.*

(like a) bump on a log An insipid simile. *dead; dormant; dull; immobile; immovable; inactive; inanimate; indolent; inert; inoperative; languid; latent; lethargic; lifeless; listless; motionless; phlegmatic; quiescent; quiet; sluggish; stagnant; static; stationary; still; stock-still; torpid; unresponsive.*

bumpy road (ahead) A moribund metaphor (see page 21). *complication; difficulty; dilemma; mess; muddle; ordeal; pickle; plight; predicament; problem; quandary; trial; trouble.*

bunch of baloney A moribund metaphor (see page 21). *balderdash; baloney; nonsense; rubbish.*

bundle of joy A moribund metaphor (see page 21). *babe; baby; child; infant; neonate; newborn; nursling; suckling; toddler; tot; weanling.*

bundle of nerves A moribund metaphor (see page 21). *agitated; anxious; eager; edgy; excitable; excited; fidgety; frantic; jittery; jumpy; nervous; ill at ease; on edge; restive; restless; skittish; uncomfortable; uneasy.*

burn a hole in (my) pocket A moribund metaphor (see page 21).

burn (your) bridges (behind) (you) A moribund metaphor (see page 21).

burning desire An inescapable pair (see page 20). *ardor; eagerness; fervor; passion; vehemence; zeal.* ■ Suppose you sell group insurance to employers, and your prospect has ten employees and a *burning desire* to expand the business. REPLACE WITH *zeal.*

(it) burns (me) up A moribund metaphor (see page 21). *acerbate; anger; annoy; bother; bristle; chafe; enrage; incense; inflame; infuriate; irk; irritate; madden; miff; provoke; rile; roil; vex.*

burn the candle at both ends A moribund metaphor (see page 21). 1. *drudge; grind; grub; labor; moil; slave; strain; strive; struggle; sweat; toil; travail; work hard.* 2. *debilitate; deplete; drain; empty; enervate; exhaust; fatigue; overdo; overwork; sap; tire; wear out; weary.* 3. *be merry; carouse; carry on; celebrate; debauch; disport; frolic; party; play; revel; riot; roister; rollick; romp; skylark.*

burn the midnight oil A moribund metaphor (see page 21). *drudge; grind; grub; labor; moil; slave; strain; strive; struggle; sweat; toil; travail; work hard; work long hours.* ■ We are indebted to our wives and families for their patience while we *burned the midnight oil.* REPLACE WITH *worked long hours.*

bursting at the seams A moribund metaphor (see page 21). 1. *aflame; agitated; animated; anxious; eager; ebullient; effervescent; enthusiastic; excitable; excited; fervent; fervid; frantic; frenzied; impassioned; impatient; lively; restless; spirited.* 2. *abounding; brimful; brimming; bursting; chock-full; congested; crammed; crowded; dense; filled; full; gorged; jammed; jam-packed; overcrowded; overfilled; overflowing; packed; replete; saturated; stuffed; swarming; teeming.*

burst on (onto) the scene A moribund metaphor (see page 21). *appear; arise; come forth; emerge; occur; originate; present itself; rise; surface; turn up.*

bur under (his) saddle A moribund metaphor (see page 21). *affliction; annoyance; bane; bother; burden; curse; difficulty; inconvenience; irritant; irritation; load; nuisance; ordeal; pain; pest; plague; problem; torment; tribulation; trouble; vexation; weight; worry.*

bury (her) head in the sand A moribund metaphor (see page 21). *cower;*

cringe; grovel; quail; recoil; shrink. ■ When confronted with negative press, school officials ought not to *bury their heads in the sand.* REPLACE WITH *cower.*

bury the hatchet A moribund metaphor (see page 21). *make peace.*

business as usual A torpid term (see page 24). ■ All too many male-dominated workplaces still are doing *business as usual* and denying women equal pay and benefits. ■ In simple terms, it means *business as usual*; specifically, all business will be conducted today as it was yesterday. SEE ALSO *politics as usual.*

> The tile floor smelled strongly of antiseptic and faintly of cat pee: Business as usual. — Jo-Ann Mapson, *The Wilder Sisters*

business is business A quack equation (see page 23).

bust (my) ass A moribund metaphor (see page 21). *attempt; drudge; endeavor; essay; exert; grind; grub; labor; moil; slave; strain; strive; struggle; sweat; toil; travail; try; work.*

(as) busy as a beaver An insipid simile. *assiduous; busy; diligent; grinding; hardworking; indefatigable; industrious; inexhaustible; sedulous; slaving; tireless; toiling; unflagging; unrelenting; untiring.*

(as) busy as a bee An insipid simile. *assiduous; busy; diligent; grinding; hardworking; indefatigable; industrious; inexhaustible; sedulous; slaving; tireless; toiling; unflagging; unrelenting; untiring.*

butterflies in (her) stomach A moribund metaphor (see page 21). 1. *agitated; anxious; eager; edgy; excitable; excited; fidgety; frantic; jittery; jumpy; nervous; ill at ease; on edge; restive; restless; skittish; uncomfortable; uneasy.* 2. *nauseated; nauseous; queasy; sick; squeamish.*

butter (them) up A moribund metaphor (see page 21). *acclaim; applaud; celebrate; commend; compliment; extol; flatter; laud; praise.*

butter wouldn't melt in (her) mouth A moribund metaphor (see page 21). *affected; artful; artificial; coy; crafty; cunning; deceitful; dishonest; demure; dissembling; dissimulating; duplicitous; fake; false; false-hearted; feigned; foxy; guileful; insincere; lying; mannered; mendacious; phony; plastic; sly; sneaky; tricky; two-faced; uncandid; underhanded; unfrank; unnatural; untrue; untruthful; wily.*

button (zip) your lip A moribund metaphor (see page 21). 1. *be silent; be still; hush; keep quiet; quiet; silence.* 2. *be closed-mouthed; be quiet; be reticent; be silent; be speechless; be taciturn; be uncommunicative.*

buy a pig in a poke A moribund metaphor (see page 21).

buy into A moribund metaphor (see page 21). *accept; adopt; advocate; affirm; agree to; assent to; back; believe in; endorse; espouse; favor; further; hold; sanction; side with; support.* ■ When others witness your confidence in an activity, they are more likely to *buy into* your plans of action. REPLACE WITH *back.*

buy the farm A moribund metaphor (see page 21). *cease to exist; depart; die; expire; pass away; pass on; perish.*

buy time A moribund metaphor (see page 21). *defer; delay; hold off; hold up; postpone; put aside; put off; set aside; shelve; suspend; table; waive.*

by a hair's breadth A moribund metaphor (see page 21). *barely; by a little; hardly; just; merely; narrowly; only just; scarcely.*

(won) by a landslide A moribund metaphor (see page 21).

by a whisker A moribund metaphor (see page 21). *barely; by a little; hardly; just; merely; narrowly; only just; scarcely.*

by fits and starts A moribund metaphor (see page 21). *convulsively; erratically; fitfully; intermittently; irregularly; paroxysmally; randomly; spasmodically; sporadically; unevenly.*

by hook or (by) crook A moribund metaphor (see page 21). *somehow; someway.*

(growing) by leaps and bounds A moribund metaphor (see page 21). *abruptly; apace; briskly; fast; hastily; hurriedly; posthaste; promptly; quickly; rapidly; rashly; speedily; straightaway; swiftly; wingedly.*

by no (not by any) stretch of the imagination A moribund metaphor (see page 21). *at no time; by no means; in no way; never; no; not; not at all; not ever; not in any way; not in the least.*

> Rubashov found that by no stretch of his imagination could he picture his neighbor's state of mind, in spite of all his practice in the art of 'thinking through others' minds'. — Arthur Koestler, *Darkness at Noon*

(go; pass) by the board A moribund metaphor (see page 21). *abandoned; completed; concluded; disappeared; discarded; done; ended; finished; forfeited; gone (by); lost; over; passed; vanished.* ■ There was a little rain, sleet, and snow, but all that has *gone by the board.* REPLACE WITH *passed.*

(go) by the book A moribund metaphor (see page 21). 1. *correctly; properly; rightly.* 2. *according to the rules.* ■ She's done everything *by the book.* REPLACE WITH *correctly.*

by the same token A wretched redundancy (see page 25). *also; and; as well; besides; beyond that (this); even; further; furthermore; in addition; likewise; moreover; more than that (this); similarly; still more; too; what is more.*

by the seat of (his) pants A moribund metaphor (see page 21). *automatically; by impulse; by instinct; by intuition; by reflex; impulsively; instinctively; intuitively; reflexively; spontaneously; unthinkingly; viscerally.*

by the skin of (his) teeth A moribund metaphor (see page 21). *barely; by a little; hardly; just; merely; narrowly; only just; scarcely.*

by the sweat of (his) brow A moribund metaphor (see page 21). *arduously; backbreakingly; burdensomely; exhaustingly;*

fatiguingly; gruelingly; laboriously; onerously; strenuously; toilfully; toilsomely; toughly; wearisomely; with difficulty.

by virtue of the fact that A wretched redundancy (see page 25). *because; considering; for; in that; since.* ■ There are a lot of people who expect too little *by virtue of the fact that* that's all they've known. REPLACE WITH *because.* SEE ALSO *because of the fact that; considering the fact that; given the fact that; in consideration of the fact that; in view of the fact that; on account of the fact that.*

C

call a halt (an end; a stop) to A wretched redundancy (see page 25). *cease; close; complete; conclude; derail; discontinue; end; finish; halt; settle; stop.* ■ Let's *call a halt to* this insanity. REPLACE WITH *end.* SEE ALSO *put a halt (an end; a stop) to.*

call a spade a spade A moribund metaphor (see page 21). 1. *be aboveboard; be artless; be candid; be forthright; be frank; be genuine; be guileless; be honest; be ingenuous; be naive; be sincere; be straightforward; be truthful; be veracious; be veridical.* 2. *be blunt; clear; be direct; be explicit; be plain; be specific.*

call into question A wretched redundancy (see page 25). *challenge; contradict; dispute; doubt; question.*

call off the dogs A moribund metaphor (see page 21).

call (out) on the carpet A moribund metaphor (see page 21). *admonish; animadvert; berate; castigate; censure; chasten; chastise; chide; condemn; criticize; denounce; denunciate; discipline; excoriate; fulminate against; imprecate; impugn; inveigh against; objurgate; punish; rebuke; remonstrate; reprehend; reprimand; reproach; reprobate; reprove; revile; scold; swear at; upbraid; vituperate.* ■ Popular sentiment indicates that *calling the president on the carpet* is not a labor the people wish to bear. REPLACE WITH *rebuking the president.* ■ She *called Starr on the carpet* as well, notably for alleged leaks to the press. REPLACE WITH *upbraided Starr.*

callow youth An inescapable pair (see page 20). *adolescent; artless; callow; green; guileless; immature; inexperienced; inexpert; ingenuous; innocent; juvenile; naive; raw; simple; undeveloped; unfledged; unskilled; unskillful; unsophisticated; untaught; untrained; unworldly; young; youthful.*

call the plays A moribund metaphor (see page 21). *administer; boss; choose; command; control; decide; determine; dictate; direct; dominate; govern; in charge; in command; in control; manage; manipulate; master; order; overpower; oversee; predominate; prevail; reign over; rule; superintend.*

call the shots A moribund metaphor (see page 21). *administer; boss; choose; command; control; decide; determine; dictate; direct; dominate; govern; in charge; in command; in control; manage; manipulate; master; order; overpower; oversee;*

predominate; prevail; reign over; rule; superintend.

> It's neither true nor fair to say I'm to blame for her predicament, but I have a long history of letting Sylvia call the shots. — Dave King, *The Ha-Ha*

(the) calm before the storm A moribund metaphor (see page 21).

calm, cool, and collected An infantile phrase (see page 20). *at ease; calm; collected; composed; controlled; cool; imperturbable; insouciant; nonchalant; placid; poised; relaxed; sedate; self-possessed; serene; tranquil; unemotional; unperturbed; unruffled.* ■ She seemed so *calm, cool, and collected* in the interview. REPLACE WITH *calm.*

(we) came, (we) saw, (we) conquered An infantile phrase (see page 20).

can chew gum and think (walk) at the same time A moribund metaphor (see page 21). *be able; be adept; be adroit; be ambidextrous; be capable; be competent; be deft; be dexterous; be nimble; be proficient; be skilled; be skillful.*

candor and frankness An inescapable pair (see page 20). *candor; frankness; honesty; openness; sincerity; truth; truthfulness; veracity.*

(you) can (can't) have your cake and eat it too A popular prescription (see page 23).

can I ask (tell) you something? A plebeian sentiment (see page 23). This is a question asked by the ignorant, by the ill-bred, not the well mannered. ■ *Can I tell you something?* I don't really like to go out. DELETE *Can I tell you something?* ■ *Can I ask you something?* Do you want me to give you a check so you can take care of that? DELETE *Can I ask you something?* SEE ALSO *let me ask you something.*

(open up a) can of worms A moribund metaphor (see page 21). *complication; difficulty; dilemma; mess; muddle; ordeal; pickle; plight; predicament; problem; quandary; trial; trouble.*

(I) can take it or leave it An infantile phrase (see page 20). *apathetic; cool; halfhearted; indifferent; insouciant; languid; laodicean; lukewarm; nonchalant; tepid; unenthusiastic.*

(I) can't complain An infantile phrase (see page 20). *all right; average; fair; fine; good; mediocre; not bad; passable; pretty good; tolerable; well.*

(we) can't help you if you don't want to be helped A popular prescription (see page 23).

(he) can't see beyond (the end of) (his) nose A moribund metaphor (see page 21). 1. *blind; eyeless; purblind; shortsighted; sightless; unseeing; unsighted; visionless.* 2. *addleheaded; bovine; cretinous; decerebrate; dense; dull; dull-witted; fatuous; fat-witted; half-witted; harebrained; hebetudinous; idiotic; ignorant; imbecilic; incogitant; insensate; mindless; moronic; muddled; nescient; obtuse; phlegmatic; slow; slow-witted; sluggish; thick; torpid; undiscerning; unintelligent; vacuous; witless.*

can't see the forest (woods) for the trees A moribund metaphor (see page 21). *nearsighted; myopic; purblind; shortsighted.*

(with) cap (hat) in hand A moribund metaphor (see page 21). *deferentially; diffidently; humbly; modestly; respectfully; sheepishly; unassumingly; unpretentiously.*

captain of industry A moribund metaphor (see page 21). *administrator; boss; brass; chief; commander; director; executive; foreman; head; headman; leader; manager; master; (high) muckamuck; officer; official; overseer; owner; president; principal; proprietor; superintendent; supervisor.*

capture the attention of A torpid term (see page 24). *absorb; attract; beguile; bewitch; captivate; charm; enamor; engage; engross; enrapture; enthrall; entice; entrance; fascinate; mesmerize; occupy.* ■ The civil rights struggle *captured the attention of* the entire nation. REPLACE WITH *captivated.*

(the) cards (deck) are stacked against (him) A moribund metaphor (see page 21).

card up (his) sleeve A moribund metaphor (see page 21).

(like) carrying coals to Newcastle An insipid simile. *barren; bootless; effete; feckless; feeble; fruitless; futile; impotent; inadequate; inconsequential; inconsiderable; ineffective; ineffectual; infertile; insignificant; inutile; meaningless; meritless; nugatory; null; of no value; pointless; powerless; profitless; purposeless; redundant; sterile; superfluous; trifling; trivial; unavailing; unimportant; unnecessary; unproductive; unprofitable; unserviceable; unworthy; useless; vain; valueless; weak; worthless.*

carry (his) own weight A moribund metaphor (see page 21).

carry the ball A moribund metaphor (see page 21).

carry the weight of the world on (my) shoulders A moribund metaphor (see page 21).

(it's a) catch-22 A moribund metaphor (see page 21). 1. *contradiction; dilemma; impasse; incongruity; paradox; plight; predicament; quandary; situation.* 2. *conundrum; enigma; puzzle; riddle.*

carte blanche A foreign phrase (see page 19).

carved (cast; fixed) in stone A moribund metaphor (see page 21). 1. *decided; determined; established; firm; fixed; resolved; set; settled.* 2. *changeless; constant; eternal; everlasting; firm; fixed; immutable; invariable; irreversible; irrevocable; permanent; rigid; stable; unalterable; unchangeable; unchanging; unending.* ■ The state's census count is not yet *fixed in stone.* REPLACE WITH *immutable.* ■ Your choice of per-server or per-seat licensing is not *cast in stone.* REPLACE WITH *unalterable.*

cash in (their) chips A moribund metaphor (see page 21). *cease to exist; decease; depart; die; expire; pass away; pass on; perish.*

cash on the barrel A moribund metaphor (see page 21).

cast a shadow over A moribund metaphor (see page 21). 1. *becloud; cloak; darken; eclipse; mask; obscure; shroud; veil.* 2. *belittle; confound;*

degrade; demean; embarrass; humiliate; lower; shame. SEE ALSO *hang like a cloud (over).*

cast in (our) lot with A moribund metaphor (see page 21). *ally; collaborate; comply; concur; conspire; cooperate; join; unite; work together.*

cast into the pot A moribund metaphor (see page 21).

castles in Spain (the air) A moribund metaphor (see page 21). *apparition; caprice; chimera; delusion; dream; fanciful idea; fancy; fantasty; fluff; frivolity; hallucination; illusion; imagination; maggot; mirage; phantasm; vagary; vision; whim; whimsy.*

cast (his) net A moribund metaphor (see page 21).

cast (your) pearls before swine A moribund metaphor (see page 21).

cast the first stone A moribund metaphor (see page 21).

catalyst for change A moribund metaphor (see page 21). ■ These are the young people who will be the *catalysts for change* in their own communities in the coming decades.

catch as catch can A moribund metaphor (see page 21). 1. *aimless; free; irregular; uncontrolled; unplanned.* 2. *by any means; however possible.*

catch forty winks A moribund metaphor (see page 21). *doze; go to bed; nap; rest; retire; sleep; slumber.*

catch in the act A moribund metaphor (see page 21). *catch; decoy; ensnare; entrap; net; trap.*

catch the wave A moribund metaphor (see page 21).

catch (him) with (his) pants down A moribund metaphor (see page 21). *catch unawares; surprise.* ■ He isn't the first president to be *caught with his pants down,* nor will he be the last. REPLACE WITH *caught unawares.*

(like a) cat on a hot tin roof An insipid simile. *agitated; anxious; eager; edgy; excitable; excited; fidgety; frantic; jittery; jumpy; nervous; ill at ease; on edge; restive; restless; skittish; uncomfortable; uneasy.*

cat's got (your) tongue A moribund metaphor (see page 21). *be closed-mouthed; be quiet; be reticent; be silent; be speechless; be taciturn; be uncommunicative.*

(the) cat's out of the bag A moribund metaphor (see page 21).

(look) (like) (the) cat that (ate) swallowed the canary An insipid simile. *complacent; gleeful; pleased; self-satisfied; smug; thrilled.* ■ On the day after an election in which President Clinton was supposed to have been chastened, many of the faces at the White House looked *like the cat that swallowed the canary.* REPLACE WITH *complacent.*

caught in the crossfire A moribund metaphor (see page 21).

> He paused from this pattern only to whisper, when an innocent — and I must admit, quite plump — regular Joe got caught in the crossfire, "That should've been me!" — Marian Keyes, *Angels*

caught red-handed A moribund metaphor (see page 21).

caught with (her) hand in the cookie jar A moribund metaphor (see page 21).

cautiously optimistic A torpid term (see page 24). *confident; encouraged; heartened; hopeful; optimistic; rosy; sanguine. Optimistic* is a perfectly vigorous word, but modified by *cautiously* or *guardedly,* as it so often is, it becomes valueless. *Cautiously optimistic* is a phrase favored by poltroons and politicians, most of whom make a point of devaluing the meaning of their words. ■ The retailer was *cautiously optimistic* about its latest report. DELETE *cautiously.* ■ When I realized that CBS was interested, I became *cautiously optimistic.* REPLACE WITH *hopeful.* ■ On the Rhode Island waterfront, the fishermen are *cautious but optimistic.* DELETE *but optimistic.* SEE ALSO *guardedly optimistic.*

cease and desist An inescapable pair (see page 20). *cease; desist; end; halt; stop.*

celebrity A suspect superlative (see page 24). As the most popular books are sometimes the least worthy of being read, so the most public people are sometimes the least worthy of being known.

If we must acknowledge these creatures — these *celebrities* — let us better understand them for who they are. All dictionary definitions of *celebrity* should include 1. a mediocrity; a vulgarian; a coxcomb. 2. a scantly talented person who through shameless self-aggrandizement and utter inanity becomes widely known. 3. a repellent person. SEE ALSO *the rich and famous.*

center around A wretched redundancy (see page 25). *center on.* ■ Concern will *center around* military governments. REPLACE WITH *center on.*

center of attention A suspect superlative (see page 24). *cynosure.* People who seek to be the *center of attention* are forever peripheral to themselves.

(take) center stage A moribund metaphor (see page 21).

c'est la vie A foreign phrase (see page 19). To this popular French expression of resignation, there are more than a few English-language equivalents. SEE ALSO *such is life; that's how (the way) it goes; that's how (the way) the ball bounces; that's how (the way) the cookie crumbles; that's life; that's life in the big city; that's show biz; what are you going to do; what can you do.*

chalk it up to experience A popular prescription (see page 23).

champing (chomping) at the bit A moribund metaphor (see page 21). *anxious; ardent; avid; craving; desiring; desirous; eager; enthusiastic; fervent; fervid; frantic; frenzied; impassioned; impatient; intent; itching; keen; longing; pining; ready; vehement; yearning; zealous.* ■ State corrections officials were *chomping* *at the bit* to show not only that the program was tightly managed but also that it was benefiting offenders and citizens alike. REPLACE WITH *eager*. ■ It leaves me *chomping at the bit* to be able to do something with these tapes. REPLACE WITH *longing*.

change (shift; switch) gear A moribund metaphor (see page 21). *alter; change; convert; metamorphose; modify; transform; transmute.*

> But the very thing I became aware of first was that time had shifted gear and was vibrating differently, and it was this that was the first assault on my own habitual pattern of substance. — Doris Lessing, *Briefing for a Descent Into Hell*

change on a dime A moribund metaphor (see page 21). *be adaptable; be flexible; be malleable; be versatile.* ■ He sees AmEx's program as an example of what the smartest marketers will be doing: creating rewards programs that can *change on a dime* based on what consumers tell them. REPLACE WITH *be flexible.*

changing of the guard A moribund metaphor (see page 21).

charity begins at home A popular prescription (see page 23).

chart a new course A moribund metaphor (see page 21).

cheap shot A moribund metaphor (see page 21).

cheek by jowl A moribund metaphor (see page 21). *attached; close; inseparable; intimate; side by side.*

chew (her) out A moribund metaphor (see page 21). *admonish; animadvert; belittle; berate; castigate; censure; chasten; chastise; chide; condemn; criticize; denounce; denunciate; discipline; excoriate; fulminate against; imprecate; impugn; inveigh against; objurgate; punish; rebuke; remonstrate; reprehend; reprimand; reproach; reprobate; reprove; revile; scold; swear at; upbraid; vituperate.*

chew the cud A moribund metaphor (see page 21). *brood; cerebrate; cogitate; consider; contemplate; deliberate; excogitate; meditate; ponder; reflect; ruminate; think.*

chew the fat (rag) A moribund metaphor (see page 21). *babble; blab; cackle; chaffer; chat; chitchat; chatter; confabulate; converse; gossip; jabber; palaver; prate; prattle; rattle; talk.*

(that's) chicken feed A moribund metaphor (see page 21). *frivolous; immaterial; inconsequential; inconsiderable; inferior; insignificant; minor; negligible; niggling; nugatory; petty; secondary; trifling; trivial; unimportant; worthless.*

chicken-or-egg (question) A moribund metaphor (see page 21).

(like a) chicken with its head cut off An insipid simile. *agitated; crazed; crazy; demented; deranged; distraught; frantic; frenetic; frenzied; insane; mad; raging; wild.*

(the) child is father of the man A popular prescription (see page 23).

children should be seen and not heard A popular prescription (see page 23).

(that's) child's play A moribund metaphor (see page 21). *apparent; basic; clear; clear-cut; conspicuous; distinct; easily done; easy; effortless; elementary; evident; explicit; facile; limpid; lucid; manifest; obvious; patent; pellucid; plain; simple; simplicity itself; straightforward; translucent; transparent; unambiguous; uncomplex; uncomplicated; understandable; unequivocal; unmistakable.*

> This was child's play for him, and he got a dollar and seventy-five cents a day for it .... — Upton Sinclair, *The Jungle*

chill to the bone (marrow) A moribund metaphor (see page 21). 1. *chill; cool; freeze; ice; refrigerate.* 2. *alarm; appall; benumb; daunt; frighten; horrify; intimidate; panic; paralyze; petrify; scare; shock; startle; terrify; terrorize.*

> The mere sight of that medley of wet nakedness chilled him to the bone. — James Joyce, *A Portrait of the Artist as a Young Man*

chink in (his) armor A moribund metaphor (see page 21). *defect; deficiency; disadvantage; failing; fault; flaw; foible; fragility; frailness; frailty; handicap; limitation; shortcoming; susceptibility; susceptibleness; vulnerability; vulnerableness; weakness.*

(a) chip off the old block A moribund metaphor (see page 21). *carbon copy; clone; double; duplicate; mirror image; replica; twin.*

chip on (her) shoulder A moribund metaphor (see page 21). *animosity; bitterness; enmity; grievance; grudge; hostility; indignation; ill will; offense; rancor; resentment; spite; umbrage.*

chock full (of) A torpid term (see page 24). *abounding; brimful; brimming; bursting; congested; crammed; crowded; dense; filled; full; gorged; jammed; jam-packed; overcrowded; overfilled; packed; replete; saturated; stuffed; swarming; teeming.*

(a) chorus of A moribund metaphor (see page 21). SEE ALSO *a barrage of.*

chrome dome An infantile phrase (see page 20). *alopecic; bald; baldheaded; baldpated; glabrous; hairless; depilated; pilgarlic; smooth; tonsured.*

Cinderella story A moribund metaphor (see page 21). *dream; fantasy.*

class A suspect superlative (see page 24). The antithesis of culture, *class* is a quality possessed by those who have neither elegance nor grace nor poise nor polish. ■ This always hurts me because I know who he is: a very intelligent, sensitive, *classy* human being. REPLACE WITH *admirable.*

Here's a description of a woman that no discerning man would ever wish to meet: ■ I am a shapely and petite, 31-year-old, exquisitely feminine, *classy* lady. REPLACE WITH *elegant.* SEE ALSO *gentleman; lady.*

(as) clean as a hound's tooth An insipid simile. *antiseptic; clean; cleansed; disinfected; germ-free; hygienic; immaculate; sanitary; sanitized; scoured; scrubbed; spotless; stainless; sterile;*

unblemished; unsoiled; unspotted; unsullied; untarnished; washed.

(as) clean as a whistle An insipid simile. *antiseptic; clean; cleansed; disinfected; germ-free; hygienic; immaculate; sanitary; sanitized; scoured; scrubbed; spotless; stainless; sterile; unblemished; unsoiled; unspotted; unsullied; untarnished; washed.*

clean bill of health A moribund metaphor (see page 21). *blooming; doing well; energetic; fit; flourishing; good; hale; hardy; healthful; healthy; hearty; robust; sound; strong; vigorous; well; well-off.*

clean (his) clock A moribund metaphor (see page 21). 1. *assail; assault; attack; batter; beat; cudgel; flagellate; flog; hit; lambaste; lash; lick; mangle; pound; pummel; strike; thrash; trounce.* 2. *beat; conquer; crush; defeat; outdo; overcome; overpower; overwhelm; prevail; quell; rout; succeed; triumph; trounce; vanquish; win.*

cleanliness is next to godliness A popular prescription (see page 23).

clear a (major) hurdle A moribund metaphor (see page 21). ■ The proposed sale and redevelopment of Lafayette Place *cleared a final hurdle* yesterday.

(a) clear and present danger An infantile phrase (see page 20). *danger; hazard; menace; peril; threat; troublemaker.* ■ He is *a clear and present danger.* REPLACE WITH *a menace.*

(as) clear as a bell An insipid simile. *audible; clarion; clear; distinct; plain; pure; sharp.*

(as) clear as crystal An insipid simile. *apparent; basic; clear; clear-cut; conspicuous; crystalline; distinct; easily done; easy; effortless; elementary; evident; explicit; facile; limpid; lucid; manifest; obvious; patent; pellucid; plain; simple; simplicity itself; straightforward; translucent; transparent; unambiguous; uncomplex; uncomplicated; understandable; unequivocal; unmistakable.*

(as) clear as day An insipid simile. *apparent; basic; clear; clear-cut; conspicuous; crystalline; distinct; easily done; easy; effortless; elementary; evident; explicit; facile; limpid; lucid; manifest; obvious; patent; pellucid; plain; simple; simplicity itself; straightforward; translucent; transparent; unambiguous; uncomplex; uncomplicated; understandable; unequivocal; unmistakable.*

(as) clear as mud An insipid simile. *ambiguous; blurred; blurry; cloudy; dim; fuzzy; hazy; indistinct; muddy; murky; nebulous; obfuscatory; obscure; opaque; unclear; vague.*

clear sailing A moribund metaphor (see page 21). *apparent; basic; clear; clear-cut; conspicuous; distinct; easily done; easy; effortless; elementary; evident; explicit; facile; limpid; lucid; manifest; obvious; patent; pellucid; plain; simple; simplicity itself; straightforward; translucent; transparent; unambiguous; uncomplex; uncomplicated; understandable; unequivocal; unmistakable.*

clear the air A moribund metaphor (see page 21).

clear the decks A moribund metaphor (see page 21).

climbing the walls A moribund metaphor (see page 21). *agitated; anxious; eager; edgy; excitable; excited; fidgety; frantic; jittery; jumpy; nervous; ill at ease; on edge; restive; restless; skittish; uncomfortable; uneasy.*

climb (move up) the ladder (of success) A moribund metaphor (see page 21). *advance; flourish; progress; prosper; rise; succeed.*

clinging vine A moribund metaphor (see page 21). *clinging; dependent; subject; subordinate; subservient.*

cling like a limpet An insipid simile. *adhere; affix; attach; bind; cleave; cling; cohere; connect; fasten; fuse; hitch; hold; join; stick.*

clip (her) wings A moribund metaphor (see page 21). *abase; chasten; debase; decrease; deflate; degrade; demean; depreciate; depress; diminish; disgrace; dishonor; embarrass; humble; humiliate; lower; mortify; puncture; shame.*

(the) clock is ticking A moribund metaphor (see page 21).

(a) cloud of A moribund metaphor (see page 21). ■ But he did so under *a cloud of* uncertainty over whether what he said could be used against him later by law enforcement officials.

close (near) at hand A moribund metaphor (see page 21). *accessible; at hand; close; close by; handy; near; nearby; neighboring; vicinal.*

close but no cigar An infantile phrase (see page 20). *almost; just about; nearly.*

closely allied An inescapable pair (see page 20).

closely guarded secret A torpid term (see page 24).

> Each year He returned and incarnated Himself in a different leading citizen whose identity was always a closely guarded secret, and with His nondenominational mysteries He brought a playful glamour to the city. — Jonathan Franzen, *The Twenty-Seventh City*

close scrutiny An inescapable pair (see page 20).

close (shut) the door on (to) A moribund metaphor (see page 21). *ban; banish; bar; block; disallow; dismiss; eliminate; exclude; hinder; ignore; impede; obstruct; preclude; prevent; prohibit; proscribe; reject; rule out.*

(hold cards) close to the chest (vest) A moribund metaphor (see page 21). *clandestine; cloaked; closed; concealed; confidential; covert; furtive; hidden; masked; mysterious; private; secretive; secret; shrouded; sly; stealthy; surreptitious; veiled.* ■ If police have any leads, they are keeping them *close to the vest.* REPLACE WITH *secret.*

clothes make the man A popular prescription (see page 23).

clutch (grasp) at straws A moribund metaphor (see page 21).

(the) coast is clear A moribund metaphor (see page 21).

cock of the walk A moribund metaphor (see page 21). *administrator; boss; brass; chief; commander; director; executive; foreman; head; headman; leader; magnate; manager; master; mogul; (high) muckamuck; notable; officer; official; overseer; patrician; personage; president; principal; ruler; superintendent; supervisor.*

cog in the wheel A moribund metaphor (see page 21). *aide; apparatchik; assistant; cog; dependent; drudge; flunky; helper; hireling; inferior; junior; minion; secondary; servant; slave; subaltern; subordinate; underling; vassal.*

cold and calculating An inescapable pair (see page 20).

> There was something cold and calculating about Elizabeth, small as she was. — Muriel Maddox, *Llantarnam*

(as) cold as a witch's tit An insipid simile. *algid; arctic; brumal; chilly; cold; cool; freezing; frigid; frosty; frozen; gelid; glacial; hibernal; hyperborean; ice-cold; icy; nippy; polar; rimy; wintry.*

(as) cold as ice An insipid simile. *algid; arctic; brumal; chilly; cold; cool; freezing; frigid; frosty; frozen; gelid; glacial; hibernal; hyperborean; ice-cold; icy; nippy; polar; rimy; wintry.*

(as) cold as marble An insipid simile. *algid; arctic; brumal; chilly; cold; cool; freezing; frigid; frosty; frozen; gelid; glacial; hibernal; hyperborean; ice-cold; icy; nippy; polar; rimy; wintry.*

cold enough to freeze the balls off a brass monkey A moribund metaphor (see page 21). *algid; arctic; brumal; chilly; cold; cool; freezing; frigid; frosty; frozen; gelid; glacial; hibernal; hyperborean; ice-cold; icy; nippy; polar; rimy; wintry.*

(get) cold feet A moribund metaphor (see page 21). *afraid; alarmed; apprehensive; cowardly; craven; diffident; fearful; frightened; pavid; pusillanimous; recreant; scared; timid; timorous; tremulous.* ■ When the woman heard that the story opened with the theft of the godparents' guns, she *got cold feet.* DELETE *became apprehensive.*

cold fish A moribund metaphor (see page 21). *apathetic; callous; chilly; cold; cool; detached; dispassionate; distant; emotionless; frigid; glacial; hard; hardhearted; harsh; heartless; hostile; icy; impassive; indifferent; passionless; pitiless; reserved; unconcerned; unemotional; unfeeling; unfriendly; unresponsive.*

cold turkey A moribund metaphor (see page 21).

collaborate together A wretched redundancy (see page 25). *collaborate.* ■ Staff from the American and European sides *collaborate together* to make the journey and the home stay a rewarding experience. DELETE *together.*

collect (gather) dust A moribund metaphor (see page 21). *fallow; idle; in abeyance; inactive; inoperative; set aside; unoccupied; unused.*

combine together A wretched redundancy (see page 25). *combine.* ■ Look at each reviewer's comments separately or *combine* them *together* for a consolidated view. DELETE *together.*

come around A moribund metaphor (see page 21). *agree; consent; feel as (we) do; support (us); think as (I) think.* ■ We believe that in the end the public is going to *come around.* REPLACE WITH *support us.*

come back to haunt A moribund metaphor (see page 21). *haunt; recoil on; redound on; return to; revisit.*

> If Maggie Feller had learned one thing in her fourteen years of dealing with members of the opposite sex, it was this: your bad hookups will always come back to haunt you. — Jennifer Weiner, *In Her Shoes*

come clean A moribund metaphor (see page 21). *acknowledge; admit; affirm; allow; avow; be forthright; be frank; be honest; be sincere; be straightforward; be truthful; be veracious; concede; confess; disclose; divulge; expose; grant; own; reveal; tell; uncover; unveil.* ■ It is time for the president to *come clean.* REPLACE WITH *be forthright.*

come forward (with) A moribund metaphor (see page 21). *advance; broach; introduce; offer; present; propose; propound; submit; suggest; tender.* ■ Nobody has *come forward with* a good argument for any way to create more jobs and raise the incomes of working people without expanding trade. REPLACE WITH *proposed.* SEE ALSO *put forward.*

come full circle A moribund metaphor (see page 21).

come hell or high water A moribund metaphor (see page 21). *no matter what; regardless.*

(chickens) come home to roost A moribund metaphor (see page 21).

come in from the cold A moribund metaphor (see page 21). ■ Alternative medicine is *coming in from the cold.* REPLACE WITH *gaining respectability.*

come in through the back door A moribund metaphor (see page 21).

come knocking (on my door) A moribund metaphor (see page 21).

come on like gangbusters An insipid simile. 1. *assertive; commanding; dynamic; emphatic; energetic; forceful; intense; mighty; potent; powerful; strong; vehement; vigorous; virile.* 2. *authoritarian; authoritative; autocratic; bossy; despotic; dictatorial; dogmatic; domineering; imperious; iron-handed; lordly; overbearing; peremptory; tyrannical.*

come on strong A moribund metaphor (see page 21). 1. *assertive; commanding; dynamic; emphatic; energetic; forceful; intense; mighty; potent; powerful; strong; vehement; vigorous; virile.* 2. *authoritarian; authoritative; autocratic; bossy; despotic; dictatorial; dogmatic; domineering; imperious; iron-handed; lordly; overbearing; peremptory; tyrannical.*

come out in the wash A moribund metaphor (see page 21).

come out of left field A moribund metaphor (see page 21).

come out of the closet A moribund metaphor (see page 21).

come (crawl) out of the woodwork A moribund metaphor (see page 21).

come out (up) smelling like a rose An insipid simile.

come out swinging A moribund metaphor (see page 21). *aggressive; antagonistic; battling; bellicose; belligerent; combative; fighting; militant; pugnacious; truculent; warlike.*

comes (goes) with the territory (turf) A moribund metaphor (see page 21). *is expected; is inescapable; is inevitable; is necessary; is unavoidable.* ■ He's got to understand that these questions *go with the territory.* REPLACE WITH *are inevitable.*

come to a boil A moribund metaphor (see page 21). *cap; climax; conclude; consummate; crest; crown; culminate; peak.*

come to a close (a halt; an end; a stop) A wretched redundancy (see page 25). *cease; close; complete; conclude; derail; discontinue; end; finish; halt; settle; stop; terminate.* ■ The days of easy credit, strong liquidity, and speculation are *coming to a close.* REPLACE WITH *ending.* SEE ALSO *bring to a close (a halt; an end; a stop); grind to a halt.*

come to (find) a happy medium A moribund metaphor (see page 21). *compromise.*

come to a head A moribund metaphor (see page 21). *cap; climax; conclude; consummate; crest; crown; culminate; peak.*

come to blows A moribund metaphor (see page 21). *battle; brawl; clash; fight; grapple; jostle; make war; scuffle; skirmish; tussle; war; wrestle; wrangle.*

> Winnie said she believed at that moment it would come to blows, though she had never seen a man strike a woman, nor a woman strike a man for that matter. — Beth Gutcheon, *More Than You Know*

come to find out An infantile phrase (see page 20). *ascertain; determine; discern; discover; find out; learn; realize.*

come to grips with A moribund metaphor (see page 21). *accept; comprehend; cope with; deal with; face; handle; struggle with; understand.*

come to pass A moribund metaphor (see page 21). *befall; come about; happen; occur; result; take place.*

come to terms with A torpid term (see page 24). *accept; comprehend; cope with; deal with; face; handle; struggle with; understand.*

come to the end of the line (road) A moribund metaphor (see page 21).

come up empty (handed) A moribund metaphor (see page 21). *find nothing.*

come up roses A moribund metaphor (see page 21).

(as) comfortable as an old shoe An insipid simile. *comfortable; cosy; habitable; homey; inhabitable; livable; safe; snug.*

coming (falling) apart at the seams A moribund metaphor (see page 21). *breaking down; collapsing; crumbling; decaying; decomposing; degenerating; deteriorating; disintegrating; dissipating; dissolving; dying; ending; fading; failing; unraveling.* ■ How do you hold it together at work when your life is *coming apart at the seams*? REPLACE WITH *disintegrating.* ■ For the last year and a half it seems the world economy has been *coming apart at the seams.* REPLACE WITH *unraveling.*

(as) common as dirt An insipid simile. *average; basic; common; commonplace; customary; everyday; normal; omnipresent; ordinary; prevalent; quotidian; regular; standard; typical; ubiquitous; unexceptional; universal; unremarkable; usual; widespread; workaday.*

common courtesy A suspect superlative (see page 24). If this expression is not heard as often as it once was, it's because courtesy is today not so common.

Genuine expressions of courtesy such as *please* and *thank you* (SEE) and *you're welcome* have been usurped by glib ones such as *have a nice day* and *I appreciate it* and *no problem.*

What's more, a vapid phrase like *how goes it* (SEE), or a vulgar one like *hey* (SEE), is more popular than an authentic *hello.*

The worsening of our speech accompanies the withering of our souls. SEE ALSO *(I) appreciate (it); have a good (nice) day (evening).*

compare and contrast A wretched redundancy (see page 25). *compare; contrast.* ■ Competition is essential to enable consumers to *compare and contrast* alternatives. REPLACE WITH *compare* or *contrast.*

(as) compared to what? An infantile phrase (see page 20). SEE ALSO *everything's (it's all) relative; (as) opposed to what?.*

complete and utter A wretched redundancy (see page 25). *absolute; compleat; complete; consummate; deadly; outright; perfect; thorough; thoroughgoing; total; unmitigated; unqualified; utter.* ■ She may be my boss, but she is also a *complete and utter* fool. REPLACE WITH *complete.*

component part A wretched redundancy (see page 25). *component; part.* ■ Denial is a *component part* of dying. REPLACE WITH *component* or *part.*

comrades in arms A moribund metaphor (see page 21).

concerted effort An inescapable pair (see page 20).

conflicted A torpid term (see page 24). *Conflicted* is a perfectly silly choice of words. It's as if to say having conflicting feelings about something — as common as that is — is more than that, more complicated or less explicable, and only a psychological-sounding term might adequately convey this.

People indefatigably mimic one another; *conflicted,* like so many other ridiculously popular terms, would have less appeal if people were more confident and inclined to think for themselves. ■ Many such parents *feel conflicted* about segregating their children in special classes but think they have no alternative. REPLACE WITH *have conflicting feelings.* ■ The single most important element to a successful production of *Julius Caesar* is to see Brutus as a truly honorable, yet *conflicted* soul whose actions belie his intentions. REPLACE WITH *torn.* ■ My guess is that you have underlying and perhaps, *conflicted* feelings about the way this change occurred. REPLACE WITH *conflicting.*

And some people use *conflicted* to mean war-torn or embattled. ■ RONCO involvement in humanitarian demining in *conflicted* countries evolves from 20 years experience with worldwide development and humanitarian assistance contracts. REPLACE WITH *embattled.* ■ The war on drugs cannot alone explain why the U.S. is sending 60 Black Hawk and Huey helicopters to this *conflicted* nation. REPLACE WITH *war-torn.*

connect together A wretched redundancy (see page 25). *connect.* ■ The next step was to *connect* these systems *together* into a system called APRS. DELETE *together.*

consensus of opinion A wretched redundancy (see page 25). *consensus.* ■ The *consensus of opinion* is that newspaper endorsements are momentum builders. REPLACE WITH *consensus.*

considering the fact that A wretched redundancy (see page 25). *because; considering; for; in that; since; when.* ■ I don't see how you can say you're not a prostitute *considering the fact that* you are paid for your time. REPLACE WITH *when.* SEE ALSO *because of the fact that; by virtue of the fact that; given the fact that; in consideration of the fact that; in view of the fact that; on account of the fact that.*

conspicuous by (his) absence A torpid term (see page 24). ■ If I didn't sing about what I was going through, it would have been *conspicuous by its absence.*

contact An overworked word (see page 22). *ask; call; inform; phone; query; question; reach; speak to; talk to; tell; write to.*

continue on A wretched redundancy (see page 25). *continue.* ■ We're going to *continue on* with more of this. DELETE *on.*

continuing refrain An inescapable pair (see page 20).

contrary to popular belief (opinion) A torpid term (see page 24). ■ *Contrary to popular opinion,* a strong dollar does not attract foreign investment to U.S. stocks but to U.S. bonds.

conventional wisdom A suspect superlative (see page 24). ■ Washington is in thrall at the moment to two competing *conventional wisdoms.*

conversation piece A plebeian sentiment (see page 23). This is an annoying little term. That people might need an object whose purpose is mainly to stimulate conversation reveals just how infertile, just how fallow, our minds are.

convicted felon A wretched redundancy (see page 25). *felon.* ■ You were a deputy sheriff and now you're a *convicted felon*? DELETE *convicted.*

cook (his) goose A moribund metaphor (see page 21).

(the) cook's tour A moribund metaphor (see page 21).

cook the books A moribund metaphor (see page 21).

(as) cool as a cucumber An insipid simile. *at ease; calm; collected; composed; controlled; cool; imperturbable; insouciant; nonchalant; placid; poised; relaxed; sedate; self-possessed; serene; tranquil; unemotional; unperturbed; unruffled.*

cool customer A moribund metaphor (see page 21). *at ease; calm; collected; composed; controlled; cool; imperturbable; insouciant; nonchalant; placid; poised; relaxed; sedate; self-possessed; serene; tranquil; unemotional; unperturbed; unruffled.*

cool (your) heels A moribund metaphor (see page 21). *be patient; hold on; relax; wait.*

cooperate together A wretched redundancy (see page 25). *cooperate.* ■ It's important that we *cooperate together* in order to resolve our problems. DELETE *together.*

cost a pretty penny A moribund metaphor (see page 21). *costly; dear; expensive; high-priced; precious; priceless; valuable.*

(I) could (should) write a book A plebeian sentiment (see page 23). If all those who proclaim *I could write a book* — or all those who are advised *You should write a book* — were to do so, we would be immersed (more than we already are) in the vengeful, petty, or everyday lamentations of hollow-headed homemakers, shameless celebrities, and failed or forgotten businesspeople. ■ *I could write a book* about the way parents pay high prices in raising a disabled child.

count (pinch) (my) pennies A moribund metaphor (see page 21). *be cheap; be economical; be frugal; be miserly; be niggardly; be parsimonious; be stingy; be thrifty.*

course of action A wretched redundancy (see page 25). *action; course; direction; intention; method; move; plan; policy; procedure; route; scheme; strategy.*

cover all the bases A moribund metaphor (see page 21).

cover a lot of ground A moribund metaphor (see page 21).

cover (his) tracks A moribund metaphor (see page 21).

crack the whip A moribund metaphor (see page 21). 1. *bully; coerce; intimidate; menace; terrorize; threaten.* 2. *castigate; chastise; discipline; penalize; punish.*

crap shoot A moribund metaphor (see page 21).

(as) crazy as a coot An insipid simile. *batty; cracked; crazy; daft; demented; deranged; fey; foolish; goofy; insane; lunatic; mad; maniacal; neurotic; nuts; nutty; psychotic; raving; silly; squirrelly; touched; unbalanced; unhinged; unsound; wacky; zany.*

(as) crazy as a loon An insipid simile. *batty; cracked; crazy; daft; demented; deranged; fey; foolish; goofy; insane; lunatic; mad; maniacal; neurotic; nuts;*

nutty; psychotic; raving; silly; squirrelly; touched; unbalanced; unhinged; unsound; wacky; zany.

> She was quite put out with him, it seemed, or else she was making her mind up that he was crazy as a loon — one of the two. — Barbara Kingsolver, *Prodigal Summer*

crazy like a fox An insipid simile. *artful; cagey; clever; conniving; crafty; cunning; foxy; guileful; shifty; shrewd; sly; smart; subtle; tricky; wily.*

(the) cream of the crop A moribund metaphor (see page 21). *best; brightest; choice; choicest; elite; excellent; finest; first-class; first-rate; foremost; greatest; highest; matchless; nonpareil; optimal; optimum; outstanding; paramount; peerless; preeminent; premium; prominent; select; superior; superlative; top; unequaled; unexcelled; unmatched; unrivaled; unsurpassed.*

crème de la crème A foreign phrase (see page 19). *best; brightest; choice; choicest; elite; excellent; finest; first-class; first-rate; foremost; greatest; highest; matchless; nonpareil; optimal; optimum; outstanding; paramount; peerless; preeminent; premium; prominent; select; superior; superlative; top; unequaled; unexcelled; unmatched; unrivaled; unsurpassed.* ■ But I have the *crème de la crème* of celebrity users. REPLACE WITH *foremost.* ■ The following list contains the *crème de la crème* of online record retailers. REPLACE WITH *best.*

crisis An overworked word (see page 22). We have a "crisis" for all occurrences. For example: *career crisis; crisis in the making; crisis in values; crisis of confidence; crisis proportions; crisis situation; crisis stage; current crisis; economic crisis; educational crisis; energy crisis; extinction crisis; family crisis; financial crisis; fiscal crisis; identity crisis; mid-life crisis; moral crisis; mounting crisis; national crisis; political crisis;* and even, incomprehensibly, *severe crisis.*

Surely, some of these crises are less than that. The terms we use to characterize events and emotions largely decide how we react to them. SEE ALSO *devastate.*

(shed) crocodile tears A moribund metaphor (see page 21).

(as) crooked as a dog's hind legs An insipid simile.

(as) cross as a bear An insipid simile. *angry; bad-tempered; bilious; cantankerous; choleric; churlish; crabby; cranky; cross; curmudgeonly; disagreeable; dyspeptic; grouchy; gruff; grumpy; ill-humored; ill-tempered; irascible; irritable; mad; peevish; petulant; quarrelsome; short-tempered; splenetic; surly; testy; vexed.*

cross (my) fingers A moribund metaphor (see page 21). *hope for; pray for; think positively; wish.*

cross (my) heart and hope to die A moribund metaphor (see page 21). *affirm; asseverate; assert; attest; aver; avow; declare; pledge; promise; swear; testify; vow; warrant.*

cross swords A moribund metaphor (see page 21). 1. *altercate; argue; disagree; dispute; feud; fight; quarrel; spat; squabble; wrangle.* 2. *battle; brawl; clash; fight; grapple; jostle; make war; scuffle; skirmish; tussle; war; wrestle.*

(we'll) cross that bridge when (we) come to it A moribund metaphor (see page 21).

cross the line A moribund metaphor (see page 21).

cross the Rubicon A moribund metaphor (see page 21).

cross to bear A moribund metaphor (see page 21). *affliction; burden; charge; cross; difficulty; encumbrance; hardship; hindrance; impediment; load; obstacle; obstruction; onus; oppression; ordeal; problem; trial; trouble; weight.*

crush like a bug An insipid simile.1. *annihilate; assassinate; butcher; destroy; exterminate; kill; massacre; murder; slaughter; slay.* 2. *beat; conquer; crush; defeat; outdo; overcome; overpower; overwhelm; prevail; quell; rout; succeed; triumph; trounce; vanquish; win.*

> It was entirely possible that one song could destroy your life. Yes, musical doom could fall on a lone human form and crush it like a bug. — Jonathan Lethem, *The Fortress of Solitude*

cry (weep) like a baby An insipid simile. *cry; howl; shriek; sob; ululate; wail; weep; whimper; whine.*

> The next morning she found him gathering eggs in the henhouse, weeping like a baby. — Jennifer Haigh, *Baker Towers*

cry over spilt milk A moribund metaphor (see page 21). *lament; mourn; sulk.*

crystal clear A moribund metaphor (see page 21). *apparent; basic; clear; clear-cut; conspicuous; crystalline; distinct; easily done; easy; effortless; elementary; evident; explicit; facile; limpid; lucid; manifest; obvious; patent; pellucid; plain; simple; simplicity itself; straightforward; translucent; transparent; unambiguous; uncomplex; uncomplicated; understandable; unequivocal; unmistakable.* ■ What seems *crystal clear* to you, and perhaps to others, is not all that obvious to me. REPLACE WITH *obvious.*

cry (say) uncle A moribund metaphor (see page 21). *abdicate; accede; acquiesce; bow; capitulate; cede; concede; give in; give up; quit; relinquish; retreat; submit; succumb; surrender; yield.*

cry wolf A moribund metaphor (see page 21).

(see) (the) cup (glass) half empty A moribund metaphor (see page 21). *despairing; hopeless; pessimistic.*

(see) (the) cup (glass) half full A moribund metaphor (see page 21). *cheerful; hopeful; optimistic; pollyanna; pollyannaish; positive; roseate; sanguine; upbeat.*

(not) (her) cup of tea A moribund metaphor (see page 21). *bent; choice; leaning; pick; inclination; predilection; preference; propensity; tendency.* ■ Choosing a logo and letterhead design from a catalog may not be everyone's *cup of tea*. REPLACE WITH *preference.*

> In any case, Edwin always felt that Norman was more Marcia's friend than he was, more her cup of tea if anyone was. — Barbara Pym, *Quartet in Autumn*

curiosity killed the cat A popular prescription (see page 23).

curse a blue streak A moribund metaphor (see page 21). *anathematize; blaspheme; condemn; curse; cuss; damn; defile; desecrate; excoriate; execrate; fulminate; imprecate; swear at.*

cushion the blow A moribund metaphor (see page 21). ■ We think that will help *cushion the blow* for some people.

(a) cut above (the rest) A moribund metaphor (see page 21). *abler; better; exceptional; greater; higher; more able (accomplished; adept; capable; competent; qualified; skilled; talented); outstanding; standout; superior; superlative.*

cut and dried (dry) A moribund metaphor (see page 21). 1. *common; commonplace; customary; everyday; normal; ordinary; quotidian; regular; routine; standard; typical; usual.* 2. *anodyne; banal; bland; boring; deadly; dry; dull; everyday; flat; humdrum; insipid; jejune; lifeless; lusterless; mediocre; monotonous; prosaic; stale; tedious; tiresome; unexciting; uninteresting; vapid; watered-down.*

cut a rug A moribund metaphor (see page 21). *dance.*

(as) cute as a button An insipid simile. *appealing; attractive; beautiful; becoming; captivating; comely; cute; dazzling; exquisite; fair; fetching; good-looking; gorgeous; handsome; lovely; nice-looking; pleasing; pretty; pulchritudinous; radiant; ravishing; seemly; stunning.*

cut (them) off at the pass A moribund metaphor (see page 21).

cut off (my) nose to spite (my) face A moribund metaphor (see page 21).

cut (its) own throat A moribund metaphor (see page 21).

cut (her) teeth (on) A moribund metaphor (see page 21). ■ Case majored in political science at Williams College and *cut his teeth* as a marketing executive at PepsiCo Inc. and Procter & Gamble.

cut the legs out from under A moribund metaphor (see page 21).

cut the mustard A moribund metaphor (see page 21). *fare well; flourish; meet expectations; prevail; progress; prosper; succeed; thrive; triumph; win.*

cutthroat competition An inescapable pair (see page 20).

cut through red tape A moribund metaphor (see page 21).

(the) cutting edge A moribund metaphor (see page 21). *advanced; ground-breaking; innovative; inventive; new; original; pioneering; progressive; radical; revolutionary; unconventional.*

cut to pieces A moribund metaphor (see page 21).1. *annihilate; assassinate; butcher; destroy; exterminate; kill; massacre; murder; slaughter; slay.* 2. *beat; conquer; crush; defeat; outdo; overcome; overpower; overwhelm; prevail; quell; rout; succeed; triumph; trounce; vanquish; win.*

cut (costs) to the bone A moribund metaphor (see page 21).

cut (stung) to the quick A moribund metaphor (see page 21). *affront; crush;*

dash; devastate; hurt; injure; insult; offend; outrage; shatter; slap; slight; upset; wound.

(could) cut (it) with a knife A moribund metaphor (see page 21).

> Amid Grandfather and I was a silence you could cut with a scimitar. — Jonathan Safran Foer, *Everything Is Illuminated*

D

damaged goods A moribund metaphor (see page 21).

dancing in the aisles (streets) A moribund metaphor (see page 21). *be merry; carouse; carry on; celebrate; debauch; disport; frolic; party; play; revel; riot; roister; rollick; romp; skylark.*

(a) dark day A moribund metaphor (see page 21).

(a) day at the beach A moribund metaphor (see page 21). 1. *easily done; easy; effortless; elementary; facile; simple; simplicity itself; straightforward; uncomplex; uncomplicated.* 2. *agreeable; beguiling; charming; delightful; enchanting; engaging; enjoyable; fun; glorious; gratifying; inviting; joyful; joyous; pleasant; pleasing; pleasurable.*

(her) day in court A moribund metaphor (see page 21).

day in (and) day out A moribund metaphor (see page 21). *ceaseless; constant; continual; continuous; daily; diurnal; endless; eternal; everlasting; evermore; every day; frequent; interminable; nonstop; permanent; perpetual; persistent; recurrent; regular; repeated; unceasing; unremitting.*

> And the day in, day out routine of school — was that a sham, too, a cunning deception perpetrated to soften us up with rational expectations and foster nonsensical feelings of trust? — Philip Roth, *The Plot Against America*

day (moment) in the sun A moribund metaphor (see page 21).

> I guess maybe my brother had his moment in the sun for the four years he was alive before Kate got diagnosed, but ever since then, we've been too busy looking over our shoulders to run headlong into growing up. — Jodi Picoult, *My Sister's Keeper*

days of wine and roses An infantile phrase (see page 20).

dead and buried An inescapable pair (see page 20). *ceased; completed; concluded; dead; deceased; defunct; departed; done; ended; exanimate; expired; extinct; extinguished; finished; gone; inanimate; lifeless; no more; over; past; perished; stopped; terminated.*

dead and gone A wretched redundancy (see page 25). *ceased; completed; concluded; dead; deceased; defunct; departed; done; ended; exanimate; expired; extinct; extinguished; finished; gone; inanimate;*

lifeless; no more; over; past; perished; stopped; terminated.

> Instead, they returned to Ireland when I was four, my brother, Malachy, three, the twins, Oliver and Eugene, barely one, and my sister, Margaret, dead and gone. — Frank McCourt, *Angela's Ashes*

(as) dead as a dodo An insipid simile. 1. *ceased; completed; concluded; dead; deceased; defunct; departed; done; ended; exanimate; expired; extinct; extinguished; finished; gone; inanimate; lifeless; no more; over; perished; stopped; terminated.* 2. *antediluvian; antiquated; archaic; dead; obsolescent; obsolete; old; old-fashioned; outdated; outmoded; out of date; out of fashion; passé; superannuated.* 3. *beat; bushed; debilitated; depleted; drained; drowsy; enervated; exhausted; fatigued; groggy; sapped; sleepy; sluggish; slumberous; somnolent; soporific; spent; tired; weary; worn out.*

(as) dead as a doornail An insipid simile. 1. *ceased; completed; concluded; dead; deceased; defunct; departed; done; ended; exanimate; expired; extinct; extinguished; finished; gone; inanimate; lifeless; no more; over; perished; stopped; terminated.* 2. *antediluvian; antiquated; archaic; dead; obsolescent; obsolete; old; old-fashioned; outdated; outmoded; out of date; out of fashion; passé; superannuated.* 3. *beat; bushed; debilitated; depleted; drained; drowsy; enervated; exhausted; fatigued; groggy; sapped; sleepy; sluggish; slumberous; somnolent; soporific; spent; tired; weary; worn out.*

> I settled on getting raised from the dead, since a big part of me still felt dead as a doornail. — Sue Monk Kidd, *The Secret Life of Bees*

dead body A wretched redundancy (see page 25). *body.* ■ Their car was abandoned on a bridge, and *dead bodies* were nowhere to be found. DELETE *dead.*

dead duck A moribund metaphor (see page 21).

deader than a doornail A moribund metaphor (see page 21). 1. *ceased; completed; concluded; dead; deceased; defunct; departed; done; ended; exanimate; expired; extinct; extinguished; finished; gone; inanimate; lifeless; no more; over; perished; stopped; terminated.* 2. *antediluvian; antiquated; archaic; dead; obsolescent; obsolete; old; old-fashioned; outdated; outmoded; out of date; out of fashion; passé; superannuated.* 3. *beat; bushed; debilitated; depleted; drained; drowsy; enervated; exhausted; fatigued; groggy; sapped; sleepy; sluggish; slumberous; somnolent; soporific; spent; tired; weary; worn out.*

dead in the water A moribund metaphor (see page 21). *dead; dormant; dull; inactive; inanimate; indolent; inert; inoperative; languid; latent; lethargic; lifeless; listless; motionless; phlegmatic; quiescent; quiet; sluggish; stagnant; static; stationary; still; stock-still; torpid.* ■ The civil rights impulse from the 1960s is *dead in the water.* REPLACE WITH *listless.*

dead on arrival A moribund metaphor (see page 21).

dead on (her) feet A moribund metaphor (see page 21). *beat; bushed; debilitated; depleted; drained; drowsy; enervated; exhausted; fatigued; groggy; sapped; sleepy; sluggish; slumberous; somnolent; soporific; spent; tired; weary; worn out.*

dead ringer A moribund metaphor (see page 21).

dead serious An inescapable pair (see page 20).

dead to the world A moribund metaphor (see page 21). 1. *asleep; dozing; napping; sleeping.* 2. *anesthetized; benumbed; comatose; insensate; insensible; insentient; oblivious; senseless; soporiferous; soporific; stuporous; unconscious.*

(as) deaf as a post An insipid simile. 1. *deaf; unhearing.* 2. *heedless; inattentive; oblivious; unmindful.*

deaf, dumb, and blind A moribund metaphor (see page 21). *anesthesized; cataleptic; comatose; insensate; insensible; insensient; numb; sensationless; unconscious; unfeeling.*

deal a (crushing; devastating; major; serious) blow to A moribund metaphor (see page 21). 1. *annihilate; assassinate; butcher; demolish; destroy; devastate; eradicate; exterminate; kill; massacre; murder; obliterate; pulverize; rack; ravage; raze; ruin; shatter; slaughter; slay; smash; undo; wrack; wreck.* 2. *beat; conquer; crush; defeat; outdo; overcome; overpower; overwhelm; prevail; quell; rout; succeed; triumph; trounce; vanquish; win.*

Still another phrase favored by journalists *deal a (crushing; devastating; major; serious) blow to,* though it tries mightily to move us, leaves us unimpressed. Drained of any force it might once have had, this dimwitticism exhausts us precisely as much as it is exhausted. ■ Falling real estate values, the stock market crash, and changes in the rules under which S&Ls operate *dealt crushing blows to* the bank's success. REPLACE WITH *vanquished.* ■ Most recently, it was Bennett who *dealt the most devastating blow* to Clinton's leadership. REPLACE WITH *most wracked.*

a deal is a deal A quack equation (see page 23).

(like) death warmed over An insipid simile. *anemic; ashen; blanched; bloodless; cadaverous; colorless; deathlike; doughy; haggard; lusterless; pale; pallid; pasty; peaked; sallow; sickly; wan; whitish.*

declare war (on) A moribund metaphor (see page 21).

deepen the wound A moribund metaphor (see page 21).

deeper in (into) the hole A moribund metaphor (see page 21).

(has) deep pockets A moribund metaphor (see page 21). *affluent; moneyed; opulent; prosperous; rich; wealthy; well-off; well-to-do.*

deep six (*v*) A moribund metaphor (see page 21). *discard; eliminate; get rid of; jettison; reject; throw away; toss out.*

definitely An overworked word (see page 22). So popular is this word that we might well marvel at the assuredness of those who use it. But, of course, the overuse of *definitely* bespeaks carelessness more than it does confidence. SEE ALSO *absolutely; most assuredly; most (very) definitely.*

degree A torpid term (see page 24). *Degree* — and the superfluity of phrases in which it is found — should be excised from almost all of our speech and writing. No sentence is made more compelling by the use of this word and its diffuse phrases. ■ I believe he has *a very high degree* of integrity and takes extreme pride in his workmanship. REPLACE WITH *a good deal.* ■ Increased employee morale would require *a lesser degree of* accuracy. REPLACE WITH *less.* ■ Their hopes are based, *to a large degree,* on signs that business activity is pulling out of its recent slowdown. REPLACE WITH *largely.* ■ *To a larger degree* than was expected, these economically stunted nations can count on help from the 12-nation organization. REPLACE WITH *More.* ■ Another realm in which schools of choice can and do differ is *the degree to which* the staff and parents are involved in the day-to-day operations of the school. REPLACE WITH *how much.* SEE ALSO *extent.*

> She knew she was sick but she didn't know the degree to which it was commonplace, a matter of spring flu, the usual malaise, passed from student to student and among faculty members. — Joyce Carol Oates, *Solstice*

déjà vu A foreign phrase (see page 19).

déjà vu all over again An infantile phrase (see page 20). ■ The police served him with a restraining order; it was *déjà vu all over again.*

delicate balance An inescapable pair (see page 20).

(a) deluge of A moribund metaphor (see page 21). SEE ALSO *a barrage of.*

den of iniquity A moribund metaphor (see page 21).

den of thieves A moribund metaphor (see page 21).

desperately seeking An infantile phrase (see page 20).

despite (in spite of) or (maybe; perhaps) because of (the fact that) An ineffectual phrase (see page 19). These phrases sound as though they have the ring of respectability to them — that is, they sound intelligent — but since the phrases are formulaic (a staple among journalists and those who write like them) and the contribution they make to a sentence uncertain (*despite* virtually nullifies *because of*), they are actually disreputable — that is, they are dimwitted. ■ *Despite* his old-fashioned style, *or perhaps because of* it, Mansfield remains an extremely popular lecturer. ■ *In spite of or, perhaps, because of the fact that* we humans are normally vision experts at a very young age, we have little intuition about how vision develops or how we accomplish seeing. ■ Excessive weight gain occurred during periods of this pregnancy *despite, or because of,* the mother's emotional problems. ■ Lately, she finds herself having a hard time falling asleep, *despite — or perhaps because of* — her exhaustion. ■ But this is what the harvest is all about, and *despite* the hard work, *or actually,* precisely *because of* it, a harvest wants to be celebrated. ■ They sustain a high level of motivation and achieve performance peak after performance peak *in spite of* (*or perhaps because of*) the lack of traditional supervision and rewards.

> Despite or perhaps because of the fact that he left us, he knows it's vital that he does nothing to undermine my self-confidence. — William Nicholson, *The Society of Others*

despite the fact that A wretched redundancy (see page 25). *although; but; even if; even though; still; though; yet.* ■ Long a critic of exorbitant executive salaries, he agreed to a 4.7 percent raise, *despite the fact that* his company's profits doubled. REPLACE WITH *even though.* ■ *Despite the fact that* no serious adverse effects have been found, there are still risks. REPLACE WITH *Although.* SEE ALSO *in spite of the fact that; regardless of the fact that.*

devastate An overworked word (see page 22). We can hardly wonder why so many of us are so easily *devastated.* This word is pervasive. Rarely are we *disconsolate*, rarely are we *flustered.* If only we would use more measured terms, we might feel less weak and woundable.

Consider these terms, all more moderate: *agitated; bothered; crestfallen; despondent; disappointed; discomposed; disconsolate; distressed; disturbed; downcast; downhearted; flustered; heartbroken; heartsick; perturbed; ruffled; unsettled; upset.* ■ When Glen was transferred to a city 100 miles away, I was *devastated.* REPLACE WITH *heartbroken.*

But if devastation it is, here are other terms that might relieve us of our reliance on this one: *atomized; crushed; demolished; desolate; destroyed; distraught; obliterated; overcome; overpowered; overwhelmed; prostrate; ravaged; ruined; shattered; undone.* ■ Dean and Jenna were *devastated* when she lost their baby. REPLACE WITH *shattered.* SEE ALSO *crisis.*

(the) devil finds work for idle hands to do A popular prescription (see page 23).

devil's disciple A moribund metaphor (see page 21).

(the) devil take the hindmost A moribund metaphor (see page 21).

devil to pay A moribund metaphor (see page 21).

develop steam A moribund metaphor (see page 21).

diametrically opposed An inescapable pair (see page 20).

(a) diamond in the rough A moribund metaphor (see page 21). *bad-mannered; coarse; common; crass; crude; ill-bred; ill-mannered; impolite; rough; rude; uncivilized; uncouth; uncultured; unrefined; unsophisticated; vulgar.*

(the) dictionary defines An infantile phrase (see page 20). ■ *Webster's New World Dictionary defines* investigate as "to search into; examine in detail; inquire into systematically." ■ *The dictionary defines* gratitude as "a feeling of thankful appreciation for favors or benefits received." SEE ALSO *as defined in (the dictionary).*

didn't miss a beat A moribund metaphor (see page 21).

> Bess didn't miss a beat. She looked up, looked Christine straight in the eye and said, "Chris, don't go cutting the fool." — Nancy Bartholomew, *Stand by Your Man*

die laughing A moribund metaphor (see page 21).

(the) die is cast A moribund metaphor (see page 21).

die (wither) on the vine A moribund metaphor (see page 21). *atrophy; be unsuccessful; bomb; break down; collapse; decay; fail; fall short; falter; fizzle; flop; flounder; fold; founder; languish; mess up; miscarry; miss; not succeed; shrivel; stumble; topple; wilt; wither.* ■ We believe Medicare is going to *wither on the vine* because we think people are going to voluntarily leave it. REPLACE WITH *founder.* ■ The history of computing is littered with great products that *withered on the vine.* REPLACE WITH *failed.*

different strokes for different folks A popular prescription (see page 23).

difficult task An inescapable pair (see page 20).

digging (your) own grave A moribund metaphor (see page 21).

dig in (his) heels A moribund metaphor (see page 21). *be adamant; be balky; be bullheaded; be cantankerous; be contrary; be contumacious; be determined; be dogged; be firm; be headstrong; be inflexible; be intractable; be mulish; be obdurate; be obstinate; be ornery; be perverse; be refractory; be resistant; be resolute; be resolved; be rigid; be stubborn; be unyielding; be willful.* ■ By then, the auto industry was *digging in its heels,* and almost as soon as the law was approved, its provisions were called too stringent. REPLACE WITH *becoming resolute.*

(a) dime a dozen A moribund metaphor (see page 21). *average; basic; common; commonplace; customary; everyday; normal; omnipresent; ordinary; prevalent; quotidian; regular; standard; typical; ubiquitous; unexceptional; universal; unremarkable; usual; widespread.* ■ Sikhs in Kenya are *a dime a dozen.* REPLACE WITH *ubiquitous.*

> What you find out in your thirties is that clever children are a dime a dozen. It's what you do later that counts, and so far I had done nothing. — Christina Schwarz, *All Is Vanity*

(a) direct line to God An infantile phrase (see page 20). ■ A pair of men spotted outside the Marshalls' house leads Dunning to the Preacher, a bookseller with questionable intentions and *a direct line to God.* ■ These nontraditionalist Christians frequently assert *a direct line to God,* purporting to know details about the consummation of the world.

> When she pictures *shefa,* she thinks of the red phone on the President's desk that is supposed to be a direct line to the Soviet Union. *Shefa* will be her red telephone, a direct line to God. — Myla Goldberg, *Bee Season*

dirt cheap A moribund metaphor (see page 21). *cheap; economical; inexpensive; low-cost; low-priced; not costly.*

dirty pool A moribund metaphor (see page 21).

(a) dirty word A moribund metaphor (see page 21). *abhorrent; abominable; a curse; an abomination; anathema; antipathetic; detestable; execrable; hateful; loathsome; monstrous; offensive; repugnant.* ■ Some in the academic community may disagree, but to working families corporate takeovers are still *a dirty word.* REPLACE WITH *anathema.*

dis An infantile phrase (see page 20). *Dis* is a prefix aspiring to be a word. Are we to allow *un* and *anti, non* and *pre* to follow? People are increasingly mono- and disyllabic as it is; let's rail against this foolishness, this affront, this dimwitted *dis.* ■ And not only does the little *dissing* contest draw the battle lines in today's best-selling music world, but it serves as a reminder of the way *Rolling Stone* manages to embody two sides without appearing totally ridiculous. REPLACE WITH *disparaging.* ■ This issue addresses five other means of *dissing* employees: buck passing, procrastination, inattentiveness, impatience and public reprimands. REPLACE WITH *disrespecting.* ■ More bad news for Leonardo DiCaprio: ABC News is *dissing* him big-time. REPLACE WITH *dismissing.* ■ Gov. Bill Owens made a media splash Monday, playing TV critic and *dissing* first lady of TV news Barbara Walters on national television. REPLACE WITH *disparaging.* ■ Watch Letterman stir up trouble with a Top 10 list or by *dissing* the soft drink Dr. Pepper as "liquid manure." REPLACE WITH *denigrating.* ■ Franzen, despised and envied by all writers for his talent, his luck, his good looks, and his marketing acumen, essentially *dissed* the Oprah award for being ... lowbrow. REPLACE WITH *dismissed.*

disappear (vanish) into thin air A moribund metaphor (see page 21). *disappear; disperse; dissolve; evaporate; fade; vanish; vaporize; volatilize.*

disappear (vanish) without a trace A moribund metaphor (see page 21). *disappear; disperse; dissolve; evaporate; fade; vanish; vaporize; volatilize.*

discretion is the better part of valor A popular prescription (see page 23).

dismal failure An inescapable pair (see page 20). ■ The mayor's attempt at improving the quality of life on Boston Common at night was a *dismal failure.*

divine intervention An inescapable pair (see page 20).

do a disappearing act A moribund metaphor (see page 21). *abscond; clear out; decamp; depart; desert; disappear; escape; exit; flee; fly; go; go away; leave; move on; part; pull out; quit; retire; retreat; run away; take flight; take off; vacate; vanish; withdraw.*

do a hatchet job on A moribund metaphor (see page 21). *asperse; badmouth; belittle; besmirch; bespatter; blacken; calumniate; defame; defile; denigrate; denounce; depreciate; deride; disparage; impugn; insult; libel; malign; profane; revile; scandalize; slander; slap; slur; smear; sully; taint; traduce; vilify; vitiate.*

do a job on A moribund metaphor (see page 21). 1. *blight; cripple; damage; deface; disable; disfigure; harm; hurt; impair; incapacitate; injure; lame; maim; mar; mess up; rack; ruin; sabotage; spoil; subvert; undermine; vitiate; wrack; wreck.* 2. *agitate; bother; disquiet; distress; disturb; fluster; jar; jolt; pain; perturb; ruffle; shake; trouble; unsettle; upset; wound.* SEE ALSO *do a number on.*

do all (everything) in (my) power A torpid term (see page 24). ■ I believe that Cashbuild has *done everything in its* *power* to cope with the changing South American environment.

do an about-face A moribund metaphor (see page 21). *apostatize; backtrack; flip-flop; recidivate; renege; reverse; tergiversate.* SEE ALSO *do a 180.*

do (make) an end run around A moribund metaphor (see page 21). *avoid; bypass; circumvent; dodge; duck; elude; evade; go around; parry; sidestep; skirt.* ■ Trying to *do an end run around* the person responsible for making purchasing decisions isn't advisable. REPLACE WITH *sidestep*.

do a number on A moribund metaphor (see page 21). 1. *blight; cripple; damage; deface; disable; disfigure; harm; hurt; impair; incapacitate; injure; lame; maim; mar; mess up; rack; ruin; sabotage; spoil; subvert; undermine; vitiate; wrack; wreck.* 2. *agitate; bother; disquiet; distress; disturb; fluster; jar; jolt; pain; perturb; ruffle; shake; trouble; unsettle; upset; wound.* SEE ALSO *do a job on.*

do a 180 A moribund metaphor (see page 21). *apostatize; backtrack; flip-flop; recidivate; renege; reverse; tergiversate.* SEE ALSO *do an about face.*

do as I say, not as I do A popular prescription (see page 23).

doctor, lawyer, Indian chief A moribund metaphor (see page 21).

dodge the bullet A moribund metaphor (see page 21).

(it) doesn't amount to a hill of beans A moribund metaphor (see page 21). *barren; bootless; effete; feckless; feeble; fruitless; futile; impotent; inadequate; inconsequential; inconsiderable; ineffective; ineffectual; infertile; insignificant; inutile; meaningless; meritless; nugatory; null; of no value; pointless; powerless; profitless; purposeless; sterile; trifling; trivial; unavailing; unimportant; unproductive; unprofitable; unserviceable; unworthy; useless; vain; valueless; weak; worthless.*

> I had too much to do, I told myself, to worry with last-minute, undoubtedly invalid last wills and testaments that probably wouldn't amount to a hill of beans. — Ann B. Ross, *Miss Julia Speaks Her Mind*

doesn't have a clue A moribund metaphor (see page 21). *addlebrained; addleheaded; addlepated; Boeotian; bovine; brainless; clueless; cretinous; decerebrate; dense; dim-witted; doltish; dull; dumb; dunderheaded; empty-headed; fatuous; fat-witted; harebrained; hebetudinous; ignorant; imbecilic; incogitant; insensate; ludicrous; mindless; moronic; muddled; nescient; obtuse; oxlike; phlegmatic; slow-witted; sluggish; stupid; torpid; unaware; unintelligent; unknowing; vacuous; witless.*

doesn't have a snowball's chance in hell A moribund metaphor (see page 21). *impossible; unachievable; unattainable; unfeasible.*

doesn't have both oars in the water A moribund metaphor (see page 21). *batty; cracked; crazy; daft; demented; deranged; fey; foolish; goofy; insane; lunatic; mad; maniacal; neurotic; nuts; nutty; psychotic; raving; silly; squirrelly; strange; touched; unbalanced; unhinged; unsound; wacky; zany.*

doesn't have two nickels to rub together A moribund metaphor (see page 21). *bankrupt; broke; destitute; distressed; impecunious; impoverished; indigent; insolvent; needy; penniless; poor; poverty- stricken; underprivileged.*

doesn't hold water A moribund metaphor (see page 21). *baseless; captious; casuistic; casuistical; erroneous; fallacious; false; faulty; flawed; groundless; illogical; inaccurate; incorrect; invalid; irrational; jesuitical; mistaken; nonsensical; non sequitur; paralogistic; senseless; sophistic; sophistical; specious; spurious; unfounded; unreasonable; unsound; untenable; untrue; unveracious; wrong.*

doesn't know (her) ass from a hole in the wall A moribund metaphor (see page 21). 1. *addlebrained; addleheaded; addlepated; Boeotian; bovine; brainless; clueless; cretinous; decerebrate; dense; dimwitted; doltish; dull; dumb; dunderheaded; empty-headed; fatuous; fat-witted; harebrained; hebetudinous; ignorant; imbecilic; incogitant; insensate; ludicrous; mindless; moronic; muddled; nescient; obtuse; oxlike; phlegmatic; slow-witted; sluggish; stupid; torpid; unaware; unintelligent; unknowing; vacuous; witless.* 2. *deficient; inadequate; inapt; incapable; incompetent; ineffective; inefficacious; inept; lacking; not able; unable; unfit; unqualified; unsatisfactory; unskilled; wanting.*

doesn't know (his) ass from (his) elbow A moribund metaphor (see page 21). 1. *addlebrained; addleheaded; addlepated; Boeotian; bovine; brainless; clueless; cretinous; decerebrate; dense; dimwitted; doltish; dull; dumb; dunderheaded; empty-headed; fatuous; fat-witted; harebrained; hebetudinous; ignorant; imbecilic; incogitant; insensate; ludicrous; mindless; moronic; muddled; nescient; obtuse; oxlike; phlegmatic; slow-witted; sluggish; stupid; torpid; unaware; unintelligent; unknowing; vacuous; witless.* 2. *deficient; inadequate; inapt; incapable; incompetent; ineffective; inefficacious; inept; lacking; not able; unable; unfit; unqualified; unsatisfactory; unskilled; wanting.*

doesn't know enough to come in out of the rain A moribund metaphor (see page 21). 1. *addlebrained; addleheaded; addlepated; Boeotian; bovine; brainless; clueless; cretinous; decerebrate; dense; dimwitted; doltish; dull; dumb; dunderheaded; empty-headed; fatuous; fat-witted; harebrained; hebetudinous; ignorant; imbecilic; incogitant; insensate; ludicrous; mindless; moronic; muddled; nescient; obtuse; oxlike; phlegmatic; slow-witted; sluggish; stupid; torpid; unaware; unintelligent; unknowing; vacuous; witless.* 2. *adolescent; artless; callow; green; guileless; immature; inexperienced; inexpert; ingenuous; innocent; juvenile; naive; raw; simple; undeveloped; unfledged; unskilled; unskillful; unsophisticated; untaught; untrained; unworldly; young; youthful.*

dog and pony show A moribund metaphor (see page 21).

(the) dog days of summer A moribund metaphor (see page 21). *boiling; hot; humid; scorching; sizzling; sweltering.*

dog-eat-dog A moribund metaphor (see page 21). *barbarous; bloodthirsty; brutal; cold-blooded; compassionless; cruel; cutthroat; feral; ferocious; fierce; hard; hard-hearted; harsh; heartless; implacable; inexorable; inhuman; merciless; murderous; rancorous; relentless;*

ruthless; savage; uncompassionate; unmerciful; unrelenting; vicious; virulent; wild.

(a) dog's age A moribund metaphor (see page 21). *ages; a long time; a long while; an age; an eternity; decades; eons; forever; months; years.*

(lead a) dog's life A moribund metaphor (see page 21). *misery; unhappiness; wretchedness.*

dollars and sense An infantile phrase (see page 20).

dollars to doughnuts A moribund metaphor (see page 21). *be certain; be sure.*

> I had no place to stay, and dollars to doughnuts, sitting in front of me was a building with a vacant apartment. — Janet Evanovich, *Ten Big Ones*

(a) done deal A infantile phrase. *absolute; completed; concluded; conclusive; consummated; definitive; final; finished.* ■ There seems to be a misconception that this is *a done deal.* REPLACE WITH *consummated.*

don't count your chickens before they're hatched A popular prescription (see page 23).

don't cry over spilled milk A popular prescription (see page 23).

don't do anything I wouldn't do An infantile phrase (see page 20).

don't get mad, get even A popular prescription (see page 23). ■ Hillary, *don't get mad, get even* — write a book.

don't get me wrong An infantile phrase (see page 20). ■ I'm not trying to condone what I've done. *Don't get me wrong.* REPLACE WITH *Don't misunderstand me.* SEE ALSO *I hear you.*

don't give up the ship A popular prescription (see page 23). *carry on; continue; ensue; go on; keep up; persevere; persist; press on; proceed.*

don't hold (your) breath A moribund metaphor (see page 21).

don't knock it until you try it A popular prescription (see page 23).

don't rock the boat A moribund metaphor (see page 21).

don't see eye to eye A moribund metaphor (see page 21). *clash; conflict; differ; disagree; think differently.*

don't start anything you can't finish A popular prescription (see page 23).

doom and gloom An inescapable pair (see page 20).

doomed to failure A torpid term (see page 24). *damned; doomed; hopeless; ill-fated.*

do or die A popular prescription (see page 23).

do's and don'ts *canon; codes; conventions; conventionality; customs; decorum; directives; etiquette; formula; formulary; guidelines; law; manners; policy; precepts; protocol; proprieties; regulations; rules; standards.*

dot the i's and cross the t's A moribund metaphor (see page 21). *careful; conscientious; exact; exacting; fastidious; finical; finicky; fussy; meticulous; nice; painstaking; particular; picky; precise; punctilious; scrupulous; thorough.*

double-edge sword A moribund metaphor (see page 21).

doubting Thomas A moribund metaphor (see page 21). *cynic; disbeliever; doubter; skeptic.*

down and out A moribund metaphor (see page 21). *bankrupt; broke; destitute; distressed; impecunious; impoverished; indigent; insolvent; needy; penniless; poor; poverty- stricken; underprivileged.*

down at the heels A moribund metaphor (see page 21). 1. *dowdy; frowzy; messy; ragged; run-down; seedy; shabby; slipshod; sloppy; slovenly; tattered; threadbare; unkempt; untidy; worn.* 2. *bankrupt; broke; destitute; distressed; impecunious; impoverished; indigent; insolvent; needy; penniless; poor; poverty-stricken; underprivileged.*

down (out) for the count A moribund metaphor (see page 21). 1. *asleep; napping; sleeping; slumbering; snoozing.* 2. *cataleptic; comatose; dormant; inactive; insensible; lifeless; out cold; passed out; unconscious; unresponsive.*

down in the dumps A moribund metaphor (see page 21). *aggrieved; blue; cheerless; dejected; demoralized; depressed; despondent; disconsolate; discouraged; disheartened; dismal; dispirited; doleful; downcast; downhearted; dreary; forlorn; funereal; gloomy; glum; grieved; low; melancholy; miserable; morose; mournful; plaintive; sad; sorrowful; unhappy; woebegone; woeful.*

down in the mouth A moribund metaphor (see page 21). *aggrieved; blue; cheerless; dejected; demoralized; depressed; despondent; disconsolate; discouraged; disheartened; dismal; dispirited; doleful; downcast; downhearted; dreary; forlorn; funereal; gloomy; glum; grieved; low; melancholy; miserable; morose; mournful; plaintive; sad; sorrowful; unhappy; woebegone; woeful.*

> Thought it was Nora, but when I opened the door, Lewis was standing there in his rumpled linen suit, looking a bit down in the mouth, not a trace of the bulldog in his face. — Richard B. Wright, *Clara Callan*

(go) down the drain A moribund metaphor (see page 21). 1. *be misused; be squandered; be thrown way; be wasted.* 2. *break down; collapse; deteriorate; die; disappear; disintegrate; disperse; dissipate; dissolve; evaporate; fade; fail; finish; forfeit; go; lose; pass; scatter; vanish; vaporize; volatilize; waste.* 3. *annihilated; crushed; demolished; destroyed; obliterated; overturned; ravaged; ruined; scuttled; shattered; smashed; undone; wrecked.* ■ One major mistake and your career is *down the drain.* REPLACE WITH *ruined.* ■ Without new revenue, our schools will *go down the drain.* REPLACE WITH *collapse.*

down the hatch A moribund metaphor (see page 21). *drink; gulp; guzzle; imbibe; quaff; swallow.*

(later on) down the line (path; pike; road) A wretched redundancy (see page

25). *at length; before long; eventually; from now; in time; later; ultimately.* ■ Even though this knowledge might not seem essential right now, it just might prove invaluable *down the line.* REPLACE WITH *later.* ■ Two players will be added to the team *later, some months down the road.* REPLACE WITH *some months later.* ■ *Later on down the line*, we did in fact marry. REPLACE WITH *At length.*

(go) down the tubes A moribund metaphor (see page 21). 1. *be despoiled; be destroyed; be devastated; be dissipated; be pillaged; be plundered; be ravaged; be ruined; break down; collapse; disintegrate; fail; fall short; flop; founder; miscarry; topple.* 2. *be misused; be squandered; be thrown way; be wasted.* ■ Her article points out a major reason why our country is *going down the tubes.* REPLACE WITH *foundering.* ■ All the money my parents spent on my braces *went down the tubes.* REPLACE WITH *was wasted.*

down to earth A moribund metaphor (see page 21). *artless; common; earthly; everyday; genuine; guileless; mortal; mundane; natural; normal; plain; secular; staid; temporal; unaffected; unassuming; unpretentious; worldly.*

(come) down to the wire A moribund metaphor (see page 21).

drag (their) feet A moribund metaphor (see page 21). *arrest; balk; block; bridle; check; dawdle; defer; delay; detain; encumber; hamper; hesitate; hinder; hold up; impede; inhibit; obstruct; pause; postpone; put off; retard; stall; stay; stonewall; suspend.* ■ The regional Bells have *dragged their feet* in rolling out DSL services. REPLACE WITH *dawdled.*

drag into (through) the mud A moribund metaphor (see page 21). *asperse; badmouth; belittle; besmirch; bespatter; blacken; calumniate; defame; defile; denigrate; denounce; depreciate; deride; disparage; impugn; insult; libel; malign; profane; revile; scandalize; slander; slap; slur; smear; sully; taint; traduce; vilify; vitiate.* ■ His name was *dragged through the mud* last week thanks to a Harvard Law School professor. REPLACE WITH *defamed.*

> He sat down again, trembling with rage; person after person was being dragged into the mud. — E. M. Forster, *A Passage to India*

drag kicking and screaming A moribund metaphor (see page 21).

draw a bead on A moribund metaphor (see page 21). 1. *aim at; focus on; sight; train on.* 2. *admonish; animadvert; berate; castigate; censure; chasten; chastise; chide; condemn; criticize; denounce; denunciate; discipline; impugn; objurgate; punish; rebuke; remonstrate; reprehend; reprimand; reproach; reprobate; reprove; revile; scold; upbraid; vituperate.*

draw a blank A moribund metaphor (see page 21). 1. *be addleheaded; be bovine; be cretinous; be decerebrated; be dense; be dull; be dull-witted; be fatuous; be fat-witted; be half-witted; be harebrained; be hebetudinous; be idiotic; be ignorant; be imbecilic; be incogitant; be insensate; be mindless; be moronic; be muddled; be nescient; be obtuse; be phlegmatic; be slow; be slow-witted; be sluggish; be thick; be torpid; be undiscerning; be unintelligent; be vacuous; be witless.* 2. *be absent-minded; be forgetful; be lethean; be oblivious.* ■ A successful attorney,

Caroline *draws a blank* when it comes to men. REPLACE WITH *is witless.*

draw a veil over A moribund metaphor (see page 21). *adumbrate; becloud; befog; camouflage; cloak; cloud; conceal; cover; disguise; dissemble; enshroud; harbor; hide; keep secret; mask; obfuscate; obscure; overshadow; screen; shroud; suppress; veil; withhold.*

draw fire (from) A moribund metaphor (see page 21).

draw in (his) horns A moribund metaphor (see page 21). *back away; back down; back off; disengage; evacuate; fall back; recede; regress; retire; retreat; withdraw.*

draw in the reins A moribund metaphor (see page 21). *bridle; check; curb; curtail; halt; restrain; stall; stay; stop.*

draw the line (at) A moribund metaphor (see page 21).

draw the long bow A moribund metaphor (see page 21). *elaborate; embellish; embroider; enhance; enlarge; exaggerate; hyperbolize; inflate; magnify; overdo; overreact; overstress; overstate; strain; stretch.*

(a) dream (fairy tale) come true A plebeian sentiment (see page 23).

dredge up dirt A moribund metaphor (see page 21).

dressed to kill A moribund metaphor (see page 21). *elaborately; elegantly; extravagantly; fashionably; flamboyantly; flashily; gaudily; lavishly; ostentatiously; profusely; richly; showily; smartly; stylishly.*

dribs and drabs An inescapable pair (see page 20). *bits; chunks; crumbs; fragments; modicums; morsels; nuggets; particles; pieces; scraps; segments; shreds; snips; snippets; specks.*

drink like a fish An insipid simile. *alcoholic; bibulous.*

drive a stake through the heart (of) A moribund metaphor (see page 21). 1. *execute; kill; massacre; murder; slaughter; slay.* 2. *annihilate; demolish; destroy; eliminate; eradicate; exterminate; liquidate; obliterate; ravage; ruin; sack; wreck.* ■ The IRB's decision *drives a stake through the heart of* the myth peddled by Carey sympathizers inside and outside the Teamsters. REPLACE WITH *slays.*

drive a wedge between A moribund metaphor (see page 21).

drive (me) bananas (crazy; nuts) A moribund metaphor (see page 21). *annoy; badger; bedevil; bother; chafe; distress; disturb; exasperate; gall; grate; harass; harry; hassle; heckle; hector; hound; irk; irritate; nag; nettle; persecute; pester; plague; provoke; rankle; rile; roil; tease; torment; vex.*

drive (me) to drink A moribund metaphor (see page 21). *annoy; badger; bedevil; bother; chafe; distress; disturb; exasperate; gall; grate; harass; harry; hassle; heckle; hector; hound; irk; irritate; nag; nettle; persecute; pester; plague; provoke; rankle; rile; roil; tease; torment; vex.*

drive (me) up the wall A moribund metaphor (see page 21). *annoy; badger; bedevil; bother; chafe; distress; disturb; exasperate; gall; grate; harass; harry; hassle; heckle; hector; hound; irk; irritate;*

nag; nettle; persecute; pester; plague; provoke; rankle; rile; roil; tease; torment; vex.

driving force A wretched redundancy (see page 25). *drive; energy; force; impetus; motivation; power.*

drop (fall) by the wayside A moribund metaphor (see page 21). 1. *abate; cease to be; diminish; disappear; dissolve; dwindle; fade; go away; recede; vanish.* 2. *be unsuccessful; fail; fall short; founder.* 3. *give in; give way; submit; succumb; surrender; yield.* ■ Social class distinctions have mostly *fallen by the wayside*, and scientists are now more likely to admit the collective nature of research. REPLACE WITH *disappeared.*

> Believe me in those days the girls were dropping by the wayside like seeds off a poppyseed bun and you learned to look at every day as a prize. — Barbara Kingsolver, *The Bean Trees*

drop-dead gorgeous A moribund metaphor (see page 21). *attractive; beautiful; comely; exquisite; fair; fetching; good looking; gorgeous; handsome; lovely; pretty; pulchritudinous; ravishing.*

(a) drop in the bucket (ocean) A moribund metaphor (see page 21). *frivolous; inappreciable; immaterial; inconsequential; inconsiderable; insignificant; meager; meaningless; negligible; next to nothing; nugatory; paltry; petty; scant; scanty; scarcely anything; slight; trifling; trivial; unimportant; unsubstantial; worthless.* ■ Relative to need, it's *a drop in the bucket.* REPLACE WITH *next to nothing.* ■ When art is part of a larger construction budget, the money is usually *a drop in the bucket* compared with overall costs. REPLACE WITH *inconsiderable.*

drop like a hot potato An insipid simile. *abandon; abdicate; desert; discard; ditch; drop; forgo; forsake; get rid of; give up; jettison; leave; quit; reject; relinquish; renounce; surrender; throw away; toss out; yield.*

drop like flies An insipid simile. *annihilate; decimate; demolish; slaughter.*

drop off the face of the earth A moribund metaphor (see page 21). *disappear; vanish.*

drop the ball A moribund metaphor (see page 21). *be unsuccessful; bomb; break down; collapse; fail; fall short; falter; fizzle; flop; fold; founder; mess up; miscarry; not succeed; stumble; topple.*

(a) drowning man will clutch at a straw A popular prescription (see page 23).

(as) drunk as a lord An insipid simile. *besotted; crapulous; drunk; inebriated; intoxicated; sodden; stupefied; tipsy.*

(as) drunk as a skunk An insipid simile. *besotted; crapulous; drunk; inebriated; intoxicated; sodden; stupefied; tipsy.*

(as) dry as a bone An insipid simile. *arid; dehydrated; desiccated; droughty; dry; exsiccated; parched; sear; shriveled; thirsty; wilted; withered.*

(as) dry as dust An insipid simile. *anodyne; banal; barren; bland; boring; deadly; dreary; dry; dull; everyday; flat; humdrum; inanimate; insipid; jejune; lifeless; lusterless; mediocre; monotonous; prosaic; routine; spiritless; stale; tedious; tiresome; unexciting; uninteresting; vapid; wearisome.*

dubious distinction An inescapable pair (see page 20). ■ Now the Cowboys are coming off a 34-0 shutout in Philadelphia while the Giants have the *dubious distinction* of being the first team to lose to Washington this season.

duck soup A moribund metaphor (see page 21). *easily done; easy; effortless; elementary; facile; simple; simplicity itself; straightforward; uncomplex; uncomplicated.*

due to circumstances beyond (our) control An ineffectual phrase (see page 19). Of those who use this phrase, we may remark that their speech is no more grammatical than their actions are genuine.

Due to, as often as not, should be *because of* or *owing to*, and only the similarly disingenuous would believe that *circumstances beyond our control* is an explanation rather than an evasion.

In the end, those who express themselves badly are less credible than those who express themselves well. ■ *Due to circumstances beyond our control,* no motel rooms are available in the area on June 25th, 26th, and 27th. ■ *Due to circumstances beyond our control,* the following items may not be available as advertised. SEE ALSO *due to popular demand.*

due to popular demand An ineffectual phrase (see page 19). There is with this phrase the same solecism and a similar suspicion as with *due to circumstances beyond (our) control* (SEE). ■ *Due to popular demand,* The Magic Show will be held over another two weeks.

due to the fact that A wretched redundancy (see page 25). *because; considering; for; in that; since.* ■ Requirements continue to decrease slowly *due to the fact that* activity generally decreases with age. REPLACE WITH *since.* ■ Could this be *due to the fact that* it is undecidable? REPLACE WITH *because.* SEE ALSO *attributable to the fact that; owing to the fact that.*

(as) dull as dishwater An insipid simile. 1. *addleheaded; bovine; cretinous; decerebrate; dense; dull; dull-witted; fatuous; fat-witted; half-witted; harebrained; hebetudinous; idiotic; ignorant; imbecilic; incogitant; insensate; mindless; moronic; muddled; nescient; obtuse; phlegmatic; slow; slow-witted; sluggish; thick; torpid; undiscerning; unintelligent; vacuous; witless.* 2. *anodyne; banal; barren; bland; boring; deadly; dreary; dry; dull; everyday; flat; humdrum; inanimate; insipid; jejune; lifeless; lusterless; mediocre; monotonous; prosaic; routine; spiritless; stale; tedious; tiresome; unexciting; uninteresting; vapid; wearisome.*

(as) dumb as a stone An insipid simile. *addlebrained; addleheaded; addlepated; Boeotian; bovine; brainless; clueless; cretinous; decerebrate; dense; dim-witted; doltish; dull; dumb; dunderheaded; empty-headed; fatuous; fat-witted; harebrained; hebetudinous; ignorant; imbecilic; incogitant; insensate; ludicrous; mindless; moronic; muddled; nescient; obtuse; oxlike; phlegmatic; slow-witted; sluggish; stupid; torpid; unaware; unintelligent; unknowing; vacuous; witless.*

(as) dumb as dirt An insipid simile. *addlebrained; addleheaded; addlepated; Boeotian; bovine; brainless; clueless; cretinous; decerebrate; dense; dim-witted; doltish; dull; dumb; dunderheaded; empty-headed; fatuous; fat-witted; hare-*

brained; hebetudinous; ignorant; imbecilic; incogitant; insensate; ludicrous; mindless; moronic; muddled; nescient; obtuse; oxlike; phlegmatic; slow-witted; sluggish; stupid; torpid; unaware; unintelligent; unknowing; vacuous; witless. ■ Frankly, I think these allegations are simply *dumb as dirt.* REPLACE WITH *Boeotian.*

during (in; over) the course of A wretched redundancy (see page 25). *during; in; over; throughout.* ■ *In the course of* a 30 minute conversation, she spoke about her married life and her plans for the future. REPLACE WITH *During.* ■ *Over the course of* a woman's life, she may experience a kaleidoscope of health concerns. REPLACE WITH *Throughout.*

> She had drunk a quantity of champagne, and during the course of her song she had decided, ineptly, that everything was very, very sad — she was not only singing, she was weeping too. — F. Scott Fitzgerald, *The Great Gatsby*

during the period (time) that A wretched redundancy (see page 25). *while.* ■ *During the time that* we were with him, he called her several uncomplimentary names. REPLACE WITH *While.*

(when) (the) dust settles A moribund metaphor (see page 21).

(like a) Dutch uncle An insipid simile.

dyed-in-the-wool A moribund metaphor (see page 21). *ardent; constant; devoted; faithful; inflexible; intractable; loyal; refractory; resolute; rigid; staunch; steadfast; unbending; unwavering; unyielding.*

(a) dying breed A moribund metaphor (see page 21). *declining; dying; moribund; waning.*

dynamic duo An infantile phrase (see page 20).

E

each and every (one) A wretched redundancy (see page 25). *all; each; everybody; everyone.* ■ Software developers have changed the way *each and every one* of us does business. REPLACE WITH *each.*

each one A wretched redundancy (see page 25). *each.* ■ The fact that these companies do have to compete for business gives *each one* an incentive to work harder and to lower prices. DELETE *one.* SEE ALSO *either one; neither one.*

each to his own A popular prescription (see page 23).

eagle eyed A moribund metaphor (see page 21). *alert; attentive; observant; vigilant; watchful.*

(the) early bird catches the worm A popular prescription (see page 23).

(the) end justifies the means A popular prescription (see page 23).

(the) exception, not (rather than) the rule A torpid term (see page 24). *aberrant; abnormal; anomalistic; anomalous; atypical; bizarre; curious; deviant; different; distinct; distinctive; eccentric; exceptional; extraordinary; fantastic; foreign; grotesque; idiosyncratic; independent; individual; individualistic; irregular; notable; noteworthy; novel; odd; offbeat; original; peculiar; puzzling; quaint; queer; rare; remarkable; separate; singular; strange; uncommon; unconventional; unexampled; unique; unnatural; unorthodox; unparalleled; unprecedented; unusual; weird.*

Most people find it easier to mimic a repeatedly used phrase like this — however wordy and inexact, however obtuse and tedious — than to remember a rarely used word like *aberrant* or *anomalous.* ■ Today, in region after region, single-town school districts are *the exception, not the rule.* REPLACE WITH *exceptional.* ■ Arrest or issuing a citation is *the exception, not the rule.* REPLACE WITH *atypical.*

(the) exception that proves the rule An infantile phrase (see page 20).

(the) exception to the rule A torpid term (see page 24). *aberrant; abnormal; anomalistic; anomalous; atypical; bizarre; curious; deviant; different; distinct; distinctive; eccentric; exceptional; extraordinary; fantastic; foreign; grotesque; idiosyncratic; independent; individual; individualistic; irregular; notable; noteworthy; novel; odd; offbeat; original; peculiar; puzzling; quaint; queer; rare; remarkable; separate; singular; strange; uncommon; unconventional; unexampled; unique; unnatural; unorthodox; unparalleled; unprecedented; unusual; weird.*

earn (his) stripes A moribund metaphor (see page 21).

(as) easy as A B C An insipid simile. *apparent; basic; clear; clear-cut; conspicuous; distinct; easily done; easy; effortless; elementary; evident; explicit; facile; limpid; lucid; manifest; obvious; patent; pellucid; plain; simple; simplicity itself; straightforward; translucent; transparent; unambiguous; uncomplex; uncomplicated; understandable; unequivocal; unmistakable.*

(as) easy as 1 2 3 An insipid simile. *apparent; basic; clear; clear-cut; conspicuous; distinct; easily done; easy; effortless; elementary; evident; explicit; facile; limpid; lucid; manifest; obvious; patent; pellucid; plain; simple; simplicity itself; straightforward; translucent; transparent; unambiguous; uncomplex; uncomplicated; understandable; unequivocal; unmistakable.*

(as) easy as pie An insipid simile. *apparent; basic; clear; clear-cut; conspicuous; distinct; easily done; easy; effortless; elementary; evident; explicit; facile; limpid; lucid; manifest; obvious; patent; pellucid; plain; simple; simplicity itself; straightforward; translucent; transparent; unambiguous; uncomplex; uncomplicated; understandable; unequivocal; unmistakable.* ■ It's *easy as pie* to strike up a conversation with the person sitting next to you. REPLACE WITH *easy.*

> It was easy as pie to slip back into my old self. — Laurie Colwin, *Goodbye Without Leaving*

easy on the eyes A moribund metaphor (see page 21). *attractive; beautiful; comely; exquisite; fair; fetching; good looking;*

gorgeous; handsome; lovely; pretty; pulchritudinous; ravishing.

> One of the four girls, the one in red, asked, "Will you be going, Michael?" An outsider, she was, but very easy on the eyes. — Anne Tyler, *The Amateur Marriage*

easy on the pocket(book) A moribund metaphor (see page 21). *affordable; cheap; economical; inexpensive; low-cost; low-priced; reasonable.*

an easy (simple) task A torpid term (see page 24). *apparent; basic; clear; clear-cut; conspicuous; distinct; easily done; easy; effortless; elementary; evident; explicit; facile; limpid; lucid; manifest; obvious; patent; pellucid; plain; simple; simplicity itself; straightforward; translucent; transparent; unambiguous; uncomplex; uncomplicated; understandable; unequivocal; unmistakable.* ■ Identifying opinion leaders is not *a simple task* since they tend to be product specific and differ over time. REPLACE WITH *easy.*

eat crow A moribund metaphor (see page 21). *be abased; be chastened; be debased; be degraded; be demeaned; be disgraced; be dishonored; be embarrassed; be humbled; be humiliated; be lowered; be mortified; be shamed.*

eat dirt A moribund metaphor (see page 21). *be abased; be chastened; be debased; be degraded; be demeaned; be disgraced; be dishonored; be embarrassed; be humbled; be humiliated; be lowered; be mortified; be shamed.*

eat, drink, and be merry A popular prescription (see page 23). *be merry; carouse; carry on; celebrate; debauch; disport; frolic; party; play; revel; riot; roister; rollick; romp; skylark.*

eat, drink, and be merry, for tomorrow we die A popular prescription (see page 23).

eat (your) heart out A moribund metaphor (see page 21). *ache; agonize; grieve; hurt; lament; mourn; pine; sorrow; suffer; worry.*

eat (live) high off (on) the hog A moribund metaphor (see page 21). *epicureanly; extravagantly; lavishly; lushly; luxuriantly; opulently; prodigally; profusely; sumptuously; very well.*

eat humble pie A moribund metaphor (see page 21). *be abased; be chastened; be debased; be degraded; be demeaned; be disgraced; be dishonored; be embarrassed; be humbled; be humiliated; be lowered; be mortified; be shamed.*

> But telling my editors they were about to be fined several thousand dollars was not a prospect I relished. So I took a deep breath and ate humble pie. — Neely Tucker, *Love in the Driest Season*

eat like a bird An insipid simile. *be abstemious.; be ascetic.*

eat like a horse An insipid simile. 1. *be esurient; be famished; be gluttonous; be greedy; be hungry; be insatiable; be omnivorous; be rapacious; be ravenous; be starved; be starving; be voracious.* 2. *glut; gorge; overdo; overeat; overfeed; overindulge; sate; satiate; stuff; surfeit.*

eat like a pig An insipid simile. 1. *be esurient; be famished; be gluttonous; be* *greedy; be hungry; be insatiable; be omnivorous; be rapacious; be ravenous; be starved; be starving; be voracious.* 2. *glut; gorge; overdo; overeat; overfeed; overindulge; sate; satiate; stuff; surfeit.*

eat out of (the palm of) (her) hand A moribund metaphor (see page 21). *abide by; acquiesce; comply with; conform; follow; obey; yield.*

eat (me) out of house and home A moribund metaphor (see page 21). 1. *be esurient; be famished; be gluttonous; be greedy; be hungry; be insatiable; be omnivorous; be rapacious; be ravenous; be starved; be starving; be voracious.* 2. *glut; gorge; overdo; overeat; overfeed; overindulge; sate; satiate; stuff; surfeit.*

eat (him) (up) alive A moribund metaphor (see page 21). 1. *consume; enclose; envelop; surround.* 2. *exploit; use.*

> We might had charged the stage to eat him up alive if he had been any more sly and enchanting and wise. — Philip Roth, *The Ghost Writer*

eat (her) words A moribund metaphor (see page 21). *disavow; recant; repudiate; retract; take back; withdraw.*

ebb and flow A moribund metaphor (see page 21). ■ Optimists try to attribute a linear progression to the *ebb and flow* of history.

effect An overworked word (see page 22). For example: *chilling effect; cumulative effect; domino effect; dramatic effect; negative effect; snowball effect; sobering effect; trickle-down effect.* ■ LeBlanc's lawyers say that would *have a chilling effect on* fraud lawsuits brought by government employees. REPLACE WITH *discourage.* ■ You can learn how to free yourself from the *destructive effects* of negative people in your workplace. REPLACE WITH *detriment.* SEE ALSO *has an effect on.*

effective and efficient An inescapable pair (see page 20). Businesspeople, in particular, seem unable to use the word *effective* without also using *efficient.* And though businesses endlessly plume themselves on how *effective and efficient* they are (and how *excellent* their products and services are), this is rarely true. In the end, the dimwitted *effective and efficient* may mean to us all what it has come to mean to businesses: 1. shoddy and inept, 2. uncaring and purblind, 3. money-grubbing and malevolent. ■ For these methods, more *effective and efficient* methods are available. REPLACE WITH *effective* or *efficient.* ■ More than an audit, the study should evaluate the *efficiency and effectiveness* of social services and public works. REPLACE WITH *efficiency* or *effectiveness.* ■ The work place should be a safe environment where one can *effectively and efficiently* perform required duties. REPLACE WITH *effectively* or *efficiently.*

effectuate A torpid term (see page 24). *bring about; carry out; cause; do; effect; execute; occasion.* SEE ALSO *eventuate.*

(with) egg on (my) face A moribund metaphor (see page 21). *abashed; ashamed; chagrined; confused; discomfited; discomposed; disconcerted; embarrassed; flustered; humbled; humiliated; mortified; nonplused; perplexed; red-faced; shamed; shamefaced; sheepish; upset.* ■ Everybody likes to see Harvard *with egg on its face.* REPLACE WITH *embarrassed.*

egregious error A*n* inescapable pair (see page 20).

either one A wretched redundancy (see page 25). *either.* ■ He doesn't care about *either one* of you. DELETE *one.* SEE ALSO *each one; neither one.*

(an) element A torpid term (see page 24). ■ Proper validation is *an* essential *element.* DELETE *an element.* ■ Black turnout was especially low, and that was *a* key *element* to her victory. DELETE *a element.* SEE ALSO *(a) factor.*

elevate to an art form A moribund metaphor (see page 21). ■ He would add to the gridlock, then compound the people's frustrations by *elevating* the blame game *to an art form.*

empty void A wretched redundancy (see page 25). *emptiness; void.* ■ I know that without me around my mother got lonely and just needed someone to fill the *empty void.* REPLACE WITH *emptiness* or *void.*

enclosed herein (herewith) A wretched redundancy (see page 25). *enclosed; here.* ■ *Enclosed herein* is the complete manuscript. REPLACE WITH *Here* or *Enclosed.*

enclosed please find A wretched redundancy (see page 25). *enclosed is; here is.* ■ *Enclosed please find* materials that you might find useful prior to your arrival. REPLACE WITH *Enclosed are.* ■ *Enclosed please find* a listing of single family properties that are available for purchase by eligible buyers. REPLACE WITH *Here is.*

endangered species A moribund metaphor (see page 21). ■ We all recognize that the nuclear family is an *endangered species.*

end of the line A moribund metaphor (see page 21). *close; completion; conclusion; culmination; consummation; end; ending; finale; finish; fulfillment; termination.*

end on a high note A moribund metaphor (see page 21).

end result A wretched redundancy (see page 25). *result.* ■ The *end result* should be that all mothers and fathers would pay what they can afford. DELETE *end.*

enjoy it while (you) can A popular prescription (see page 23).

enough is enough A quack equation (see page 23). Though often used to conclude an argument, *enough is enough* is the least compelling of summations. No one can argue *enough is enough* and expect to be persuasive. The phrase convinces us only that its user reasons ineffectually and unremarkably.

equally as A wretched redundancy (see page 25). *as; equally.* ■ *Equally as* important, this program provides comprehensive preventive coverage. REPLACE WITH *As* or *Equally.*

ere A withered word (see page 24). *before.* ■ So I avoided the hole and assumed it might likely be June *ere* it was patched. REPLACE WITH *before.*

ergo A withered word (see page 24). *consequently; hence; therefore.*

establishment A torpid term (see page 24). *business; club; company; firm; outlet; shop; store.* ■ You should park close to the entrance of the *establishment* you are shopping at. REPLACE WITH *store.*

et cetera (etc., etc.; et cetera, et cetera) A grammatical gimmick (see page 19). ■ I'm very outgoing and adaptable, *et cetera, et cetera.* DELETE *et cetera, et cetera.* ■ She told me he was everything she was looking for, *et cetera, et cetera.* DELETE *et cetera, et cetera.* ■ Dr. Holmes was a man of brilliant conversational gifts — one of the most notable of that noted circle which composed the "Saturday Club" in Boston — Longfellow, Emerson, Lowell, Whittier, Thoreau, Bayard Taylor, *etc., etc.* DELETE *etc., etc.*

When thoughts stumble and then stop, words, or at least intelligible words, do as well. As often as not, *et cetera* is a means of expressing, without having to admit to its meaning, all those words only dimly thought. SEE ALSO *blah, blah, blah; and so on, and so forth.*

et tu, Brute A foreign phrase (see page 19).

even Steven An infantile phrase (see page 20).

even the score A moribund metaphor (see page 21).

eventuate A torpid term (see page 24). *befall; come about; end; happen; occur; result; take place.* SEE ALSO *effectuate.*

ever and anon A withered word (see page 24). *now and then; occasionally.*

everybody and (his) brother (mother) An infantile phrase (see page 20). *all; everybody; everyone.* ■ *Everybody and their mother* is on line today. REPLACE WITH *Everybody.* ■ It's like *everybody and their brother* is having a hearing on Enron.

everybody talks about the weather, but nobody does anything about it An infantile phrase (see page 20).

every cloud has a silver lining A popular prescription (see page 23).

every effort is being made A suspect superlative (see page 24). This phrase, disembodied though it is, serves to disarm people as it dismisses them. ■ *Every effort is being made* to find the perpetrators of this heinous crime. ■ *Every effort has been made* to make this verification as simple and painless as possible. ■ During this time, please be patient as *every effort is being made* to process your order in a timely manner. ■ First, we want to be sure that *every effort is being made* to spot, recover, preserve, identify and deliver any human remains to the families of the victims. SEE ALSO *that's interesting; that's nice.*

every nook and cranny A moribund metaphor (see page 21). *all around; all over; all through; everyplace; everywhere; throughout.*

every single (solitary) A wretched redundancy (see page 25). *every.* ■ *Every single solitary* night we see people dying. REPLACE WITH *Every.*

every step of the way A moribund metaphor (see page 21). 1. *always; ceaselessly; constantly; continually; continuous-*

ly; endlessly; eternally; everlastingly; evermore; forever; forevermore; frequently; interminably; nonstop; permanently; perpetually; persistently; recurrently; regularly; repeatedly; unceasingly; unremittingly. 2. *all during; all over; all through; everywhere; throughout.*

everything but the kitchen sink A moribund metaphor (see page 21). *aggregate; all; all things; entirety; everything; gross; lot; sum; total; totality; whole.*

everything happens for a reason A popular prescription (see page 23).

everything's coming up roses An infantile phrase (see page 20). *be auspicious; be encouraging; be good; be hopeful; be optimistic; be promising; be propitious; be rosy.*

everything's (it's all) relative An infantile phrase (see page 20). SEE ALSO *(as) compared to what? (as) opposed to what?*

everything under the sun A moribund metaphor (see page 21). *all; all things; everything.* ■ I tried *everything under the sun* to get her to shape up. REPLACE WITH *everything.*

everything (it) will turn out for the best A popular prescription (see page 23).

everything you always wanted to know about ... but were afraid to ask An infantile phrase (see page 20).

every time (you) turn around A moribund metaphor (see page 21). *always; ceaselessly; constantly; continually; continuously; endlessly; eternally; everlastingly; evermore; forever; forevermore; frequently; interminably; often; permanently; perpetually; persistently; recurrently; regularly; repeatedly; unceasingly; unremittingly.*

every Tom, Dick, and Harry A moribund metaphor (see page 21). *all; citizenry; commonage; commonalty; common people; crowd; everybody; everyone; herd; hoi polloi; masses; mob; multitude; plebeians; populace; proletariat; public; rabble.* ■ I am not advocating that you tip *every Tom, Dick, and Harry.* REPLACE WITH *everyone.*

every trick in the book A moribund metaphor (see page 21). ■ They're pulling *every trick in the book* to keep this amendment off the 1992 ballot.

excellence An overworked word (see page 22). The word is overworked, and the concept undervalued. Too much, today, passes for *excellence.* Too much of our work is shoddy, too much of our wisdom, suspect, too much of our worth, unsure. ■ With your help, we will continue that tradition of *excellence.* SEE ALSO *pursue (strive for) excellence.*

excess verbiage A wretched redundancy (see page 25). *verbiage.*

excruciating pain An inescapable pair (see page 20). ■ This medication was initially prescribed to soothe the *excruciating pain* that I was suffering.

excuse me? An infantile phrase (see page 20). No longer exclusively a polite way of signifying that you did not hear what a person has said, *excuse me* is also — especially among the young and stupidly egoistic — an impolite way of signifying that you did not like what a person has said. With an autocratic intonation, the person expresses hostility to what he hears. This phrase is particularly loathsome, for those who use it dare not be openly angry or upset; they try to disguise their anger and arrogance behind a mantle of mannerliness. SEE ALSO *I'm sorry; thank you; whatever.*

expert opinion A suspect superlative (see page 24).

expletive deleted An infantile phrase (see page 20).

explore every avenue A moribund metaphor (see page 21).

(an) explosion of A moribund metaphor (see page 21). SEE ALSO *a barrage of.*

express (concern) A torpid term (see page 24). Phrases like *express concern, express doubt, express opposition, express thanks* make any sentence instantly sodden. ■ Officials *express concern* about the slow pace of economic growth. REPLACE WITH *worry.* ■ House Democrats continue to *express anger* about the state's ethics and campaign finance laws. REPLACE WITH *fume.* ■ I want to *express my appreciation to* all of you who have lent us a hand in this endeavor. REPLACE WITH *thank.*

extend (hold out) the olive branch A moribund metaphor (see page 21). *be accommodating; be agreeable; be conciliatory; be obliging; be peaceable; be propitiatory.*

extent A torpid term (see page 24). Like *degree,* the word *extent,* along with the phrases in which it is found, is best avoided.

These are lifeless expressions, and it is listless people who use them. ■ In some cases, they've been transformed *to such an extent* that you can no longer recognize them. REPLACE WITH *so much.* ■ The study said that women, *to a greater extent* than men, manage by personal interactions with their subordinates. REPLACE WITH *more.* ■ Resources are always used *to the optimum extent.* REPLACE WITH *optimally.* ■ Sooner or later, we will see *to what extent* the central banks are prepared to back up words with actions. REPLACE WITH *how far.* ■ *The extent to which* these practices are seen as flowing in one direction, down from headquarters to subsidiaries, may influence *the extent to which* these practices are adopted and *to what extent* the behavior, beliefs, and values of the corporate culture are incorporated or even complied with. REPLACE WITH *How much, how much,* and *how much.* SEE ALSO *degree.*

extenuating circumstances A torpid term (see page 24).

> It was a lovely apology for missing drinks the previous evening due to extenuating circumstances, you know, my job. — Michele Mitchell, *The Latest Bombshell*

(an) eye for an eye (and a tooth for a tooth) A popular prescription (see page 23).

(his) eyes are bigger than (his) stomach A moribund metaphor (see page 21).

eyes are the windows of the soul A moribund metaphor (see page 21).

(has) eyes in the back of (his) head A moribund metaphor (see page 21). *alert; attentive; aware; eagle-eyed; heedful; keen; observant; perceptive; vigilant; wakeful; watchful.*

eyes (are) wide open A moribund metaphor (see page 21). *alert; attentive; aware; cognizant; conscious; eagle-eyed; heedful; keen; observant; perceptive; vigilant; wakeful; watchful.*

F

fabulous An overworked word (see page 22). As still another synonym for *very good* or *extremely pleasing*, *fabulous* is indeed overused. In its sense of *hard to believe* or *astounding*, it is now and again used, and in its sense of *like a fable* or *legendary*, it is woefully unused.

(the) face that launched a thousand ships A moribund metaphor (see page 21).

face the music A moribund metaphor (see page 21). *pay; suffer.*

> Not to be a member of the communion of saints or gods or demigods or fathers or mothers or grandfathers or grandmothers or brothers or sisters or brethren of any kind, germane to me through consanguinity, affinity, or any other kind of linear or genitive or collateral bond. To face the music at last. — Edna O'Brien, *Night*

(the) (plain; simple) fact is (that) An ineffectual phrase (see page 19). ■ *The fact is* at least the govenor is trying. DELETE *The fact is.* ■ *The simple fact is* we are now spending nearly $1 trillion on health care. DELETE *The simple fact is.* ■ *The plain fact is* American women are buying guns like they've never bought them before. DELETE *The plain fact is.*

(the) (simple) fact of the matter is An ineffectual phrase (see page 19). ■ *The fact of the matter is* the police took the children from you. DELETE *The fact of the matter is.* ■ Despite her behavior, *the simple fact of the matter is* I still love her. DELETE *the simple fact of the matter is.* SEE ALSO *the truth of the matter is.*

(the) fact remains (that) An ineffectual phrase (see page 19). ■ We call this campaign a "snoozer," but *the fact remains* both candidates did behave responsibly. DELETE *the fact remains.* ■ Whether one prefers the proverb's optimism or Euripides' pessimism, *the fact remains that* the way in which investigations are conducted can have a significant impact on the outcome of any case. DELETE *the fact remains that.*

(the) fact that An ineffectual phrase (see page 19). ■ *The fact that* many more computers are in communication with one another increases concern that users' privacy will be violated. REPLACE WITH *That.* ■ *The fact that* she was rather attractive did not escape their notice. REPLACE WITH *That.*

> In other rooms, in other houses, all over the world, other bodies devoted to sex, or compost, or holism, or Marxism, are forming

thousands of similar wheels: but what makes these wheels so fatally different from the one now running at Hyde's Mortimer is the fact that all the others are running in wrong directions. — Nigel Dennis, *Cards of Identity*

(a) factor A torpid term (see page 24). ■ I think the TV show was *a* contributing *factor* to this tragedy. REPLACE WITH *contributed.* ■ They thought the biggest problem we were dealing with was *a* jealousy *factor.* REPLACE WITH *jealousy.* ■ The key *factor* in the decline appears to be the Irish-American voter's willingness to vote for candidates from other ethnic groups. REPLACE WITH *key to.* SEE ALSO *(an) element.* ■ The presence of a long umbilical cord is *a* contributory *factor* to the occurrence of nuchal cord. REPLACE WITH *contributes.*

facts and figures An inescapable pair (see page 20).

facts and information A wretched redundancy (see page 25). *data; facts; information.*

fade into the sunset A moribund metaphor (see page 21). *disappear; disperse; dissolve; evaporate; fade; vanish; vaporize; volatilize.*

fade into the woodwork A moribund metaphor (see page 21). *depart; disappear; disperse; dissolve; evaporate; fade; vacate; vanish; vaporize; volatilize; withdraw.* ■ It is easy to *fade into the woodwork* and never have to deal with those problems. REPLACE WITH *disappear.*

fading fast A moribund metaphor (see page 21). *beat; bushed; debilitated; depleted; drained; drowsy; enervated; exhausted; fatigued; groggy; sapped; sleepy; sluggish; slumberous; somnolent; soporific; spent; tired; weary; worn out.*

fair and equitable An inescapable pair (see page 20). *equitable; fair; just.* ■ The key to maintaining that system is ensuring that you are treated *fairly and equitably.* REPLACE WITH *equitably* or *fairly.*

fair and square An inescapable pair (see page 20). *aboveboard; creditable; equitable; fair; honest; honorable; just; lawful; legitimate; open; proper; reputable; respectable; right; square; straightforward; upright; veracious; veridical.*

fair game A moribund metaphor (see page 21).

fair is fair A quack equation (see page 23).

fair share A torpid term (see page 24). *allocation; allotment; allowance; amount; apportionment; dole; lot; measure; part; piece; portion; quota; ration; share.* ■ We are setting out to get our *fair share* of the residential real estate mortgage business.

fair to middling A wretched redundancy (see page 25). *average; common; fair; mediocre; middling; moderate; ordinary; passable; tolerable.*

fait accompli A foreign phrase (see page 19).

fall between (through) the cracks A moribund metaphor (see page 21). *be discounted; be disregarded; be elided; be forgotten; be ignored; be left out; be missed; be neglected; be omitted; be overlooked; be skipped; be slighted; be* *snubbed; elapse; end; fail; go by; lapse; slid; slip.* ■ Such a caring environment is particularly important for students who have few other sources of support and who might well *fall through the cracks* in a less personalized school setting. REPLACE WITH *be forgotten.* ■ Between groping for meaningful full-time employment and anguishing over the political state of our country, I've allowed some things to *fall between the cracks.* REPLACE WITH *lapse.*

fall flat on (its) face A moribund metaphor (see page 21). *be unsuccessful; blunder; bomb; break down; bungle; collapse; fail; fall short; falter; fizzle; flop; fold; founder; mess up; miscarry; not succeed; stumble; topple.* ■ Some professional investors are betting the company will *fall flat on its face.* REPLACE WITH *fail.*

fall from grace A moribund metaphor (see page 21). *collapse; decline; downfall; failure; fall; misadventure; misfortune; offense; peccadillo; ruin; sin; transgression; wrongdoing.*

fall in (into) line (place) A moribund metaphor (see page 21). *abide by; accede; accommodate; accord; acquiesce; adapt; adhere to; agree; behave; comply; concur; conform; correspond; follow; harmonize; heed; mind; obey; observe; submit; yield.*

fall into (my) lap A moribund metaphor (see page 21). ■ It just kind of *fell into my lap.*

fall on deaf ears A moribund metaphor (see page 21). *disregard; ignore.*

fall through the floor A moribund metaphor (see page 21). *collapse; crash; decline; decrease; descend; dip; drop; ebb; fall; plummet; plunge; recede; sink; slide; slip; subside; topple; tumble.* ■ But Cellucci said the bond rating *fell through the floor* in the late 1980s during the fiscal crisis. REPLACE WITH *collapsed.*

fame and fortune A suspect superlative (see page 24). SEE ALSO *the rich and famous.*

familiarity breeds contempt A popular prescription (see page 23).

> When we first discussed my working on the books' pages, Nathan argued that, if I ever achieved my ambition to become the books editor, I would end up hating books. Familiarity bred contempt.
> — Elizabeth Buchan, *Revenge Of The Middle-Aged Woman*

(the) family that prays together stays together A popular prescription (see page 23).

fan (fuel) the fire (flames) A moribund metaphor (see page 21). *activate; agitate; animate; arouse; awaken; encourage; enkindle; enliven; exacerbate; excite; feed; foment; ignite; impassion; incite; inflame; intensify; invigorate; make worse; nourish; prod; provoke; rejuvenate; revitalize; revive; rouse; shake up; stimulate; stir up; vitalize; worsen.*

far and away A wretched redundancy (see page 25). *by far; much.*

far and wide An inescapable pair (see page 20). *all around; all over; all through; broadly; everyplace; everywhere; extensively; throughout; ubiquitously; universally; widely.* SEE ALSO *high and wide; left and right.*

far-reaching consequences (implications) An inescapable pair (see page 20).

fashion statement A plebeian sentiment (see page 23). Making a *fashion statement* is the concern of adolescents and addle-brained adults who have yet to fashion for themselves a sense of identity. Their habiliments interest them more than does their humanity.

People so intent on being fashionable make only misstatements. They but blither.

fast and furious An inescapable pair (see page 20).

(as) fast as (her) legs can carry (her) An insipid simile. *abruptly; apace; at once; briskly; directly; expeditiously; fast; forthwith; hastily; hurriedly; immediately; instantaneously; instantly; posthaste; promptly; quickly; rapidly; rashly; right away; speedily; straightaway; swiftly; wingedly.*

fasten your seat belts A moribund metaphor (see page 21).

faster than a speeding bullet (more powerful than a locomotive, able to leap small buildings at a single bound) An infantile phrase (see page 20).

fast track A moribund metaphor (see page 21).

fast trigger finger A moribund metaphor (see page 21).

(as) fat as a cow An insipid simile. *ample; big; bulky; chubby; chunky; colossal; corpulent; dumpy; enormous; fat; flabby; fleshy; gigantic; heavy; hefty; huge; immense; large; mammoth; massive; obese; plump; portly; pudgy; rotund; round; squat; stocky; stout.*

(as) fat as a pig An insipid simile. *ample; big; bulky; chubby; chunky; colossal; corpulent; dumpy; enormous; fat; flabby; fleshy; gigantic; heavy; hefty; huge; immense; large; mammoth; massive; obese; plump; portly; pudgy; rotund; round; squat; stocky; stout.*

fat cat A moribund metaphor (see page 21). *billionaire; capitalist; financier; magnate; materialist; millionaire; mogul; multimillionaire; nabob; plutocrat; tycoon.*

(the) fat's in the fire A moribund metaphor (see page 21).

fear and trembling An inescapable pair (see page 20). *alarm; anxiety; apprehension; consternation; dismay; dread; fear; foreboding; fright; horror; panic; terror; trembling; trepidation.*

feast or famine An inescapable pair (see page 20).

(a) feather in (his) cap A moribund metaphor (see page 21). *accomplishment; achievement; feat; success; triumph; victory.*

> But I can remember that from quite early on, for some reason, Isabel decided that Edith was rather a feather in her cap, someone that little bit special to be fed to her country neighbours in rationed morsels. — Julian Fellowes, *Snobs*

feather (their) nest A moribund metaphor (see page 21). ■ He repeatedly denied allegations that he used his three years at the Denver-based thrift to *feather his* own *nest.*

feed (you) a line A moribund metaphor (see page 21). *deceive; dissemble; distort; equivocate; falsify; fib; lie; misconstrue; mislead; misrepresent; pervert; prevaricate.*

feedback A torpid term (see page 24). *answers; data; feelings; ideas; information; recommendations; replies; responses; suggestions; thoughts; views.* ■ Your *feedback* helps us continually improve. REPLACE WITH *suggestions.* ■ And as *feedback* is obtained, it is the duty of the firm's leaders to convey it to all members of the firm. REPLACE WITH *ideas.* SEE ALSO *(the) bottom line; input; interface; output; parameters.*

feeling no pain A moribund metaphor (see page 21). *besotted; crapulous; drunk; inebriated; intoxicated; sodden; stupefied; tipsy.*

feeling (his) oats A moribund metaphor (see page 21). *active; alive; animated; dynamic; energetic; exuberant; frisky; indefatigable; inexhaustible; invigorated; lively; peppy; spirited; sprightly; spry; tireless; unflagging; vibrant; vigorous; vivacious; zestful; zesty.*

(the) feeling's mutual An infantile phrase (see page 20).

feel the pinch A moribund metaphor (see page 21).

feel the heat A moribund metaphor (see page 21).

fertile ground A moribund metaphor (see page 21).

few and far between A wretched redundancy (see page 25). *exiguous; limited; inadequate; infrequent; meager; rare; scant; scanty; scarce; sparse; uncommon; unusual.* ■ Role models are *few and far between* in those groups. REPLACE WITH *scarce.*

(has a) few screws loose A moribund metaphor (see page 21). *batty; cracked; crazy; daft; demented; deranged; fey; foolish; goofy; insane; lunatic; mad; maniacal; neurotic; nuts; nutty; psychotic; raving; silly; squirrelly; strange; touched; unbalanced; unhinged; unsound; wacky; zany.*

(the) first step is always the hardest A popular prescription (see page 23).

(bid) a fond farewell An infantile phrase (see page 20).

(a) fool and his money are soon parted A popular prescription (see page 23).

(a) force to be reckoned with An infantile phrase (see page 20). *adversary; antagonist; challenger; competitor; contender; contestant; force; opponent; rival.* ■ The combination of Walsh, the broadcast of Celtics games this season, and hot Fox network programming will make WFXT *a force to be reckoned with.* REPLACE WITH *a contender.*

(the) four corners of the earth (world) A moribund metaphor (see page 21). *all over; everyplace; everywhere; the world over; throughout (the land); universally; worldwide.* ■ These changes will affect our American patients as well as those who come to the clinic from the *four* *corners of the world.* REPLACE WITH *the world over.*

fiddle while Rome burns A moribund metaphor (see page 21).

(a) fifth wheel A moribund metaphor (see page 21). *excessive; extra; extraneous; immaterial; incidental; inconsequential; insignificant; irrelevant; needless; nonessential; superabundant; superfluous; unimportant; unnecessary.* ■ With his mother doing the cooking and other household chores, I would feel like *a fifth wheel.* REPLACE WITH *superfluous.*

fight a losing battle A moribund metaphor (see page 21).

fight fire with fire A moribund metaphor (see page 21).

fight like cats and dogs An insipid simile 1. *altercate; argue; disagree; dispute; feud; fight; quarrel; spat; squabble; wrangle.* 2. *battle; brawl; clash; fight; grapple; jostle; make war; scuffle; skirmish; tussle; war; wrestle.*

filled to bursting (overflowing) A moribund metaphor (see page 21). *abounding; brimful; brimming; bursting; chock-full; congested; crammed; crowded; dense; filled; full; gorged; jammed; jam-packed; overcrowded; overfilled; overflowing; packed; replete; saturated; stuffed; swarming; teeming.*

filled to the brim A moribund metaphor (see page 21). *abounding; brimful; brimming; bursting; chock-full; congested; crammed; crowded; dense; filled; full; gorged; jammed; jam-packed; overcrowded; overfilled; packed; replete; saturated; stuffed; swarming; teeming.*

> I recall the scent of some kind of toilet powder — I believe she stole it from her mother's Spanish maid — a sweetish, lowly, musky perfume. It mingled with her own biscuity odor, and my senses were suddenly filled to the brim; a sudden commotion in a nearby bush prevented them from overflowing .... — Vladimir Nabokov, *Lolita*

fill in the blanks An infantile phrase (see page 20).

fill (his) shoes A moribund metaphor (see page 21).

fill the bill A moribund metaphor (see page 21). 1. *be appropriate; be apt; be befitting; be felicitous; be fit; be fitting; be happy; be meet; be proper; be right; be seemly; be suitable; be suited.* 2. *be acceptable; be adequate; be qualified; be satisfactory; be sufficient.*

fill to capacity A wretched redundancy (see page 25). *fill.* ■ Our free public facilities are *filled to capacity*, and there are long waiting lists for some programs. REPLACE WITH *filled.*

filthy lucre A moribund metaphor (see page 21). *money; riches; wealth.*

final and irrevocable An inescapable pair (see page 20). *final; firm; irrevocable; unalterable.*

final chapter A moribund metaphor (see page 21). *close; completion; conclusion; consummation; culmination; denouement; end; ending; finale; finish; termination.*

final conclusion A wretched redundancy (see page 25). ■ We have made no *final conclusions* on responsibility for the attacks in Kenya and Tanzania. DELETE *final.*

final culmination A wretched redundancy (see page 25). culmination. ■ Owning a farm was the *final culmination* of all our efforts. DELETE *final.*

final decision A wretched redundancy (see page 25). *decision.* ■ That's one of the things we have under consideration, but no final *decision* has been made. DELETE *final.*

(the) final (last) frontier A moribund metaphor (see page 21).

(that's) the final (last) straw A moribund metaphor (see page 21).

finalize A torpid term (see page 24). *complete; conclude; consummate; end; execute; finish; fulfill; made final; terminate.* ■ Delays in *finalizing* the state budget and its allocations to cities and towns make a special town meeting necessary. REPLACE WITH *completing.* SEE ALSO utilize.

finder's keepers, loser's weepers An infantile phrase (see page 20).

find (some) middle ground A moribund metaphor (see page 21). *compromise.*

fine and dandy An inescapable pair (see page 20). *all right; excellent; fine; good; O.K.; well.* SEE ALSO *well and good.*

(a) fine (pretty) kettle of fish A moribund metaphor (see page 21). *complication; difficulty; dilemma; mess; muddle; ordeal; pickle; plight; predicament; problem; quandary; trial; trouble.*

fine line A moribund metaphor (see page 21). ■ There is a very *fine line* between vision and delusion.

fingers on the pulse of A moribund metaphor (see page 21).

fire (launch) a salvo A moribund metaphor (see page 21).

(all) fired (hopped, psyched) up A moribund metaphor (see page 21). *afire; aflame; anxious; ardent; burning; eager; enthusiastic; excited; fanatic; fanatical; fervent; fervid; fiery; impassioned; inflamed; intense; perfervid; keen; passionate; vehement; zealous.*

fire in (his) belly A moribund metaphor (see page 21). *ambitious; ardent; determined; dogged; driven; eager; enthusiastic; fervent; impassioned; motivated; passionate; persistent; pushy; resolute; strong-willed.*

(a) firestorm of A moribund metaphor (see page 21). ■ That decision unleashed *a firestorm of* protest in the Capitol. SEE ALSO *a barrage of.*

firmly establish An inescapable pair (see page 20). Adverbs often modify other words needlessly. Here, firmly is superfluous, for establish means "to make firm." ■ The play *firmly established* him as a dramatist. DELETE *firmly.*

first and foremost A wretched redundancy (see page 25). *chief; chiefly; first; foremost; initial; initially; main; mainly;*

most important; mostly; primarily; primary; principal; principally. ■ *First and foremost* these people must have a commitment to public service. REPLACE WITH *Most important.* SEE ALSO *first and most important.*

first and most important A wretched redundancy (see page 25). *chief; chiefly; first; foremost; initial; initially; main; mainly; most important; mostly; primarily; primary; principal; principally.* SEE ALSO *first and foremost.*

first begin (start) A wretched redundancy (see page 25). *begin; start.* ■ When we *first started* exploring the idea, we didn't even know if it was possible to do. DELETE *first.*

first line of defense A moribund metaphor (see page 21).

first of all A wretched redundancy (see page 25). *first.* ■ *First of all,* I am delighted about our progress in that area. REPLACE WITH *First.* SEE ALSO *second of all.*

first (highest; number-one; top) priority A torpid term (see page 24). Nothing soulful can be said using these expressions, so when a U.S. cardinal dreariy sermonizes "The protection of children must be our number-one priority," we are hardly convinced that this is his or the church's principal concern. When we read, in some corporate promotional piece, "Your satisfaction is our number-one priority," we are likewise, and for good reason, suspicious. Mechanical expressions like *first (highest; number-one; top) priority* defy tenderness, resist compassion, and counter concern. SEE ALSO *reach epidemic proportions.*

fish or cut bait A moribund metaphor (see page 21).

(like a) fish out of water An insipid simile. *awkward; blundering; bumbling; bungling; clumsy; gawky; gauche; ham-handed; heavy-handed; inapt; inept; lubberly; lumbering; maladroit; uncoordinated; uncouth; ungainly; ungraceful; unhandy; unskillful; unwieldy.*

(bigger; other) fish to fry A moribund metaphor (see page 21).

> Now, I wish I could remember Daddy's reply to all her nagging, but I had bigger fish to fry that weekend and didn't much care that Missy had inexplicably fallen in love with her own uncle .... — Janis Owens, *The Schooling of Claybird Catts*

(as) fit as a fiddle An insipid simile. *athletic; beefy; brawny; energetic; fit; good; hale; hardy; healthful; healthy; hearty; husky; lanky; lean; manly; muscular; powerful; robust; shapely; sinewy; slender; solid; sound; stalwart; stout; strong; sturdy; thin; trim; vigorous; virile; well; well-built.*

fit for a king A moribund metaphor (see page 21). *august; awe-inspiring; distinguished; elegant; eminent; exalted; exquisite; extraordinary; extravagant; glorious; grand; great; impressive; kingly; luxurious; magnificent; majestic; monarchical; nobel; opulent; princely; regal; royal; sovereign; splendid; stately; sumptuous.*

fitting and proper An inescapable pair (see page 20). *appropriate; apt; befitting; felicitous; fit; fitting; happy; meet; proper; right; seemly; suitable; suited.* ■ And it is generally regarded as *fitting and proper* for women to do this. REPLACE WITH *fitting*.

fit to be tied A moribund metaphor (see page 21). *angry; cross; enraged; fuming; furious; incensed; indignant; infuriated; irate; mad; outraged; raging; wrathful.*

fix (her) wagon A moribund metaphor (see page 21). 1. *castigate; censure; chasten; chastise; chide; criticize; discipline; penalize; punish; rebuke; reprove; scold.* 2. *spank.*

flaming inferno An infantile phrase (see page 20). *blaze; conflagration; fire; inferno.*

flash in the pan A moribund metaphor (see page 21). *brief; ephemeral; evanescent; fleeting; momentary; short; short-lived; short-term; temporary; transient; transitory.*

(as) flat as a board An insipid simile. *even; flat; flush; horizontal; level; plane; smooth.*

(as) flat as a pancake An insipid simile. *even; flat; flush; horizontal; level; plane; smooth.*

flat on (his) back A moribund metaphor (see page 21). *afflicted; ailing; crippled; debilitated; defenseless; disabled; diseased; feeble; fragile; helpless; ill; incapacitated; indisposed; infirm; not (feeling) well; sick; sickly; unhealthy; unwell; valetudinarian; weak.*

(my) (own) flesh and blood A moribund metaphor (see page 21). 1. *brother; child; daughter; father; kin; mother; parent; relative; sibling; sister; son.* 2. *depth; reality; substance.*

flight of fancy A moribund metaphor (see page 21). *caprice; chimera; crotchet; daydream; delusion; dream; fancy; fantasy; hallucination; humor; illusion; imagination; notion; phantasm; vagary; whim; whimsy.*

flip (her) lid A moribund metaphor (see page 21). *bellow; bluster; clamor; explode; fulminate; fume; holler; howl; rage; rant; rave; roar; scream; shout; storm; thunder; vociferate; yell.*

(on the) flip side (of the coin) A moribund metaphor (see page 21). 1. *antithesis; contrary; converse; opposite; reverse.* 2. *but; in contrast; conversely; however; inversely; whereas; yet.*

(whatever) floats your boat A moribund metaphor (see page 21).

(a) flood of A moribund metaphor (see page 21). ■ The evidence indicates NAFTA will lead to *a flood of* auto exports from the United States to Mexico. ■ Should the doctors win, labor leaders predict *a flood of* physicians signing up with unions. SEE ALSO *a barrage of.*

flotsam and jetsam An inescapable pair (see page 20). 1. *debris; litter; rack; refuse; rubbish; rubble; wrack; wreckage.* 2. *bits; fragments; modicums; odds and ends; particles; pieces; remnants; scraps; shreds; snippets; trifles.* 3. *itinerants; rovers; tramps; vagabonds; vagrants; wanderers.*

flowing with milk and honey A moribund metaphor (see page 21).

fly (ride) below (under) the radar (of) A moribund metaphor (see page 21). 1. *disregarded; hidden; ignored; imperceptible; indiscernible; invisible; overlooked; undetectable; undetected; unheard of; unknown; unnoticeable; unnoticed; unobserved; unperceived; unrevealed; unseen.* 2. *discreet; inconspicuous; self-effacing; unassuming; understated; unobtrusive.* ■ The sport isn't exactly *riding under the radar* in the United States anymore, thanks in large part to Lance Armstrong's dominant reign in the Tour de France. REPLACE WITH *unnoticed.* ■ *Flying under the radar* are the Russians, who may just be warming up for the medal round. REPLACE WITH *Unassuming.*

fly-by-night A moribund metaphor (see page 21). *irresponsible; undependable; unreliable; untrustworthy.*

fly by the seat of (his) pants A moribund metaphor (see page 21). *be extemporaneous; be instinctive; be spontaneous; impromptu; improvise.* ■ Administrators who *fly by the seat of their pants* typically rely on trial and error because there are no overarching objectives and guidelines. REPLACE WITH *are instinctive.*

flying high A moribund metaphor (see page 21). 1. *advantageous; auspicious; blessed; charmed; enchanted; favored; felicitous; flourishing; fortuitous; fortunate; golden; happy; in luck; lucky; propitious; prosperous; successful; thriving.* 2. *blissful; blithe; buoyant; cheerful; delighted; ecstatic; elated; enraptured; euphoric; exalted; excited; exhilarated; exultant; gay; glad; gleeful; good-humored; happy; intoxicated; jolly; jovial; joyful; joyous; jubilant; merry; mirthful; overjoyed; pleased; rapturous; thrilled.*

fly in the face of A moribund metaphor (see page 21). *buck; challenge; contradict; defy; disobey; dispute; disregard; flout; go against; ignore; militate against; neglect; oppose; overlook; resist; violate.* ■ This is nonsensical and *flies in the face of* history and basic economic principles. REPLACE WITH *contradicts.*

fly in the ointment A moribund metaphor (see page 21). *bar; barrier; block; blockage; catch; check; deterrent; difficulty; encumbrance; handicap; hindrance; hitch; hurdle; impediment; interference; obstacle; obstruction; rub; snag.*

fly off the handle A moribund metaphor (see page 21). *bellow; blow up; bluster; clamor; explode; fulminate; fume; holler; howl; rage; rant; rave; roar; scream; shout; storm; thunder; vociferate; yell.* ■ To tell the truth, investors are *flying off the handle* everywhere you look. REPLACE WITH *howling.* ■ Meditation makes me a much calmer person; I don't *fly off the handle* so much. REPLACE WITH *rant.*

fly the coop A moribund metaphor (see page 21). *abscond; clear out; decamp; depart; desert; disappear; escape; exit; flee; fly; go; go away; leave; move on; part; pull out; quit; retire; retreat; run away; take flight; take off; vacate; vanish; withdraw.*

fly (too) close to the sun A moribund metaphor (see page 21). *chance; dare; endanger; gamble; hazard; imperil; jeopardize; make bold; peril; risk; venture.*

(a) flurry of A moribund metaphor (see page 21). ■ The U.S. stock market's strong recovery in the last months of 1998 prompted *a flurry of* charitable giving in December. SEE ALSO *a barrage of.*

(a) fly on the wall A moribund metaphor (see page 21).

foaming (frothing) at the mouth A moribund metaphor (see page 21). *angry; berserk; convulsive; crazed; delirious; demented; demoniac; deranged; enraged; feral; ferocious; fierce; frantic; frenzied; fuming; furious; hysterical; infuriated; in hysterics; insane; incensed; irate; mad; maddened; maniacal; murderous; possessed; rabid; raging; ranting; raving; savage; seething; wild; wrathful.*

focus attention (concentration) on A wretched redundancy (see page 25). *concentrate on; focus on.* ■ Microsoft has always *focused its attention on* software products and software standards. REPLACE WITH *focused on.* ■ It is hardly magic to *focus concentration on* success instead of failure. REPLACE WITH *concentrate on.* SEE ALSO *focus effort (energy) on.*

focus effort (energy) on A wretched redundancy (see page 25). *concentrate on; focus on.* ■ This downsizing will cut our expenses and allow us to *focus our efforts on* serving our customers. REPLACE WITH *focus on.* ■ Owners can *focus their energy on* expanding the business to a point where it can function outside of a "nurtured" environment. REPLACE WITH *focus on.* SEE ALSO *focus attention (concentration) on.*

focus in on A wretched redundancy (see page 25). *focus on.* ■ I have to *focus in on* what I want to accomplish. DELETE *in.*

fold (their) tent A moribund metaphor (see page 21). *abscond; clear out; decamp; depart; desert; disappear; escape; exit; flee; fly; go; go away; leave; move on; part; pull out; quit; retire; retreat; run away; take flight; take off; vacate; vanish; withdraw.*

follow in (her) footsteps A moribund metaphor (see page 21).

follow suit A moribund metaphor (see page 21). *copy; do as much; follow; imitate; mimic.* ■ NYNEX is expected to *follow suit* in the near future. REPLACE WITH *do as much.* ■ When American Airlines slashed fares, TWA *followed suit.* REPLACE WITH *did as much.*

follow the crowd A moribund metaphor (see page 21). *abide by; accede; accommodate; accord; acquiesce; adapt; adhere to; agree; behave; comply; concur; conform; correspond; follow; harmonize; heed; mind; obey; observe; submit; yield.*

follow your instincts A popular prescription (see page 23).

food for thought A moribund metaphor (see page 21). SEE ALSO *(it's) something to think about.*

food for worms A moribund metaphor (see page 21). *dead; deceased; defunct; departed; exanimate; expired; extinct; extinguished; finished; gone; inanimate; lifeless; no more; perished; terminated.*

fools rush in where angels fear to tread A popular prescription (see page 23).

footloose and fancy free A moribund metaphor (see page 21). *at liberty; autonomous; free; independent; self-reliant; unattached; unbound; unconfined; unconstrained; unencumbered; unentangled; unfettered; uninhibited; unrestrained; unrestricted; unshackled; untied.*

footprints in the sands of time A moribund metaphor (see page 21).

foot the bill A moribund metaphor (see page 21). *pay (for).*

> To argue would mean she was offering to foot the bill, something she had done so often over their years of living together that it had become expected of her. — Amy Tan, *The Bonesetter's Daughter*

for all intents and purposes A wretched redundancy (see page 25). *effectively; essentially; in effect; in essence; practically; virtually.* ■ *For all intents and purposes*, the civil rights acts of 1964 and 1965 signified the demise of official segregation in the United States. REPLACE WITH *In effect.* SEE ALSO *for all practical purposes; to all intents and purposes; to all practical purposes.*

for all practical purposes A wretched redundancy (see page 25). *effectively; essentially; in effect; in essence; practically; virtually.* ■ Services are, *for all practical purposes*, sold as products to end users, so the distinction between services and goods is artificial at best. REPLACE WITH *essentially.* SEE ALSO *for all intents and purposes; to all intents and purposes; to all practical purposes.*

for all (he was) worth A moribund metaphor (see page 21).

for a song A moribund metaphor (see page 21). *cheaply; economically; inexpensively.*

> A real beauty, with wood-spoke wheels and navy mohair upholstery. He was getting it for a song, from a widow who'd never learned to drive her husband's car. — Anita Shreve, *Sea Glass*

for better or for worse A torpid term (see page 24).

> But the family room, the only room where any of us has ever spent any time, has always been, for better or for worse, the ultimate reflection of our true inclinations. — Dave Eggers, *A Heartbreaking Work of Staggering Genius*

forever and a day A moribund metaphor (see page 21). *always; ceaselessly; constantly; continually; continuously; endlessly; eternally; everlastingly; evermore; forever; forevermore; immortally; indefinitely; interminably; permanently; perpetually; persistently; unceasingly; unremittingly.*

for every action there's an equal and opposite reaction A popular prescription (see page 23).

for every negative there is a positive A popular prescription (see page 23).

for everything there is a season A popular prescription (see page 23).

forewarn A wretched redundancy (see page 25). *warn.* ■ *Forewarn* your clients that they might be stared at by locals. REPLACE WITH *Warn.* SEE ALSO *advance warning; warn in advance.*

forewarned is forearmed A quack equation (see page 23).

for free A wretched redundancy (see page 25). *free.*

forgive and forget A popular prescription (see page 23).

fork in the road A moribund metaphor (see page 21).

formative years A torpid term (see page 24). *adolescence; childhood; immaturity; juvenility.*

forsooth A withered word (see page 24). *actually; indeed; in fact; in faith; in reality; in truth; truly.*

(it's) for the birds A moribund metaphor (see page 21). 1. *absurd; asinine; childish; comical; farcical; fatuous; flighty; foolhardy; foolish; frivolous; giddy; idiotic; immature; inane; laughable; ludicrous; nonsensical; preposterous; ridiculous; senseless; silly.* 2. *barren; bootless; effete; feckless; feeble; fruitless; futile; impotent; inadequate; inconsequential; inconsiderable; ineffective; ineffectual; infertile; insignificant; inutile; meaningless; meritless; nugatory; null; of no value; pointless; powerless; profitless; purposeless; sterile; trifling; trivial; unavailing; unimportant; unproductive; unprofitable; unserviceable; unworthy; useless; vain; valueless; weak; worthless.*

for the (simple) fact that A wretched redundancy (see page 25). *because; considering; for; in that; since.* ■ Women received some assistance in the colonial period *for the simple fact that* American Protestants strongly favored "peaceable" and intact families. REPLACE WITH *because.* SEE ALSO *for the (simple) reason that.*

for the most part A wretched redundancy (see page 25). *almost all; chiefly; commonly; generally; greatly; in general; largely; mainly; most; mostly; most often; much; nearly all; overall; normally; typically; usually.* ■ The search for solutions to these crises has focused *for the most part* on the legal system. REPLACE WITH *largely.*

for (with) the purpose of -ing A wretched redundancy (see page 25). *for (-ing); so as to; to.* ■ These analyses have been used *for the purpose of criticizing* the shortcomings of Western management. REPLACE WITH *for criticizing* or *to criticize.* ■ The other was the development in 1923 of a comparison microscope that could be used *for the purpose of determining* whether or not a bullet found at the scene of a crime was fired by a particular gun. REPLACE WITH *for determining* or *to determine.*

for the (simple) reason that A wretched redundancy (see page 25). *because; considering; for; in that; since.* ■ Polls dominate political discourse *for the simple reason that* "Everyone else has an opinion; the pollster has a fact." REPLACE WITH *because.* SEE ALSO *for the (simple) fact that.*

for your information An ineffectual phrase (see page 19). ■ *For your information,* he loves me, and I love him. DELETE *For your information.*

foul up (gum up; screw up) the works A moribund metaphor (see page 21). 1. *agitate; confuse; disorder; disorganize; disquiet; disrupt; disturb; fluster; jar; jinx;*

jolt; jumble; mix up; muddle; perturb; rattle; ruffle; shake up; stir up; unnerve; unsettle; upset. 2. *blight; cripple; damage; disable; harm; hurt; impair; incapacitate; lame; mar; mess up; rack; ruin; sabotage; spoil; subvert; undermine; vitiate; wrack; wreck.*

free and easy An inescapable pair (see page 20). *casual; carefree; easygoing; informal; insouciant; lighthearted; nonchalant; relaxed; untroubled.*

free and gratis An infantile phrase (see page 20). *free.*

(as) free as a bird An insipid simile. *autonomous; free; independent; self-reliant; unattached; unbound; unconfined; unconstrained; unencumbered; unentangled; unfettered; uninhibited; unrestrained; unrestricted; unshackled; untied.*

(as) free as the wind An insipid simile. *autonomous; free; independent; self-reliant; unattached; unbound; unconfined; unconstrained; unencumbered; unentangled; unfettered; uninhibited; unrestrained; unrestricted; unshackled; untied.*

free gift A wretched redundancy (see page 25). *gift.* ■ With every renewal, you will receive a *free gift.* DELETE *free.*

(no) free lunch A moribund metaphor (see page 21).

free ride A moribund metaphor (see page 21).

freezing cold An inescapable pair (see page 20). *algid; arctic; brumal; chilly; cold; cool; freezing; frigid; frosty; frozen; gelid; glacial; hibernal; hyperborean; ice-cold; icy; nippy; polar; rimy; wintry.*

(as) fresh as a daisy An insipid simile. *active; alive; animated; blooming; dynamic; energetic; fresh; healthy; hearty; lively; peppy; refreshed; rested; rosy; ruddy; spirited; sprightly; spry; vibrant; vigorous; vivacious.*

fret and fume An inescapable pair (see page 20).

a friend in need (is a friend indeed) A popular prescription (see page 23).

frighten by (his) own shadow A moribund metaphor (see page 21). *alarm; appall; benumb; daunt; frighten; horrify; intimidate; panic; paralyze; petrify; scare; shock; startle; terrify; terrorize; unnerve.*

frighten (scare) out of (her) wits A moribund metaphor (see page 21). *alarm; appall; benumb; daunt; frighten; horrify; intimidate; panic; paralyze; petrify; scare; shock; startle; terrify; terrorize; unnerve.*

frighten the life out of A moribund metaphor (see page 21). *alarm; appall; benumb; daunt; frighten; horrify; intimidate; panic; paralyze; petrify; scare; shock; startle; terrify; terrorize; unnerve.*

(go) from a simmer to a hard boil A moribund metaphor (see page 21).

from A to Z A moribund metaphor (see page 21). 1. *all during; all over; all through; throughout.* 2. *altogether; completely; entirely; fully; perfectly; quite; roundly; thoroughly; totally; unreservedly; utterly; wholly.*

from beginning to end A moribund metaphor (see page 21). 1. *always; ceaselessly; constantly; continually; continuously; endlessly; eternally; everlastingly; evermore; forever; forevermore; frequently; interminably; nonstop; permanently; perpetually; persistently; recurrently; regularly; repeatedly; unceasingly; unremittingly.* 2. *all during; all over; all through; throughout.* 3. *altogether; completely; entirely; fully; perfectly; quite; roundly; thoroughly; totally; unreservedly; utterly; wholly.*

from (the) cradle to (the) grave A moribund metaphor (see page 21). 1. *always; ceaselessly; constantly; continually; continuously; endlessly; eternally; everlastingly; evermore; forever; forevermore; frequently; interminably; nonstop; permanently; perpetually; persistently; recurrently; regularly; repeatedly; unceasingly; unremittingly.* 2. *all during; all over; all through; throughout.*

from darkness to light A moribund metaphor (see page 21).

> No longer a pariah, you were now a desired guest at parties, where you were supposed to speak eloquently about the struggle, to tear up and talk about the walk from the darkness into the light. — Lisa Fugard, *Skinner's Drift*

from dawn to (until) dusk A moribund metaphor (see page 21). *all day; all the time; always; ceaselessly; constantly; continually; continuously; endlessly; eternally; everlastingly; evermore; forever; forevermore; frequently; interminably; nonstop; permanently; perpetually; persistently; recurrently; regularly; repeatedly; unceasingly; unremittingly.* ■ She has to put up with this kind of stuff *from dawn to dusk.* REPLACE WITH *endlessly.*

(the) (date) from hell A moribund metaphor (see page 21).

from hence A wretched redundancy (see page 25). *hence.*

from pillar to post A moribund metaphor (see page 21). ■ You can't let your convictions be shaken, or you'll jump *from pillar to post* the moment times become difficult.

from rags to riches A moribund metaphor (see page 21).

from soup to nuts A moribund metaphor (see page 21). *all; all things; everything.*

from start to finish A moribund metaphor (see page 21). 1. *always; ceaselessly; constantly; continually; continuously; endlessly; eternally; everlastingly; evermore; forever; forevermore; frequently; interminably; nonstop; permanently; perpetually; persistently; recurrently; regularly; repeatedly; unceasingly; unremittingly.* 2. *all during; all over; all through; throughout.*

from stem to stern A moribund metaphor (see page 21). 1. *all during; all over; all through; throughout.* 2. *altogether; completely; entirely; fully; perfectly; quite; roundly; thoroughly; totally; unreservedly; utterly; wholly.*

from the bottom (depths) of (my) heart A moribund metaphor (see page 21). *earnestly; fervently; genuinely; heartily; honestly; sincerely; unreservedly; wholeheartedly.*

from the frying pan into the fire A moribund metaphor (see page 21).

(straight) from the horse's mouth A moribund metaphor (see page 21).

from the word *go* An infantile phrase (see page 20).

> Even my life so far has been plain. More Daisy than Elizabeth from the word go. — Meg Rosoff, *How I Live Now*

from tip to toe A moribund metaphor (see page 21). 1. *all during; all over; all through; throughout.* 2. *altogether; completely; entirely; fully; perfectly; quite; roundly; thoroughly; totally; unreservedly; utterly; wholly.*

from top to bottom A moribund metaphor (see page 21). 1. *all during; all over; all through; throughout.* 2. *altogether; completely; entirely; fully; perfectly; quite; roundly; thoroughly; totally; unreservedly; utterly; wholly.*

from whence A wretched redundancy (see page 25). *whence.* ■ The dolphins were judged sufficiently healthy to be taken back to the sea *from whence* they came. DELETE *from.* ■ And it all boiled over on talk radio — *from whence* it moved into the nation's high schools and junior highs and into late-night television. DELETE *from.*

front and center An inescapable pair (see page 20). *foremost; high; leading; main; major; prominent; salient; top.*

> John and I used to talk about how the current phase of the moon as well as the names of trees and flowers and birds — at least the local ones! — should be front and center in people's brains; maybe such a connection to nature would help to make us more civilized. — Elizabeth Berg, *The Year of Pleasures*

(on the) front burner A moribund metaphor (see page 21). *cardinal; chief; foremost; head; important; leading; main; paramount; predominant; primary; principal; prominent; topmost; uppermost.* ■ Preserving Yellowstone is probably a priority for most Americans, but at the moment it's not *on anyone's front burner.* REPLACE WITH *paramount.* ■ Procter & Gamble was faced with a *front-burner* actor suffering from a mysterious ailment. REPLACE WITH *leading.*

fuel the fire of A moribund metaphor (see page 21). 1. *fire; ignite; inflame; kindle.* 2. *galvanize; goad; incite; induce; needle; poke; prod; prompt; provoke; spur; stimulate; urge.* 3. *activate; animate; arouse; electrify; energize; enliven; excite; inspirit; invigorate; motivate; quicken; stimulate; stir; vitalize; vivify.*

full capacity A wretched redundancy (see page 25). *capacity.* ■ Buses are running closer to *full capacity* than at any time since the strike began. DELETE *full.*

full frontal assault A moribund metaphor (see page 21).

full of (herself) A moribund metaphor (see page 21). *egocentric; egoistic; egotistic; egotistical; narcissistic; self-absorbed; selfish; solipsistic.*

full of beans A moribund metaphor (see page 21). 1. *active; alive; animated; dynamic; energetic; exuberant; frisky; indefatigable; inexhaustible; invigorated; lively; peppy; spirited; sprightly; spry; tireless; unflagging; vibrant; vigorous; vivacious; zestful; zesty.* 2. *amiss; astray; deceived; deluded; erring; erroneous; fallacious; false; faulty; inaccurate; incorrect; in error; misguided; misinformed; mislead; mistaken; not correct; not right; wrong.*

full of holes A moribund metaphor (see page 21). 1. *defective; faulty; flawed; impaired; imperfect; marred; tainted.* 2. *baseless; captious; casuistic; casuistical; erroneous; fallacious; false; faulty; flawed; groundless; illogical; inaccurate; incorrect; invalid; irrational; jesuitic; jesuitical; mistaken; nonsensical; non sequitur; paralogistic; senseless; sophistic; sophistical; specious; spurious; unfounded; unreasonable; unsound; untenable; untrue; unveracious; wrong.*

full of hot air A moribund metaphor (see page 21). 1. *aggrandizing; blustering; boasting; bragging; coloring; crowing; elaborating; embellishing; embroidering; exaggerating; fanfaronading; gloating; hyperbolizing; magnifying; overstating; swaggering.* 2. *amiss; astray; deceived; deluded; erring; erroneous; fallacious; false; faulty; inaccurate; incorrect; in error; misguided; misinformed; mislead; mistaken; not correct; not right; wrong.*

full of piss and vinegar A moribund metaphor (see page 21). *active; alive; animated; dynamic; energetic; hearty; indefatigable; inexhaustible; lively; peppy; spirited; sprightly; spry; tireless; unflagging; vibrant; vigorous; vivacious.*

full of vim and vigor A moribund metaphor (see page 21). *active; alive; animated; dynamic; energetic; hearty; indefatigable; inexhaustible; lively; peppy; spirited; sprightly; spry; tireless; unflagging; vibrant; vigorous; vivacious.*

full plate A moribund metaphor (see page 21). *booked; busy; employed; engaged; involved; obligated; occupied.*

full potential A wretched redundancy (see page 25). *potential.* ■ Youngsters with talents that range from mathematical to musical are not challenged to work to their *full potential.* DELETE *full.*

(at) full speed (ahead) A moribund metaphor (see page 21). *abruptly; apace; at once; briskly; directly; expeditiously; fast; forthwith; hastily; hurriedly; immediately; instantaneously; instantly; posthaste; promptly; quickly; rapidly; rashly; right away; speedily; straightaway; swiftly; wingedly.*

(at) full steam (ahead) A moribund metaphor (see page 21). *abruptly; apace; at once; briskly; directly; expeditiously; fast; forthwith; hastily; hurriedly; immediately; instantaneously; instantly; posthaste; promptly; quickly; rapidly; rashly; right away; speedily; straightaway; swiftly; wingedly.*

a funny thing happened to me on the way to An infantile phrase (see page 20). ■ But *a funny thing happened on the way to* the Memorial Plaza.

G

gain a foothold A moribund metaphor (see page 21).

gain an advantage over A torpid term (see page 24). *beat; conquer; crush; defeat; outdo; overcome; overpower; overwhelm; prevail; quell; rout; succeed; triumph; trounce; vanquish; win.*

gain steam A moribund metaphor (see page 21).

game plan A moribund metaphor (see page 21). *action; course; direction; intention; method; move; plan; policy; procedure; route; scheme; strategy.*

game, set, and match A moribund metaphor (see page 21).

garden variety A moribund metaphor (see page 21). *average; common; commonplace; customary; everyday; fair; mediocre; middling; normal; ordinary; passable; plain; quotidian; regular; routine; simple; standard; tolerable; typical; uneventful; unexceptional; unremarkable; usual; workaday.*

gather together A wretched redundancy (see page 25). *gather.* ■ This summer's training provided all 1,500 youth an opportunity to *gather together* from around the country and to develop their skills and knowledge. DELETE *together.*

(I) gave (him) the best years of (my) life A plebeian sentiment (see page 23).

gaze into a crystal ball A moribund metaphor (see page 21). *anticipate; augur; divine; envision; forebode; forecast; foreknow; foresee; foretell; predict; prognosticate; prophesy; vaticinate.*

general consensus A wretched redundancy (see page 25). *consensus.* ■ The *general consensus* is that house prices have hit bottom. DELETE *general.*

(the) genie is out of the bottle A moribund metaphor (see page 21).

(as) gentle as a lamb An insipid simile. *affable; agreeable; amiable; amicable; compassionate; friendly; gentle; goodhearted; good-natured; humane; kind; kind-hearted; kindly; personable; pleasant; tender; tolerant.*

gentleman A suspect superlative (see page 24). Slipshod usage has reduced *gentleman* to a vulgarism. Common or crude people say *gentleman* when *man* would serve; though *gentleman* may sound dignified, it is actually dimwitted. Moreover, any man who doesn't, in revulsion, quiver at being called a *gentleman* is likely in jeopardy of becoming as vulgar as the word. ■ I am seeking a professional *gentleman* with diversified interests. REPLACE WITH *man.* ■ One *gentleman* told me it is a fantasy world and not to believe everything I hear. REPLACE WITH *man.* SEE ALSO *lady.*

(the) genuine article A moribund metaphor (see page 21). *actual; authentic; genuine; legitimate; pure; real; sterling; true; unadulterated; unalloyed; veritable.*

> He had constantly to be reassured. *Was* this the genuine article? *Was* this the real guaranteed height of a Good Time? — Christopher Isherwood, *Goodbye to Berlin*

get (our) act together An infantile phrase (see page 20). ■ They don't have the luxury of five years to *get their act together*.

get (has) a fix on A moribund metaphor (see page 21). *ascertain; assess; comprehend; determine; evaluate; learn; understand.*

get (has) a handle on A moribund metaphor (see page 21). 1. *cope with; deal with.* 2. *ascertain; assess; comprehend; determine; evaluate; learn; understand.*

get a life An infantile phrase (see page 20).

get away with murder A moribund metaphor (see page 21).

get (my) back up A moribund metaphor (see page 21). *acerbate; anger; annoy; bother; bristle; chafe; enrage; exasperate; gall; incense; inflame; infuriate; irk; irritate; madden; miff; pique; provoke; rile; roil; vex.*

get (his) dander up A moribund metaphor (see page 21). *acerbate; anger; annoy; bother; bristle; chafe; enrage; exasperate; gall; incense; inflame; infuriate; irk; irritate; madden; miff; pique; provoke; rile; roil; vex.*

get down to brass tacks A moribund metaphor (see page 21).

get (put) (all) (your) ducks in a row A moribund metaphor (see page 21). *arrange; categorize; classify; order; organize; prepare; ready; sort.*

> Everywhere they're smoothing down imperfections, putting hairs in place, putting ducks in a row, replacing divots. — Jonathan Lethem, *Motherless Brooklyn*

get (their) feet wet A moribund metaphor (see page 21).

get (your) foot in the door A moribund metaphor (see page 21).

get (my) goat A moribund metaphor (see page 21). *acerbate; anger; annoy; bother; bristle; chafe; enrage; incense; inflame; infuriate; irk; irritate; madden; miff; provoke; rile; roil; vex.* ■ "In denial" is one of those politically correct terms that *gets my goat*. REPLACE WITH *infuriates me.*

get (her) hackles up A moribund metaphor (see page 21). *acerbate; anger; annoy; bother; bristle; chafe; enrage; incense; inflame; infuriate; insult; irk; irritate; madden; miff; offend; provoke; rile; roil; vex.*

get (your) house in order A moribund metaphor (see page 21).

get in (my) hair A moribund metaphor (see page 21). *annoy; badger; bedevil; bother; chafe; distress; disturb; gall; grate; harass; harry; hassle; heckle; hector; hound; irk; irritate; nag; nettle; persecute; pester; plague; provoke; rankle; rile; roil; tease; torment; vex.*

get into the act A moribund metaphor (see page 21).

get in touch with (your) feelings A popular prescription (see page 23). *be aware; be cognizant; be conscious; be insightful; be mindful; be perceptive; be sensitive.*

get off (my) back A moribund metaphor (see page 21).

get (it) off (your) chest A moribund metaphor (see page 21). *acknowledge; admit; affirm; allow; avow; concede; confess; disclose; divulge; expose; grant; own; reveal; tell; uncover; unveil.*

get off on the wrong foot A moribund metaphor (see page 21).

get off the dime A moribund metaphor (see page 21). 1. *be certain; be decided; be decisive; be determined; be positive; be resolute; be sure.* 2. *budge; move; stir.*

get off the ground A moribund metaphor (see page 21). *begin; commence; embark on; inaugurate; initiate; introduce; launch; originate; start.* ■ Like all true entrepreneurs, they were eager to *get* another project *off the ground.* REPLACE WITH *launch.*

get on (my) nerves A moribund metaphor (see page 21). *annoy; badger; bedevil; bother; chafe; distress; disturb; gall; grate; harass; harry; hassle; heckle; hector; hound; irk; irritate; nag; nettle; persecute; pester; plague; provoke; rankle; rile; roil; tease; torment; vex.*

get on the stick A moribund metaphor (see page 21). *be active; be lively; move; stir.*

get (go) on with (my) life A popular prescription (see page 23). SEE ALSO *put (it) behind (us).*

get out of Dodge A moribund metaphor (see page 21). *abscond; clear out; decamp; depart; desert; disappear; escape; exit; flee; fly; go; go away; leave; move on; part; pull out; quit; retire; retreat; run away; take flight; take off; vacate; vanish; withdraw.* ■ The most sensible thing to do was *get out of Dodge.* REPLACE WITH *leave.*

get (it) out of (your) system A moribund metaphor (see page 21). *acknowledge; admit; affirm; allow; avow; concede; confess; disclose; divulge; expose; grant; own; reveal; tell; uncover; unveil.*

(don't) get (your) panties in a bunch A moribund metaphor (see page 21). 1. *agitated; anxious; aroused; displeased; disquieted; excited; flustered; perturbed; troubled; upset; worried.* 2. *acerbated; angered; annoyed; bothered; disturbed; exasperated; galled; irked; irritated; miffed; nettled; provoked; rankled; riled; roiled; upset; vexed.*

get (your) skates on A moribund metaphor (see page 21). *accelerate; advance; bestir; bustle; charge; dash; go faster; hasten; hurry; quicken; run; rush; speed up; sprint.*

get the ax A moribund metaphor (see page 21). *canned; discharged; dismissed; fired; let go; ousted; released; sacked; terminated.*

get (start) the ball rolling A moribund metaphor (see page 21). *begin; commence; embark on; inaugurate; initiate; introduce; launch; originate; start.*

get the better of A moribund metaphor (see page 21). 1. *beat; conquer; crush; defeat; outdo; overcome; overpower; overwhelm; prevail; quell; rout; succeed; triumph; trounce; vanquish; win.* 2. *outmaneuver; outsmart; outwit.*

> My body had got the better of me and could no longer be trusted. — Christina Schwarz, *Drowning Ruth*

get (give) the bum's rush A moribund metaphor (see page 21). *chuck; eject; expel; fling; throw out.*

(I) get the picture A moribund metaphor (see page 21). *appreciate; apprehend; comprehend; discern; fathom; grasp; know; perceive; realize; recognize; see; understand.*

get the word out A moribund metaphor (see page 21). *advertise; announce; broadcast; disseminate; proclaim; promote; promulgate; publicize; publish; trumpet.*

(let's) get this show on the road A moribund metaphor (see page 21). *begin; commence; embark; inaugurate; initiate; launch; originate; start.*

get to the bottom of (this) A moribund metaphor (see page 21). *appreciate; apprehend; comprehend; discern; fathom; grasp; know; perceive; realize; recognize; see; understand.*

get under (my) skin A moribund metaphor (see page 21). *acerbate; anger; annoy; bother; bristle; chafe; disturb; exasperate; gall; grate; irk; irritate; miff; nettle; provoke; rankle; rile; roil; upset; vex.*

get-up-and-go A moribund metaphor (see page 21). *ambition; bounce; dash; drive; dynamism; élan; energy; enthusiasm; initiative; liveliness; motivation; spirit; verve; vigor; vim; vitality; vivacity; zeal.*

(full of) get up and go A moribund metaphor (see page 21). 1. *active; alive; animated; dynamic; energetic; exuberant; frisky; indefatigable; inexhaustible; invigorated; lively; peppy; spirited; sprightly; spry; tireless; unflagging; vibrant; vigorous; vivacious; zestful; zesty.* 2. *ambitious; assiduous; busy; determined; diligent; hard-working; industrious; motivated; perseverant; persevering; persistent; sedulous.*

get up on the wrong side of the bed A moribund metaphor (see page 21). *bad-tempered; cantankerous; crabby; cranky; cross; disagreeable; grouchy; ill-humored; ill-natured; ill-tempered; irascible; irritable; quarrelsome; peevish; petulant; splenetic; sullen; surly; testy.*

get (her) walking papers A moribund metaphor (see page 21). *canned; discharged; dismissed; fired; let go; ousted; released; sacked; terminated.*

get wind of A moribund metaphor (see page 21). *ascertain; become aware of; discover; find out; hear about; learn.*

get (our) wires crossed A moribund metaphor (see page 21). *baffle; befuddle; bewilder; confound; confuse; disconcert; flummox; mix up; muddle; nonplus; perplex; puzzle.*

(it'll) get worse before it gets better A plebeian sentiment (see page 23). ■ Things will *get worse* at the bank *before they get better.*

gild (paint) the lily A moribund metaphor (see page 21). *overdo; overstate.*

give (her) a bum steer A moribund metaphor (see page 21). *bamboozle; befool; beguile; betray; bilk; bluff; cheat; con; deceive; defraud; delude; dupe; feint; fool; gyp; hoodwink; lead astray; misdirect; misguide; misinform; mislead; spoof; swindle; trick.*

give (her) a dose (taste) of (her) own medicine A moribund metaphor (see page 21).

give and take An inescapable pair (see page 20). *collaboration; cooperation; exchange; reciprocity.*

give (them) an inch and (they'll) take a mile A moribund metaphor (see page 21).

give (them) a piece of (his) mind A moribund metaphor (see page 21). *admonish; animadvert; berate; castigate; censure; chasten; chastise; chide; condemn; criticize; denounce; denunciate; discipline; impugn; objurgate; punish; rebuke; remonstrate; reprehend; reprimand; reproach; reprobate; reprove; revile; scold; upbraid; vituperate.*

> She didn't come down to give them a piece of her mind because it was no use fighting; they were sometimes able to get me some small job or other, through the influence of Jimmy's uncle Tambow, who delivered the vote of his relatives in the ward and was a pretty big wheel in Republican ward politics. — Saul Bellow, *The Adventures of Augie March*

give (him) a run for (his) money A moribund metaphor (see page 21).

give away the store A moribund metaphor (see page 21).

give (her) a wide berth (to) A moribund metaphor (see page 21). *avoid; bypass; circumvent; dodge; elude; evade; shun; sidestep; skirt.*

give birth (to) A moribund metaphor (see page 21). *bring about; cause; effect; generate; give rise to; inaugurate; initiate; introduce; occasion; produce; provoke; result in.*

give credit where credit is due A popular prescription (see page 23).

give (my) eyeteeth (right arm) for A moribund metaphor (see page 21).

give it a rest A moribund metaphor (see page 21). 1. *be silent; be still; hush; keep quiet; quiet; silence.* 2. *cease; close; complete; conclude; derail; desist; discontinue; end; finish; halt; quit; settle; stop; terminate.*

give it a shot (whirl) A moribund metaphor (see page 21). *aim; attempt; endeavor; essay; exert; labor; moil; strain; strive; struggle; toil; try hard; undertake; work at.*

give it (take) (your) best shot A moribund metaphor (see page 21). *aim; attempt; endeavor; essay; exert; labor; moil; strain; strive; struggle; toil; try; try hard; undertake; work at; work hard.*

> It was all very well to tell yourself, as he had been doing for years, that all you could do was give it your best shot. — Jane Smiley, *Moo*

given the fact that A wretched redundancy (see page 25). *because; considering; for; in that; since; when.* ■ *Given the fact that* all kibbutz youth were inducted into the army and commingled with tens of thousands of potential mates from outside their kibbutz before they got married, the rate of 200 marriages from within the same kibbutz is far more than could be expected by chance. REPLACE WITH *Since.* ■ I'd be interested in being a guest, but I gather you can't even consider it *given the fact that* I live in Cancun. REPLACE WITH *since.* SEE ALSO *because of the fact that; by virtue of the fact that; considering the fact that; in consideration of the fact that; in view of the fact that; on account of the fact that.*

(it) gives (me) something to do A plebeian sentiment (see page 23). SEE ALSO *(it) keeps (me) busy; (it) keeps (me) out of trouble; (it's) something to do.*

give (him) the back of (my) hand A moribund metaphor (see page 21). *abuse; affront; disdain; insult; offend; outrage; scorn; slap.*

give (her) the brush (brush-off) A moribund metaphor (see page 21). *abuse; affront; avoid; disdain; disregard; ignore; insult; neglect; offend; outrage; overlook; rebuff; reject; scorn; shun; sidestep; slap; slight; slur; skirt; sneer; snub; spurn.*

give (him) the business A moribund metaphor (see page 21). *admonish; animadvert; berate; castigate; censure; chasten; chastise; chide; condemn; criticize; denounce; denunciate; discipline; impugn; objurgate; punish; rebuke; remonstrate; reprehend; reprimand; reproach; reprobate; reprove; revile; scold; upbraid; vituperate.*

give (him) the cold shoulder A moribund metaphor (see page 21). *abuse; affront; avoid; disdain; disregard; ignore; insult; neglect; offend; outrage; overlook; rebuff; reject; scorn; shun; sidestep; slap; slight; slur; skirt; sneer; snub; spurn.*

give the devil his due A moribund metaphor (see page 21).

give (her) the pink slip A moribund metaphor (see page 21). *discharge; dismiss; fire; lay off; sack; suspend; terminate; throw out.*

give (him) the runaround A moribund metaphor (see page 21). *avoid; dodge; doubletalk; equivocate; evade; fence; hedge; palter; prevaricate; quibble; shuffle; sidestep; tergiversate; waffle.*

give (him) the third degree A moribund metaphor (see page 21). *catechize; cross-examine; examine; grill; inquire; interrogate; pump; question; quiz; test.*

give the thumbs down (sign) A moribund metaphor (see page 21). *decline; deny; disallow; disapprove; forbid; nix; prohibit; proscribe; refuse; reject; rule out; say no; turn down; veto.*

give the thumbs up (sign) A moribund metaphor (see page 21). *accredit; affirm; allow; approve; authorize; back; bless; certify; countenance; endorse; favor; permit; ratify; sanction; support.*

give (me) the time of day A moribund metaphor (see page 21). *be affable; be approachable; be cordial; be friendly; be genial; be pleasant; be polite; be receptive; be responsive; be sociable.*

> In about an hour, I would be sitting across the table from the most attractive woman who had ever stooped so low as to give me the time of day. — Don Keith, *The Forever Season*

give up the ghost A moribund metaphor (see page 21). *cease to exist; decease; depart; die; expire; pass away; pass on; perish.*

(a) glimmer of hope A moribund metaphor (see page 21). *anticipation; expectancy; expectation; hope; hopefulness; optimism; possibility; promise; prospect; sanguinity.*

gloom and doom An inescapable pair (see page 20).

go against the grain (of) A moribund metaphor (see page 21). *buck; challenge; contradict; defy; disobey; dispute; disregard; flout; go against; ignore; neglect; oppose; overlook; resist; violate.* ■ Does the message *go against the grain of* corporate philosophy? REPLACE WITH *flout.*

> It is not in our makeup to intervene. This goes against the grain, is entirely out of our character. — Kate Walbert, *Our Kind*

go ahead, make my day An infantile phrase (see page 20).

go belly up A moribund metaphor (see page 21). *break down; collapse; disintegrate; fail; fall short; flop; founder; miscarry; topple.* ■ All the biotech start-ups in the Bioventures portfolio would likely *go belly up* if the veterinary school is shut down. REPLACE WITH *fail.*

God is love A quack equation (see page 23).

go downhill A moribund metaphor (see page 21). *decay; decline; degenerate; destroy; deteriorate; disintegrate; ebb; erode; fade; fall off; languish; lessen; plummet; ruin; wane; weaken; wither; worsen.* ■ The bad news is that during the second night, everybody's performance *went downhill.* REPLACE WITH *deteriorated.*

(he) goes An infantile phrase (see page 20). Only the adolescent or the addle-brained prefer this gruesome *goes* to *acknowledge; admit; announce; assert; asseverate; aver; avow; comment; confess; cry; declare; disclose; divulge; exclaim; mention; note; observe; proclaim; pronounce; remark; reveal; say; state; utter.* ■ They say they don't know anything, and then they *go,* "if we hear anything, we'll call you." REPLACE WITH *say.* ■ He walked into the room, and she *goes,* "Guess what?" REPLACE WITH *exclaims.* ■ I asked what do you like about her, and he *went,* "I don't know." REPLACE WITH *confessed.* ■ And then he *goes,* "I don't want to see you any more." REPLACE WITH *announces.*

go for the gold An infantile phrase (see page 20).

go for the gusto An infantile phrase (see page 20).

go forward A torpid term (see page 24). 1. *advance; continue; develop; go on; grow; happen; improve; increase; make headway; make progress; move on; occur; proceed; progress; take place.* 2. *shall; will;* delete.

■ The way in which this is drafted will allow those takeovers to *go forward,* which would allow for a greater efficiency and productivity. REPLACE WITH *proceed.* ■ It is still our expectation that the summit will *go forward* and be productive. REPLACE WITH *occur.* ■ We look forward to *going forward.* REPLACE WITH proceeding. SEE ALSO *a step forward; a step (forward) in the right direction; move forward; move (forward) in the right direction; proceed forward.*

Going forward is replacing auxiliary verbs like *will* and *shall,* which to the politicians and businesspeople who now rely on *going forward,* do not convey futurity as effectively. *Going forward,* to these dimwitted thinkers, seems to reveal the future more forcefully; yet distinctions in tense, mood, and voice may be forfeited along with a subtle, yet indispensable, sense of what it means to be human.

■ This highlights perhaps the greatest risk to the economy *going forward.* DELETE *going forward.* ■ We need to train more Iraqi troops *going forward.* DELETE *going forward.* ■ I can't wait to share ideas about what we can do *going forward.* DELETE *going forward.* ■ *Going forward,* as the company has more mature branches, its profit margins should benefit and widen a bit more. DELETE *going forward.* ■ The company will continue to face challenges *going forward.* DELETE *going forward.* ■ This is an excellent opportunity for both companies and we look forward to maintaining positive momentum *going forward.* DELETE *going forward.*

going, going, gone An infantile phrase (see page 20).

going great guns A moribund metaphor (see page 21).

going on (19) An infantile phrase (see page 20). ■ I'm 69 *going on 70.* ■ I've been there 5 years, *going on 6 years.*

> Elizabeth Costello is a writer, born in 1928, which makes her sixty-six years old, going on sixty-seven. —J. M. Coetzee, *Elizabeth Costello*

going to hell in a handbasket A moribund metaphor (see page 21). *collapse; corrode; crumble; decay; decline; degenerate; destroy; deteriorate; disintegrate; ebb; erode; fade; fail; fall off; fester; flag; languish; lessen; plummet; putrefy; regress; rot; ruin; stagnate; ulcerate; wane; weaken; wither; worsen.* ■ The typical reaction people seem to have is that public education is *going to hell in a handbasket.* REPLACE WITH *deteriorating.*

going (have) to live with that for the rest of my life A plebeian sentiment (see page 23).

go (send) into a tailspin A moribund metaphor (see page 21). 1. *be unsuccessful; bomb; break down; collapse; fail; fall short; falter; fizzle; flop; fold; founder; mess up; miscarry; not succeed; stumble; topple.* 2. *be ailing; be anxious; be unhealthy; be ill; be sick; be sickly; be unwell.*

go into orbit A moribund metaphor (see page 21). 1. *be delighted; be ecstatic; be elated; be enraptured; be euphoric; be exalted; be excited; be exhilarated; be exultant; be gay; be glad; be gleeful; be good-*

humored; be happy; be intoxicated; be jolly; be jovial; be joyful; be joyous; be jubilant; be merry; be mirthful; be overjoyed; be pleased; be rapturous; be thrilled. 2. *be angry; be annoyed; be enraged; be exasperated; be furious; be incensed; be infuriated; be irate; be irked; be irritated; be mad; be raging; be wrathful.*

go kicking and screaming A moribund metaphor (see page 21). *antagonistically; defiantly; disagreeably; grudgingly; recalcitrantly; reluctantly; renitently; resistantly; resistingly; unconsentingly; unwillingly.*

golden opportunity An inescapable pair (see page 20). ■ We have a *golden opportunity* to prevent this cycle from continuing.

(a) goldmine of (information) A moribund metaphor (see page 21). SEE ALSO *a barrage of.* ■ His diary is nonetheless *a goldmine of information* about earlier American gay social life.

go (run) like the wind An insipid simile. *abruptly; apace; at once; briskly; directly; expeditiously; fast; forthwith; hastily; hurriedly; immediately; instantaneously; instantly; posthaste; promptly; quickly; rapidly; rashly; right away; speedily; straightaway; swiftly; wingedly.*

(has) gone with the wind A moribund metaphor (see page 21). 1. *be forgotten; dead; disappeared; dissolved; evaporated; past; vanished.* 2. *ephemeral; evanescent; fleeting; flitting; fugacious; fugitive; short-lived; transient; transitory; volatile.* ■ I would retain some of what I read, and then it would very likely *be gone with the wind.* REPLACE WITH *vanish.*

good and sufficient An inescapable pair (see page 20). *adequate; good; satisfactory; sufficient.*

(as) good as gold An insipid simile. *best; excellent; exceptional; fine; finest; first-class; first-rate; good; great; optimal; optimum; superior; superlative.*

good, bad, and (or) indifferent A torpid term (see page 24). ■ We really don't know what the effect will be; it could be *good, bad, or indifferent.*

(the) good, (the) bad, and (the) ugly An infantile phrase (see page 20). ■ Teach yourself to open up more and share with your readership by forcing yourself to look at *the good, bad, and ugly* of your life.

(the) good doctor An infantile phrase (see page 20). ■ I think everything *the good doctor* has said is hogwash.

good egg A moribund metaphor (see page 21). *agreeable; decent; ethical; forthright; honest; just; moral; righteous; straight; trustworthy; upright; virtuous.*

(a) good man is hard to find A popular prescription (see page 23).

(the) good news is (that) An infantile phrase (see page 20). ■ *The good news is that* most students report that speaking gets easier as the term progresses.

(the) good old days A suspect superlative (see page 24). *antiquity; history; the past; yesterday.* ■ We're going back to *the good old days* on gas prices.

(a) good read An infantile phrase (see page 20). This is a hideous expression that only the very badly read — those, that is, who read merely to be entertained — could possibly verbalize. The people who use this phrase are the people who read *best-selling authors* (SEE) ■ This bookstore caters to those looking for *a good read in paperback*. REPLACE WITH *a readable paperback*. ■ While Foley's piece on football stadiums was *a good read*, it is entirely off the mark in terms of the proposed megaplex. REPLACE WITH *entertaining*. ■ It is hard to make air-conditioning repair *a good read*. REPLACE WITH *captivating*. SEE ALSO *a (must) read*.

good riddance to bad rubbish An infantile phrase (see page 20).

good (great) stuff When we need to use the word *stuff* to describe something we like, something we also call *good* or *great*, we might wonder if we have lost all sense of what is likable and what not.

Stuff best describes the nondescript and uneventful, the poor, the ordinary, and the pathetic.

good things come in small packages A popular prescription (see page 23).

(and a) good time was had by all An infantile phrase (see page 20).

go off half-cocked A moribund metaphor (see page 21). *careless; emotional; foolhardy; hasty; headlong; heedless; impulsive; incautious; indiscreet; precipitate; rash; reckless; thoughtless; unmindful; unthinking.*

go off the deep end A moribund metaphor (see page 21). 1. *be careless; be emotional; be foolhardy; be hasty; be headlong; be heedless; be impulsive; be incautious; be indiscreet; be precipitate; be rash; be reckless; be thoughtless; be unmindful; be unthinking.* 2. *acerbate; anger; annoy; bother; bristle; chafe; enrage; incense; inflame; infuriate; irk; irritate; madden; miff; provoke; rile; roil; vex.*

go (her) one better A moribund metaphor (see page 21). *beat; best; better; defeat; eclipse; exceed; excel; outclass; outdo; outflank; outmaneuver; outpace; outperform; outplay; outrank; outrival; outsmart; outstrip; outthink; outwit; overcome; overpower; overshadow; prevail; rout; surpass; top; triumph; trounce; vanquish; whip; win.*

goose egg A moribund metaphor (see page 21). *cipher; naught; zero.*

(his) goose is cooked A moribund metaphor (see page 21).

(kill) (the) goose that lays the golden egg A moribund metaphor (see page 21).

go overboard A moribund metaphor (see page 21). *exaggerate; hyperbolize; overdo; overreact; overstress; overstate.*

go (send) over the edge A moribund metaphor (see page 21). 1. *be unsuccessful; bomb; break down; collapse; fail; fall short; falter; fizzle; flop; fold; founder; mess up; miscarry; not succeed; stumble; topple.* 2. *be ailing; be anxious; be unhealthy; be ill; be sick; be sickly; be unwell.* 3. *acerbate; anger; annoy; bother; bristle; chafe; enrage; incense; inflame; infuriate; irk; irritate; madden; miff; provoke; rile; roil; vex.*

> Jack is their guide: young and irreverent, thank God. Reverence would send Paul over the edge. — Julia Glass, *Three Junes*

go (head) south A moribund metaphor (see page 21). *collapse; crash; decline; decrease; descend; dip; drop; ebb; fail; fall; plummet; plunge; recede; regress; retire; sink; slide; slip; subside; topple; tumble.* ■ And it is possible that the market may *go south* before the shares can be offered. REPLACE WITH *fall.* ■ Obviously, any of these could cause your spirits to *go south* temporarily. REPLACE WITH *ebb.* ■ He expressed some concern for her job if the relationship should *go south.* REPLACE WITH *fail.*

go the extra mile A moribund metaphor (see page 21). ■ Average citizens who regularly *go the extra mile* to make this a better world are everywhere.

go their separate ways A moribund metaphor (see page 21). *break up; divorce; part; separate; split up.*

go the way of all flesh A moribund metaphor (see page 21). *cease to exist; decease; depart; die; end; expire; pass away; pass on; perish.*

go the way of the dinosaur A moribund metaphor (see page 21). *become extinct; cease to exist; disappear; vanish.*

go the whole hog An infantile phrase (see page 20). *do completely; do entirely; do fully; do thoroughly; do totally; do utterly; do wholly; do wholeheartedly.*

> Perhaps it was that if I was going to have a predawn wedding in a crimson dress, I might as well go the whole hog and be hovering at an unsuspecting witness's bedside as he woke. — Suzannah Dunn, *The Queen of Subtleties*

go through the ceiling (roof) A moribund metaphor (see page 21). *bellow; bluster; clamor; explode; fulminate; fume; holler; howl; rage; rant; rave; roar; scream; shout; storm; thunder; vociferate; yell.*

go through the mill A moribund metaphor (see page 21).

go (shoot) through the roof A moribund metaphor (see page 21). *ascend; balloon; billow; bulge; climb; escalate; expand; go up; grow; improve; increase; inflate; mount; multiply; rise; skyrocket; soar; surge; swell.* ■ Some people thought it was an extravagance at a time when billings aren't exactly *going through the roof.* REPLACE WITH *soaring.* ■ My quality of life has *gone through the roof* since he quit his job. REPLACE WITH *improved immeasurably.*

go to bat for A moribund metaphor (see page 21). *abet; advance; advocate; aid; assist; back; bolster; champion; defend; espouse; fight for; further; help; support; uphold.* ■ All I want to say is that it is easier to *go to bat for* people when they recognize they're wrong. REPLACE WITH *defend.*

go toe to toe with A moribund metaphor (see page 21). *battle; compete; contend; fight; struggle; vie.*

(we) got off on the wrong foot A moribund metaphor (see page 21).

go to pieces A moribund metaphor (see page 21). *decay; decline; degenerate; destroy; deteriorate; disintegrate; ebb; erode; fade; fall off; languish; lessen; ruin; wane; weaken; wither; worsen.*

go to pot A moribund metaphor (see page 21). *decay; decline; degenerate; destroy; deteriorate; disintegrate; ebb; erode; fade; fall off; languish; lessen; ruin; wane; weaken; wither; worsen.*

go to (her) reward A moribund metaphor (see page 21). *cease to exist; decease; depart; die; expire; pass away; pass on; perish.*

go (run) to seed A moribund metaphor (see page 21). *decay; decline; degenerate; deteriorate; devitalize; disintegrate; ebb; erode; fade; fall off; languish; lessen; ruin; wane; weaken; wither; worsen.*

go to the dogs A moribund metaphor (see page 21). *decay; decline; degenerate; destroy; deteriorate; disintegrate; ebb; erode; fade; fall off; languish; lessen; ruin; wane; weaken; wither; worsen.*

go to the mat (for) A moribund metaphor (see page 21). 1. *battle; brawl; clash; fight; grapple; jostle; scuffle; skirmish; tussle; war; wrestle.* 2. *advocate; aid; assist; back; champion; defend; espouse; help; protect; shield; support; uphold.* 3. *argue; dispute; fight; quarrel; wrangle.*

go up in flames A moribund metaphor (see page 21). *annihilate; break down; crumble; demolish; destroy; deteriorate; die; disintegrate; dissolve; end; eradicate; exterminate; obliterate; pulverize; rack; ravage; raze; ruin; shatter; smash; undo; wrack; wreck.*

go up (the chimney) in smoke A moribund metaphor (see page 21). *annihilate; break down; crumble; demolish; destroy; deteriorate; die; disappear; disintegrate; dissipate; dissolve; end; eradicate; evaporate; exterminate; fade; obliterate; pulverize; rack; ravage; raze; ruin; shatter; smash; undo; vanish; vaporize; volatilize; wrack; wreck.* ■ Everything I worked for over the last ten years is *going up in smoke.* REPLACE WITH *evaporating.*

go with the flow A moribund metaphor (see page 21). *abide by; accede to; accept; accommodate; acquiesce; adapt to; adhere to; adjust to; agree to; assent; be agreeable; be complacent; bend; be resigned; bow; comply with; concede to; concur; conform; consent to; fit; follow; reconcile; submit; succumb; yield.* ■ We have to *go with the flow.* REPLACE WITH *acquiesce.*

(as) graceful as a swan An insipid simile. *agile; graceful; limber; lissome; lithe; lithesome; nimble; supple.*

grace (us) with (his) presence A torpid term (see page 24). ■ Most of these essays first appeared in *The New Yorker,* which Liebling *graced with his presence* between 1935 and 1963.

(like) Grand Central Station An insipid simile. 1. *abounding; brimful; brimming; bursting; chock-full; congested; crammed; crowded; dense; filled; full; gorged; jammed; jam-packed; overcrowded; overfilled; overflowing; packed; replete; saturated; stuffed; swarming; teeming.* 2. *busy; hectic.*

(the) grass is (always) greener (on the other side of) A popular prescription (see page 23).

(pure) gravy A moribund metaphor (see page 21). 1. *benefit; earnings; gain; money; proceeds; profit.* 2. *a benefit; a bonus; a dividend; a gift; a gratuity; a* *lagniappe; an extra; a perk; a perquisite; a pourboire; a premium; a tip.*

> And he'd like being told the good news. He'd smile, maybe. Anything you win for nothing, anything that falls into your lap, it's all gravy, right? — Joyce Carol Oates, *Blonde*

gravy train A moribund metaphor (see page 21).

grease (her) palm with silver A moribund metaphor (see page 21). 1. *bribe; induce; pay; suborn.* 2. *compensate; pay; recompense; tip.*

grease the skids A moribund metaphor (see page 21). *arrange; get ready; organize; prepare; set up.*

great A suspect superlative (see page 24). That which is called *great* is seldom more than *good,* and that which is *good* is scarcely mentionable. *Great expectations* often turn out to be slight realizations, and *great stuff* is seldom more than stuff.

Great is also, of course, a hugely overworked word. Consider this laughable sentence: ■ When I think of their golf course, the first word that comes to mind is *great.*

Alternatives to the quotidian *great* include *consequential; considerable; consummate; distinguished; eminent; excellent; exceptional; exemplary; exquisite; extraordinary; fine; flawless; grand; ideal; illustrious; impeccable; imposing; impressive; magnificent; marvelous; matchless; momentous; nonpareil; notable; noteworthy; perfect; preeminent; remarkable; select; splendid; superb; superior; superlative; supreme; transcendent; weighty; wonderful.*

(the) great American novel A suspect superlative (see page 24).

(the) great beyond A moribund metaphor (see page 21). *afterlife; eternity; everlastingness.*

(go) great guns A moribund metaphor (see page 21). *abruptly; briskly; expeditiously; fast; hastily; hurriedly; posthaste; promptly; quickly; rapidly; speedily; straightaway; swiftly; wingedly.*

green around the gills A moribund metaphor (see page 21). 1. *afflicted; ailing; diseased; ill; indisposed; infirm; not (feeling) well; sick; sickly; suffering; unhealthy; unsound; unwell; valetudinarian.* 2. *nauseated; nauseous; queasy; sick; squeamish; vomiting.*

(as) green as grass An insipid simile. 1. *aquamarine; emerald; green; greenish; teal; verdant; virescent.* 2. *adolescent; artless; awkward; callow; green; guileless; immature; inexperienced; inexpert; ingenuous; innocent; juvenile; naive; raw; simple; undeveloped; unfledged; unseasoned; unskilled; unskillful; unsophisticated; untaught; untrained; unworldly; young; youthful.*

green-eyed monster A moribund metaphor (see page 21). *envy; jealousy.*

green light A moribund metaphor (see page 21). *allowance; approval; assent; authority; authorization; blessing; consent; freedom; leave; liberty; license; permission; permit; power; sanction; warrant.*

Like *red light,* the expression *green light* appeals to people who grasp the meaning of colorful visuals and expressive pictures more easily than they do polysyllabic words and complicated thoughts. Some people upgrade simple or straightforward ideas to unintelligible ones; others degrade substantive or nuanced ideas to unsophisticated ones. *Green light* is an example of the latter, but both tactics suggest an insincere mind, an unknowable heart.

■ The Baby Bells — which already have *the green light* to go into just about any other venture — have railed against the remaining restrictions since they were imposed. REPLACE WITH *permission*. ■ The FBI was given *the green light* by the Justice Department to continue its investigation. REPLACE WITH *authorization*. ■ Why would we be surprised when others take that message as a *green light* to lie, cheat, steal, and do whatever will benefit them? REPLACE WITH *license*. SEE ALSO *red light*.

green with envy A moribund metaphor (see page 21). *covetous; desirous; envious; grudging; jealous; resentful.*

grim reaper A moribund metaphor (see page 21). *death.*

grin and bear it A popular prescription (see page 23).

grind to a halt A moribund metaphor (see page 21). *cease; close; complete; conclude; end; finish; halt; settle; stop; terminate.* ■ Once it becomes apparent that no payment is forthcoming, construction activity can quickly *grind to a halt*. REPLACE WITH *halt*.

grist for the mill A moribund metaphor (see page 21).

gross exaggeration An inescapable pair (see page 20). *embellishment; exaggeration; hyperbole; overstatement.*

(get in on the) ground floor A moribund metaphor (see page 21).

ground zero A moribund metaphor (see page 21).

grow (spread) like a cancer An insipid simile. *augment; breed; duplicate; grow; increase; metastasize; multiply; mushroom; procreate; proliferate; propagate; reproduce; snowball; spread; swell.*

(doesn't) grow on trees A moribund metaphor (see page 21). *exiguous; limited; inadequate; infrequent; meager; rare; scant; scanty; scarce; sparse; uncommon; unusual.*

gruesome twosome An infantile phrase (see page 20).

guardedly optimistic A torpid term (see page 24). *confident; encouraged; heartened; hopeful; optimistic; rosy; sanguine.* ■ Firefighters are *guardedly optimistic* that they have the blaze under control. DELETE *guardedly*. ■ We're *guardedly optimistic* that this synthetic compound may work. DELETE *guardedly*. SEE ALSO *cautiously optimistic.*

guardian angel A suspect superlative (see page 24). *liberator; redeemer; rescuer; savior.*

guesstimate An infantile phrase (see page 20). *appraisal; assessment; estimate; estimation; guess; impression; opinion.* ■ If you would like a *guesstimate* of time required for your site, we would be happy to give you one. REPLACE WITH *estimate*. ■ Yet with just a few moments of thought you can make a surprisingly good *guesstimate*. REPLACE WITH *guess*. ■ They were asked to guess what the contents were and *guesstimate* how many objects were in the envelope. REPLACE WITH *guess*.

Guesstimate is a perfectly ridiculous merger that people who are uncomfortable with using *guess* will turn to. Most of us prefer knowing to not knowing, or at least we prefer letting others believe we are knowledgeable. *Guesstimate*, these people reason, adds intelligence and respectability to their wild *guess*, their unsubstantiated *estimate*.

(as) guilty as sin An insipid simile. *at fault; blamable; blameful; blameworthy; censurable; condemnable; culpable; guilty; in error; reprehensible.*

(a) guilty conscience needs no accuser A popular prescription (see page 23).

H

(a) hailstorm of A moribund metaphor (see page 21). ■ Thus, President Gerald R. Ford's 1974 pardon of former President Richard M. Nixon provoked *a hailstorm of* criticism and may have contributed to Mr. Ford's defeat two years later by Jimmy Carter. SEE ALSO *a barrage of.*

hale and hearty An inescapable pair (see page 20). *energetic; fine; fit; good; hale; healthful; healthy; hearty; robust; sound; strong; vigorous; well.*

(anyone with) half a brain A moribund metaphor (see page 21).

half a loaf is better than none A moribund metaphor (see page 21).

half-baked (idea) A moribund metaphor (see page 21). *bad; blemished; defective; deficient; faulty; flawed; ill-conceived; imperfect; inadequate; incomplete; inferior; malformed; poor; unsound.*

(go at it) hammer and tongs A moribund metaphor (see page 21). *actively; aggressively; dynamically; emphatically; energetically; fast; ferociously; fervently; fiercely; forcefully; frantically; frenziedly; furiously; hard; intensely; intently; mightily; passionately; powerfully; robustly; savagely; spiritedly; strenuously; strongly; vehemently; viciously; vigorously; violently; wildly; with vigor.*

> He'd always been of the hammer-and-tongs school. She taught him sexual stealth, the occasional necessity of stillness. — Ian McEwan, *Amsterdam.*

handed to (her) on a silver platter A moribund metaphor (see page 21).

hand and (in) glove A moribund metaphor (see page 21). *amiable; amicable; attached; brotherly; chummy; close; confidential; devoted; familiar; friendly; inseparable; intimate; loving; thick.*

(goes) hand in hand A moribund metaphor (see page 21). *be indissoluble; be indivisible; be inseparable; be together.*

> New churches were established in the surrounding villages and a few schools with them. From the very

beginning religion and education went hand in hand. — Chinua Achebe, *Things Fall Apart*

hand over fist A moribund metaphor (see page 21). *apace; briskly; expeditiously; fast; hastily; hurriedly; posthaste; quickly; rapidly; speedily; swiftly; wingedly.*

(my) hands are tied A moribund metaphor (see page 21).

(the) hand that rocks the cradle (rules the world) A popular prescription (see page 23).

handwriting (is) on the wall A moribund metaphor (see page 21). *divination; foreboding; forewarning; indication; omen; portent; prediction; premonition; presage; presentiment; sign; signal; warning.*

hang (hold) (on) by a thread A moribund metaphor (see page 21). ■ The small towns in western Massachusetts are *holding on by a thread.*

hang fire A moribund metaphor (see page 21). 1. *be delayed; be slow.* 2. *be undecided; be unsettled.*

hang (your) hat on A moribund metaphor (see page 21).

hang (our) hats A moribund metaphor (see page 21). *dwell; inhabit; live; reside; stay.*

It is not the same as Hoving Road where we all once hung our hats, but things change in ways none of us can expect, no matter how damn much we know or how smart and good-intentioned each of us is or thinks he is. — Richard Ford, *The Sportswriter*

hang in there A moribund metaphor (see page 21). *carry on; get along; manage; succeed.* ■ Even though profits remain down, most firms are still *hanging in there.* REPLACE WITH *succeeding.* ■ I'm *hanging in there.* REPLACE WITH *managing.*

hang like a cloud (over) An insipid simile. 1. *becloud; cloak; darken; eclipse; mask; obscure; shroud; veil.* 2. *belittle; confound; degrade; demean; embarrass; humiliate; lower; shame.* ■ Their parents' divorce *hangs like a cloud over* their lives. REPLACE WITH *beclouds.* ■ There is nothing that Jesus does not understand about the heartache that *hangs like a cloud over* the history of our lives. REPLACE WITH *darkens.* ■ The aftermath of the bitter July incident *hangs like a cloud over* professors, students, and administrators alike. REPLACE WITH *embarrasses.* SEE ALSO *cast a shadow (over).*

hang on every word A moribund metaphor (see page 21). *attend to; hark; hear; hearken; heed; listen; pay attention; pay heed.*

hang over (our) heads A moribund metaphor (see page 21). *hang over; impend; loom; menace; overhang; overshadow; threaten; tower over.*

(these things) happen to other people, not to (me) A plebeian sentiment (see page 23).

(as) happy as a clam (at high tide) An insipid simile. *blissful; blithe; buoyant;*

cheerful; delighted; ecstatic; elated; enraptured; euphoric; exalted; excited; exhilarated; exultant; gay; glad; gleeful; good-humored; happy; intoxicated; jolly; jovial; joyful; joyous; jubilant; merry; mirthful; overjoyed; pleased; rapturous; thrilled.

(as) happy as a lark An insipid simile. *blissful; blithe; buoyant; cheerful; delighted; ecstatic; elated; enraptured; euphoric; exalted; excited; exhilarated; exultant; gay; glad; gleeful; good-humored; happy; intoxicated; jolly; jovial; joyful; joyous; jubilant; merry; mirthful; overjoyed; pleased; rapturous; thrilled.*

> They are happy as larks, they shine with their luck, their joy. — Audrey Niffenegger, *The Time Traveler's Wife*

(as) happy as Larry An insipid simile. *blissful; blithe; buoyant; cheerful; delighted; ecstatic; elated; enraptured; euphoric; exalted; excited; exhilarated; exultant; gay; glad; gleeful; good-humored; happy; intoxicated; jolly; jovial; joyful; joyous; jubilant; merry; mirthful; overjoyed; pleased; rapturous; thrilled.*

happy camper An infantile phrase (see page 20). *blissful; blithe; buoyant; cheerful; delighted; ecstatic; elated; enraptured; euphoric; exalted; excited; exhilarated; exultant; gay; glad; gleeful; good-humored; happy; intoxicated; jolly; jovial; joyful; joyous; jubilant; merry; mirthful; overjoyed; pleased; rapturous; thrilled.* ■ The six families who bought in to the project, all at full price, are not *happy campers* these days. REPLACE WITH *pleased.*

(a) hard (tough) act to follow A moribund metaphor (see page 21).

hard and fast (rule) A moribund metaphor (see page 21). *absolute; binding; certain; defined; dogmatic; entrenched; established; exact; exacting; fast; firm; fixed; hard; immutable; inflexible; invariable; permanent; resolute; rigid; set; severe; solid; steadfast; strict; stringent; unalterable; unbending; uncompromising; unyielding.* ■ Events are happening too quickly in Eastern Europe to make *hard and fast* plans at this point. REPLACE WITH *firm.*

(as) hard as a rock An insipid simile. 1. *adamantine; firm; granitelike; hard; petrified; rock-hard; rocklike; rocky; solid; steellike; steely; stonelike; stony.* 2. *athletic; beefy; brawny; burly; firm; fit; hale; hardy; hearty; husky; manly; mighty; muscular; powerful; puissant; robust; rugged; sinewy; solid; stalwart; stout; strapping; strong; sturdy; tough; vigorous; virile; well-built.* 3. *constant; dependable; determined; faithful; fast; firm; fixed; inexorable; inflexible; loyal; obdurate; resolute; resolved; rigid; solid; stable; staunch; steadfast; steady; stern; tenacious; unflinching; unwavering; unyielding.*

(as) hard as nails An insipid simile. 1. *athletic; beefy; brawny; burly; firm; fit; hale; hardy; hearty; husky; manly; mighty; muscular; powerful; puissant; robust; rugged; sinewy; solid; stalwart; stout; strapping; strong; sturdy; tough; vigorous; virile; well-built.* 2. *constant; dependable; determined; faithful; fast; firm; fixed; inexorable; inflexible; loyal; obdurate; resolute; resolved; rigid; solid; stable; staunch; steadfast; steady; stern; tenacious; unflinching; unwavering; unyielding.*

hard (tough) nut to crack A moribund metaphor (see page 21). 1. *arduous; backbreaking; burdensome; difficult;*

exhausting; fatiguing; hard; herculean; laborious; not easy; onerous; severe; strenuous; toilful; toilsome; tough; troublesome; trying; wearisome. 2. *impenetrable; incomprehensible; inexplicable; inscrutable; mysterious; obscure; unexplainable; unfathomable; ungraspable; unintelligible; unknowable.*

hard (rough) on the eyes A moribund metaphor (see page 21). *coarse; homely; ill-favored; plain; ugly; unattractive; unbeautiful; uncomely; unsightly.*

hard (tough) row to hoe A moribund metaphor (see page 21). *arduous; backbreaking; burdensome; difficult; exhausting; fatiguing; hard; herculean; laborious; not easy; onerous; severe; strenuous; toilful; toilsome; tough; troublesome; trying; wearisome.*

hard to believe A torpid term (see page 24). *beyond belief; beyond comprehension; doubtful; dubious; farfetched; implausible; improbable; incomprehensible; inconceivable; incredible; inexplicable; questionable; remote; unbelievable; unimaginable; unlikely; unrealistic.*

hard (tough) to swallow A moribund metaphor (see page 21). 1. *beyond belief; beyond comprehension; doubtful; dubious; farfetched; implausible; improbable; incomprehensible; inconceivable; incredible; inexplicable; questionable; remote; unbelievable; unimaginable; unlikely; unrealistic.* 2. *disagreeable; distasteful; indigestible; unpalatable; unpleasant.*

has a finger in every pie A moribund metaphor (see page 21).

has a heart as big as all outdoors An insipid simile. *beneficent; benevolent; compassionate; big-hearted; generous; good-hearted; humane; kind; kind-hearted; kindly; sensitive; sympathetic; understanding.*

has a heart of gold A moribund metaphor (see page 21). *beneficent; benevolent; compassionate; big-hearted; generous; good-hearted; good-natured; humane; kind; kind-hearted; kindly; sensitive; sympathetic; understanding.*

has a heart of stone A moribund metaphor (see page 21). *apathetic; callous; chilly; cold; cool; detached; dispassionate; distant; emotionless; frigid; glacial; hard; hardhearted; harsh; heartless; hostile; icy; impassive; indifferent; passionless; pitiless; reserved; unconcerned; unemotional; unfeeling; unfriendly; unresponsive.*

has an effect on A wretched redundancy (see page 25). *acts on; affects; bears on; influences; sways; works on.* ■ That's one of the problems that *has an effect on* everyone's quality of life. REPLACE WITH *affects*. SEE ALSO *effect*.

has an impact on A wretched redundancy (see page 25). *acts on; affects; bears on; influences; sways; works on.* ■ That too *had an impact on* the jury. REPLACE WITH *swayed*. SEE ALSO *impact*.

has a swelled head A moribund metaphor (see page 21). *arrogant; cavalier; conceited; disdainful; egocentric; egotistic; egotistical; haughty; lofty; pompous; pretentious; proud; narcissistic; self-centered; self-important; self-satisfied; supercilious; superior; vain.*

has both feet on the ground A moribund metaphor (see page 21). *busi-*

nesslike; careful; cautious; circumspect; expedient; judicious; politic; practical; pragmatic; prudent; realistic; reasonable; sensible; utilitarian.

has (his) hands full A moribund metaphor (see page 21). *booked; busy; employed; engaged; involved; obligated; occupied.*

has (him) in the palm of (my) hand A moribund metaphor (see page 21). *be in charge; be in command; be in control.*

has the patience of Job A moribund metaphor (see page 21). *accepting; accommodating; acquiescent; complacent; complaisant; compliant; cowed; deferential; docile; dutiful; easy; forbearing; gentle; humble; long-suffering; meek; mild; obedient; passive; patient; prostrate; quiet; reserved; resigned; stoical; submissive; subservient; timid; tolerant; tractable; unassuming; uncomplaining; yielding.*

has to do with A wretched redundancy (see page 25). *concerns; deals with; is about; pertains to; regards; relates to.* ■ The most recent academy committee mission *has to do with* climate-monitoring satellites. REPLACE WITH *concerns.*

has two left feet A moribund metaphor (see page 21). *awkward; blundering; bumbling; bungling; clumsy; gawky; gauche; ham-handed; heavy-handed; inapt; inept; lubberly; lumbering; maladroit; uncoordinated; uncouth; ungainly; ungraceful; unhandy; unskillful; unwieldy.*

has (him) under (her) thumb A moribund metaphor (see page 21). *administer; boss; command; control; dictate; direct; dominate; domineer; govern; in charge; in command; in control; manage; manipulate; master; misuse; order; overpower; oversee; predominate; prevail; reign over; rule; superintend; tyrannize; use.*

hat in hand A moribund metaphor (see page 21). *diffidently; humbly; meekly; modestly; respectfully; unassumingly.*

haul (rake) over the coals A moribund metaphor (see page 21). *admonish; animadvert; berate; castigate; censure; chasten; chastise; chide; condemn; criticize; denounce; denunciate; discipline; excoriate; fulminate against; imprecate; impugn; inveigh against; objurgate; punish; rebuke; remonstrate; reprehend; reprimand; reproach; reprobate; reprove; revile; scold; swear at; upbraid; vituperate.*

have a conniption (fit) A moribund metaphor (see page 21). *bellow; bluster; clamor; explode; fulminate; fume; holler; howl; rage; rant; rave; roar; scream; shout; storm; thunder; vociferate; yell.*

have a good (nice) day (evening) A plebeian sentiment (see page 23). We are bovine creatures who find that formulas rather than feelings suit us well enough; indeed, they suit us mightily. How pleasant it is not to have to think of a valid sentiment when a vapid one does so nicely; how effortless to rely on triteness rather than on truth.

Dimwitticisms veil our true feelings and avert our real thoughts. SEE ALSO *common courtesy.*

have a hemorrhage A moribund metaphor (see page 21). *bellow; bluster; clamor; explode; fulminate; fume; holler; howl; rage; rant; rave; roar; scream; shout; storm; thunder; vociferate; yell.*

have (take) a listen An infantile phrase (see page 20). *listen.* As inane as it is insulting, *have (take) a listen* obviously says nothing that *listen* alone does not. Journalists and media personalities who use this offensive phrase ought to be silenced; businesspeople, dismissed; public officials, pilloried.

■ But some fans will take a walk and *take a listen* to the sales pitch, intrigued by such generous offers and possibility of making such a huge profit. REPLACE WITH *listen.* ■ It has been far too long since I have had the opportunity to hear the Seneca Chamber Orchestra, so I went over to Christ Church United Methodist to *have a listen,* and boy, has it grown. REPLACE WITH *listen.* ■ *Take a listen* and decide for yourself. REPLACE WITH *Listen.* ■ But first we will *take a listen* to attorney Frederic Woocher arguing against the law. REPLACE WITH *listen.*

have (me) by the ears A moribund metaphor (see page 21). *clasp; cleave (to); clench; clutch; grab; grasp; grip; hold; secure; seize.*

> In spite of the recent falls in the value of the Nasdaq index and the value of Amazon stock, the new technology had the city by the ears .... — Salman Rushdie, *Fury*

(the) have-nots A moribund metaphor (see page 21). *bankrupt; broke; destitute; distressed; impecunious; impoverished; indigent; insolvent; needy; penniless; poor; poverty- stricken; underprivileged.* ■ You, me, and many others can afford to pay a little more for health insurance if it gives some to the *have-nots.* REPLACE WITH *indigent.*

(the) haves A moribund metaphor (see page 21). *affluent; comfortable; moneyed; opulent; privileged; prosperous; rich; wealthy; well-off; well-to-do.*

(you) have to learn to walk before (you) can run A popular prescription (see page 23).

(you) have to love (yourself) before (you) can love another A popular prescription (see page 23).

(you) have (your) whole life ahead of (you) A popular prescription (see page 23).

(stand) head and shoulders above (the rest) A moribund metaphor (see page 21). *abler; better; exceptional; greater; higher; more able (accomplished; adept; capable; competent; qualified; skilled; talented); outstanding; standout; superior; superlative.* ■ By now, a few names should clearly be *heads and shoulders above* all others. REPLACE WITH *better than.*

head for the hills A moribund metaphor (see page 21). *abscond; clear out; decamp; depart; desert; disappear; escape; exit; flee; fly; go; go away; leave; move on; part; pull out; quit; retire; retreat; run away; take flight; take off; vacate; vanish; withdraw.*

head in the clouds and feet on the ground A moribund metaphor (see page 21).

head into the home stretch A moribund metaphor (see page 21).

(has a good) head on (his) shoulders A moribund metaphor (see page 21).

able; adroit; apt; astute; bright; brilliant; capable; clever; competent; discerning; effective; effectual; efficient; enlightened; insightful; intelligent; judicious; keen; knowledgeable; learned; logical; luminous; perceptive; perspicacious; quick; rational; reasonable; sagacious; sage; sapient; sensible; sharp; shrewd; smart; sound; understanding; wise.

head on the block A moribund metaphor (see page 21).

head over heels A moribund metaphor (see page 21). *altogether; ardently; completely; deeply; earnestly; entirely; fervently; fully; intensely; passionately; perfectly; quite; roundly; thoroughly; totally; unreservedly; utterly; wholly; zealously.*

head over heels (in love) A moribund metaphor (see page 21). *besotted; crazed; haunted; infatuated; lovesick; mad; obsessed; possessed; smitten.*

> Even in his Mammon days, he always leaned to the general while I tumbled head over heels into the particular; he loved ideas and I personalities; he was all for argument and I yearned for gossip. — Louis Auchincloss, *The Rector of Justin*

(as) healthy as a horse An insipid simile. *athletic; beefy; brawny; energetic; fine; fit; good; hale; hardy; hearty; healthful; healthy; husky; lanky; lean; manly; muscular; powerful; robust; shapely; sinewy; slender; solid; sound; stalwart; strong; sturdy; thin; trim; vigorous; virile; well; well-built.*

heap dirt (scorn) on A moribund metaphor (see page 21). *asperse; badmouth; belittle; besmirch; bespatter; blacken; calumniate; defame; defile; denigrate; denounce; depreciate; deride; disparage; impugn; insult; libel; malign; profane; revile; scandalize; slander; slap; slur; smear; sully; taint; traduce; vilify; vitiate.*

hear by (via) the grapevine A moribund metaphor (see page 21).

heart and soul A moribund metaphor (see page 21). 1. *altogether; completely; entirely; fully; perfectly; quite; roundly; thoroughly; totally; unreservedly; utterly; wholly.* 2. *earnestly; fervently; genuinely; heartily; honestly; sincerely; unreservedly; wholeheartedly.*

(a) heartbeat away A moribund metaphor (see page 21).

(my) heart bleeds for (you) A moribund metaphor (see page 21). *commiserate; empathize; feel bad; feel sorry; pity; sympathize.*

(his) heart is in the right place A moribund metaphor (see page 21). *be well-intentioned.*

(you) hear what I'm saying? An ineffectual phrase (see page 19). ■ She's the one who did it, not me. *You hear what I'm saying?* DELETE *You hear what I'm saying?* SEE ALSO *(you) know what I mean? (you) know what I'm saying; (you) know what I'm telling you? (do) you know?.*

(I) hear you An infantile phrase (see page 20). *appreciate; apprehend; comprehend; grasp; see; understand.*

(the) heat is on A moribund metaphor (see page 21). *be coerced; be compelled; be forced; be pressured.*

heaven on earth A moribund metaphor (see page 21). *ambrosial; angelic; beatific; blissful; delightful; divine; enchanting; glorious; godlike; godly; heavenly; joyful; magnificent; resplendent; splendid; sublime.*

(as) heavy as lead An insipid simile. *bulky; heavy; hefty; weighty.*

(through) hell and high water A moribund metaphor (see page 21). *adversity; affliction; calamity; catastrophe; difficulty; distress; hardship; misadventure; misfortune; ordeal; trial; tribulation; trouble; woe.*

hell (hellbent) for leather A moribund metaphor (see page 21). *breakneck; brisk; fast; hasty; hurried; immediate; madcap; prompt; quick; rapid; rash; speedy; swift; wild; winged.* ■ Connors clearly thought that he had more to gain by pursuing his *hell-for-leather* expansion in the region.

hell has no fury like (a woman scorned) An insipid simile.

hell on earth A moribund metaphor (see page 21). *chthonian; chthonic; hellish; impossible; infernal; insufferable; insupportable; intolerable; painful; plutonic; sulfurous; unbearable; uncomfortable; unendurable; unpleasant; stygian; tartarean.* ■ Being a stepmother is *hell on earth.* REPLACE WITH *hellish.* SEE ALSO *a living hell.*

hell on wheels A moribund metaphor (see page 21). 1. *boisterous; disorderly; feral; obstreperous; rambunctious; riotous; roistering; rowdy; uncontrolled; undisciplined; unrestrained; unruly; untamed; wild.* 2. *angry; bad-tempered; bilious; cantankerous; choleric; churlish; crabby; cranky; cross; curmudgeonly; disagreeable; dyspeptic; grouchy; gruff; grumpy; ill-humored; ill-tempered; irascible; irritable; mad; peevish; petulant; quarrelsome; short-tempered; splenetic; surly; testy; vexed.*

hem and haw An inescapable pair (see page 20). *dally; dawdle; hesitate; vacillate; waver.*

hemorrhage red ink A moribund metaphor (see page 21).

(like a) herd of elephants An insipid simile.

(right) here and now An inescapable pair (see page 20). *currently; now; nowadays; presently; the present; today.*

here's the thing An ineffectual phrase (see page 19). ■ *Here's the thing,* whoever is mayor must be able to work with the community. DELETE *Here's the thing.* ■ *Here's the thing,* men don't even know that we're different. DELETE *Here's the thing.* SEE ALSO *that's the thing; the thing about (of) it is; the thing is.*

here, there, and everywhere A wretched redundancy (see page 25). *all over; everywhere; omnipresent; ubiquitous.*

here today, gone tomorrow An infantile phrase (see page 20). *brief; ephemeral; evanescent; fleeting; flitting; fugacious; fugitive; impermanent; momentary; passing; short; short-lived; temporary; transient; transitory; volatile.* ■ I still love it even though nothing is as *here today, gone tomorrow* as a job in TV. REPLACE WITH *fleeting.* ■ In politics, issues *that* *are here today are gone tomorrow.* REPLACE WITH *are ephemeral.*

here to stay An infantile phrase (see page 20). *constant; deep-rooted; enduring; entrenched; established; everlasting; fixed; lasting; long-lived; permanent; secure; stable; unending.* ■ They questioned whether ability grouping is *here to stay*. REPLACE WITH *permanent.*

hero A suspect superlative (see page 24). Seldom someone who strives valorously to achieve a noble goal, *hero* has come to mean anyone who simply does his job or, perhaps, doing it, dies. As often, *hero* is used to describe a person who behaves ethically or suitably — merely, as he was told or taught.

Only comic book characters and cartoon creatures, today, define the word well.

■ The brother of former POW Jessica Lynch is calling his sister a *hero.* ■ A two-year-old boy who dialed 999 after his mother suffered an epileptic fit was today hailed a "little *hero*" by police in England. ■ Juventus goal *hero* David Trezeguet says his teammates are confident they can reach the Champions League final after last night's 2-1 defeat by Real Madrid. ■ A Brazilian bulldozer driver has become a national *hero* after refusing to knock down a house shared by a single mother and her seven children. ■ A male nurse who died of SARS was yesterday given a *hero's* funeral attended by Chief Executive Tung Chee-hwa.

hey An infantile phrase (see page 20). As a substitute for *hello* or *hi, hey* is a cheerless one. Perhaps the best way to discourage people from using *hey* is to respond with a hearty *diddle, diddle?*

■ You have a sharp mind for business and know how to relate to those who are self-employed or who work in unconventional careers (because, *hey*, you're part of the group!).

hide (their) heads in the sand A moribund metaphor (see page 21). *brush aside; avoid; discount; disregard; dodge; duck; ignore; neglect; omit; pass over; recoil from; shrink from; shun; shy away from; turn away from; withdraw from.* ■ Even when informed of the problem, some denominations are continuing to *hide their heads in the sand.*

(neither) hide nor (or) hair A moribund metaphor (see page 21). *nothing; sign; soupçon; trace; vestige.*

(left) high and dry An inescapable pair (see page 20). *abandoned; alone; deserted; forgotten; helpless; left; powerless; stranded.*

> His voice trailed off, he didn't know where; it left him high and dry, just staring at Ikmen like a fool. — Barbara Nadel, *Belshazzar's Daughter*

high and low An inescapable pair (see page 20). *all around; all over; all through; broadly; everyplace; everywhere; extensively; throughout; ubiquitously; universally; widely.* SEE ALSO *far and wide; left and right.*

high and mighty An inescapable pair (see page 20). *arrogant; cavalier; conceited; condescending; contemptuous; despotic; dictatorial; disdainful; dogmatic; domineering; haughty; imperious; insolent; lofty; overbearing; overweening; patronizing; pompous; pretentious; scornful; self-*

important; supercilious; superior; vainglorious.

(as) high as a kite An insipid simile. 1. *agitated; aroused; ebullient; effusive; enthused; elated; excitable; excited; exhilarated; expansive; impassioned; inflamed; overwrought; stimulated.* 2. *besotted; crapulous; drunk; inebriated; intoxicated; sodden; stupefied; tipsy.*

high (top) man on the totem pole A moribund metaphor (see page 21). *administrator; boss; brass; chief; commander; director; executive; foreman; head; headman; leader; manager; master; (high) muckamuck; officer; official; overseer; president; principal; superintendent; supervisor.*

(give) high marks A moribund metaphor (see page 21).

high on the hog A moribund metaphor (see page 21). *extravagantly; lavishly; luxuriantly.* ■ It's the state officials who are living *high on the hog.* REPLACE WITH *extravagantly.*

high-water mark A moribund metaphor (see page 21).

highway robbery A moribund metaphor (see page 21).

hindsight is 20/20 A quack equation (see page 23).

hired gun A moribund metaphor (see page 21). 1. *assassin; killer; mercenary; murderer.* 2. *adviser; authority; consultant; counselor; expert; guru; specialist.*

hit a home run A moribund metaphor (see page 21). *advance; fare well; flourish; prevail; progress; prosper; succeed; thrive; triumph; win.*

hit (strike; touch) a nerve A moribund metaphor (see page 21).

hit (him) (straight) between the eyes A moribund metaphor (see page 21). *amaze; astonish; astound; awe; dazzle; dumbfound; flabbergast; overpower; overwhelm; shock; startle; stun; stupefy; surprise.*

hit (rock) bottom A moribund metaphor (see page 21). *bankrupt; broke; destitute; distressed; impecunious; impoverished; indigent; insolvent; penniless; poor; poverty-stricken.*

hitch (your) wagon to a star A moribund metaphor (see page 21). *be ambitious; be determined; be motivated; be striving.*

hit (close to) home A moribund metaphor (see page 21).

hit (me) like a ton of bricks An insipid simile. *amaze; astonish; astound; awe; confound; daze; dazzle; dumbfound; flabbergast; overpower; overwhelm; shock; stagger; startle; stun; stupefy; surprise.* ■ The report *hit Congress like a ton of bricks.* REPLACE WITH *overwhelmed Congress.*

hit or miss A moribund metaphor (see page 21). *aimless; arbitrary; capricious; casual; erratic; haphazard; incidental; inconsistent; infrequent; irregular; lax; loose; occasional; odd; offhand; random; sporadic; uncontrolled; unplanned.*

hit over the head A moribund metaphor (see page 21).

hit pay dirt A moribund metaphor (see page 21). *flourish; get rich; prevail; prosper; succeed; thrive; triumph; win.*

hit the ceiling A moribund metaphor (see page 21). *bellow; bluster; clamor; explode; fulminate; fume; holler; howl; rage; rant; rave; roar; scream; shout; storm; thunder; vociferate; yell.*

hit the ground running A moribund metaphor (see page 21). ■ I get up in the morning and *hit the ground running.*

hit the hay A moribund metaphor (see page 21). *doze; go to bed; nap; rest; retire; sleep; slumber.*

hit the jackpot A moribund metaphor (see page 21). *flourish; get rich; prevail; prosper; succeed; thrive; triumph; win.*

hit the nail (squarely) on the head A moribund metaphor (see page 21). *be correct; be right.*

hit the road A moribund metaphor (see page 21). *abscond; clear out; decamp; depart; desert; disappear; escape; exit; flee; fly; go; go away; leave; move on; part; pull out; quit; retire; retreat; run away; take flight; take off; vacate; vanish; withdraw.*

hit the roof A moribund metaphor (see page 21).1. *be angry; be annoyed; be enraged; be exasperated; be furious; be incensed; be infuriated; be irate; be irked; be irritated; be mad; be raging; be wrathful.* 2. *bellow; bluster; clamor; explode; fulminate; fume; holler; howl; rage; rant; rave; roar; scream; shout; storm; thunder; vociferate; yell.* ■ He *hit the roof.* REPLACE WITH *became enraged.*

hit the sack A moribund metaphor (see page 21). *doze; go to bed; nap; rest; retire; sleep; slumber.*

hit the skids A moribund metaphor (see page 21). *decay; decline; degenerate; destroy; deteriorate; disintegrate; ebb; erode; fade; fall off; languish; lessen; ruin; wane; weaken; wither; worsen.*

hit (him) while (he's) down A moribund metaphor (see page 21).

(as) hoarse as a crow An insipid simile. *grating; gravelly; gruff; guttural; harsh; hoarse; rasping; raspy; throaty.*

hoist with (his) own petard A moribund metaphor (see page 21).

(can't) hold a candle (to) A moribund metaphor (see page 21). 1. *compare; equal; equate; liken; match; measure up; meet; rival.* 2. *be inferior.* ■ Various third-party utilities are available to improve this situation, but only one of them *holds a candle to* the NetWare SALVAGE utility. REPLACE WITH *rivals.* ■ When it comes to hosting wackos, the oft-maligned Web can't *hold a candle to* AM radio. REPLACE WITH *compare to.*

hold a gun to A moribund metaphor (see page 21). *coerce; command; compel; constrain; demand; dictate; force; insist; make; order; pressure; require.*

hold all the cards A moribund metaphor (see page 21). *administer; boss; command; control; dictate; direct; dominate; govern; in charge; in command; in control; manage; manipulate; master; order; overpower; oversee; predominate; prevail; reign over; rule; superintend.*

hold (their) feet to the fire A moribund metaphor (see page 21). *coerce; command; compel; constrain; demand; enforce; force; goad; impel; importune; incite; induce; insist; instigate; make; oblige; press; pressure; prod; push; require; spur; urge.* ■ The task now for those senators who truly support reform is to *hold their colleagues' feet to the fire* and bring this bill up again and again. REPLACE WITH *pressure their colleagues.* ■ He campaigns by movement-building: helping candidates, running ads to promote tax cuts, and *holding congressional Republicans' feet to the fire.* REPLACE WITH *prodding congressional Republicans.*

hold (your) fire A moribund metaphor (see page 21). 1. *be silent; be still; hush; keep quiet; quiet; silence.* 2. *be closed-mouthed; be quiet; be reticent; be silent; be speechless; be taciturn; be uncommunicative.*

hold (their) ground A moribund metaphor (see page 21). 1. *hold fast; stand firm.* 2. *assert; command; decree; dictate; insist; order; require.*

hold (my) hand A moribund metaphor (see page 21). *accompany; escort; guide.* ■ The intent of this text is to *hold your hand* through the learning process. REPLACE WITH *guide you.*

hold (her) head up (high) A moribund metaphor (see page 21). *be proud; show self-respect.*

hold on for dear life A torpid term (see page 24). *clutch; grab; grasp; hold; seize.*

hang (hold) on to your hat A moribund metaphor (see page 21). *be careful; be cautious; be prepared; be wary; look out; take heed; watch out.*

hold the fort A moribund metaphor (see page 21). 1. *defend; guard; protect.* 2. *look after.*

hold the phone A moribund metaphor (see page 21). *be patient; hold on; pause; slow down; wait.*

hold the purse strings A moribund metaphor (see page 21). *administer; boss; command; control; dictate; direct; dominate; govern; in charge; in command; in control; manage; manipulate; master; order; overpower; oversee; predominate; prevail; reign over; rule; superintend.*

hold (my) breath A moribund metaphor (see page 21). *agitated; anxious; eager; edgy; excitable; excited; fidgety; frantic; jittery; jumpy; nervous; ill at ease; on edge; restive; restless; skittish; uncomfortable; uneasy.*

> Still, though I'd already unlatched the door for her, I felt unprepared for her arrival, needing to back away and sit again in my leather chair. I was holding my breath, waiting for her to go away. — Elizabeth Rosner, *The Speed of Light*

hold (your) tongue A moribund metaphor (see page 21). 1. *be silent; be still; hush; keep quiet; quiet; silence.* 2. *be closed-mouthed; be quiet; be reticent; be silent; be speechless; be taciturn; be uncommunicative.*

hold true A wretched redundancy (see page 25). *hold.* ■ What *holds true* for them may not *hold true* for others. DELETE *true.*

hold water A moribund metaphor (see page 21). *hold; is true; is valid.* ■ We have to ask if the ancient ideas of the roles of bonds still *hold water.* REPLACE WITH *hold.*

hold your horses A moribund metaphor (see page 21). *be patient; calm down; hang on; hold on; pause; slow down; wait.*

home free A moribund metaphor (see page 21). *guarded; protected; safe; secure; sheltered; shielded; undamaged; unharmed; unhurt; unscathed.*

home is where the heart is A popular prescription (see page 23).

homely as a mud fence An insipid simile. *coarse; homely; ill-favored; plain; ugly; unattractive; unbeautiful; uncomely; unsightly.*

(down) (the) home stretch A moribund metaphor (see page 21).

(as) honest as the day is long An insipid simile. *aboveboard; blunt; candid; direct; earnest; faithful; forthright; frank; genuine; honest; reliable; sincere; straightforward; trustworthy; truthful; upright; veracious; veridical.*

honest truth A wretched redundancy (see page 25). *honesty; truth.* ■ If you want the *honest truth,* I am in love with him. REPLACE WITH *truth.*

honestly and truly An inescapable pair (see page 20). ■ I *honestly and truly* believed he was the best I could hope for. REPLACE WITH *honestly* or *truly.*

honesty is the best policy A popular prescription (see page 23).

(the) honeymoon is over A moribund metaphor (see page 21).

hook, line, and sinker A moribund metaphor (see page 21). *altogether; completely; entirely; fully; perfectly; roundly; quite; thoroughly; totally; unreservedly; utterly; wholly.*

hoot and holler An inescapable pair (see page 20). *bay; bawl; bellow; blare; caterwaul; clamor; cry; holler; hoot; howl; roar; screak; scream; screech; shout; shriek; shrill; squawk; squeal; vociferate; wail; whoop; yell; yelp; yowl.*

hope and expect (expectation) A wretched redundancy (see page 25). *hope; expect (expectation); trust.* ■ I *hope and expect* you'll be seeing a lot more of this. REPLACE WITH *expect* or *hope.*

hope and pray An inescapable pair (see page 20). ■ I *hope and pray* that in future features of this sort, the *Globe* puts the emphasis where it belongs.

hope for the best A popular prescription (see page 23). *be confident; be encouraged; be heartened; be hopeful; be optimistic; be positive; be rosy; be sanguine.*

hope for the best but expect the worst A popular prescription (see page 23). ■ Since governments can never know how stable the oil-exporting countries are, governments of importing countries should *hope for the best but prepare for the worst.*

(just) hope (it'll) go away A popular prescription (see page 23).

hopeless romantic An inescapable pair (see page 20).

hopes and dreams An inescapable pair (see page 20).

hope springs eternal A popular prescription (see page 23). *confident; encouraged; heartened; hopeful; optimistic; rosy; sanguine.*

hopping mad An inescapable pair (see page 20). *agitated; alarmed; angry; annoyed; aroused; choleric; enraged; fierce; fuming; furious; incensed; inflamed; infuriated; irate; irritable; mad; maddened; raging; splenetic.*

(a) hop, skip, and a jump A moribund metaphor (see page 21).

hornet's nest A moribund metaphor (see page 21). *complexity; complication; difficulty; dilemma; entanglement; imbroglio; labyrinth; maze; muddle; perplexity; plight; predicament; problem; puzzle; quagmire; tangle.* ■ Senator Dodd called the jurisdictional issue a *hornet's nest* but said he was ready to tackle it. REPLACE WITH *imbroglio.*

horse of a different (another) color A moribund metaphor (see page 21). *aberrant; abnormal; anomalistic; anomalous; atypical; bizarre; curious; deviant; different; distinct; distinctive; eccentric; exceptional; extraordinary; fantastic; foreign; grotesque; idiosyncratic; independent; individual; individualistic; irregular; novel; odd; offbeat; original; peculiar; puzzling; quaint; queer; rare; remarkable; separate; singular; uncommon; unconventional; unexampled; unique; unnatural; unorthodox; unparalleled; unprecedented; unusual; weird.*

(the) hostess with the mostess An infantile phrase (see page 20).

hot air A moribund metaphor (see page 21). *aggrandizement; bluster; boasting; braggadocio; bragging; bravado; crowing; elaboration; embellishment; embroidery; exaggeration; fanfaronade; gasconade; gloating; hyperbole; overstatement; rodomontade; swaggering.*

hot and bothered An inescapable pair (see page 20). *agitated; anxious; aroused; bothered; displeased; disquieted; disturbed; excited; flustered; perturbed; troubled; upset; worried.*

hot and heavy An inescapable pair (see page 20). *aggressive; dynamic; emphatic; energetic; ferocious; fervent; fierce; forceful; frantic; frenzied; furious; intense; mighty; passionate; powerful; robust; savage; spirited; strenuous; strong; vehement; vicious; vigorous; violent.*

(as) hot as fire An insipid simile. *aflame; blazing; blistering; boiling; burning; fiery; flaming; heated; hot; ovenlike; roasting; scalding; scorching; searing; simmering; sizzling; steaming; sweltering; torrid; tropical; warm.*

(as) hot as hades (hell) An insipid simile. *aflame; blazing; blistering; boiling; burning; fiery; flaming; heated; hot; ovenlike; roasting; scalding; scorching; searing; simmering; sizzling; steaming; sweltering; torrid; tropical; warm.*

hot little hands A moribund metaphor (see page 21).

hotly contested An inescapable pair (see page 20).

hot potato A moribund metaphor (see page 21). *card; character; eccentric; exception; original.*

hot ticket A moribund metaphor (see page 21). *card; character; eccentric; exception; original.*

hot to trot A moribund metaphor (see page 21). 1. *concupiscent; horny; lascivious; lecherous; lewd; libidinous; licentious; lustful; prurient.* 2. *anxious; eager; impatient; ready; willing.*

hot under the collar A moribund metaphor (see page 21). *agitated; alarmed; angry; annoyed; aroused; choleric; enraged; fierce; fuming; furious; incensed; inflamed; infuriated; irate; irritable; mad; maddened; raging; splenetic.*

(a) house divided against itself cannot stand A popular prescription (see page 23).

(like a) house of cards An insipid simile. *breakable; broken-down; crumbly; decrepit; dilapidated; flimsy; fragile; frangible; friable; precarious; ramshackle; rickety; shabby; shaky; tottering; unsound; unstable; unsteady; unsure; wobbly.* ■ He argued that the government's case against them is *a house of cards*. REPLACE WITH *rickety*.

how could this have happened? A plebeian sentiment (see page 23).

how did (I) get into this? A plebeian sentiment (see page 23).

how goes it? (how's it going? how you doing?) An ineffectual phrase (see page 19). These phrases are uttered by the unalert and inert. *How goes it? how's it going?* and *how you doing?* are gratuitous substitutes for a gracious *hello.*

how much (do) you want to bet? An infantile phrase (see page 20).

hue and cry An inescapable pair (see page 20). *clamor; commotion; din; hubbub; noise; outcry; protest; racket; shout; tumult; uproar.*

huff and puff An inescapable pair (see page 20). 1. *blow; breathe heavily; gasp; huff; pant; puff; wheeze.* 2. *bellow; bluster; clamor; explode; fulminate; fume; holler; howl; rage; rant; rave; roar; scream; shout; storm; thunder; vent; vociferate; yell.*

> Finally as she stood there huffing and puffing, while he was near apoplectic, she would agree to a compromise. — J. P. Donleavy, *The Saddest Summer of Samuel S*

huge throng A wretched redundancy (see page 25). *throng.* ■ A *huge throng* of young people attended the concert. DELETE *huge.*

hugs and kisses An inescapable pair (see page 20).

human nature being what it is An ineffectual phrase (see page 19) ■ *Human nature being what it is,* most of us would rather speak our own mind than listen to what someone else says. DELETE *Human nature being what it is.* ■ *Human nature being what it is,* when people place demands on others, their initial reaction is to rebel. DELETE *Human nature being what it is.* ■ *Human nature being what it is*, getting an extra day made everybody slow down. DELETE *Human nature being what it is.*

(my) humble abode An infantile phrase (see page 20). ■ I recently had the opportunity to visit CMD's headquarters in Boulder, Colorado, not far from my *humble abode.* REPLACE WITH *home.*

humongous An infantile phrase (see page 20). *big; brobdingnagian; colossal; elephantine; enormous; gargantuan; giant; gigantic; grand; great; huge; immense; large; mammoth; massive; monstrous; prodigious; stupendous; titanic; tremendous; vast.*

Not quite a misusage, *humongous* is altogether a monstrosity. And though it's not fair to say that people who use the word are monstrous as well, at some point we come to be — or at the least are known by — what we say, what we write.

■ My appetite was *humongous.* REPLACE WITH *enormous.* ■ We were up against a *humongous* insurance company. REPLACE WITH *colossal.* ■ My feeling is that there is a *humongous* gap between justice for the rich and the poor and working class. REPLACE WITH *huge.* ■ The players should recognize the exception for what it is: a *humongous* bargaining chip. REPLACE WITH *titanic.*

> Before you know it you are paying a humongous divorce settlement to a woman who had more than once declared that she was an innocent who had no understanding of money matters. — Saul Bellow, *Ravelstein*

(as) hungry as a bear An insipid simile. *esurient; famished; gluttonous; greedy; hungry; insatiable; omnivorous; rapacious; ravenous; starved; starving; voracious.*

(as) hungry as a horse An insipid simile. *esurient; famished; gluttonous; greedy; hungry; insatiable; omnivorous; rapacious; ravenous; starved; starving; voracious.*

hunt with the hounds and run with the hares A moribund metaphor (see page 21).

hurdle to clear A moribund metaphor (see page 21). *bar; barrier; block; blockage; check; deterrent; difficulty; encumbrance; handicap; hindrance; hurdle; impediment; interference; obstacle; obstruction.*

hurl insults A moribund metaphor (see page 21).

hustle and bustle An inescapable pair (see page 20). *bustle; commotion; hustle; stir.* ■ Macau presents a restful alternative to the *hustle and bustle* of Hong Kong. REPLACE WITH *bustle* or *hustle.*

I

I can't believe I'm telling you this A plebeian sentiment (see page 23). Only the foolish or the unconscious, unaware of or ambivalent about the words they use or why they use them, can exclaim *I can't believe I'm telling you this.* Language use, the essence of being human, entails certain responsibilities — care and consciousness among them; otherwise, it's all dimwitted. SEE ALSO *I don't know why I'm telling you this.*

I can't get no satisfaction An infantile phrase (see page 20).

icing on the cake A moribund metaphor (see page 21). *a benefit; a bonus; a dividend; a gift; a gratuity; a lagniappe; an extra; a perk; a perquisite; a pourboire; a premium; a tip.* ■ Accreditation is still only *icing on the cake* and does not guarantee a department any rewards beyond the recognition of peers. REPLACE WITH *a perquisite.*

> Dr. Pierce and Deena had returned to our Sunday school class, buoying my spirits. And several of the alumni from the Live Free or Die class had stopped attending, which was icing on the cake. — Philip Gulley, *Life Goes On: A Harmony Novel*

(an) idea whose time has come An infantile phrase (see page 20). ■ The good-news section is *an idea whose time has come.*

idle rich An inescapable pair (see page 20).

I don't know A plebeian sentiment (see page 23). ■ New passion is sweet, but after you know someone for a while, it fades. *I don't know.* ■ I know who I am — I have a good sense of that — but I will never know you, or anyone else, as well. *I don't know.*

For a person to conclude his expressed thoughts and views with *I don't know* would nullify all he seemed to know if it weren't that *I don't know* is less an admission of not knowing than it is an apology for presuming to.

I don't know if (whether) I'm coming or going A moribund metaphor (see page 21). *baffled; befuddled; bewildered; confounded; confused; disconcerted; flummoxed; mixed up; muddled; perplexed; puzzled.*

I don't know, what do you want to do? An infantile phrase (see page 20).

I don't know why I'm telling you this A plebeian sentiment (see page 23). SEE ALSO *I can't believe I'm telling you this.*

I (just) don't think about it A plebeian sentiment (see page 23). SEE ALSO *you think too much.*

if and when A wretched redundancy (see page 25). *if; when.* ■ *If and when* a conflict should arise, it should be taken care of as soon as possible to protect the harmonious environment. REPLACE WITH *If* or *when.* SEE ALSO *if, as, and when; when and if; when and whether; when, as, and if; whether and when.*

if, as, and when A wretched redundancy (see page 25). *if; when.* SEE ALSO *if and when; when and if; when, as, and if; when and whether; whether and when.*

if at first you don't succeed (try, try again) A popular prescription (see page 23).

I feel (understand) your pain The people who spout about how empathic they are (*I feel your pain; I know how you feel*) are often the same people who have scant notion of what it is to be sensitive, kindhearted, even responsive. The emphasis is on showing empathy, which we do more for our own welfare than for others'; it's socially obligatory to be, or pretend to be, empathic. Ultimately, empathy will be thought no more highly of than sympathy now is. SEE ALSO *I'm sorry.*

if it ain't broke, don't fix it A popular prescription (see page 23).

if it feels good, it can't be bad A popular prescription (see page 23).

if it isn't one thing, it's another A plebeian sentiment (see page 23). SEE ALSO *it's one thing after another.*

if it's (not) meant to be, it's (not) meant to be A popular prescription (see page 23).

if it sounds too good to be true, it (probably) is A popular prescription (see page 23).

if the shoe fits (wear it) A moribund metaphor (see page 21).

if the truth be (were) known (told) An ineffectual phrase (see page 19).

if you can't beat them, join them A popular prescription (see page 23).

if you can't say something nice, don't say anything A plebeian sentiment (see page 23). SEE ALSO *be nice.*

if you can't stand the heat, stay out of the kitchen A popular prescription (see page 23).

if you don't know, I'm not going to tell you An infantile phrase (see page 20).

ignorance is bliss A plebeian sentiment (see page 23).

I (I've) got to (have to) tell you (something) An ineffectual phrase (see page 19). Like *I'll tell you (something), I'll tell you what, I'm telling you*, and *let me tell you (something), I (I've) got to (have to) tell you (something)* is a mind-numbing expression spoken only by people who are unaware of how foolish they sound — and of how foolish they are. These are the same people who are wont to begin other sentences with *Look* or *Listen, Hey* or *Okay.* ■ *I got to tell you*, he was the only person I could discuss my frustrations with. DELETE *I got to tell you.* ■ *I've got to tell you something*, I'm so proud of you. DELETE *I've got to tell you something.* ■ *I have to tell you*, the emerging country rates are up 21 percent. DELETE *I have to tell you.*

I just work here A plebeian sentiment (see page 23).

I'll bet you any amount of money An infantile phrase (see page 20).

ill-gotten gains An inescapable pair (see page 20).

I'll tell you (something) An ineffectual phrase (see page 19). This phrase — like *I got to (have to) tell you (something); I'll tell you what; I'm telling you; let me tell you (something)* — is mouthed by unimpressive men and irritating women, the one no more able, no more elegant than the other. ■ You got off easy, *I'll tell you.* DELETE *I'll tell you.* ■ *I'll tell you something,* they look like the greatest team ever. DELETE *I'll tell you something.* ■ *I'll tell you something,* if it doesn't work out, you've always got a job here. DELETE *I'll tell you something.* ■ The publisher got a sharp letter from me, *I'll tell you.* DELETE *I'll tell you.* SEE ALSO *I got to (have to) tell you (something); I'll tell you what; I'm telling you; let me tell you (something).*

I'll tell you what An ineffectual phrase (see page 19). ■ *I'll tell you what,* let's pause for a commercial and then you can tell us your story. DELETE *I'll tell you what.* ■ *I'll tell you what,* I'm not bitter against women, but I sure judge them quicker now. DELETE *I'll tell you what.* SEE ALSO *I got to (have to) tell you (something); I'll tell you (something); I'm telling you; let me tell you (something).*

I love (him) but I'm not in love with (him) A popular prescription (see page 23). The need to distinguish between loving someone and being *in* love with someone is fundamentally false. That there are different kinds of love is nothing that any discerning person has to be reminded of.

Some who make such a distinction may do so to ease their conscience, to absolve themselves for not loving someone who likely loves them and whom they surely feel gratitude or obligation to. In these instances, saying *I love (him) but I'm not in love with (him)* is simply a way of feeling good about having made someone feel bad.

Love, like few other words, ought not to be trifled with. ■ *I love him but I'm not in love with him.* REPLACE WITH *I love him.* SEE ALSO *be nice; excuse me?*

I'm bored (he's boring) A plebeian sentiment (see page 23). Being boring is preferable to being bored. The boring are often thoughtful and imaginative; the bored, thoughtless and unimaginative.

We would do well to shun those who whine about how bored they are or how boring another is. It's they, these bored ones, who in their eternal quest for entertainment and self-oblivion are most suited to causing trouble, courting turmoil, and coercing talk. SEE ALSO *(it) keeps (me) busy.*

I mean A grammatical gimmick (see page 19). Elliptical for "what I mean to say," *I mean* is said by those who do not altogether know what they mean to say. ■ Nobody deserves to die like that. *I mean,* he didn't stand a chance. DELETE *I mean.* ■ *I mean,* being in the entertainment field is not easy; *I mean,* I work hard at my job and still have performances to give. DELETE *I mean.* ■ I enjoy the outdoors; *I mean,* how can you live here and not enjoy it? DELETE *I mean.* ■ *I mean,* if you were in the movies or on TV, *I mean,* many more people would be interested. DELETE *I mean.*

imitation is the sincerest form of flattery A popular prescription (see page 23).

I'm not perfect (you know) A plebeian sentiment (see page 23). Even though *(I'm) a perfectionist* (SEE) is A suspect superlative (see page 24) — meaning that people who proclaim this do not easily disabuse themselves of the notion of being perfect — *I'm not perfect (you know)* is A plebeian sentiment (see page 23) — meaning that people who proclaim this all too easily excuse themselves for being imperfect. ■ I have some deep-seated anger. Hey, *I'm not perfect, you know*. SEE ALSO *(I'm) a perfectionist; nobody's perfect.*

I'm not stupid (you know) A plebeian sentiment (see page 23). ■ *I'm not stupid, you know*; I'm 24 years old, and I've been around.

impact (on) (*v*) An overworked word (see page 22). *act on; affect; bear on; influence; sway; work on.* ■ Let's look at two important trends that may *impact* the future of those languages. REPLACE WITH *influence.* ■ Everybody's district is *impacted* in a different way. REPLACE WITH *affected.* SEE ALSO *has an impact on.*

implement An overworked word (see page 22). *accomplish; achieve; carry out; complete; execute; fulfill; realize.*

I'm sorry A plebeian sentiment (see page 23). No simple apology, the plebeian *I'm sorry* pretends to soothe while it actually scolds. Even though it may seem like an apology — often for something that requires nothing of the sort — *I'm sorry* is said, unapologetically, in a tone of resentment.

Traditionally, a woman's emotion — for women have been, more than men, reluctant to express anger, bare and unbounded — resentment more and more of late finds favor with men and women alike.

■ Nine years old is too young to be left alone, *I'm sorry*. ■ I have to disagree. *I'm sorry*. ■ I know you guys are going to blow up after I'm done talking, but *I'm sorry*. SEE ALSO *excuse me?; nice; thank you.*

Another common usage of *I'm sorry* is when people hear another speak of some difficulty. This is the height of dimwitted English, for the people who say *I'm sorry* — an expression precisely as untrue as it is trite — likely have no more empathy in their hearts than there are syllables in the sentence. SEE ALSO *I feel (understand) your pain.*

I'm telling you An ineffectual phrase (see page 19). ■ It has more twists and turns than Route 66, *I'm telling you.* DELETE *I'm telling you.* ■ *I'm telling you*, there are people who take this seriously. DELETE *I'm telling you.* SEE ALSO *I got to (have to) tell you (something); I'll tell you (something); I'll tell you what; let me tell you (something).*

in a big (major) way A torpid term (see page 24). *acutely; a great deal; badly; consumedly; enormously; exceedingly; extremely; greatly; hugely; immensely; intensely; largely; mightily; prodigiously; seriously; strongly; very much.* ■ He wants to meet me *in a big way.* REPLACE WITH *very much.* ■ It hurt me *in a big way.* REPLACE WITH *badly.* SEE ALSO *in the worst way.*

> The photographer had barked "Smile!" I'd overcompensated in a big way. — Susan Isaacs, *After All These Years*

in a bind A moribund metaphor (see page 21). *at risk; endangered; hard-pressed; imperiled; in a bind; in a dilemma; in a fix; in a jam; in a predicament; in a quandary; in danger; in difficulty; in jeopardy; in peril; in trouble; jeopardized.*

in (the) absence of A wretched redundancy (see page 25). *absent; having no; lacking; minus; missing; not having; with no; without.* ■ *In the absence of* these articulated linkages, changes introduced will be difficult to monitor. REPLACE WITH *Absent.*

in a class by (itself) A moribund metaphor (see page 21). *different; exceptional; extraordinary; incomparable; inimitable; matchless; nonpareil; notable; noteworthy; novel; odd; original; peculiar; peerless; remarkable; singular; special; strange; uncommon; unequaled; unexampled; unique; unmatched; unparalleled; unrivaled; unusual; without equal.*

(head) in a (the) cloud(s) A moribund metaphor (see page 21). *absent; absent-minded; absorbed; abstracted; bemused; captivated; daydreaming; detached; distracted; distrait; dreamy; engrossed; enraptured; faraway; fascinated; immersed; inattentive; in thought; lost; mesmerized; oblivious; preoccupied; rapt; spellbound.*

> It brought it all back to me. Celia Langley. Celia Langley standing in front of me, her hands on her hips and her head in a cloud. — Andrea Levy, *Small Island*

in a delicate condition A moribund metaphor (see page 21). *anticipating; enceinte; expectant; expecting; gravid; parturient; pregnant; with child.*

in a dog's age A moribund metaphor (see page 21).

in advance of A wretched redundancy (see page 25). *ahead of; before.* ■ *In advance of* introducing our guest, let me tell you why he's here. REPLACE WITH *Before.* SEE ALSO *in advance of; previous to; subsequent to.*

in a (the) family way A moribund metaphor (see page 21). *anticipating; enceinte; expectant; expecting; gravid; parturient; pregnant; with child.*

in a (blue) funk A moribund metaphor (see page 21). *aggrieved; blue; cheerless; dejected; demoralized; depressed; despondent; disconsolate; discouraged; disheartened; dismal; dispirited; doleful; downcast; downhearted; dreary; forlorn; funereal; gloomy; glum; grieved; low; melancholy; miserable; morose; mournful; plaintive; sad; sorrowful; unhappy; woebegone; woeful.*

in a good mood A torpid term (see page 24). *blissful; blithe; buoyant; cheerful; cheery; content; contented; delighted; elated; excited; gay; glad; gleeful; happy; jolly; joyful; joyous; merry; pleased; sanguine; satisfied.* SEE ALSO *positive feelings.*

in a heartbeat A moribund metaphor (see page 21). *abruptly; apace; at once; briskly; directly; expeditiously; fast; forthwith; hastily; hurriedly; immediately; instantaneously; instantly; posthaste; promptly; quickly; rapidly; rashly; right away; speedily; straightaway; swiftly; wingedly.*

> Bless me, father, for I have sinned, I have lied to my husband, left him never knowing he will have a child, and would do it all again in a heartbeat. — Ann Patchett, *Patron Saint of Liars*

in a jam A moribund metaphor (see page 21). *at risk; endangered; hard-pressed; imperiled; in a bind; in a dilem-*

ma; in a fix; in a jam; in a predicament; in a quandary; in danger; in difficulty; in jeopardy; in peril; in trouble; jeopardized.

in a lather A moribund metaphor (see page 21). *agitated; distraught; disturbed; excited; nervous; shaken; uneasy; upset.*

in a manner of speaking A wretched redundancy (see page 25). *as it were; in a sense; in a way; so to speak.* ■ Your contractor is correct *in a manner of speaking.* REPLACE WITH *in a sense.*

in and of itself (themselves) A wretched redundancy (see page 25). *as such; in itself (in themselves).* ■ This trend is interesting *in and of itself* but is also quite instructive. REPLACE WITH *in itself.* ■ All the benefits are worthwhile *in and of themselves,* but they have the additional benefit of translating into improved cost efficiency. REPLACE WITH *in themselves.*

in a nutshell A moribund metaphor (see page 21). *briefly; concisely; in brief; in short; in sum; succinctly; tersely.*

> One thing leads to another; that is, houses lead to commodes, and then commodes lead to houses, which lead to land, which leads to dairy cattle, which lead to cheese, which leads to pizza pies, which lead to manicotti and veal Parmesan, which lead to wine, which leads to love, which leads to babies, houses, and commodes. That was Gordon Baldwin in a nutshell. — Jane Smiley, *Good Faith*

in any way, shape, form, or fashion An infantile phrase (see page 20). *at all; in any way; in some way; in the least; somehow; someway.* That anyone uses this expression is wondrous. To discerning listeners and readers, *in any way, shape, form, or fashion,* as well as similar assemblages, is as rickety as it is ridiculous.

■ If students are asked to leave the University, their return certainly should not be celebrated *in any way, shape, form, or fashion.* DELETE *in any way, shape, form, or fashion.* ■ Do you feel being on television will help you *in any way, shape, or form?* REPLACE WITH *somehow.* ■ That control is no longer there, not *in any way, shape, or form.* REPLACE WITH *at all.* ■ He wants something that doesn't resemble the landmark *in any way, shape, or fashion.* REPLACE WITH *in the least.* SEE ALSO *in every way, shape, and (or) form; in no way, shape, form, or fashion.*

in a pickle A moribund metaphor (see page 21). *at risk; endangered; hard-pressed; imperiled; in a bind; in a dilemma; in a fix; in a jam; in a predicament; in a quandary; in danger; in difficulty; in jeopardy; in peril; in trouble; jeopardized.*

> Well, if he was in a pickle in regard to his followers, why the hell should she make it easy for him? — Susan Isaacs, *Red, White and Blue*

in a pig's eye A moribund metaphor (see page 21). *at no time; by no means; hardly; in no way; never; no; not at all; not ever; not in any way; not in the least; scarcely; unlikely.*

(stuck) in a rut A moribund metaphor (see page 21). *bogged down; caught; cornered; enmeshed; ensnared; entangled;*

entrapped; netted; mired; snared; stuck; trapped.

in a (constant) state of flux A torpid term (see page 24). *capricious; changeable; erratic; ever-changing; fluid; variable.*

in a timely fashion (manner; way) A wretched redundancy (see page 25). *in time; promptly; quickly; rapidly; right away; shortly; soon; speedily; swiftly; timely.* ■ He believes in getting the job done *in a timely fashion* and is very committed to achieving that goal.

(off) in a world of (his) own A moribund metaphor (see page 21). *absent; absent-minded; absorbed; abstracted; bemused; captivated; daydreaming; detached; distracted; distrait; dreamy; engrossed; enraptured; faraway; fascinated; immersed; inattentive; lost; mesmerized; oblivious; preoccupied; rapt; spellbound.*

in (her) birthday suit A moribund metaphor (see page 21). *bare; disrobed; naked; nude; stripped; unclothed; uncovered; undressed.*

in close (near) proximity to A wretched redundancy (see page 25). *close by; close to; in proximity; near; nearby.* ■ Cities were born out of the desire and necessity of human beings to live and work *in close proximity to* each other. REPLACE WITH *close to.* ■ In those cases, the verb will be in agreement with the subject that is *closest in proximity to* the verb. REPLACE WITH *closest to.*

in (the) clover A moribund metaphor (see page 21). *affluent; moneyed; opulent; prosperous; rich; successful; wealthy; well-off; well-to-do.*

in cold blood A moribund metaphor (see page 21). *deliberately; intentionally; knowingly; mindfully; on purpose; premeditatively; willfully.*

in connection with A wretched redundancy (see page 25). *about; as for; as to; concerning; for; in; of; on; over; regarding; respecting; to; toward; with.* ■ The police wanted to talk to him *in connection with* a fur store robbery. REPLACE WITH *about.* ■ *In connection with* the hiring incidents, this was the first time he denied any wrongdoing. REPLACE WITH *Concerning.*

in consideration of the fact that A wretched redundancy (see page 25). *because; considering; for; in that; since.* ■ *In consideration of the fact that* we have to have something submitted by January 15, we have get to started on this. REPLACE WITH *Since.* SEE ALSO *because of the fact that; considering the fact that; by virtue of the fact that; given the fact that; in view of the fact that; on account of the fact that.*

in (my) corner A moribund metaphor (see page 21).

incredible An overworked word (see page 22). 1. *beyond belief; beyond comprehension; doubtful; dubious; implausible; imponderable; improbable; incomprehensible; inconceivable; inexplicable; questionable; unfathomable; unimaginable; unthinkable.* 2. *astonishing; astounding; breathtaking; extraordinary; fabulous; fantastic; marvelous; miraculous; overwhelming; prodigious; sensational; spectacular; wonderful; wondrous.*

Like the platitudinous *unbelievable* (SEE), this word is very much overused.

One of the hallmarks of dimwitted

language is the unimaginativeness of those who use it. We would do well to try to distinguish ourselves through our speech and writing rather than rely on the words and phrases that so many others are wont to use. Those who speak as others speak, inescapably, think as others think. ■ But that someone would shoot a two-year-old child is *incredible*. REPLACE WITH *unimaginable*. ■ All these people are *incredibly* brave. REPLACE WITH *astonishingly*.

incumbent upon A torpid term (see page 24). *binding; compelling; compulsory; essential; imperative; mandatory; necessary; obligatory; required; requisite; urgent.*

in (his) cups A moribund metaphor (see page 21). *besotted; crapulous; drunk; inebriated; intoxicated; sodden; stupefied; tipsy.*

indebtedness A torpid term (see page 24). *debt.*

indelible impression An inescapable pair (see page 20). To describe something considered unforgettable with a cliché — an unoriginal, a forgettable, phrase — is indeed dimwitted. ■ The tundra will make an *indelible impression* on you. ■ War has made an *indelible impression* on international art movements, as well as on Australian art.

> It was never published, but I saw it once and it made an indelible impression on my mind. — Sherwood Anderson, *Winesburg, Ohio*

in-depth analysis An inescapable pair (see page 20).

indicate A torpid term (see page 24). *Indicate* has virtually devoured every word that might be used instead of it.

More designative words include *acknowledge; admit; affirm; allow; announce; argue; assert; avow; bespeak; betoken; claim; confess; comment; concede; contend; declare; disclose; divulge; expose; feel; hint; hold; imply; insinuate; intimate; maintain; make known; mention; note; point out; profess; remark; reveal; say; show; signal; signify; state; suggest; tell; uncover; unveil.* ■ He *indicated* that he would be fine. REPLACE WITH *said*. ■ People have provided us with documents that *indicate* that veterans were exposed. REPLACE WITH *reveal*. ■ They have *indicated* that they do not understand the managed competition proposals and don't want to. REPLACE WITH *confessed*. ■ Last week's decision of the Federal Reserve Board *indicated* that minority-lending records will be an issue for many years to come. REPLACE WITH *signaled*.

individual(s) (*n*) A torpid term (see page 24). *anybody; anyone; everybody; everyone; man; men; people; person; somebody; someone; those; woman; women; you.* ■ This *individual* needs to be stopped. REPLACE WITH *woman*. ■ He seemed like a friendly enough *individual*. REPLACE WITH *person*.

in due course (time) A torpid term (see page 24). *at length; eventually; in time; ultimately; yet.*

in each others' pocket A moribund metaphor (see page 21). 1. *indissoluble; indivisible; inseparable; involved; together.* 2. *dependent; reliant.*

in every way, shape, form, or fashion An infantile phrase (see page 20). *altogether; completely; entirely; fully; quite; roundly; thoroughly; in all ways; in every way; perfectly; totally; unreservedly; utterly; wholly.* ■ For centuries, since the first African ancestors were brought here, whites have tried to imitate blacks *in every way, shape, form, or fashion* and I'm tired of it. REPLACE WITH *in all ways.* ■ He supports her *in every way, shape, and form.* REPLACE WITH *thoroughly.* SEE ALSO *in any way, shape, form, or fashion; in no way, shape, form, or fashion.*

in excess of A wretched redundancy (see page 25). *above; better than; beyond; faster than; greater than; larger than; more than; over; stronger than.* ■ *In excess of* 10 candidates wanted to make the town of Andover both their profession and their home. REPLACE WITH *More than.* ■ Police said Mr. Howard was driving *in excess of* 90 miles per hour. REPLACE WITH *faster than.*

in extremis A foreign phrase (see page 19). *decaying; declining; deteriorating; disintegrating; dying; ebbing; expiring; fading; failing; near death; sinking; waning.*

inextricably tied An inescapable pair (see page 20). ■ In good times and in bad, our future and our fortunes are *inextricably tied* together.

in fine fettle A moribund metaphor (see page 21). *energetic; fine; fit; good; hale; hardy; healthful; healthy; hearty; robust; sound; strong; trim; vigorous; well.*

in for a rude awakening (shock) A torpid term (see page 24). ■ The companies that still think the only ones who are going to make it are Caucasian males are *in for a rude awakening.*

in for a (pleasant) surprise A torpid term (see page 24). ■ If she had set out to write a story about a spoiled brat, she was *in for a surprise.*

in full swing A moribund metaphor (see page 21).

in harm's way A moribund metaphor (see page 21). *exposed; insecure; obnoxious; unguarded; unprotected; unsafe; unsheltered; unshielded; vulnerable.*

in high gear A moribund metaphor (see page 21). *abruptly; apace; briskly; directly; expeditiously; fast; hastily; hurriedly; immediately; instantaneously; instantly; posthaste; promptly; quickly; rapidly; rashly; speedily; swiftly; wingedly.*

> Rosemary was in high gear. She was mounting a campaign to woo the chairman of the committee that would vote the bill out to the full Senate or decide to let it die ignominiously. — Marge Piercy, *The Third Child*

in hot water A moribund metaphor (see page 21). *at risk; endangered; hard-pressed; imperiled; in danger; in difficulty; in jeopardy; in peril; in trouble; jeopardized.*

in its (their) entirety A wretched redundancy (see page 25). *all; complete; completely; entire; entirely; every; full; fully; roundly; whole; wholly.* ■ This would leave Wednesday, either partially or *in its entirety*, for coordination. REPLACE WITH *entirely.*

inject (new) life into A moribund metaphor (see page 21). *animate; energize; enliven; inspirit; invigorate; vitalize.*

in less than no time A moribund metaphor (see page 21). *abruptly; apace; at once; briskly; directly; expeditiously; fast; forthwith; hastily; hurriedly; immediately; instantaneously; instantly; posthaste; promptly; quickly; rapidly; rashly; right away; speedily; straightaway; suddenly; swiftly; unexpectedly; wingedly.*

(keep) (us) in line A moribund metaphor (see page 21). *acquiescent; amenable; behaving; biddable; compliant; docile; dutiful; in conformity; law abiding; obedient; pliant; submissive; tame; tractable; yielding.*

in loco parentis A foreign phrase (see page 19).

in (our) midst A wretched redundancy (see page 25). *amid; among.* ■ There are growing numbers of crazy people *in our midst.* REPLACE WITH *among us.*

in nature A wretched redundancy (see page 25). ■ He said the diaries are personal *in nature.* DELETE *in nature.* ■ Laws governing freedom to protest politically obviously are political *in nature.* DELETE *in nature.*

(as) innocent as a newborn babe (child) An insipid simile. *artless; guileless; ingenuous; innocent; naïve; simple.*

in nothing (no time) flat A torpid term (see page 24). *abruptly; apace; at once; briskly; directly; expeditiously; fast; forthwith; hastily; hurriedly; immediately; instantaneously; instantly; posthaste; promptly; quickly; rapidly; rashly; right away; speedily; straightaway; suddenly; swiftly; unexpectedly; wingedly.*

in no way, shape, form, or fashion An infantile phrase (see page 20). *at no time; by no means; in no way; never; no; not; not at all; not ever; not in any way; not in the least.* ■ The gas contributed *in no way, shape, or form* to the fire. REPLACE WITH *not at all.* ■ *In no way, shape, or form* did she resemble a 63-year-old woman. REPLACE WITH *In no way.* ■ *In no way, shape, form, or fashion* was there any wrongdoing or misappropriation of funds. REPLACE WITH *Never.* SEE ALSO *in any way, shape, form, or fashion; in every way, shape, and (or) form.*

in one ear and out the other A moribund metaphor (see page 21). *forgetful; heedless; inattentive; lethean; neglectful; negligent; oblivious; remiss; thoughtless; unmindful; unthinking.*

> I hand them over, glad to be relieved of them. Maybe she'll understand them better than I. Anchee's explanations, I'm afraid, went in one ear and out the other.
> — Dennis Danvers, *The Watch*

(get) in on the ground floor A moribund metaphor (see page 21).

in over (my) head A moribund metaphor (see page 21). 1. *overburdened; overextended; overloaded; overwhelmed.* 2. *in arrears; in debt.*

(he's) in (his) own world A moribund metaphor (see page 21). *self-absorbed; self-involved; solipsistic.*

in point of fact A wretched redundancy (see page 25). *actually; indeed; in fact;*

in faith; in reality; in truth; truly. ■ *In point of fact,* we do all the wrong things, and we have for years. REPLACE WITH *In fact.* ■ *In point of fact,* Krakatoa is west of Java, but east apparently sounded better to Hollywood. REPLACE WITH *Actually.* ■ There aren't, *in point of fact,* one or two buildings; there are two exactly. DELETE *in point of fact.*

input A torpid term (see page 24). *data; feelings; ideas; information; recommendations; suggestions; thoughts; views.* ■ We would appreciate *input* from anyone who has knowledge in the above areas. REPLACE WITH *information.* ■ Of course, discretion must be used in evaluating their *inputs* since sales reps are biased toward lowering prices and pushing volume. REPLACE WITH *suggestions.* SEE ALSO *(the) bottom line; feedback; interface; output; parameters.*

inquiring minds (want to know) An infantile phrase (see page 20).

in (with) reference to A wretched redundancy (see page 25). *about; as for; as to; concerning; for; in; of; on; over; regarding; respecting; to; toward; with.* ■ *With reference to* the latest attempt to forge statehood for the District of Columbia, I favor our ancestors' concept that the District ought to be an entity unto itself. REPLACE WITH *As for.*

in (with) regard to A wretched redundancy (see page 25). *about; as for; as to; concerning; for; in; of; on; over; regarding; respecting; to; toward; with.* ■ *With regard to* the *StataQuest,* I am expecting the first six chapters sometime this week. REPLACE WITH *Regarding.*

in (high) relief A moribund metaphor (see page 21). *clearly; conspicuously; distinctly; manifestly; markedly; noticeably; obviously; perceptibly; plainly; prominently; unmistakably; visibly.*

in (with) respect to A wretched redundancy (see page 25). *about; as for; as to; concerning; for; in; of; on; over; regarding; respecting; to; toward; with.* ■ Some history *with respect to* the origins and evolution of the AS/400 will then be discussed. REPLACE WITH *on.*

in seventh heaven A moribund metaphor (see page 21). *blissful; blithe; buoyant; cheerful; delighted; ecstatic; elated; enraptured; euphoric; exalted; excited; exhilarated; exultant; gay; glad; gleeful; good-humored; happy; intoxicated; jolly; jovial; joyful; joyous; jubilant; merry; mirthful; overjoyed; pleased; rapturous; thrilled.*

in short order A torpid term (see page 24). *abruptly; apace; at once; briskly; directly; expeditiously; fast; forthwith; hastily; hurriedly; immediately; instantaneously; instantly; posthaste; promptly; quickly; rapidly; rashly; right away; speedily; straightaway; swiftly; wingedly.*

in short supply A torpid term (see page 24). *exiguous; inadequate; meager; rare; scant; scanty; scarce; sparse; uncommon; unusual.*

inside (and) out A moribund metaphor (see page 21). *altogether; completely; entirely; fully; perfectly; quite; roundly; thoroughly; totally; unreservedly; utterly; wholly.*

(an) inspiration to us all A suspect superlative (see page 24). How inspirational could anyone be when he is described with such an uninspired expression? ■ He's been *an inspiration to us all.*

in spite of the fact that A wretched redundancy (see page 25). *although; but; even if; even though; still; though; yet.* ■ This is true *in spite of the fact that* a separate symbol has been designated for input and output operations. REPLACE WITH *even though.* SEE ALSO *despite the fact that; regardless of the fact that.*

> Right away after the move I longed for it, in spite of the fact that I'd been in a conspicuous position, the kid of a proselytizing socialist schoolteacher and a city-slicker piano-playing mother. — Jane Hamilton, *Disobedience*

in (within) striking distance A moribund metaphor (see page 21).

integral part An inescapable pair (see page 20). This is another example of one word modifying another to little or no purpose.

integrate together A wretched redundancy (see page 25). *integrate.* ■ The cost of the transmitters can be significantly reduced if all the lasers can be *integrated together* on a single substrate. DELETE *together.*

interesting An overworked word (see page 22). *absorbing; alluring; amusing; arresting; bewitching; captivating; charming; curious; diverting; enchanting; engaging; engrossing; entertaining; enthralling; enticing; exciting; fascinating; gripping; intriguing; invigorating; inviting; pleasing; provocative; refreshing; riveting; spellbinding; stimulating; taking; tantalizing.*

Not only An overworked word (see page 22), *interesting* is also a worsened one, for it connotes uninteresting as often as it denotes interesting. SEE ALSO *that's interesting.*

interface A torpid term (see page 24). SEE ALSO *(the) bottom line; feedback; input; output; parameters.*

in terms of A wretched redundancy (see page 25). This phrase is most often a plodding replacement for words like *about; as for; as to; concerning; for; in; of; on; regarding; respecting; through; with.* And with some slight thought, the phrase frequently can be pared from a sentence. ■ *In terms of* what women need to know about men, I have learned a lot. REPLACE WITH *Regarding.* ■ A key element *in terms of* quality health care is going to be having the best *in terms of the* education and continuing educational abilities to train the best in this country. REPLACE WITH *of;* DELETE *in terms of the.* ■ For further information, you would want to read outside sources that analyze *your competitors in terms of their products.* REPLACE WITH *your competitors' products.*

intestinal fortitude An infantile phrase (see page 20). *boldness; bravery; courage; daring; determination; endurance; fearlessness; firmness; fortitude; grit; guts; hardihood; hardiness; intrepidity; mettle; nerve; perseverance; resolution; resolve; spirit; spunk; stamina; steadfastness; tenacity.* ■ It takes a little luck and a lot of *intestinal fortitude* to break into a game. REPLACE WITH *daring.* ■ Voters will need *intestinal fortitude* to make it to election day. REPLACE WITH *fortitude.*

in the affirmative A wretched redundancy (see page 25). *affirmatively; favorably; positively; yes.* ■ The answer is *in the affirmative.* REPLACE WITH *yes.*

in the altogether A moribund metaphor (see page 21). *bare; disrobed; naked; nude; stripped; unclothed; uncovered; undressed.*

in the arms of Morpheus A moribund metaphor (see page 21). *asleep; dozing; dreaming; napping; sleeping; slumbering; unconscious.*

in the back of (my) mind A moribund metaphor (see page 21). *subconsciously; subliminally.* ■ I always knew, *in the back of my mind,* that something was bothering him. REPLACE WITH *subconsciously.*

(it's) in the bag A moribund metaphor (see page 21). *assured; certain; definite; guaranteed; incontestable; incontrovertible; indisputable; indubitable; positive; secure; sure; unquestionable.*

in the ballpark of A moribund metaphor (see page 21). *about; around; close to; more or less; near; nearly; or so; roughly; some.* ■ Estimates put the cost of each TAO work time gained or lost *in the ballpark of* $3 million per year. REPLACE WITH *around.* SEE ALSO *in the neighborhood of; in the vicinity of.*

in the black A moribund metaphor (see page 21). *debt-free; debtless.*

in the blink of an eye A moribund metaphor (see page 21). *abruptly; apace; at once; briskly; directly; expeditiously; fast; forthwith; hastily; hurriedly; immediately; instantaneously; instantly; posthaste; promptly; quickly; rapidly; rashly; right away; speedily; straightaway; suddenly; swiftly; unexpectedly; wingedly.* ■ Self-indulgent, run-on sentences will *earn you a rejection slip in the blink of an eye.* REPLACE WITH *quickly earn you a rejection slip.*

in the buff A moribund metaphor (see page 21). *bare; disrobed; naked; nude; stripped; unclothed; uncovered; undressed.*

in (on) the cards A moribund metaphor (see page 21). *certain; destined; expected; fated; foreordained; foreseeable; imminent; impending; liable; likely; possible; probable; ordained; prearranged; predestined; predetermined; predictable; sure.* ■ I think that kind of complexity is not *in the cards.* REPLACE WITH *likely.*

in the chips A moribund metaphor (see page 21). *affluent; moneyed; opulent; prosperous; rich; wealthy; well-off; well-to-do.*

in the clear A moribund metaphor (see page 21). 1. *absolved; acquitted; blameless; clear; excused; exonerated; faultless; guiltless; inculpable; innocent; irreproachable; unblamable; unblameworthy; vindicated.* 2. *guarded; protected; safe; secure; sheltered; shielded.* 3. *debt-free; debtless.*

in the closet A moribund metaphor (see page 21). *clandestine; concealed; confidential; covert; hidden; private; secret; secluded; shrouded; surreptitious; undercover; unspoken; veiled.*

in the cold light of reason A moribund metaphor (see page 21).

(keep) in the dark A moribund metaphor (see page 21). *ignorant; incognizant; insensible; mystified; nescient; unacquainted; unadvised; unapprised; unaware; unenlightened; unfamiliar; uninformed; uninitiated; uninstructed; unintelligent; unknowing; unschooled; untaught; unversed.* ■ They told me everything; I was never *kept in the dark*. REPLACE WITH *uninformed.*

in the dead of night A moribund metaphor (see page 21).

> Some of it she told him anyway, that it was extremely urgent she communicate with a friend in Tijuana, that quite possibly it was a matter of life and death, which is why she had taken it upon herself to wake him in the dead of night and for that, together with the breaking of his window, she had apologized profusely. — Kem Nunn, *Tijuana Straits*

in the depths of depression (despair) A moribund metaphor (see page 21). *aggrieved; blue; cheerless; dejected; demoralized; depressed; despondent; disconsolate; discouraged; disheartened; dismal; dispirited; doleful; downcast; downhearted; dreary; forlorn; funereal; gloomy; glum; grieved; low; melancholy; miserable; morose; mournful; plaintive; sad; sorrowful; unhappy; woebegone; woeful.*

in the distant future A wretched redundancy (see page 25). *at length; eventually; finally; in the end; in time; later; one day; over the (months); over time; someday; sometime; ultimately; with time.* ■ A similar agreement with Mexico could result in a true North American common market *in the distant future*. REPLACE WITH *one day*. SEE ALSO *in the immediate future; in the near future; in the not-too-distant future.*

in the doghouse A moribund metaphor (see page 21). *in disfavor; in disgrace.*

in the doldrums A moribund metaphor (see page 21). 1. *dead; dormant; dull; immobile; immovable; inactive; inanimate; indolent; inert; inoperative; languid; latent; lethargic; lifeless; listless; motionless; phlegmatic; quiescent; quiet; sluggish; stagnant; static; stationary; still; stock-still; torpid; unresponsive.* 2. *aggrieved; blue; cheerless; dejected; demoralized; depressed; despondent; disconsolate; discouraged; disheartened; dismal; dispirited; doleful; downcast; downhearted; dreary; forlorn; funereal; gloomy; glum; grieved; low; melancholy; miserable; morose; mournful; plaintive; sad; sorrowful; unhappy; woebegone; woeful.*

in the driver's seat A moribund metaphor (see page 21). *administer; boss; command; control; dictate; direct; dominate; govern; in charge; in command; in control; manage; manipulate; master; order; overpower; oversee; predominate; prevail; reign over; rule; superintend.* ■ Buyers are most definitely *in the driver's seat*. REPLACE WITH *in charge*. ■ Unlike traditional pension plans, which your employer controls, 401(k) plans put you *in the driver's seat*. REPLACE WITH *in control.*

(down) in the dumps A moribund metaphor (see page 21). *aggrieved; blue; cheerless; dejected; demoralized; depressed; despondent; disconsolate; discouraged; disheartened; dismal; dispirited; doleful; downcast; downhearted; dreary; forlorn; funereal; gloomy; glum; grieved; low;*

melancholy; miserable; morose; mournful; plaintive; sad; sorrowful; unhappy; woebegone; woeful.

in the event (that) A wretched redundancy (see page 25). *if; should.* ■ *In the event* you think I am overreacting, let me call attention to the realities of the contemporary workplace. REPLACE WITH *If* or *Should.*

in the final (last) analysis A wretched redundancy (see page 25). *in the end; ultimately.*

in the first place A wretched redundancy (see page 25). *first.* ■ *In the first place,* I don't want to, and *in the second place,* I can't afford to. REPLACE WITH *First; second.* SEE ALSO *in the second place.*

in the flesh A moribund metaphor (see page 21). 1. *alive.* 2. *in person; present.*

in the fullness of time A moribund metaphor (see page 21). *at length; eventually; in time; ultimately; yet.*

> Here in the fullness of time would lie Kaiser himself. — Evelyn Waugh, *The Loved One*

in the heat of battle A moribund metaphor (see page 21).

in the heat of the moment A moribund metaphor (see page 21).

in the immediate future A wretched redundancy (see page 25). *at once; at present; before long; currently; directly; immediately; in a (week); next (month); now; presently; quickly; shortly; soon; straightaway; this (month).* ■ I will, *in the immediate future,* contact my fellow mayor in New York and ask him to make a decision. REPLACE WITH *this week.* SEE ALSO *in the distant future; in the near future; in the not-too-distant future.*

in (on) the issue (matter; subject) of A wretched redundancy (see page 25). *about; as for; as to; concerning; for; in; of; on; over; regarding; respecting; to; toward; with.* ■ This state used to be a leader *on the issue of* health reform. REPLACE WITH *in.* ■ *On the matter of* quality in teaching, he proposed a more symbiotic relationship between classroom time and research. REPLACE WITH *As for.*

in the know A moribund metaphor (see page 21). 1. *able; adept; apt; capable; competent; conversant; deft; dexterous; experienced; expert; familiar; practiced; proficient; seasoned; skilled; skillful; veteran.* 2. *adroit; astute; bright; brilliant; clever; discerning; effective; effectual; efficient; enlightened; insightful; intelligent; judicious; keen; knowledgeable; learned; logical; luminous; perceptive; perspicacious; quick; rational; reasonable; sagacious; sage; sapient; sensible; sharp; shrewd; smart; sound; understanding; wise.*

(live) in the lap of luxury A moribund metaphor (see page 21). *affluent; moneyed; opulent; prosperous; rich; wealthy; well-off; well-to-do.*

in (over) the long run (term) A wretched redundancy (see page 25). *at length; eventually; finally; in the end; in time; later; long-term; one day; over the (months); over time; someday; sometime; ultimately; with time.* ■ *In the long run,* that may be the most important thing. REPLACE WITH *Over time.* SEE ALSO *in (over) the short run (term).*

in the market for A moribund metaphor (see page 21). *able to afford; desire; looking for; need; ready to buy; require; seeking; want; wish for.*

in the midst of A wretched redundancy (see page 25). *amid; among; between; encircled by; encompassed by; in; inside; in the middle of; surrounded by.* ■ The United States, *in the midst of* increasing tension over Korea, is softening its tone on China. REPLACE WITH *amid.* ■ My profound conviction is that anytime we are together, Christ is *in the midst of* us. REPLACE WITH *among.*

in the money A moribund metaphor (see page 21). *affluent; moneyed; opulent; prosperous; rich; wealthy; well-off; well-to-do.*

in the near future A wretched redundancy (see page 25). *before long; directly; eventually; in time; later; one day; presently; quickly; shortly; sometime; soon.* ■ I'm looking forward to the possibility that you might review my work *in the near future.* REPLACE WITH *soon.* SEE ALSO *in the distant future; in the immediate future; in the not-too-distant future.*

in the neighborhood of A wretched redundancy (see page 25). *about; around; close to; more or less; near; nearly; or so; roughly; some.* ■ The rebels may have killed *in the neighborhood of* ten people. REPLACE WITH *close to.* SEE ALSO *in the ballpark of; in the vicinity of.*

in the not-too-distant future A wretched redundancy (see page 25). *before long; directly; eventually; in time; later; one day; presently; quickly; shortly; sometime; soon.* ■ *In the not-too-distant future,* Americans will have the telephone equivalent of a superhighway to every home and business. REPLACE WITH *Before long.* SEE ALSO *in the distant future; in the immediate future; in the near future.*

in the not-too-distant past A wretched redundancy (see page 25). *before; earlier; formerly; not long ago; once; recently.* ■ *In the not-too-distant past,* women were expected to be home, be nice, be sexy, and be quiet. REPLACE WITH *Not long ago.* SEE ALSO *in the past; in the recent past.*

in the offing A moribund metaphor (see page 21). *approaching; at hand; close; coming; expected; forthcoming; imminent; impending; looming; near; nearby.*

in the past A wretched redundancy (see page 25). ■ I'm just saying what we did do *in the past.* DELETE *in the past.* ■ We can remember *in the past* when we sometimes had two or three representatives. DELETE *in the past.* SEE ALSO *in the not-too-distant past; in the recent past.*

in the picture A moribund metaphor (see page 21). SEE ALSO *not in the picture.*

in the pink A moribund metaphor (see page 21). *energetic; fine; fit; good; hale; hardy; healthful; healthy; hearty; robust; sound; strong; vigorous; well.*

in the pipeline A moribund metaphor (see page 21).

in the process of -ing A wretched redundancy (see page 25). *as; while;* delete. Even though *in the process of* seems to add significance to what is being said — and to who is saying it — it plainly subtracts from both. ■ The hurricane is *in the process of* making a slow turn to the northeast. DELETE *in the process of.* ■ I'm *in the process of* going on a lot of interviews. DELETE *in the process of.* ■ The office is still *in the process of* collecting facts. DELETE *in the process of.*

> In the process of taking his jacket off, the Artiste thrust his thick chest forward. — Tom Wolfe, *A Man in Full*

in (within) the realm of possibility A wretched redundancy (see page 25). *believable; conceivable; conjecturable; doable; feasible; imaginable; likely; plausible; possible; practicable; supposable; thinkable; workable.* ■ Appointment of a "civilian" generalist public administrator possessing some public safety background is also *within the realm of possibility.* REPLACE WITH *possible.* ■ I'm afraid it is *within the realm of possibility* that that many warheads may be missing. REPLACE WITH *conceivable.*

in the recent past A wretched redundancy (see page 25). *before; earlier; formerly; lately; not long ago; of late; once; recent; recently.* ■ *In the recent past,* such performers were on the fringes of American culture. REPLACE WITH *Recently.* SEE ALSO *in the not-too-distant past; in the past.*

in the red A moribund metaphor (see page 21). *in arrears; in debt.*

in the right direction A torpid term (see page 24). ■ Furthermore, when onerous regulations are brought to the attention of senior officials, the government has taken steps *in the right direction.* REPLACE WITH *to make them less unwieldy.*

in the right place at the right time An infantile phrase (see page 20). SEE ALSO *in the wrong place at the wrong time.*

in the saddle A moribund metaphor (see page 21). *administer; boss; command; control; dictate; direct; dominate; govern; in charge; in command; in control; manage; manipulate; master; order; overpower; oversee; predominate; prevail; reign over; rule; superintend.*

in the same boat A moribund metaphor (see page 21).

> They might all be in the same boat — sharing a comparatively small plot of land — but that didn't mean it was necessary to socialize. — Katie Fforde, *Wild Designs*

in the second place A wretched redundancy (see page 25). *second.* ■ *In the second place,* I sincerely believe that the merger has given it another chance to become the quality institution these students deserve. REPLACE WITH *Second.* SEE ALSO *in the first place.*

in (over) the short run (term) A wretched redundancy (see page 25). *at present; before long; currently; directly; eventually; in time; later; next (month); now; one day; presently; quickly; shortly; short-term; sometime; soon; this (month).* ■ I hope we're able to do something about this *in the short term.* REPLACE WITH *soon.* SEE ALSO *in (over) the long run (term).*

in the soup A moribund metaphor (see page 21). *at risk; endangered; hard-pressed; imperiled; in a bind; in a dilemma; in a fix; in a jam; in a predicament; in a quandary; in danger; in difficulty; in jeopardy; in peril; in trouble; jeopardized.*

in the spotlight A moribund metaphor (see page 21).

in the swim A moribund metaphor (see page 21). *absorbed; active; busy; employed; engaged; engrossed; immersed; involved; occupied; preoccupied; wrapped up in.*

in the swing of things A moribund metaphor (see page 21). *in step; in sync; in tune.*

in the thick of (it) A moribund metaphor (see page 21). 1. *amid; among; encircled; encompassed; in the middle; surrounded.* 2. *absorbed; active; busy; employed; engaged; engrossed; immersed; involved; occupied; preoccupied; wrapped up in.*

in the trenches A moribund metaphor (see page 21).

in the twinkling (wink) of an eye A moribund metaphor (see page 21). *abruptly; apace; at once; briskly; directly; expeditiously; fast; forthwith; hastily; hurriedly; immediately; instantaneously; instantly; posthaste; promptly; quickly; rapidly; rashly; right away; speedily; straightaway; suddenly; swiftly; unexpectedly; wingedly.*

> It actually struck the Minister-President on the shoulder as he stooped over his dying servant, then falling between his feet exploded with a terrific concentrated violence, striking him dead to the ground, finishing the wounded man and practically annihilating the empty sledge in the twinkling of an eye. — Joseph Conrad, *Under Western Eyes*

in the vicinity of A wretched redundancy (see page 25). *about; around; close to; more or less; near; nearly; or so; roughly; some.* ■ The final phase prohibits smoking anywhere *in the vicinity of* the main building's entrance. REPLACE WITH *near.* ■ The public puts its approval of Clinton's conduct *in the vicinity of* 70 percent. REPLACE WITH *around.* SEE ALSO *in the ballpark of; in the neighborhood of.*

in the wake of A moribund metaphor (see page 21). *after; behind; ensuing; following; succeeding.* SEE ALSO *(hot) on the heels of; reach epidemic proportions.*

in the wastebasket A moribund metaphor (see page 21). *abandoned; discarded; dismissed; jettisoned; rejected; repudiated; thrown out; tossed out.*

in the way of A wretched redundancy (see page 25). ■ They don't think they'll meet much *in the way of* resistance. DELETE *in the way of.* ■ The result is a staggering investment in foreign-oriented training with little *in the way of* return on investment. DELETE *in the way of.* ■ They didn't have much *in the way of* money. DELETE *in the way of.* ■ The result is that this disorganized interview usually provides little *in the way of* valuable information. DELETE *in the way of.*

in the worst (possible) way A torpid term (see page 24). *acutely; a great deal; badly; consumedly; exceedingly; extremely; greatly; hugely; immensely; intensely; mightily; prodigiously; seriously; very much.* ■ The Eagles want to win *in the worst way.* REPLACE WITH *very much.* SEE ALSO *in a big way.*

in the wrong place at the wrong time An infantile phrase (see page 20). An ascription of meaningfulness for those who unhappily speak it, it is an accedence to meaninglessness for those who sadly hear it. Along with *in the right place at the right time* (SEE), this phrase is evidence of what reason has been reduced to. ■ That little girl was just *in the wrong place at the wrong time.*

in this day and age A moribund metaphor (see page 21). *at present; currently; now; presently; these days; today.* ■ *In this day and age*, we need to train medical students to see beyond the front door of the hospital and to see the broader issues. REPLACE WITH *Today.*

in (their) time of need A torpid term (see page 24). ■ The ultimate beneficiaries are those who turn to the Clinic *in their time of need.*

in two shakes (of a lamb's tail) A moribund metaphor (see page 21). *abruptly; apace; at once; briskly; directly; expeditiously; fast; forthwith; hastily; hurriedly; immediately; instantaneously; instantly; posthaste; promptly; quickly; rapidly; rashly; right away; speedily; straightaway; suddenly; swiftly; unexpectedly; wingedly.*

in view of the fact that A wretched redundancy (see page 25). *because; considering; for; in that; since.* ■ *In view of the fact that* you couldn't pay your bills, you became a prostitute? REPLACE WITH *Because.* SEE ALSO *because of the fact that; considering the fact that; by virtue of the fact that; given the fact that; in consideration of the fact that; on account of the fact that.*

(a lot of) irons in the fire A moribund metaphor (see page 21). 1. *assignments; chores; duties; involvements; jobs; projects; responsibilities; tasks.* 2. *possibilities; potentialities; prospects.*

I second that emotion An infantile phrase (see page 20).

I shall return An infantile phrase (see page 20).

(money) isn't everything A popular prescription (see page 23). ■ Price is important, but *price isn't everything.*

it doesn't take (you don't have to be) a rocket scientist (an Einstein; a PhD) to (know) An infantile phrase (see page 20). We can be reasonably certain that the people who use this expression are not rocket scientists, not Einsteins, not PhDs. We can be less certain that the people who use this phrase are not dull-witted, not obtuse, not brainless. ■ *It doesn't take a rocket scientist to* see that a brutal police attack on a peaceful march is unacceptable and outrageous. ■ *It doesn't take a rocket scientist to* understand that high standards and a quality education should rank over diversity. ■ *It doesn't take an Einstein to* know that when kids see Mark McGwire they're going to head to the mall and buy the supplements. ■ *It doesn't take a rocket scientist to* figure out what's going on here. ■ *It doesn't take a PhD to* realize that the problem with the lagoon is what it contains — trash and polluted water. SEE ALSO *alive and kicking.*

it felt (seemed) like a lifetime An insipid simile. SEE ALSO *it felt (seemed) like an eternity.*

it felt (seemed) like an eternity An insipid simile. ■ Although it took 10 hours to convince the man to come down, *it felt like an eternity*. SEE ALSO *it felt (seemed) like a lifetime.*

it has been brought to (my) attention An ineffectual phrase (see page 19). ■ *It has been brought to my attention* that we have no record of your order. REPLACE WITH *I have been told.* SEE ALSO *it has come to (my) attention.*

it has come to (my) attention An ineffectual phrase (see page 19). ■ *It has come to our attention* that the number 3 is very popular. REPLACE WITH *We have learned.* ■ *It has come to my attention that* your deposit was received too late to be disbursed to your creditors this month. DELETE *It has come to my attention that.* SEE ALSO *it has been brought to (my) attention.*

it is important to note (that) An ineffectual phrase (see page 19). Attachments like *it is important to note (that)* and *it is interesting to note (that)* suggest that whatever follows them is probably not so important or interesting. Only people who mistrust the import or interest of their own statements use phrases like these — clear signals that their meaning is likely without merit, their message likely without allure. ■ *It is important to note that* you can change these settings for any document. DELETE *It is important to note that.* SEE ALSO *it is interesting to note (that); it is significant to note (that).*

it is important to realize (that) An ineffectual phrase (see page 19). ■ *It is important to realize that* analogical reasoning is used to explain and clarify, whereas causal reasoning is used to prove. DELETE *It is important to realize that.*

it is important to remember (that) An ineffectual phrase (see page 19). ■ *It is important to remember that* all three phases are important to your success. DELETE *It is important to remember that.*

it is important to understand (that) An ineffectual phrase (see page 19). ■ *It is important to understand that* turning the grid lines on and off changes only the display on the monitor and not the printout. DELETE *It is important to understand that.* SEE ALSO *you have to understand (that).*

it is interesting to note (that) An ineffectual phrase (see page 19). ■ *It is interesting to note that* although the sex hormone makes men more subject to baldness than women, it is more acceptable for women to wear wigs. DELETE *It is interesting to note that.* ■ *It is interesting to note that* in America bylines were largely an outcome of false reporting in another war, the Civil War. DELETE *It is interesting to note that.* SEE ALSO *it is important to note (that); it is significant to note (that).*

(so) ... it isn't (even) funny An infantile phrase (see page 20). ■ We've got so much overcapacity in the securities business *it isn't funny.* ■ I'm so sick of her *it isn't funny.*

it isn't over till it's over A popular prescription (see page 23).

it is significant to note (that) An ineffectual phrase (see page 19). ■ *It is significant to note that* the original database has not been altered. DELETE *It is significant to note that.* SEE ALSO *it is important to note (that); it is interesting to note (that).*

it is what it is A quack equation (see page 23).

it is worth noting (that) An ineffectual phrase (see page 19). ■ *It is worth noting that* he regarded her as "one of the finest writers of fiction." DELETE *It is worth noting that.*

it just happened An infantile phrase (see page 20). As an explanation for how circumstances or incidents unfold, none is more puerile. And though we might excuse children such a sentiment, it is rarely they who express it.

It just happened is a phrase used by those too slothful or too fearful to know what has happened. ■ It wasn't something I planned; *it just happened.* ■ What can I say? *It just happened.* SEE ALSO *because (that's why); whatever happens happens.*

it makes you (stop and) think A plebeian sentiment (see page 23).

it must (should) be mentioned (that) An ineffectual phrase (see page 19). ■ *It should be mentioned that* hiperspace is used by authorized programs only. DELETE *It should be mentioned that.*

it must (should) be noted (that) An ineffectual phrase (see page 19). ■ *It should be noted that* not all parents require an extensive interview. DELETE *It should be noted that.* ■ In terms of who conducts investigations, *it should be noted that* patrol personnel also may be used as investigators. DELETE *it should be noted that.*

it must (should) be pointed out (that) An ineffectual phrase (see page 19). ■ *It should be pointed out that* when you send this type of letter you must follow through with the filing in the court, or it can be looked on as a threat. DELETE *It should be pointed out that.*

it must (should) be realized (that) An ineffectual phrase (see page 19). ■ *It should be realized that* uncoupling is complete when the partners have defined themselves and are defined by others as separate and independent of each other. DELETE *It should be realized that.*

it must (should) be understood (that) An ineffectual phrase (see page 19). ■ *It should be understood that* a quitting concern assumption would be clearly disclosed on the financial statement. DELETE *It should be understood that.*

it never ends A plebeian sentiment (see page 23).

it never rains, but it pours A moribund metaphor (see page 21).

I told you (so) An infantile phrase (see page 20).

it's a bird, it's a plane, (it's Superman) An infantile phrase (see page 20).

it's a dirty job, but someone's got to do it A popular prescription (see page 23).

it's a dream come true A moribund metaphor (see page 21). ■ To be mentioned in the same sentence as Bette Davis — *it's a dream come true.*

it's a free country An infantile phrase (see page 20). This expression is one that only fettered thinkers could possibly use. One of the difficulties with dimwitticisms is that, because they are so familiar, people will most often use them thoughtlessly. Manacled as people are to these well-worn phrases, original thoughts and fresh words are often unreachable. ■ If owners of eating establishments want to allow smoking, let them do so — *it's a free country.* ■ *It's a free country.* It's what makes America great. ■ *It's a free country,* and no one tells me what to say!

it's a jungle (out there) A moribund metaphor (see page 21).

it's all Greek to me An infantile phrase (see page 20). *abstract; abstruse; ambiguous; arcane; blurred; blurry; cloudy; confusing; cryptic; deep; dim; esoteric; impenetrable; inaccessible; incoherent; incomprehensible; indecipherable; indistinct; muddy; murky; nebulous; obscure; puzzling; recondite; unclear; unfathomable; unintelligible; vague.*

it's a long story A torpid term (see page 24). *It's a long story* — cipher for *I don't want to tell you* — is a mannerly expression that we use to thwart the interest of a person in whom we are not much interested. SEE ALSO *that's for me to know and you to find out.*

it's always darkest just before dawn A popular prescription (see page 23).

it's always something A plebeian sentiment (see page 23).

it's an art A suspect superlative (see page 24). ■ Parallel parking is not easy; *it's an art.* ■ Creating a seamless event involves skill and experience; *it's an art.* ■ Congress is involved with changing the bankruptcy system; *it's an art* with no exact formula. ■ Admissions is not a precise science, *it's an art.*

it's a nice place to visit but I wouldn't want to live there A popular prescription (see page 23).

it's a two-way street A moribund metaphor (see page 21).

it's a whole different ballgame A moribund metaphor (see page 21).

it's better than nothing A popular prescription (see page 23).

it's better to have loved and lost than never to have loved at all A popular prescription (see page 23).

it's like a death in the family An insipid simile.

it's like losing a member of the family An insipid simile.

it's more fun than a barrel of monkeys A moribund metaphor (see page 21). *amusing; comical; entertaining; funny; hilarious; humorous; hysterical; riotous; risible; side-splitting.*

it's not over till (until) it's over A quack equation (see page 23). People say *it's not over till (until) it's over* in earnest, as if it were a weighty remark, a solemn truth when, of course, it's nothing but dimwitted. We might have an occasional insight, even a revelation, if we didn't persistently speak, and think in terms of, this kind of rubbish. ■ But *it isn't over till it's over*, and right now we have a statement from Dubai Ports World and little else.

it's not over till (until) the fat lady sings An infantile phrase (see page 20).

it's (been) one of those days A plebeian sentiment (see page 23).

it's one thing after another A plebeian sentiment (see page 23). SEE ALSO *if it isn't one thing, it's another.*

it's the same old story A torpid term (see page 24).

it's what's inside that counts A popular prescription (see page 23).

it takes all kinds A popular prescription (see page 23).

it takes one to know one An infantile phrase (see page 20).

it takes two A popular prescription (see page 23).

it takes two to tango A popular prescription (see page 23).

it was a dark and stormy night An infantile phrase (see page 20).

it will all come out in the wash A moribund metaphor (see page 21).

it works both ways A popular prescription (see page 23).

J

(made) (her) jaw drop A moribund metaphor (see page 21). *amaze; astonish; astound; awe; confound; dumbfound; flabbergast; jar; jolt; overwhelm; shock; start; startle; stun; stupefy; surprise.* ■ There are a couple levels that are truly inspired, though there's nothing that will *make your jaw drop.* REPLACE WITH *astound you.* ■ But Jabra, a company that usually doesn't let us down with its Bluetooth headsets, has rolled out a model that *made our jaw drop.* REPLACE WITH *stunned us.*

> She found herself living again a moment at her mother's funeral, which at the time had made her jaw drop with amazement. — Rebecca West, *Sunflower*

(has) (his) jaw set A moribund metaphor (see page 21). *be determined; be firm; be fixed; be inexorable; be inflexible; be obdurate; be resolute; be resolved; be rigid; be tenacious; be unflinching; be unwavering; be unyielding.* ■ Both Frist and DeLay seem to *have their jaws set* on this one. REPLACE WITH *be firm.*

(Dr.) Jekyll-(Mr.) Hyde (personality) A moribund metaphor (see page 21). *capricious; changeable; erratic; fickle; fitful; flighty; fluctuating; haphazard; inconsistent; inconstant; intermittent; irregular; mercurial; occasional; random; sometime; spasmodic; sporadic; unpredictable; unsettled; unstable; unsteady; vacillating; volatile; wavering; wayward.*

je ne sais quoi A foreign phrase (see page 19).

John Hancock A moribund metaphor (see page 21). *signature.*

Johnny-come-lately A moribund metaphor (see page 21). *climber; latecomer; newcomer; parvenu; upstart.*

joie de vivre A foreign phrase (see page 19).

join at the hip A moribund metaphor (see page 21). *indissoluble; indivisible; inseparable; together.*

join forces A moribund metaphor (see page 21). *ally; collaborate; comply; concur; conspire; cooperate; join; unite; work together.*

join together A wretched redundancy (see page 25). *join.* ■ ASA *joins* a powerful job scheduler *together* with select elements of automated operations to create a unique software system. DELETE *together.*

judge not, lest you be judged A popular prescription (see page 23).

juggling act A moribund metaphor (see page 21).

jump all over A moribund metaphor (see page 21). *admonish; anathematize; berate; blame; castigate; censure; chastise; chide; condemn; criticize; curse; decry; denounce; execrate; imprecate; inculpate; indict; rebuke; reprimand; reproach; reprove; scold; upbraid.*

jump down (her) throat A moribund metaphor (see page 21). *admonish; animadvert; berate; castigate; censure; chasten; chastise; chide; condemn; criticize; denounce; denunciate; discipline; excoriate; fulminate against; imprecate; impugn; inveigh against; objurgate; punish; rebuke; remonstrate; reprehend; reprimand; reproach; reprobate; reprove; revile; scold; swear at; upbraid; vituperate.*

jump for joy A moribund metaphor (see page 21). *be blissful; be blithe; be buoyant; be cheerful; be delighted; be ecstatic; be elated; be enraptured; be euphoric; be exalted; be excited; be exhilarated; be exultant; be gay; be glad; be gleeful; be good-humored; be happy; be intoxicated; be jolly; be jovial; be joyful; be joyous; be jubilant; be merry; be mirthful; be overjoyed; be pleased; be rapturous; be thrilled.*

jump from the frying pan into the fire A moribund metaphor (see page 21).

jump in with both feet A moribund metaphor (see page 21).

> I wanted to jump in with both feet, but something stopped me. — Jessica Speart, *Coastal Disturbance*

jumping-off point A moribund metaphor (see page 21).

jump on the bandwagon A moribund metaphor (see page 21). *be included; be involved; enlist; enroll; join; sign up; take part.* ■ Once everyone in an industry has learned about something that works, there's a tendency to *jump on the bandwagon.*

jump out of (her) skin A moribund metaphor (see page 21). *be amazed; be astonished; be astounded; be awed; be flabbergasted; be jarred; be jolted; be overwhelmed; be shocked; be started; be startled; be stunned; be stupefied; be surprised.*

jump ship A moribund metaphor (see page 21). *abandon; desert; forsake; leave; quit.*

jump the gun A moribund metaphor (see page 21).

jump through hoops A moribund metaphor (see page 21).

(the) jury is still out A moribund metaphor (see page 21). *be arguable; be debatable; be disputable; be doubtful; be dubious; be in doubt; be moot; be open; be questionable; be uncertain; be unclear; be undecided; be undetermined; be unknown; be unresolved; be unsettled; be unsolved; be unsure.*

Still another way to express not knowing or being undecided, *the jury is still out,* used figuratively, is as foolish a phrase as it is a meaning. Any sentence in which this dimwitticism is used is sentenced to being forgettable.

just exactly A wretched redundancy (see page 25). *exactly; just.* ■ *Just exactly* what do you mean? REPLACE WITH *Just* or *Exactly.*

just recently A wretched redundancy (see page 25). *just; recently.* ■ I *just recently* completed my bachelor's degree. REPLACE WITH *just* or *recently.*

just what the doctor ordered A moribund metaphor (see page 21).

just when you thought it was safe to An infantile phrase (see page 20).

keep a (the) lid on A moribund metaphor (see page 21). *bridle; check; constrain; control; curb; govern; harness; hold back; inhibit; muzzle; repress; restrain; stifle; suppress.* ■ Its leaders have said they cannot *keep a lid on* popular anger if the government does not begin to respond to citizens' demands. REPLACE WITH *restrain.*

> Buster had declined, of course, but there was talk that he got some of his employees to join and keep the lid on things. — Loraine Despres, *The Scandalous Summer of Sissy LeBlanc*

keep a low profile A moribund metaphor (see page 21).

keep an ear to the ground A moribund metaphor (see page 21). *be alert; be attentive; be awake; be aware; be eagle-eyed; be heedful; be informed; be keen; be* *observant; be vigilant; be wakeful; be watchful.*

keep an eye out for A moribund metaphor (see page 21). *be alert; be attentive; be awake; be aware; be eagle-eyed; be heedful; be informed; be keen; be observant; be vigilant; be wakeful; be watchful; hunt; look for; search.*

keep a stiff upper lip A moribund metaphor (see page 21). *be brave; be courageous; be determined; be resolute.*

keep (them) at arm's length A moribund metaphor (see page 21). ■ In some cases, you need to *keep hurtful people at arm's length* so they can't continue hurting you.

keep a watchful eye on A moribund metaphor (see page 21). *be alert; be attentive; be awake; be aware; be eagle-eyed; be heedful; be informed; be keen; be observant; be vigilant; be wakeful; be watchful.*

keep body and soul together A moribund metaphor (see page 21). *endure; exist; keep alive; live; manage; subsist; survive.*

keep (your) chin up A moribund metaphor (see page 21). *be brave; be courageous; be determined; be resolute.*

keep (his) cool A moribund metaphor (see page 21). *be calm; be composed; be patient; be self-possessed; be tranquil.*

keep (our) distance A moribund metaphor (see page 21). *be aloof; be chilly; be cool; be reserved; be standoffish; be unamiable; be unamicable; be uncompanionable; be uncongenial; be unfriendly; be unsociable; be unsocial.*

keep (his) eye on the ball A moribund metaphor (see page 21). 1. *be alert; be attentive; be awake; be aware; be eagle-eyed; be heedful; be observant; be vigilant; be wakeful; be watchful.* 2. *be able; be adroit; be apt; be astute; be bright; be brilliant; be capable; be clever; be competent; be discerning; be effective; be effectual; be efficient; be enlightened; be insightful; be intelligent; be judicious; be keen; be knowledgeable; be learned; be logical; be luminous; be perceptive; be perspicacious; be quick; be rational; be reasonable; be sagacious; be sage; be sapient; be sensible; be sharp; be shrewd; be smart; be sound; be understanding; be wise.*

keep (your) eyes (open) peeled A moribund metaphor (see page 21). *be alert; be attentive; be awake; be aware; be eagle-eyed; be heedful; be observant; be vigilant; be wakeful; be watchful.*

keep (its) finger on the pulse of A moribund metaphor (see page 21). ■ The Chinese government has been able to *keep its finger on the pulse of* technology acquisition activities.

keep (your) fingers crossed A moribund metaphor (see page 21). *hope for; pray for; think positively; wish.*

keep (me) glued to (my) seat A moribund metaphor (see page 21).

keep (my) head above water A moribund metaphor (see page 21). *be solvent; exist; live; subsist; survive.*

keep (your) head on (your) shoulders A moribund metaphor (see page 21). *be calm; be composed; be patient; be self-possessed; be tranquil.*

keep (your) nose clean A moribund metaphor (see page 21). *behave.*

keep (your) nose to the grindstone A popular prescription (see page 23). *drudge; grind; grub; labor; moil; slave; strain; strive; struggle; sweat; toil; travail; work hard.*

keep on a short leash A moribund metaphor (see page 21).

keep (your) pants (shirt) on A moribund metaphor (see page 21). *be calm; be composed; be patient; be self-possessed; be tranquil; calm down; hold on; wait.*

(it) keeps (me) busy A plebeian sentiment (see page 23). SEE ALSO *(he's) boring; (it) gives (me) something to do; (it) keeps (me) out of trouble; (it's) something to do.*

(it) keeps (me) going A plebeian sentiment (see page 23).

keep smiling A plebeian sentiment (see page 23). *Keep smiling* is insisted on by ghoulish brutes who would rob us of our gravity, indeed, steal us from ourselves.

(it) keeps (me) out of trouble A plebeian sentiment (see page 23). SEE ALSO *(it) gives (me) something to do; (it) keeps (me) busy; (it's) something to do.*

keep the ball rolling A moribund metaphor (see page 21). *continue; go on; keep on; move on; persevere; persist; proceed.*

keep the faith A popular prescription (see page 23). *be confident; be encouraged; be heartened; be hopeful; be optimistic; be positive; be sanguine.*

keep the home fires burning A moribund metaphor (see page 21).

keep the wolves at bay A moribund metaphor (see page 21).

keep under (his) hat A moribund metaphor (see page 21). *camouflage; cloak; conceal; cover; disguise; enshroud; harbor; hide; keep secret; mask; screen; shroud; suppress; veil; withhold.*

keep under lock and key A moribund metaphor (see page 21). 1. *confine; detain; hold; imprison; intern; jail; lock up; restrain.* 2. *lock up; protect; secure.*

keep up appearances A plebeian sentiment (see page 23).

> She desired children, decorum, an establishment; she desired to avoid waste, she desired to keep up appearances. — Ford Madox Ford, *The Good Soldier*

keep up with the Joneses A plebeian sentiment (see page 23).

(a) kick in the pants A moribund metaphor (see page 21). 1. *encouragement; fillip; goad; impetus; impulse; incentive; incitation; incitement; inducement; jolt; motivation; motive; prod; provocation; push; shove; spur; stimulation; stimulus; thrust; urge.* 2. *animation; ebullience; elation; enthusiasm; excitement; exhilaration; exultation; jubilance; jubilation; liveliness; rapture; stimulation; vivacity.* 3. *admonishment; castigation; censure; chastisement; disapprobation; disapproval; rebuke; remonstrance; reprimand; reproof; scolding; upbraiding.*

(a) kick in the teeth A moribund metaphor (see page 21). *abuse; affront; contempt; contumely; derision; disappointment; disdain; impertinence; indignity; insult; offense; outrage; rebuff; rebuke; rejection; scorn; slap; slight; slur; sneer; snub.* ■ We have received a judgment that has been *a kick in the teeth.* REPLACE WITH *an insult.*

kick the bucket A moribund metaphor (see page 21). *cease to exist; decease; depart; die; expire; pass away; pass on; perish.*

> So when I put my phone to my ear and heard her choke out "He's gone" who could blame me for thinking that Dad had kicked the bucket and that now it was only her and me. — Marian Keyes, *The Other Side of the Story*

kick up (our) heels A moribund metaphor (see page 21). *be merry; carouse; carry on; cavort; celebrate; debauch; disport; frolic; gambol; party; play; revel; riot; roister; rollick; romp; skylark.*

(like a) kid in a candy shop (store) An insipid simile.

kill (them) by inches A moribund metaphor (see page 21). *afflict; agonize; crucify; excruciate; harrow; martyr; persecute; rack; torment; torture.*

kill the goose that lays the golden egg A moribund metaphor (see page 21).

kill two birds with one stone A moribund metaphor (see page 21).

kill (her) with kindness A moribund metaphor (see page 21).

kind (and) gentle An inescapable pair (see page 20). *affable; agreeable; amiable; amicable; compassionate; friendly; gentle; good-hearted; good-natured; humane; kind; kind-hearted; personable; pleasant; tender; tolerant.*

(a) ... kind (sort; type) of thing A grammatical gimmick (see page 19). ■ It was *a* spur-of-the-moment *kind of thing.* DELETE *a ... kind of thing.* ■ It's *a* very upsetting *sort of thing.* DELETE *a ... sort of thing.* ■ It's difficult to find a person to commit to in terms of a long-term relationship *type of thing.* DELETE *type of thing.*

kiss and make up A moribund metaphor (see page 21).

> You have to be careful when criticizing a friend's partner because the second they kiss and make up, *you* are the baddie who slagged off the love of her life. — Anna Maxted, *Running in Heels*

kiss and tell A moribund metaphor (see page 21).

kiss (him) goodbye A moribund metaphor (see page 21). *abandon; abdicate; cede; desert; forfeit; forgo; give up; lose (out on); relinquish; renounce; sacrifice; surrender; waive; yield.* ■ Without a new government-funded convention center, Boston will *kiss major gatherings and tourist events goodbye.* REPLACE WITH *forfeit major gatherings and tourist events.*

kiss of death A moribund metaphor (see page 21).

(the) (whole) kit and caboodle A moribund metaphor (see page 21). *aggregate; all; all things; entirety; everything; gross; lot; sum; total; totality; whole.*

kith and kin An inescapable pair (see page 20).
acquaintances; family; friends; kin; kindred; kinfolk; kinsman; kith; relatives.

knee-high to a grasshopper A moribund metaphor (see page 21). 1. *diminutive; dwarfish; elfin; elfish; lilliputian; little; miniature; minikin; petite; pygmy; short; small; teeny; tiny*. 2. *young; youthful.*

knee-jerk reaction A moribund metaphor (see page 21). *automatic; habitual; instinctive; inveterate; mechanical; perfunctory; reflex; spontaneous; unconscious; unthinking.*

knight in shining armor A moribund metaphor (see page 21).

knock-down, drag-out fight A moribund metaphor (see page 21). 1. *altercation; argument; disagreement; discord; disputation; dispute; feud; fight; misunderstanding; quarrel; rift; row; spat; squabble.* 2. *battle; brawl; clash; fight; grapple; jostle; make war; scuffle; skirmish; tussle; war; wrestle.*

knock (me) down with a feather A moribund metaphor (see page 21). *amaze; astonish; astound; awe; dazzle; dumbfound; flabbergast; overpower; overwhelm; shock; startle; stun; stupefy; surprise.*

knock (throw) for a loop A moribund metaphor (see page 21). *amaze; astonish; astound; awe; dazzle; dumbfound; flabbergast; overpower; overwhelm; shock; startle; stun; stupefy; surprise.*

knock off (his) feet A moribund metaphor (see page 21). *amaze; astonish; astound; awe; dazzle; dumbfound; flabbergast; overpower; overwhelm; shock; startle; stun; stupefy; surprise.*

knock on wood A moribund metaphor (see page 21). *hope for; pray for; think positively; wish.*

knock (himself) out A moribund metaphor (see page 21). *aim; attempt; endeavor; essay; exert; exhaust; labor; moil; strain; strive; struggle; toil; try hard; undertake; work at.*

knock-out punch A moribund metaphor (see page 21).

knock (her) socks off A moribund metaphor (see page 21). 1. *amaze; astonish; astound; awe; dazzle; dumbfound; flabbergast; overpower; overwhelm; shock; startle; stun; stupefy; surprise.* 2. *beat; better; conquer; defeat; exceed; excel; outclass; outdo; outflank; outmaneuver; outperform; outplay; overcome; overpower; prevail; rout; succeed; surpass; top; triumph; trounce; vanquish; whip; win.*

knock the bottom out of A moribund metaphor (see page 21). *belie; confute; contradict; controvert; counter; debunk; deny; disprove; discredit; dispute; expose; invalidate; negate; rebut; refute; repudiate.*

knock the spots off A moribund metaphor (see page 21). *beat; better;*

conquer; defeat; exceed; excel; outclass; outdo; outflank; outmaneuver; outperform; outplay; overcome; overpower; prevail; rout; succeed; surpass; top; triumph; trounce; vanquish; whip; win.

know for a fact An infantile phrase (see page 20). ■ I *know for a fact* that he was there with her. DELETE *for a fact.* ■ I'm sure they do; I *know for a fact* they do. DELETE *for a fact.*

(don't) know ... from Adam A moribund metaphor (see page 21). *unacquainted; unconversant; unfamiliar; unknown.*

(know) ... inside (and) out A moribund metaphor (see page 21). *completely; comprehensively; deeply; exhaustively; expertly; fully; in depth; in detail; profoundly; thoroughly; well.*

> They came here because they *knew* this place. They knew it inside and out. — Zadie Smith, *White Teeth*

knowledge is power A quack equation (see page 23).

know all the angles A moribund metaphor (see page 21). 1. *able; adept; apt; capable; competent; deft; dexterous; experienced; expert; practiced; proficient; seasoned; skilled; skillful; veteran.* 2. *adroit; astute; bright; brilliant; clever; discerning; effective; effectual; efficient; enlightened; insightful; intelligent; judicious; keen; knowledgeable; learned; logical; luminous; perceptive; perspicacious; quick; rational; reasonable; sagacious; sage; sapient; sensible; sharp; shrewd; smart; sound; understanding; wise.*

(a man is) known by the company (he) keeps A popular prescription (see page 23).

(you) know something? An ineffectual phrase (see page 19). ■ *You know something?* I'm going to do whatever is in my power to end this relationship. DELETE *You know something?* ■ *You know something?* I never loved you either. DELETE *You know something?* SEE ALSO *(you) know what?*

know what's what An infantile phrase (see page 20). 1. *able; adept; apt; capable; competent; deft; dexterous; experienced; expert; practiced; proficient; seasoned; skilled; skillful; veteran.* 2. *adroit; astute; bright; brilliant; clever; discerning; effective; effectual; efficient; enlightened; insightful; intelligent; judicious; keen; knowledgeable; learned; logical; luminous; perceptive; perspicacious; quick; rational; reasonable; sagacious; sage; sapient; sensible; sharp; shrewd; smart; sound; understanding; wise.*

know which side (her) bread is buttered on A moribund metaphor (see page 21).

know thyself A popular prescription (see page 23).

(you) know what? An ineffectual phrase (see page 19). ■ *You know what?* When we return, you'll meet her mother. DELETE *You know what?* ■ She broke up with me, and *you know what?*, I've got a career now, which is good. DELETE *you know what?* SEE ALSO *(you) know something?*

(you) know what I mean? An ineffectual phrase (see page 19). ■ Some people have to work at it more than others. *Know what I mean?* DELETE *Know what I mean?* ■ How can you not be depressed if you don't remember things. *You know what I mean?* DELETE *You know what I mean?* SEE ALSO *(you) hear what I'm saying? (you) know what I'm saying? (you) know what I'm telling you? (do) you know?*

(you) know what I'm saying? An ineffectual phrase (see page 19). ■ It was an association that wasn't based on any fact. *You know what I'm saying?* DELETE *You know what I'm saying?* ■ I want a girl that's real. *You know what I'm saying?* DELETE *You know what I'm saying?* SEE ALSO *(you) hear what I'm saying? (you) know what I mean? (you) know what I'm telling you? (do) you know?*

(you) know what I'm telling you? An ineffectual phrase (see page 19). ■ I don't know; I can't think of the words. *You know what I'm telling you?* DELETE *You know what I'm telling you?* ■ I like to be with a woman who has the same mindset as I do. *You know what I'm telling you?* DELETE *You know what I'm telling you?* SEE ALSO *(you) hear what I'm saying? (you) know what I mean? (you) know what I'm saying? (do) you know?*

knuckle under A moribund metaphor (see page 21). *abdicate; accede; acquiesce; bow; capitulate; cede; concede; give in; give up; quit; relinquish; retreat; submit; succumb; surrender; yield.*

kudos A foreign phrase (see page 19).

L

(a) labor of love A moribund metaphor (see page 21).

> It has been a true labor of love, and something more — the only thing that has kept her calm during the long winter months of waiting for the hearing to begin. — Anita Shreve, *Fortune's Rocks*

lack of A torpid term (see page 24). Whatever happened to our negative words, to the prefixes *dis-, il-, im-, in-, ir-, mis-, non-,* and *un-*? No doubt many people say *absence of* or *lack of* because they know so few negative forms of the words that follow these phrases. These people will say *lack of moderation* instead of *immoderation* and *absence of pleasure* instead of *displeasure.*

Others subscribe to society's oral imperative that all things negative be left unsaid. To these people, *lack of respect* is somehow preferable to, and more positive than, *disrespect.* ■ These reports by the media reflect a *lack of sensitivity* to basic human decency. REPLACE WITH *insensitivity.* ■ It was her *lack of judgment* that lost us the sale. REPLACE WITH *misjudgment.* SEE ALSO *absence of; less than (enthusiastic).*

lady A suspect superlative (see page 24). *Lady* has become a pejorative term. No longer does it suggest a cultured, sophisticated woman; rather, it suggests a woman hopelessly common, forever coarse. ■ If you wanted to sweep one of these *ladies* off her feet, what would you do? REPLACE WITH *women.* ■ I am a *lady*, and I like to be treated as such. REPLACE WITH *well-bred woman.* ■ I have a question for both of you *ladies.* DELETE *ladies.* SEE ALSO *class; gentleman.*

(the) land of milk and honey A moribund metaphor (see page 21).

(the) land of nod A moribund metaphor (see page 21). *sleep; slumber.*

land on (her) feet A moribund metaphor (see page 21). *come through; continue; endure; hold on; persevere; persist; remain; survive.*

landslide victory A moribund metaphor (see page 21).

last but (by) no means least An infantile phrase (see page 20). This term, like *last but not least*, needs to be retired. It's a drab, depressing formula used by forlorn people, by *team players* (SEE) and troglodytes alike, by hacks and hirelings all.

last but not least An infantile phrase (see page 20).

> They were concerned for the newcomer, and they were concerned for themselves; midwives, barber-surgeons, nannies, priest and, last but not least, solicitors crowded around the event in droves. — Peter Esterhazy, *Celestial Harmonies*

lasting An overworked word (see page 22). For example: *lasting consequence; lasting contribution; lasting impact; lasting impression; lasting lesson; lasting peace.*

last nail in (his) coffin A moribund metaphor (see page 21).

last of the Mohicans An infantile phrase (see page 20).

(for a) laugh A plebeian sentiment (see page 23). This expression is spoken by people who tally their giggles and count their guffaws, people who value numbers and sums more than they do words and concepts, people who consider laughter a commodity and life a comedy. ■ I need *a laugh.* ■ Sue and I want to do these silly things to you *for a laugh.* ■ I'm always looking *for a laugh.* SEE ALSO *avid reader; on a scale of 1 to 10.*

laughing (my) head off A moribund metaphor (see page 21). *cachinnate; cackle; chortle; chuckle; convulse; guffaw; hoot; howl; laugh; roar; shriek.*

laughing on the outside and crying on the inside A moribund metaphor (see page 21).

laughter is the best medicine A popular prescription (see page 23).

launching pad (for) A moribund metaphor (see page 21). *base; beginning; foundation; springboard; start*

laundry list A moribund metaphor (see page 21).

lavishly illustrated An inescapable pair (see page 20).

(the) law is the law A quack equation (see page 23).

law of the jungle A moribund metaphor (see page 21).

(don't) lay a finger (hand) on A moribund metaphor (see page 21). *caress; feel; finger; fondle; handle; pat; paw; pet; rub; stroke; touch.*

lay an egg A moribund metaphor (see page 21). *abort; blunder; bomb; fail; fall short; falter; flop; flounder; go wrong; miscarry; not succeed; slip; stumble; trip.*

lay at (their) door A moribund metaphor (see page 21). *accredit to; ascribe to; assign to; associate to; attribute to; blame on; charge to; connect with; correlate to; credit to; equate to; impute to; link to; relate to; trace to.*

lay a trap for A moribund metaphor (see page 21). *catch; decoy; ensnare; entrap; net; trap.*

lay at the door (feet) of A moribund metaphor (see page 21). *accredit to; ascribe to; assign to; associate to; attribute to; blame on; charge to; connect with; correlate to; credit to; equate to; impute to; link to; relate to; trace to.* ■ It doesn't seem that all this volatility can be *laid at the feet of* foreigners. REPLACE WITH *blamed on.*

lay (put) (your) cards on the table A moribund metaphor (see page 21). *be aboveboard; be candid; be forthright; be frank; be honest; be open; be straightforward; be truthful.*

lay down the law A moribund metaphor (see page 21). 1. *assert; command; decree; dictate; insist; order; require.* 2. *admonish; berate; castigate; censure; chastise; chide; condemn; criticize; decry; rebuke; reprimand; reproach; reprove; scold; upbraid.*

lay (spread) it on thick A moribund metaphor (see page 21). 1. *elaborate; embellish; embroider; enhance; enlarge; exaggerate; hyperbolize; inflate; magnify; overdo; overreact; overstress; overstate; strain; stretch.* 2. *acclaim; applaud; celebrate; commend; compliment; congratulate; eulogize; extol; flatter; hail; laud; panegyrize; praise; puff; salute.*

lay (it) on the line A moribund metaphor (see page 21). *be aboveboard; be candid; be forthright; be frank; be honest; be open; be straightforward; be truthful.*

lay (her) out in lavendar A moribund metaphor (see page 21). *admonish; animadvert; berate; castigate; censure; chasten; chastise; chide; condemn; criticize; denounce; denunciate; discipline; excoriate; fulminate against; imprecate; impugn; inveigh against; lecture; objurgate; punish; rebuke; remonstrate; reprehend; reprimand; reproach; reprobate; reprove; revile; scold; swear at; upbraid; vituperate.*

lay the groundwork (for) A moribund metaphor (see page 21). *arrange; groom; make ready; plan; prepare; prime; ready.*

lead (her) by the nose A moribund metaphor (see page 21). *administer; boss; command; control; dictate; direct; dominate; domineer; govern; in charge; in command; in control; manage; manipulate; master; misuse; order; overpower; oversee; predominate; prevail; reign over; rule; superintend; tyrannize; use.*

lead down the garden path A moribund metaphor (see page 21). *bamboozle; befool; beguile; bilk; bluff; cheat; con; deceive; defraud; delude; dupe; feint; fool; gyp; hoodwink; lead astray; misdirect; misguide; misinform; mislead; spoof; swindle; trick; victimize.*

leader of the pack A moribund metaphor (see page 21). 1. *administrator; boss; brass; chief; commander; director; executive; foreman; head; headman; leader; manager; master; (high) muckamuck; officer; official; overseer; president; principal; superintendent; supervisor.* 2. *aristocrat; dignitary; eminence; lord; luminary; magnate; mogul; notable; patrician; personage; ruler; sovereign; worthy.*

(put) lead in your pencil A moribund metaphor (see page 21). *energy; force; life; power; punch; spirit; strength; verve; vigor; vim; vitality; zest.*

leak like a sieve An insipid simile. 1. *leaky; permeable.* 2. *forgetful; heedless; inattentive; lethean; neglectful; negligent; oblivious; remiss; thoughtless; unmindful; unthinking.*

lean and hungry (look) A moribund metaphor (see page 21).

lean and mean An inescapable pair (see page 20).

leaps off the page A moribund metaphor (see page 21).

learn the ropes A moribund metaphor (see page 21).

> She was left sitting until a slight, sparrow-like woman, with bright fringed hair and round blue eyes, came past and remarked warningly that she should keep her eyes open and learn the ropes. — Doris M. Lessing, *Martha Quest*

leave a bad taste in (my) mouth A moribund metaphor (see page 21).

leave a little (a lot; much; something) to be desired A torpid term (see page 24). *be deficient; be inadequate; be insufficient; be lacking; be substandard; be wanting.* ■ In the area of health, the U.S. position *leaves much to be desired.* REPLACE WITH *is sickly.* ■ The plan was great; it was the execution that *left a little to be desired.* REPLACE WITH *was not.* ■ Sorry about that, my handwriting *leaves something to be desired.* REPLACE WITH *is scarcely legible.*

leave holding the bag A moribund metaphor (see page 21). *abandon; depart from; desert; exclude; forsake; leave; quit; withdraw from.*

leave (out) in the cold A moribund metaphor (see page 21). *abandon; ban; banish; bar; desert; exclude; exile; forsake; ostracize; shut out.*

leave (him) in the dust A moribund metaphor (see page 21). *beat; best; better; defeat; eclipse; exceed; excel; outclass; outdo; outflank; outmaneuver; outpace; outperform; outplay; outrank; outrival; outsmart; outstrip; outthink; outwit; overcome; overpower; overshadow; prevail; rout; surpass; top; triumph; trounce; van-*

quish; whip; win. ■ It is here where Homo sapiens *leaves* other species *in the dust*, and the hands usually make it possible. REPLACE WITH *surpasses.*

leave (hanging) in the lurch A moribund metaphor (see page 21). *abandon; depart from; desert; exclude; forsake; leave; quit; withdraw from.* ■ We don't want to *leave* parents *hanging in the lurch*. REPLACE WITH *abandon.*

> Today, Jorie has once again left her poor friend Charlotte in the lurch, with no explanations or apologies.
> — Alice Hoffman, *Blue Diary*

leave no stone unturned A moribund metaphor (see page 21). *analyze; canvass; comb; examine; explore; filter; forage; hunt; inspect; investigate; look for; probe; quest; ransack; rummage; scour; scrutinize; search; seek; sieve; sift; winnow.*

leave the door (wide) open (for) A moribund metaphor (see page 21). ■ The remainder of the majority *left the door open for* a return to capital punishment.

leave well enough alone A popular prescription (see page 23).

left and right An inescapable pair (see page 20). *all around; all over; all through; broadly; everyplace; everywhere; extensively; throughout; ubiquitously; universally; widely.* SEE ALSO *far and wide; high and low.*

(a) legend in (his) own mind An infantile phrase (see page 20).

leg to stand on A moribund metaphor (see page 21).

(has a) leg up on A moribund metaphor (see page 21). *advantage (over); predominance over; superiority to; supremacy over.* ■ This is expected to give auto makers *a natural leg up*. REPLACE WITH *a natural advantage.* ■ Even I have *a leg up on* him in that department. REPLACE WITH *an advantage over.*

lend a (helping) hand (to) A moribund metaphor (see page 21). *aid; assist; benefit; favor; help; oblige; succor.* ■ During this holiday season, it is fitting for all of us to be thinking of *lending a helping hand to* those in need. REPLACE WITH *aiding.* ■ These writers believe it's their mission to *lend a hand* wherever there is a need. REPLACE WITH *help.*

lend an ear A moribund metaphor (see page 21). *attend to; heed; listen; note.*

(a) leopard cannot change his spots A popular prescription (see page 23).

leopards don't lose their spots A moribund metaphor (see page 21).

(the) lesser of two evils A torpid term (see page 24).

less is more A quack equation (see page 23).

(the) less said, the better A popular prescription (see page 23).

less than (enthusiastic) A torpid term (see page 24). ■ When Fred told his wife about the unbelievable opportunity, he was shocked at her *less than enthusiastic* response. REPLACE WITH *unenthusiastic.* ■ The response from their neighbors has been *less than hospitable.*

REPLACE WITH *inhospitable.* SEE ALSO *absence of; lack of.*

let bygones be bygones A popular prescription (see page 23).

let go of the past A popular prescription (see page 23).

let grass grow under (your) feet A moribund metaphor (see page 21). *be idle; be inactive; be lazy; be unemployed; be unoccupied; dally; dawdle; delay; hesitate; linger; loaf; loiter; loll; lounge; pause; relax; repose; rest; tarry; unwind; wait; waste time.*

let (take) (her) hair down A moribund metaphor (see page 21). *be casual; be free; be informal; be loose; be natural; be open; be relaxed; be unbound; be unconfined; be unrestrained; be unrestricted.*

let (him) have it with both barrels A moribund metaphor (see page 21). *admonish; animadvert; berate; castigate; censure; chasten; chastise; chide; condemn; criticize; denounce; denunciate; discipline; excoriate; fulminate against; imprecate; impugn; inveigh against; objurgate; punish; rebuke; remonstrate; reprehend; reprimand; reproach; reprobate; reprove; revile; scold; swear at; upbraid; vituperate.*

let it all hang out A moribund metaphor (see page 21). *acknowledge; admit; affirm; allow; avow; concede; confess; disclose; divulge; expose; grant; own; reveal; tell; uncover; unveil.*

let it be A popular prescription (see page 23).

let me ask you something An ineffectual phrase (see page 19). ■ *Let me ask you something,* is there anything about school that you like? DELETE *Let me ask you something.* ■ *Let me ask you something:* What would you think if I met three women tonight? DELETE *Let me ask you something.* SEE ALSO *can I ask (tell) you something?*

let me tell you (something) An ineffectual phrase (see page 19). Of course the people who use this phrase seldom enunciate *let me*; they mutter *lemme,* an inauspicious sign, we might reasonably believe, of what is to come. *Let me tell you (something)* is a vulgarity, very nearly an insult. It unveils a person, only crudely conscious of what he utters, who has as much respect for the language as he does for his listeners.

■ This is really class, *let me tell you.* DELETE *let me tell you.* ■ It's been one of those days, *let me tell you.* DELETE *let me tell you.* ■ *Let me tell you,* there is nothing scarier than being in hurricane force winds and hearing huge clangs and thumps and shattering of glass or metal. DELETE *Let me tell you.* SEE ALSO *I got to (have to) tell you (something); I'll tell you (something); I'll tell you what; I'm telling you.*

let nature take its course A popular prescription (see page 23).

let sleeping dogs lie A popular prescription (see page 23). *avoid; discount; disregard; dodge; duck; ignore; neglect; omit; pass over; shun; shy away from; turn away from; withdraw from.*

let the cat out of the bag A moribund metaphor (see page 21). *reveal secrets.*

let the chips fall where they may A moribund metaphor (see page 21).

let there be no mistake A torpid term (see page 24). SEE ALSO *make no mistake (about it).*

let your fingers do the walking An infantile phrase (see page 20).

let your mind run wild A moribund metaphor (see page 21).

(a) level playing field A moribund metaphor (see page 21). *equality; equitableness; equity; fairness; impartiality; justice; justness.* ■ If you live in a democracy, there has to be *a level playing field.* REPLACE WITH *equality.* ■ Many people of goodwill sincerely, but mistakenly, believe that today we have achieved *a level playing field.* REPLACE WITH *fairness.*

level the playing field A moribund metaphor (see page 21). *balance; equalize; even out; level; make equal; make level.* ■ The chief aim of the bill is to *level the playing field* so that challengers and incumbents will have an equal opportunity to get their message across. ■ We're not out to hurt anybody, we're just out to *level the playing field.* SEE ALSO *a level playing field.*

lick (his) chops A moribund metaphor (see page 21).

lick into shape A moribund metaphor (see page 21). *drill; instruct; perfect; train.*

lick (your) wounds A moribund metaphor (see page 21).

lie down on the job A moribund metaphor (see page 21). *be idle; be inactive; be lazy; be unemployed; be unoccupied; dally; dawdle; linger; loaf; loiter; loll; lounge; malinger; tarry.*

lie like a rug An insipid simile. *deceive; dissemble; distort; equivocate; falsify; fib; lie; misconstrue; mislead; misrepresent; pervert; prevaricate.*

> He had the press, he had the money, and he would lie like a rug in order to manipulate people into helping him. — Diane Jessup, *The Dog Who Spoke With Gods*

lie low A moribund metaphor (see page 21). 1. *be closed-mouthed; be quiet; be reticent; be silent; be speechless; be still; be taciturn; be uncommunicative; keep quiet.* 2. *disappear; hide; hole up.*

lie through (his) teeth A moribund metaphor (see page 21). *deceive; dissemble; distort; equivocate; falsify; fib; lie; misconstrue; mislead; misrepresent; pervert; prevaricate.*

life begins at forty A popular prescription (see page 23).

life goes on A popular prescription (see page 23).

life in a fishbowl A moribund metaphor (see page 21).

life in the fast lane A moribund metaphor (see page 21).

life is a cabaret A moribund metaphor (see page 21).

life is for the living A popular prescription (see page 23).

life isn't (always) fair A popular prescription (see page 23).

life is short A quack equation (see page 23).

(live a) life of luxury A moribund metaphor (see page 21). *affluent; moneyed; opulent; prosperous; rich; wealthy; well-off; well-to-do.*

(live) (the) life of Reilly A moribund metaphor (see page 21). 1. *be affluent; be moneyed; be opulent; be prosperous; be rich; be wealthy; be well-off; be well-to-do.* 2. *be extravagant; be lavish; be lush; be luxuriant; be sumptuous; be very well.* ■ It was *the life of Reilly*, but something was missing.

lift a finger A moribund metaphor (see page 21). *aid; assist; benefit; favor; help; oblige; succor.*

light a fire under A moribund metaphor (see page 21). *arouse; awaken; excite; galvanize; goad; impel; incite; induce; motivate; prompt; provoke; push; rouse; spur; stimulate; stir; urge.* ■ May the bishops' counsel encourage those husbands already living their words and *light a fire under* those dozing. REPLACE WITH *rouse*.

(as) light as a feather An insipid simile. *airy; buoyant; delicate; ethereal; feathery; gaseous; gauzy; gossamer; light; lightweight; slender; slight; sylphid; thin; vaporous; weightless.*

(as) light as air An insipid simile. *airy; buoyant; delicate; ethereal; feathery; gaseous; gauzy; gossamer; light; lightweight; slender; slight; sylphid; thin; vaporous; weightless.*

light at the end of the tunnel A moribund metaphor (see page 21). *anticipation; expectancy; expectation; hope; hopefulness; optimism; possibility; promise; prospect; sanguinity.* ■ When the opportunity arose that he could work for the government, we saw *light at the end of the tunnel.* REPLACE WITH *possibility.*

(a) light went off (in my head) A moribund metaphor (see page 21). *afflatus; brainwave; breakthrough; flash; idea; insight; inspiration; revelation.*

like An infantile phrase (see page 20). A cachet of all who are grievously adolescent, *like* mars the meaning of every sentence in which it is used. ■ Our family is *like* very open. DELETE *like.* ■ They lived together for *like* twelve years. DELETE *like.* ■ I should, *like*, get up and do something. DELETE *like.* ■ It's *like* just a habit. DELETE *like.* ■ *Like*, you can't really overuse words. DELETE *Like.* ■ My mom said, "Why not circulate a petition and see what happens," which is what I did, but, *like*, I still can't believe it worked. DELETE *like.*

(know) (her) like a book An insipid simile. *altogether; completely; entirely; fully; perfectly; quite; roundly; thoroughly; totally; unreservedly; utterly; wholly.*

(works) like a charm An insipid simile. *accurately; easily; exactly; excellently; faultlessly; flawlessly; flowingly; impeccably; indefectibly; methodically; perfectly; precisely; regularly; smoothly; systematically; well.*

like a deer caught in the headlights An insipid simile. *afraid; alarmed; anxious; apprehensive; fearful; frightened; panicky; scared; terrified; timid; timorous.*

■ Tom looked *like a deer caught in the headlights.* REPLACE WITH *terrified.*

> Mark was fiddling with a brightly colored train, but, every so often, he glanced up at the television with the fascination of a rabbit caught in the headlights. — Elizabeth Buchan, *Revenge of the Middle-Aged Woman*

(take to it) like a duck to water An insipid simile. *easily; effortlessly; fluently; naturally; smoothly; with ease.*

(fits) like a glove An insipid simile. *accurately; easily; exactly; excellently; faultlessly; flawlessly; flowingly; impeccably; indefectibly; methodically; perfectly; precisely; regularly; smoothly; systematically; well.* ■ By having a single, reliable technology solution that fits all of our companies *like a glove,* we are delivering the best technology at the best price to our associates. REPLACE WITH *faultlessly.*

like a hole in the head An insipid simile. *by no means; hardly; in no way; not at all; not in any way; not in the least; scarcely.*

> Kate needed water like a hole in the head. Whisky: that might just help. — Judith Cutler, *Power on Her Own*

(go over) like a lead balloon An insipid simile. *badly; poorly; unsatisfactorily; unsuccessfully.*

like clockwork An insipid simile. *accurately; easily; exactly; excellently; faultlessly; flawlessly; flowingly; impeccably; indefectibly; methodically; perfectly; precisely; regularly; smoothly; systematically; well.*

like comparing dollars to doughnuts A moribund metaphor (see page 21). *different; discordant; discrepant; dissimilar; dissonant; divergent; incommensurable; incommensurate; incomparable; incompatible; incongruent; incongruous; inconsistent; inconsonant; inharmonious; unlike.*

like crazy (mad) An insipid simile. 1. *actively; aggressively; dynamically; emphatically; energetically; ferociously; fervently; fiercely; forcefully; frantically; frenziedly; furiously; hard; intensely; intently; mightily; passionately; powerfully; robustly; savagely; spiritedly; strenuously; strongly; vehemently; viciously; vigorously; violently; wildly; with vigor;* 2. *ardently; devotedly; eagerly; enthusiastically; fervently; fervidly; passionately; spiritedly; zealously.* 3. *hastily; hurriedly; posthaste; promptly; quickly; rapidly; speedily; swiftly; very fast; wingedly.* ■ He is also eating *like crazy.* REPLACE WITH *zealously.*

like hell An insipid simile. 1. *actively; aggressively; dynamically; emphatically; energetically; ferociously; fervently; fiercely; forcefully; frantically; frenziedly; furiously; hard; intensely; intently; mightily; passionately; powerfully; robustly; savagely; spiritedly; strenuously; strongly; vehemently; viciously; vigorously; violently; wildly; with vigor.* 2. *ardently; devotedly; eagerly; enthusiastically; fervently; fervidly; passionately; spiritedly; zealously.* 3. *hastily; hurriedly; posthaste; promptly; quickly; rapidly; speedily; swiftly; very fast; wingedly.*

(selling) like hotcakes An insipid simile. *briskly; fast; quickly; rapidly; speedily; swiftly; very well; wingedly.* ■ Their current album is selling *like hotcakes.* REPLACE WITH *swiftly.*

like it's going out of style An insipid simile. 1. *actively; aggressively; dynamically; emphatically; energetically; ferociously; fervently; fiercely; forcefully; frantically; frenziedly; furiously; hard; intensely; intently; mightily; passionately; powerfully; robustly; savagely; spiritedly; strenuously; strongly; vehemently; viciously; vigorously; violently; wildly; with vigor.* 2. *hastily; hurriedly; posthaste; promptly; quickly; rapidly; speedily; swiftly; very fast; wingedly.* ■ I've been taking aspirin *like it's going out of style.* REPLACE WITH *aggressively.* SEE ALSO *like there's no tomorrow.*

like (a streak of; greased) lightning An insipid simile. *abruptly; apace; at once; briskly; directly; expeditiously; fast; forthwith; hastily; hurriedly; immediately; instantaneously; instantly; posthaste; promptly; quickly; rapidly; rashly; right away; speedily; straightaway; swiftly; wingedly.*

(works) like magic An insipid simile. *amazingly; astonishingly; astoundingly; extraordinarily; inexplicably; magically; miraculously; mysteriously; phenomenally; remarkably; wondrously.*

like nobody's business An insipid simile. 1. *beautifully; brilliantly; consummately; dazzlingly; excellently; exceptionally; expertly; exquisitely; extraordinarily; fabulously; flawlessly; grandly; magnificently; marvelously; perfectly; remarkably; splendidly; superbly; superlatively; supremely; transcendently; very well; wonderfully; wondrously.* 2. *actively; aggressively; dynamically; emphatically; energetically; ferociously; fervently; fiercely; forcefully; frantically; frenziedly; furiously; hard; intensely; intently; mightily; passionately; powerfully; robustly; savagely; spiritedly; strenuously; strongly; vehemently; viciously; vigorously; violently; wildly; with vigor.* ■ Here was the one and only Kronos Quartet in town again, playing — as always — *like nobody's business.* REPLACE WITH *superbly.* ■ He can play the piano *like nobody's business.* REPLACE WITH *beautifully.*

like seeing (looking) ... through rose-colored glasses A moribund metaphor (see page 21). *hopeful; optimistic; pollyanna; pollyannaish; positive; roseate; sanguine; upbeat.* ■ Life then becomes *like seeing the world through rose-colored glasses*: beautiful and warm. REPLACE WITH *pollyannish.*

(sounds) like something out of a novel An insipid simile.

> Bluey had started by thinking they were like something out of a novel herself, the sort of novel set in another, intriguing age and society. — Joanna Trollope, *The Men and the Girls*

like the back of (my) hand An insipid simile. *altogether; completely; entirely; fully; perfectly; quite; roundly; thoroughly; totally; unreservedly; utterly; wholly.*

like there's no tomorrow An insipid simile. 1. *actively; aggressively; dynamically; emphatically; energetically; ferociously; fervently; fiercely; forcefully; frantically; frenziedly; furiously; hard; intensely; intently; mightily; passionately; powerfully; robustly; savagely; spiritedly; strenuously; strongly; vehemently; viciously; vigorously; violently; wildly; with vigor.* 2. *hastily; hurriedly; posthaste; promptly; quickly; rapidly; speedily; swiftly; very fast; wingedly.* SEE ALSO *like it's going out of style.*

like the shifting sands An insipid simile. *brief; ephemeral; evanescent; fleeting; flitting; fugacious; fugitive; impermanent; momentary; passing; short; short-lived; temporary; transient; transitory; volatile.*

like watching paint dry An insipid simile. *anodyne; banal; barren; bland; boring; deadly; dreary; dry; dull; everyday; flat; humdrum; inanimate; insipid; jejune; lifeless; lusterless; mediocre; monotonous; prosaic; routine; spiritless; stale; tedious; tiresome; unexciting; uninteresting; vapid; wearisome.*

like watching the grass grow An insipid simile. 1. *anodyne; banal; barren; bland; boring; deadly; dreary; dry; dull; everyday; flat; humdrum; inanimate; insipid; jejune; lifeless; lusterless; mediocre; monotonous; prosaic; routine; spiritless; stale; tedious; tiresome; unexciting; uninteresting; vapid; wearisome.* 2. *crawling; dallying; dawdling; deliberate; dilatory; faltering; hesitant; laggardly; lagging; leisurely; methodical; plodding; procrastinating; slothful; slow; slow-paced; sluggardly; sluggish; snaillike; systematic; tardy; tortoiselike; unhurried.*

like water An insipid simile. *abundantly; copiously; freely; generously; liberally; profusely; unreservedly.*

> It might seem strange that a successful Hollywood lady would go for a nomadic gent who ran through passports like water, could spout off funny if lewd phrases in thirty languages, and never would be financially secure. — David Baldacci, *The Christmas Train*

like water (rolling) off a duck's back An insipid simile. *to no avail; with no result; without effect.*

like wildfire An insipid simile. 1. *briskly; fast; hastily; hurriedly; quickly; promptly; rapidly; speedily; swiftly.* 2. *actively; aggressively; dynamically; emphatically; energetically; ferociously; fervently; fiercely; forcefully; frantically; frenziedly; furiously; hard; intensely; intently; mightily; passionately; powerfully; robustly; savagely; spiritedly; strenuously; strongly; vehemently; viciously; vigorously; violently; wildly; with vigor.*

(draw [a] the) line in the sand A moribund metaphor (see page 21). *border; bound; boundary; frontier; limit; perimeter.*

> For the time being he could see the line in the sand: on one side of it, all he had; on the other, all he'd lose. — Martin Amis, *Yellow Dog*

line of fire A moribund metaphor (see page 21).

lines are drawn A moribund metaphor (see page 21).

lining (his) pockets A moribund metaphor (see page 21).

link together A wretched redundancy (see page 25). *link.* ■ This business will *link together* the telephone, the television, and the computer. DELETE *together.*

(the) lion's share A moribund metaphor (see page 21). *almost all; most; much; nearly all.* ■ The company was late to develop HMOs, and it let competitors grab *the lion's share* of the market. REPLACE WITH *most.*

(my) lips are sealed A moribund metaphor (see page 21).

liquid refreshment An infantile phrase (see page 20). *beverage; drink; refreshment.*

litany of complaints A moribund metaphor (see page 21).

literary event A suspect superlative (see page 24).

(a) little bird told me An infantile phrase (see page 20).

(the) little boy's (girl's) room An infantile phrase (see page 20). *bathroom; lavatory; restroom; toilet.*

(like) (the) little engine (that could) An insipid simile.

(a) little (honesty) goes a long way A popular prescription (see page 23).

(a) little knowledge is a dangerous thing A popular prescription (see page 23).

little old lady from Dubuque A moribund metaphor (see page 21). *boor; bumpkin; commoner; common man; common person; conventional person; peasant; philistine; pleb; plebeian; vulgarian; yokel.* ■ By the time the contest was over, *little old ladies in Dubuque* could probably discourse on the subject.

(the) little woman An infantile phrase (see page 20). *consort; helpmate; helpmeet; mate; spouse; wife.*

lit to the gills A moribund metaphor (see page 21). *besotted; crapulous; drunk; inebriated; intoxicated; sodden; stupefied; tipsy.*

lit up like a Christmas tree An insipid simile.

live and learn A popular prescription (see page 23).

live and let live A popular prescription (see page 23).

live as though each day were your last A popular prescription (see page 23).

live dangerously A popular prescription (see page 23).

live each day to the fullest A popular prescription (see page 23).

live for the moment A popular prescription (see page 23).

live happily ever after A suspect superlative (see page 24).

live high off (on) the hog A moribund metaphor (see page 21).

live in a pigsty A moribund metaphor (see page 21).

live one day at a time A popular prescription (see page 23).

live wire A moribund metaphor (see page 21). *card; character; eccentric; exception; original.*

(learn to) live with it A popular prescription (see page 23).

(a) living hell A moribund metaphor (see page 21). *chthonian; chthonic; hellish; impossible; infernal; insufferable; insupportable; intolerable; painful; plutonic; sulfurous; unbearable; uncomfortable; unendurable; unpleasant; stygian; tartarean.*

The force and colorfulness of this metaphor is no longer evident. An uncommonly used word — such as *chthonic, insupportable, plutonic, sulfurous, stygian,* or *tartarean* — is often more potent and captivating than a commonly used metaphor. SEE ALSO *hell on earth.*

(a) living legend A suspect superlative (see page 24).

loaded for bear A moribund metaphor (see page 21). 1. *eager; prepared; primed; ready; set.* 2. *angry; bad-tempered; bilious; cantankerous; choleric; churlish; crabby; cranky; cross; curmudgeonly; disagreeable; dyspeptic; grouchy; gruff; grumpy; ill-humored; ill-tempered; irascible; irritable; mad; peevish; petulant; quarrelsome; riled; roiled; short-tempered; splenetic; surly; testy; vexed.*

lo and behold A withered word (see page 24).

location, location, location An infantile phrase (see page 20).

lock horns with A moribund metaphor (see page 21). *battle; brawl; clash; fight; grapple; jostle; make war; scuffle; skirmish; tussle; war; wrestle.*

lock, stock, and barrel A moribund metaphor (see page 21). *aggregate; all; all things; entirety; everything; gross; lot; sum; total; totality; whole.*

long and hard A torpid term (see page 24). *aggressively; dynamically; emphatically; energetically; ferociously; fervently; fiercely; forcefully; frantically; frenziedly; furiously; hard; intensely; intently; mightily; passionately; powerfully; robustly; savagely; spiritedly; strenuously; strongly; vehemently; viciously; vigorously; violently; wildly; with vigor.* ■ The compromise would be a partial victory for Baybanks, which has fought *long and hard* against the legislation. REPLACE WITH *mightily.*

(the) long and (the) short of (it) A wretched redundancy (see page 25). *basis; center; core; crux; essence; gist; heart; kernel; pith; substance.*

long in the tooth A moribund metaphor (see page 21). *aged; aging; ancient; antediluvian; antique; archaic; elderly; hoary; hoary-headed; old; patriarchal; prehistoric; seasoned; superannuated.*

> Notice these are all attractive, smart, funny women who happen to be a little long in the tooth. — Patricia Gaffney, *The Saving Graces*

long overdue An inescapable pair (see page 20). ■ This legislation is *long overdue.*

long road ahead A moribund metaphor (see page 21).

(a) long shot A moribund metaphor (see page 21). *doubtful; dubious; far-fetched; implausible; improbable; remote; unlikely; unrealistic.* ■ Something that might happen is *a longer shot* than something that may happen. REPLACE WITH *less likely.*

long time no see An infantile phrase (see page 20).

look a fright A moribund metaphor (see page 21). *disheveled; dowdy; frowzy; messy; ragged; run-down; scruffy; seedy; shabby; sloppy; slovenly; tattered; tousled; unkempt; untidy.*

(don't) look a gift horse in the mouth A popular prescription (see page 23).

look before you leap A popular prescription (see page 23). *be careful; be cautious; be circumspect; be prudent; be safe; be wary.*

look down (her) nose (at) A moribund metaphor (see page 21). *contemn; deride; despise; detest; disdain; jeer at; laugh at; mock; ridicule; scoff at; scorn; shun; slight; sneer; snub; spurn.*

look into a crystal ball A moribund metaphor (see page 21). *forecast; foreshadow; foretell; portend; predict; prefigure; presage; prognosticate; prophesy.*

look like a drowned rat An insipid simile. *bedraggled; drenched; dripping; saturated; soaked; sopping; wet.*

look over (our) shoulders A moribund metaphor (see page 21). *be anxious; be apprehensive; be fearful; be frightened; be insecure; be nervous; be panicky; be scared; be timid; be timorous; be uneasy.*

looks aren't everything A popular prescription (see page 23).

(take a) look see A infantile phrase. This phrase is one of the new illiteracies. Expressions like *a good read, a must have,* and *a look see* are favored today by the "illiterati" — smart, articulate people who find it fashionable to speak unintelligibly. SEE ALSO *a good read; (a) must have; (a) must see; a (must) read.*

(she) looks like a million bucks (dollars) An insipid simile. 1. *appealing; attractive; beautiful; becoming; captivating; comely; cute; dazzling; exquisite; fair; fetching; good-looking; gorgeous; handsome; lovely; nice-looking; pleasing; pretty; pulchritudinous; radiant; ravishing; seemly; stunning.* 2. *energetic; fine; fit; good; hale; hardy; healthful; healthy; hearty; robust; sound; strong; vigorous; well.* 3. *affluent; moneyed; opulent; prosperous; rich; successful; wealthy; well-off; well-to-do.*

look the other way A moribund metaphor (see page 21). *brush aside; avoid; discount; disregard; dodge; duck; ignore; neglect; omit; pass over; recoil from; shrink from; shun; shy away from; turn away from; withdraw from.*

look what the tide brought in A moribund metaphor (see page 21).

look who's talking An infantile phrase (see page 20).

look what (who) the cat dragged in A moribund metaphor (see page 21).

loose cannon A moribund metaphor (see page 21). *capricious; changeable; erratic; fickle; fluctuating; inconsistent; inconstant; mercurial; unpredictable; unstable; unsteady; variable; volatile; wavering.*

lose (her) head (over) A moribund metaphor (see page 21). 1. *alarm; appall; benumb; daunt; frighten; horrify;*

intimidate; panic; paralyze; petrify; scare; shock; startle; terrify; terrorize. 2. *infatuated.*

lose (his) marbles (mind) A moribund metaphor (see page 21). *batty; cracked; crazy; daft; demented; deranged; fey; foolish; goofy; insane; lunatic; mad; maniacal; neurotic; nuts; nutty; psychotic; raving; silly; squirrelly; touched; unbalanced; unhinged; unsound; wacky; zany.*

> I'd had older men look at me that way since I'd lost my baby fat, but they usually didn't lose their marbles over me when I was wearing my royal blue parka and yellow elephant bell-bottoms — Alice Sebold, *The Lovely Bones*

lose steam A moribund metaphor (see page 21).

(a) losing battle A moribund metaphor (see page 21). *hopeless; impossible; incurable; irreclaimable; irredeemable; irremediable; irreparable; irretrievable; remediless.*

> And now the dog was dead, and Morris was saying that, as the dog should have known, his was a losing battle, and that that not given in love would be redressed in blood. — David Mamet, *The Old Religion*

lost in the shuffle A moribund metaphor (see page 21). *be discounted; be disregarded; be forgotten; be ignored; be neglected; be omitted; be passed over; be shunned.* ■ There is so much to teach that is writing related, that sometimes the writing itself can *get lost in the shuffle.* REPLACE WITH *be neglected.*

(a) lot of times A wretched redundancy (see page 25). *frequently; often.* ■ *A lot of times* people have a tendency to think that others are controlling their destiny. REPLACE WITH *Often.*

loud and clear An inescapable pair (see page 20). *apparent; audible; clear; conspicuous; definite; distinct; emphatic; evident; explicit; graphic; lucid; manifest; obvious; patent; pellucid; plain; sharp; translucent; transparent; unambiguous; uncomplex; uncomplicated; understandable; unequivocal; unmistakable; vivid.*

love and cherish An inescapable pair (see page 20).

love conquers all A popular prescription (see page 23).

love is blind A quack equation (see page 23).

love it or leave it An infantile phrase (see page 20).

love moves mountains A moribund metaphor (see page 21).

low blow A moribund metaphor (see page 21). *dishonorable; foul; inequitable; unconscientious; underhanded; unethical; unfair; unjust; unprincipled; unscrupulous; unsportsmanlike.*

lower the boom A moribund metaphor (see page 21). 1. *admonish; animadvert; berate; castigate; censure; chasten; chastise; chide; condemn; criticize; denounce; denunciate; discipline; excoriate; fulminate against; imprecate; impugn; inveigh against; objurgate; punish; rebuke; remonstrate; reprehend; reprimand; reproach; reprobate; reprove; revile; scold; swear at;*

upbraid; vituperate. 2. *abort; annul; arrest; cancel; cease; check; conclude; derail; discontinue; end; halt; nullify; quash; quell; revoke; squelch; stop; suspend; terminate.*

lowest common denominator A torpid term (see page 24). For some — copycat journalists, delicate marketing people, and feeble-minded social scientists perhaps — *lowest common denominator* is a long-winded, short-sighted way of avoiding more telling words.

■ Instead of disseminating the best in our culture, television too often panders to the *lowest common denominator.* REPLACE WITH *worst.* ■ If you fear making anyone mad, then you ultimately probe for the *lowest common denominator* of human achievement. REPLACE WITH *nadir.* ■ In that environment, each show tried to appeal to the *lowest common denominator.* REPLACE WITH *masses.* ■ The J.D. InterPrizes' *lowest common denominator* design concept allows for the widest possible viewing audience. REPLACE WITH *readily accessible.* ■ So movies must imitate the familiar and be pitched to the *lowest common denominator,* causing most of them to be flat, stale and familiar. REPLACE WITH *dull-minded.*

low (man) on the totem pole A moribund metaphor (see page 21). *inferior; junior; lesser; low ranking; minor; second rate; secondary; subordinate.* ■ If you're a freshman member, regardless of what party you're in, you're *low on the totem pole* to be sure. REPLACE WITH *low ranking.*

> Everyone in Emerson House had a job of some sort, and as low man on the totem pole Cal got the job nobody else wanted: dishwasher. — Orland Outland, *Different People*

(a) lump in (her) throat A moribund metaphor (see page 21).

M

(as) mad as a hatter An insipid simile. *batty; cracked; crazy; daft; demented; deranged; fey; foolish; goofy; insane; lunatic; mad; maniacal; neurotic; nuts; nutty; psychotic; raving; silly; squirrelly; touched; unbalanced; unhinged; unsound; wacky; zany.*

(as) mad as a hornet An insipid simile. *angry; berserk; convulsive; crazed; delirious; demented; demoniac; deranged; enraged; feral; ferocious; fierce; frantic; frenzied; fuming; furious; hysterical; infuriated; in hysterics; insane; incensed; irate; mad; maddened; maniacal; murderous; possessed; rabid; raging; ranting; raving; savage; seething; wild; wrathful.*

> She always wanted to get to the game in time to hear the National Anthem, and she'd get mad as a hornet at Irv when he'd insist they leave early to beat the bridge traffic if the game was in hand one way or the other. — Pam Houston, *Sight Hound*

(as) mad as a March hare An insipid simile. *batty; cracked; crazy; daft; demented; deranged; fey; foolish; goofy; insane; lunatic; mad; maniacal; neurotic; nuts; nutty; psychotic; raving; silly; squirrelly; touched; unbalanced; unhinged; unsound; wacky; zany.*

(as) mad as a wet hen An insipid simile. *angry; berserk; convulsive; crazed; delirious; demented; demoniac; deranged; enraged; feral; ferocious; fierce; frantic; frenzied; fuming; furious; hysterical; infuriated; in hysterics; insane; incensed; irate; mad; maddened; maniacal; murderous; possessed; rabid; raging; ranting; raving; savage; seething; wild; wrathful.*

(he) made (me) an offer (I) couldn't refuse An infantile phrase (see page 20). ■ We'd still be here today if Bally's hadn't *made us an offer we couldn't refuse.*

(you) made my day A plebeian sentiment (see page 23). Often a response to being complimented, *you made my day* appeals to the mass of people who rely on others for their opinion of themselves.

And if they embrace others' approval, so they bow to their criticism.

made of money A moribund metaphor (see page 21). *affluent; moneyed; opulent; prosperous; rich; successful; wealthy; well-off; well-to-do.*

magic bullet A moribund metaphor (see page 21). *answer; solution.*

(the) main event A moribund metaphor (see page 21).

major An overworked word (see page 22). For example: *major blow; major breakthrough; major commitment; major concern; major consideration; major defeat; major disaster; major new writer; major opportunity; major player; major ramifications; major road block; major setback; major thrust.*

(a) (the) ... majority (of) A torpid term (see page 24). This phrase and others like it — *a large majority; an overwhelming majority; the vast majority* — are indispensable to those who luxuriate in circumlocutory language. They seldom mean more than an unpretentious *almost all, most,* or *nearly all.* ■ *The vast majority* of those people don't receive death sentences. REPLACE WITH *Most.* ■ Within two years, *the overwhelming majority of* Americans will have health coverage. REPLACE WITH *nearly all.* ■ *A large majority of* the participatory lenders have now joined the major banks in supporting our plan. REPLACE WITH *Almost all.* SEE ALSO *a ... number (of).*

make a clean breast of A moribund metaphor (see page 21). *acknowledge; admit; affirm; allow; avow; concede; confess; disclose; divulge; expose; grant; own; reveal; tell; uncover; unveil.*

make a concerted effort A wretched redundancy (see page 25). *aim; attempt; endeavor; essay; labor; moil; seek; strive; toil; try; undertake; venture; work.* ■ True change will come only when those in power *make a concerted effort* to promote large numbers of women and blacks to high-status jobs. REPLACE WITH *try.*

make a conscious attempt (effort) A wretched redundancy (see page 25). *aim; attempt; endeavor; essay; labor; moil;*

seek; strive; toil; try; undertake; venture; work. ■ We *made a conscious effort* not to do what most companies do. REPLACE WITH *strived.* ■ Wash your hands and *make conscious attempts* not to touch your face, nose, and eyes. REPLACE WITH *try.*

make a conscious choice (decision) A wretched redundancy (see page 25). *Make a conscious choice* means no more than *choose*, and *make a conscious decision* no more than *decide*. Of course, this phrase suggests that those who use it may not otherwise be conscious of what they choose or decide, or even, it could be, do or say. ■ We *made a conscious decision* that this sort of legal terrorism would not affect the way we operate. REPLACE WITH *decided.* ■ They *made a conscious choice* not to have any bedroom scenes in this movie. REPLACE WITH *chose.* SEE ALSO *make an informed choice (decision).*

make a decision A wretched redundancy (see page 25). *conclude; decide; determine; resolve.* ■ It's difficult to *make a decision* at this time. REPLACE WITH *decide.* ■ If he *made a decision* not to use protection, he should *make a decision* to support the child. REPLACE WITH *resolved* and *resolve.*

make a determination A wretched redundancy (see page 25). *conclude; decide; determine; resolve.* ■ We want the SJC to look at it and *make a determination* to clearly state what is permissible and impermissible. REPLACE WITH *determine.*

make a difference (about; on) A suspect superlative (see page 24). Many of us speak of making a difference, some of us strive to make a difference, and few of us succeed in making a difference. 1. *be climacteric; be consequential; be considerable; be critical; be crucial; be effective; be effectual; be helpful; be important; be significant; be useful; be vital; count; matter.* 2. *act on; affect; bear on; influence; sway; work on.* 3. *aid; assist; help.* ■ She is part of a great tradition in U.S. society, in which ordinary individuals voice their concerns in order to *make a difference about* issues that matter to them. REPLACE WITH *influence.* ■ You need to have a sense of humor and to recognize that there's hope, not only despair, in the world — and you need to know that you can *make a difference.* REPLACE WITH *be helpful.* ■ Your answers are important, and they do *make a difference.* REPLACE WITH *matter.*

make a federal case out of A moribund metaphor (see page 21). *elaborate; embellish; embroider; enhance; enlarge; exaggerate; hyperbolize; inflate; magnify; overdo; overreact; overstress; overstate; strain; stretch.*

make a getaway A moribund metaphor (see page 21). *abscond; clear out; decamp; depart; desert; disappear; escape; exit; flee; fly; go; go away; leave; move on; part; pull out; quit; retire; retreat; run away; take flight; take off; vacate; vanish; withdraw.*

make a monkey out of A moribund metaphor (see page 21). *abase; chasten; debase; degrade; demean; deride; disgrace; dishonor; dupe; embarrass; humble; humiliate; mock; mortify; ridicule; shame.*

> You make a money out of one of them and he jumps on your back and stays there for life, but let one make a money out of you and all

you can do is kill him or disappear. — Flannery O'Connor, *Everything That Rises Must Converge*

make a mountain out of a molehill A moribund metaphor (see page 21). *elaborate; embellish; embroider; enhance; enlarge; exaggerate; hyperbolize; inflate; magnify; overdo; overreact; overstress; overstate; strain; stretch.*

make an informed choice (decision) A wretched redundancy (see page 25). *choose; decide.* SEE ALSO *make a conscious choice (decision).*

make a pig of (myself) A moribund metaphor (see page 21). *cloy; cram; glut; gorge; overdo; overeat; overfeed; overindulge; sate; satiate; stuff; surfeit.*

make a quick exit A moribund metaphor (see page 21). *abscond; clear out; decamp; depart; desert; disappear; escape; exit; flee; fly; go; go away; leave; move on; part; pull out; quit; retire; retreat; run away; take flight; take off; vacate; vanish; withdraw.*

make a silk purse out of a sow's ear A moribund metaphor (see page 21).

make (my) blood boil A moribund metaphor (see page 21). *acerbate; anger; annoy; bother; bristle; chafe; enrage; incense; inflame; infuriate; irk; irritate; madden; miff; provoke; rile; roil; vex.*

make (both) ends meet A moribund metaphor (see page 21). *economize; endure; exist; live; manage; subsist; survive.* ■ Older people are having a tough enough time trying to *make ends meet.* REPLACE WITH *survive.*

make eyes at A moribund metaphor (see page 21). *flirt.*

make false statements A wretched redundancy (see page 25). *lie.* ■ The indictment alleges that he *made false statements* to the FEC and obstructed proceedings. REPLACE WITH *lied.*

make (my) flesh creep (crawl) A moribund metaphor (see page 21). *alarm; appall; disgust; frighten; horrify; nauseate; panic; repel; repulse; revolt; scare; shock; sicken; startle; terrify.*

make (my) hair stand on end A moribund metaphor (see page 21). *alarm; appall; disgust; frighten; horrify; nauseate; panic; repel; repulse; revolt; scare; shock; sicken; startle; terrify.*

make hay while the sun shines A moribund metaphor (see page 21). *capitalize on; exploit; take advantage.*

make heads or tails of A moribund metaphor (see page 21). *appreciate; apprehend; comprehend; discern; fathom; grasp; know; make sense of; perceive; realize; recognize; see; understand.* ■ His failures in punctuation make it almost impossible to *make heads or tails of* his convoluted sentences. REPLACE WITH *understand.*

make it big A moribund metaphor (see page 21). *prevail; succeed; triumph; win.*

make mincemeat (out) of A moribund metaphor (see page 21). *crush; defeat; demolish; destroy; devastate; hammer; obliterate; overpower; overwhelm; rack; ravage; rout; ruin; shatter; slaughter; smash; thrash; undo; wrack; wreck.*

make no bones (about it) A moribund metaphor (see page 21). *avidly; eagerly; enthusiastically; heartily; promptly; readily; unconditionally; unhesitatingly; unreservedly; unwaveringly; wholeheartedly.*

> She made no bones about accepting her client's invitation to dine, and showed no surprise when he confidentially murmured that he had a little proposition to put before her. — Dorothy L. Sayers, *Strong Poison*

make no mistake (about it) An ineffectual phrase (see page 19). ■ *Make no mistake about it,* if we were to leave, other nations would leave, too, and chaos would resume. ■ *Make no mistake,* Jacksonville is not a bad team. ■ *Make no mistake about it,* this impeachment issue has become a battle for who controls the Republican party. SEE ALSO *let there be no mistake.*

make (yourself) scarce An infantile phrase (see page 20). *abscond; clear out; decamp; depart; desert; disappear; escape; exit; flee; fly; go; go away; leave; move on; part; pull out; quit; retire; retreat; run away; take flight; take off; vacate; vanish; withdraw.*

make (me) see red A moribund metaphor (see page 21). *acerbate; anger; annoy; bother; bristle; chafe; enrage; incense; inflame; infuriate; irk; irritate; madden; miff; provoke; rile; roil; vex.*

(try to) make the best (most) of it A popular prescription (see page 23).

make the feathers (fur) fly A moribund metaphor (see page 21). *battle; brawl; clash; fight; grapple; jostle; make war; scuffle; skirmish; tussle; war; wrestle; wrangle.*

> When the flying fur from the divorce settled, I found myself with a grown daughter, a full-time university job (after years of part-time teaching), a modest securities portfolio, and an entire future to invent. — Frances Mayes, *Under the Tuscan Sun*

make the grade A moribund metaphor (see page 21). 1. *accomplish; achieve; make good; succeed.* 2. *be able; be accomplished; be adept; be adequate; be capable; be competent; be deft; be equal to; be equipped; be fitted; be proficient; be qualified; be skilled; be skillful; be suited; measure up.*

make up (his) mind A wretched redundancy (see page 25). *choose; conclude; decide; determine; pick; resolve; select; settle.*

make tracks A moribund metaphor (see page 21). *abscond; clear out; decamp; depart; desert; disappear; escape; exit; flee; fly; go; go away; leave; move on; part; pull out; quit; retire; retreat; run away; take flight; take off; vacate; vanish; withdraw.*

make waves A moribund metaphor (see page 21). *agitate; disrupt; disturb; perturb; rattle; ruffle; shake up; stir up; unsettle.*

(a) man's home is his castle A popular prescription (see page 23).

(the) man in the street A moribund metaphor (see page 21). *citizen; commoner; everyman; pleb; plebeian; vulgarian.*

(the) manner (means; mechanism; method; procedure; process) by (in) which A wretched redundancy (see page 25). These magisterial-sounding phrases should be replaced by one of the least stately of words: *how.* ■ I'm not going to discuss *the methods by which* we achieved that. REPLACE WITH *how.* ■ The philosophical methodology specifies *the procedure by which* concepts will be used to construct a theory. REPLACE WITH *how.* ■ It does less well in explaining *the process by which* a particular firm decides to implement a price change. REPLACE WITH *how.* ■ Virtually all of them have been critical of *the manner in which* the administration dealt with the situation. REPLACE WITH *how.*

(the) man who came to dinner An infantile phrase (see page 20).

many of my closest friends (are) A plebeian sentiment (see page 23). ■ *Many of my closest friends* are Italian.

marching orders A moribund metaphor (see page 21).

(a) marriage made in heaven A suspect superlative (see page 24). *ideal; model; perfect; wonderful.*

mass exodus A wretched redundancy (see page 25). *exodus.*

(it's a) matter of life and death A moribund metaphor (see page 21). *critical; crucial; essential; imperative; important; necessary; pressing; urgent; vital.*

maybe, maybe not An infantile phrase (see page 20).

maybe yes, maybe no An infantile phrase (see page 20).

may (might) possibly A wretched redundancy (see page 25). *may (might).* ■ I *might possibly* be there when you are. DELETE *possibly.*

mea culpa A foreign phrase (see page 19).

meal ticket A moribund metaphor (see page 21).

meaningful An overworked word (see page 22). So elusive is meaning in our lives that we think we must modify scores of words with the word *meaningful.* Though we may struggle not to believe that emptiness is all, attaching *meaningful* to words like *action, change, dialogue, discussion, experience* is no sound solution. *Meaningful* describes that which has meaning, and derides that which has none. SEE ALSO *significant.*

(...) means never having to say you're sorry An infantile phrase (see page 20).

meat and potatoes A moribund metaphor (see page 21). *basal; basic; elementary; essential; fundamental; primary; rudimentary.*

(the) medium is the message A quack equation (see page 23).

(as) meek as a lamb An insipid simile. *accepting; accommodating; acquiescent; complacent; complaisant; compliant; cowed; deferential; docile; dutiful; easy; forbearing; gentle; humble; long-suffering; meek; mild; obedient; passive; patient; prostrate; quiet; reserved; resigned; stoical;*

submissive; subservient; timid; tolerant; tractable; unassuming; uncomplaining; yielding.

(as) meek as Moses An insipid simile. *accepting; accommodating; acquiescent; complacent; complaisant; compliant; cowed; deferential; docile; dutiful; easy; forbearing; gentle; humble; long-suffering; meek; mild; obedient; passive; patient; prostrate; quiet; reserved; resigned; stoical; submissive; subservient; timid; tolerant; tractable; unassuming; uncomplaining; yielding.*

> Having embarrassed himself, he went in, meek as Moses, to the Judge. — Carson McCullers, *Clock Without Hands*

(the) meek shall inherit the earth A popular prescription (see page 23).

meeting of (the) minds A moribund metaphor (see page 21). *accord; accordance; agreement; common view; compatibility; concord; concordance; concurrence; consensus; harmony; unanimity; understanding; unison; unity.* ■ We're talking to him to see if we can have a *meeting of minds*. REPLACE WITH *agreement.*

meet (his) Waterloo A moribund metaphor (see page 21).

meet your maker A moribund metaphor (see page 21). *die.*

me, myself, and I An infantile phrase (see page 20).

mend fences A moribund metaphor (see page 21). *reconcile.* ■ Please continue to tell your readers it's never too late to try to *mend those fences*. REPLACE WITH *reconcile.*

(the) men in white coats A moribund metaphor (see page 21).

meteoric rise An inescapable pair (see page 20). ■ His approach has struck a chord with the American people — hence his unprecedented and *meteoric rise* to prominence.

methodology A torpid term (see page 24). A favorite among dimwitted academicians, this polysyllabic word means no more than *method*. ■ How did research *methodologies* change over time in the articles of the *American Journal of Psychology* between 1887 and 1930? REPLACE WITH *methods.*

Mickey-Mouse An infantile phrase (see page 20). *inferior; poor; second-class; second-rate; shoddy; subordinate; substandard.*

(the) Midas touch A moribund metaphor (see page 21).

middle-of-the-road A moribund metaphor (see page 21). 1. *average; common; conservative; conventional; everyday; mediocre; middling; normal; ordinary; quotidian; second-rate; standard; traditional; typical; uneventful; unexceptional; unremarkable; usual.* 2. *careful; cautious; circumspect; prudent; safe; wary.*

might makes right A popular prescription (see page 23).

(a) mile a minute A moribund metaphor (see page 21). *apace; briskly; expeditiously; fast; hastily; hurriedly; posthaste; quickly; rapidly; speedily; swiftly; wingedly.*

(a) mile wide and an inch deep A moribund metaphor (see page 21). 1. *blowhard; boaster; braggadocio; braggart; know-it-all; showoff; swaggerer; trumpeter; windbag.* 2. *glib; silver-tongued; slick; smooth-tongued.*

(the) milk of human kindness A moribund metaphor (see page 21). *commiseration; compassion; sympathy; understanding.*

milk the last drop out of A moribund metaphor (see page 21).

(a) million miles away A moribund metaphor (see page 21). *absent; absent-minded; absorbed; abstracted; bemused; captivated; daydreaming; detached; distracted; distrait; dreamy; engrossed; enraptured; faraway; fascinated; immersed; inattentive; lost; mesmerized; oblivious; preoccupied; rapt; spellbound.*

millstone around (my) neck A moribund metaphor (see page 21). *burden; duty; encumbrance; hardship; hindrance; impediment; obligation; obstacle; obstruction; onus; responsibility.*

(has a) mind like a sieve An insipid simile. *forgetful; heedless; inattentive; lethean; neglectful; negligent; oblivious; remiss; thoughtless; unmindful; unthinking.*

mind like a steel trap An insipid simile. *adroit; astute; bright; brilliant; clever; discerning; enlightened; insightful; intelligent; judicious; keen; knowledgeable; learned; logical; luminous; perceptive; perspicacious; quick; rational; reasonable; sagacious; sage; sapient; sensible; sharp; shrewd; smart; sound; understanding; wise.*

mind (your) P's and Q's A moribund metaphor (see page 21). *be accurate; be careful; be exact; be meticulous; be particular; be precise.*

mindset An overworked word (see page 22). *attitude; bent; bias; cast; disposition; habit; inclination; leaning; outlook; penchant; perspective; point of view; position; predilection; predisposition; prejudice; proclivity; slant; stand; standpoint; temperament; tendency; view; viewpoint; way of thinking.* ■ You don't have these huge organizations built on patronage anymore, but the *mindset* is still there. REPLACE WITH *predisposition.* ■ What we are doing is changing people's *mindset.* REPLACE WITH *views.* ■ The report is critical of the *mindset* of those in charge of the pipeline. REPLACE WITH *attitude.*

mind the store A moribund metaphor (see page 21).

mirabile dictu A foreign phrase (see page 19).

miracle of miracles An infantile phrase (see page 20). *astonishingly; astoundingly; breathtakingly; extraordinarily; fabulously; fantastically; marvelously; miraculously; overwhelmingly; prodigiously; sensationally; spectacularly; wonderfully; wondrously.*

■ *Miracle of miracles,* it works because of two things: Keanu Reeves and theology. REPLACE WITH *Miraculously.* ■ *Miracle of miracles,* in our second at-bat, with the brace strapped on tight, we homered against the Mets. REPLACE WITH *Amazingly.* ■ I was cleaning the house the other day, and, *miracle of miracles,* my kids were actually helping. REPLACE WITH *astonishingly.*

> And maybe if she closed her eyes she could see a time — miracle of miracles — when Helen Bober was enrolled here, not just a stranger on the run, pecking at a course or two at night, and tomorrow morning back at Levenspiel's Louisville Panties and Bras. — Bernard Malamud, *The Assistant*

misery loves company A popular prescription (see page 23).

mission accomplished An infantile phrase (see page 20).

a miss is as good as a mile A popular prescription (see page 23).

miss the boat A moribund metaphor (see page 21). *be deprived of; forego; forfeit; give up; lose out; miss out; sacrifice; surrender.* ■ If we define success in terms of material things, we *miss the boat.* REPLACE WITH *lose out.*

mix and mingle An inescapable pair (see page 20). *associate; consort; hobnob; fraternize; keep company; mingle; mix; socialize.*

mixed bag A moribund metaphor (see page 21).

> Usually he was entertained by Tokyo Station, the mixed bag of commuters in three-piece suits and farmers in cone-shaped hats of straw. — Martin Cruz Smith, *December 6*

moan and groan An inescapable pair (see page 20). *bawl; bemoan; bewail; blubber; cry; groan; moan; snivel; sob; wail; weep; whimper; whine.*

modus operandi A foreign phrase (see page 19).

modus vivendi A foreign phrase (see page 19).

Monday morning quarterback(ing) A moribund metaphor (see page 21).

money can't buy everything A popular prescription (see page 23).

(like) money in the bank An insipid simile. *absolute; assured; certain; definite; guaranteed; sure; sure-fire.*

money is the root of all evil A popular prescription (see page 23).

money (making) machine A moribund metaphor (see page 21).

money talks A moribund metaphor (see page 21).

money to burn A moribund metaphor (see page 21).

monkey on (my) back A moribund metaphor (see page 21). 1. *addiction; fixation; habit; obsession.* 2. *complication; difficulty; dilemma; mess; muddle; ordeal; pickle; plight; predicament; problem; quandary; trial; trouble.*

monkey see, monkey do An infantile phrase (see page 20).

(a) month of Sundays A moribund metaphor (see page 21). *ages; a long time; a long while; an age; an eternity; decades; eons; forever; months; years.*

mop (wipe) the floor with A moribund metaphor (see page 21). 1. *assail;*

assault; attack; batter; beat; cudgel; flagellate; flog; hit; lambaste; lash; lick; mangle; pound; pummel; strike; thrash; trample; trounce. 2. *beat; conquer; crush; defeat; outdo; overcome; overpower; overwhelm; prevail; quell; rout; subdue; succeed; triumph; trounce; vanquish; win.* ■ Amazon.com has *mopped the floor with* barnesandnoble.com. REPLACE WITH *routed.*

more is better A quack equation (see page 23).

more preferable A wretched redundancy (see page 25). *preferable.* ■ While the patient is still at risk to hemorrhage during that time, waiting may be *more preferable* to surgery. DELETE *more.*

more than (I) bargained for A torpid term (see page 24).

more ... than you could shake a stick at A moribund metaphor (see page 21). *countless; dozens of; hundreds of; incalculable; inestimable; innumerable; many; numerous; scores of; thousands of; untold.* ■ He had *more* women in his life *than you could shake a stick at.* REPLACE WITH *untold.*

(the) more the merrier A quack equation (see page 23).

(the) more things change, the more they stay the same A popular prescription (see page 23).

more times than I care to admit A torpid term (see page 24).

> I've been married twice, done in more times than I care to admit.
> — Sue Grafton, *E Is for Evidence*

most assuredly An infantile phrase (see page 20). *assuredly; certainly; decidedly; definitely; positively; surely; undoubtedly; unequivocally; unhesitatingly; unquestionably.* ■ The customer will *most assuredly* notify the maitre d' if he or she is expecting someone else. REPLACE WITH *certainly.* SEE ALSO *absolutely; definitely; most (very) definitely.*

most (very) definitely An infantile phrase (see page 20). It is irredeemably dimwitted to say *most definitely* when the more moderate, indeed, the more civilized *certainly, I (am), indeed; just so, quite right, surely, that's right,* or *yes* will do. ■ And you feel your daughter was unjustly treated?
Most definitely. REPLACE WITH *I do.* ■ So whoever you meet has to accommodate your needs? *Very definitely.* REPLACE WITH *Yes.* ■ So when you're sitting around, you are the only white person there? *Most definitely.* REPLACE WITH *Just so.*

As a synonym for words like *assuredly; certainly; decidedly; definitely; positively; surely; undoubtedly; unequivocally; unhesitatingly; unquestionably;* the phrase *most definitely* is ridiculously redundant. ■ Getting this magazine out is a labor of love, but it is *most definitely* labor. REPLACE WITH *decidedly.* ■ Colder weather is *most definitely* on the way. REPLACE WITH *unquestionably.* ■ Would you do it again? *Most definitely.* REPLACE WITH *Unhesitatingly.* SEE ALSO *absolutely; definitely; most assuredly.*

motivating force A wretched redundancy (see page 25). *drive; energy; force; impetus; motivation; power.*

motley crew An inescapable pair (see page 20).

a mountain of A moribund metaphor (see page 21). SEE ALSO *a barrage of.* ■ Since January, Starr has assembled *a mountain of* evidence.

move forward A torpid term (see page 24). *advance; continue; develop; go on; grow; happen; improve; increase; make headway; make progress; move on; occur; proceed; progress; take place.* Politicos and spokespeople endlessly spout fuzzy phrases like *move forward* and *go forward* and *proceed forward* and even *move forward in the right direction.* Pellucid words like *advance, further, improve, proceed,* and *progress* seem to completely elude their intellects. ■ I believe that it was contact with the United States that has *moved* the process of economic reform *forward,* and hopefully some day will *move* the process of political reform *forward.* REPLACE WITH *advanced* and *advance.* ■ What we need is to empower the city in order to *move* it *forward.* REPLACE WITH *improve.* ■ As the company *moves forward,* it's very important that we hold on to those values. REPLACE WITH *grows.* ■ Serious hurdles remain to make this workable and complete, but this agreement today gives us a way to *move forward.* REPLACE WITH *proceed.* ■ Even if Congress decides they want to play politics this year, we can *move forward and* make progress. DELETE *move forward and.* ■ Using these components as our groundwork, we can now *move forward and* examine how to apply them in your web application. DELETE *move forward and.*

And here is a truly ludicrous example: ■ As the year *moves forward,* we will see more *forward movement* in global and domestic environmental issues. REPLACE WITH *advances* and *progress.* SEE ALSO *a step forward; a step (forward) in the right direction; go forward; move (forward) in the right direction; proceed forward.*

move heaven and earth A moribund metaphor (see page 21). *aim; attempt; endeavor; essay; exert; exhaust; labor; moil; strain; strive; struggle; toil; try hard; undertake; work at.*

> Even then I begged my grandfather to see that my testimony was published; but the Michaelises also belong to those old families that move heaven and earth to keep their names out of the papers. — Thornton Wilder, *Theophilus North*

move (forward) in the direction (of) -ing A torpid term (see page 24). *advance; continue; develop; go on; grow; happen; improve; increase; make headway; make progress; move on; occur; proceed; progress; take place.* ■ We've decided to *move in the direction of helping* the claimants make an educated choice. REPLACE WITH *help.*

move (forward) in the right direction A torpid term (see page 24). *advance; continue; develop; go on; grow; happen; improve; increase; make headway; make progress; move on; occur; proceed; progress; take place.*

Only the least eloquent speakers use *move forward* or *move forward in the right direction.* These expressions are wholly unable to move us. They dull our minds and immobilize our actions.

■ I know the company will resolve its problems and *move forward in the right direction.* REPLACE WITH *grow.* ■ All the numbers are looking pretty good and *moving in the right direction.*

REPLACE WITH *increasing.* ■ We are *moving in the right direction,* and I want to keep *moving in the right direction.* REPLACE WITH *making progress* and *making progress.*

Often, formulaic phrases like *move in the right direction* are simply bluster, as in this nearly nonsensical sentence: ■ I'm ready, willing, and able to bring people together and get everybody *moving in the right direction forward.*

Like slander and excessive swearing, *move (forward) in the right direction* exposes a person of questionable character and certain inarticulacy. SEE ALSO *a step forward; a step (forward) in the right direction; go forward; move forward; proceed forward.*

move it or lose it An infantile phrase (see page 20).

move mountains A moribund metaphor (see page 21). *aim; attempt; endeavor; essay; exert; exhaust; labor; moil; strain; strive; struggle; toil; try hard; undertake; work at.*

mover and shaker A moribund metaphor (see page 21). 1. *administrator; boss; brass; chief; commander; director; executive; foreman; head; headman; leader; manager; master; (high) muckamuck; officer; official; overseer; president; principal; superintendent; supervisor.* 2. *aristocrat; dignitary; eminence; lord; luminary; magnate; mogul; notable; patrician; personage; ruler; sovereign; worthy.*

moving target A moribund metaphor (see page 21).

(make) much ado about nothing An infantile phrase (see page 20). *elaborate; embellish; embroider; enhance; enlarge; exaggerate; hyperbolize; inflate; magnify; overdo; overestimate; overrate; overreact; overstress; overstate; strain; stretch.* ■ If you think this discussion about apostrophes is *much ado about nothing,* tell that to the Apostrophe Protection Society. REPLACE WITH *overstated.*

muck and mire An inescapable pair (see page 20).

muddy the waters A moribund metaphor (see page 21). *becloud; blur; complicate; confuse; muddy; obscure.*

> Still, Swenson can't muddy the waters by asking him to look at two books. — Francine Prose, *Blue Angel*

muscle in on A moribund metaphor (see page 21). *break in; encroach; infiltrate; intrude; penetrate; pierce.*

music to (my) ears A moribund metaphor (see page 21).

(a) must (miss) An infantile phrase (see page 20). Like all badly made terms, *(a) must (miss)* is no sooner said than it sounds stale, no sooner read than it sours. In all its variations — *a must have; a must read; a must see;* and so on — this phrase is altogether too *musty.*

■ A good soundtrack, but a dull story, bad acting and weak special effects make this *a must-miss.* ■ Phone interviewing skills are *a must* for most human resource professionals spend a good portion of their day on the phone. ■ Is that business trip *a must*? ■ It is a *must-stop* location for portfolio-toting high school and college students from across the country. ■ Over 200 *must-do* summer events are listed. ■ Aux Delices is *a must stop* for chowhounds. ■ If ever the Lightning faced *a must-win* game, this was it.

(a) must have An infantile phrase (see page 20). *compulsory; critical; essential; imperative; important; indispensable; mandatory; necessary; needed; obligatory; required; requisite; vital.* ■ His book is a student's friend, a professional's ally, a *must-have* reference. REPLACE WITH *indispensable.* ■ No application has yet emerged to make a miniaturized computer *a must-have.* REPLACE WITH *essential.* ■ Microsoft Services for NetWare is *a must-have* for any administrator who is managing a network that includes both types of users. REPLACE WITH *vital.* ■ This software is *a must have* in any web marketing company's toolbox. REPLACE WITH *mandatory.* SEE ALSO *(take) a look see; a (absolute) must; (a) must (miss); (a) must see; a (definite) plus.*

(a) must read An infantile phrase (see page 20). Colloquial usage such as this leads only to everyday thoughts and commonplace actions; few insights, fewer epiphanies, can be had with mediocre language. In essence, *a (must) read* is an expression that secures the banality of what it describes. ■ Tom Wolfe's *Bonfire of the Vanities* is *an enormously entertaining read.* REPLACE WITH *enormously entertaining.* ■ This book is *a tough read* but one of the most important recent accounts of personal identity. REPLACE WITH *tough to understand.* ■ There are a few books on the list that I feel are clearly *easy reads.* REPLACE WITH *easy to read.* ■ There are thousands of great books out there, but how many are *must reads*? REPLACE WITH *compelling.* ■ It's a very challenging *read.* REPLACE WITH *book.* ■ Is it Tolstoy? is it Dostoyevsky? no, but it is a wonderfully satisfying *read.* REPLACE WITH *story.* ■ The manuscript is 312 pages long and *a pretty easy read.* REPLACE WITH *easily readable.* ■ But the problem with the "ho-hum" approach to a life story is that it makes for *a tiresome read.* REPLACE WITH *tiresome reading.* ■ *I'm having a quiet read.* REPLACE WITH *I'm reading quietly.* SEE ALSO *a good read; (take) a look see; (a) must (miss); (a) must have; (a) must see.*

(a) must see An infantile phrase (see page 20). 1. *compulsory; critical; essential; imperative; important; indispensable; mandatory; necessary; needed; obligatory; required; requisite; vital.* 2. *compelling; powerful.* ■ This is *must-see* TV. REPLACE WITH *compelling.* ■ It is the *must-see* event of the season. REPLACE WITH *obligatory.* SEE ALSO *(take) a look see; a (absolute) must; (a) must (miss); (a) must have; a (definite) plus.*

mutual admiration society An infantile phrase (see page 20). *affinity with.*

mutually exclusive An inescapable pair (see page 20). A phrase from the thoughtless person's formulary, *mutually exclusive* reduces the readability of any sentence in which it is used. *Mutually exclusive* screams a fallow imagination, a barren intellect, a cowering spirit.

■ It has managed to prove that Islam and democracy are not *mutually exclusive.* ■ Being selective and being aggressive are not *mutually exclusive.* ■ The two wildly different stories that jurors will be presented with in some ways are not *mutually exclusive.* ■ As Ferrari, Pegoretti and Cipollini all prove, a powerful engine and a sexy profile are not *mutually exclusive.*

N

nagging doubts An inescapable pair (see page 20).

nail (their) colors (flag) to the mast A moribund metaphor (see page 21).

(like) nailing jelly to a tree (the wall) An insipid simile. *barren; bootless; effete; feckless; feeble; fruitless; futile; impotent; inadequate; inconsequential; inconsiderable; ineffective; ineffectual; infertile; insignificant; inutile; meaningless; meritless; nugatory; null; of no value; pointless; powerless; profitless; sterile; trifling; trivial; unavailing; unimportant; unproductive; unprofitable; unserviceable; unworthy; useless; vain; valueless; weak; worthless.*

nail (him) to the wall A moribund metaphor (see page 21). 1. *admonish; anathematize; berate; blame; castigate; censure; chastise; chide; condemn; criticize; curse; decry; denounce; execrate; imprecate; inculpate; indict; rebuke; reprimand; reproach; reprove; scold; upbraid.* 2. *beat; better; conquer; defeat; exceed; excel; outclass; outdo; outflank; outmaneuver; outperform; outplay; overcome; overpower; prevail; rout; succeed; surpass; top; triumph; trounce; vanquish; whip; win.*

> But if he was a bad guy, I'd nail him to the wall. — Jane Heller, *Lucky Stars*

(as) naked as a jaybird An insipid simile. *bare; disrobed; naked; nude; stripped; unclothed; uncovered; undressed.*

(my) name is mud A moribund metaphor (see page 21).

name of the game A moribund metaphor (see page 21). *basis; center; core; crux; essence; gist; heart; kernel; pith; substance.*

(as) narrow as an arrow An insipid simile. *asthenic; attenuated; bony; cachectic; emaciated; gaunt; lank; lanky; lean; narrow; rail-thin; scraggy; scrawny; skeletal; skinny; slender; slight; slim; spare; spindly; svelte; sylphid; thin; trim; wispy.*

national pastime A moribund metaphor (see page 21). *baseball.*

neat and tidy An inescapable pair (see page 20). *neat; orderly; tidy.*

(as) neat as a pin An insipid simile. *methodical; neat; ordered; orderly; organized; systematic; tidy; trim; well-organized.*

necessary evil A torpid term (see page 24). ■ Their staunch refusal to concede that new taxes are, at the least, a *necessary evil*, could shut them out of the budget process altogether.

(a) necessary prerequisite A wretched redundancy (see page 25). *necessary; prerequisite.* ■ An understanding of expressions is *a necessary prerequisite* to learning any command language. DELETE *necessary*. ■ The transfer of information is *a necessary prerequisite* for the effective transfer of technology. DELETE *a prerequisite.*

necessary requirement A wretched redundancy (see page 25). *necessary; requirement.* ■ Because of the labor problems that we have been having with the police patrolmen's union, we will be unable to meet the *necessary requirements* by the deadline. DELETE *necessary.*

necessity is the mother of invention A popular prescription (see page 23).

neck and neck A moribund metaphor (see page 21). *abreast; close; equal; tied.*

> Up till a moment ago we were neck and neck but then my peel broke and I had to refind my purchase. — Janni Visman, *Yellow*

(our) neck of the woods A moribund metaphor (see page 21). *area; community; country; county; district; domain; environment; environs; locale; locality; milieu; neighborhood; part; region; section; sector; surroundings; territory; vicinity; zone.*

> Now, they don't read a lot of books in this neck of the woods. — Will Ferguson, *Happiness*

need(s) and want(s) An inescapable pair (see page 20).

(like) (finding; looking for a) needle in a haystack A moribund metaphor (see page 21).

negative (*n*) A torpid term (see page 24). *burden; deterrence; deterrent; disadvantage; drawback; encumbrance; frailty; hardship; hindrance; liability; limitation; obstacle; onus; shortcoming; weakness.* ■ I don't see how it's a *negative* to the United States to be supporting a democratic government. REPLACE WITH *disadvantage.* SEE ALSO *positive.*

negative effect (impact) A torpid term (see page 24). SEE ALSO *positive effect (impact).* ■ The committee is concerned with both short-term and long-term *negative effects.* REPLACE WITH *disruptions.* ■ Imaging helps to overcome the *negative effects* produced by generalizations. REPLACE WITH *inaccuracies.*

negative feelings A torpid term (see page 24). This expression tells us how little we listen to how we feel. In our quest for speed and efficiency, we have forfeited our feelings. The niceties of emotion — *anger, animosity, anxiety, depression, despair, displeasure, disquiet, distrust, fear, frustration, fury, gloom, grief, guilt, hatred, hopelessness, hostility, ill will, insecurity, jealousy, malice, melancholy, rage, resentment, sadness, shame, sorrow, stress,* and so on — have been sacrificed to a pointless proficiency. ■ It was reported that IAM headquarters failed to renew a $1 million bond that matured in June, due to their *negative feelings* toward El Al's actions. REPLACE WITH *displeasure.* ■ *Negative feelings* can trigger a cascade of stress hormones that accelerate the heart rate, shut down the immune system, and encourage blood clotting. REPLACE WITH *Resentment or anger.* ■ But *those negative feelings* can work against you if they render you unwilling or unable to act the next time you face a major decision. REPLACE WITH *anger and embarrassment.* ■ Though little is known about the effects of negative emotions on your heart, there are a few theories about why *negative feelings* can do so much damage. REPLACE WITH *stress and depression.* SEE ALSO *positive feelings.*

neither a borrower nor a lender be A popular prescription (see page 23).

neither fish nor fowl A moribund metaphor (see page 21). *indefinite; indeterminate; indistinct; undefined; undetermined.*

neither here nor there A moribund metaphor (see page 21). *extraneous; immaterial; impertinent; inapplicable; irrelevant.*

neither one A wretched redundancy (see page 25). *neither.* ■ *Neither one* of these choices is exclusive of the other. DELETE *one.* SEE ALSO *each one; either one.*

ne plus ultra A foreign phrase (see page 19).

nerves of steel A moribund metaphor (see page 21). *bold; brave; courageous; dauntless; fearless; intrepid; stouthearted; unafraid.*

nest egg A moribund metaphor (see page 21). *assets; finances; funds; resources; savings.*

never (not) in a million years An infantile phrase (see page 20). *at no time; by no means; in no way; never; no; not; not at all; not ever; not in any way; not in the least.* ■ I would never have imagined — *not in a million years* — feeling compelled to come to the defense of that grande dame of the administration, the president's wife. DELETE *not in a million years.*

never in my wildest dreams An infantile phrase (see page 20). *at no time; by no means; in no way; never; no; not; not at all; not ever; not in any way; not in the least.* ■ *Never in my wildest dreams* did I imagine that Pinochet would be arrested here in London. DELETE *in my wildest dreams.*

never say die A popular prescription (see page 23).

never say never A popular prescription (see page 23).

new and improved A suspect superlative (see page 24).

new and innovative An inescapable pair (see page 20). *innovative; new.* ■ We used some *new and innovative* manufacturing techniques. REPLACE WITH *innovative* or *new.*

(a) (whole) new (different) ballgame A moribund metaphor (see page 21). ■ Although the procedure is basically the same, recording a macro is slightly different in Word and PowerPoint than in Excel, and creating a macro in Access is *a whole different ballgame.* REPLACE WITH *wholly different.*

new deck (pack) of cards A moribund metaphor (see page 21).

(the) new kid on the block A moribund metaphor (see page 21). ■ Being *the new kid on the block* does not excuse them from their responsibilities.

(a) new lease on life A moribund metaphor (see page 21). *animated; energized; enlivened; inspired; inspirited; invigorated; refreshed; reinvigorated; rejuvenated; revitalized; revived; roused; stimulated; stired; vitalized.*

(like) new wine in old bottles An insipid simile.

nice An overworked word (see page 22). *affable; agreeable; amiable; amicable; companionable; compassionate; congenial; cordial; delightful; friendly; genial; good; good-hearted; good-natured; humane; kind; kind-hearted; likable; neighborly; personable; pleasant; pleasing; sociable; tender; tolerant.*

The word *nice* we might reserve for its less well-known definitions of *fastidious* and *subtle.*

(as) nice as pie An insipid simile. *affable; agreeable; amiable; amicable; companionable; compassionate; congenial; cordial; delightful; friendly; genial; good; good-hearted; good-natured; humane; kind; kind-hearted; likable; neighborly; personable; pleasant; pleasing; sociable; tender; tolerant.*

> And then once more her eyes glaze, her body deadens, and she cries out again and again, 'Who are you? Who are you? Who are you?' and she is crying and this time I simply want to escape this strange circle, and I get up and hastily pull on my clothes, and the Conga all the time saying, as nice as pie, genuinely upset, 'But why? Why are you going?' — Richard Flanagan, *Gould's Book of Fish*

nice work if you can get it A plebeian sentiment (see page 23).

nickel-and-dime A moribund metaphor (see page 21). 1. *cheap; economical; inexpensive; low-cost; low-priced.* 2. *cheap; frugal; miserly; niggardly; parsimonious; stingy; thrifty.* 3. *inconsequential; insignificant; minor; negligible; paltry; petty; small; small-time; trifling; trivial; unimportant.* ■ The banks were shoveling money into every *nickel-and-dime* developer that walked in. REPLACE WITH *insignificant.*

nickel-and-dime (him) to death A moribund metaphor (see page 21). ■ Many governors have begun to *nickel-and-dime taxpayers to death* with fees, fines, tolls, and excise taxes. SEE ALSO *to death.*

(like) night and day An insipid simile. *antipodal; antipodean; antithetical; contrary; converse; diametric; diametrical; different; inverse; opposite; reverse.*

(it's a) nightmare A moribund metaphor (see page 21). How impoverished our imaginations are. Nightmares ought to be terrifying, but this metaphor — so popular has it become — is hopelessly tame. *It was a nightmare* instills in us as little compassion as it does interest; it makes us yawn rather than yell. No longer is there terror to it.

Though an incident might well be *agonizing, alarming, appalling, awful, disgusting, disquieting, distressing, disturbing, dreadful, excruciating, frightening, frightful, ghastly, grisly, gruesome, harrowing, hideous, horrendous, horrible, horrid, horrific, horrifying, monstrous, nauseating, nightmarish, petrifying, repellent, repulsive, revolting, shocking, sickening, terrifying, tormenting, traumatic,* saying *it was a nightmare* makes it sound as though it were no more than an annoyance, no more than a mere inconvenience.

It was a nightmare, the metaphor, has hardly the force of a sweet dream. ■ It was *a nightmare.* REPLACE WITH *ghastly.* ■ If the birth mother shows up, it's *a nightmare* for the adopting mother. REPLACE WITH *disquieting.*

Altogether remarkable about this expression is that people use it to describe something that tormented or terrified them. They describe an extraordinary event with an ordinary phrase. How can we not doubt the sincerity of their words, the terror of their experience? Is this then what it is to be human, to be able to use language, expressing ourselves in platitudes to illustrate what affects us most deeply? Are so many of us still scribblers? SEE ALSO *(every person's) worst nightmare.*

nip and tuck A moribund metaphor (see page 21).

nip (it) in the bud A moribund metaphor (see page 21). *abort; annul; arrest; balk; block; cancel; check; contain; crush; derail; detain; end; extinguish; foil; frustrate; halt; hinder; impede; neutralize; nullify; obstruct; prevent; quash; quell; repress; restrain; retard; squash; squelch; squish; stall; stay; stifle; stop; subdue; suppress; terminate; thwart.* ■ Another reader in California has found a sure-fire method for *nipping travel stress in the bud.* REPLACE WITH *squelching travel stress.*

nipping at (your) heels A moribund metaphor (see page 21).

> Then he ran off behind his brother, as if embarrassment were nipping at his heels. — Patricia Jones, *Red on a Rose*

no big deal An infantile phrase (see page 20). *inappreciable; inconsequential; inconsiderable; insignificant; minor; negligible; niggling; nugatory; petty; trifling; trivial; unimportant; unsubstantial.*

nobody but nobody An infantile phrase (see page 20). *nobody; nobody at all; none; no one; no one at all.*

nobody's perfect A popular prescription (see page 23). SEE ALSO *(I'm) a perfectionist; I'm not perfect (you know).*

no easy task A torpid term (see page 24). *arduous; backbreaking; burdensome; difficult; exhausting; fatiguing; hard; herculean; laborious; not easy; onerous; severe; strenuous; toilful; toilsome; tough; troublesome; trying; wearisome.* ■ Getting this place ready has been *no easy task.* REPLACE WITH *backbreaking.*

no great shakes A moribund metaphor (see page 21). 1. *average; common; commonplace; customary; everyday; fair; mediocre; middling; normal; ordinary; passable; quotidian; regular; routine; standard; tolerable; typical; uneventful; unexceptional; unremarkable; usual.* 2. *inappreciable; inconsequential; inconsiderable; insignificant; minor; negligible; niggling; nugatory; petty; trifling; trivial; unimportant; unsubstantial.*

no guts, no glory A popular prescription (see page 23).

no holds barred A moribund metaphor (see page 21). *candidly; explicitly; openly; overtly; without restraint.*

no ifs, ands, ors, or buts An infantile phrase (see page 20). SEE ALSO *period.*

no man is an island A popular prescription (see page 23).

non compos mentis A foreign phrase (see page 19). *batty; cracked; crazy; cretinous; daft; demented; deranged;*

insane; lunatic; mad; maniacal; neurotic; nuts; nutty; psychotic; raving; squirrelly; touched; unbalanced; unhinged; unsound.

none of the above An infantile phrase (see page 20). ■ Do you want to talk to me or argue with me? *None of the above.* REPLACE WITH *Neither.* SEE ALSO *all of the above.*

no news is good news A quack equation (see page 23). ■ There is a new breed of progressive administrators who do not believe that *no news is good news.*

no offense (intended) An infantile phrase (see page 20).

> And I say that with no offence to the good people of Sydney intended. — Nick Hornby, *A Long Way Down*

(every) nook and cranny A moribund metaphor (see page 21). *complexities; details; fine points; intricacies; minutiae; niceties; particulars.* ■ There is lots of time in which to explore the *nooks and crannies* of virtually any topic on AM radio. REPLACE WITH *intricacies.*

no pain, no gain A popular prescription (see page 23).

no problem An infantile phrase (see page 20). 1. *you're welcome.* 2. *not at all; not in the least.* 3. *I'd be glad to; I'd be happy to.* 4. *it's O.K.; that's all right.* 5. *easy; easily; effortlessly; readily.* ■ Thanks very much. *No problem.* REPLACE WITH *You're welcome.* ■ Can you do it? *No problem.* REPLACE WITH *Easily.* SEE ALSO *common courtesy.*

no pun intended An infantile phrase (see page 20).

nose out of joint A moribund metaphor (see page 21). 1. *acerbated; angry; annoyed; bothered; cross; displeased; enraged; furious; grouchy; incensed; inflamed; infuriated; irate; irked; irritated; mad; miffed; peeved; provoked; riled; roiled; testy; upset; vexed.* 2. *covetous; desirous; envious; grudging; jealous; resentful.*

(it's) no skin off (my) nose A moribund metaphor (see page 21).

no small feat (task) A torpid term (see page 24). *arduous; backbreaking; burdensome; difficult; exhausting; fatiguing; hard; herculean; laborious; not easy; onerous; severe; strenuous; toilful; toilsome; tough; troublesome; trying; wearisome.*

(I'm) no spring chicken A moribund metaphor (see page 21). *aged; aging; ancient; antediluvian; antique; archaic; elderly; hoary; hoary-headed; old; patriarchal; prehistoric; seasoned; superannuated.*

no strings attached A moribund metaphor (see page 21). *unconditionally; unreservedly.*

no sweat A moribund metaphor (see page 21). *easily done; easy; effortless; elementary; facile; simple; simplicity itself; straightforward; uncomplex; uncomplicated.*

not a Chinaman's chance A moribund metaphor (see page 21). 1. *doubtful; dubious; farfetched; implausible; improbable; remote; unlikely; unrealistic.* 2. *hopeless; impossible; impracticable; impractical; infeasible; unrealizable; unworkable.*

not a ghost of a chance A moribund metaphor (see page 21). 1. *doubtful; dubious; farfetched; implausible; improbable; remote; unlikely; unrealistic.* 2. *hopeless; impossible; impracticable; impractical; infeasible; unrealizable; unworkable.*

not a hope in hell A moribund metaphor (see page 21). 1. *doubtful; dubious; farfetched; implausible; improbable; remote; unlikely; unrealistic.* 2. *hopeless; impossible; impracticable; impractical; infeasible; unrealizable; unworkable.*

not all (what) (it's) cracked up to be A torpid term (see page 24). *deficient; disappointing; discouraging; dissatisfying; inadequate; inapt; incapable; incompetent; ineffective; inferior; insufficient; lacking; unfit; unqualified; unsatisfactory; wanting.*

not a mean bone in (her) body A moribund metaphor (see page 21). *affable; agreeable; amiable; amicable; compassionate; friendly; gentle; good-hearted; good-natured; humane; kind; kind-hearted; personable; pleasant; tender; tolerant.*

not a snowball's chance in hell A moribund metaphor (see page 21). 1. *doubtful; dubious; farfetched; implausible; improbable; remote; unlikely; unrealistic.* 2. *hopeless; impossible; impracticable; impractical; infeasible; unrealizable; unworkable.*

not by a long shot A moribund metaphor (see page 21). *at no time; by no means; in no way; never; no; not; not at all; not ever; not in any way; not in the least.*

notch in (his) belt A moribund metaphor (see page 21). *achievement; attainment; success.*

not for all the tea in China A moribund metaphor (see page 21). *at no time; by no means; in no way; never; no; not; not at all; not ever; not in any way; not in the least.*

not for anything in the world A moribund metaphor (see page 21). *at no time; by no means; in no way; never; no; not; not at all; not ever; not in any way; not in the least.*

not for love or money A moribund metaphor (see page 21). *at no time; by no means; in no way; never; no; not; not at all; not ever; not in any way; not in the least.*

not for the world A moribund metaphor (see page 21). *at no time; by no means; in no way; never; no; not; not at all; not ever; not in any way; not in the least.*

nothing could be further from the truth A torpid term (see page 24). 1. *by no means; in no way; never; no; not; not at all; not ever; nothing of the sort; not in any way; not in the least.* 2. *be amiss; be astray; be deceived; be deluded; be erring; be erroneous; be fallacious; be false; be faulty; be inaccurate; be incorrect; be in error; be misguided; be misinformed; be mislead; be mistaken; be not correct; be not right; be untrue; be wrong.*

You would think that anyone who uses this phrase — anyone, that is, whose words or actions were being questioned or whose honor was being impugned — would choose to speak more eloquently. You would think that unfair or inaccurate accusations would elicit profound and persuasive expressions of denial. When they do not, as they certainly do not when a person resorts to *nothing could be further from the truth,* we have to wonder who is telling the truth and who is not. Formulaic responses like this may make us doubt the sincerity of those who use them

■ The premise put forth by the administration that employment must be sacrificed to protect the environment *could not be further from the truth.* REPLACE WITH *is erroneous.* ■ I know there will be Republicans who will try to say that because I'm not with you today in Chicago that I'm trying to distance myself from you, but *nothing could be further from the truth.* REPLACE WITH *they are mistaken.* ■ W. R. Grace makes use of my "model citizen" sound bite as though it were some sort of blanket absolution. *Nothing could be further from the truth.* REPLACE WITH *It is not.*

> They had been credited with attempting to stir up rebellion among the animals on neighbouring farms. Nothing could be further from the truth! — George Orwell, *Animal Farm*

nothing lasts forever A popular prescription (see page 23).

nothing to sneeze at A moribund metaphor (see page 21). *consequential; considerable; meaningful; momentous; significant; substantial; weighty.* ■ Two hundred thousand jobs is *nothing to sneeze at.* REPLACE WITH *considerable.*

nothing to write home about A moribund metaphor (see page 21). 1. *average; common; commonplace; customary; everyday; fair; mediocre; middling; normal; ordinary; passable; quotidian; regular; standard; tolerable; typical; uneventful; unexceptional; unexciting; unremarkable; usual; workaday.* 2. *anodyne; banal; barren; bland; boring; deadly; dreary; dry; dull; everyday; flat; humdrum; inanimate; insipid; jejune; lifeless; lusterless; mediocre; monotonous; prosaic; routine; spiritless; stale; tedious; tiresome; unexciting; uninteresting; vapid; wearisome.*

nothing ventured, nothing gained A popular prescription (see page 23).

not in (this) lifetime A moribund metaphor (see page 21). *at no time; by no means; in no way; never; no; not; not at all; not ever; not in any way; not in the least.*

not in (out of) the picture A moribund metaphor (see page 21). Some metaphors — so bloodless have they become — accommodate many different meanings. *Not in (out of) the picture* is one of them, for this pale expression could easily mean *dead* or *departed*, conceivably mean *forgotten* or *forgettable*, or imaginably mean *unmentionable* or *nameless.* SEE ALSO *in the picture.*

not on your life A moribund metaphor (see page 21). *at no time; by no means; in no way; never; no; not; not at all; not ever; not in any way; not in the least.*

not what (it) used to be A torpid term (see page 24). *deficient; disappointing; discouraging; dissatisfying; inadequate; inapt; incapable; incompetent; ineffective; inferior; insufficient; lacking; unfit; unqualified; unsatisfactory; wanting.*

not with a bang but with a whimper An infantile phrase (see page 20).

not worth a continental A moribund metaphor (see page 21). *barren; bootless; effete; feckless; feeble; fruitless; futile; impotent; inadequate; inconsequential; inconsiderable; ineffective; ineffectual; infertile; insignificant; inutile; meaningless; meritless; nugatory; null; of no value; pointless; powerless; profitless; sterile; trifling; trivial; unavailing; unimportant; unproductive; unprofitable; unserviceable; unworthy; useless; vain; valueless; weak; worthless.*

not worth a (tinker's) damn A moribund metaphor (see page 21). *barren; bootless; effete; feckless; feeble; fruitless; futile; impotent; inadequate; inconsequential; inconsiderable; ineffective; ineffectual; infertile; insignificant; inutile; meaningless; meritless; nugatory; null; of no value; pointless; powerless; profitless; sterile; trifling; trivial; unavailing; unimportant; unproductive; unprofitable; unserviceable; unworthy; useless; vain; valueless; weak; worthless.*

not worth a plugged nickel A moribund metaphor (see page 21). *barren; bootless; effete; feckless; feeble; fruitless; futile; impotent; inadequate; inconsequential; inconsiderable; ineffective; ineffectual; infertile; insignificant; inutile; meaningless; meritless; nugatory; null; of no value; pointless; powerless; profitless; sterile; trifling; trivial; unavailing; unimportant; unproductive; unprofitable; unserviceable; unworthy; useless; vain; valueless; weak; worthless.*

not worth a straw A moribund metaphor (see page 21). *barren; bootless; effete; feckless; feeble; fruitless; futile; impotent; inadequate; inconsequential; inconsiderable; ineffective; ineffectual; infertile; insignificant; inutile; meaningless; meritless; nugatory; null; of no value; pointless; powerless; profitless; sterile; trifling; trivial; unavailing; unimportant; unproductive; unprofitable; unserviceable; unworthy; useless; vain; valueless; weak; worthless.*

not worth the paper it's written (printed) on A moribund metaphor (see page 21). *barren; bootless; effete; feckless; feeble; fruitless; futile; impotent; inadequate; inconsequential; inconsiderable; ineffective; ineffectual; infertile; insignificant; inutile; meaningless; meritless; nugatory; null; of no value; pointless; powerless; profitless; sterile; trifling; trivial; unavailing; unimportant; unproductive; unprofitable; unserviceable; unworthy; useless; vain; valueless; weak; worthless.* ■ I say to you that the governor's budget is *not worth the paper it's written on.* REPLACE WITH *useless.* ■ He went on to say that he did not believe in the United States Constitution, and that it was *not worth the paper it's printed on.* REPLACE WITH *nugatory.*

no use crying over spilt milk A popular prescription (see page 23).

no way An infantile phrase (see page 20). *at no time; by no means; in no way; never; no; not; not at all; not ever; not in any way; not in the least.*

no way José An infantile phrase (see page 20). *at no time; by no means; in no way; never; no; not; not at all; not ever; not in any way; not in the least.*

now it's my time (turn) A plebeian sentiment (see page 23). ■ I've done my family duty and brought up my children, and *now it's my turn.*

now you see it, now you don't An infantile phrase (see page 20).

null and void An inescapable pair (see page 20). *abolished; annulled; canceled; countermanded; invalid; null; nullified; recalled; repealed; rescinded; revoked; void; withdrawn; worthless.* ■ We aren't sure what the terms of the deal are, or what may be expected of them, or what may make them *null and void.* REPLACE WITH *invalid.*

(her) number is up A moribund metaphor (see page 21).

> Ach, just my luck! Then the old fellow's number is up. — Isaac Babel, *Red Cavalry*

number-one A moribund metaphor (see page 21). *chief; foremost; leading; main; primary; prime; principal.*

number one (two) A wretched redundancy (see page 25). *first (second).* ■ *Number one,* I don't feel that qualifies her as black. *Number two,* a person's color shouldn't be worn on their sleeve. REPLACE WITH *First; Second.*

nuts and bolts A moribund metaphor (see page 21). *basics; essentials; facts; foundation; fundamentals; principles.* ■ In this text, we explore the *nuts and bolts* of radio production. REPLACE WITH *essentials.*

nuttier than a fruitcake A moribund metaphor (see page 21). *batty; cracked; crazy; daft; demented; deranged; fey; foolish; goofy; insane; lunatic; mad; maniacal; neurotic; nuts; nutty; psychotic; raving; silly; squirrelly; touched; unbalanced; unhinged; unsound; wacky; zany.*

object of one's affection An infantile phrase (see page 20). *admirer; beau; beloved; boyfriend (girlfriend); companion; darling; dear; flame; infatuate; inamorato (inamorata); lover; paramour; steady; suiter; swain; sweetheart; wooer.* SEE ALSO *significant other.*

obscene An overworked word (see page 22). *abhorrent; abominable; accursed; appalling; atrocious; awful; beastly; blasphemous; detestable; disagreeable; disgusting; dreadful; execrable; frightening; frightful; ghastly; grisly; gruesome; hateful; horrendous; horrible; horrid; horrifying; indecent; indelicate; inhuman; insulting; loathesome; monstrous; obnoxious; odious; offensive; repellent; repugnant; repulsive; revolting; tasteless; terrible; terrifying; unspeakable; unutterable; vulgar.* ■ Certain levels of expenditure are *obscene* and do a great injustice to our concept of social justice. REPLACE WITH *offensive.* ■ It's an *obscene* scenario that's being played out. REPLACE WITH *unspeakable.*

obviate the need for A wretched redundancy (see page 25). *obviate.* ■ If indicated, create a limited-access, safe unit to *obviate the need for* activity restriction. DELETE *the need for.*

(an) ocean of A moribund metaphor (see page 21). SEE ALSO *a barrage of.*

oceans of ink A moribund metaphor (see page 21).

> Those journalists who professed science, at war with those who professed wit, spilled oceans of ink in this memorable campaign .... — Jules Verne, *Twenty Thousand Leagues Under the Seas*

of biblical (epic) proportions A moribund metaphor (see page 21). *colossal; elephantine; enormous; epical; gargantuan; giant; gigantic; great; grand; huge; immense; impressive; legendary; mammoth; massive; monstrous; prodigious; stupendous; titanic; tremendous; vast.* ■ It has been called *a comeback of epic proportions.* REPLACE WITH *an epical comeback.* ■ He created a landmark television character whose suffering was *of biblical proportions.* REPLACE WITH *prodigious.*

> As if she'd made a cosmic announcement, her last word was followed by a trumpet blast of Biblical proportions that shook the windows. — Jill Churchill, *The Merchant of Menace*

(woman) of easy virtue A moribund metaphor (see page 21). *dissolute; immoral; licentious; loose; promiscuous; wanton.*

off and running A moribund metaphor (see page 21).

off base A moribund metaphor (see page 21). *amiss; astray; deceived; deluded; erring; erroneous; fallacious; false; faulty; inaccurate; incorrect; in error; misguided; misinformed; mislead; mistaken; not correct; not right; wrong.* ■ Given all the uncertainty surrounding the nation's economic future, no one is prepared to say the administration is *off base.* REPLACE WITH *incorrect.*

off (her) rocker A moribund metaphor (see page 21). *batty; cracked; crazy; daft; demented; deranged; fey; foolish; goofy; insane; lunatic; mad; maniacal; neurotic; nuts; nutty; psychotic; raving; silly; squirrelly; touched; unbalanced; unhinged; unsound; wacky; zany.*

off the beaten path (track) A moribund metaphor (see page 21). 1. *aberrant; abnormal; anomalistic; anomalous; atypical; bizarre; curious; deviant; different; distinct; distinctive; eccentric; exceptional; extraordinary; fantastic; foreign; grotesque; idiosyncratic; independent; individual; individualistic; irregular; novel; odd; offbeat; original; peculiar; queer; strange; uncommon; unconventional; unexampled; unique; unnatural; unorthodox; unusual; weird.* 2. *inaccessible; isolated; remote; secluded; unreachable.* ■ A lot of smaller towns of 800 to 3000 people are *off the beaten path.* REPLACE WITH *remote.*

off the cuff A moribund metaphor (see page 21). *extemporaneous; extempore; impromptu; improvised; spontaneous; unprepared; unprompted; unrehearsed.*

(go) off the deep end A moribund metaphor (see page 21). *batty; cracked; crazy; daft; demented; deranged; fey; foolish; goofy; insane; lunatic; mad; maniacal; neurotic; nuts; nutty; psychotic; raving; silly; squirrelly; touched; unbalanced; unhinged; unsound; wacky; zany.*

(let) off the hook A moribund metaphor (see page 21). *absolve; acquit; clear; condone; exculpate; excuse; exonerate; forgive; overlook; pardon; remit; vindicate.* ■ Confronting sexual issues is so taboo in most African culture that rapists are frequently *let off the hook* because few families will endure the public shame of acknowledging the abuse. REPLACE WITH *acquitted.* ■ But as news events in the scandal coverage ebb, the media have had to find new ways to *let Clinton off the hook*. REPLACE WITH *absolve Clinton.* ■ Now she's calling for Nicaragua and Honduras to be *let off the hook* for at least two years. REPLACE WITH *excused.*

off the record A moribund metaphor (see page 21). *classified; confidential; personal; private; privy; restricted; secret.*

off the top of (my) head A moribund metaphor (see page 21). *extemporaneous; extempore; impromptu; improvised; spontaneous; unprepared; unprompted; unrehearsed.*

off the wall A moribund metaphor (see page 21). *aberrant; abnormal; anomalistic; anomalous; atypical; bizarre; curious; deviant; different; distinct; distinctive; eccentric; exceptional; extraordinary; fantastic; foreign; grotesque; idiosyncratic; independent; individual; individualistic; irregular; novel; odd; offbeat; original; peculiar; puzzling; quaint; queer; rare; remarkable; separate; singular; strange; uncommon; unconventional; unexampled; unique; unorthodox; unparalleled; unprecedented; unusual; weird.*

off to the races A moribund metaphor (see page 21).

(goes) off track A moribund metaphor (see page 21). *amiss; astray; deceived; deluded; erring; erroneous; fallacious; false; faulty; inaccurate; incorrect; in error; misguided; misinformed; mislead; mistaken; not correct; not right; wrong.*

> An intelligent and beautiful girl from a loving family grows up in Orangetown, Ontario, her mother's a writer, her father's a doctor, and then she goes off the track. — Carol Shields, *Unless*

off (her) trolley A moribund metaphor (see page 21). *batty; cracked; crazy; daft; demented; deranged; fey; foolish; goofy; insane; lunatic; mad; maniacal; neurotic; nuts; nutty; psychotic; raving; silly; squirrelly; touched; unbalanced; unhinged; unsound; wacky; zany.*

oftentimes A wretched redundancy (see page 25). *frequently; often; repeatedly.* ■ *Oftentimes*, this results in overloading the office staff with the added responsibility of planning the company's meetings and events. REPLACE WITH *Often.*

(time is) of the essence A torpid term (see page 24). *critical; crucial; essential; important; key; significant; vital.*

> Time was of the essence — not only because of what those rival companies were up to, but also (and the Rani lowered her voice mysteriously) for Other Reasons. — Aldous Huxley, *Island*

of the first water A moribund metaphor (see page 21). *best; brightest; choice; choicest; elite; excellent; finest; first-class; first-rate; foremost; greatest; highest; highest quality; matchless; non-*

pareil; optimal; optimum; outstanding; paramount; peerless; preeminent; premium; prominent; select; superior; superlative; top; unequaled; unexcelled; unmatched; unrivaled; unsurpassed.

off (his) trolley A moribund metaphor (see page 21). *batty; cracked; crazy; daft; demented; deranged; fey; foolish; goofy; insane; lunatic; mad; maniacal; neurotic; nuts; nutty; psychotic; raving; silly; squirrelly; touched; unbalanced; unhinged; unsound; wacky; zany.*

ofttimes A withered word (see page 24). *frequently; often; repeatedly.*

of two minds A moribund metaphor (see page 21). *ambivalent; confused; divided; indecisive; in doubt; irresolute; neutral; torn; uncertain; uncommitted; undecided; unsure.*

O.K.? An infantile phrase (see page 20). ■ I don't have a lot of respect for people who judge others by their skin tone, *O.K.?* DELETE *O.K.?* ■ I have a master's degree, *O.K.?* but if I dress bad or speak bad, I'm treated bad, *O.K.?* DELETE *O.K.?* ■ Once that sperm hits that egg, *O.K.?* you have no rights after that, *O.K.?* DELETE *O.K.?* ■ What I did was wrong, *O.K.?* I shouldn't have done it, *O.K.?* I did my time for it, *O.K.?* DELETE *O.K.?*

old adage A wretched redundancy (see page 25). *adage.* ■ The *old adage* "The first half of our lives is ruined by our parents and the last half by our children" need not be and should not be. DELETE *old.*

old and decrepit An inescapable pair (see page 20).

(as) old as Adam An insipid simile. *aged; aging; ancient; antediluvian; antique; archaic; elderly; hoary; hoary-headed; old; patriarchal; prehistoric; seasoned; superannuated; venerable.*

(as) old as the hills An insipid simile. *aged; aging; ancient; antediluvian; antique; archaic; elderly; hoary; hoary-headed; old; patriarchal; prehistoric; seasoned; superannuated; venerable.*

(as) old as time An insipid simile. *aged; aging; ancient; antediluvian; antique; archaic; elderly; hoary; hoary-headed; old; patriarchal; prehistoric; seasoned; superannuated; venerable.*

> The family! Here was the old blackmail tactic, old as Time. — Joyce Carol Oates, *The Tattooed Girl*

old-boy network A moribund metaphor (see page 21).

old cliché A wretched redundancy (see page 25). *cliché.* ■ Working for these guys I feel like the *old cliché* "a cog in the wheel." DELETE *old.*

old enough to know better An infantile phrase (see page 20).

old enough to know better but young enough not to care An infantile phrase (see page 20).

(an) old hand A moribund metaphor (see page 21). *ablé; adept; apt; capable; competent; deft; dexterous; experienced; expert; practiced; proficient; seasoned; skilled; skillful; veteran.*

oldest story in the book A moribund metaphor (see page 21).

old habits never die A popular prescription (see page 23).

> Old habits never die. And when you've once been in the business of granting wishes, the impulse never quite leaves you. — Joanne Harris, *Chocolat.*

old hat A moribund metaphor (see page 21). 1. *antediluvian; antiquated; archaic; dead; obsolescent; obsolete; old; old-fashioned; outdated; outmoded; out of date; out of fashion; passé; superannuated.* 2. *anodyne; banal; barren; bland; boring; deadly; dreary; dry; dull; everyday; flat; humdrum; inanimate; insipid; jejune; lifeless; lusterless; mediocre; monotonous; prosaic; routine; spiritless; stale; tedious; tiresome; unexciting; uninteresting; vapid; wearisome.*

old maxim A wretched redundancy (see page 25). *maxim.* ■ A number of studies indicate that, in deciding what punishment is appropriate for different crimes, individuals typically rely on an *old maxim*: Let the punishment fit the crime. DELETE *old.*

old saw A wretched redundancy (see page 25). *saw.* ■ The claim is similar to the *old saw* from the tobacco industry, now proven false, that there is no direct link between cancer and smoking. DELETE *old.*

old saying A wretched redundancy (see page 25). *saying.* ■ The *old saying* "A picture is worth a thousand words" is usually true. DELETE *old.*

old wives' tale A moribund metaphor (see page 21).

on a ... basis A wretched redundancy (see page 25). ■ Meat production is the major use of goats *on a worldwide basis.* REPLACE WITH *worldwide.* ■ I am tortured *on a daily basis.* REPLACE WITH *daily.* ■ I see him for my treatment *on a regular basis.* REPLACE WITH *regularly.* ■ You meet the students *on a weekly basis.* REPLACE WITH *weekly.* ■ We should look at these issues *on a case by case basis.* REPLACE WITH *case by case.*

on account of the fact that A wretched redundancy (see page 25). *because; considering; for; given; in that; since.* ■ The former Beatle refused the award *on account of the fact that* he believes he is too young to receive it and does not want to be perceived as a washed-up has been. REPLACE WITH *because.* SEE ALSO *because of the fact that; considering the fact that; by virtue of the fact that; given the fact that; in view of the fact that; on account of the fact that.*

on a collision course A moribund metaphor (see page 21).

on a different wavelength A moribund metaphor (see page 21). *conflict; differ; disagree; disharmonize; feel differently; think unalike.*

on a dime A moribund metaphor (see page 21). *cheaply; economically; inexpensively.* ■ When it comes to interior design or decorating *on a dime,* you've got hundreds of tips and tricks to share with readers. REPLACE WITH *economically.*

(working) on all cylinders A moribund metaphor (see page 21). 1. *able; adept; apt; capable; competent; conversant; deft; dexterous; experienced; expert; familiar; practiced; proficient; seasoned; skilled; skillful; veteran.* 2. *adroit; astute; bright; brilliant; clever; discerning; effective; effectual; efficient; enlightened; insightful; intelligent; judicious; keen; knowledgeable; learned; logical; luminous; perceptive; perspicacious; quick; rational; reasonable; sagacious; sage; sapient; sensible; sharp; shrewd; smart; sound; understanding; wise.* ■ This rapid growth cycle is a challenge opportunity and needs good *people working on all cylinders* to take advantage of it. REPLACE WITH *capable people.*

on all fours (with) A moribund metaphor (see page 21). *analogous (to); equal (to); equivalent (to); identical (to).* ■ There's no circumstance in history that fits identically *on all fours* with subsequent circumstances. DELETE *on all fours.*

on an even keel A moribund metaphor (see page 21). *balanced; even; firm; fixed; stable; steadfast; steady; unfaltering; unwavering.*

on a ... note A wretched redundancy (see page 25). ■ *On a personal note,* I would not be all that appalled if my children were to perform well only 99 percent of the time. REPLACE WITH *Personally.*

on a roll A moribund metaphor (see page 21). *doing well; flourishing; prospering; succeeding; thriving.*

on a scale of 1 to 10 An infantile phrase (see page 20). The popularity of this phrase is further evidence of the delight some people have with numbers and counting and the distaste they have for words and concepts.

Of course, their fondness for numbers may not go much beyond the count of 10 — so too, perhaps, the number of words in their vocabulary.

■ *On a scale of 1 to 10,* how much does uncertainty surrounding laws and regulations in [COUNTRY] increase the risk of equities in that country? ■ *On a scale of 1 to 10,* just how good a student are you? ■ *On a scale of 1 to 10* (1 being the lowest, 10 being the highest) please rank the usefulness and intuitiveness of the website's navigational elements. ■ How would you rank your programming skills (in your best language) *on a scale of 1 to 10,* with 1 being lowest and 10 being highest? SEE ALSO *(for) a laugh; avid reader.*

on a shoestring A moribund metaphor (see page 21). *cheaply; economically; inexpensively.*

> He had been everywhere and he knew everything about traveling on a shoestring. — Laura Kalpakian, *Steps and Exes: A Novel of Family*

on automatic pilot A moribund metaphor (see page 21). *automatic; habitual; mechanical; routine.*

(come) on board A moribund metaphor (see page 21). ■ Some doctors are starting to *come on board,* but many haven't got a clue what's going on. REPLACE WITH *take alternative medicine seriously.*

on both sides (either side) of the equation A moribund metaphor (see page 21). ■ I believe there is little trust *on either side of the equation.* ■ Merrills tempers the super-cycle view to some extent however, by suggesting simply that there are risks *on either side of the equation.* ■ There is already a writer and producer attached to our first project, working *on both sides of the equation* — game and movie. ■ I have likewise seen the disconnect between people of color and law enforcement — the misconceptions *on both sides of the equation.*

on both sides of the fence A moribund metaphor (see page 21). *ambivalent; divided; indecisive; in doubt; irresolute; neutral; torn; uncertain; uncommitted; undecided; unsure.*

once bitten (burned), twice shy A popular prescription (see page 23).

once (and) for all A torpid term (see page 24). *conclusively; decisively; finally.* ■ Our broken judicial confirmation process must *be fixed once and for all.* REPLACE WITH *finally be fixed.*

once in a blue moon A moribund metaphor (see page 21). *hardly; infrequently; not often; occasionally; rarely; scarcely; seldom; sporadically; uncommonly.*

once in a lifetime (opportunity) A moribund metaphor (see page 21). *different; exceptional; extraordinary; incomparable; inimitable; matchless; nonpareil; notable; noteworthy; novel; odd; original; peculiar; peerless; rare; remarkable; singular; special; strange; uncommon; unequaled; unexampled; unique; unmatched; unparalleled; unrivaled; unusual; without equal.* ■ This is a *once in a lifetime* opportunity. REPLACE WITH *singular.*

once upon a time An infantile phrase (see page 20).

> Once upon a time, in the rural South, there were farmhouses and farm wives who set tables where almost any passing stranger, a traveling preacher, a knife-grinder, an itinerant worker, was welcome to sit down to a hearty midday meal. — Truman Capote, *Music for Chameleons*

on cloud nine A moribund metaphor (see page 21). *blissful; blithe; buoyant; cheerful; delighted; ecstatic; elated; enraptured; euphoric; exalted; excited; exhilarated; exultant; gay; glad; gleeful; good-humored; happy; intoxicated; jolly; jovial; joyful; joyous; jubilant; merry; mirthful; overjoyed; pleased; rapturous; thrilled.*

on (our) doorstep A moribund metaphor (see page 21). *approaching; at hand; close; coming; expected; forthcoming; imminent; impending; looming; near; nearby.*

(the) one and only A wretched redundancy (see page 25). *one; only; sole.* ■ In the early days of any business, the *one and only* thing you understand is that the customer is king. REPLACE WITH *one* or *only.*

one and the same A wretched redundancy (see page 25). *identical; one; the same.* ■ Are you saying that submission and competition are *one and the same?* REPLACE WITH *the same.* ■ Some people believe that marketing and advertising are *one and the same*. REPLACE WITH *identical.*

on easy street A moribund metaphor (see page 21). *affluent; moneyed; opulent; prosperous; rich; wealthy; well-off; well-to-do.*

one big, happy family A suspect superlative (see page 24).

one foot in and one foot out A moribund metaphor (see page 21). *ambivalent; divided; indecisive; irresolute; torn; uncertain; uncommitted; undecided; unsure.*

(put) one foot in front of the other A moribund metaphor (see page 21).

one foot in the grave A moribund metaphor (see page 21). *decaying; declining; deteriorating; disintegrating; dying; ebbing; expiring; fading; failing; moribund; near death; sinking; very ill; waning.*

> She only used to marvel how so old and flabby a man, with one foot in the grave, came to be possessed of so fertile an imagination. — Esther Singer Kreitman, *Deborah*

one for the books A moribund metaphor (see page 21). *different; exceptional; extraordinary; incomparable; inimitable; matchless; nonpareil; notable; noteworthy; novel; odd; original; peculiar; peerless; remarkable; singular; special; strange; uncommon; unequaled; unexampled; unique; unmatched; unparalleled; unrivaled; unusual; without equal.*

one good turn deserves another A popular prescription (see page 23).

one hundred (100) percent An infantile phrase (see page 20). *absolutely; altogether; categorically; completely; entirely; fully; perfectly; positively; quite; roundly; thoroughly; totally; unconditionally; unreservedly; utterly; wholly.* ■ I agree with you *one hundred percent*. REPLACE WITH *unreservedly.*

one in a million A moribund metaphor (see page 21). *different; exceptional; extraordinary; incomparable; inimitable; matchless; nonpareil; notable; noteworthy; novel; odd; original; peculiar; peerless; remarkable; singular; special; strange; uncommon; unequaled; unexampled; unique; unmatched; unparalleled; unrivaled; unusual; without equal.* ■ One teacher commented that Philip is *one in a million*. REPLACE WITH *peerless.*

one man's meat is another man's poison A popular prescription (see page 23).

one man's trash is another man's treasure A popular prescription (see page 23).

one of a kind A torpid term (see page 24). *different; exceptional; extraordinary; incomparable; inimitable; matchless; nonpareil; notable; noteworthy; novel; odd; original; peculiar; peerless; remarkable; singular; special; strange; uncommon; unequaled; unexampled; unique; unmatched; unparalleled; unrivaled; unusual; without equal.*

one size fits all An infantile phrase (see page 20). *procrustean.* ■ We do not advocate a *one-size-fits-all* approach in making decisions about how students should be educated. REPLACE WITH *procrustean.*

one step at a time A popular prescription (see page 23).

(well) one thing led to another A grammatical gimmick (see page 19).

one-two punch A moribund metaphor (see page 21).

one-way street A moribund metaphor (see page 21).

one-way ticket to A moribund metaphor (see page 21).

on firm (solid) ground A moribund metaphor (see page 21). *firm; solid; sound; stable; sturdy.*

ongoing An overworked word (see page 22). *Ongoing* has superseded practically all of its synonyms. We have *ongoing basis; ongoing care; ongoing commitment; ongoing destruction; ongoing discussions; ongoing education; ongoing effort; ongoing investigation; ongoing plan; ongoing process; ongoing program; ongoing relationship; ongoing service; ongoing support;* and so many more.

Consider these synonyms: *ceaseless; constant; continual; continuing; continuous; endless; enduring; incessant; lifelong; long-lived; nonstop; progressing; unbroken; unceasing; unremitting.* ■ With this new rehabilitation center, patients will no longer have to travel outside the community to receive the *ongoing* care they need. DELETE *ongoing.* ■ Establishing paternity also may force more women into *ongoing* relationships with fathers who are abusive or violent. REPLACE WITH *lifelong.*

(up) on (her) high horse A moribund metaphor (see page 21). *arrogant; cavalier; condescending; contemptuous; despotic; dictatorial; disdainful; dogmatic; domineering; haughty; imperious; insolent; lofty; overbearing; overweening; patronizing; pompous; pretentious; scornful; self-important; supercilious; superior; vainglorious.*

on (its) last legs A moribund metaphor (see page 21). 1. *decaying; declining; deteriorating; disappearing; disintegrating; dying; ebbing; expiring; fading; failing; moribund; near death; sinking; vanishing; waning.* 2. *beat; bushed; debilitated; depleted; drained; drowsy; enervated; exhausted; fatigued; groggy; sapped; sleepy; sluggish; slumberous; somnolent; soporific; spent; tired; weary; worn out.* ■ The battle for a smoke-free environment is hardly *on its last legs.* REPLACE WITH *moribund.*

(high) on (my) list of priorities A torpid term (see page 24).

> You were living with Amanda in New York and marriage wasn't high on your list of priorities, although on Amanda's it was. — Jay McInerney, *Bright Lights, Big City*

(the) only good (cat) is a dead (cat) A quack equation (see page 23).

only the strong survive A popular prescription (see page 23).

on (his) part A wretched redundancy (see page 25). *among; by; for; from; of; -s.* ■ I think this is really irresponsible *on your part.* REPLACE WITH *of you.* ■ I guess this is selfish *on my part.* REPLACE

WITH *of me*. ■ It's an incredible sacrifice *on her part and her family's part*. REPLACE WITH *from her and her family*. ■ This single one-page assignment made the point that Wilder's attitudes toward Native Americans and toward African Americans are problematic, and made it better than any amount of lecturing *on my part* could have done. REPLACE WITH *I*. SEE ALSO *on the part of*.

> All but Lucia, that is to say, whose throne had, quite unintentionally on Olga's part, been pulled smartly from under her, and her scepter flew in one direction, and her crown in another. — E. F. Benson, *Lucia in London*

on pins and needles A moribund metaphor (see page 21). *agitated; anxious; apprehensive; disquieted; distressed; disturbed; edgy; fretful; ill at ease; impatient; in suspense; nervous; on edge; restive; restless; troubled; uneasy; unquiet; unsettled; worried*. ■ Democrats — already *on pins and needles* over the release of Clinton's grand jury testimony — were scrambling yesterday with how to cope over the second tape. REPLACE WITH *uneasy*.

on (her) plate A moribund metaphor (see page 21). *awaiting (her); before (her); pending*.

on safe ground A moribund metaphor (see page 21). *guarded; protected; safe; secure; sheltered; shielded*.

on shaky ground A moribund metaphor (see page 21). *indefensible; shaky; unsound; unsustainable*.

on speaking terms A wretched redundancy (see page 25). *speaking*.

> For reasons they could no longer define clearly, Colin and Mary were not on speaking terms. — Ian McEwan, *The Comfort of Strangers*

(right) on target A moribund metaphor (see page 21). *accurate; correct; exact; irrefutable; precise; right; true*. ■ The Jan. 19 editorial identifying the inconsistent, but vociferous, antitax group as "the haters" is *right on target*. REPLACE WITH *irrefutable*.

on tenterhooks A moribund metaphor (see page 21). *agitated; anxious; apprehensive; disquieted; distressed; disturbed; edgy; fretful; ill at ease; impatient; in suspense; nervous; on edge; restive; restless; troubled; uneasy; unquiet; unsettled; worried*.

> Mick sat on tenterhooks, leaning forward in his chair, glaring at her almost hysterically: and whether he was more anxious out of vanity for her to say Yes! or whether he was more panic-stricken for fear she *should* say Yes! — who can tell? — D. H. Lawrence, *Lady Chatterley's Lover*

on the back burner A moribund metaphor (see page 21). *in abeyance; on hold; pending; suspended*.

on the ball A moribund metaphor (see page 21). 1. *alert; attentive; awake; aware; eagle-eyed; heedful; observant; vigilant; wakeful; watchful*. 2. *able; adroit; apt; astute; bright; brilliant; capable; clever; competent; discerning; effective;*

effectual; efficient; enlightened; insightful; intelligent; judicious; keen; knowledgeable; learned; logical; luminous; perceptive; perspicacious; quick; rational; reasonable; sagacious; sage; sapient; sensible; sharp; shrewd; smart; sound; understanding; wise.

on the basis of A wretched redundancy (see page 25). *after; based on; because of; by; due to; for; from; in; on; owing to; through; via; with.* ■ NABCO chooses material for this site *on the basis of* its timely and useful content. REPLACE WITH *based on.* ■ Exemption from IRB review and approval is determined *on the basis of* the risks associated with the study. REPLACE WITH *by.* ■ There shall be no discrimination against any individual *on the basis of* ethnic group, race, religion, gender, sexual orientation, age, or record of public offense. REPLACE WITH *because of.*

on the blink A moribund metaphor (see page 21). *broken; defective; in disrepair; not working; not functioning; out of order.*

on the brink of A moribund metaphor (see page 21). *about to; (very) close (to); (very) near (to).*

(right) on the button A moribund metaphor (see page 21). *accurate; correct; exact; irrefutable; precise; right; true.*

on the chopping block A moribund metaphor (see page 21). *at risk; endangered; imperiled; in danger; in jeopardy; in peril; in trouble; jeopardized.*

(ride) on the coattails of A moribund metaphor (see page 21).

on the cuff A moribund metaphor (see page 21). *on credit.*

on the cutting (leading) edge A moribund metaphor (see page 21). *first; forefront; foremost; leading; vanguard.*

on the day A torpid term (see page 24). *today;* delete. ■ He scored 16 points *on the day.* REPLACE WITH *today.* ■ The euro was flat *on the day* at 133.85 yen after it rose nearly 0.6 percent on Wednesday. REPLACE WITH *today.* ■ Even late in the fourth set, I was up a break to take it into a fifth set, and I just didn't quite play the big points as well as he did *on the day.* DELETE *on the day.*

Sports writers, known for mismanaging words, and financial analysts, known for mismanaging money, are especially fond of the expression *on the day.*

on the dot A moribund metaphor (see page 21). *on time; precisely; promptly; punctually.*

> They must be clean and neat about their persons and clothes and show up promptly — on the dot — and in good condition for the work every day. — Theodore Dreiser, *An American Tragedy*

on the drawing board A moribund metaphor (see page 21). ■ The university now has seven new schools *on the drawing board.*

on the edge of (their) seats A moribund metaphor (see page 21). *absorb; arrest; bewitch; captivate; charm; curious; divert; enchant; engage; engross; entertain; enthrall; entice; excite; fascinate; intrigue; rivet; spellbind; stimulate; tantalize.* ■

People are *on the edge of their seats* about this report. REPLACE WITH *fascinated.*

on the fast track A moribund metaphor (see page 21).

(sit) on the fence A moribund metaphor (see page 21). *ambivalent; divided; impartial; indecisive; irresolute; neutral; noncommittal; torn; uncertain; uncommitted; undecided; unsettled; unsure.*

on the firing line A moribund metaphor (see page 21).

on the fly A moribund metaphor (see page 21). *ad-lib; extemporize; improvise.*

on the fritz A moribund metaphor (see page 21). *broken; defective; in disrepair; not working; not functioning; out of order.*

on the front burner A moribund metaphor (see page 21). ■ While lawmakers continue their work, the governor is visiting schools across the state to keep the issue *on the front burner.*

on the front lines A moribund metaphor (see page 21).

on the go A moribund metaphor (see page 21). *absorbed; active; busy; employed; engaged; engrossed; going; immersed; involved; moving; occupied; preoccupied; wrapped up in.*

(hot) on the heels of A moribund metaphor (see page 21). *after; behind; ensuing; following; succeeding.* SEE ALSO *in the wake of.*

on the horizon A moribund metaphor (see page 21). *approaching; at hand; close; coming; expected; forthcoming; imminent; impending; near; nearby.*

(caught) on the horns of a dilemma A moribund metaphor (see page 21). *at risk; endangered; hard-pressed; imperiled; in a bind; in a dilemma; in a fix; in a jam; in a predicament; in a quandary; in danger; in difficulty; in jeopardy; in peril; in trouble; jeopardized.*

(take it) on the lam A moribund metaphor (see page 21). *abscond; clear out; decamp; depart; desert; disappear; escape; exit; flee; fly; go; go away; leave; move on; part; pull out; quit; retire; retreat; run away; take flight; take off; vacate; vanish; withdraw.*

on the level A torpid term (see page 24). *aboveboard; creditable; equitable; fair; genuine; honest; honorable; just; lawful; legitimate; open; proper; reputable; respectable; right; sincere; square; straightforward; truthful; upright; veracious; veridical.*

on the loose A torpid term (see page 24). *at large; at liberty; free; loose; unattached; unbound; unconfined; unrestrained; unrestricted.*

on the mark A moribund metaphor (see page 21). *accurate; correct; exact; precise; right; true.*

on the mend A torpid term (see page 24). *ameliorating; amending; coming round; convalescent; convalescing; gaining strength; getting better; healing; improving; looking up; meliorating; mending; rallying; recovering; recuperating; refreshing; renewing; reviving; strengthening.*

(right) on the money A moribund metaphor (see page 21). *accurate; correct; exact; fact; irrefutable; precise; right; true.* ■ I think it was *right on the money.* REPLACE WITH *irrefutable.*

on the nose A moribund metaphor (see page 21). *accurate; correct; exact; irrefutable; precise; right; true.*

> As usual, he gives me two hours with him, what will be two hours on the nose. — Binnie Kirshenbaum, *A Disturbance in One Place*

(on the) other side of the coin A moribund metaphor (see page 21). 1. *antithesis; contrary; converse; opposite; reverse.* 2. *but; in contrast; conversely; however; inversely; whereas; yet.* ■ *On the other side of the coin,* if you're astute you can occasionally buy them at big discounts. REPLACE WITH *But.*

on the part of A wretched redundancy (see page 25). *among; by; for; from; of; -s. On the part of* is a preposition phrase that apparently appeals to bombastic men and women who may not fully consider what they say, for they certainly do not consider how they say it. People use *on the part of* when they're too lazy to think of the proper, or even a better, word. This is a thoughtless person's phrase. ■ As a result, and following vigorous lobbying *on the part of* CFS victims, the disease is now called chronic fatigue immunodeficiency syndrome. REPLACE WITH *by.* ■ Open-ended questions require much more effort *on the part of* the person answering them. REPLACE WITH *from.* ■ There is some cultural resistance *on the part of* some U.S. racial and ethnic groups to government-sponsored contraceptive programs. REPLACE WITH *from.* ■ *Misconduct on the part of the police* sometimes also violates the criminal law. REPLACE WITH *Police misconduct.* ■ It has also sometimes been attributed to an attitude *on the part of* health counselors that the poor are charity cases who should be satisfied with whatever they get since they are probably not paying for their own care. REPLACE WITH *among.* ■ If we are to get over the current crisis, *sacrifices on the part of everyone will have to be made.* REPLACE WITH *everyone will have to make sacrifices.* ■ Exhaustive questions reduce the *frustration on the part of the respondents.* REPLACE WITH *respondents' frustrations.* SEE ALSO *on (his) part.*

on the Q.T. A moribund metaphor (see page 21). *clandestinely; confidentially; covertly; furtively; mysteriously; in private; in secret; privately; quietly; secludedly; secretly; slyly; stealthily; surreptitiously; undercover.*

on the razor's edge A moribund metaphor (see page 21). *at risk; endangered; hard-pressed; imperiled; in danger; in difficulty; in jeopardy; in peril; in trouble; jeopardized.*

(start) on the right foot A moribund metaphor (see page 21). *auspiciously; favorably; positively; propitiously; well.*

on the right track A moribund metaphor (see page 21). *on target; on track.*

on the road A moribund metaphor (see page 21). *traveling.*

on the road to recovery A moribund metaphor (see page 21). *ameliorating; amending; coming round; convalescent; convalescing; feeling better; gaining strength; getting better; healing; improving; looking up; meliorating; mending; rallying; recovering; recuperating; refreshing; renewing; reviving; strengthening.* ■ His wife has been ill, but she's *on the road to recovery*. REPLACE WITH *improving.*

on the rocks A moribund metaphor (see page 21). *at risk; collapsing; endangered; failing; imperiled; in danger; in difficulty; in jeopardy; in peril; in trouble; jeopardized.* ■ Our marriage is *on the rocks*. REPLACE WITH *imperiled.*

on the ropes A moribund metaphor (see page 21). 1. *at risk; endangered; hard-pressed; imperiled; in danger; in difficulty; in jeopardy; in peril; in trouble; jeopardized.* 2. *defenseless; helpless; impotent; powerless.*

on the same page A moribund metaphor (see page 21). *agree; concur; feel similarly; harmonize; (be) in accord; (be) in agreement; (be) in harmony; like-minded; match; mesh; think alike. On the same page* is spoken or written by pawns and puppets who cannot think for themselves, who rely on others for how they should speak and what they should think; who prize the ease of agreement more than they do the entanglement of dissent; who turn few pages and read fewer books.

■ I believe we're all *on the same page.* REPLACE WITH *thinking alike.* ■ It gives us direction — everybody is *on the same page,* everybody knows where we want to get and how we want to get there. REPLACE WITH *in harmony.* ■ He usually gets his way, but we're usually *on the same page*. REPLACE WITH *in agreement.*

> He figured since Franklin hadn't responded to the idea with a gasp or an indignant speech they were on the same page. — Bill Fitzhugh, *Fender Benders*

on the same wavelength A moribund metaphor (see page 21). *agree; concur; feel similarly; harmonize; (be) in accord; (be) in agreement; (be) in harmony; like-minded; match; mesh; think alike.*

> He was the typical teacher on the same wavelength as his kids, since he himself didn't look a day over thirty, and the best part of it was that he wasn't some half-ass .... — Zoe Valdes, *Dear First Love*

on the ... side A wretched redundancy (see page 25). ■ Tuesday will be *on the chilly side*. REPLACE WITH *chilly.* ■ She is *on the thin side*. REPLACE WITH *thin.* ■ That means the 550,000 estimate is probably *on the low side*. REPLACE WITH *low.*

on the sly A torpid term (see page 24). *clandestinely; confidentially; covertly; furtively; mysteriously; in private; in secret; privately; quietly; secludedly; secretly; slyly; stealthily; surreptitiously; undercover.*

on the spot A torpid term (see page 24). 1. *at once; directly; forthwith; immediately; instantly; momentarily; promptly; right away; straightaway; summarily; without delay.* 2. *at risk; endangered; hard-pressed; imperiled; in danger; in difficulty; in jeopardy; in peril; in trouble; jeopardized.*

on the spur of the moment A wretched redundancy (see page 25). *impetuously; impulsively; spontaneously; suddenly; unexpectedly; without warning.*

on the table A moribund metaphor (see page 21). *before us; being considered; being discussed; considerable; discussable; under discussion.* Whoever speaks this expression speaks words scarcely worth hearing. Whoever writes this expression writes words scarcely worth reading. There are words that stir, words that persuade, words that compel; the expression *on the table* is not and is never among them.

■ A healthy dialog on value systems when there is no pressing issue *on the table* may help clear the air. REPLACE WITH *before us.* ■ There is nothing that is not *on the table.* REPLACE WITH *being considered.* ■ The White House could withdraw his nomination but say that option isn't *on the table.* REPLACE WITH *being discussed.*

(out) on the town A moribund metaphor (see page 21). *be merry; carouse; carry on; celebrate; debauch; disport; frolic; party; play; revel; riot; roister; rollick; romp; skylark.*

on the up-and-up A torpid term (see page 24). *aboveboard; creditable; equitable; fair; honest; honorable; just; lawful; legitimate; open; proper; reputable; respectable; right; sincere; square; straightforward; upright; veracious; veridical.*

on the warpath A moribund metaphor (see page 21). 1. *angry; bad-tempered; bilious; cantankerous; choleric; churlish; crabby; cranky; cross; curmudgeonly; disagreeable; dyspeptic; grouchy; gruff; grumpy; ill-humored; ill-tempered; irascible; irritable; mad; peevish; petulant; quarrelsome; riled; roiled; short-tempered; splenetic; surly; testy; vexed.* 2. *aggressive; antagonistic; arguing; argumentative; battling; bellicose; belligerent; bickering; brawling; clashing; combative; contentious; fighting; militant; pugnacious; quarrelsome; querulous; squabbling; truculent; warlike; wrangling.*

on the wings of the wind A moribund metaphor (see page 21). *abruptly; apace; at once; briskly; directly; expeditiously; fast; forthwith; hastily; hurriedly; immediately; instantaneously; instantly; posthaste; promptly; quickly; rapidly; rashly; right away; speedily; straightaway; swiftly; wingedly.*

(start) on the wrong foot A moribund metaphor (see page 21). *adversely; inauspiciously; negatively; unfavorably; unpropitiously.*

on the wrong track A moribund metaphor (see page 21). *amiss; astray; deceived; deluded; erring; erroneous; fallacious; false; faulty; inaccurate; incorrect; in error; misguided; misinformed; mislead; mistaken; not correct; not right; wrong.*

(skate) on thin ice A moribund metaphor (see page 21). *chance; dare; endanger; gamble; hazard; imperil; jeopardize; make bold; peril; risk; venture.*

(keep) on (his) toes A moribund metaphor (see page 21). *(be) alert; (be) attentive; (be) awake; (be) aware; (be) heedful; (be) vigilant; (be) wakeful.*

(sitting) on top of the world A moribund metaphor (see page 21). 1. *advantageous; auspicious; blessed; charmed;*

enchanted; favored; felicitous; flourishing; fortuitous; fortunate; golden; in luck; lucky; propitious; prosperous; successful; thriving. 2. *blissful; blithe; buoyant; cheerful; delighted; ecstatic; elated; enraptured; euphoric; exalted; excited; exhilarated; exultant; gay; glad; gleeful; good-humored; happy; intoxicated; jolly; jovial; joyful; joyous; jubilant; merry; mirthful; overjoyed; pleased; rapturous; thrilled.*

onward and upward An inescapable pair (see page 20).

open and aboveboard A moribund metaphor (see page 21). *aboveboard; creditable; equitable; fair; honest; honorable; just; lawful; legitimate; open; proper; reputable; respectable; right; square; straightforward; upright; veracious; veridical.*

(an) open-and-shut case A moribund metaphor (see page 21). *apparent; clear; evident; open; plain; straightforward; unambiguous; uncomplex; uncomplicated.*

open (up) a Pandora's box A moribund metaphor (see page 21).

(an) open book A moribund metaphor (see page 21). 1. *apparent; clear; clear-cut; crystalline; evident; explicit; limpid; lucid; manifest; obvious; open; patent; pellucid; plain; translucent; transparent; unambiguous; uncomplex; uncomplicated; understandable; unequivocal; unmistakable.* 2. *aboveboard; artless; blunt; candid; direct; forthright; frank; genuine; guileless; honest; ingenuous; naive; sincere; straightforward; truthful; veracious; veridical.*

(the) opening (latest) salvo A moribund metaphor (see page 21).

(a) (an) (wide) open question A wretched redundancy (see page 25). *a question; debatable; disputable; moot; open; questionable; uncertain; unclear; undecided; undetermined; unknown; unsettled; unsure.* ■ Whether it's still possible for us to complete the project by next season is *an open question* at this point. REPLACE WITH *questionable.*

open the door for (on; to) A moribund metaphor (see page 21). *bring about; cause; create; effect; generate; give rise to; inaugurate; initiate; introduce; lead to; occasion; produce; provoke; result in; usher in.* ■ This breakthrough could *open the door to* a wide range of new varieties of important crops. REPLACE WITH *result in.* ■ Human embryo cells have been isolated and grown in the test tube for the first time, a development that could *open the door to* new drug therapies. REPLACE WITH *lead to.*

open the floodgates A moribund metaphor (see page 21).

operative A torpid term (see page 24). ■ The *operative* philosophy is spelled out early on: Winning is the most important thing in life.

opportunity knocks only once A popular prescription (see page 23).

(as) opposed to what? An infantile phrase (see page 20). SEE ALSO *(as) compared to what?; everything's (it's all) relative.*

opposites attract A popular prescription (see page 23).

or anything A grammatical gimmick (see page 19). ■ I didn't go beat her up, *or anything.* DELETE *or anything.* ■ Not to be rude *or anything,* but I don't think we should talk to each other. DELETE *or anything.* SEE ALSO *or anything like that.*

or anything like that A grammatical gimmick (see page 19). ■ He wasn't my first boyfriend *or anything like that.* DELETE *or anything like that.* ■ He didn't go out and say, "Who goes there?" *or anything like that.* DELETE *or anything like that.* ■ I really apologize if I was inappropriate or upset you *or anything like that.* DELETE *or anything like that.* SEE ALSO *or anything.*

(an) orgy of A moribund metaphor (see page 21). SEE ALSO *a barrage of.*

or (a; the) lack thereof A torpid term (see page 24). ■ He was ousted because the majority of voters believe he didn't do a good job as mayor — not because of his skin color, but because of his merit *or lack thereof.*

or something A grammatical gimmick (see page 19). As there are phrases that help us begin sentences, like *I'll tell you (something),* so there are phrases that help us end them. *Or something, or something like that, or something or other* extricate us from having to conclude our thoughts clearly. Said as a person's thoughts end, but before his words do, *or something,* like its many relations, is a thoughtless phrase that reminds us only of our trembling humanity.

■ This is like something I'd wear in third grade, *or something.* DELETE *or something.* ■ It makes you mad when they make them sound like they're vicious people — that if you walk the street, they're going to grab you *or something.* DELETE *or something.* SEE ALSO *or something like that; or something or other.*

or something like that A grammatical gimmick (see page 19). ■ Why couldn't they have shot him in his arm or leg *or something like that?* DELETE *or something like that.* SEE ALSO *or something; or something or other.*

or something or other A grammatical gimmick (see page 19). ■ We might go to the movies *or something or other.* DELETE *or something or other.* SEE ALSO *or something; or something like that.*

or what A grammatical gimmick (see page 19). ■ Did you see an opportunity for escape, or plan it for a long time, *or what?* DELETE *or what.* ■ Was he being vulgar *or what?* DELETE *or what.* ■ Did you make enough money so you can retire *or what?* REPLACE WITH *or not.*

or whatever A grammatical gimmick (see page 19). ■ They say he corrupted my mind *or whatever.* DELETE *or whatever.* ■ Is it a good thing, is it a bad thing, is it useless, *or whatever?* DELETE *or whatever.* ■ She just wants the extra attention, *or whatever.* DELETE *or whatever.* ■ You can call this arrogance or way too much self-assurance *or whatever.* DELETE *or whatever.* ■ The percent remembered is the same whether the audience is a business audience, a college audience, a PTA audience, *or whatever.* DELETE *or whatever.*

or words to that effect A grammatical gimmick (see page 19).

(an) ounce of prevention A moribund metaphor (see page 21).

(an) ounce of prevention is worth a pound of cure A popular prescription (see page 23).

out and out A torpid term (see page 24). *absolute; compleat; complete; consummate; deadly; outright; perfect; thorough; thoroughgoing; total; unmitigated; unqualified; utter.*

out at the elbows A moribund metaphor (see page 21). 1. *disheveled; dowdy; frowzy; messy; ragged; run-down; seedy; shabby; slipshod; sloppy; slovenly; tattered; threadbare; unkempt; untidy; worn.* 2. *bankrupt; broke; destitute; distressed; impecunious; impoverished; indigent; insolvent; needy; penniless; poor; poverty-stricken; underprivileged.*

out for blood A moribund metaphor (see page 21). *revengeful; ruthless; vengeful; vindictive.*

out in left field A moribund metaphor (see page 21). 1. *amiss; astray; confused; deceived; deluded; erring; erroneous; fallacious; false; faulty; inaccurate; incorrect; in error; misguided; misinformed; mislead; mistaken; not correct; not right; uninformed; wrong.* 2. *ignorant; incognizant; insensible; nescient; unacquainted; unadvised; unapprised; unaware; unenlightened; unfamiliar; unintelligent; unknowing; unschooled; untaught; unversed.* ■ On this issue, feminists are truly *out in left field.* REPLACE WITH *misguided.*

(they're) out in the cold A moribund metaphor (see page 21). *abandoned; alone; assailable; attackable; defenseless; deserted; exposed; forsaken; obnoxious; penetrable; pregnable; stranded; undefended; unguarded; unprotected; unshielded; vulnerable.*

out in the sun too much A moribund metaphor (see page 21). *bewildered; confounded; confused; dazed; mixed up; muddled; perplexed.*

out like a light An insipid simile. 1. *asleep; dozing; napping; sleeping.* 2. *anesthetized; benumbed; comatose; insensate; insensible; insentient; oblivious; senseless; soporiferous; soporific; stuporous; unconscious.*

out of a clear blue sky A moribund metaphor (see page 21). *by surprise; suddenly; unexpectedly; without warning.*

out of circulation A moribund metaphor (see page 21). 1. *broken; defective; in disrepair; not working; not functioning; out of order.* 2. *afflicted; ailing; diseased; ill; indisposed; infirm; not (feeling) well; sick; sickly; suffering; unhealthy; unsound; unwell; valetudinarian.*

out of commission A moribund metaphor (see page 21). 1. *broken; defective; in disrepair; not working; not functioning; out of order.* 2. *afflicted; ailing; diseased; ill; indisposed; infirm; not (feeling) well; sick; sickly; suffering; unhealthy; unsound; unwell; valetudinarian.*

out of gas A moribund metaphor (see page 21). *beat; bushed; debilitated; depleted; drained; drowsy; enervated; exhausted; fatigued; groggy; sapped; sleepy; sluggish; slumberous; somnolent; soporific; spent; tired; weary; worn out.*

out of harm's way A moribund metaphor (see page 21). *guarded; protected; safe; secure; sheltered; shielded; undamaged; unharmed; unhurt; unscathed.*

out of it A moribund metaphor (see page 21). *ignorant; incognizant; insensi-*

ble; nescient; unacquainted; unadvised; unapprised; unaware; unenlightened; unfamiliar; uninformed; unintelligent; unknowing; unschooled; untaught; unversed.

out of kilter A moribund metaphor (see page 21). 1. *askew; awry; cockeyed; misaligned; skewed.* 2. *shaky; unbalanced; unsettled; unsound; unstable; wobbly.* 3. *broken; defective; in disrepair; not working; not functioning; out of order.*

> In a further aside, I should just like to add here that I have observed in my sixty-four years that passion both erodes and enhances character in equal measure, and not slowly but instantly, and in such a manner that what is left is not in balance but is thrown desperately out of kilter in both directions. — Anita Shreve, *All He Ever Wanted*

out of line A moribund metaphor (see page 21).
1. *improper; inappropriate; inapt; indecorous; unbefitting; uncalled for; unfit; unfitting; unsuitable; unsuited.* 2. *boisterous; contrary; contumacious; disobedient; disorderly; fractious; insubordinate; misbehaving; obstreperous; rebellious; recalcitrant; refractory; rowdy; uncontrolled; undisciplined; unruly.*

out of reach A moribund metaphor (see page 21). 1. *inaccessible; remote; unapproachable; unreachable.* 2. *impossible; impracticable; improbable; unfeasible; unlikely; unworkable.*

out of sorts A moribund metaphor (see page 21). *angry; annoyed; cheerless; cross; dejected; depressed; despondent; discouraged; dispirited; displeased; downcast; enraged; furious; gloomy; glum; grouchy; irate; irritated; mad; morose; peevish; riled; roiled; sad; testy; troubled; uneasy; unhappy; upset; vexed; worried.*

out of sync A moribund metaphor (see page 21). 1. *askew; awry; cockeyed; misaligned; skewed.* 2. *shaky; unbalanced; unsettled; unsound; unstable; wobbly.* 3. *broken; defective; in disrepair; not working; not functioning; out of order.*

out of the blue A moribund metaphor (see page 21). *by surprise; suddenly; unexpectedly; without warning.*

out of the frying pan and into the fire A moribund metaphor (see page 21). *aggravate; complicate; exacerbate; heighten; increase; intensify; irritate; make worse; worsen.*

out of the game A moribund metaphor (see page 21).

out of the realm of possibility A wretched redundancy (see page 25). *implausible; imponderable; impossible; impracticable; inconceivable; infeasible; not likely; unbelievable; unconjecturable; unimaginable; unsupposable; unthinkable; unworkable.* ■ It's not *out of the realm of possibility* that he wants to embarrass the president. REPLACE WITH *unthinkable.*

out of the running A moribund metaphor (see page 21). *noncontender; not competing; not contending.*

out of the woods A moribund metaphor (see page 21). *guarded; protected; safe; secure; sheltered; shielded; undamaged; unharmed; unhurt; unscathed.*

out of thin air A moribund metaphor (see page 21).

out of this world A moribund metaphor (see page 21). *consummate; distinguished; eminent; excellent; exceptional; exemplary; exquisite; extraordinary; fabulous; fantastic; flawless; grand; great; ideal; illustrious; magnificent; marvelous; matchless; nonpareil; perfect; preeminent; remarkable; splendid; superb; superior; superlative; supreme; terrific; transcendent; tremendous; wonderful; wondrous.*

out of whack A moribund metaphor (see page 21). 1. *askew; awry; cockeyed; misaligned; skewed.* 2. *shaky; unbalanced; unsettled; unsound; unstable; wobbly.* 3. *broken; defective; in disrepair; not working; not functioning; out of order.*

(create) out of (the) whole cloth A moribund metaphor (see page 21). *fabricated; fake; false; falsified; fictional; fictitious; forged; invented; made-up; untrue.*

> She considered that she had created this man out of whole cloth, had thought him up, and she was sure that she could do a better job if she had to do it again. — John Steinbeck, *The Moon Is Down*

(go) out on a limb A moribund metaphor (see page 21). 1. *at risk; endangered; hard-pressed; imperiled; in a bind; in a dilemma; in a fix; in a jam; in a predicament; in a quandary; in danger; in difficulty; in jeopardy; in peril; in trouble; jeopardized.* 2. *abandoned; alone; assailable; attackable; defenseless; deserted; exposed; forsaken; obnoxious; penetrable; pregnable; stranded; undefended; unguarded; unprotected; unshielded; vulnerable.* 3. *be adventuresome; be adventurous; be bold; be daring.*

output A torpid term (see page 24). SEE ALSO *(the) bottom line; feedback; input; interface; parameters.*

out the window A moribund metaphor (see page 21). 1. *abandoned; discarded; dismissed; jettisoned; rejected; repudiated; thrown out; tossed out.* 2. *dead; disappeared; dissolved; dispersed; evaporated; finished; forfeited; gone; inapplicable; inappropriate; inoperative; insignificant; irrelevant; lost; no longer applicable (apply); over; passed; scattered; unimportant; vanished.* ■ It's just that old rules are *out the window*, like most of last year's assumptions about Europe. REPLACE WITH *inapplicable.* ■ It's 1999 in America, a land where common sense *went out the window* long ago. REPLACE WITH *was jettisoned.*

out to lunch A moribund metaphor (see page 21). 1. *absent-minded; absorbed; abstracted; bemused; daydreaming; distrait; dreamy; faraway; lost; preoccupied.* 2. *forgetful; heedless; inattentive; lethean; neglectful; oblivious; unmindful.* 3. *ignorant; incognizant; insensible; nescient; unacquainted; unadvised; unapprised; unaware; unenlightened; unfamiliar; unintelligent; unknowing; unschooled; untaught; unversed.* 4. *amiss; astray; confused; deceived; deluded; erring; erroneous; fallacious; false; faulty; inaccurate; incorrect; in error; misguided; misinformed; mislead; mistaken; not correct; not right; uninformed; wrong.*

(put) out to pasture A moribund metaphor (see page 21). *discharge; dismiss; fire; lay off; let go; release; retire;*

sack; set aside; shelve. ■ Motors Inc. said Joe will be *put out to pasture* when it introduces next year's lineup of vehicles. REPLACE WITH *retired.*

over a barrel A moribund metaphor (see page 21). *defenseless; helpless; impotent; powerless.*

over and done with A wretched redundancy (see page 25). *completed; concluded; done; ended; finished; over; passed; through.* ■ But in reality, it is the same old story, one we'd like to think of as *over and done with.* REPLACE WITH *concluded.*

over (my) dead body A moribund metaphor (see page 21). *at no time; by no means; in no way; never; no; not; not at all; not ever; not in any way; not in the least*

overplay (his) hand A moribund metaphor (see page 21).

(go) over the edge A moribund metaphor (see page 21). *batty; cracked; crazy; daft; demented; deranged; fey; foolish; goofy; insane; lunatic; mad; maniacal; neurotic; nuts; nutty; psychotic; raving; silly; squirrelly; touched; unbalanced; unhinged; unsound; wacky; zany.*

over the hill A moribund metaphor (see page 21). *aged; aging; ancient; antediluvian; antique; archaic; elderly; hoary; hoary-headed; old; patriarchal; prehistoric; seasoned; superannuated; venerable.*

over the moon A moribund metaphor (see page 21). *blissful; blithe; buoyant; cheerful; delighted; ecstatic; elated; enraptured; euphoric; exalted; excited; exhilarated; exultant; gay; glad; gleeful; good-humored; happy; intoxicated; jolly; jovial; joyful; joyous; jubilant; merry; mirthful; overjoyed; pleased; rapturous; thrilled.*

> Over breakfast, expecting her to be over the moon, Paul had told her that she could give her notice in at the nursery, he'd fix her up a half share in a smart little business with the girlfriend of a friend of his. — Elizabeth Young, *Asking for Trouble*

over the transom A moribund metaphor (see page 21).

overworked and understaffed An inescapable pair (see page 20).

owing to the fact that A wretched redundancy (see page 25). *because; considering; for; in that; since.* ■ *Owing to the fact that* many companies are members of more than one EDI system, it is helpful if they all change in recognizable ways. REPLACE WITH *Since.* SEE ALSO *attributable to the fact that; due to the fact that.*

> In the past she and I had seldom spoken to each other, owing to the fact that her 'one remaining joy' — her charming little Karl — had never succeeded in kindling into flame those sparks of maternity which are supposed to grow in great numbers upon the altar of every respectable female heart .... — Katherine Mansfield, *In a German Pension*

P

pack a punch (wallop) A moribund metaphor (see page 21). *cogent; convincing; dynamic; effective; effectual; emotional; energetic; ferocious; fierce; forceful; formidable; gripping; hard-hitting; herculean; impassioned; inspiring; intense; lively; mighty; moving; passionate; persuasive; potent; powerful; strong; vehement; vigorous; vital.* ■ No doubt hurricane Bonnie is still *packing a punch.* REPLACE WITH *mighty.*

packed in (trapped) like sardines (in a can) An insipid simile. *abounding; brimful; brimming; bursting; chock-full; congested; crammed; crowded; dense; filled; full; gorged; jammed; jam-packed; overcrowded; overfilled; overflowing; packed; replete; saturated; stuffed.*

> She gave me a rather disparaging look and took out a tin of Golden Virginia, which she opened to reveal a layer of tiny neat joints packed in like sardines. — Kate Atkinson, *Emotionally Weird*

pack to the gills A moribund metaphor (see page 21). *abounding; brimful; brimming; bursting; chock-full; congested; crammed; crowded; dense; filled; full; gorged; jammed; jam-packed; overcrowded; overfilled; overflowing; packed; replete; saturated; stuffed; swarming; teeming.* ■ Maybe we'll visit the Museum of Science, which will surely be *packed to the gills* and most unpleasant. REPLACE WITH *overcrowded.*

pack to the rafters A moribund metaphor (see page 21). *abounding; brimful; brimming; bursting; chock-full; congested; crammed; crowded; dense; filled; full; gorged; jammed; jam-packed; overcrowded; overfilled; overflowing; packed; replete; saturated; stuffed; swarming; teeming.*

pack up and leave A moribund metaphor (see page 21). *abscond; clear out; decamp; depart; desert; disappear; escape; exit; flee; fly; go; go away; leave; move on; part; pull out; quit; retire; retreat; run away; take flight; take off; vacate; vanish; withdraw.*

paddle (my) own canoe A moribund metaphor (see page 21). *be autonomous; be free; be independent; be self-reliant; be self-sufficient.* ■ I like to *paddle my own canoe* in life, but when you have holes in your canoe, it's hard to know what to do. REPLACE WITH *be self-reliant.*

pain and suffering An inescapable pair (see page 20). *agony; anguish; distress; grief; misery; pain; suffering; torment; worry.*

painfully shy An inescapable pair (see page 20). *afraid; apprehensive; bashful; coy; demure; diffident; distant; fearful; humble; introverted; meek; modest; pavid; quiet; reserved; reticent; retiring; sheepish; shrinking; shy; timid; timorous; tremulous; unassuming; unobtrusive; unsociable; unsocial; withdrawn.*

(a) pain in the ass (butt; rear) A moribund metaphor (see page 21). *affliction; annoyance; bane; bother; burden; curse; difficulty; inconvenience; irritant; irritation; load; nuisance; ordeal; pain; pest; plague; problem; torment; tribulation; trouble; vexation; weight; worry.*

(a) pain in the neck A moribund metaphor (see page 21). *affliction; annoyance; bane; bother; burden; curse; difficulty; inconvenience; irritant; irritation; load; nuisance; ordeal; pain; pest; plague; problem; torment; tribulation; trouble; vexation; weight; worry.*

> The do-gooder, the bleeding heart, the concerned citizen, the militant reformer: what a pain in the neck they are: always making us feel guilty about something. — Edward Abbey, *The Fool's Progress: An Honest Novel*

paint a (rosy) picture of A moribund metaphor (see page 21). *delineate; demonstrate; depict; describe; document; draw; evince; illustrate; indicate; paint; picture; portray; present; report; represent; reveal; show.* ■ The document will *paint a picture of* the nation's worsening financial system and warn that many large banks are near insolvency. REPLACE WITH *describe.* ■ Together, they *paint a picture of* hard times ahead. REPLACE WITH *portray.*

paint (himself) into a corner A moribund metaphor (see page 21). *at bay; catch; corner; enmesh; ensnare; entangle; entrap; net; snare; trap.*

paint the town red A moribund metaphor (see page 21). *be merry; carouse; carry on; celebrate; debauch; disport; frolic; party; play; revel; riot; roister; rollick; romp; skylark.*

paint with a broad brush A moribund metaphor (see page 21). *generalize; universalize.*

pair of (two) twins A wretched redundancy (see page 25). *twins.* ■ There were *two twins* at the mall who came up to him and asked him out. DELETE *two.*

(as) pale as death An insipid simile. *anemic; ashen; blanched; bloodless; cadaverous; colorless; deathlike; doughy; haggard; lusterless; pale; pallid; pasty; peaked; sallow; sickly; wan; whitish.*

> Her skin had turned as pale as death, after she'd been stuck in that blasted compartment of hers with a shade that only went up halfway, while the train rattled and shook, rattled and shook, day after day after day across the country. — John Sedgwick, *The Education of Mrs. Bemis*

(as) pale as a ghost An insipid simile. *anemic; ashen; blanched; bloodless; cadaverous; colorless; deathlike; doughy; haggard; lusterless; pale; pallid; pasty; peaked; sallow; sickly; wan; whitish.*

parameter An overworked word (see page 22). 1. *boundary; guideline; guidepost; limit; limitation; perimeter.* 2. *characteristic; factor.* ■ At this time, potential funding *parameters* may change in a variety of ways. REPLACE WITH *characteristics.* ■ We would like to send you our most recent catalog to see if any of our books fit within your reviewing *parameters.* REPLACE WITH *guidelines.* SEE ALSO *(the) bottom line; feedback; input; interface; output.*

pardon my French An infantile phrase (see page 20).

par excellence A foreign phrase (see page 19). *incomparable; preeminent.*

par for the course A moribund metaphor (see page 21). The people who say *par for the course* are *average; common; commonplace; customary; everyday; mediocre; middling; normal; ordinary; quotidian; regular; routine; standard; typical; uneventful; unexceptional; unremarkable; usual* users of the English language.

Though sports and even the word *sports* may make us imagine action and excitement, sports metaphors are among the most prosaic expressions available to us. Those who use them are precisely as dull and uninspired as are their words. ■ That is *par for the course* for foreign businesses here, which have descended upon the Soviet Union much as they descended upon China. REPLACE WITH *normal.* ■ It's *par for the course* for this administration to blame all of its troubles on someone else. REPLACE WITH *customary.*

> I'd heard of cleaning ladies with filthy houses, and of divorced marriage counselors, so maybe this was par for the course. — Susan Coll, *Rockville Pike*

part and parcel An inescapable pair (see page 20). *component; element; factor; part; portion.*

parting is such sweet sorrow A popular prescription (see page 23).

parting of the ways A moribund metaphor (see page 21). *altercation; argument; conflict; disagreement; discord; disputation; dispute; feud; fight; misunderstanding; quarrel; rift; row; spat; squabble.*

partner in crime A moribund metaphor (see page 21). *abettor; accessory; accomplice; affiliate; ally; assistant; associate; co-conspirator; cohort; collaborator; colleague; compatriot; compeer; comrade; confederate; consort; co-worker; crony; partner; peer.*

part of the landscape A moribund metaphor (see page 21). *average; common; conventional; customary; everyday; expected; familiar; habitual; natural; normal; ordinary; regular; routine; standard; usual; traditional; typical.* ■ In the Bay Area, bad traffic's *part of the landscape.* REPLACE WITH *expected.* ■ When does an exotic species become *part of the landscape*? REPLACE WITH *familiar.*

pass the buck A moribund metaphor (see page 21). *ascribe; assign; attribute; impute.*

pass the time of day A moribund metaphor (see page 21). *babble; blab; cackle; chaffer; chat; chitchat; chatter; confabulate; converse; gossip; jabber; palaver; prate; prattle; rattle; talk.*

pass with flying colors A moribund metaphor (see page 21). *ace; do well; excel; shine.*

past experience A wretched redundancy (see page 25). *experience.* ■ I know from *past experience* that a lot of you are not going to like what I have to say. DELETE *past.*

past history A wretched redundancy (see page 25). *history.* ■ We did not anticipate that the town would attempt to live off of its *past history.* DELETE *past.*

past (his) prime A torpid term (see page 24). *aged; aging; ancient; antediluvian; antique; archaic; elderly; hoary; hoary-headed; old; patriarchal; prehistoric; seasoned; superannuated; venerable.*

past the point of no return A moribund metaphor (see page 21).

> Until that last time, when I knew I had to go, when I knew that if I told my son I'd broken my nose, blacked my eyes, split my lip, by walking into the dining-room door in the dark, that I would have gone past some point of no return. — Anna Quindlen, *Black and Blue*

(as) patient as Job An insipid simile. *accepting; accommodating; acquiescent; complacent; complaisant; compliant; cowed; deferential; docile; dutiful; easy; forbearing; gentle; humble; long-suffering; meek; mild; obedient; passive; patient; prostrate; quiet; reserved; resigned; stoical; submissive; subservient; timid; tolerant; tractable; unassuming; uncomplaining; yielding.*

pat on the back A moribund metaphor (see page 21). *acclaim; accolade; acknowledgment; applause; appreciation; approval; compliment; congratulation; felicitation; homage; honor; plaudits; praise; recognition; tribute.* ■ The selections are a nice *pat on the back* for our talented staff around the world. REPLACE WITH *compliment.* ■ To me, it's *a pat on the back* for hard work well done. REPLACE WITH *an acknowledgment.*

pat (myself) on the back A moribund metaphor (see page 21). *acclaim; applaud; celebrate; cheer; commend; compliment; congratulate; extol; flatter; hail; honor; laud; plume; praise; puff; salute; self-congratulate.* ■ After *patting himself on the back*, he incidentally points out that many other people may have had something to do with it. REPLACE WITH *congratulating himself.*

pave the way (for) A moribund metaphor (see page 21). 1. *arrange; groom; make ready; plan; prepare; prime; ready.* 2. *bring about; cause; create; effect; generate; give rise to; inaugurate; initiate; introduce; lead to; occasion; produce; provoke; result in; usher in.* ■ Chartering all schools *paves the way* for a new way to organize public education. REPLACE WITH *prepares.*

pay (their) debt to society A moribund metaphor (see page 21).

pay (my) dues A moribund metaphor (see page 21).

pay the fiddler (piper) A moribund metaphor (see page 21). *pay; suffer.*

pay the price A moribund metaphor (see page 21). *pay; suffer.*

pay the ultimate price Like other euphemisms, other ludicrous expressions for death and dying, *pay the ultimate price* — for *be executed; be killed; be murdered; die* — diminishes death, often an avenging, merciless death. There is no reverence for the dead, or for death, in this dimwitted expression.

pay through the nose A moribund metaphor (see page 21). *costly; dear; excessive; exorbitant; expensive; high-priced.*

peace and harmony A wretched redundancy (see page 25). *harmony; peace.* ■ I want there to be *peace and harmony* between us. REPLACE WITH *harmony* or *peace.*

> When Ada reached the story's conclusion, and the old lovers after long years together in peace and harmony had turned to oak and linden, it was full dark. — Charles Frazier, *Cold Mountain*

peace and quiet An inescapable pair (see page 20). *calm; calmness; composure; equanimity; peace; peacefulness; poise; quiet; quietude; repose; rest; serenity; silence; stillness; tranquility.*

peaches and cream (complexion) A moribund metaphor (see page 21).

pea in (my) shoe A moribund metaphor (see page 21). *affliction; annoyance; bane; bother; burden; curse; difficulty; inconvenience; irritant; irritation; load; nuisance; ordeal; pain; pest; plague; problem; torment; tribulation; trouble; vexation; weight; worry.*

peaks and valleys A moribund metaphor (see page 21). *alterations; changes; erraticism; fluctuations; fortuitousness; inconstancies; shifts; uncertainties; vacillations; variations; vicissitudes.*

peanut gallery An infantile phrase (see page 20). *audience; spectators; viewers.*

pearls of wisdom A moribund metaphor (see page 21). *acumen; astuteness; erudition; insight; intelligence; perspicacity; sagacity; wisdom.* ■ In addition to the $50,000 fee, his *pearls of wisdom* will cost three first-class airplane tickets. REPLACE WITH *insights.*

pearly whites A moribund metaphor (see page 21). *teeth.*

> Then I saw him out of the corner of my eye, a little flash of pearly whites, a curl of chestnut hair, jawbones that could cut glass, and an entourage bigger than the crowd at my last birthday party. — Eric Garcia, *Cassandra French's Finishing School for Boys*

pencil pusher A moribund metaphor (see page 21). 1. *assistant; clerk; office worker; recorder; scribe; secretary; typist.* 2. *drudge; menial; scullion; toiler.*

(the) pen is mightier than the sword A moribund metaphor (see page 21).

penny pinching A moribund metaphor (see page 21). *cheap; economical; frugal; miserly; niggardly; parsimonious; stingy; thrifty.*

(a) penny saved is a penny earned A popular prescription (see page 23).

people are who (what) they are A quack equation (see page 23).

people who live in glass houses shouldn't throw stones A popular prescription (see page 23).

(as) per (your request) A torpid term (see page 24). *according to; as.* Quintessentially dimwitted, *(as) per (your request)* is used by brainless people who cannot manage to sustain an original thought. These are the people who rely on ready-made phrases and formulas; the people who unquestioningly do as they're told; the people who join mass movements because they themselves cannot bear the burden of making decisions; the people who hate on instruction and fear forever.

■ *As per your request,* you have been unsubscribed. REPLACE WITH *As you requested.* ■ Enclosed are chapters 1 through 6, *as per your request.* REPLACE WITH *as you requested.* ■ *As per usual,* he refuses to choose between his chief of staff and his chief of budget. REPLACE WITH *As usual.* ■ *Per our discussion,* please substitute the version developed in the earlier tool for all but the last two sentences of this. REPLACE WITH *As we discussed.* ■ OPEC crude production in the first half of 1989 was supposed to be 18.5 million b/d, *as per* the November 1988 agreement. REPLACE WITH *as stated in.* ■ *As per* the Semiconductor Industry Association, U.S. manufacturers accounted for nearly $137 billion in revenues during the year 1997. REPLACE WITH *According to.*

perception is reality A quack equation (see page 23). Perception is too often purblind for there to be much reality to this quack equation. Still, it is a formula, uttered by mountebanks and managers alike, that has done much to disturb the life and livelihood of people.

perchance A withered word (see page 24). 1. *conceivably; feasibly; maybe; perhaps; possibly.* 2. *accidentally; by chance.*

perennially popular An inescapable pair (see page 20).

(I'm a) perfectionist A suspect superlative (see page 24). Anyone who declares he is a perfectionist is most often someone who can barely manage his life, someone who trips over trying. SEE ALSO *I'm not perfect (you know); nobody's perfect.*

period An infantile phrase (see page 20). ■ The lesson of the women's movement is clearly that no one makes it on their own. *Period.* DELETE *period.* ■ I know some professional, single women who would not date married men. *Period.* DELETE *period.* SEE ALSO *no ifs, ands, or buts.*

period of time A wretched redundancy (see page 25). *period; time; while.* ■ I've been wanting to watch this movie for a long *period of time.* REPLACE WITH *time.* ■ Over a considerable *period of time,* this therapy gradually provides immunization. REPLACE WITH *period.*

> He enjoyed these exercises in increasing intimacy and was warmed by the knowledge that he would be able to remain for a period of time in the vicinity of the natural references that would move him. — Jane Urquhart, *A Map of Glass*

perish the thought An infantile phrase (see page 20).

> Perish the thought — such dark thoughts were too cynical and bleak to entertain. — Robert Traver, *Anatomy of a Murder*

personal friend A suspect superlative (see page 24). A *personal friend* is but a friend, and a friend, more often than not, but an acquaintance.

persona non grata A foreign phrase (see page 19). *undesirable.*

(as) phony (queer) as a three-dollar bill An insipid simile. *artificial; bogus; counterfeit; ersatz; fake; false; feigned; fic-*

titious; forged; fraudulent; imitation; mock; phony; pseudo; sham; simulated; spurious; synthetic.

phony baloney An infantile phrase (see page 20). *artificial; bogus; counterfeit; ersatz; fake; false; feigned; fictitious; forged; fraudulent; imitation; mock; phony; pseudo; sham; simulated; spurious; synthetic.*

physician, heal thyself A popular prescription (see page 23).

pick and choose An inescapable pair (see page 20). *choose; cull; decide; determine; elect; pick; select.* ■ For years, we could *pick and choose* where our students worked. REPLACE WITH *select.*

pick of the litter A moribund metaphor (see page 21). *best; choice; elite; excellent; finest; first-class; first-rate; foremost; greatest; highest; matchless; nonpareil; optimal; optimum; outstanding; paramount; peerless; preeminent; premium; prominent; select; superior; superlative; top; unequaled; unexcelled; unmatched; unrivaled; unsurpassed.*

pick up speed A moribund metaphor (see page 21). *accelerate; advance; bestir; bustle; hasten; hurry; precipitate; quicken; rush; speed up.*

pick up steam A moribund metaphor (see page 21). 1. *accelerate; advance; bestir; bustle; hasten; hurry; precipitate; quicken; rush; speed up.* 2. *advance; awaken; better; expand; flourish; gain; gain strength; grow; heal; improve; increase; pick up; progress; prosper; rally; recover; recuperate; refresh; renew; revive; rouse; strengthen; thrive.*

pick up (take) the ball (and run with it) A moribund metaphor (see page 21). *activate; bring about; cause; create; effect; enter on; generate; give rise to; inaugurate; initiate; instigate; introduce; lead to; occasion; produce; provoke; usher in.*

pick up the pace A moribund metaphor (see page 21). *accelerate; advance; bestir; bustle; charge; dash; go faster; hasten; hurry; quicken; run; rush; speed up; sprint.*

> Today, I'm running behind Greta, who picks up the pace just as we hit the twisted growth at the base of the mountain. — Jodi Picoult, *Vanishing Acts*

pick up the pieces A moribund metaphor (see page 21).

pick up the tab A moribund metaphor (see page 21). *pay (for).*

(a) picture is worth a thousand words A popular prescription (see page 23).

> If one picture's worth a thousand words, that's the first two thousand right there, two thousand minus the hi howareya nicetameetcha. — Francine Prose, *A Changed Man*

picture of health A moribund metaphor (see page 21). *fit; good; hale; hardy; healthful; healthy; hearty; robust; sound; strong; well.*

picture perfect A moribund metaphor (see page 21). *absolute; beautiful; consummate; excellent; exemplary; exquisite; faultless; flawless; ideal; impeccable; lovely; magnificent; matchless; nonpareil;*

model; peerless; perfect; pretty; pure; sublime; superb; supreme; transcendent; ultimate; unblemished; unequaled; unexcelled; unrivaled; unsurpassed; untarnished.

pièce de résistance A foreign phrase (see page 19).

(a) piece of cake A moribund metaphor (see page 21). *apparent; basic; clear; clear-cut; conspicuous; distinct; easily done; easy; effortless; elementary; evident; explicit; facile; limpid; lucid; manifest; obvious; patent; pellucid; plain; simple; simplicity itself; straightforward; translucent; transparent; unambiguous; uncomplex; uncomplicated; understandable; unequivocal; unmistakable.* Evoking only the silliest of images, *a piece of cake* ought to tell us that those who use this expression have nothing serious to say, and perhaps little thoughtful to think.

■ Choosing the menu for the wedding reception isn't always *a piece of cake*. REPLACE WITH *easy*. ■ Setting up a Palm device to use GoType! is *a piece of cake*. REPLACE WITH *simplicity itself*. ■ At my high school, preparing for college is not *a piece of cake*. REPLACE WITH *effortless*.

> Her job at UGP is a piece of cake, a lot of financial paper shuffling and occasional simultaneous interpreting of meetings between the polite and cold Swiss men in dark suits who run the front office and the hostile and sneering Arabs — known, I regret to say, as "towel heads" — who secretly control everything. — Katharine Weber, *Objects in Mirror Are Closer Than They Appear*

(a) piece of the action An infantile phrase (see page 20). ■ Similar to the U.S. model, it will give companies the capital and technology they need while giving employees a *piece of the action* and establishing a constituency for capitalism.

(a) piece (slice) of the pie A moribund metaphor (see page 21).

(a) piece of the puzzle A moribund metaphor (see page 21). *clue; hint; inkling; pointer; sign.*

(a) piece of work A moribund metaphor (see page 21). *aberrant; abnormal; anomalistic; anomalous; atypical; bizarre; curious; deviant; different; distinct; distinctive; eccentric; exceptional; extraordinary; fantastic; foreign; grotesque; idiosyncratic; independent; individual; individualistic; irregular; novel; odd; offbeat; original; peculiar; puzzling; quaint; queer; rare; remarkable; separate; singular; strange; uncommon; unconventional; unexampled; unique; unnatural; unorthodox; unparalleled; unprecedented; unusual; weird.*

pie in the sky A moribund metaphor (see page 21). *artificial; capricious; chimeric; chimerical; delusive; dreamy; fanciful; fantastical; fictitious; frivolous; hallucinatory; illusory; imaginary; maggoty; phantasmal; phantasmic; unreal; whimsical.* ■ The only alternatives to testing she proposes are scarcely more than *pie in the sky*. REPLACE WITH *illusory*. ■ Other predictions were laughably *pie-in-the-sky*. REPLACE WITH *chimerical*.

pillar of society (the church; the community) A suspect superlative (see page 24). It is the pillars of society —

whether powerful, knowledgeable, or moneyed — who are often the most wobbly among us.

Few who have power do not misapply it, few who have knowledge do not misuse it, and few who have money do not misspend it.

For these reasons and others, before long and before others, pillars totter and then topple.

■ But beware — you'll be going up against the well-informed dealer who might be viewed as *a pillar of the community.*

pillar (tower) of strength A moribund metaphor (see page 21). *constant; dependable; determined; faithful; fast; firm; fixed; inexorable; inflexible; loyal; obdurate; reliable; resolute; resolved; rigid; solid; stable; staunch; steadfast; steady; stern; strong; supportive; tenacious; true; trustworthy; trusty; unflinching; unwavering; unyielding.*

pin (his) ears back A moribund metaphor (see page 21). 1. *beat; better; cap; defeat; exceed; excel; outclass; outdo; outflank; outmaneuver; outperform; outplay; outrank; outsmart; outthink; outwit; overcome; overpower; prevail over; surpass; top; triumph over; trounce; whip; win out.* 2. *admonish; animadvert; berate; castigate; censure; chasten; chastise; chide; condemn; criticize; denounce; denunciate; discipline; impugn; objurgate; punish; rebuke; remonstrate; reprehend; reprimand; reproach; reprobate; reprove; revile; scold; upbraid; vituperate.*

pin the blame on A moribund metaphor (see page 21). *accuse; blame; censure; charge; condemn; criticize; implicate; incriminate; inculpate; rebuke; reprimand; reproach; reprove; scold.*

(the) pits A moribund metaphor (see page 21). 1. *abhorrent; abominable; appalling; atrocious; awful; beastly; detestable; disagreeable; disgusting; dreadful; frightening; frightful; ghastly; grisly; gruesome; horrendous; horrible; horrid; horrifying; inhuman; loathesome; objectionable; obnoxious; odious; offensive; repellent; repugnant; repulsive; revolting; terrible; terrifying; unspeakable; unutterable.* 2. *calamitous; deplorable; depressing; distressing; disturbing; grievous; lamentable; unfortunate; upsetting; sad; tragic; woeful.*

(a) place for everything and everything in its place A popular prescription (see page 23).

place the blame on (her) shoulders A moribund metaphor (see page 21). *accuse; blame; censure; charge; condemn; criticize; implicate; incriminate; inculpate; rebuke; reprimand; reproach; reprove; scold.*

plain and simple An inescapable pair (see page 20). *apparent; basic; clear; clear-cut; conspicuous; distinct; easily done; easy; effortless; elementary; evident; explicit; facile; limpid; lucid; manifest; obvious; patent; pellucid; plain; simple; simplicity itself; straightforward; translucent; transparent; unambiguous; uncomplex; uncomplicated; understandable; unequivocal; unmistakable.*

(as) plain as a pikestaff An insipid simile. *apparent; basic; clear; clear-cut; conspicuous; distinct; easily done; easy; effortless; elementary; evident; explicit; facile; limpid; lucid; manifest; obvious; patent; pellucid; plain; simple; simplicity itself; straightforward; translucent; transparent; unambiguous; uncomplex; uncomplicated;*

understandable; unequivocal; unmistakable.

(as) plain as day An insipid simile. *apparent; basic; clear; clear-cut; conspicuous; distinct; easily done; easy; effortless; elementary; evident; explicit; facile; limpid; lucid; manifest; obvious; patent; pellucid; plain; simple; simplicity itself; straightforward; translucent; transparent; unambiguous; uncomplex; uncomplicated; understandable; unequivocal; unmistakable.*

> To a person that knew B. from hill's foot, it was just as plain as day that if that card laid on there in the office, Mr. Brightman would miss that important meeting in St. Louis in the morning. — Kate Chopin, *A Vocation and a Voice*

(as) plain as the nose on (your) face An insipid simile. *apparent; basic; clear; clear-cut; conspicuous; distinct; easily done; easy; effortless; elementary; evident; explicit; facile; limpid; lucid; manifest; obvious; patent; pellucid; plain; simple; simplicity itself; straightforward; translucent; transparent; unambiguous; uncomplex; uncomplicated; understandable; unequivocal; unmistakable.*

plain (smooth) sailing A moribund metaphor (see page 21). *apparent; basic; clear; clear-cut; conspicuous; distinct; easily done; easy; effortless; elementary; evident; explicit; facile; limpid; lucid; manifest; obvious; patent; pellucid; plain; simple; simplicity itself; smooth; straightforward; translucent; transparent; unambiguous; uncomplex; uncomplicated; understandable; unequivocal; unmistakable.*

plain vanilla A moribund metaphor (see page 21). *basic; common; conservative; conventional; customary; general; normal; ordinary; quotidian; regular; routine; standard; traditional; typical; uncreative; undaring; unimaginative; usual.* ■ He was uninterested in staying now that the bank has been limited to *plain vanilla* banking. REPLACE WITH *basic.*

plan ahead A wretched redundancy (see page 25). *plan.* ■ It's important that you *plan ahead* for your retirement. DELETE *ahead.*

plan for the worst, but hope for the best A popular prescription (see page 23).

plan of action A torpid term (see page 24). *action; course; direction; intention; method; move; plan; policy; procedure; route; scheme; strategy.*

plans and specifications A wretched redundancy (see page 25). *plans; specifications.* ■ Allowed expenditures include architectural and engineering services and related costs for *plans and specifications* for the renovation. USE *plans* or *specifications.*

play ball A moribund metaphor (see page 21). *agree; assent; collaborate; comply; concur; conspire; cooperate; join in; participate; work together.*

play both ends against the middle A moribund metaphor (see page 21).

play (your) cards right A moribund metaphor (see page 21).

play cat and mouse A moribund metaphor (see page 21). *fool; tease.*

play catch up A moribund metaphor (see page 21).

play (his cards) close to the chest (vest) A moribund metaphor (see page 21). *be clandestine; be confidential; be covert; be furtive; be mysterious; be private; be secretive; be secret; be sly; be stealthy; be surreptitious.*

play cupid A moribund metaphor (see page 21).

play fast and loose (with) A moribund metaphor (see page 21). *be careless; be dishonest; be disloyal; be false; be undependable; be unpredictable; be unreliable; be untrue; be untrustworthy.*

play games (with) A moribund metaphor (see page 21). *confuse; deceive; trick.*

play hardball A moribund metaphor (see page 21). *be demanding; be hard-hitting; be harsh; be rough; be severe; be stern; be strict; be tough.*

play hard to get A moribund metaphor (see page 21). *be coy; be fickle.*

play (raise) havoc with A moribund metaphor (see page 21). *disturb; mess up; devastate; rack; ravage; ruin; shatter; smash; undo; upset; wrack; wreck.*

play hell (the devil) with A moribund metaphor (see page 21). *disturb; mess up; devastate; rack; ravage; ruin; shatter; smash; undo; upset; wrack; wreck.*

play hide and seek A moribund metaphor (see page 21).

(like) playing Russian roulette An insipid simile. ■ Licensees who sell on Sundays in violation of state law are *playing Russian roulette* with their licenses.

(will it) play in Peoria A moribund metaphor (see page 21).

play it by ear A moribund metaphor (see page 21). *ad-lib; extemporize; improvise.*

play musical chairs A moribund metaphor (see page 21).

play out A torpid term (see page 24). 1. *carry out; execute; perform; play.* 2. *develop; evolve; unfold.* ■ We will report to you how all this *plays out.* REPLACE WITH *unfolds.*

play possum A moribund metaphor (see page 21).

> On other occasions, I had learned at great cost that it is always wiser, with grownups and with a crowd, to play possum, as if beneath the snout of a fierce animal. — Albert Memmi, *The Pillar of Salt*

play second fiddle A moribund metaphor (see page 21). *be ancillary; be inferior; be lesser; be lower; be middling; be minor; be second; be secondary; be second-rate; be subordinate; be subservient; be substandard.*

play the field A moribund metaphor (see page 21). *date.*

play the fool A moribund metaphor (see page 21). *be silly; clown; fool around; mess around.*

play the game A moribund metaphor (see page 21). *abide by; accommodate; accord; acquiesce; act fairly; adapt; adhere to; agree; behave; comply; concur; conform; correspond; follow; harmonize; heed; mind; obey; observe; submit; yield.*

play the waiting game A moribund metaphor (see page 21). *be patient; wait.*

play to the crowd A moribund metaphor (see page 21). *perform; play up; posture; show off.*

play (your) trump card A moribund metaphor (see page 21).

play with fire A moribund metaphor (see page 21). *chance; dare; endanger; gamble; hazard; imperil; jeopardize; make bold; peril; risk; venture.*

pleasant surprise An inescapable pair (see page 20).

(as) pleased as Punch An insipid simile. *blissful; buoyant; cheerful; delighted; elated; excited; gay; glad; gladdened; gleeful; good-humored; gratified; happy; jolly; jovial; joyful; joyous; jubilant; merry; mirthful; pleased; tickled.*

pleasingly plump An inescapable pair (see page 20). *ample; big; bulky; chubby; chunky; colossal; corpulent; dumpy; enormous; fat; flabby; fleshy; gigantic; heavy; hefty; huge; immense; large; mammoth; massive; obese; plump; portly; pudgy; rotund; round; squat; stocky; stout.*

plow new ground A moribund metaphor (see page 21). 1. *arrange; groom; make ready; plan; prepare; prime; ready.* 2. *bring about; cause; create; effect; generate; give rise to; inaugurate; initiate; introduce; lead to; occasion; produce; provoke; result in; usher in.*

(5:00) p.m. ... (in the) afternoon (evening) A wretched redundancy (see page 25). *(5:00) p.m.; (in the) afternoon (evening).* ■ The city school legislature was called to order at *2 p.m.* on a Monday *afternoon.* DELETE *afternoon.*

(he's) (a) poet but (he) doesn't know it An infantile phrase (see page 20).

poetry in motion A moribund metaphor (see page 21). *agile; graceful; limber; lissome; lithe; lithesome; nimble; supple.*

(a) point in time A wretched redundancy (see page 25). *a time.* ■ There comes *a point in time* when we all pass into adulthood. REPLACE WITH *a time.*

(the) point of no return A moribund metaphor (see page 21).

point the finger (of blame) at A moribund metaphor (see page 21). *accuse; blame; censure; charge; condemn; criticize; implicate; incriminate; inculpate; rebuke; reprimand; reproach; reprove; scold.* ■ When the problem is that severe, regulators have to *point the finger at* someone. REPLACE WITH *blame.*

poke (her) nose into A moribund metaphor (see page 21). *encroach; entrench; infringe; interfere; intrude; invade; meddle; pry; tamper; trespass.*

politics as usual A torpid term (see page 24). This is but a euphemism, a politic phrase, for words like *cheating; deceit; deceitfulness; deception; dishonesty; duplicity; falsehood; fraudulence; lying; mendacity; perfidy; self-interest; selfishness; tergiversation; treachery* or *backbiting; bad-mouthing; calumny; cruelty; defamation; denigration; infighting; insult; malevolence; malice; meanness; nastiness; slander; slur; spite; spitefulness; viciousness; vilification; vindictiveness.* ■ In the course of this election, there has been too much *politics as usual.* REPLACE WITH *dishonesty.* ■ Democrats have been somewhat more restrained than Republicans in returning to *politics as usual,* apparently because they don't want to be seen as undermining Bush during wartime. REPLACE WITH *backbiting.*

pomp and circumstance An inescapable pair (see page 20). *array; ceremony; circumstance; dazzle; display; fanfare; grandeur; magnificence; ostentation; pageantry; panoply; parade; pomp; resplendence; ritual; show; spectacle; splendor.*

(as) poor as a churchmouse An insipid simile. *bankrupt; broke; destitute; distressed; impecunious; impoverished; indigent; insolvent; needy; penniless; poor; poverty- stricken; underprivileged.*

(as) poor as sin An insipid simile. *bankrupt; broke; destitute; distressed; impecunious; impoverished; indigent; insolvent; needy; penniless; poor; poverty-stricken; underprivileged.*

> They would be poor as sin on his military pay, and then Teddy would just get himself killed and leave her stranded in California with nothing — or worse, with a baby. — Maile Meloy, *Liars and Saints*

poor cousin to A moribund metaphor (see page 21). ■ Independent TV stations were once viewed as *poor cousins to* network-owned stations and affiliates.

pose no immediate (imminent) danger (threat) A torpid term (see page 24). ■ And though the radioactive fuel may *pose no immediate threat,* the canisters continue to deteriorate.

positive (*n*) A torpid term (see page 24). *advantage; asset; benefit; gain; good; strength.* SEE ALSO *negative.*

positive effect (impact) A torpid term (see page 24). ■ The breakup doesn't undo any of the *positive effects,* and it doesn't mean I revert to the way I was 10 years ago. REPLACE WITH *goodness.* ■ A small but growing number of school programs on problem solving show *positive effects* in preventing depression. REPLACE WITH *success.* ■ It's a defeat for minority children who can't afford to attend private schools through grade 6, thus missing out on the *positive effect* of a private school education. REPLACE WITH *benefit.* SEE ALSO *negative effect (impact).*

positive feelings A torpid term (see page 24). As the following variety of synonyms shows, *positive feelings* is a pulpous expression that arouses only our inattention: *affection; approval; blissfulness; courage; delectation; delight; ecsta-*

sy; enjoyment; fondness; friendliness; friendship; generosity; goodwill; happiness; hope; joy; kindness; lightheartedness; like; liking; love; loyalty; merriment; passion; peace; pleasure; rapture; relish; respect; warmth. ■ I feel she may have *positive feelings* for me, and I'd like to know for sure. REPLACE WITH *affection.* ■ The goal is to capture the *positive feelings* about making special purchases. REPLACE WITH *delectation.* ■ The better in touch you are with your *positive feelings* for each other, the less likely you are to act contemptuous of your spouse when you have a difference of opinion. REPLACE WITH *fondness and admiration.* SEE ALSO *in a good mood; negative feelings.*

(like) (the) pot calling the kettle black An insipid simile.

pot of gold A moribund metaphor (see page 21). *affluence; fortune; money; opulence; prosperity; riches; treasure; wealth.*

(exact) (a) pound of flesh A moribund metaphor (see page 21).

pound the pavement A moribund metaphor (see page 21). *hunt; look for; quest; ransack; rummage; scour; search; seek.*

pouring (down) rain A wretched redundancy (see page 25). *pouring; raining; storming.*

pour oil on troubled waters A moribund metaphor (see page 21). *allay; alleviate; appease; assuage; calm; compose; ease; mitigate; mollify; pacify; palliate; quiet; relieve; soothe; still; tranquilize.*

pour (rub) salt on (our) wounds A moribund metaphor (see page 21). *aggravate; complicate; exacerbate; heighten; increase; intensify; irritate; make worse; worsen.*

(the) power of the purse A moribund metaphor (see page 21).

practice makes perfect A popular prescription (see page 23).

practice what (you) preach A popular prescription (see page 23).

praise (them) to the skies A moribund metaphor (see page 21). *acclaim; applaud; celebrate; commend; compliment; congratulate; eulogize; extol; flatter; hail; laud; panegyrize; praise; puff; salute.*

precarious position An inescapable pair (see page 20).

pretty An overworked word (see page 22). *adequately; amply; enough; fairly; moderately; quite; rather; reasonably; somewhat; sufficiently; tolerably.* ■ She's a *pretty* bright woman. REPLACE WITH *reasonably.* ■ We're suffering some *pretty* devastating effects right now. DELETE *pretty.*

Pretty, in these senses, proclaims its users have a vocabulary of little more than disyllabic words. For a person who says *pretty* also says *little* and *logy, really* and *leery, input* and *impact.* And with so few words, only so much can be known, only so much can be conveyed.

(as) pretty as a picture An insipid simile. *appealing; attractive; beautiful; becoming; captivating; comely; cute; dazzling; exquisite; fair; fetching; good-looking; gorgeous; handsome; lovely; nice-look-*

ing; pleasing; pretty; pulchritudinous; radiant; ravishing; seemly; stunning.

(a) pretty picture A moribund metaphor (see page 21).

prevailing winds of A moribund metaphor (see page 21).

previous to A torpid term (see page 24). *before.* ■ *Previous to* meeting her, I showed no interest in women. REPLACE WITH *Before.* SEE ALSO *in advance of; previous to; subsequent to.*

prick (puncture) (his) balloon A moribund metaphor (see page 21). *abase; chasten; debase; decrease; deflate; degrade; demean; depreciate; depress; diminish; disgrace; dishonor; embarrass; humble; humiliate; lower; mortify; puncture; shame.*

prick up (her) ears A moribund metaphor (see page 21). *attend to; hark; hear; hearken; heed; listen; pay attention; pay heed.*

> I pricked up my ears, for it was positively the first time I had ever heard a foreign tongue. — Willa Cather, *My Antonia*

pride and joy An inescapable pair (see page 20).

prim and proper An inescapable pair (see page 20).

primrose path A moribund metaphor (see page 21).

(a) prince among men A suspect superlative (see page 24).

prince charming An infantile phrase (see page 20).

princely price An inescapable pair (see page 20). *costly; dear; excessive; exorbitant; expensive; high-priced.*

prioritize A torpid term (see page 24). *arrange; classify; list; order; place; put; rank; rate.* ■ He *prioritizes* this relationship above all his "after high school plans," such as going to college. REPLACE WITH *ranks.*

prior to A torpid term (see page 24). *before.* ■ Select only the cells to be printed *prior to* selecting the Print command. REPLACE WITH *before.* ■ Certain verbs in English require the use of a pronoun *prior to* and after an infinitive phrase. REPLACE WITH *before.* SEE ALSO *in advance of; previous to; subsequent to.*

prize(d) possession An inescapable pair (see page 20). ■ In an era of spiraling costs, a good indirect cost rate is a *prized possession.*

proactive A torpid term (see page 24). 1. *anticipatory; involved; participatory.* 2. *aggressive; assertive; enterprising.* ■ To educate parents to take this more *proactive* role in the education of their children, the board has authorized the creation of a parent-controlled Family Education Resources Center. REPLACE WITH *participatory.* ■ It is vital to obtain sell-through information from retailers so that you can take *proactive* steps to get a new order. REPLACE WITH *aggressive.* ■ A school needs a PR person to develop a *proactive* approach that anticipates problems before they develop. REPLACE WITH *enterprising.* ■ Smaller, specialty firms, such as Bath & Body

Works, or apparel stores, such as Bloomingdale's, Nordstrom, and Canada's famed Harry Rosen, teach their employees to *proactively* ask customers if they need assistance. DELETE *proactively*.

proceeded to A torpid term (see page 24). ■ The team *proceeded to develop* the recently generated ideas into a concrete curriculum. REPLACE WITH *developed*. ■ He then *proceeded to declare* his undying love for me. REPLACE WITH *declared*.

proceed forward A torpid term (see page 24). *advance; continue; develop; go on; grow; happen; improve; increase; make headway; make progress; move on; occur; proceed; progress; take place*. ■ Reducing operating losses in this business will give us increased flexibility to *proceed forward* with other endeavors. REPLACE WITH *proceed*. SEE ALSO *a step forward; a step (forward) in the right direction; go forward; move forward; move (forward) in the right direction*.

(the) promised land A moribund metaphor (see page 21). *Eden; El Dorado; Elysian Fields; Elysium; heaven; kingdom come; nirvana; paradise; utopia; Valhalla*.

(a) promise is a promise A quack equation (see page 23).

(the) proof of the pudding (is in the eating) A popular prescription (see page 23).

(as) proud as a peacock An insipid simile. *arrogant; cavalier; conceited; disdainful; egocentric; egotistic; egotistical; haughty; lofty; pompous; pretentious; prideful; proud; narcissistic; self-centered; self-important; self-satisfied; supercilious; superior; vain*.

proud parent An inescapable pair (see page 20).

pull a fast one A moribund metaphor (see page 21). *bamboozle; befool; beguile; bilk; bluff; cheat; con; deceive; defraud; delude; dupe; feint; fool; gyp; hoodwink; lead astray; misdirect; misguide; misinform; mislead; spoof; swindle; trick; victimize*.

pull a rabbit out of the hat A moribund metaphor (see page 21). *be creative; be ingenious; be inventive; be resourceful*.

pull (yank) (her) chain A moribund metaphor (see page 21). *bamboozle; befool; beguile; bilk; bluff; cheat; con; deceive; defraud; delude; dupe; feint; fool; gyp; hoodwink; jest; joke; kid; lead astray; misdirect; misguide; misinform; mislead; rib; spoof; swindle; tease; trick; trifle with*.

pull (my) leg A moribund metaphor (see page 21). *bamboozle; befool; beguile; bilk; bluff; cheat; con; deceive; defraud; delude; dupe; feint; fool; gyp; hoodwink; jest; joke; kid; lead astray; misdirect; misguide; misinform; mislead; rib; spoof; swindle; tease; trick; trifle with*.

(like) pulling teeth An insipid simile. *arduous; backbreaking; burdensome; difficult; exhausting; fatiguing; hard; herculean; laborious; not easy; onerous; severe; strenuous; toilful; toilsome; tough; troublesome; trying; wearisome*. ■ Getting these people to level with reporters is often *like pulling teeth*. REPLACE WITH *arduous*.

pull no punches A moribund metaphor (see page 21). *be blunt; be candid; be direct; be forthright; be frank; be open; be outspoken; be straightforward.*

pull (it) off A moribund metaphor (see page 21). *accomplish; bring about; do; carry out; perform; succeed.*

pull out all the stops A moribund metaphor (see page 21). *aim; attempt; endeavor; essay; exert; exhaust; labor; moil; strain; strive; struggle; toil; try hard; undertake; work at.*

pull strings A moribund metaphor (see page 21).

pull the plug (on) A moribund metaphor (see page 21). *abandon; abort; annul; arrest; ban; cancel; cease; check; conclude; derail; desert; desist; discontinue; end; forsake; halt; invalidate; leave; quit; repeal; rescind; revoke; stop; suspend; terminate; withdraw.* ■ Organizers say they'll *pull the plug* on the parade if a gay and lesbian group is allowed to participate. REPLACE WITH *cancel.* ■ Cellucci *pulled the plug on* the PAC last summer after learning it was being organized by inmates at some of the states' toughest prisons. REPLACE WITH *banned.*

> He thought about it, wondering if he really could pull the plug. — Christopher Bram, *Lives of the Circus Animals*

pull the rug out from under A moribund metaphor (see page 21). *capsize; founder; invert; overset; overthrow; overturn; reverse; sink; tip; topple; tumble; upend; upset.*

> For once the big dick of the law and government would not pull the rug out from under me. — Tim Miller, *Shirts & Skin*

pull the wool over (his) eyes A moribund metaphor (see page 21). *bamboozle; befool; beguile; bilk; bluff; cheat; con; deceive; defraud; delude; dupe; fake; feign; feint; fool; gyp; hoodwink; lead astray; lie; misdirect; misguide; misinform; mislead; misrepresent; pretend; spoof; swindle; trick; victimize.* ■ You also have a built-in B.S. detector, and you can tell if someone is attempting to *pull the wool over your eyes.* REPLACE WITH *mislead you.*

pull (yourself) up by (your) own bootstraps A moribund metaphor (see page 21).

pull up stakes A moribund metaphor (see page 21). *abscond; clear out; decamp; depart; desert; disappear; escape; exit; flee; fly; go; go away; leave; move on; part; pull out; quit; retire; retreat; run away; take flight; take off; vacate; vanish; withdraw.*

(can't) punch (his) way out of a paper bag A moribund metaphor (see page 21). *ham-fisted; inadequate; incapable; incompetent; ineffective; ineffectual; inefficacious; inept; lacking; not able; unable; unfit; unqualified; unskilled; useless; wanting.*

pure and simple An inescapable pair (see page 20). *basic; elementary; fundamental; pure; simple; straightforward; uncomplicated.*

(as) pure as the driven snow An insipid simile. 1. *decent; ethical; exemplary; good; honest; honorable; just; moral;*

pure; righteous; straight; upright; virtuous; wholesome. 2. *celibate; chaste; immaculate; maidenly; modest; snowy; spotless; stainless; unblemished; unsoiled; untarnished; virgin; virginal; virtuous.*

pursuant to A torpid term (see page 24). *according to; by; following; under.*

pursue (strive for) excellence A suspect superlative (see page 24). ■ *Striving for excellence* is not just a goal but a way of life. ■ The recipients had to prepare brief statements on what inspires them to *strive for excellence.* SEE ALSO *excellence.*

push and shove An inescapable pair (see page 20). *bulldoze; drive; propel; push; shove; thrust.*

(when) push comes to shove A moribund metaphor (see page 21).

push the envelope A moribund metaphor (see page 21). 1. *be adventuresome; be adventurous; be bold; be daring.* 2. *beat; exceed; outdo; outstrip; surpass; top.*

Like thousands of English idioms, *push the envelope* helps ensure that any article, any book in which it appears is mediocre and unmemorable.

Literature does not allow worn metaphors like this; bestsellers demand them.

> I push the envelope and put my right hand gently, softly, on his upper arm, inches away from his chin. — Alix Strauss, *The Joy of Funerals*

push the panic button A moribund metaphor (see page 21). *be alarmed; be anxious; be excited; be frightened; be jumpy; be nervous; be panicky; be panic-stricken; be scared; be unnerved.*

push the right buttons A moribund metaphor (see page 21).

pushed (me) to the wall A moribund metaphor (see page 21). 1. *coerced; compelled; constrained; dictated; enforced; enjoined; forced; made; ordered; pressed; pressured; required.* 2. *at bay; caught; cornered; enmeshed; ensnared; entangled; entrapped; netted; snared; trapped.*

put a bug in (his) ear A moribund metaphor (see page 21). *allude to; clue; connote; cue; hint; imply; indicate; insinuate; intimate; prompt; suggest; tip off.*

put a damper on A moribund metaphor (see page 21). *check; dampen; deaden; depress; discourage; hinder; impede; inhibit; obstruct; repress; restrain.*

put a gun to (my) head A moribund metaphor (see page 21). *coerce; command; compel; constrain; demand; dictate; enforce; enjoin; force; insist; make; order; pressure; require.* ■ Nobody *put a gun to your head.* REPLACE WITH *forced you.*

put a halt (an end; a stop) to A wretched redundancy (see page 25). *cease; close; complete; conclude; derail; discontinue; end; finish; halt; settle; stop.* ■ It's time we *put a stop to* all the violence. REPLACE WITH *stop.* SEE ALSO *call a halt (an end; a stop) to.*

put a lid on (it) A moribund metaphor (see page 21). 1. *abandon; abort; annul; arrest; ban; cancel; cease; check; conclude; desert; desist; discontinue; end; forsake;*

halt; leave; quit; stop; suspend; terminate. 2. *censor; hush up; muffle; quash; smother; squash; squelch; stifle.* 3. *be closed-mouthed; be quiet; be reticent; be silent; be speechless; be still; be taciturn; be uncommunicative; hush (up); keep quiet; shut up.* ■ *Put a lid on it.* REPLACE WITH *Be quiet.*

(don't) put all (your) eggs in one basket A moribund metaphor (see page 21).

put a sock in (it) A moribund metaphor (see page 21). *be closed-mouthed; be quiet; be reticent; be silent; be speechless; be still; be taciturn; be uncommunicative; hush (up); keep quiet; shut up.*

> I listened patiently to all this minutiae, never once wishing he'd put a sock in it. — Jane Heller, *Female Intelligence*

put a spin on A moribund metaphor (see page 21).

put (it) behind (us) A moribund metaphor (see page 21). ■ She is eager to testify before the grand jury and to *put this part of the investigation behind her.* SEE ALSO *get (go) on with (my) life.*

put (his) best foot forward A moribund metaphor (see page 21).

put (your) finger on A moribund metaphor (see page 21). *detect; discern; discover; distinguish; find; identify; know; locate; make out; note; notice; perceive; pick out; pinpoint; place; point out; recall; recognize; recollect; remember; see; specify; spot; think of.*

put (her) foot down A moribund metaphor (see page 21). 1. *hold fast; stand firm.* 2. *assert; command; decree; dictate; insist; order; require.* 3. *deny; disallow; forbid; prohibit; refuse; reject.* ■ I *put my foot down.* REPLACE WITH *refused.*

put (his) foot in (his) mouth A moribund metaphor (see page 21).

put forward A torpid term (see page 24). *advance; broach; introduce; offer; present; propose; propound; submit; suggest; tender.* ■ There is speculation that he opposed Moynihan's plan so he could *put forward* his own. REPLACE WITH *propose.* SEE ALSO *come forward (with).*

put (his) head in the lion's mouth A moribund metaphor (see page 21). *chance; dare; endanger; gamble; hazard; imperil; jeopardize; make bold; peril; risk; venture.*

put (our) heads together A moribund metaphor (see page 21). *collaborate; conspire; cooperate; work together.*

put (your) house (back) in order A moribund metaphor (see page 21). *correct; rectify; redress; remedy; restore; right.* ■ Ravaged by losses after it lost direction in a period of rapid growth, Phoenix is attempting to *put its house back in order.* REPLACE WITH *right itself.*

put in a plug for A moribund metaphor (see page 21). *acclaim; applaud; celebrate; commend; compliment; congratulate; eulogize; extol; flatter; hail; laud; panegyrize; praise; puff; salute.*

put (him) in bad light A moribund metaphor (see page 21).

put in cold storage A moribund metaphor (see page 21). *defer; delay; forget; hold off; hold up; ignore; pigeonhole; postpone; procrastinate; put aside; put off; set aside; shelve; suspend; table; waive.*

put in motion A moribund metaphor (see page 21). *begin; commence; embark; inaugurate; initiate; launch; originate; start; undertake.*

put (her) in (her) place A moribund metaphor (see page 21). *abase; chasten; debase; decrease; deflate; degrade; demean; depreciate; depress; diminish; disgrace; dishonor; embarrass; humble; humiliate; lower; mortify; puncture; shame.*

> Whenever he first spoke, whatever he said, one of us would have to put him in his place. — Karen Joy Fowler, *The Jane Austen Book Club*

put (yourself) in (her) place A moribund metaphor (see page 21). *be sorry for; commiserate; empathize; feel for; feel sorry for; identify with; pity; sympathize; understand.*

put (myself) in (his) shoes A moribund metaphor (see page 21). *be sorry for; commiserate; empathize; feel for; feel sorry for; identify with; pity; sympathize; understand.*

put (your) life on the line A moribund metaphor (see page 21). *chance; dare; endanger; gamble; hazard; imperil; jeopardize; make bold; peril; risk; venture.*

put money on A moribund metaphor (see page 21). *bet; gamble; wager.*

put (his) neck on the line A moribund metaphor (see page 21). *chance; dare; endanger; gamble; hazard; imperil; jeopardize; make bold; peril; risk; venture.*

put new life into A moribund metaphor (see page 21). *animate; energize; enliven; inspire; inspirit; invigorate; refresh; reinvigorate; rejuvenate; revitalize; revive; rouse; stimulate; stir; vitalize.*

put on airs A moribund metaphor (see page 21). *be affected; be arrogant; be conceited; be condescending; be contumelious; be disdainful; be egotistic; be egotistical; be haughty; be high-handed; be magisterial; be overbearing; be pompous; be pretentious; be proud; be prideful; be self-important; be snobbish; be supercilious; be superior.*

put on an act A moribund metaphor (see page 21). *affect; fake; feign; make believe; pretend; simulate.*

put (her) on a pedestal A moribund metaphor (see page 21). *adore; cherish; esteem; eulogize; exalt; extol; glorify; honor; idealize; idolize; laud; love; panegyrize; prize; revere; treasure; venerate; worship.*

put one over on (her) A moribund metaphor (see page 21). *bamboozle; befool; beguile; bilk; bluff; cheat; con; deceive; defraud; delude; dupe; feint; fool; gyp; hoodwink; lead astray; misdirect; misguide; mislead; spoof; swindle; trick; victimize.*

put on hold A torpid term (see page 24). *defer; delay; forget; hold off; hold up; ignore; pigeonhole; postpone; procrastinate; put aside; put off; set aside; shelve; suspend; table; waive.* ■ The agreement had been scheduled to go into effect on Tuesday, after being *put on hold* for 30 days. REPLACE WITH *delayed.*

put on ice A moribund metaphor (see page 21). *defer; delay; forget; hold off; hold up; ignore; pigeonhole; postpone; procrastinate; put aside; put off; set aside; shelve; suspend; table; waive.*

put on the back burner A moribund metaphor (see page 21). *defer; delay; forget; hold off; hold up; ignore; pigeonhole; postpone; procrastinate; put aside; put off; set aside; shelve; suspend; table; waive.* ■ She understands the necessity of *putting* her own emotional needs *on the back burner* when these would otherwise interfere with her goal. REPLACE WITH *waiving.*

put on the front burner A moribund metaphor (see page 21). *advance.* ■ They are all familiar with the lonesome efforts of Rev. Ladi Thompson's Macedonian Initiative which has strove for years to *put* the plight of northern Christians *on the front burner.*

put (us) on the map A moribund metaphor (see page 21). ■ At the time analysts thought Ames was just the tonic Zayre needed, and the deal *put* the 30-year-old Ames *on the map.*

put (it) on the table A moribund metaphor (see page 21). *be aboveboard; be candid; be forthright; be frank; be honest; be open; be straightforward; be truthful.*

put (it) out of (its) misery A moribund metaphor (see page 21). 1. *destroy; kill; murder; slay.* 2. *cease; close; end; finish; halt; shut off; stop; terminate; turn off.*

> She applied the parking brake, gently put the engine out of its misery, then held on for dear life as it convulsed, sputtered, and died with a sigh. — Rob Kean, *The Pledge*

put out to pasture A moribund metaphor (see page 21). 1. *cast off; discard; dismiss; drop; dump; eliminate; exclude; expel; jettison; lay aside; reject; retire; set aside; shed.* 2. *ax; discharge; dismiss; fire; let go; retire.* ■ Playing a hot-blooded parent helps you feel like you haven't yet been *put out to pasture.* REPLACE WITH *dismissed.*

put (his) pants on one leg at a time A moribund metaphor (see page 21). *average; common; commonplace; conservative; conventional; customary; everyday; mediocre; middling; normal; ordinary; quotidian; regular; routine; standard; traditional; typical; uneventful; unexceptional; unremarkable; usual.*

put pen to paper A moribund metaphor (see page 21). *author; compose; indite; inscribe; jot down; pen; scrabble; scratch; scrawl; scribble; scribe; write.*

put (your) shoulder to the wheel A moribund metaphor (see page 21). *drudge; grind; grub; labor; moil; slave; strain; strive; struggle; sweat; toil; travail; work hard.*

put (your) stamp of approval on A moribund metaphor (see page 21). *approve of; authorize; certify; endorse; sanction.* ■ To portray our community as *putting a stamp of approval on* the execution is inaccurate. REPLACE WITH *approving of.*

put that in your pipe and smoke it A moribund metaphor (see page 21).

put the brakes on A moribund metaphor (see page 21). *abandon; abort; arrest; block; bridle; cancel; cease; check; conclude; control; curb; derail; desert; desist; discontinue; disturb; end; forsake; halt; interrupt; leave; obstruct; quit; repress; restrain; stop; suppress; suspend; terminate.* ■ The parent's problems with its retail divisions effectively *put the brakes on* the project and helped stall other downtown projects as well. REPLACE WITH *stopped.* ■ It *put the brakes on* the decline of political talk radio. REPLACE WITH *checked.*

put the cart before the horse A moribund metaphor (see page 21). *backward; counterclockwise; inside-out; inverted; reversed; upside-down.*

put the best face on A moribund metaphor (see page 21). ■ In the aftermath, AT&T management tried to *put the best face on* an embarrassing and costly mix-up.

put the fear of God into (them) A torpid term (see page 24). *alarm; appall; benumb; daunt; frighten; horrify; intimidate; panic; paralyze; petrify; scare; shock; startle; terrify; terrorize.*

put the finger on A moribund metaphor (see page 21). *betray; deliver up; inform on; turn in.*

put the finishing touches on A moribund metaphor (see page 21). *complete; conclude; consummate; finish.*

put the genie back in the bottle A moribund metaphor (see page 21).

put the kibosh on A moribund metaphor (see page 21). *abort; annul; arrest; balk; block; bridle; cancel; check; derail; detain; end; foil; frustrate; halt; harness; neutralize; nullify; restrain; retard; stall; stay; stop; terminate; thwart.*

put the screws to A moribund metaphor (see page 21). *bulldoze; bully; coerce; compel; constrain; demand; drive; enforce; enjoin; goad; force; impel; incite; intimidate; make; necessitate; obligate; oblige; order; press; pressure; prod; require; threaten; tyrannize; urge.*

put the skids on A moribund metaphor (see page 21). *abandon; abort; arrest; cancel; cease; check; conclude; derail; desert; desist; discontinue; end; forsake; halt; leave; quit; stop; suspend; terminate.*

put through (her) paces A moribund metaphor (see page 21). *catechize; cross-examine; examine; grill; inquire; interrogate; pump; question; quiz; test.*

put through the wringer A moribund metaphor (see page 21). *catechize; cross-examine; examine; grill; inquire; interrogate; pump; question; quiz; test.*

put together the pieces of the puzzle A moribund metaphor (see page 21). *clear up; decipher; disentangle; explain; explicate; figure out; resolve; solve; unravel; untangle; work out.*

put (them) to the test A torpid term (see page 24). *catechize; cross-examine; examine; grill; inquire; interrogate; pump; question; quiz; test.*

put two and two together A moribund metaphor (see page 21). *comprehend; conclude; decipher; deduce; discern; draw;*

fathom; figure out; gather; grasp; infer; interpret; perceive; realize; reason; see; understand.

(like) putty in (my) hands An insipid simile. *accommodating; acquiescent; adaptable; agreeable; amenable; complacent; complaisant; compliant; deferential; docile; ductile; elastic; flexible; malleable; manageable; moldable; obedient; obliging; persuasible; pliant; responsive; submissive; tractable; trained; yielding.*

put up or shut up An infantile phrase (see page 20).

Q

queer fish A moribund metaphor (see page 21). *aberrant; abnormal; anomalistic; anomalous; atypical; bizarre; curious; deviant; different; distinct; distinctive; eccentric; exceptional; extraordinary; fantastic; foreign; grotesque; idiosyncratic; independent; individual; individualistic; irregular; novel; odd; offbeat; original; peculiar; puzzling; quaint; queer; rare; remarkable; separate; singular; strange; uncommon; unconventional; unexampled; unique; unnatural; unorthodox; unparalleled; unprecedented; unusual; weird.*

(as) quick and dirty An inescapable pair (see page 20). *crude; haphazard; improvised; makeshift; provisional; slapdash; temporary; tentative.*

(the) quick and the dead A moribund metaphor (see page 21).

(as) quick as a bunny An insipid simile. *brisk; expeditious; fast; fleet; hasty; hurried; immediate; instant; instantaneous; prompt; quick; rapid; speedy; spry; sudden; swift; winged.*

(as) quick as a flash An insipid simile. *brisk; expeditious; fast; fleet; hasty; hurried; immediate; instant; instantaneous; prompt; quick; rapid; speedy; spry; sudden; swift; winged.*

(as) quick as a wink An insipid simile. *brisk; expeditious; fast; fleet; hasty; hurried; immediate; instant; instantaneous; prompt; quick; rapid; speedy; spry; sudden; swift; winged.*

> I showed her everything, and she got a job quick as a wink in my same factory, in a section where they made flexible mounts for the fifty-calibers. — Nancy E. Turner, *The Water and the Blood*

(as) quick as lightning An insipid simile. *brisk; expeditious; fast; fleet; hasty; hurried; immediate; instant; instantaneous; prompt; quick; rapid; speedy; spry; sudden; swift; winged.*

quick on (his) feet A moribund metaphor (see page 21). 1. *brisk; expeditious; fast; fleet; hasty; hurried; immediate; instant; instantaneous; prompt; quick; rapid; speedy; spry; sudden; swift; winged.* 2. *able; adroit; alert; apt; astute; bright; brilliant; capable; clever; competent; discerning; enlightened; insightful; intelligent; judicious; keen; knowledgeable; learned; logical; luminous; perceptive; perspicacious; quick; rational; reason-*

able; sagacious; sage; sapient; sensible; sharp; shrewd; smart; sound; understanding; wise; witty.

quick on the draw A moribund metaphor (see page 21). *fast; fast-acting; quick; rapid; speedy; swift.*

quid pro quo A foreign phrase (see page 19).

(as) quiet as a mouse An insipid simile. *dumb; hushed; motionless; mum; mute; noiseless; quiet; reticent; silent; speechless; stationary; still; stock-still; subdued; taciturn; unmoving; voiceless; wordless.*

quiet desperation An inescapable pair (see page 20).

> There was a look of quiet desperation on her face, just weeks into this new life, one she hadn't wanted. — Kathleen Cambor, *In Sunlight, in a Beautiful Garden*

quit the scene A torpid term (see page 24). *abscond; clear out; decamp; depart; desert; disappear; escape; exit; flee; fly; go; go away; leave; move on; part; pull out; quit; retire; retreat; run away; take flight; take off; vacate; vanish; withdraw.*

quit while (you're) ahead A popular prescription (see page 23).

quote, unquote An infantile phrase (see page 20). *as it were; so-called; so to speak; such as it is.* ■ It's too soon in the *quote, unquote* relationship for that. REPLACE WITH *so-called.* ■ I was referred to them by a friend of mine, *quote, unquote.* REPLACE WITH *as it were.*

R

(a) race to the finish (line) A moribund metaphor (see page 21).

(gone to) rack (wrack) and ruin An inescapable pair (see page 20). *broken down; crumbly; decayed; deteriorated; dilapidated; run-down; shabby.*

rack (wrack) (my) brains A moribund metaphor (see page 21). *endeavor; exert; labor; moil; slave; strain; strive; struggle; toil; try; work.*

radiantly happy An inescapable pair (see page 20). *blissful; blithe; buoyant; cheerful; delighted; ecstatic; elated; enraptured; euphoric; exalted; excited; exhilarated; exultant; gay; glad; gleeful; good-humored; happy; intoxicated; jolly; jovial; joyful; joyous; jubilant; merry; mirthful; overjoyed; pleased; rapturous; thrilled.*

> And both were radiantly happy because of old times' sake. — Theodore Dreiser, *An American Tragedy*

raid the cookie jar A moribund metaphor (see page 21). *filch; pilfer; pinch; purloin; rob; steal; take; thieve.*

raining cats and dogs A moribund metaphor (see page 21). *pouring; raining; storming.*

raining pitchforks A moribund metaphor (see page 21). *pouring; raining; storming.*

rain on (your) parade A moribund metaphor (see page 21). *blight; cripple; damage; disable; disrupt; disturb; harm; hurt; impair; incapacitate; lame; mar; mess up; rack; ruin; sabotage; spoil; subvert; undermine; vitiate; wrack; wreck.*

(come) rain or shine A moribund metaphor (see page 21). *no matter what; regardless.*

raise a (red) flag A moribund metaphor (see page 21). *alert; apprise; caution; forewarn; inform; notify; signal; warn.*

raise a stink A moribund metaphor (see page 21).

> What did trouble him was that he might not lie enough or in the right way to suit Washington, and that some eager beaver, or numbskull, or stooge might raise a stink that would cost Benny his job. — Patricia Highsmith, *Tales of Natural and Unnatural Catastrophes*

raise Cain A moribund metaphor (see page 21). 1. *bellow; bluster; clamor; complain; explode; fulminate; fume; holler; howl; object; protest; rage; rant; rave; roar; scream; shout; storm; thunder; vociferate; yell.* 2. *be merry; carouse; carry on; celebrate; debauch; disport; frolic; party; play; revel; riot; roister; rollick; romp; skylark.*

raise (some) eyebrows (of) A moribund metaphor (see page 21). *amaze; astonish; astound; awe; dumbfound; flabbergast; jar; jolt; shock; start; startle; stun; stupefy; surprise.* ■ An executive at one financial institution that participated in the bailout said Goldman Sachs's dual role *raised the eyebrows of* some participants. REPLACE WITH *surprised.*

raise hell A moribund metaphor (see page 21). 1. *bellow; bluster; clamor; complain; explode; fulminate; fume; holler; howl; object; protest; rage; rant; rave; roar; scream; shout; storm; thunder; vociferate; yell.* 2. *be merry; carouse; carry on; celebrate; debauch; disport; frolic; party; play; revel; riot; roister; rollick; romp; skylark.*

raise the dead A moribund metaphor (see page 21). *be merry; carouse; carry on; celebrate; debauch; disport; frolic; party; play; revel; riot; roister; rollick; romp; skylark.*

raise the flag A moribund metaphor (see page 21). *be delighted; be elated; be glad; be overjoyed; be pleased; celebrate; cheer; exult; glory; jubilate; rejoice; triumph.*

raise the hackles A moribund metaphor (see page 21). *acerbate; anger; annoy; bother; bristle; chafe; enrage; incense; inflame; infuriate; insult; irk; irritate; madden; miff; nettle; offend; provoke; rile; roil; vex.*

raise the roof A moribund metaphor (see page 21). 1. *bellow; bluster; clamor; complain; explode; fulminate; fume; holler; howl; object; protest; rage; rant; rave; roar; scream; shout; storm; thunder; vociferate; yell.* 2. *be merry; carouse; carry on; celebrate; debauch; disport; frolic; party; play; revel; riot; roister; rollick; romp; skylark.*

raison d'être A foreign phrase (see page 19).

rake over the coals A torpid term (see page 24). *admonish; animadvert; berate; castigate; censure; chasten; chastise; chide; condemn; criticize; denounce; denunciate;*

discipline; impugn; objurgate; punish; rebuke; remonstrate; reprehend; reprimand; reproach; reprobate; reprove; revile; scold; upbraid; vituperate.

rally 'round the flag A moribund metaphor (see page 21).

rank and file A moribund metaphor (see page 21). *all; citizenry; commonage; commonalty; common people; crowd; everybody; everyone; followers; herd; hoi polloi; laborers; masses; mob; multitude; plebeians; populace; proletariat; public; rabble; workers.*

rant and rave An inescapable pair (see page 20). *bellow; bluster; clamor; explode; fulminate; fume; holler; howl; rage; rant; rave; roar; scream; shout; storm; thunder; vent; vociferate; yell.*

rap (his) knuckles A moribund metaphor (see page 21). *admonish; animadvert; berate; castigate; censure; chasten; chastise; chide; condemn; criticize; denounce; denunciate; discipline; impugn; objurgate; punish; rebuke; remonstrate; reprehend; reprimand; reproach; reprobate; reprove; revile; scold; upbraid; vituperate.*

rara avis A foreign phrase (see page 19). *aberrant; abnormal; anomalistic; anomalous; atypical; bizarre; curious; deviant; different; distinct; distinctive; eccentric; exceptional; extraordinary; fantastic; foreign; grotesque; idiosyncratic; independent; individual; individualistic; irregular; novel; odd; offbeat; original; peculiar; puzzling; quaint; queer; rare; remarkable; separate; singular; strange; uncommon; unconventional; unexampled; unique; unnatural; unorthodox; unparalleled; unprecedented; unusual; weird.*

rarely (seldom) ever A wretched redundancy (see page 25). *rarely (seldom).* ■ We are brothers, but we *rarely ever* speak. DELETE *ever.*

rat race A moribund metaphor (see page 21).

(like) rats abandoning a ship An insipid simile.

rattle (their) cage A moribund metaphor (see page 21). 1. *agitate; disquiet; disturb; excite; stir up; trouble; upset; work up.* 2. *goad; incite; inflame; needle; provoke; rouse; spur.* 3. *acerbate; anger; annoy; bother; bristle; chafe; enrage; incense; inflame; infuriate; insult; irk; irritate; madden; miff; nettle; offend; provoke; rile; roil; vex.*

> Never, *never* had she met anyone who could rattle her cage with such quick thoroughness. — Susan Anderson, *Obsessed*

rave reviews A suspect superlative (see page 24). ■ The new LapLink for Windows is already getting *rave reviews* from both industry experts and users like you. ■ But it turned out *Maximumrocknroll* gave it a *rave review.* ■ In 1995, CeCe got *rave reviews* for her solo debut.

raving lunatic An inescapable pair (see page 20).

(a) ray of light (sunshine) A moribund metaphor (see page 21). *anticipation; expectancy; expectation; hope; hopefulness; optimism; possibility; promise; prospect; sanguinity.* ■ I don't see any *ray of sunshine* when we have all these interplaying forces in conflict. REPLACE WITH *hope.*

reach epidemic proportions A torpid term (see page 24). This phrase and journalistic junk of its kind — for example, *(breathe; heave) a collective sigh of relief* (SEE); *an uphill battle (fight)* (SEE); *deal a (crushing; devastating; major; serious) blow to* (SEE); *first (number-one; top) priority* (SEE); *grind to a halt* (SEE); *in the wake of; send a message (signal)* (SEE); *shocked (surprised) and saddened (dismayed)* (SEE); *weather the storm (of)* (SEE) — ensure the writers of them will never be seriously read, and the readers of them never thoroughly engaged.

■ The availability of guns on the street has *reached epidemic proportions.* ■ Dog bites among children are reportedly *reaching epidemic proportions.*

reach for the sky A moribund metaphor (see page 21). *exceed; excel; outclass; outdo; outrival; outshine; outstrip; shine; stand; surpass.*

reach out and touch (someone) An infantile phrase (see page 20).

> She sat in silence for a long moment, afraid he would reach out and touch her. — Tim Farrington, *The Monk Downstairs*

reach the end of (our) rope (tether) A moribund metaphor (see page 21). *exhausted; frazzled; harassed; stressed; stressed out; tense; weary; worn out.*

read between the lines A moribund metaphor (see page 21). *assume; conclude; conjecture; deduce; gather; guess; hypothesize; imagine; infer; presume; speculate; suppose; surmise; theorize; venture.*

read it and weep An infantile phrase (see page 20).

read (her) like a (an open) book An insipid simile. *empathize; identify with; know; sympathize; understand.*

read my lips An infantile phrase (see page 20).

read (him) the riot act A moribund metaphor (see page 21). *admonish; animadvert; berate; castigate; censure; chasten; chastise; chide; condemn; criticize; denounce; denunciate; discipline; excoriate; fulminate against; imprecate; impugn; inveigh against; objurgate; punish; rebuke; remonstrate; reprehend; reprimand; reproach; reprobate; reprove; revile; scold; swear at; upbraid; vituperate.*

ready, willing, and able An infantile phrase (see page 20). ■ She described her client as being *ready, willing, and able* to testify. REPLACE WITH *willing.* ■ We have a lot of social problems that need to be addressed, and I'm *ready, willing, and able* to do that. REPLACE WITH *ready.*

re- again A wretched redundancy (see page 25). *re-.* ■ I divorced him, and then I *remarried again.* DELETE *again.* ■ We missed the first ten minutes of his talk, so he *repeated* it *again* for us. DELETE *again.*

real An overworked word (see page 22). For example: *real contribution; real difference; real obvious; real possibility; real progress; real tragedy.*

reality check An infantile phrase (see page 20).

real, live An infantile phrase (see page 20).

really An overworked word (see page 22). If such an intensive is needed at all, alternatives to the word *really* include *consumedly; enormously; especially; exceedingly; exceptionally; extraordinarily; extremely; genuinely; particularly; remarkably; specially; truly; uncommonly; very.*

Often, however, such highlighting seems only to moderate the value of our statements. ■ At the *London Review* we take serious pride in our role as one of the *really* significant participants in the international exchange of ideas and information. DELETE *really.* ■ He did a *really* good job of convincing us to buy. DELETE *really.* ■ This speechlessness is *really* affecting his moods, his behavior, and his mental state. DELETE *really.* SEE ALSO *very.*

really? An infantile phrase (see page 20). SEE ALSO *you're kidding; you've got to be kidding.*

really (and) truly An infantile phrase (see page 20). ■ I *really and truly* love being in love. DELETE *really and truly.* ■ Do you *really truly* believe that your mom thinks you're a whore? DELETE *really.* ■ They *really and truly* thought I would never make it. DELETE *really and.* ■ She was, *really and truly,* only following orders. DELETE *really and truly.* ■ *Star* magazine is reporting that not only is Demi Moore *really and truly* pregnant with Ashton Kutcher's child, she's having a boy! DELETE *really and truly.*

> There I was with my parents and my sister and a serving plate layered with skewers of shish kabob, and I thought I was going to be ill. Really and truly ill. — Chris Bohjalian, *Before You Know Kindness*

(the) real McCoy A moribund metaphor (see page 21). *actual; authentic; genuine; legitimate; pure; real; sterling; true; unadulterated; unalloyed; veritable.* ■ When you are talking about classical scholarship, he is *the real McCoy.*

rear (its) (ugly) head A moribund metaphor (see page 21). *appear; emerge; materialize; surface.* ■ That hypocritical axiom, "Do as I say, not as I do" seems to have *reared its ugly head* on the editorial pages of the *Globe* once again. ■ None of us knows for sure whether there is another problem in this volatile environment which could *rear its ugly head* soon.

reasonable facsimile An inescapable pair (see page 20).

(the) reason (why) is because A wretched redundancy (see page 25). *because; reason is (that).* ■ One of *the reasons why* people keep this to themselves *is because of* the stigma. REPLACE WITH *the reasons ... is.*

(the) reason why A wretched redundancy (see page 25). *reason.* ■ There is a *reason why* she is the way she is. DELETE *why.* ■ The researchers are not certain as to the *reason why.* DELETE *why.*

receive back A wretched redundancy (see page 25). *receive.* ■ DPL now communicates with Excel, sending the input values and *receiving back* the output value Profit. DELETE *back*.

reckless abandon An inescapable pair (see page 20).

record-breaking A wretched redundancy (see page 25). *record.* ■ We'll take a look at some *record-breaking* snowfalls. REPLACE WITH *record.* SEE ALSO *all-time record; record-high.*

record-high A wretched redundancy (see page 25). *record.* ■ In Concord, it was a *record-high* 12 degrees. REPLACE WITH *record.* SEE ALSO *all-time record; record-breaking.*

(as) red as a beet An insipid simile. 1. *beet-red; blood-red; burgundian; burgundy; cardinal; carmine; cerise; cherry; crimson; fire-engine-red; maroon; purple; purplish; red; reddish; rose; rose-colored; rosy; rubefacient; rubescent; rubicund; rubied; rubiginous; ruby; ruddy; rufescent; rufous; russet; sanguine; sanguineous; scarlet; vermilion; wine; wine-colored.* 2. *abashed; ashamed; blushing; chagrined; confused; discomfited; discomposed; disconcerted; embarrassed; flushed; flustered; mortified; nonplused; perplexed; red-faced; shamed; shamefaced; sheepish.*

(as) red as a cherry An insipid simile. 1. *beet-red; blood-red; burgundian; burgundy; cardinal; carmine; cerise; cherry; crimson; fire-engine-red; maroon; purple; purplish; red; reddish; rose; rose-colored; rosy; rubefacient; rubescent; rubicund; rubied; rubiginous; ruby; ruddy; rufescent; rufous; russet; sanguine; sanguineous; scarlet; vermilion; wine; wine-colored.* 2. *abashed; ashamed; blushing; chagrined; confused; discomfited; discomposed; disconcerted; embarrassed; flushed; flustered; mortified; nonplused; perplexed; red-faced; shamed; shamefaced; sheepish.*

(as) red as a rose An insipid simile. 1. *beet-red; blood-red; burgundian; burgundy; cardinal; carmine; cerise; cherry; crimson; fire-engine-red; maroon; purple; purplish; red; reddish; rose; rose-colored; rosy; rubefacient; rubescent; rubicund; rubied; rubiginous; ruby; ruddy; rufescent; rufous; russet; sanguine; sanguineous; scarlet; vermilion; wine; wine-colored.* 2. *abashed; ashamed; blushing; chagrined; confused; discomfited; discomposed; disconcerted; embarrassed; flushed; flustered; mortified; nonplused; perplexed; red-faced; shamed; shamefaced; sheepish.*

(as) red as a ruby An insipid simile. 1. *beet-red; blood-red; burgundian; burgundy; cardinal; carmine; cerise; cherry; crimson; fire-engine-red; maroon; purple; purplish; red; reddish; rose; rose-colored; rosy; rubefacient; rubescent; rubicund; rubied; rubiginous; ruby; ruddy; rufescent; rufous; russet; sanguine; sanguineous; scarlet; vermilion; wine; wine-colored.* 2. *abashed; ashamed; blushing; chagrined; confused; discomfited; discomposed; disconcerted; embarrassed; flushed; flustered; mortified; nonplused; perplexed; red-faced; shamed; shamefaced; sheepish.*

red herring A moribund metaphor (see page 21). *decoy; distraction; diversion; lure; ploy; trick.*

red in the face A moribund metaphor (see page 21). *abashed; ashamed; blushing; chagrined; confused; discomfited; discomposed; disconcerted; embarrassed; flushed; flustered; mortified; nonplused; perplexed; red-faced; shamed; shamefaced; sheepish.*

They laughed together understandingly; then, bending forward, he kissed her hastily on the cheek and went out, leaving her red in the face as if she were a young lass. — Catherine Cookson, *The Glass Virgin*

red-letter day A moribund metaphor (see page 21).

red light A moribund metaphor (see page 21). *ban; disallowance; enjoinment; exclusion; interdiction; prohibition; proscription; veto.* SEE ALSO *green light.*

red tape A moribund metaphor (see page 21). *bureaucracy; formalities; paperwork; procedures; regulations; rules.*

refer back A wretched redundancy (see page 25). *refer.* ■ *Refer back* to Chapter 4. DELETE *back.*

reflect back A wretched redundancy (see page 25). *reflect.* ■ Part of the energy is *reflected back* into medium 1 as a reflected ray, and the remainder passes into medium 2 as a refracted ray. DELETE *back.*

regardless of the fact that A wretched redundancy (see page 25). *although; but; even if; even though; still; though; yet.* ■ *Regardless of the fact that* these products are low in sucrose, they still contain energy from other nutrients. REPLACE WITH *Though.* SEE ALSO *despite the fact that; in spite of the fact that.*

(as) regular as clockwork An insipid simile. *cyclic; established; fixed; habitual; periodic; recurrent; recurring; regular; repetitive; rhythmic; rhythmical.*

And week after week, regular as clockwork, LaShawndra comes over and raids Mother's kitchen like it's the Piggly Wiggly. — Tina McElroy Ansa, *You Know Better*

reinvent the wheel A moribund metaphor (see page 21).

relate back A wretched redundancy (see page 25). *relate.* ■ Like the Chicago School, anomie theory *relates back* to the European sociology of the 1800s. DELETE *back.*

relic of the past A wretched redundancy (see page 25). *relic.* ■ The very idea of a single, domestic market has become a *relic of the past.* REPLACE WITH *relic.*

(it) remains to be seen A torpid term (see page 24). *I don't know; (it's) not (yet) known; (that's) uncertain; (that's) unclear; (it's) unknown.* This phrase is often euphemistic for *(I) don't know* and similar admissions. ■ So much *remains to be seen.* REPLACE WITH *is unknown.* ■ *It remains to be seen* whether dietary soybeans can protect women against breast cancer. REPLACE WITH *We do not know.* ■ How the French public, fond of both cigarettes and alcohol, will respond *remains to be seen.* REPLACE WITH *is not yet known.* SEE ALSO *your guess is as good as mine; (just have to) wait and see.*

remedy the situation A torpid term (see page 24). Like all torpid terms, *remedy the situation* neither moves nor motivates us; its use practically ensures that nothing will be righted, nothing remedied.

An ill we might be moved to correct, a problem we might be inspired to solve, but a situation we might never be roused to remedy.

■ If the decisions actually turn out to hamper civil rights enforcement, obviously I would want to take steps to *remedy the situation.* ■ To *remedy the situation* — and make the process fairer, the SEC should require that voting be strictly confidential. ■ One issue has been bothering management for quite a while, but they feel somewhat helpless to *remedy the situation.* ■ The report again called on the government to *remedy this intolerable situation.* SEE ALSO *(a) situation.*

reminisce about the past A wretched redundancy (see page 25). *reminisce.* ■ She's now 89 years old and she spends most of her time *reminiscing about the past.* DELETE *about the past.*

remove the cotton from (my) ears A moribund metaphor (see page 21).

repay back A wretched redundancy (see page 25). *repay.* ■ She is *repaying* her debt *back* to society. DELETE *back.*

replace back A wretched redundancy (see page 25). *replace.* ■ When a change needs to be made, a developer reserves that file from the library, makes the change, and then *replaces* it *back.* DELETE *back.*

reports of (my) death are greatly exaggerated An infantile phrase (see page 20).

represent(s) A torpid term (see page 24). Increasingly, *represents* is being used for a sad, simple *is* (and *represent* for *are*). ■ The budgeted capacity level *represents* the level of expected business activity under normal operating conditions. REPLACE WITH *is.* ■ Newstar and BASYS currently *represent* the major newsroom computer systems in the broadcasting field. REPLACE WITH *are.* ■ Radiosurgery *represents* a major step forward in our ability to treat tumors that previously have been untreatable. REPLACE WITH *is.* ■ I think Ginger, Patty, and I *represent* three very hard-working, committed faculty members. REPLACE WITH *are.*

respond back A wretched redundancy (see page 25). *respond.* ■ The OPP will review each request and *respond back* within ten business days. DELETE *back.*

rest and relaxation An inescapable pair (see page 20). *calm; calmness; leisure; peace; peacefulness; quiet; quietude; relaxation; repose; rest; serenity; stillness; tranquility.*

(and) (the) rest is history An infantile phrase (see page 20).

rest on (her) laurels A moribund metaphor (see page 21).

restore back A wretched redundancy (see page 25). *restore.* ■ The new Undo feature allows you to *restore* the disk *back* to its original state. DELETE *back.*

return back A wretched redundancy (see page 25). *return.* ■ When SEU is exited, the user will be *returned back* to the Programmer Menu. DELETE *back.*

revenge is sweet A quack equation (see page 23).

revert back A wretched redundancy (see page 25). *revert.* ■ Scientists speculate that the rapid spread of the disease may be due to farmland *reverting back* to woodland. DELETE *back*. ■ Not knowing what to do, I would *revert right back* to my old eating habits. DELETE *right back*.

revolving door policy A moribund metaphor (see page 21).

(the) rich and famous A suspect superlative (see page 24). *The rich and famous* infatuate only foolish people, who are as boring to themselves as they are barren of themselves. ■ It has become a summer hideaway for *the rich and famous*. SEE ALSO *celebrity; fame and fortune*.

(as) rich as Croesus An insipid simile. *affluent; moneyed; opulent; prosperous; rich; wealthy; well-off; well-to-do*.

richly deserves An inescapable pair (see page 20). ■ Instead of vilifying him, we should be giving him the encouragement and support he *richly deserves*.

rich man, poor man, beggarman, thief A moribund metaphor (see page 21). ■ It doesn't matter whether you are *rich man, poor man, beggar, or thief*, if you are black, there's an artificial ceiling on your ambition.

ride herd on A moribund metaphor (see page 21). *control; direct; guard; manage; mind; watch over*.

ride off into the sunset A moribund metaphor (see page 21). *abscond; clear out; decamp; depart; desert; disappear; escape; exit; flee; fly; go; go away; leave; move on; part; pull out; quit; retire; retreat; run away; take flight; take off; vacate; vanish; withdraw*.

ride on (her) coattails A moribund metaphor (see page 21).

ride out the storm A moribund metaphor (see page 21).

ride roughshod over A moribund metaphor (see page 21). *boss; browbeat; brutalize; bully; dictate; domineer; enslave; master; oppress; overpower; overrule; reign over; repress; rule; subjugate; suppress; tyrannize*.

(as) right as rain An insipid simile. 1. *accurate; correct; exact; irrefutable; precise; right; true*. 2. *fit; good; hale; hardy; healthful; healthy; hearty; robust; sound; strong; well*.

(a case of) (the) right hand not knowing what the left hand is doing A moribund metaphor (see page 21).

(what's) right is right A quack equation (see page 23).

right off the bat A moribund metaphor (see page 21). *abruptly; apace; at once; briskly; directly; expeditiously; fast; forthwith; hastily; hurriedly; immediately; instantaneously; instantly; posthaste; promptly; quickly; rapidly; rashly; right away; speedily; straightaway; swiftly; wingedly*.

(on the) right track A moribund metaphor (see page 21).

ring a bell A moribund metaphor (see page 21). *be familiar; remind; sound familiar*.

ring down the curtain (on) A moribund metaphor (see page 21). *cease; close; complete; conclude; discontinue; end; finish; halt; settle; stop*.

ringing endorsement An inescapable pair (see page 20).

ringing off the hook A moribund metaphor (see page 21). *ceaselessly; constantly; continually; continuously; nonstop; perpetually; steadily.* ■ The phones are *ringing off the hook.* REPLACE WITH *constantly ringing.*

rip (tear) to shreds A moribund metaphor (see page 21). *demolish; destroy; devastate; obliterate; rack; ravage; ruin; shatter; smash; undo; wrack; wreck.*

rise from the ashes A moribund metaphor (see page 21). *rise anew.*

rise to the bait A moribund metaphor (see page 21). *get angry; react; rejoin; respond; retort.*

> My job was to look respectfully attentive without rising to his bait. — Gail Godwin, *Queen of the Underworld*

(a) rising tide of A moribund metaphor (see page 21). ■ The report found in the nation's public schools *a rising tide of* mediocrity. SEE ALSO *a barrage of.*

road less traveled A moribund metaphor (see page 21).

(the) road to hell is paved with good intentions A popular prescription (see page 23).

road to ruin A moribund metaphor (see page 21). ■ To permit lying is a step down the *road to ruin.*

roar (in) like a lion An insipid simile. *growl; roar.*

rob Peter to pay Paul A moribund metaphor (see page 21).

(the) rock of Gibraltar A moribund metaphor (see page 21). 1. *beefy; brawny; burly; energetic; firm; fit; hale; hardy; healthful; healthy; hearty; husky; manly; mighty; muscular; powerful; puissant; robust; rugged; sinewy; solid; sound; stalwart; stout; strapping; strong; sturdy; tough; vigorous; virile; well-built.* 2. *constant; dependable; determined; faithful; fast; firm; fixed; inexorable; inflexible; loyal; obdurate; resolute; resolved; rigid; solid; stable; staunch; steadfast; steady; stern; strong; tenacious; unflinching; unwavering; unyielding.*

rock the boat A moribund metaphor (see page 21). *agitate; confuse; disorder; disorganize; disquiet; disrupt; disturb; fluster; jar; jolt; jumble; mess up; mix up; muddle; perturb; rattle; ruffle; shake up; stir up; trouble; unnerve; unsettle; upset.*

(a) rogue's gallery of A moribund metaphor (see page 21).

(positive) role model A torpid term (see page 24). *archetype; example; exemplar; good example; good man (woman); guide; hero; ideal; inspiration; model; paragon; prototype.*

(like) (a) (an emotional) roller-coaster (ride) A moribund metaphor (see page 21). Without relentless amusement, endless diversions, people might manage to speak tolerably well. As it is, the need to be entertained so overcomes us that we can speak in little but laughable images. The expression *(like) a (an emotional) roller-coaster (ride)*, one such image, results from and gives rise to only carnival-like conversation, sideshow prose. ■ But the next season, it's the same thing, a game filled with ups and downs; it really is *like a roller coaster ride.* ■ The stock market is *like a roller coaster ride.* ■ If you find that the everyday activities of your daily life are being interrupted by intense emotions or *a roller coaster* of emotions, call EAP Preferred to schedule a session. ■ When I started TTC again, I knew that this pregnancy would be a bit of *an emotional roller coaster,* but I had no idea just how terrified I would be.

> And so before it's too late I want to get it down for good: this roller-coaster ride of a single gene through time. — Jeffrey Eugenides, *Middlesex*

rolling in money A moribund metaphor (see page 21). *affluent; moneyed; opulent; prosperous; rich; wealthy; well-off; well-to-do.*

rolling over (smiling; turning over) in (his) grave A moribund metaphor (see page 21).

(a) rolling stone gathers no moss A popular prescription (see page 23).

roll in the aisles A moribund metaphor (see page 21). *cachinnate; cackle; chortle; chuckle; convulse; guffaw; hoot; howl; laugh; roar; shriek; whoop.*

roll out the red carpet A moribund metaphor (see page 21). *esteem; honor; respect; venerate; welcome.*

roll up (her) sleeves A moribund metaphor (see page 21). *drudge; grind; grub; labor; moil; slave; strain; strive; struggle; sweat; toil; travail; work hard.*

roll with the punches A moribund metaphor (see page 21). *abide by; accede to; accept; accommodate; acquiesce; adapt to; adhere to; adjust to; agree to; assent; be agreeable; be complacent; bend; be resigned; bow; comply with; concede to; concur; conform; consent to; fit; follow; reconcile; submit; succumb; yield.*

romantic interlude A suspect superlative (see page 24). *intercourse; love-making; sex.*

Rome wasn't built in a day A popular prescription (see page 23).

(the) roof fell in A moribund metaphor (see page 21). *break down; break up; collapse; crash; crumple; disintegrate; end; fail; fall apart; fold; stop.*

(a) roof over (their) heads A moribund metaphor (see page 21). *asylum; cover; harbor; harborage; haven; housing; lodging; protection; refuge; retreat; safety; sanctuary; shelter.*

root cause A wretched redundancy (see page 25). *cause; origin; reason; root; source.* ■ It does not truly solve the problem of rising health care costs since it does not address the *root cause* of the problem. REPLACE WITH *root.*

rootin', tootin', shootin' An infantile phrase (see page 20).

(money is) (the) root of all evil A popular prescription (see page 23).

(a) rose by any other name (would smell as sweet) A popular prescription (see page 23).

(a) rose is a rose (is a rose) A quack equation (see page 23).

rotten apple A moribund metaphor (see page 21). *bastard; blackguard; cad; charlatan; cheat; cheater; fake; fraud; impostor; knave; mountebank; phony; pretender; quack; rascal; rogue; scoundrel; swindler; undesirable; villain.*

rotten to the core A moribund metaphor (see page 21). *bad; base; contemptible; corrupt; crooked; deceitful; despicable; dishonest; evil; immoral; iniquitous; malevolent; mean; miserable; nefarious; pernicious; praetorian; rotten; sinister; underhanded; unethical; untrustworthy; venal; vicious; vile; wicked.*

rough and ready An inescapable pair (see page 20).

rough and tumble A moribund metaphor (see page 21). *boisterous; disorderly; raucous; riotous; rough; tempestuous; tumultuous; turbulent; uproarious; violent; wild.*

rough around the edges A moribund metaphor (see page 21). 1. *bad-mannered; boorish; coarse; crude; ill-mannered; loutish; oafish; rough; rude; uncouth; uncultured; unrefined; unsophisticated; vulgar.* 2. *imperfect; incomplete; unfinished.*

(a) round peg in a square hole A moribund metaphor (see page 21). *curiosity; deviant; eccentric; iconoclast; individual; individualist; maverick; misfit; nonconformist; oddball; oddity; renegade; undesirable.*

rousing success An inescapable pair (see page 20).

rub elbows (shoulders) with A moribund metaphor (see page 21). *associate; be involved with; consort; fraternize; frequent; hobnob; keep company; mingle; mix; see; socialize.*

rub (me) the wrong way A moribund metaphor (see page 21). 1. *acerbate; anger; annoy; chafe; gall; grate; irk; irritate; miff; nettle; provoke; rankle; rile; roil; upset; vex.* 2. *affront; agitate; bother; disrupt; disturb; fluster; insult; jar; offend; perturb; rattle; ruffle; shake up; stir up; trouble; unnerve; unsettle; upset.* ■ I wouldn't want to do anything that would *rub her the wrong way*. REPLACE WITH *annoy her*.

ruffle (her) feathers A moribund metaphor (see page 21). *affront; agitate; bother; disrupt; disturb; fluster; insult; jar; offend; perturb; rattle; ruffle; shake up; stir up; trouble; unnerve; unsettle; upset.*

(a) rule is a rule A quack equation (see page 23).

rules and regulations An inescapable pair (see page 20). *regulations; rules.* ■ You may have a player that's disappointed, but we're adhering to our *rules and regulations*. REPLACE WITH *regulations* or *rules*.

rules are made to be broken A popular prescription (see page 23).

(the) rule rather than the exception A torpid term (see page 24). *basic; common; commonplace; conventional; customary; general; normal; ordinary; quotidian; regular; routine; standard; typical; uneventful; unexceptional; unremarkable; usual.* ■ New advertising campaigns costing $5 million or even $10 million are becoming *the rule rather than the exception.* REPLACE WITH *common.*

(the) rules of the game A moribund metaphor (see page 21).

(the) rules of the road A moribund metaphor (see page 21).

rule the roost A moribund metaphor (see page 21). *administer; be in charge; be in command; be in control; boss; command; control; dictate; direct; dominate; govern; lead; manage; manipulate; master; order; overpower; oversee; predominate; preponderate; prevail; reign over; rule; superintend.* ■ High school football no longer *rules the roost.* REPLACE WITH *predominates.*

> Each of the stories Ma told us about Papa reinforced the message that he was the boss, that he ruled the roost, that what he said went.
> — Wally Lamb, *I Know This Much Is True*

rule with an iron fist (hand) A moribund metaphor (see page 21). *authoritarian; authoritative; autocratic; cruel; despotic; dictatorial; dogmatic; domineering; hard; harsh; imperious; iron-handed; lordly; oppressive; overbearing; peremptory; repressive; rigorous; severe; stern; strict; tough; tyrannical.*

run a tight ship A moribund metaphor (see page 21). *controlled; ordered; organized; structured.*

run circles (rings) around A moribund metaphor (see page 21). *beat; better; cap; defeat; exceed; excel; outclass; outdo; outflank; outmaneuver; outperform; outplay; outrank; outsmart; outstrip; outthink; outwit; overcome; overpower; prevail over; surpass; top; triumph over; trounce; whip; win out.*

(a) run for (his) money A moribund metaphor (see page 21).

run (it) into the ground A moribund metaphor (see page 21).

running on empty A moribund metaphor (see page 21). *be exhausted; be fatigued; be spent; be tired; be weary; be worn out.*

running on fumes A moribund metaphor (see page 21).

run off at the mouth A moribund metaphor (see page 21). *babbling; blathering; chatty; facile; fluent; garrulous; glib; jabbering; logorrheic; long-winded; loquacious; prolix; talkative; verbose; voluble; windy.*

run of the mill A moribund metaphor (see page 21). *average; common; commonplace; customary; everyday; fair; mediocre; middling; normal; ordinary; passable; plain; quotidian; regular; routine; simple; standard; tolerable; typical; uneventful; unexceptional; unremarkable; usual; workaday.*

run out of steam A moribund metaphor (see page 21). *be exhausted; be fatigued; conclude; decline; deteriorate; die; droop; dwindle; end; expire; fade; fail; finish; flag; languish; perish; quit; regress; stop; tire; weaken; wear out.* ■ Market rallies within ongoing bear markets tend to *run out of steam* as soon as the market climbs back up to the vicinity of its 200-day moving average. REPLACE WITH *languish.*

(money) runs through (his) fingers A moribund metaphor (see page 21).

run the gauntlet A moribund metaphor (see page 21). *bear; endure; experience; face; suffer; undergo.*

run the show A moribund metaphor (see page 21). *administer; boss; command; control; dictate; direct; dominate; govern; in charge; in command; in control; manage; manipulate; master; order; overpower; oversee; predominate; prevail; reign over; rule; superintend.*

> He had called me sir more than enough times for me to have no hallucinations about who was running the show, and so I did leave, and, as I say, that was the end of it. — Philip Roth, *The Human Stain*

run with the pack A moribund metaphor (see page 21). *abide by; accommodate; accord; acquiesce; adapt; adhere to; agree; behave; comply; concur; conform; correspond; follow; harmonize; heed; mind; obey; observe; submit; yield.*

run with the hare and hunt with the hounds A moribund metaphor (see page 21).

S

sacred cow A moribund metaphor (see page 21).

sacrificial lamb A moribund metaphor (see page 21). *sacrifice; victim.*

safe and sound An inescapable pair (see page 20). *all right; unharmed; uninjured; safe.*

> They were going to pray that he come home safe and sound, with a minimum of mosquito bites. — William Kowalski, *The Adventures of Flash Jackson*

safe haven A wretched redundancy (see page 25). *asylum; haven; refuge; sanctuary; shelter.* ■ Massachusetts, which likes to think of itself as a liberal mecca, is no *safe haven.* REPLACE WITH *haven.*

safety net A moribund metaphor (see page 21).

said A withered word (see page 24). *that; the; these; this; those;* delete. ■ Therefore, the relative pronouns used to introduce clauses will retain *said* function. REPLACE WITH *this.*

sail (too) close to the wind A moribund metaphor (see page 21). *chance; dare; endanger; gamble; hazard; imperil; jeopardize; make bold; peril; risk; venture.*

sail under false colors A moribund metaphor (see page 21). *bamboozle;*

befool; beguile; belie; bilk; bluff; cheat; color; con; deceive; defraud; delude; disguise; dissemble; dissimulate; dupe; fake; falsify; feign; feint; fool; gyp; hoodwink; lead astray; masquerade; misdirect; misguide; misinform; mislead; misrepresent; pretend; simulate; spoof; swindle; trick.

(the) salt of the earth A moribund metaphor (see page 21).

(the) same A torpid term (see page 24). *it; one; them.* ■ Gemini critique partners are eager to assist, but steel yourself against their tendency to fire-off suggestions without consideration of your emotional reaction to *the same.* REPLACE WITH *them.* ■ Provide access aisle for first accessible parking space which lacks *same.* REPLACE WITH *it.*

(the) same but different An infantile phrase (see page 20). SEE ALSO *same difference.*

sans A withered word (see page 24). *bereft; lacking; without.* ■ He has a reckless streak, as revealed in his tendency to go swimming *sans* suit. REPLACE WITH *without a.* ■ Using this button will allow you to see what the dialog box will look like to the user, *sans* any personal or company information that you'll eventually add to it. REPLACE WITH *without.*

save A withered word (see page 24). *but; except.* ■ The room was quiet during his performance, *save* when he would take a deep breath and let out some of it. REPLACE WITH *except.* ■ In 1990, the Emirate of Kuwait — tiny in all respects *save* its role in oil affairs — was invaded by fellow OPEC and Arab League member Iraq. REPLACE WITH *but.*

saved by the bell An infantile phrase (see page 20).

save (it) for a rainy day A moribund metaphor (see page 21).

save (his) neck (skin) A moribund metaphor (see page 21).

save your breath A moribund metaphor (see page 21). *be quiet; be silent; be still; hush; keep quiet; keep still.*

(as) scarce (scarcer) as hen's teeth An insipid simile. *exiguous; inadequate; meager; rare; scant; scanty; scarce; sparse; uncommon; unusual.*

scare the (living) daylights out of (me) A moribund metaphor (see page 21). *alarm; appall; benumb; daunt; frighten; horrify; intimidate; panic; paralyze; petrify; scare; shock; startle; terrify; terrorize.*

scare the pants off (me) A moribund metaphor (see page 21). *alarm; appall; benumb; daunt; frighten; horrify; intimidate; panic; paralyze; petrify; scare; shock; startle; terrify; terrorize.*

scare to death A moribund metaphor (see page 21). *alarm; appall; benumb; daunt; frighten; horrify; intimidate; panic; paralyze; petrify; scare; shock; startle; terrify; terrorize.* SEE ALSO *to death.*

school of hard knocks A moribund metaphor (see page 21).

(just) scratch the surface A moribund metaphor (see page 21).

scream and yell An inescapable pair (see page 20). *bay; bawl; bellow; blare;*

caterwaul; clamor; cry; holler; hoot; howl; roar; screak; scream; screech; shout; shriek; shrill; squawk; squeal; vociferate; wail; whoop; yell; yelp; yowl. ■ If parents are *screaming and yelling* at each other, that causes fear in children. REPLACE WITH *yelling.* ■ It's very flattering that women *scream and yell* when you walk on stage. REPLACE WITH *scream.* SEE ALSO *yell and scream.*

scream (yell) at the top of (my) lungs A moribund metaphor (see page 21). *bay; bawl; bellow; blare; caterwaul; clamor; cry; holler; hoot; howl; roar; screak; scream; screech; shout; shriek; shrill; squawk; squeal; vociferate; wail; whoop; yell; yelp; yowl.*

scream (yell) bloody murder A moribund metaphor (see page 21). 1. *bay; bawl; bellow; blare; caterwaul; clamor; cry; holler; hoot; howl; roar; screech; shout; shriek; shrill; squawk; squeal; vociferate; wail; whoop; yell; yelp; yowl.* 2. *clamor; complain; explode; fulminate; fume; fuss; gripe; grumble; holler; howl; object; protest; rage; rant; rave; remonstrate; roar; scream; shout; storm; thunder; vociferate; yell.* ■ The Jones lawyers would have *screamed bloody murder*, and rightly so. REPLACE WITH *protested.*

screech to a halt A moribund metaphor (see page 21). *cease; close; complete; conclude; derail; discontinue; end; finish; halt; settle; stop.* ■ Work in 535 congressional offices *screeched to a halt.* REPLACE WITH *ceased.*

(a) sea of A moribund metaphor (see page 21). ■ He was surrounded by *a sea of* concerned women. DELETE *a sea of.* SEE ALSO *a barrage of.*

(the) second American Revolution A moribund metaphor (see page 21).

second banana A moribund metaphor (see page 21). *aide; assistant; associate; inferior; junior; minion; secondary; subordinate; underling.* ■ Murphy's greatest political need is to convince the public that she is a leader, and not just the governor's long-suffering *second banana.*

second of all A wretched redundancy (see page 25). *second.* ■ *Second of all*, you're going to get hurt if you continue this behavior. REPLACE WITH *Second.* SEE ALSO *first of all.*

second to none A torpid term (see page 24). *best; different; exceptional; extraordinary; finest; first; greatest; highest; incomparable; inimitable; matchless; nonpareil; notable; noteworthy; novel; odd; optimal; optimum; original; outstanding; peculiar; peerless; remarkable; singular; special; strange; superlative; uncommon; unequaled; unexampled; unique; unmatched; unparalleled; unrivaled; unusual; without equal.*

(plant) (the) seeds of A moribund metaphor (see page 21).

see eye to eye A moribund metaphor (see page 21). *agree; concur; think alike.* ■ We *see eye to eye* on most all matters. REPLACE WITH *agree.*

seeing is believing A quack equation (see page 23).

seek and you shall find A popular prescription (see page 23).

see red A moribund metaphor (see page 21). *acerbate; anger; annoy; bother; bris-*

tle; chafe; enrage; incense; inflame; infuriate; irk; irritate; madden; miff; provoke; rile; roil; vex.

see the glass half empty A moribund metaphor (see page 21). *cynical; dark; despairing; doubtful; gloomy; hopeless; morbid; pessimistic; sullen.*

see the light A moribund metaphor (see page 21). *appreciate; apprehend; comprehend; discern; fathom; grasp; know; make sense of; perceive; realize; recognize; see; understand.*

see the light of day A moribund metaphor (see page 21). 1. *be actualized; be carried out; be implemented; be initiated; be instituted; be realized; be undertaken.* 2. *be accomplished; be achieved; be completed; be consummated; be executed; be finished; be fulfilled.* ■ The proposal will never *see the light of day.* REPLACE WITH *be realized.*

seething mass of humanity A moribund metaphor (see page 21).

self-fulfilling prophecy A torpid term (see page 24). ■ If retailers think negatively and pessimistically in terms of Christmas, it's going to be a *self-fulfilling prophecy.*

sell (him) a bill of goods A moribund metaphor (see page 21). *cheat; deceive; defraud; dupe; fool; lie to; swindle; trick; victimize.* ■ We realize that we've been *sold a bill of goods.* REPLACE WITH *swindled.*

sell (him) down the river A moribund metaphor (see page 21). *betray; deliver up; inform on; turn in.*

send a (loud) message (signal) A torpid term (see page 24). This phrase is a favorite among journalists and politicians — scrawlers and stammerers — who are accustomed to expressing themselves with dead and indifferent words. And from such words, only the faintest of feelings and the shallowest of thoughts can be summoned.

■ The patent system that protects new drugs from competition *sends a message* to pharmaceutical companies: if you invest enough money and come up with a hit, you can make a killing. REPLACE WITH *says.* ■ We want to *send a message* that this kind of behavior will not be tolerated. REPLACE WITH *make clear.* ■ The police department *sent out a message* that we would not allow such looting to occur again. REPLACE WITH *made it known.* ■ By agreeing to act now, we are *sending a signal* that we do not want this plan to fail. REPLACE WITH *announcing.* ■ I think the MFA, by hosting this exhibit, is *sending the wrong message to* the public. REPLACE WITH *misguiding.* ■ A triple-spaced term paper *sends the loud message* that the writer probably has very little to say. REPLACE WITH *proclaims.* SEE ALSO *reach epidemic proportions.*

send chills (shivers) down (my) spine A moribund metaphor (see page 21). 1. *agitate; disquiet; disrupt; disturb; fluster; jar; jolt; perturb; rattle; ruffle; shake up; stir up; trouble; unnerve; unsettle; upset.* 2. *alarm; appall; benumb; daunt; frighten; horrify; intimidate; panic; paralyze; petrify; scare; shock; startle; terrify; terrorize.*

send (them) packing A moribund metaphor (see page 21). *discard; dismiss; discharge.*

send shock waves (through) A moribund metaphor (see page 21). *agitate; arouse; astound; bother; confuse; discomfit; disconcert; disquiet; disrupt; disturb; excite; jolt; shock; startle; stimulate; stir; stun; unsettle; upset.* ■ When Swiss pharmaceutical giant Roche Holding Ltd. announced that it would buy 60 percent of Genentech Inc., it *sent shock waves through* the biotechnology community. REPLACE WITH *shocked.*

send up a trial balloon A moribund metaphor (see page 21). *assess; check; explore; inspect; investigate; look into; probe; test; try.*

separate and distinct A wretched redundancy (see page 25). *distinct; separate.* ■ Nor are the stages *separate and distinct*; they may occur at the same time. REPLACE WITH *distinct.*

separate and independent A wretched redundancy (see page 25). *independent; separate.* ■ Since the audio and video in an Interactive Multipoint videoconference travel over *separate and independent* paths, the audio must be delayed to synchronize it with the video. REPLACE WITH *separate.*

separate out A wretched redundancy (see page 25). *separate.* ■ I don't think you can *separate out* those two things. DELETE *out.* ■ Our objective was to *separate out* the NLR from the continuum emission by subtracting the different filter images. DELETE *out.* ■ One of the things that became very clear to us early on was that you simply can't *separate out* issues like curriculum and teachers' professional development and learning and instruction. DELETE *out.*

separate the men from the boys A moribund metaphor (see page 21). *choose; cull; differentiate; discriminate; distinguish; divide; filter; isolate; pick; screen; segregate; select; separate; sieve; sift; sort; strain; weed out; winnow.*

separate the sheep from the goats A moribund metaphor (see page 21). *choose; cull; differentiate; discriminate; distinguish; divide; filter; isolate; pick; screen; segregate; select; separate; sieve; sift; sort; strain; weed out; winnow.*

separate the wheat from the chaff A moribund metaphor (see page 21). *choose; cull; differentiate; discriminate; distinguish; divide; filter; isolate; pick; screen; segregate; select; separate; sieve; sift; sort; strain; weed out; winnow.*

serious reservations An inescapable pair (see page 20).

set in concrete A moribund metaphor (see page 21). *eternal; everlasting; firm; immutable; invariable; irreversible; irrevocable; permanent; rigid; stable; unalterable; unchangeable; unchanging.*

set (her) teeth on edge A moribund metaphor (see page 21). 1. *acerbate; anger; annoy; bristle; chafe; enrage; incense; inflame; infuriate; irk; irritate; madden; miff; nettle; offend; provoke; rile; roil; vex.* 2. *agitate; bother; disconcert; disturb; fluster; perturb; unnerve; upset.*

> The music runs clear up my spine and sets my teeth on edge. — Michael Lee West, *Crazy Ladies*

set the record straight A torpid term (see page 24). ■ There are a lot of things I can do in my book in terms of *setting* *the record straight.* ■ EPA believes it's time to *set the record straight* about an indisputable fact: secondhand smoke is a real and preventable health risk.

set the stage (for) A moribund metaphor (see page 21). *arrange; groom; make ready; plan; prepare; prime; ready.*

set the wheels in motion A moribund metaphor (see page 21). *begin; commence; embark; inaugurate; initiate; launch; originate; start; undertake.*

set the world on fire A moribund metaphor (see page 21). *amaze; animate; awe; captivate; dazzle; electrify; excite; exhilarate; fascinate; impress; intoxicate; thrill; overwhelm.*

settle the score A moribund metaphor (see page 21).

seventh heaven A moribund metaphor (see page 21). *bliss; delight; ecstasy; joy; rapture.*

(he's a) shadow of (his) former self A moribund metaphor (see page 21). *apparition; specter; wraith.*

shake to its foundations A moribund metaphor (see page 21). *agitate; disquiet; disrupt; disturb; fluster; jar; jerk; jolt; perturb; quake; quiver; rattle; ruffle; shake up; shudder; stir up; unnerve; unsettle; tremble; upset.*

shaking in (his) boots A moribund metaphor (see page 21). 1. *afraid; alarmed; apprehensive; cowardly; craven; diffident; faint-hearted; fearful; frightened; pavid; pusillanimous; recreant; scared; terror-striken; timid; timorous; tremulous.* 2. *jittery; jumpy; nervous; quivering; shaking; shivering; shivery; shuddering; skittish; trembling.*

shaking like a leaf An insipid simile. 1. *jittery; jumpy; nervous; quivering; shaking; shivering; shivery; shuddering; skittish; trembling.* 2. *afraid; alarmed; apprehensive; cowardly; craven; diffident; faint-hearted; fearful; frightened; pavid; pusillanimous; recreant; scared; terror-striken; timid; timorous; tremulous.*

shank's mare A moribund metaphor (see page 21). *by foot.*

share and share alike A popular prescription (see page 23).

(as) sharp as a razor An insipid simile. *able; adroit; apt; astute; bright; brilliant; capable; clever; competent; discerning; enlightened; insightful; intelligent; judicious; keen; knowledgeable; learned; logical; luminous; perceptive; perspicacious; quick; rational; reasonable; sagacious; sage; sapient; sensible; sharp; shrewd; smart; sound; understanding; wise.*

(as) sharp as a tack An insipid simile. 1. *dapper; neat; smart; trim; well dressed; well groomed.* 2. *able; adroit; apt; astute; bright; brilliant; capable; clever; competent; discerning; enlightened; insightful; intelligent; judicious; keen; knowledgeable; learned; logical; luminous; perceptive; perspicacious; quick; rational; reasonable; sagacious; sage; sapient; sensible; sharp; shrewd; smart; sound; understanding; wise.*

shed (throw) light on A moribund metaphor (see page 21). *clarify; clear up; describe; disentangle; elucidate; enlighten; explain; explicate; illume; illuminate; interpret; make clear; make plain; reveal; simplify.*

> But he had little faith that Dohmler would throw much light on the matter; he himself was the incalculable element involved. — F. Scott Fitzgerald, *Tender is the Night*

shift (swing) into high gear A moribund metaphor (see page 21). ■ The lawyer is *shifting into high gear*, summoning all his persuasive powers for a rhetorical flourish that will dazzle the jury and save his client a multimillion-dollar court award.

ship of fools A moribund metaphor (see page 21).

(like) (two) ships passing in the night An insipid simile.

> She became a ship passing in the night — an emblem of the loneliness of human life, an occasion for queer confidences and sudden appeals for sympathy. — Virginia Woolf, *The Voyage Out*

(my) ship to come in A moribund metaphor (see page 21).

(cost) (the) shirt off (my) back A moribund metaphor (see page 21).

shocked (surprised) and saddened (dismayed) A torpid term (see page 24). These are formulas that people — especially spokespeople and journalists it seems — use to express indignation. And, as formulas, the *shock and sadness,* the *shock and dismay,* the *shock and outrage* is scarcely heartfelt.

■ Gilda Radner's death from cancer *shocked and saddened* Hollywood. ■ I was *shocked and saddened* by the news of his death. ■ Shoppers and shop owners were also *shocked and saddened* by Mr. Stuart's suicide. ■ Relatives were *shocked and dismayed* by what they saw today. ■ When Kissinger was selected instead of the banking mogul, Rockefeller's staff were *shocked and dismayed.* ■ Sullivan says she is *surprised and saddened* by the recent turn of events. ■ We are *saddened and outraged* by the tragic death of a young man just starting to fulfill his life promise. ■ We are terribly *shocked and dismayed;* Ed was an active and important member of our community who will be missed by his colleagues. ■ Needless to say, my dear husband was, and is, *shocked and saddened.* ■ I am *shocked and saddened* by these allegations. ■ I want to begin by saying that Hillary and I are profoundly *shocked and saddened* by the tragedy today in Littleton. ■ The man who was at the heart of the Cape Verdean neighborhood leaves behind a wife, five children, and a *shocked and saddened* community.

A newspaper editor who has just learned of the mutilation of one of his female reporters in a strife-torn country remarks he is *saddened and distressed* by her death. This is the same soulless formula; anyone who has not surrendered to this dimwitticism would surely have said it differently. SEE ALSO *reach epidemic proportions.*

> Shocked and surprised as I was I agreed without hesitation, prompted both by curiosity as to his own feelings and a desire to discuss the transaction which concerned the child. — Lawrence Durrell, *Justine*

(the) shoe is on the other foot A moribund metaphor (see page 21).

shoot down A moribund metaphor (see page 21). *belie; confute; contradict; controvert; counter; debunk; deny; disprove; discredit; dispute; expose; invalidate; negate; rebut; refute; repudiate.*

shoot from the hip A moribund metaphor (see page 21). 1. *be aboveboard; be artless; be blunt; be candid; be direct; be forthright; be frank; be genuine; be guileless; be honest; be ingenuous; be naive; be outspoken; be sincere; be straightforward.* 2. *hasty; headlong; heedless; hot-headed; impetuous; impulsive; incautious; precipitate; rash; reckless; thoughtless; unthinking.* ■ Congress is feeling very ambivalent, there are very complicated questions of government here, and these *shoot-from-the-hip* folks already have their opinion locked in cement. REPLACE WITH *incautious.*

shoot full of holes A moribund metaphor (see page 21). *belie; confute; contradict; controvert; counter; debunk; deny; disprove; discredit; dispute; expose; invalidate; negate; rebut; refute; repudiate.*

(like) shooting fish in a barrel An insipid simile. *easily done; easy; effortless; elementary; facile; simple; simplicity itself; straightforward; uncomplex; uncomplicated.*

shoot the breeze (bull) A moribund metaphor (see page 21). *babble; blab; cackle; chaffer; chat; chitchat; chatter; confabulate; converse; gossip; jabber; palaver; prate; prattle; rattle; talk.* ■ He would come down every couple of weeks just to *shoot the breeze.* REPLACE WITH *chat.*

shoot the messenger A moribund metaphor (see page 21).

shoot the works A moribund metaphor (see page 21).

shop till you drop A moribund metaphor (see page 21).

short and sweet An inescapable pair (see page 20). *brief; compact; concise; condensed; curt; laconic; pithy; short; succinct; terse.*

short and to the point A torpid phrase. *brief; compact; concise; condensed; curt; laconic; pithy; short; succinct; terse.*

short end of the stick A moribund metaphor (see page 21).

(a) shot across the bow A moribund metaphor (see page 21). *admonition; caution; warning.*

shot heard around the world A moribund metaphor (see page 21).

shot (himself) in the foot A moribund metaphor (see page 21).

(a) shot in the arm A moribund metaphor (see page 21). *boost; encouragement; fillip; goad; impetus; impulse; incentive; incitation; incitement; inducement; jolt; motivation; motive; prod;*

provocation; push; shove; spur; stimulus; thrust; urge. ■ Their success will give *a shot in the arm* to the rest of the economy. REPLACE WITH *a thrust.*

(a) shot in the dark A moribund metaphor (see page 21). *appraisal; assessment; assumption; conjecture; estimate; estimation; guess; hypothesis; impression; opinion; presumption; speculation; supposition; surmise.*

shot to hell A moribund metaphor (see page 21). 1. *demolished; destroyed; devastated; obliterated; racked; ruined; shattered; smashed; wracked; wrecked.* 2. *damaged; decayed; decrepit; deteriorated; dilapidated; ragged; shabby; shopworn; tattered; worn.*

(stand) shoulder to shoulder A moribund metaphor (see page 21). *collaborate; comply; concur; conspire; cooperate; work together.*

shout (it) from the housetops (rooftops) A moribund metaphor (see page 21). *advertise; announce; broadcast; cry out; declaim; disseminate; exclaim; proclaim; promulgate; publicize; publish; shout; trumpet; yell.*

shove down (their) throats A moribund metaphor (see page 21). *bulldoze; bully; coerce; compel; constrain; demand; drive; enforce; enjoin; goad; force; impel; incite; intimidate; make; necessitate; obligate; oblige; order; press; pressure; prod; require; threaten; tyrannize; urge.*

show me a ... and I'll show you a ... An infantile phrase (see page 20). ■ *Show me a* person who's lived a normal, conventional life, *and I'll show you a* dullard.

(the) show must go on A popular prescription (see page 23).

(not a) shred of (evidence) A moribund metaphor (see page 21). ■ There was not a *shred of evidence* to support his contentions.

shrinking violet A moribund metaphor (see page 21). *diffident; quiet; reserved; retiring; self-effacing; shy; timid.*

shut (his) eyes to A moribund metaphor (see page 21). *brush aside; avoid; discount; disregard; dodge; duck; ignore; neglect; omit; pass over; recoil from; shrink from; shun; shy away from; turn away from; withdraw from.*

sick and tired (of) An inescapable pair (see page 20). 1. *annoyed; bored; discouraged; disgusted; exasperated; exhausted; fatigued; fed up; impatient; irked; irritated; sick; sickened; tired; wearied; weary.* 2. *cloyed; glutted; gorged; jaded; sated; satiated; surfeited.* ■ I'm *sick and tired* of seeing the welfare bashing in the newspaper. REPLACE WITH *weary.* ■ No matter how desperate and *sick and tired* and lonely I felt, I was also vibrant and alive. REPLACE WITH *discouraged.*

(as) sick as a dog An insipid simile. 1. *afflicted; ailing; diseased; ill; indisposed; infirm; not (feeling) well; sick; sickly; suffering; unhealthy; unsound; unwell; valetudinarian.* 2. *nauseated; nauseous; queasy; sick; squeamish; vomiting.*

sick to death A moribund metaphor (see page 21). *annoyed; bored; discouraged; disgusted; exasperated; exhausted; fatigued; fed up; impatient; irked; irritated; sick; sickened; tired; wearied; weary.* SEE ALSO *to death.*

(breathe; exhale; heave) a (collective) sigh of relief A torpid term (see page 24). *be allayed; be alleviated; be assuaged; be calmed; be comforted; be mollified; be palliated; be relieved; be soothed; calm down; quiet down; relax; rest; unwind.* People who *breathe a collective sigh of relief* also *welcome a breath of fresh air* (SEE). They expire fetid words and inspire foolish thoughts.

■ Investors *breathed a sigh of relief* there was nothing more in the report than they expected. REPLACE WITH *were relieved.* ■ Emergency workers were *breathing a collective sigh of relief.* REPLACE WITH *relieved.* ■ Every morning when I come in and see them, I *breathe a sigh of relief.* REPLACE WITH *relax.* ■ After holding its breath for days, the city finally *exhaled a sigh of relief.* REPLACE WITH *relaxed.* ■ You are probably *breathing a sigh of relief knowing* that you won't have to mangle code any longer to render a display of a list within a list. REPLACE WITH *relieved to know.* SEE ALSO *reach epidemic proportions.*

(a) sight for sore eyes A moribund metaphor (see page 21).

signed, sealed, and delivered A moribund metaphor (see page 21). *completed; concluded; consummated; ended; executed; finished; fulfilled; made final; terminated.*

significant An overworked word (see page 22). For example: *significant development; significant effect; significant impact; significant progress.* SEE ALSO *meaningful.*

significant other A torpid term (see page 24). The use of this dispassionate expression will likely result in a bloodless relationship with whomever it is used to describe. Any one of the following words is a far better choice: *admirer; beau; beloved; boyfriend (girlfriend); companion; confidant; darling; dear; dearest; familiar; family member; flame; friend; husband (wife); inamorata (inamorato); infatuate; intimate; love; lover; paramour; partner; spouse; steady; suitor; swain; sweetheart.*

The term *significant other* (SO) gives rise to sentiments like this:

Lover: I love you SO.

Loved: I love you so, SO.

■ Whether it be with instructors, *significant others,* children, or bosses, you practice the art of gentle persuasion continually. REPLACE WITH *spouses.* ■ My *significant other* is always calling me a spoil sport because I won't compromise on things. REPLACE WITH *lover.* ■ Men trying to use it to cheat on their *significant others* should know that a pager number will work on a woman for only a short time. REPLACE WITH *girlfriends or wives.* ■ I am being stalked by a former *significant other.* REPLACE WITH *boyfriend.* SEE ALSO *object of one's affection.*

(a) significant part (portion; proportion) A wretched redundancy (see page 25). *a good (great) deal; a good (great) many; almost all; many; most; much; nearly all.* ■ Many programmers spend *a significant portion* of their working day maintaining software. REPLACE WITH *a good deal.* SEE ALSO *a substantial part (portion; proportion).*

silence is golden A quack equation (see page 23).

(as) silent as the dead An insipid simile. *dumb; hushed; mum; mute; noiseless; quiet; reticent; silent; speechless; still; stock-still; taciturn; voiceless; wordless.*

(the) silent majority A moribund metaphor (see page 21). *all; citizenry; commonage; commonalty; common people; crowd; everybody; everyone; followers; herd; hoi polloi; masses; mob; multitude; plebeians; populace; proletariat; public; rabble.*

(as) silly as a goose An insipid simile. *absurd; asinine; childish; comical; farcical; fatuous; flighty; foolhardy; foolish; frivolous; giddy; idiotic; immature; inane; laughable; ludicrous; nonsensical; ridiculous; senseless; silly.*

silver lining A moribund metaphor (see page 21).

simultaneously at the same time A wretched redundancy (see page 25). *at the same time; simultaneously.* ■ This machine does four welds *simultaneously at the same time.* REPLACE WITH *at the same time* or *simultaneously.* SEE ALSO *while at the same time; while simultaneously.*

(a) sine qua non A foreign phrase (see page 19). *critical essential; indispensable; necessary; requisite; vital.* ■ A comprehensive neurologic assessment is *a sine qua non* in assessing cases of cerebral palsy. REPLACE WITH *indispensable.*

sing a different tune A moribund metaphor (see page 21).

singe (your) wings A moribund metaphor (see page 21). *be harmed; be injured; be wounded.*

sing for (her) supper A moribund metaphor (see page 21).

sing from the same hymn sheet A moribund metaphor (see page 21).

single best (biggest; greatest; highest; largest; most) A wretched redundancy (see page 25). *best (most).* This expression is a good example of how people pay scant attention to what they say or write. Idiom or no, superlatives like *best* and *most* need not be qualified by the word *single.* People attend more to what others say — copying, as they do, one another's words — than to what they themselves say.

■ The *single most* important problem is discrimination among one another. DELETE *single.* ■ Good records are the *single best* way to avoid having deductions disallowed in the event you are audited. DELETE *single.* ■ The *single biggest* issue is the cost of upgrading a substandard system. DELETE *single.* ■ The school committee and the superintendent place student safety as their *single highest* priority. DELETE *single.*

sing like a bird An insipid simile. *dulcet; harmonious; melodic; melodious; pleasant-sounding; sonorous; sweet.*

sing (his) praises A torpid term (see page 24). *acclaim; applaud; celebrate; commend; compliment; congratulate; eulogize; extol; flatter; hail; laud; panegyrize; praise; puff; salute.*

(enough to) sink a ship A moribund metaphor (see page 21). *a big (brobdingnagian; colossal; enormous; gargantuan; giant; gigantic; grand; great; huge; immense; large; massive; monstrous; prodigious; tremendous; vast) amount; a great deal; a lot.*

sink or swim A moribund metaphor (see page 21).

sink (my) teeth into A moribund metaphor (see page 21). 1. *absorb; engage; engross; immerse; involve; plunge; submerge.* 2. *brood over; cogitate on; consider; contemplate; deliberate on; dwell on; excogitate on; meditate on; mull over; ponder; reflect on; study; think about.* ■ If you can *sink your teeth into* a good role, and the end result is anything like what you hope it's going to be, it's really satisfying. REPLACE WITH *plunge into.* ■ Rarely does a recording of such grace and elegance also offer so much to *sink your teeth into.* REPLACE WITH *contemplate.*

> She can' t get into it. It' s not at all like sinking your teeth into a foreign language. — Nancy Zafris, *The Metal Shredders*

sit on (her) duff A moribund metaphor (see page 21). *be idle; be inactive; be lazy; be unemployed; be unoccupied; dally; dawdle; loaf; loiter; loll; lounge; relax; repose; rest.*

sit on (their) hands A moribund metaphor (see page 21). *be idle; be inactive; be lazy; be unemployed; be unoccupied; dally; dawdle; loaf; loiter; loll; lounge; relax; repose; rest.*

sit on the fence A moribund metaphor (see page 21). *ambivalent; divided; indecisive; in doubt; irresolute; neutral; torn; uncertain; uncommitted; undecided; unsure.* ■ If you're *sitting on the fence* or your answer is yes, you're in luck. REPLACE WITH *undecided.*

sit tight A moribund metaphor (see page 21). *be patient; hold on; wait.*

(a) sitting duck A moribund metaphor (see page 21).

sitting on a gold mine A moribund metaphor (see page 21).

(a) situation An overworked word (see page 22). For example: *crisis situation; difficult situation; life-threatening situation; push-pull situation; no-lose situation; no-win situation; open-ended situation; problematic situation; sad situation; tragic situation; win-win situation.* ■ It's really *a* pathetic *situation.* DELETE *a situation.* ■ If there is an emergency *situation,* then that person can exit as well. DELETE *situation.* ■ It's nice to be *in a situation where you are* recognized for the work you're doing. DELETE *in a situation where you are.* ■ The *air conditioning situation* is currently under repair. DELETE *situation* or REPLACE WITH *air conditioner.* ■ The network approach *is a win-win situation for* all involved. REPLACE WITH *benefits.* SEE ALSO *remedy the situation.*

(sit) with (his) head in (his) hands A moribund metaphor (see page 21). *brood; despair; despond; mope.*

(it's) six of one, half dozen of the other A moribund metaphor (see page 21). *either; either way; it doesn't matter; no matter.*

(the) $64,000 question An infantile phrase (see page 20). ■ That's *the $64,000 question* for a number of people.

skate on thin ice A moribund metaphor (see page 21). *chance; dare; endanger; gamble; hazard; imperil; jeopardize; make bold; peril; risk; venture.*

skeletons in the closet (cupboard) A moribund metaphor (see page 21). *secret; surprise.*

(all) skin and bones A moribund metaphor (see page 21). *asthenic; attenuated; bony; cachectic; emaciated; gaunt; lank; lanky; lean; narrow; rail-thin; scraggy; scrawny; skeletal; skinny; slender; slight; slim; spare; spindly; svelte; sylphid; thin; trim; wispy.*

(as) skinny as a stick An insipid simile. *asthenic; attenuated; bony; cachectic; emaciated; gaunt; lank; lanky; lean; narrow; rail-thin; scraggy; scrawny; skeletal; skinny; slender; slight; slim; spare; spindly; svelte; sylphid; thin; trim; wispy.*

(the) sky's the limit A moribund metaphor (see page 21).

(a) slap in the face A moribund metaphor (see page 21). *abuse; affront; contempt; contumely; derision; disappointment; disdain; dishonor; impertinence; indignity; insult; offense; outrage; rebuff; rebuke; rejection; scorn; slap; slight; slur; sneer; snub.* ■ Megan's mother called the judge's decision *a slap in the face.* REPLACE WITH *an insult.* ■ The document is *a slap in the face* to the democratic principles that Americans expect their leaders to uphold. REPLACE WITH *an affront.*

> The fact that my father would spend even a nickel more than necessary was a slap in the face for all of the effort my mother put in trying to support us. — Brett Ellen Block, *The Grave of God's Daughter*

slap on the wrist A moribund metaphor (see page 21). *admonish; animadvert; berate; castigate; censure; chastise; chide; condemn; criticize; denounce; discipline; objurgate; punish; rebuke; remonstrate; reprehend; reprimand; reproach; reprobate; reprove; revile; scold; upbraid; vituperate.* ■ When the story proved false, Oliver and Smith were fired, but Arnett was *slapped on the wrist* and retained by CNN. REPLACE WITH *chided.*

sleep like a log An insipid simile. *doze; nap; rest; sleep; slumber.*

sleep like a top An insipid simile. *doze; nap; rest; sleep; slumber.*

sleep the sleep of the just A moribund metaphor (see page 21). *doze; nap; rest; sleep; slumber.*

slice of life A moribund metaphor (see page 21).

slim and trim An inescapable pair (see page 20). *asthenic attenuated; bony; cachectic; emaciated; gaunt; lank; lanky; lean; narrow; rail-thin; scraggy; scrawny; skeletal; skinny; slender; slight; slim; spare; spindly; svelte; sylphid; thin; trim; wispy.*

slings and arrows A moribund metaphor (see page 21). 1. *assault; attack; blow.* 2. *adversity; bad luck; calamity; catastrophe; hardship; ill for-*

tune; misadventure; mischance; misfortune; mishap; reversal; setback.

(the) slings and arrows of outrageous fortune A moribund metaphor (see page 21).

slip of the lip (tongue) A moribund metaphor (see page 21). *blunder; error; gaffe; mistake; slip.*

> It sometimes happens that when you make a slip of the tongue you don't want to correct it. You try to pretend that what you said was what you meant. — V. S. Naipaul, *Half a Life*

slipped (my) mind A moribund metaphor (see page 21). *be forgetful; be heedless; be inattentive; be lethean; be neglectful; be negligent; be oblivious; be remiss; be thoughtless; be unmindful; be unthinking.*

> An appointment was made with a counselor but the day came and went and they both pretended it had slipped their minds. — Kevin Guilfoile, *Cast of Shadows*

(as) slippery as an eel An insipid simile. 1. *elusive; ephemeral; evanescent; evasive; fleeting; fugitive; passing; short-lived; slippery; volatile.* 2. *crafty; cunning; deceitful; dishonest; foxy; shifty; slick; tricky; wily.*

slippery character (customer) A moribund metaphor (see page 21). *bastard; blackguard; cad; charlatan; cheat; cheater; fake; fraud; impostor; knave; mountebank; phony; pretender; quack; rascal; rogue; scoundrel; swindler; undesirable; villain.*

slippery slope A moribund metaphor (see page 21). *declivity.*

slip through (our) fingers A moribund metaphor (see page 21). *abscond; clear out; decamp; depart; desert; disappear; escape; exit; flee; fly; go; go away; leave; move on; part; pull out; quit; retire; retreat; run away; take flight; take off; vacate; vanish; withdraw.*

slip through the cracks A moribund metaphor (see page 21). *discount; disregard; elide; ignore; leave out; miss; neglect; omit; overlook; slight.*

slow and steady wins the race A popular prescription (see page 23).

(as) slow as molasses (in January) An insipid simile. *crawling; dallying; dawdling; deliberate; dilatory; faltering; hesitant; laggardly; lagging; leisurely; methodical; plodding; procrastinating; slothful; slow; slow-paced; sluggardly; sluggish; snaillike; systematic; tardy; tortoiselike; unhurried.*

(a) slow boat to China (nowhere) A moribund metaphor (see page 21).

slow(ly) but sure(ly) An inescapable pair (see page 20).

slower than molasses (in January) A moribund metaphor (see page 21). *crawling; dallying; dawdling; deliberate; dilatory; faltering; hesitant; laggardly; lagging; leisurely; methodical; plodding; procrastinating; slothful; slow; slow-paced; sluggardly; sluggish; snaillike; systematic; tardy; tortoiselike; unhurried.*

smack dab in the middle of An infantile phrase (see page 20). ■ It puts readers *smack dab in the middle of* the action.

(a) small army of A moribund metaphor (see page 21). ■ *A small army of* labor leaders came to Washington for a final assault against the agreement. SEE ALSO *a barrage of.*

small potatoes A moribund metaphor (see page 21). *immaterial; inappreciable; inconsequential; inconsiderable; insignificant; meaningless; minor; negligible; niggling; nugatory; petty; trifling; trivial; unimportant; unsubstantial.* ■ And 10,000 cases is *no small potatoes.* REPLACE WITH *not insignificant.*

(as) smart as a whip An insipid simile. *able; adroit; alert; apt; astute; bright; brilliant; capable; clever; competent; discerning; enlightened; intelligent; judicious; keen; knowledgeable; learned; logical; luminous; perceptive; perspicacious; quick; quick-witted; rational; reasonable; sagacious; sage; sapient; sensible; sharp; shrewd; smart; sound; understanding; wise.*

smart cookie A moribund metaphor (see page 21). *able; adroit; apt; astute; bright; brilliant; capable; clever; competent; discerning; enlightened; intelligent; judicious; keen; knowledgeable; learned; logical; luminous; perceptive; perspicacious; quick; rational; reasonable; sagacious; sage; sapient; sensible; sharp; shrewd; smart; sound; understanding; wise.*

smell a rat A moribund metaphor (see page 21).

smell fishy A moribund metaphor (see page 21). *doubtful; dubious; questionable; shady; shaky; suspect; suspicious.*

smoke and mirrors A moribund metaphor (see page 21). *artfulness; artifice; chicanery; cover-up; cozenage; craftiness; cunning; deceit; deceiving; deception; dissembling; dissimulation; duplicity; feigning; fraud; guile; pretense; shamming; trickery; wile.*

smokes like a chimney An insipid simile.

smoking gun A moribund metaphor (see page 21). *evidence; proof.*

(as) smooth as glass An insipid simile. 1. *burnished; even; glassy; glossy; greasy; lustrous; oily; polished; satiny; silky; sleek; slick; slippery; smooth; velvety.* 2. *apparent; basic; clear; clear-cut; conspicuous; distinct; easily done; easy; effortless; elementary; evident; explicit; facile; limpid; lucid; manifest; obvious; patent; pellucid; plain; simple; simplicity itself; smooth; straightforward; translucent; transparent; unambiguous; uncomplex; uncomplicated; understandable; unequivocal; unmistakable.*

(as) smooth as silk An insipid simile. 1. *burnished; even; glassy; glossy; greasy; lustrous; oily; polished; satiny; silky; sleek; slick; slippery; smooth; velvety.* 2. *apparent; basic; clear; clear-cut; conspicuous; distinct; easily done; easy; effortless; elementary; evident; explicit; facile; limpid; lucid; manifest; obvious; patent; pellucid; plain; simple; simplicity itself; smooth; straightforward; translucent; transparent; unambiguous; uncomplex; uncomplicated; understandable; unequivocal; unmistakable.*

smooth (her) feathers A moribund metaphor (see page 21). *allay; appease; assuage; calm; comfort; compose; concili-*

ate; console; moderate; modulate; mollify; pacify; placate; propitiate; quiet; soften; soothe; still; temper; tranquilize.

snake in the grass A moribund metaphor (see page 21). *animal; barbarian; beast; brute; degenerate; fiend; knave; lout; monster; rake; rascal; reptile; rogue; ruffian; savage; scamp; scoundrel; villain.*

snatch victory from the jaws of defeat A moribund metaphor (see page 21).

snow job A moribund metaphor (see page 21). *deception; dishonesty.*

(as) snug as a bug in a rug An insipid simile. *comfortable; cosy; habitable; homey; inhabitable; livable; safe; snug.*

(like a) soap opera An insipid simile. *exaggerated; excessive; histrionic; hyperbolic; maudlin; mawkish; melodramatic; overblown; overdone; overemotional; sensational; sentimental; soppy.*

(as) sober as a judge An insipid simile. 1. *dignified; earnest; formal; grave; pensive; reserved; sedate; self-controlled; self-restrained; serious; severe; sober; solemn; somber; staid; stern; strict; subdued; thoughtful.* 2. *abstemious; sober; teetotal; temperate.*

social butterfly A moribund metaphor (see page 21). *fin-lover; gadabout; pleasure-seeker.*

(as) soft as velvet An insipid simile. *delicate; downy; feathery; fine; fluffy; satiny; silken; silky; smooth; soft; velvety.*

soft landing A moribund metaphor (see page 21). ■ The airline industry's problem is trying to determine whether this is a *soft landing* for the economy or a recession.

soft touch A moribund metaphor (see page 21).

(as) solid as a rock An insipid simile. 1. *adamantine; firm; granitelike; hard; petrified; rock-hard; rocklike; rocky; solid; steellike; steely; stonelike; stony.* 2. *athletic; beefy; brawny; burly; firm; fit; hale; hardy; hearty; husky; manly; mesomorphic; mighty; muscular; powerful; puissant; robust; rugged; sinewy; solid; stalwart; stout; strapping; strong; sturdy; tough; vigorous; virile; well-built.* 3. *constant; dependable; determined; faithful; fast; firm; fixed; inexorable; inflexible; loyal; obdurate; resolute; resolved; rigid; solid; stable; staunch; steadfast; steady; stern; strong; tenacious; unflinching; unwavering; unyielding.*

some of my best friends are A plebeian sentiment (see page 23).

(thirty)-something An infantile phrase (see page 20). ■ But they're not the typical self-absorbed, *30-something* crowd. ■ If you give a speech on social security, your purpose will vary for audiences made up of *twenty-something, forty-something,* or *seventy-something* individuals.

(there's) something in the wind A moribund metaphor (see page 21).

(there's) something rotten in the state of Denmark A moribund metaphor (see page 21).

(like) something out of a (Norman Rockwell painting) An insipid simile. ■ Li River cruises can take your clients past dreamlike rock formations; they *look like something out of a Salvador Dali painting.*

(it's) something to do A plebeian sentiment (see page 23). SEE ALSO *(it) gives (me) something to do; (it) keeps (me) busy; (it) keeps (me) out of trouble.*

(it's) something to look forward to A plebeian sentiment (see page 23). Those who use this phrase acknowledge the future appeals to them more than does the present, as they do the apparent pallor of their lives.

(it's) something to think about A plebeian sentiment (see page 23). SEE ALSO *food for thought.*

(a) sometime thing A torpid term (see page 24). *erratic; fitful; haphazard; inconsistent; intermittent; irregular; occasional; random; sometime; spasmodic; sporadic; unpredictable.*

song and dance A moribund metaphor (see page 21). 1. *pattern; routine.* 2. *deception; dissimulation; duplicity; equivocation; evasion; excuse; fabrication; falsehood; fib; invention; lie; mumbo-jumbo; nonsense; prevarication.*

son of a gun A moribund metaphor (see page 21). *brute; degenerate; fiend; knave; lout; rake; rascal; rogue; ruffian; scamp; scoundrel; villain.*

sooner rather than later A torpid term (see page 24). 1. *before long; presently; shortly; soon.* 2. *abruptly; apace; at once; briskly; directly; expeditiously; fast; forthwith; hastily; hurriedly; immediately; instantaneously; instantly; posthaste; promptly; quickly; rapidly; rashly; right away; speedily; straightaway; swiftly; wingedly.* ■ These people will die unless help arrives *sooner rather than later.* REPLACE WITH *soon.* ■ That, more than BSE or foot and mouth disease, is why McDonald's is pushing so hard to get an animal ID system in place *sooner rather than later.* REPLACE WITH *swiftly.*

(the) sooner the better A quack equation (see page 23).

sorely missed An inescapable pair (see page 20). Let us not die only to have it said we will be *sorely missed.* We should prefer silence to such insipidity. More disturbing still is that we should be spoken of so blandly, so, indeed, badly. This is hardly the wording of a tribute, hardly an encomium. ■ He is going to be *sorely missed* by his teammates. ■ He will be *sorely missed* by those of us who were privileged to call him our friend. ■ He will be *sorely missed* by his family, friends and neighbors.

sound and fury An infantile phrase (see page 20).

> It seemed a poor catch, for all their sound and fury, and Mr. Murphy would be glad to let them have it.
> — Kevin Baker, *Dreamland*

(as) sound as a bell An insipid simile. 1. *cogent; convincing; intelligent; judicious; just; logical; prudent; rational; reasonable; sensible; sound; telling; valid; well-founded; well-grounded; wise.* 2. *athletic; beefy; brawny; energetic; fit; good; hale; hardy; healthful; healthy; hearty; lanky; lean; manly; mesomorphic; muscular; powerful; robust; shapely; sinewy; slender; solid; sound; stalwart; strong; sturdy; thin; trim; vigorous; virile; well; well-built.*

(as) sound as a dollar An insipid simile. 1. *cogent; convincing; intelligent; judicious; just; logical; prudent; rational; reasonable; sensible; sound; telling; valid; well-founded; well-grounded; wise.* 2. *athletic; beefy; brawny; energetic; fit; good; hale; hardy; healthful; healthy; hearty; lanky; lean; manly; mesomorphic; muscular; powerful; robust; shapely; sinewy; slender; solid; sound; stalwart; strong; sturdy; thin; trim; vigorous; virile; well; well-built.*

(she) sounds like a broken record An insipid simile.

(as) sour as vinegar An insipid simile.

sour grapes A moribund metaphor (see page 21). *bile; bitterness; resentment; umbrage.*

sour note A moribund metaphor (see page 21).

so what else is new? An infantile phrase (see page 20).

sow the seeds of A moribund metaphor (see page 21). *circulate; disseminate; distribute; propagate; sow; spread.*

sow (his) wild oats A moribund metaphor (see page 21). *be dissolute; be licentious; be wild; have sex.*

spare the rod and spoil the child A popular prescription (see page 23).

(a) spate of A moribund metaphor (see page 21). ■ The legislation was proposed in response to *a spate of* violent incidents. SEE ALSO *a barrage of.*

speaks volumes A moribund metaphor (see page 21).

(she's) special A suspect superlative (see page 24).

(that) special someone A suspect superlative (see page 24). *admirer; amorist; beau; boyfriend; flame; gallant; girlfriend; inamorata; inamorato; lover; paramour; steady; suitor; swain; sweetheart; wooer.* ■ I still haven't met *that special someone*, but I am confident it will happen soon. REPLACE WITH *a girlfriend.*

(the) specter of A moribund metaphor (see page 21). ■ The Troika's standard response to all who raised *the specter of* diminished social services has been insult, invective, and ire.

spick and span An inescapable pair (see page 20). *antiseptic; clean; cleansed; disinfected; germ-free; hygienic; immaculate; neat; orderly; sanitary; sanitized; scoured; scrubbed; spotless; spruce; stainless; sterile; tidy; unblemished; unsoiled; unspotted; unsullied; untarnished; washed.*

> He was secretly orderly and in person spick and span — his friends declared that they had never seen his hair rumpled. — F. Scott Fitzgerald, *The Beautiful and Damned*

spilled milk A moribund metaphor (see page 21).

spill (his) guts A moribund metaphor (see page 21). *broadcast; confess; disclose; divulge; expose; make known; proclaim; publicize; reveal; talk; tell; uncover; unveil.*

> Nor do I covet the mute commiseration of friends who *don't know what to say* and so leave me to spill my guts by way of making conversation. — Lionel Shriver, *We Need to Talk About Kevin*

spill the beans A moribund metaphor (see page 21). *confess; disclose; divulge; leak; make known; reveal; tell.*

spinning (my) wheels A moribund metaphor (see page 21). *mired; stalled; stuck.*

spit and image (spitting image) An inescapable pair (see page 20). *clone; copy; counterpart; doppelgänger; double; duplicate; exact likeness; match; twin.*

spit and polish A moribund metaphor (see page 21).

spoil rotten A moribund metaphor (see page 21). *coddle; gratify; humor; indulge; mollycoddle; overindulge; overprotect; pamper; spoil.*

spread (himself) too thin A moribund metaphor (see page 21).

sprout up like mushrooms An insipid simile. *breed; multiply; proliferate; propagate; reproduce; spread.*

(on the) spur of the moment A moribund metaphor (see page 21). *abrupt; extemporaneous; extempore; immediate; impromptu; improvised; impulsive; instant; quick; rash; spontaneous; sudden; unexpected; unprepared; unprompted; unrehearsed.*

square peg in a round hole A moribund metaphor (see page 21). *aberrant; abnormal; anomalistic; anomalous; atypical; bizarre; curious; deviant; different; distinct; distinctive; eccentric; exceptional; extraordinary; fantastic; foreign; grotesque; idiosyncratic; independent; individual; individualistic; irregular; novel; odd; offbeat; original; peculiar; puzzling; quaint; queer; rare; remarkable; separate; singular; uncommon; unconventional; unexampled; unique; unnatural; unorthodox; unparalleled; unprecedented; unusual; weird.*

squeaky clean A moribund metaphor (see page 21). *high-minded; moralistic; principled; strait-laced; upright; upstanding.*

(the) squeaky wheel gets the grease A popular prescription (see page 23).

stab (her) in the back A moribund metaphor (see page 21). 1. *assail; attack; badmouth; complain; criticize; denounce; knock; put down.* 2. *abuse; harm; hurt; injure; maltreat; mistreat; wound.* ■ If I stop trusting people because they may *stab me in the back*, I could miss out on some valuable and enriching friendships. REPLACE WITH *mistreat me.*

stack the cards (deck) A moribund metaphor (see page 21). ■ While such efforts must invariably fail, the climate of distrust and fear *stacks the deck* against individuals who must move into a hostile environment.

(the) staff of life A moribund metaphor (see page 21). *bread.*

(the) stage has been set A moribund metaphor (see page 21). ■ *The stage has been set* for a contract that will have to contain genuine reforms.

(old) stamping (stomping) ground A moribund metaphor (see page 21). *hangout; haunt; rendezvous.*

stamp of approval A moribund metaphor (see page 21). *approval; authorization; certification; endorsement; sanction.*

stand (their) ground A moribund metaphor (see page 21). 1. *hold fast; persevere; persist; stand firm; stick with.* 2. *be adamant; be balky; be bullheaded; be cantankerous; be contrary; be contumacious; be dogged; be headstrong; be inflexible; be intractable; be mulish; be obdurate; be obstinate; be ornery; be perverse; be refractory; be resolute; be rigid; be stubborn; be unyielding; be willful.*

stand on (his) own two feet A moribund metaphor (see page 21). *assured; confident; independent; self-assured; self-confident; self-contained; self-governing; self-reliant; self-ruling; self-sufficient; self-supporting; sure.*

stand on the sidelines A moribund metaphor (see page 21). ■ Surgeons who have been *standing on the sidelines* are beginning to take up the procedure themselves.

stand out from (in) the crowd (pack) A moribund metaphor (see page 21). *aberrant; abnormal; anomalistic; anomalous; atypical; bizarre; curious; deviant; different; distinct; distinctive; eccentric; exceptional; extraordinary; fantastic; foreign; grotesque; idiosyncratic; independent; individual; individualistic; irregular; novel; odd; offbeat; original; peculiar; puzzling; quaint; queer; rare; remarkable; separate; singular; strange; uncommon; unconventional; unexampled; unique; unnatural; unorthodox; unparalleled; unprecedented; unusual; weird.*

stand (stick) out like a sore thumb An insipid simile. *apparent; arresting; blatant; conspicuous; evident; flagrant; glaring; gross; manifest; noticeable; observable; obtrusive; obvious; outstanding; patent; prominent; salient.*

(his) star is on the rise A moribund metaphor (see page 21).

(has) stars in her eyes A moribund metaphor (see page 21). *dreamy; happy; idealistic; optimistic; starry-eyed.*

start the ball rolling A moribund metaphor (see page 21). *begin; commence; enter on; initiate.*

start with a clean slate A moribund metaphor (see page 21). *begin anew; start afresh; start over.*

state of siege A moribund metaphor (see page 21).

staying power A moribund metaphor (see page 21). *determination; durability; endurance; firmness; fortitude; permanence; permanency; perseverance; resolution; resolve; spunk; stability; stamina; steadfastness; tenacity.*

stay on target A moribund metaphor (see page 21).

stay the course A moribund metaphor (see page 21). *advance; continue; go on; grow; make progress; move on; occur; press on; proceed; progress.*

■ Maeng says she knows that West Point, the oldest military academy in the country, will be challenging; however, she plans to *stay the course.* ■ The congressman wants to *stay the course* until the farm bill comes up for its scheduled review in a few years. ■ If parents *stay the course* and recognize God's confidence and trust in their parenting skills, then life will be fine throughout the world.

> There was nothing to do but patch himself up as well as he could, stay the course, not be depressed. — Jonathan Franzen, *The Corrections*

(as) steady as a rock An insipid simile. *constant; dependable; determined; faithful; fast; firm; fixed; inexorable; inflexible; loyal; obdurate; reliable; resolute; resolved; rigid; solid; stable; staunch; steadfast; steady; stern; strong; supportive; tenacious; true; trustworthy; trusty; unflinching; unwavering; unyielding.*

steal the show A moribund metaphor (see page 21).

steal (her) thunder A moribund metaphor (see page 21).

steer clear (of) A moribund metaphor (see page 21). *avoid; bypass; circumvent; dodge; elude; evade; shun; sidestep; skirt.* ■ It was a signal to the new mayor to *steer cleer of* divisiveness and cliquishness. REPLACE WITH *shun.*

steer wrong A moribund metaphor (see page 21). *beguile; betray; deceive; lead astray; misdirect; misguide; mislead.* ■ I trust that you won't *steer* them *wrong.* REPLACE WITH *mislead.*

stem the flow A moribund metaphor (see page 21). *abort; arrest; block; check; curb; decelerate; delay; end; halt; hamper; hinder; impede; obstruct; plug; quash; quell; retard; slow; squash; stay; stem; stop; suspend; terminate.*

stem the tide A moribund metaphor (see page 21). *abort; arrest; block; check; curb; decelerate; delay; end; halt; hamper; hinder; impede; obstruct; plug; quash; quell; retard; slow; squash; stay; stem; stop; suspend; terminate.* ■ But twenty years of effort have failed to *stem the tide of* environmental degradation. REPLACE WITH *retard.*

> It was the inability to speak openly about them, and thus to devise ways and means to stem the tide until they could re-form their ranks. — Lawrence Durrell, *Constance*

(a) step backward A torpid term (see page 24). *backset; reversal; setback.*

(a) step forward A torpid term (see page 24). *advancement; betterment; development; furtherance; growth; headway; improvement; progress.* ■ This is *a step forward* for us all. REPLACE WITH *betterment.* For some writers, *a step forward* isn't positive enough: ■ Although the IFS interface is *a positive step forward* for DOS, it remains in a sort of twilight zone. REPLACE WITH *an advancement.* SEE ALSO *a step (forward) in the right direction; go forward; move forward;*

move (forward) in the right direction; proceed forward.

(a) step (forward) in the right direction A torpid term (see page 24). *advancement; betterment; development; furtherance; growth; headway; improvement; progress.* Like many dimwitticisms, *a step forward in the right direction* is an ungainly creation. The English language is wonderfully expressive and infinitely flexible, but this phrase is stiff, wooden, awkward. ■ Incentives to attract and retain nurses would be *a step in the right direction.* REPLACE WITH *an improvement.* ■ Mr Singh described the arrests of Mr Saeed and other militants as *a step forward in the right direction* but said more action was necessary. REPLACE WITH *progress.* SEE ALSO *a step forward; go forward; move forward; move (forward) in the right direction; proceed forward.*

step on (his) toes A moribund metaphor (see page 21). *abuse; affront; anger; annoy; bother; displease; harm; hurt; insult; irk; irritate; offend; outrage; provoke; rile; roil; slap; slight; smart; trouble; upset; vex; wound.* ■ During his five months as acting mayor, he *stepped on many people's toes.* REPLACE WITH *offended many people.*

step up to the plate A moribund metaphor (see page 21). 1. *aim for; attempt; endeavor; engage; participate; pursue; seek; strive for; try.* 2. *advance; appear; approach; come forth; come forward; emerge; rise; show; surface; transpire.* 3. *act; perform; speak; talk.* 4. *be accountable; be answerable; be responsible.* ■ Rumors of an imminent buyout circulated, but no one *stepped up to the plate.* REPLACE WITH *came forward.* ■ Industry is *stepping up to the plate on this.* REPLACE WITH *pursuing.* ■ Because his public presence has been tainted greatly, she's going to have to *step up to the plate* and do more. REPLACE WITH *come forward.*

stewed to the gills A moribund metaphor (see page 21). *besotted; crapulous; drunk; inebriated; intoxicated; sodden; stupefied; tipsy.*

stew in (her) own juice A moribund metaphor (see page 21). *brood; fret; mope; stew; worry.*

stick in (my) craw (throat) A moribund metaphor (see page 21). *acerbate; anger; annoy; bother; bristle; chafe; enrage; envenom; exacerbate; gall; incense; inflame; infuriate; insult; irk; irritate; madden; miff; nettle; offend; provoke; rankle; rile; roil; vex.*

stick (your) neck out A moribund metaphor (see page 21). *chance; dare; endanger; gamble; hazard; imperil; jeopardize; make bold; peril; risk; venture.* ■ They do not *stick their necks out* to initiate change — they are followers. REPLACE WITH *venture.*

sticks and stones will break my bones, but words will never hurt me An infantile phrase (see page 20).

stick to (your) guns A moribund metaphor (see page 21). 1. *hold fast; persevere; persist; stand firm; stick with.* 2. *be adamant; be balky; be bullheaded; be cantankerous; be contrary; be contumacious; be dogged; be headstrong; be inflexible; be intractable; be mulish; be obdurate; be obstinate; be ornery; be perverse; be refractory; be resolute; be rigid; be stubborn; be unyielding; be willful.*

stick to (your) ribs A moribund metaphor (see page 21). *fill; sate; satiate; satisfy.*

stick to the knitting A moribund metaphor (see page 21).

sticky wicket A moribund metaphor (see page 21). *affliction; annoyance; bane; bother; burden; curse; difficulty; inconvenience; irritant; irritation; load; nuisance; ordeal; pain; pest; problem; tribulation; trouble; vexation; weight; worry.*

(as) stiff as a board An insipid simile. 1. *firm; inelastic; inflexible; rigid; stiff; unbending; unmalleable; unpliable; unyielding.* 2. *awkward; ceremonious; constrained; formal; precise; priggish; prim; proper; prudish; punctilious; puritanical; reserved; starched; stiff; stilted; strait-laced; stuffy; unrelaxed; uptight.*

still and all A wretched redundancy (see page 25). *even so; still; yet.* ■ *Still and all,* I love her. REPLACE WITH *Even so* or *Still.*

(as) still as a mouse An insipid simile. *dead; dormant; dull; immobile; immovable; inactive; inanimate; indolent; inert; inoperative; languid; latent; lethargic; lifeless; listless; motionless; noiseless; phlegmatic; quiescent; quiet; silent; sluggish; soundless; stagnant; static; stationary; still; stock-still; torpid; unresponsive.*

To placate him, I sit as still as a harvest mouse (*Micromys minutus*), and after about fifteen minutes of silent work he relents. — Sally Beauman, *The Sisters Mortland*

(as) still as death An insipid simile. *dead; dormant; dull; immobile; immovable; inactive; inanimate; indolent; inert; inoperative; languid; latent; lethargic; lifeless; listless; motionless; noiseless; phlegmatic; quiescent; quiet; silent; sluggish; soundless; stagnant; static; stationary; still; stock-still; torpid; unresponsive.*

still kicking A moribund metaphor (see page 21). *alive; animate; breathing; live; living.*

still waters run deep A popular prescription (see page 23).

stink like hell An insipid simile. *reek; smell; stink.*

stir up a hornet's nest A moribund metaphor (see page 21). SEE ALSO *hornet's nest.*

stitch in time A moribund metaphor (see page 21).

(a) stitch in time saves nine A popular prescription (see page 23).

(a) stone's throw (away) A moribund metaphor (see page 21). *accessible; at hand; close; close by; handy; near; nearby; neighboring; not far from; vicinal.*

stop and smell the flowers (roses) A moribund metaphor (see page 21). *be idle; be inactive; be lazy; be unemployed; be unoccupied; dally; dawdle; loaf; loiter; loll; lounge; relax; repose; rest.*

stop (him) (dead) in (his) tracks A moribund metaphor (see page 21). *arrest; check; freeze; halt; hold; immobilize; restrain; stop.*

> But there was one photo that stopped me in my tracks, that had me standing unsmiling before it for a long time. — Elizabeth Berg, *The Art of Mending*

stop the world I want to get off An infantile phrase (see page 20).

storm brewing A moribund metaphor (see page 21).

(a) storm of A moribund metaphor (see page 21). SEE ALSO *a barrage of.*

(the) story of (my) life A plebeian sentiment (see page 23). ■ I've always felt like an outcast; it's *the story of my life.*

straddle the fence A moribund metaphor (see page 21). *ambivalent; divided; indecisive; in doubt; irresolute; neutral; torn; uncertain; uncommitted; undecided; unsure.*

(the) straight and narrow (path) A moribund metaphor (see page 21). *decent; ethical; exemplary; good; honest; honorable; just; moral; pure; righteous; straight; upright; virtuous; wholesome.*

(as) straight as an arrow An insipid simile. 1. *direct; lineal; linear; straight.* 2. *decent; ethical; exemplary; good; honest; honorable; just; moral; pure; righteous; straight; upright; virtuous; wholesome.*

straight from the horse's mouth A moribund metaphor (see page 21).

straight from the shoulder A moribund metaphor (see page 21). *bluntly; candidly; directly; forthrightly; frankly; man to man; openly; outspokenly; plainly; straightforwardly; unambiguously; unequivocally.*

straight shooter A moribund metaphor (see page 21). *decent; ethical; forthright; honest; just; moral; righteous; straight; trustworthy; upright; virtuous.*

strange An overworked word (see page 22). *aberrant; abnormal; anomalistic; anomalous; atypical; bizarre; curious; deviant; different; distinct; distinctive; eccentric; exceptional; extraordinary; fantastic; foreign; grotesque; idiosyncratic; independent; individual; individualistic; irregular; novel; odd; offbeat; original; peculiar; puzzling; quaint; queer; rare; remarkable; separate; singular; uncommon; unconventional; unexampled; unique; unnatural; unorthodox; unparalleled; unprecedented; unusual; weird.* SEE ALSO *weird.*

strange bedfellows A moribund metaphor (see page 21).

(the) straw that broke the camel's back A moribund metaphor (see page 21).

stretch the point (truth) A moribund metaphor (see page 21). *elaborate; embellish; embroider; enhance; enlarge; exaggerate; hyperbolize; inflate; magnify; overdo; overstress; overstate; strain; stretch.*

strike (touch) a chord A moribund metaphor (see page 21). *be familiar; remind; sound familiar.* ■ These words *struck a familiar chord* with many of the 6,000 conference participants.

strike gold A moribund metaphor (see page 21).

strike while the iron is hot A moribund metaphor (see page 21). *capitalize on; exploit.*

strings attached A moribund metaphor (see page 21). *conditions; limitations; preconditions; prerequisites; provisions; qualifications; requirements; stipulations; terms.*

stroll down memory lane A moribund metaphor (see page 21). *be nostalgic; recall; recollect; remember; reminisce; think back.*

(as) strong as a horse An insipid simile. *athletic; beefy; brawny; burly; energetic; fit; hale; hardy; healthful; healthy; hearty; husky; manly; mesomorphic; mighty; muscular; powerful; puissant; robust; rugged; sinewy; solid; sound; stalwart; stout; strapping; strong; sturdy; vigorous; virile; well-built.*

(a) stroll (walk) in the park A moribund metaphor (see page 21). 1. *casual; easily done; easy; effortless; elementary; facile; simple; simplicity itself; straightforward; uncomplex; uncomplicated.* 2. *agreeable; beguiling; charming; delightful; enchanting; engaging; enjoyable; fun; glorious; gratifying; inviting; joyful; joyous; pleasant; pleasing; pleasurable.* ■ Building high-rise buildings, dams, and bridges isn't exactly *a walk in the park.* REPLACE WITH *simple.* ■ Compared to NetWare 3.x, installing Windows NT Server is *a stroll in the park.* REPLACE WITH *effortless.*

(as) strong as a lion An insipid simile. *athletic; beefy; brawny; burly; energetic; fit; hale; hardy; healthful; healthy; hearty; husky; manly; mesomorphic; mighty; muscular; powerful; puissant; robust; rugged; sinewy; solid; sound; stalwart; stout; strapping; strong; sturdy; vigorous; virile; well-built.*

(as) strong as an ox An insipid simile. *athletic; beefy; brawny; burly; energetic; fit; hale; hardy; healthful; healthy; hearty; husky; manly; mesomorphic; mighty; muscular; powerful; puissant; robust; rugged; sinewy; solid; sound; stalwart; stout; strapping; strong; sturdy; vigorous; virile; well-built.*

(as) stubborn as a mule An insipid simile. *adamant; balky; bullheaded; cantankerous; contrary; contumacious; dogged; headstrong; inflexible; intractable; mulish; obdurate; obstinate; ornery; perverse; refractory; resolute; rigid; stubborn; unyielding; willful.*

stuff and nonsense An inescapable pair (see page 20). *absurdity; fatuousness; folly; foolishness; ludicrousness; nonsense; preposterousness; ridiculousness; rubbish; silliness.*

(the) stuff dreams (legends) are made of A moribund metaphor (see page 21).

(the) stuff of (legends) A moribund metaphor (see page 21). ■ His mumbo-jumbo about the war on terror was *the stuff of* prime time television. ■ The abuse of this child truly is *the stuff of* nightmares. ■ Lance Armstrong's record seventh win of the Tour de France is *the stuff of* true legends. ■ Being in the Hambletonian is *the stuff of* dreams — and obituaries.

> That was the stuff of others' lives. — Annie Proulx, *The Shipping News*

stuff to the gills A moribund metaphor (see page 21). *abounding; brimful; brimming; bursting; chock-full; congested; crammed; crowded; dense; filled; full;*

gorged; jammed; jam-packed; overcrowded; overfilled; overflowing; packed; replete; saturated; stuffed; swarming; teeming.

(major) stumbling block A moribund metaphor (see page 21). *barrier; hindrance; hurdle; impediment; obstacle; obstruction.* ■ Modernization of the Chinese HRM system is fraught with significant *stumbling blocks.* REPLACE WITH *obstacles.*

stupid An overworked word (see page 22). This epithet, along with others as common, is much overused. Let's do our best to convince *stupid* people that they are by calling them, instead, *addlebrained; addleheaded; addlepated; Boeotian; bovine; cretinous; decerebrate; doltish; dull-witted; dunderheaded; fatuous; fat-witted; harebrained; hebetudinous; imbecilic; incogitant; insensate; ludicrous; moronic; muddled; nescient; obtuse; oxlike; pedestrian; phlegmatic; sluggish; torpid; vacuous; witless.*

(as) sturdy as an oak An insipid simile. *athletic; beefy; brawny; burly; energetic; fit; hale; hardy; healthful; healthy; hearty; husky; manly; mesomorphic; mighty; muscular; powerful; puissant; robust; rugged; sinewy; solid; sound; stalwart; stout; strapping; strong; sturdy; vigorous; virile; well-built.*

subsequent to A torpid term (see page 24). *after; following.* ■ *Subsequent to* the initiation of the Ethics Committee investigation, the senator took back some tapes in my possession which I had not yet transcribed. REPLACE WITH *Following.* SEE ALSO *in advance of; previous to; subsequent to.*

(a) substantial part (portion; proportion) A wretched redundancy (see page 25). *a good (great) deal; a good (great) many; almost all; many; most; much; nearly all.* ■ It is unconscionable that *a substantial proportion* of our population does not have adequate access to health care. REPLACE WITH *much.* ■ I assume that Boston will be eligible for *a substantial portion* of the distressed communities fund. REPLACE WITH *a good deal.* SEE ALSO *a significant part (portion; proportion).*

such is life A plebeian sentiment (see page 23). SEE ALSO *that's how (the way) it goes; that's how (the way) the ball bounces; that's how (the way) the cookie crumbles; that's life; that's life in the big city; that's show biz; what are you going to do; what can you do.*

suck the life out of A moribund metaphor (see page 21). *bleed dry; deplete; drain; exhaust; sap; suck dry.*

suddenly and without warning A wretched redundancy (see page 25). *impetuously; impulsively; spontaneously; suddenly; unexpectedly; without warning.*

sufficient enough A wretched redundancy (see page 25). *enough; sufficient.* ■ Just tell them your new number, and that should be *sufficient enough.* REPLACE WITH *sufficient* or *enough.* SEE ALSO *adequate enough.*

(a) sufficient number (of) A wretched redundancy (see page 25). *enough.* ■ Effective groups contain *a sufficient number of* members to ensure good interaction. REPLACE WITH *enough.* SEE ALSO *a ... number (of).*

sugar and spice A moribund metaphor (see page 21).

sum and substance An inescapable pair (see page 20). *basis; center; core; crux; essence; gist; heart; kernel; pith; substance; sum.*

(the) summer (winter) of (our) discontent A moribund metaphor (see page 21).

(the) sun, the moon, and the stars A moribund metaphor (see page 21).

(as) sure as death An insipid simile. *assured; certain; destined; established; fated; fixed; foreordained; ineluctable; inescapable; inevitable; inexorable; irresistible; irreversible; irrevocable; ordained; prearranged; predestined; predetermined; sure; unalterable; unavoidable; unchangeable; unpreventable; unstoppable.*

(as) sure as death and taxes An insipid simile. *assured; certain; destined; established; fated; fixed; foreordained; ineluctable; inescapable; inevitable; inexorable; irresistible; irreversible; irrevocable; ordained; prearranged; predestined; predetermined; sure; unalterable; unavoidable; unchangeable; unpreventable; unstoppable.*

survival of the fittest A popular prescription (see page 23).

swallow (her) pride A moribund metaphor (see page 21). *abase; chasten; debase; degrade; demean; disgrace; dishonor; embarrass; humble; humiliate; lower; mortify; shame.*

swan song A moribund metaphor (see page 21). *farewell; good-bye.*

swear by all that's holy A moribund metaphor (see page 21). *affirm; asseverate; assert; attest; aver; avow; declare; pledge; promise; swear; testify; vow; warrant.*

swear like a sailor (trooper) An insipid simile. *abusive; blackguardly; coarse; crude; fescennine; foul-mouthed; indecent; lewd; obscene; profane; ribald; scurrilous; thersitical; vulgar.*

swear on a stack of bibles A moribund metaphor (see page 21). *affirm; asseverate; assert; attest; aver; avow; declare; pledge; promise; swear; testify; vow; warrant.*

sweat bullets A moribund metaphor (see page 21). 1. *excrete; exude; ooze; perspire; sweat; swelter; wilt.* 2. *be afraid; be agitated; be anxious; be apprehensive; be distraught; be distressed; be fearful; be fretful; be impatient; be nervous; be panicky; be tense; be uneasy; be worried.* 3. *drudge; grind; grub; labor; moil; slave; strain; strive; struggle; sweat; toil; travail; work hard.*

sweep off (her) feet A moribund metaphor (see page 21). *amaze; astonish; astound; awe; dazzle; dumbfound; flabbergast; overpower; overwhelm; shock; startle; stun; stupefy; surprise.*

sweep (it) under the (carpet) rug A moribund metaphor (see page 21). 1. *brush aside; avoid; discount; disregard; dodge; duck; ignore; neglect; omit; pass over; recoil from; shrink from; shun; shy away from; turn away from; withdraw from.* 2. *camouflage; cloak; conceal; cover; disguise; enshroud; harbor; hide; keep secret; mask; screen; shroud; suppress; veil; withhold.* ■ The strategy was to *sweep it under the rug.* REPLACE WITH *ignore it.*

sweep (it) under the table A moribund metaphor (see page 21). 1. *brush aside; avoid; discount; disregard; dodge; duck; ignore; neglect; omit; pass over; recoil from; shrink from; shun; shy away from; turn away from; withdraw from.* 2. *camouflage; cloak; conceal; cover; disguise; enshroud; harbor; hide; keep secret; mask; screen; shroud; suppress; veil; withhold.* ■ We see the word *anti-Semitism* every day in our secular newspapers, but the word *anti-Catholic* is *swept under the table.* REPLACE WITH *brushed aside.*

(as) sweet as honey An insipid simile. 1. *honeyed; luscious; saccharine; sugary; sweet; sweetened; syrupy.* 2. *agreeable; ambrosial; beguiling; celestial; charming; delectable; delicious; delightful; divine; enchanting; engaging; enjoyable; fun; heavenly; glorious; gratifying; inviting; joyful; joyous; luscious; pleasant; pleasing; pleasurable.*

(as) sweet as pie An insipid simile. 1. *honeyed; luscious; saccharine; sugary; sweet; sweetened; syrupy.* 2. *agreeable; ambrosial; beguiling; celestial; charming; delectable; delicious; delightful; divine; enchanting; engaging; enjoyable; fun; heavenly; glorious; gratifying; inviting; joyful; joyous; luscious; pleasant; pleasing; pleasurable.*

sweeten the pot A moribund metaphor (see page 21). *add to; augment; enhance; improve; increase; supplement.*

sweeter than honey A moribund metaphor (see page 21). 1. *honeyed; luscious; saccharine; sugary; sweet; sweetened; syrupy.* 2. *agreeable; ambrosial; beguiling; celestial; charming; delectable; delicious; delightful; divine; enchanting; engaging; enjoyable; fun; heavenly; glorious; gratifying; inviting; joyful; joyous; luscious; pleasant; pleasing; pleasurable.*

sweet smell of success A moribund metaphor (see page 21).

(as) swift as an arrow An insipid simile. *brisk; expeditious; fast; fleet; hasty; hurried; immediate; instant; instantaneous; prompt; quick; rapid; speedy; spry; sudden; swift; winged.*

swim against the current (tide) A moribund metaphor (see page 21). 1. *drudge; grind; grub; labor; moil; slave; strain; strive; struggle; sweat; toil; travail; work hard.* 2. *battle; fight; tussle; wrestle.*

swim like a fish An insipid simile.

swim upstream A moribund metaphor (see page 21).

swim with the tide A moribund metaphor (see page 21).

T

tabula rasa A foreign phrase (see page 19).

(a case of) (the) tail wagging the dog A moribund metaphor (see page 21). *backward; in reverse.*

take a back seat A moribund metaphor (see page 21). *be ancillary; be inferior; be lesser; be lower; be minor; be second; be* *secondary; be subordinate; be subservient.* ■ Just a few years after this work, machine learning *took a back seat* to expert knowledge systems. REPLACE WITH *became subordinate.* ■ As in most races for most offices, issues have *taken a back seat* to personality, image, footwork, money, and most important, field organization. REPLACE WITH *became ancillary.* ■ Power based on expertise frequently *takes a back seat* to power based on position. REPLACE WITH *is second.*

take a bath A moribund metaphor (see page 21). *lose money.*

take a beating A moribund metaphor (see page 21). 1. *be beaten; be conquered; be crushed; be defeated; be outdone; be overcome; be overpowered; be overwhelmed; be quelled; be routed; be trounced; be vanquished.* 2. *be assailed; be assaulted; be attacked; be battered; be beaten; be cudgeled; be flagellated; be flogged; be hit; be lambasted; be lashed; be licked; be mangled; be pounded; be pummeled; be struck; be thrashed; be trounced.*

take a breather An infantile phrase (see page 20). *be idle; be inactive; be lazy; be unemployed; be unoccupied; dally; dawdle; loaf; loiter; loll; lounge; relax; repose; rest.*

> She stops to take a breather, picks up the ringing phone. — Kate Moses, *Wintering*

take a dim view of A moribund metaphor (see page 21). *deprecate; disapprove; dislike; frown on; object; protest.*

take a fancy (shine) to A moribund metaphor (see page 21). *delight in; enjoy; fancy; like; relish.*

take a front seat A moribund metaphor (see page 21). *prevail; rise above; surmount; triumph.*

> Yesterday she way ready to pick up the phone, call Jeff, and tell him off for all he was worth. This morning, family took a front seat. — Margaret Johnson-Hodge, *Warm Hands*

take a gander (at) An infantile phrase (see page 20). *gaze; glance; glimpse; look; observe; stare; watch.*

take a haircut A moribund metaphor (see page 21). *lose money.* ■ He suggested what has been plain for some time — that holders of $1.7 billion in junk bonds would probably *take a haircut.* REPLACE WITH *lose money.*

take a hit A moribund metaphor (see page 21). *be assailed; be assaulted; be attacked; be battered; be beaten; be cudgeled; be flagellated; be flogged; be hit; be lambasted; be lashed; be licked; be mangled; be pounded; be pummeled; be struck; be thrashed; be trounced.*

take a leaf (page) out of (their) book A moribund metaphor (see page 21). *copy; duplicate; emulate; follow; imitate; mimic.*

take a load off (your) mind A moribund metaphor (see page 21). *acknowledge; admit; affirm; allow; avow; concede; confess; disclose; divulge; expose; grant; own; reveal; tell; uncover; unveil.*

take a long, hard look (at) A torpid term (see page 24). *analyze; assay; check out; delve into; examine; investigate; probe; scrutinize; study.* ■ We need leaders with the will and the determination to *take a long, hard look at* the structure of our government. REPLACE WITH *examine.*

take a nose dive A moribund metaphor (see page 21). *collapse; crash; dive; drop; fall; nose-dive; plummet; plunge.*

take a powder A moribund metaphor (see page 21). *abscond; clear out; decamp; depart; desert; disappear; escape; exit; flee; fly; go; go away; leave; move on; part; pull out; quit; retire; retreat; run away; take flight; take off; vacate; vanish; withdraw.*

take a turn for the better A moribund metaphor (see page 21). *ameliorate; amend; come round; convalesce; gain strength; get better; heal; improve; look up; meliorate; mend; rally; recover; recuperate; refresh; regain strength; renew; revive; strengthen.*

take a turn for the worse A moribund metaphor (see page 21). *decay; decline; degenerate; deteriorate; disintegrate; ebb; erode; fade; fall off; languish; lessen; wane; weaken; wither; worsen.*

take (my) ball (toys) and go home An infantile phrase (see page 20).

take (your) breath away A moribund metaphor (see page 21). *amaze; astonish; astound; awe; dazzle; dumbfound; flabbergast; overpower; overwhelm; shock; startle; stun; stupefy; surprise.*

take by storm A moribund metaphor (see page 21). *amaze; animate; awe; captivate; dazzle; electrify; excite; exhilarate; fascinate; impress; intoxicate; thrill; overwhelm.* ■ In the two years since it was introduced as the newest drug for depression, Prozac has *taken* the mental health community *by storm.* REPLACE WITH *captivated.*

take each day as it comes A popular prescription (see page 23).

take exception to A wretched redundancy (see page 25). *challenge; demur; disagree with; disapprove of; dispute; find fault with; object to; oppose; protest; question; resent.* ■ I *take exception to* your analysis of his difficulties. REPLACE WITH *disagree with.* SEE ALSO *take issue with.*

take (him) for a ride A moribund metaphor (see page 21). *bamboozle; befool; beguile; bilk; bluff; cheat; con; deceive; defraud; delude; dupe; feint; fool; gyp; hoodwink; lead astray; misdirect; misguide; misinform; mislead; spoof; swindle; trick; victimize.*

take (my) hat off to A moribund metaphor (see page 21). *acclaim; applaud; commend; compliment; congratulate; extol; hail; laud; praise.*

take (a lot of) heat A moribund metaphor (see page 21).

take into account A wretched redundancy (see page 25). *allow for; consider; contemplate; examine; inspect; investigate; look at; ponder; provide for; regard; scrutinize; study; think over; weigh.* ■ The character of the army is also an important factor to be *taken into account.* REPLACE WITH *considered.* SEE ALSO *take into consideration.*

take into consideration A wretched redundancy (see page 25). *allow for; consider; contemplate; examine; inspect;*

investigate; look at; ponder; provide for; regard; scrutinize; study; think over; weigh. ■ All this will be *taken into consideration*, and financial analysis will be done. REPLACE WITH *examined.* SEE ALSO *take into account.*

take issue with A wretched redundancy (see page 25). *challenge; demur; disagree with; disapprove of; dispute; find fault with; object to; oppose; protest; question; resent.* ■ Some *take issue with* the state requiring people to use seat belts. REPLACE WITH *object to.* SEE ALSO *take exception to.*

take it as it comes A popular prescription (see page 23).

(I) take it (that) back An infantile phrase (see page 20). 1. *be incorrect; be in error; be misguided; be misinformed; be mislead; be mistaken; be not right; be wrong.* 2. *disavow; recant; renounce; repudiate; retract; withdraw.* ■ Joanie is in third place; no, *I take it back* — it's another runner. REPLACE WITH *I'm wrong.* ■ I always wanted to be with someone more respectable; not respectable, *I take that back*, professional. REPLACE WITH *I retract that.*

take it one day (step) at a time A popular prescription (see page 23).

take it on the chin A moribund metaphor (see page 21). 1. *be beaten; be conquered; be crushed; be defeated; be flattened; be outdone; be overcome; be overpowered; be trampled; be trounced; be vanquished.* 2. *abide; accept; bear; brook; endure; stand; stomach; suffer; take; tolerate; withstand.*

take (her) life in (her) hands A moribund metaphor (see page 21). *chance; dare; endanger; gamble; hazard; imperil; jeopardize; make bold; peril; risk; venture.*

take (his) lumps A moribund metaphor (see page 21). ■ We fought our way back to profitability after *taking our lumps.*

take (their) medicine A moribund metaphor (see page 21).

taken aback A moribund metaphor (see page 21). *amazed; astonished; astounded; flabbergasted; shocked; staggered; stunned; surprised.*

take off the table A moribund metaphor (see page 21). *dismiss; not consider; reject; set aside; shelve.* ■ I don't think we should ever *take* a nuclear response *off the table.*

take the bait A moribund metaphor (see page 21).

> I almost take the bait and then decide, no, if I start talking about the boss, taking him apart, it will never quit. — Louise Erdrich, *Tales of Burning Love*

take the bit between (in) (her) teeth A moribund metaphor (see page 21). *defy; disobey; rebel; resist; revolt; take charge; take control.*

take the bitter with the sweet A popular prescription (see page 23).

take the bull by the horns A moribund metaphor (see page 21). *meet head-on.*

take the cake A moribund metaphor (see page 21). 1. *be best; be finest; be first; be first-rate; be outstanding; win.* 2. *be absurd; be disgraceful; be inane; be lowest; be outrageous; be poorest; be preposterous; be ridiculous; be worst.* ■ I am accustomed to being shocked by John Ellis, but "Beyond manifest destiny" *takes the cake.* REPLACE WITH *is outrageous.*

take the high road A moribund metaphor (see page 21). 1. *be beneficent; be benevolent; be broad-minded; be charitable; be civil; be courteous; be gracious; be high-minded; be kind; be liberal; be magnanimous; be noble.* 2. *be decent; be ethical; be exemplary; be good; be honest; be honorable; be just; be moral; be pure; be respectful; be righteous; be straight; be upright; be virtuous; be wholesome.*

take the money and run A moribund metaphor (see page 21). *abscond; clear out; decamp; depart; desert; disappear; escape; exit; flee; fly; go; go away; leave; make off; move on; part; pull out; quit; retire; retreat; run away; steal away; take flight; take off; vacate; vanish; withdraw.*

take the plunge A moribund metaphor (see page 21). *dive in; do it; jump in.*

take the wind out of (his) sails A moribund metaphor (see page 21). 1. *abase; chasten; debase; decrease; deflate; degrade; demean; depreciate; depress; diminish; disgrace; dishonor; embarrass; humble; humiliate; lower; mortify; puncture; shame.* 2. *arrest; balk; block; bridle; check; curb; derail; detain; end; foil; frustrate; halt; harness; hold up; impede; inhibit; obstruct; restrain; retard; slow; stall; stay; stop; suppress; terminate; thwart.*

(to) take this opportunity (to) An ineffectual phrase (see page 19). On the podium and before others, people speak what they're expected to say. Alone and on their deathbeds, they moan that no one knew who they were. *(To) take this opportunity (to)* is one of the phrases that people learn to mimic before they know to moan.

■ I would like *to take this opportunity* to apologize to my family and friends. DELETE *to take this opportunity.* ■ I'd like *to take this opportunity* to renew our commitment to you — to provide you with superior service. DELETE *to take this opportunity.* ■ Let me *take this opportunity to* thank our most inspirational guest. DELETE *take this opportunity to.* ■ As we wind down the current year, I would like to *take this opportunity to* thank you for your hard work on the Tech Communications Workshop this past academic year. DELETE *take this opportunity to.*

take to (his) heels A moribund metaphor (see page 21). *abscond; clear out; decamp; depart; desert; disappear; escape; exit; flee; fly; go; go away; leave; move on; part; pull out; quit; retire; retreat; run away; take flight; take off; vacate; vanish; withdraw.*

take (him) to task A torpid term (see page 24). *admonish; animadvert; berate; blame; castigate; censure; chasten; chastise; chide; condemn; criticize; denounce; denunciate; discipline; impugn; objurgate; punish; rebuke; remonstrate; reprehend; reprimand; reproach; reprobate; reprove; revile; scold; upbraid; vituperate.* ■ In polite, carefully chosen words, the auditors *take* management *to task* for a multitude of sins. REPLACE WITH *censure.*

take (her) to the cleaners A moribund metaphor (see page 21).

take (them) to the woodshed A moribund metaphor (see page 21). *admonish; animadvert; berate; castigate; censure; chasten; chastise; chide; condemn; criticize; denounce; denunciate; discipline; excoriate; fulminate against; imprecate; impugn; inveigh against; objurgate; punish; rebuke; remonstrate; reprehend; reprimand; reproach; reprobate; reprove; revile; scold; swear at; upbraid; vituperate.*

take with a grain (pinch) of salt A moribund metaphor (see page 21). *be suspicious; be wary; disbelieve; distrust; doubt; have doubts; have misgivings; have reservations; mistrust; question; suspect; wonder.* ■ But this pane's data should be *taken with a grain of salt.* REPLACE WITH *doubted.*

> But Tim Paddy hinted that this story should be taken with a pinch of salt. — William Trevor, *Fools of Fortune*

(like) taking candy from a baby An insipid simile. *apparent; basic; clear; clear-cut; conspicuous; distinct; easily done; easy; effortless; elementary; evident; explicit; facile; limpid; lucid; manifest; obvious; patent; pellucid; plain; simple; simplicity itself; straightforward; translucent; transparent; unambiguous; uncomplex; uncomplicated; understandable; unequivocal; unmistakable.*

> It was a situation tailor-made for Eden, who would've considered it just slightly more challenging than taking candy from a baby and then pushing the buggy off a cliff. — Antoinette Stockenberg, *Safe Harbor*

(like) taking lambs to the slaughter An insipid simile.

a tale never loses in the telling A popular prescription (see page 23).

(tell) tales out of school A moribund metaphor (see page 21). ■ A lot of people thought they were *telling tales out of school.*

> I oughtn't to tell tales out of school but it's a long time ago now and I'm glad Sarah has found happiness, but in those days it was well-known in Pankot that Susan was always pinching her elder sister's young men .... — Paul Scott, *Staying On*

talk a blue streak A moribund metaphor (see page 21). *babbling; blathering; chatty; facile; fluent; garrulous; glib; jabbering; logorrheic; long-winded; loquacious; prolix; talkative; verbose; voluble; windy.*

talk (my) ear (head) off A moribund metaphor (see page 21). *babbling; blathering; chatty; facile; fluent; garrulous; glib; jabbering; logorrheic; long-winded; loquacious; prolix; talkative; verbose; voluble; windy.*

talk is cheap A quack equation (see page 23).

talk (speak) out of both sides of (his) mouth A moribund metaphor (see page 21). *be ambivalent; be indecisive; be irresolute; be uncertain; be unsure; be wishy-washy; dodge; doubletalk; equivocate; evade; fence; hedge; palter; prevaricate; quibble; shuffle; sidestep; tergiversate; waffle.*

(he) talks a good game A moribund metaphor (see page 21).

talk through (his) hat A moribund metaphor (see page 21). *babble; blather; jabber; prate; prattle.*

talk turkey A moribund metaphor (see page 21).

tan (warm) (her) hide A moribund metaphor (see page 21). *spank.*

tar and feather A moribund metaphor (see page 21). *admonish; animadvert; berate; castigate; censure; chasten; chastise; chide; condemn; criticize; denounce; denunciate; discipline; impugn; objurgate; punish; rebuke; remonstrate; reprehend; reprimand; reproach; reprobate; reprove; revile; scold; upbraid; vituperate.*

tar (him) with the same brush A moribund metaphor (see page 21).

teach (me) the ropes A moribund metaphor (see page 21). *coach; educate; initiate; instruct; teach; train; tutor.*

team player A suspect superlative (see page 24). This term is much favored by those in the business world for an employee who thinks just as others do and behaves just as he is expected to. A *team player* is a person who has not the spirit to think for or be himself.

Of course, nothing new, nothing innovative is likely to be realized by insisting, as the business world does, on objectivity and consensus.

A team player is often no more than a *bootlicker;* no more than a *fawner,* a *flatterer,* a *follower;* no more than a *lackey,* a *minion,* a *stooge;* no more than a *sycophant,* a *toady,* a *yes-man.* ■ Mulvey, whose termination is perhaps the most striking — he was one of the bank's stellar performers — was not regarded as a *team player.*

tear (out) (my) hair A moribund metaphor (see page 21). 1. *acerbated; angry; annoyed; bothered; cross; displeased; enraged; furious; grouchy; incensed; inflamed; infuriated; irate; irked; irritated; mad; miffed; peeved; provoked; riled; roiled; testy; upset; vexed.* 2. *agitated; anxious; apprehensive; distraught; distressed; fearful; frustrated; nervous; panicky; stressed; stressful; tense; tormented; troubled; uneasy; worried.*

teeter on the brink (of) A moribund metaphor (see page 21).

tell it like it is An infantile phrase (see page 20). *be blunt; be candid; be forthright; be frank; be honest; be open; be truthful.* ■ He's not whining; he's just *telling it like it is.* REPLACE WITH *being honest.* ■ These videos may be informative and *tell it like it is* but are far too explicit and do not belong in a coed classroom. REPLACE WITH *truthful.*

tell it to the Marines A moribund metaphor (see page 21).

tell (her) off A torpid term (see page 24). *admonish; animadvert; berate; castigate; censure; chasten; chastise; chide; condemn; criticize; denounce; denunciate; discipline; impugn; objurgate; punish; rebuke; remonstrate; reprehend; reprimand; reproach; reprobate; reprove; revile; scold; upbraid; vituperate.*

tell (them) where to get off A torpid term (see page 24). *admonish; animadvert; berate; castigate; censure; chasten;*

chastise; chide; condemn; criticize; denounce; denunciate; discipline; impugn; objurgate; punish; rebuke; remonstrate; reprehend; reprimand; reproach; reprobate; reprove; revile; scold; upbraid; vituperate.

tempest in a teapot A moribund metaphor (see page 21).

terra firma A foreign phrase (see page 19).

terrific An overworked word (see page 22). *Terrific* means *causing terror* or *terrifying*, but of late, it means only *very bad* or, annoyingly, *very good.* ■ I have a *terrific* stomachache. REPLACE WITH *very bad.* ■ We had a *terrific* time at the party. REPLACE WITH *very good.* SEE ALSO *awesome; awful.*

(the) temper of our time A moribund metaphor (see page 21).

test the waters A moribund metaphor (see page 21).

thank goodness it's Friday An infantile phrase (see page 20).

thanks but no thanks An infantile phrase (see page 20). *thanks; thanks all the same; thanks anyway; thanks just the same.*

thank you A plebeian sentiment (see page 23). Even *thank you* — once a sure sign of civility — becomes part of the plebeian patois when it is spoken mechanically.

Only a spectacularly thoughtless person would thank others for having been abused or berated by them, for having been refused or rejected by them. SEE ALSO *excuse me?; I'm sorry.*

thank(ing) you in advance A plebeian sentiment (see page 23). These phrases are more than plebeian, they are impudent. Only the lowbred or harebrained would presume to thank another for something while requesting it of him. ■ We *thank you in advance* for your understanding in this situation. ■ *Thank you in advance* for taking the time to help us. ■ *Thanks in advance* for your cooperation. ■ I have contacted the folks at ArtistDirect as well, and wanted to *thank you in advance* for your compliance in this matter.

And now variations of this phrase are being used in other, even more facile and sillier, constructions: ■ If I offend any man, woman, beast, or anything in between, *I apologize in advance.* ■ *He apologizes in advance* to those with a more normal sense of humor.

that makes two of us An infantile phrase (see page 20). *as I do; I do too; neither do I; no more do I; nor do I; so do I.*

that's for me to know and you to find out An infantile phrase (see page 20). SEE ALSO *it's a long story.*

that's how (the way) it goes A plebeian sentiment (see page 23). *That's how (the way) it goes* and other expressions of resignation are often spoken by some people and rarely, if at all, spoken by others.

It is dimwitted people who are too often resigned when they should be complaining, too often resigned when they should be demanding, too often resigned when they should be raging. SEE ALSO *such is life; that's how (the way) the ball bounces; that's how (the way) the cookie crumbles; that's life; that's life in the big city; that's show biz; what are you going to do; what can you do.*

> The window was open so the skinny bird flew in. Flappity-flap with its frazzled black wings. That's how it goes. — Bernard Malamud, *Idiots First*

that's how (the way) the ball bounces A plebeian sentiment (see page 23). SEE ALSO *such is life; that's how (the way) it goes; that's how (the way) the cookie crumbles; that's life; that's life in the big city; that's show biz; what are you going to do; what can you do.*

that's how (the way) the cookie crumbles A plebeian sentiment (see page 23). SEE ALSO *such is life; that's how (the way) it goes; that's how (the way) the ball bounces; that's life; that's life in the big city; that's show biz; what are you going to do; what can you do.*

that's interesting A plebeian sentiment (see page 23). *That's interesting*, like *that's nice* (SEE), is most often a witless response to what a person has said. As such, it is no more than an acknowledgment of having been bored, an admission of not having listened, or a confession of having nothing clever to say. SEE ALSO *every effort is being made; interesting.*

that's life A plebeian sentiment (see page 23). SEE ALSO *such is life; that's how (the way) it goes; that's how (the way) the ball bounces; that's how (the way) the cookie crumbles; that's life in the big city; that's show biz; what are you going to do; what can you do.*

that's life in the big city A plebeian sentiment (see page 23). SEE ALSO *such is life; that's how (the way) it goes; that's how (the way) the ball bounces; that's how (the way) the cookie crumbles; that's life; that's show biz; what are you going to do; what can you do.*

that's nice A plebeian sentiment (see page 23). This phrase is used to dismiss what a person has said. *That's nice* is a perfunctory response that, though it suggests interest in a person, actually reveals indifference to the person. SEE ALSO *every effort is being made; that's interesting.*

that's show biz A plebeian sentiment (see page 23). SEE ALSO *such is life; that's how (the way) it goes; that's how (the way) the ball bounces; that's how (the way) the cookie crumbles; that's life; that's life in the big city; what are you going to do; what can you do.*

that's the thing An ineffectual phrase (see page 19). SEE ALSO *here's the thing; the thing about (of) it is; the thing is.*

that's what it's all about A popular prescription (see page 23). ■ It's the little things, not the big things — like playing with my son — *that's what it's all about.*

that's where (you) enter the picture A moribund metaphor (see page 21).

that would be An infantile phrase (see page 20). ■ So, how much carbon does a typical car add to the atmosphere each year, anyway? *That would be* about 30 pounds. DELETE *That would be.* ■ Who is the tour guide? *That would be* me. DELETE *That would be.* ■ In a state that still flies the Confederate battle flag on its statehouse grounds, could a

Democratic governor grant clemency to a white man convicted of killing a black man? *That would be* a big no. DELETE *That would be.* ■ Do you recognize the handwriting and initials? *That would be* my handwriting. *That would be* my initials. USE *That is; These are.* ■ What is the first storm of the season? *That would be* Arthur. DELETE *That would be* ■ Who sat back here? Oh *that would be* Charles Thomas. DELETE *that would be.*

thence A withered word (see page 24). 1. *from that place; from there.* 2. *from that time.* 3. *hence; therefore; thus.* ■ Saudi Arabia pumps some crude through the IPSA pipeline to the Red Sea and *thence* through the Suez canal. REPLACE WITH *from there.*

there are no words to describe (express) A plebeian sentiment (see page 23). There are many more words than people seem to think, and far more is expressible with them than people seem to imagine.

Those who depend on dimwitticisms to convey thought and feeling are more apt to believe *there are no words to describe* ..., for these people are, necessarily, most frustrated by the limits of language.

Dimwitticisms do permit us to describe our most universal feelings, our most banal thoughts, but they prevent us from describing more individual feelings, more brilliant thoughts. These are reserved for a language largely unknown to everyday speakers and writers. SEE ALSO *words cannot describe (express).*

there are other fish in the sea A moribund metaphor (see page 21).

there are two sides to every (question) story A popular prescription (see page 23).

thereby hangs a tale A torpid term (see page 24).

there's a first time for everything A popular prescription (see page 23).

there's a time and a place for everything A popular prescription (see page 23).

there's more than one way to skin a cat A popular prescription (see page 23).

there's no accounting for taste A popular prescription (see page 23).

there's no fool like an old fool A popular prescription (see page 23).

there's no (such thing as a) free lunch A popular prescription (see page 23).

there's no going back A popular prescription (see page 23).

there's no harm in trying A popular prescription (see page 23).

there's no place like home A popular prescription (see page 23).

there's no rest for the weary A popular prescription (see page 23).

there's nothing new under the sun A popular prescription (see page 23).

there's no time like the present A popular prescription (see page 23). ■ They say *there's no time like the present* and that's never been truer.

there's nowhere to go but up A popular prescription (see page 23).

there's safety (strength) in numbers A popular prescription (see page 23).

thick and fast An inescapable pair (see page 20).

> Lenina was left to face the horrors of Malpais unaided. They came crowding in on her thick and fast. — Aldous Huxley, *Brave New World*

(as) thick as molasses An insipid simile. *concentrated; congealed; gelatinous; gluey; glutinous; gooey; gummy; inspissated; jellied; jellified; jellylike; mucilaginous; sticky; thick; viscid; viscous.*

(as) thick as thieves An insipid simile. *amiable; amicable; attached; brotherly; chummy; close; confidential; devoted; familiar; friendly; inseparable; intimate; loving; thick.*

(as) thin as a reed An insipid simile. *asthenic; attenuated; bony; cachectic; emaciated; gaunt; lank; lanky; lean; narrow; rail-thin; scraggy; scrawny; skeletal; skinny; slender; slight; slim; spare; spindly; svelte; sylphid; thin; trim; wispy.*

(as) thin as a rail An insipid simile. *asthenic attenuated; bony; cachectic; emaciated; gaunt; lank; lanky; lean; narrow; rail-thin; scraggy; scrawny; skeletal; skinny; slender; slight; slim; spare; spindly; svelte; sylphid; thin; trim; wispy.*

(the) thin end of the wedge A moribund metaphor (see page 21).

(a) thing An overworked word (see page 22). ■ The mind is *an* amazing *thing.* DELETE *an thing.* ■ It's *a* very important *thing.* DELETE *a thing.* ■ We have won the battle, but the war is *an* ongoing *thing.* DELETE *an thing.* ■ I think that change is *a* good *thing.* DELETE *a thing.* ■ You do this by comparing something your listeners know a lot about with something they know little or nothing about in order to make the unfamiliar *thing* clear. DELETE *thing.*

(the) thing about (of) it is An ineffectual phrase (see page 19). ■ *The thing about it is* it's humiliating and destructive to the psyche to be hit. DELETE *The thing about it is.* ■ *The thing about it is* what they say or do has no influence on what I do. DELETE *The thing about it is.* ■ *The thing about it is* I could never tell her anything. DELETE *The thing about it is.* SEE ALSO *here's the thing; that's the thing; the thing is.*

(the) thing is An ineffectual phrase (see page 19). ■ *The thing is* we know sexual orientation is discovered prior to adolescence. DELETE *The thing is.* ■ *The thing is* I work two jobs, and when I get home I want to relax. DELETE *The thing is.* ■ But *the thing is,* there's always someone who knows where they are. DELETE *the thing is.* SEE ALSO *here's the thing; that's the thing; the thing about (of) it is.*

(a) thing of beauty is a joy forever A popular prescription (see page 23).

(a) thing of the past A torpid term (see page 24). 1. *ceased; completed; concluded; dead; deceased; defunct; departed; done; ended; exanimate; expired; extinct; extinguished; finished; gone; inanimate; lifeless; no more; over; perished; stopped; termi-*

nated. 2. *antediluvian; antiquated; archaic; dead; obsolescent; obsolete; old; old-fashioned; outdated; outmoded; out of date; out of fashion; passé; superannuated.* ■ All agree that the days of students being able to work their way through college are *a thing of the past.* REPLACE WITH *over.* ■ The 8-hour day has become *a thing of the past.* REPLACE WITH *obsolete.* ■ Is the civil rights movement still alive in the United States or *a thing of the past*? REPLACE WITH *dead.*

> He was often on our campus, invited to address Municipal Government seminars on corruption. He told students that corruption was a thing of the past. — Saul Bellow, *More Die of Heartbreak*

think outside the box A torpid term (see page 24). *be creative; be innovative; be inventive; be original.*

Think outside the box is an uninspired way of saying *be creative.* Using it is the antithesis of what is means to be clever. Only the dull and hopeless use *think outside the box.*

thinly veiled An inescapable pair (see page 20).

> There is a thinly veiled tremble in her voice that tells him she is anything but okay. — John Searles, *Strange But True*

this and that A grammatical gimmick (see page 19).

this can't be happening (to me) A plebeian sentiment (see page 23).

this is the first day of the rest of your life A popular prescription (see page 23).

this is to inform you that An ineffectual phrase (see page 19). ■ *This is to inform you that* your credit application has been approved and your account is now open. DELETE *This is to inform you that.* SEE ALSO *(please) be advised that; (please) be informed that.*

thorn in (my) flesh (side) (of) A moribund metaphor (see page 21). *affliction; annoyance; bane; blight; bother; burden; curse; difficulty; inconvenience; irritant; irritation; load; nuisance; ordeal; pain; pest; plague; problem; torment; tribulation; trouble; vexation; weight; worry.* ■ Inventory collateral valuations have been *a thorn in the side of* the agricultural industry for years. REPLACE WITH *bane to.*

> Professor Emerson Sillerton was a thorn in the side of Newport society .... — Edith Wharton, *The Age of Innocence*

those who can, do; those who can't, teach A popular prescription (see page 23).

(the) three musketeers An infantile phrase (see page 20).

three sheets to the wind A moribund metaphor (see page 21). *besotted; crapulous; drunk; inebriated; intoxicated; sodden; stupefied; tipsy.*

> At Holtzman's place, in the two webbed lawn chairs they had set up on the sparse grass of the front lawn because the low steps where they had sat for so many nights when they were young were now too hard on their aging backs and sent pins and needles into their legs, Billy leaned forward, three sheets to the wind, and told Dennis that bitterness, then, was all that was left to it. — Alice McDermott, *Charming Billy*

three strikes and you're out An infantile phrase (see page 20).

thrilled to death A moribund metaphor (see page 21). *blissful; blithe; buoyant; cheerful; delighted; ecstatic; elated; enraptured; euphoric; exalted; excited; exhilarated; exultant; gay; glad; gleeful; good-humored; happy; intoxicated; jolly; jovial; joyful; joyous; jubilant; merry; mirthful; overjoyed; pleased; rapturous; thrilled.* SEE ALSO *to death.*

> Eveline was thrilled to death, but they got Eric Egstrom to come along too, on account of Frenchmen having such a bad reputation. — John Dos Passos, *The 42nd Parallel*

thrills and chills An inescapable pair (see page 20).

through thick and thin A moribund metaphor (see page 21).

throw (a dog) a bone A moribund metaphor (see page 21).

throw (her) a curve A moribund metaphor (see page 21). *bamboozle; befool; beguile; bilk; bluff; cheat; con; deceive; defraud; delude; dupe; feint; fool; gyp; hoodwink; lead astray; misdirect; misguide; misinform; mislead; spoof; swindle; trick; victimize.*

throw a monkey wrench into the works A moribund metaphor (see page 21). 1. *agitate; confuse; disorder; disorganize; disquiet; disrupt; disturb; fluster; jar; jinx; jolt; jumble; mix up; muddle; perturb; rattle; ruffle; shake up; stir up; trouble; unnerve; unsettle; upset.* 2. *blight; cripple; damage; disable; harm; hurt; impair; incapacitate; lame; mar; mess up; rack; ruin; sabotage; spoil; subvert; undermine; vitiate; wrack; wreck.*

throw a wet blanket on A moribund metaphor (see page 21). *bridle; check; constrain; contain; curb; curtail; dampen; discourage; foil; harness; hinder; impede; inhibit; obstruct; quell; repress; restrain; restrict; retard; stifle; subdue; suppress; thwart; weaken.* SEE ALSO *throw cold water on.*

throw caution to the wind A moribund metaphor (see page 21). 1. *be adventuresome; be adventurous; be audacious; be bold; be brave; be courageous; be daring; be dauntless; be fearless; be intrepid; be mettlesome; be plucky; be stalwart; be unafraid; be valiant; be valorous; be venturesome.* 2. *be careless; be foolhardy; be hasty; be heedless; be impetuous; be incautious; be precipitate; be rash; be reckless; be thoughtless.*

throw cold water on A moribund metaphor (see page 21). *bridle; check; constrain; contain; curb; curtail; dampen; discourage; foil; harness; hinder; impede; inhibit; obstruct; quell; repress; restrain; restrict; retard; stifle; subdue; suppress;*

thwart; weaken. SEE ALSO *throw a wet blanket on.*

throw down the gauntlet (glove) A moribund metaphor (see page 21). *affront; brave; call; challenge; confront; dare; defy; encounter; face; meet.*

throw dust in (your) eyes A moribund metaphor (see page 21). *bamboozle; befool; beguile; bilk; bluff; cheat; con; deceive; defraud; delude; dupe; feint; fool; gyp; hoodwink; lead astray; misdirect; misguide; misinform; mislead; spoof; swindle; trick; victimize.*

throw enough dirt, and some will stick A moribund metaphor (see page 21).

throw for a loop A moribund metaphor (see page 21). *amaze; astonish; astound; awe; dazzle; dumbfound; flabbergast; overpower; overwhelm; shock; startle; stun; stupefy; surprise.*

throw (toss) (his) hat in the ring A moribund metaphor (see page 21). 1. *join; run.* 2. *commence; begin; enter into; start; undertake.*

throw (toss) in the sponge (towel) A moribund metaphor (see page 21). *abdicate; accede; acquiesce; bow; capitulate; cede; concede; give in; give up; quit; relinquish; retreat; submit; succumb; surrender; yield.* ■ The bloated bureaucracy remains unscathed, spending continues uncontrolled, and the House leadership has *thrown in the towel* to the governor. REPLACE WITH *acquiesced.* ■ If I get any more overwhelmed, I'm going to *throw in the towel.* REPLACE WITH *quit.*

throw (them) off the scent A moribund metaphor (see page 21). *bamboozle; befool; beguile; bilk; bluff; cheat; con; hoodwink; lead astray;; deceive; defraud; delude; dupe; feint; fool; gyp; misdirect; misguide; misinform; mislead; spoof; swindle; trick.*

throw out the baby with the bath water A moribund metaphor (see page 21).

throw (toss) out the window A moribund metaphor (see page 21). *abandon; chuck; discard; dismiss; dump; jettison; reject; repudiate; throw out; toss out.* ■ Everything I tried to teach them about getting along and togetherness has been *thrown out the window.* REPLACE WITH *jettisoned.*

throw the book at A moribund metaphor (see page 21). *admonish; animadvert; berate; castigate; censure; chasten; chastise; chide; condemn; criticize; denounce; denunciate; discipline; excoriate; fulminate against; imprecate; impugn; inveigh against; objurgate; penalize; punish; rebuke; remonstrate; reprehend; reprimand; reproach; reprobate; reprove; revile; scold; swear at; upbraid; vituperate.*

throw (them) to the dogs (wolves) A moribund metaphor (see page 21). 1. *forfeit; sacrifice; surrender.* 2. *endanger; imperil; jeopardize.*

> I remember his ex-partner at the hospital saying he'll be thrown to the hounds, and I can only hope he's wrong, that the guards will look out for one of their own, though I feel like I'm lying to myself thinking this. — Andre Dubus III, *House of Sand and Fog*

throw (his) weight around A moribund metaphor (see page 21). *awe; browbeat; bully; frighten; intimidate; menace; push around; scare; threaten; torment.*

thumb (his) nose (at) A moribund metaphor (see page 21). *contemn; deride; despise; detest; disdain; jeer at; laugh at; mock; ridicule; scoff at; scorn; shun; slight; sneer; snub; spurn.* ■ We burden our own banks with record keeping and reporting while offshore bankers *thumb their noses* at us. REPLACE WITH *mock.*

> He's breaking the rules, under their noses, thumbing his nose at them, getting away with it. — Margaret Atwood, *The Handmaid's Tale*

(turn) thumbs down A moribund metaphor (see page 21). *decline; deny; disallow; disapprove; forbid; nix; prohibit; proscribe; refuse; reject; rule out; say no; turn down; veto.*

thunderous applause An inescapable pair (see page 20).

tickled pink A moribund metaphor (see page 21). *blissful; buoyant; cheerful; delighted; elated; excited; gay; glad; gladdened; gleeful; good-humored; gratified; happy; jolly; jovial; joyful; joyous; jubilant; merry; mirthful; pleased; tickled.*

tickled to death A moribund metaphor (see page 21). *blissful; buoyant; cheerful; delighted; elated; excited; gay; glad; gladdened; gleeful; good-humored; gratified; happy; jolly; jovial; joyful; joyous; jubilant; merry; mirthful; pleased; tickled.* SEE ALSO *to death.*

(a) tidal wave of A moribund metaphor (see page 21). ■ There's just *a tidal wave of* vital information that gets delivered by telephone. SEE ALSO *a barrage of.*

(the) tide of A moribund metaphor (see page 21). SEE ALSO *a barrage of.*

tied to (her) apron strings A moribund metaphor (see page 21). *clinging; dependent; subject; subordinate; subservient.*

tie the knot A moribund metaphor (see page 21). *marry; wed.*

tie up loose ends A moribund metaphor (see page 21).

(as) tight as a drum An insipid simile. *firm; snug; strained; stretched; taut; tense; tight.*

tighten (our) belts A moribund metaphor (see page 21). *reduce costs; save money.* ■ We are constantly looking for ways to *tighten our belts.* REPLACE WITH *save money.*

tighten the screws A moribund metaphor (see page 21). *coerce; command; compel; constrain; demand; dictate; enforce; enjoin; force; insist; make; order; press; pressure; push.*

tight rein on A moribund metaphor (see page 21).

(talk) till (I'm) blue in the face A moribund metaphor (see page 21). *always; ceaselessly; constantly; continually; continuously; endlessly; eternally; everlastingly; evermore; forever; forevermore; immortally; indefinitely; interminably; permanently; perpetually; persistently; unceasingly; unremittingly.*

till (until) (her) dying days A moribund metaphor (see page 21). *always; ceaselessly; constantly; continually; continuously; endlessly; eternally; everlastingly; evermore; forever; forevermore; immortally; indefinitely; interminably; permanently; perpetually; persistently; unceasingly; unremittingly.*

till (until) hell freezes over A moribund metaphor (see page 21). *always; ceaselessly; constantly; continually; continuously; endlessly; eternally; everlastingly; evermore; forever; forevermore; immortally; indefinitely; interminably; permanently; perpetually; persistently; unceasingly; unremittingly.*

till (until) it's coming out (of) (my) ears A moribund metaphor (see page 21). *excessively; exorbitantly; extravagantly; immoderately; in excess; inordinately; profligately; unrestrainedly.*

till kingdom come A moribund metaphor (see page 21). *always; ceaselessly; constantly; continually; continuously; endlessly; eternally; everlastingly; evermore; forever; forevermore; immortally; indefinitely; interminably; permanently; perpetually; persistently; unceasingly; unremittingly.*

> I let out a great bellow such as cattle do and would have gone on bellowing till Kingdom Come had not some sinner taken my ear and turned me to look under Johnson's devilish table. — Jeanette Winterson, *Sexing the Cherry*

till (until) the cows come home A moribund metaphor (see page 21). *always; ceaselessly; constantly; continually; continuously; endlessly; eternally; everlastingly; evermore; forever; forevermore; immortally; indefinitely; interminably; permanently; perpetually; persistently; unceasingly; unremittingly.* ■ You can press Escape *until the cows come home*, and it will do nothing. REPLACE WITH *unceasingly.*

tilt at windmills A moribund metaphor (see page 21).

time and effort An inescapable pair (see page 20). ■ He still puts a lot of *time and effort* into his commercials.

time and energy An inescapable pair (see page 20). ■ Boiling water also is cheaper than buying bottled water, but it takes more *time and energy.*

time and tide wait for no man A popular prescription (see page 23).

time flies when you're having fun A popular prescription (see page 23).

(the) time has come A torpid term (see page 24). ■ *The time has come* to recognize that personal diaries must be accorded greater protection than business records.

time heals all wounds A popular prescription (see page 23).

time is a great healer A popular prescription (see page 23).

time is money A quack equation (see page 23).

time period A wretched redundancy (see page 25). *period; time.* ■ Would you go along with this for a *time period*? REPLACE WITH *period* or *time.*

time was when A torpid term (see page 24). *before; earlier; formerly; long ago; once; previously.*

(the) time will come A torpid term (see page 24).

time will tell A moribund metaphor (see page 21). ■ We have made many changes in attitude and practice, and only *time will tell* whether these are for the ultimate good or merely more mischief.

tip (my) hat to A moribund metaphor (see page 21). 1. *acknowledge; flag; greet; hail; recognize; salute; wave to; welcome.* 2. *acclaim; applaud; cheer; commend; compliment; congratulate; hail; praise; salute; support; toast.* ■ I *tip my hat to* Mayor Menino for having the vision to see that Boston does not require a professional football team to remain a world-class city. REPLACE WITH *salute.* ■ I'd also like to *tip my hat to* Jeff Staples for his fast editing and feedback. REPLACE WITH *acknowledge.*

(a) tip of the hat A moribund metaphor (see page 21).

tip of the iceberg A moribund metaphor (see page 21). *beginning; commencement; foundation; inauguration; inception; least of it; onset; start.* The monstrous and omnipresent *tip of the iceberg,* like so many other dimwitted usages, alerts us to an inarticulate speaker, a tentative writer. ■ We have just seen the *tip of the iceberg* of corporations that have loaded up with too much debt and gone broke because of the merger and takeover wars. REPLACE WITH *beginning.* ■ I feel these issues and programs are just the *tip of the iceberg.* REPLACE WITH *start.*

And here are a couple of examples no less than wonderful: ■ It's difficult to tell whether my study is the iceberg and the tip is yet to be found, or whether my study was the *tip of the iceberg.* ■ These attacks are only the *tip of the iceberg;* they are the part of the iceberg that is visible above the water, in clear view — but as everyone knows, the largest part of the iceberg, and possibly the most dangerous, lies beneath the surface of the water and is difficult to detect.

tip the scales A moribund metaphor (see page 21).

(as) tired as a dog An insipid simile. *beat; bushed; debilitated; depleted; drained; drowsy; enervated; exhausted; fatigued; groggy; sapped; sleepy; sluggish; slumberous; somnolent; soporific; spent; tired; weary; worn out.*

to all intents and purposes A wretched redundancy (see page 25). *effectively; essentially; in effect; in essence; practically; virtually.* ■ *To all intents and purposes,* you were dating two women at a time. REPLACE WITH *In effect.* SEE ALSO *for all intents and purposes; for all practical purposes; to all intents and purposes; to all practical purposes.*

to all practical purposes A wretched redundancy (see page 25). *effectively; essentially; in effect; in essence; practically; virtually.* ■ The ruling Unionist party is, *to all practical purposes,* a Protestant party. REPLACE WITH *in essence.* SEE ALSO *for all intents and purposes; for all practical purposes; to all intents and purposes.*

(the) toast of the town A moribund metaphor (see page 21).

to a T A moribund metaphor (see page 21). *accurately; correctly; exactly; faultlessly; flawlessly; ideally; just right; perfectly; precisely; rightly; strictly; to perfection; unerringly; very well.*

> Like all Whiting males, C.B. was a short man who disliked drawing attention to the fact, so the low-slung Spanish architecture suited him to a T. — Richard Russo, *Empire Falls*

to beat the band A moribund metaphor (see page 21). *actively; aggressively; dynamically; emphatically; energetically; fast; ferociously; fervently; fiercely; forcefully; frantically; frenziedly; furiously; hard; intensely; intently; mightily; passionately; powerfully; robustly; savagely; spiritedly; strenuously; strongly; vehemently; viciously; vigorously; violently; wildly; with vigor.* ■ When you wake up, it should be snowing *to beat the band.* REPLACE WITH *mightily.*

to burn A moribund metaphor (see page 21). 1. *enormous; great; huge; immense; large; massive; monstrous; prodigious; tremendous; vast.* 2. *excessive; exorbitant; extreme; immoderate; inordinate; undue.* ■ And Mrs. Dole has *Southern charm to burn.* REPLACE WITH *immense Southern charm.*

today is the first day of the rest of (your) life A popular prescription (see page 23).

to death A moribund metaphor (see page 21). *consumedly; enormously; exceedingly; excessively; exorbitantly; extraordinarily; extremely; greatly; hugely; immensely; immoderately; inordinately; intemperately; intensely; mightily; prodigiously; unreasonably; unrestrainedly; very much.* ■ I love him *to death.* REPLACE WITH *prodigiously.*

And as if *to death* were not persuasive enough: ■ The DoD and VA appeared content to study Gulf War illnesses *literally to death.* REPLACE WITH *unrestrainedly.*

to each (his) own A popular prescription (see page 23).

to err is human A popular prescription (see page 23).

to err is human, to forgive divine A popular prescription (see page 23).

toe the line (mark) A moribund metaphor (see page 21). *abide by; accede; accommodate; accord; acquiesce; adapt; adhere to; agree; behave; comply; concur; conform; correspond; follow; harmonize; heed; mind; obey; observe; submit; yield.*

(leveraged) to (their) eyebrows A moribund metaphor (see page 21).

(smell) to high heaven A moribund metaphor (see page 21). *decidedly; mightily; greatly; forcefully; hugely; powerfully; strongly; terribly; tremendously.*

to make a long story short A torpid term (see page 24). *briefly; concisely; in brief; in short; in sum; succinctly; tersely.*

(with) tongue in cheek A moribund metaphor (see page 21). *facetiously; humorously; in fun; in jest; in play; jocosely; jokingly; kiddingly; playfully; teasingly.*

(set) tongues wagging A moribund metaphor (see page 21). *babble; blab; cackle; chaffer; chat; chitchat; chatter; confabulate; converse; gossip; jabber; palaver; prate; prattle; rattle; talk.*

too big for (his) breeches A moribund metaphor (see page 21). *arrogant; cavalier; condescending; contemptuous; despotic; dictatorial; disdainful; dogmatic; domineering; haughty; imperious; insolent; lofty; overbearing; overweening; patronizing; pompous; pretentious; scornful; self-important; supercilious; superior; vainglorious.*

(she's) too good for (him) A suspect superlative (see page 24).

too hot to handle A moribund metaphor (see page 21).

(you) took the words (right) out of (my) mouth A moribund metaphor (see page 21).

too many chiefs (and not enough Indians) A moribund metaphor (see page 21).

too many cooks spoil the broth (brew) A popular prescription (see page 23).

too smart for (his) own good A plebeian sentiment (see page 23).

(fight) tooth and nail A moribund metaphor (see page 21). *actively; aggressively; dynamically; emphatically; energetically; ferociously; fervently; fiercely; forcefully; frantically; frenziedly; furiously; hard; intensely; intently; mightily; passionately; powerfully; robustly; savagely; spiritedly; strenuously; strongly; vehemently; viciously; vigorously; violently; wildly; with vigor.* ■ Bank of Boston, the state's largest bank, lobbied *tooth and nail* against the interstate law. REPLACE WITH *intensely.*

toot (your) own horn A moribund metaphor (see page 21). *acclaim; applaud; bluster; boast; brag; celebrate; cheer; commend; compliment; congratulate; crow; extol; flatter; gloat; hail; honor; laud; praise; puff; salute; self-congratulate; strut; swagger.* ■ Engineers are the world's worst at *tooting their own horn.* REPLACE WITH *applauding themselves.* ■ Even so, the group president of Lucent Technologies' Global Service Provider business division isn't the type to *toot her own horn.* REPLACE WITH *boast.*

top brass A moribund metaphor (see page 21). *administrator; boss; brass; chief; commander; director; executive; foreman; head; headman; leader; manager; master; (high) muckamuck; officer; official; overseer; president; principal; superintendent; supervisor.*

(a) torrent of A moribund metaphor (see page 21). SEE ALSO *a barrage of.*

> They crossed the street and O'Keefe bought an Irish Times and moved jauntily over the bridge, both filled with a torrent of words bled from O'Keefe's excitement and memories of Dublin. — J. P. Donleavy, *The Ginger Man*

toss and turn An inescapable pair (see page 20).

> Heaven knew how he missed her and how many nights he remained awake tossing and turning while thinking about her. — Ha Jin, *Waiting*

to tell you the truth An ineffectual phrase (see page 19).

(march) to the beat of a different drummer A moribund metaphor (see page 21). *aberrant; abnormal; anomalistic; anomalous; atypical; bizarre; curious; deviant; different; distinct; distinctive; eccentric; exceptional; extraordinary; fantastic; foreign; grotesque; idiosyncratic; independent; individual; individualistic; irregular; novel; odd; offbeat; original; peculiar; puzzling; quaint; queer; rare; remarkable; separate; singular; strange; uncommon; unconventional; unexampled; unique; unnatural; unorthodox; unparalleled; unprecedented; unusual; weird.*

to the bone A moribund metaphor (see page 21). *altogether; completely; entirely; fully; perfectly; quite; roundly; thoroughly; totally; unreservedly; utterly; wholly.*

to the ends (far reaches) of the earth A moribund metaphor (see page 21). 1. *always; ceaselessly; constantly; continually; continuously; endlessly; eternally; everlastingly; evermore; forever; forevermore; frequently; interminably; nonstop; permanently; perpetually; persistently; recurrently; regularly; repeatedly; unceasingly; unremittingly.* 2. *all during; all over; all through; everyplace; everywhere; throughout.*

(up) to the hilt A moribund metaphor (see page 21). *altogether; completely; entirely; fully; perfectly; quite; roundly; thoroughly; totally; unreservedly; utterly; wholly.*

to the letter A moribund metaphor (see page 21). *accurately; correctly; exactly; faultlessly; flawlessly; ideally; just right; perfectly; precisely; rightly; strictly; to perfection; unerringly.*

(dressed) (up) to the nines A moribund metaphor (see page 21). *elaborately; elegantly; extravagantly; fashionably; flamboyantly; flashily; gaudily; lavishly; ostentatiously; profusely; richly; showily; smartly; stylishly.* ■ The house was decorated *to the nines.* REPLACE WITH *lavishly.*

> Happily enough, it did not rain next day, and after morning school everybody dressed up to the nines. — Evelyn Waugh, *Decline and Fall*

to the point of (that; where) A wretched redundancy (see page 25). *so; so far (that); so much (that); so that; to; to when; to where.* ■ It's gotten *to the point that* I even flirt with operators. REPLACE WITH *so that.* ■ But it has now evolved *to the point where* they do it all the time. REPLACE WITH *to where.*

to the teeth A moribund metaphor (see page 21). *altogether; completely; entirely; fully; perfectly; quite; roundly; thoroughly; totally; unreservedly; utterly; wholly.*

to the tune of A wretched redundancy (see page 25). ■ It cost him *to the tune of* $4,500 to buy his new computer system. DELETE *to the tune of.*

to the victor belong the spoils A popular prescription (see page 23).

to thine own self be true A popular prescription (see page 23).

touch and go A moribund metaphor (see page 21). *dangerous; precarious; risky; uncertain.*

touch base with A moribund metaphor (see page 21).

(as) tough as leather An insipid simile. 1. *athletic; beefy; brawny; burly; energetic; firm; fit; hale; hardy; hearty; healthful; healthy; husky; leathery; manly; mesomorphic; mighty; muscular; powerful; puissant; robust; rugged; sinewy; solid; sound; stalwart; stout; strapping; strong; sturdy; tough; vigorous; virile; well-built.* 2. *constant; dependable; determined; faithful; fast; firm; fixed; inexorable; inflexible; loyal; obdurate; resolute; resolved; rigid; solid; stable; staunch; steadfast; steady; stern; strong; tenacious; unflinching; unwavering; unyielding.*

(as) tough as nails An insipid simile. 1. *athletic; beefy; brawny; burly; energetic; firm; fit; hale; hardy; healthful; healthy; hearty; leathery; manly; mesomorphic; mighty; muscular; powerful; puissant; robust; rugged; sinewy; solid; sound; stalwart; stout; strapping; strong; sturdy; tough; vigorous; virile; well-built.* 2. *constant; dependable; determined; faithful; fast; firm; fixed; inexorable; inflexible; loyal; obdurate; resolute; resolved; rigid; solid; stable; staunch; steadfast; steady; stern; strong; tenacious; unflinching; unwavering; unyielding.*

tough sledding A moribund metaphor (see page 21). *arduous; backbreaking; burdensome; difficult; exhausting; fatiguing; hard; herculean; laborious; not easy; onerous; severe; strenuous; toilful; toilsome; tough; troublesome; trying; wearisome.*

(it's) tough to teach an old dog new tricks A moribund metaphor (see page 21).

towering inferno An infantile phrase (see page 20). *blaze; conflagration; fire; holocaust; inferno.*

(proven) track record A moribund metaphor (see page 21).

tread water A moribund metaphor (see page 21). ■ He is now *treading water*, deciding what to do next.

treat (us) like royalty An insipid simile.

très A foreign phrase (see page 19). *very.* ■ She is *très* happy now that she is working. REPLACE WITH *very.* ■ Two New Yorkers we recently sent out on a discount shopping spree were *très* impressed with the hippness quotient. REPLACE WITH *very.*

trials and tribulations An inescapable pair (see page 20). *adversity; affliction; calamity; catastrophe; difficulty; distress; hardship; misadventure; misfortune; ordeal; trial; tribulation; trouble; woe.* ■ It also presents a first-hand account of the *trials and tribulations* of living in a lesbian family. REPLACE WITH *ordeal.*

tried and true An inescapable pair (see page 20). 1. *constant; dependable; faithful; firm; loyal; reliable; solid; staunch; steadfast; strong; true; trustworthy; trusty.*

2. *authentic; authenticated; established; reliable; substantiated; sound; verified; well-founded; well-grounded.*

trim (her) sails A moribund metaphor (see page 21).

trip the light fantastic A moribund metaphor (see page 21). *dance.*

triumphant return An inescapable pair (see page 20).

trouble in paradise A moribund metaphor (see page 21).

(a) trouble shared is a trouble halved A popular prescription (see page 23).

true blue A moribund metaphor (see page 21). *constant; dependable; faithful; firm; loyal; reliable; solid; staunch; steadfast; strong; true; trustworthy; trusty.*

true facts A wretched redundancy (see page 25). *facts; truth.* ■ Sometimes I wish the papers would print the *true facts*. REPLACE WITH *facts* or *truth*.

true love A suspect superlative (see page 24).

(the course of) true love never runs smooth A popular prescription (see page 23).

truthfully honest A wretched redundancy (see page 25). *honest; truthful.* ■ To be *truthfully honest,* I do want to be her friend. REPLACE WITH *truthful.*

truth is stranger than fiction A popular prescription (see page 23).

truth, justice, and the American way An infantile phrase (see page 20).

(the) truth of the matter is An ineffectual phrase (see page 19). ■ *The truth of the matter is* half of the people who get married end up divorced. DELETE *The truth of the matter is.* ■ *The truth of the matter is,* I don't understand it, but I'm against it. DELETE *The truth of the matter is.* SEE ALSO *(the) fact of the matter is.*

(the) truth will set you free A popular prescription (see page 23).

(a) tug of war A moribund metaphor (see page 21). ■ There's *a tug of war* between people who like the economy and people who are afraid.

(a) turn on A moribund metaphor (see page 21). *animating; arousing; bracing; enlivening; exciting; exhilarating; inspiring; inspiriting; invigorating; provoking; refreshing; rousing; stimulating; vivifying.*

try it, you'll like it An infantile phrase (see page 20).

try, try again A popular prescription (see page 23).

turn a blind eye to (toward) A moribund metaphor (see page 21). *brush aside; avoid; discount; disregard; dodge; duck; ignore; look away from; neglect; omit; overlook; pass over; shrink from; shun; shy away from; turn away from; withdraw from.* ■ And Chile, at least, is learning the risks of *turning a blind eye* to the past. REPLACE WITH *ignoring.* ■ Yet some of Bolt's advertisers, while lured by the site's demographics, may be *turning a blind eye* to content they normally find questionable in other media.

REPLACE WITH *overlooking*. ■ The donors have *turned a blind eye* toward allegations of corruption. REPLACE WITH *disregarded.*

> The scholarly badger, who hated contradiction and despised the Socratic method, would cast a blind eye to the twitching braid until her pupil's gasps became too insistent to ignore. — George Hagen, *The Laments*

turnabout is fair play A popular prescription (see page 23).

turn a (the) corner A moribund metaphor (see page 21). 1. *advance; awaken; better; expand; flourish; gain; gain strength; grow; heal; improve; increase; pick up; progress; prosper; rally; recover; recuperate; refresh; renew; revive; rouse; strengthen; thrive.* 2. *adjust; alter; change; modify; transform.* ■ Our No. 1 goal is to reestablish reliability and customer satisfaction, and we think we have started *to turn the corner*. REPLACE WITH *improve*.

> Two weeks was only one day more than thirteen days, but I felt we'd turned a corner that shouldn't have been turned, and I couldn't get myself out of bed. — Ann Packer, *The Dive From Clausen's Pier*

turn a deaf ear to A moribund metaphor (see page 21). *brush aside; avoid; discount; disregard; dodge; duck; ignore; neglect; omit; pass over; recoil from; shrink from; shun; shy away from; turn away from; withdraw from.* ■ Wilson should *turn a deaf ear to* HMO lobbyists and sign it. REPLACE WITH *disregard.* ■ Congress has *turned a deaf ear to* the public and taken the next step to unplug PBS and NPR. REPLACE WITH *ignored.*

turn a negative into a positive A torpid term (see page 24). ■ The revolution in traditional family ties has *turned a negative into a positive* for most singles today. SEE ALSO *negative*; *positive*.

turn (their) back on A moribund metaphor (see page 21). *abandon; abdicate; avoid; brush aside; deny; desert; disavow; discount; disinherit; disown; disregard; dodge; drop; duck; forgo; forsake; give up; ignore; leave; neglect; omit; pass over; quit; recoil from; reject; relinquish; renounce; shrink from; shun; shy away from; snub; surrender; turn away from; withdraw from; yield.* ■ It will be unfortunate, indeed, if the countries of Western Europe *turn their backs on* their Eastern neighbors. REPLACE WITH *disregard.*

turn back the clock (of time) A moribund metaphor (see page 21).

turn (your) dreams into reality A popular prescription (see page 23).

turn inside out A moribund metaphor (see page 21). *agitate; confuse; disorder; disorganize; disquiet; disrupt; disturb; fluster; jar; jolt; jumble; mess up; mix up; muddle; perturb; rattle; ruffle; shake up; stir up; trouble; unnerve; unsettle; upset.*

turn into (to) stone A moribund metaphor (see page 21). *calcify; fossilize; harden; petrify; solidify.*

turn like the weather An insipid simile. *capricious; changeable; erratic; fickle;*

fitful; flighty; fluctuating; haphazard; inconsistent; inconstant; intermittent; irregular; mercurial; occasional; random; sometime; spasmodic; sporadic; unpredictable; unsettled; unstable; unsteady; vacillating; volatile; wavering; wayward.

(another) turn of the screw A moribund metaphor (see page 21).

turn over a new leaf A moribund metaphor (see page 21). *alter; begin again; change; convert; improve; metamorphose; modify; reform; remake; remodel; rethink; transform.*

turn sour A moribund metaphor (see page 21). ■ Banks caught in the euphoria of a construction boom have watched the economy *turn sour.*

turn (my) stomach A moribund metaphor (see page 21). *appall; disgust; horrify; nauseate; offend; outrage; repel; repulse; revolt; shock; sicken.*

turn tail A moribund metaphor (see page 21). *abscond; clear out; decamp; depart; desert; disappear; escape; exit; flee; fly; go; go away; leave; move on; part; pull out; quit; retire; retreat; run away; take flight; take off; vacate; vanish; withdraw*

turn the other cheek A moribund metaphor (see page 21).

turn the tables (on) A moribund metaphor (see page 21).

turn the tide A moribund metaphor (see page 21).

turn up (her) nose A moribund metaphor (see page 21). *contemn; deride; despise; detest; disdain; jeer at; laugh at; mock; ridicule; scoff at; scorn; shun; slight; sneer; snub; spurn.*

turn up the heat A moribund metaphor (see page 21). *coerce; command; compel; constrain; demand; enforce; force; goad; impel; importune; incite; induce; insist; instigate; make; oblige; press; pressure; prod; push; spur; urge.*

(the) twelfth of never An infantile phrase (see page 20).

24/7 An infantile phrase (see page 20). *always; ceaselessly; constantly; continually; continuously; endlessly; eternally; everlastingly; evermore; forever; forevermore; frequently; interminably; nonstop; permanently; perpetually; persistently; recurrently; regularly; repeatedly; unceasingly; unremittingly.*

Nothing recommends this silly phrase — especially when so many other words, true words, mean as much. *24/7* is favored by people who find words unwieldy and thought distasteful.

(sit and) twiddle (our) thumbs A moribund metaphor (see page 21). *be idle; be inactive; be lazy; be unemployed; be unoccupied; dally; dawdle; loaf; loiter; loll; lounge; relax; repose; rest.*

twilight zone A moribund metaphor (see page 21).

twist (his) arm A moribund metaphor (see page 21). *bulldoze; bully; coerce; compel; constrain; demand; drive; enforce; enjoin; exhort; goad; force; impel; incite; insist; intimidate; make; necessitate; obligate; oblige; order; press; pressure; prod; require; threaten; tyrannize; urge.*

twist (wrap) (him) around (her) little finger A moribund metaphor (see page 21). *administer; boss; command; control; dictate; direct; dominate; domineer; govern; in charge; in control; in command; manage; manipulate; master; misuse; order; overpower; oversee; predominate; prevail; reign over; rule; superintend; tyrannize; use.*

twist of fate A moribund metaphor (see page 21).

twists and turns (of fate) A moribund metaphor (see page 21).

twist slowly in the wind A moribund metaphor (see page 21). *afflict; agonize; crucify; excruciate; harrow; martyr; persecute; rack; torment; torture.*

two heads are better than one A popular prescription (see page 23).

(like) two peas in a pod An insipid simile. *akin; alike; correspondent; corresponding; equal; equivalent; identical; indistinguishable; kindred; like; matching; one; same; selfsame; similar; twin.*

two's company, three's a crowd A popular prescription (see page 23).

two-way street A moribund metaphor (see page 21).

two wrongs don't make a right A popular prescription (see page 23).

U

(as) ugly as a toad An insipid simile. *deformed; disfigured; disgusting; displeasing; distorted; freakish; frightful; ghastly; gorgonian; grisly; grotesque; gruesome; hideous; homely; horrendous; horrible; horrid; monstrous; offensive; plain; repellent; repulsive; revolting; ugly; unsightly.*

(as) ugly as sin An insipid simile. *deformed; disfigured; disgusting; displeasing; distorted; freakish; frightful; ghastly; gorgonian; grisly; grotesque; gruesome; hideous; homely; horrendous; horrible; horrid; monstrous; offensive; plain; repellent; repulsive; revolting; ugly; unsightly.*

ugly duckling A moribund metaphor (see page 21). *deformed; disfigured; disgusting; displeasing; distorted; freakish; frightful; ghastly; gorgonian; grisly; grotesque; gruesome; hideous; homely; horrendous; horrible; horrid; monstrous; offensive; plain; repellent; repulsive; revolting; ugly; unsightly.*

unbeknownst A withered word (see page 24). *unbeknown; unknown.* ■ *Unbeknownst* to his girlfriend, he made a videotape of them having sex. REPLACE WITH *Unknown.*

unbelievable An overworked word (see page 22). 1. *beyond belief; beyond comprehension; doubtful; dubious; implausible; imponderable; improbable; incomprehensible; inconceivable; inexplicable; questionable; unfathomable; unimaginable; unthinkable.* 2. *astonishing;*

astounding; breathtaking; extraordinary; fabulous; fantastic; marvelous; miraculous; overwhelming; prodigious; sensational; spectacular; wonderful; wondrous.

uncharted waters A moribund metaphor (see page 21).

under a cloud A moribund metaphor (see page 21). *discredited; disfavored; disgraced; dishonored; distrusted; in disfavor; in disgrace; in disrepute; in ignominy; in shame; suspect; under suspicion.* ■ He became the only vice president to leave *under a cloud.* REPLACE WITH *in disgrace.* ■ He left the police department *under a cloud of suspicion.* REPLACE WITH *under suspicion.*

under (my) belt A moribund metaphor (see page 21). *background; education; experience; grooming; grounding; instruction; learning; knowledge; maturity; practice; preparation; qualifications; schooling; seasoning; skill; teaching; training.*

(come) under fire A moribund metaphor (see page 21). *be admonished; be assailed; be attacked; be castigated; be censured; be chastised; be chided; be condemned; be criticized; be denounced; be rebuked; be reprimanded; be reproached; be reproved; be scolded; be set on; be upbraided.*

(keep) under lock and key A moribund metaphor (see page 21). 1. *confined; imprisoned; in jail; locked up.* 2. *guarded; protected; safe; secure; sheltered; shielded.*

under (his) own steam A moribund metaphor (see page 21).

understaffed and overworked An inescapable pair (see page 20).

under the gun A moribund metaphor (see page 21). *be at risk; be at stake; be endangered; be imperiled; be in danger; be in jeopardy; be jeopardized; be menaced; be threatened.* ■ The American way of life, long taken for granted, was *under the gun.* REPLACE WITH *being threatened.*

under the same roof A moribund metaphor (see page 21). *be as one; be indissoluble; be indivisible; be inseparable; be together.* ■ The who's who of world power, gathered *under the same roof* in a public place, poses an unparalleled security headache for Italian authorities. REPLACE WITH *together.* ■ While he understands those living in the house could live anywhere in the community, he sees a danger in putting them all together *under the same roof.* DELETE *under the same roof.*

> I hold it singular, as I look back, that I should never have doubted for a moment that the sacred relics were there; never have failed to feel a certain joy at being under the same roof with them. — Henry James, *The Aspern Papers*

under the sun A moribund metaphor (see page 21). *in existence; known.*

under the table A moribund metaphor (see page 21). *clandestinely; confidentially; covertly; furtively; mysteriously; in private; in secret; privately; quietly; secludedly; secretly; slyly; stealthily; surreptitiously; undercover.*

under the weather A moribund metaphor (see page 21). 1. *afflicted; ail-*

ing; debilitated; diseased; enervated; feeble; frail; ill; indisposed; infirm; not (feeling) well; sick; sickly; suffering; unhealthy; unsound; unwell; valetudinarian. 2. *besotted; crapulous; drunk; inebriated; intoxicated; sodden; stupefied; tipsy.* ■ It doesn't matter if some days I'm feeling a little low or *under the weather.* REPLACE WITH *unwell.*

under the wire A moribund metaphor (see page 21).

under (his) thumb A moribund metaphor (see page 21). *dependent; subject; subordinate; subservient; under.*

under (his) wing A moribund metaphor (see page 21).

(keep) under wraps A moribund metaphor (see page 21). *camouflage; clandestine; cloak; conceal; cover; covert; disguise; enshroud; harbor; hide; out of sight; secret; mask; screen; shroud; suppress; surreptitious; veil; withhold.* ■ Radcliffe tried, and failed, to keep its list *under wraps.* REPLACE WITH *hidden.* ■ Negotiations have been kept largely *under wraps.* REPLACE WITH *secret.*

uneasy calm An inescapable pair (see page 20). ■ By midafternoon, an *uneasy calm* returned to much of the capital.

uneasy lies the head that wears a crown A popular prescription (see page 23).

united we stand (divided we fall) A popular prescription (see page 23).

unite in holy wedlock (marriage) A wretched redundancy (see page 25). *marry; wed.*

unless and (or) until A wretched redundancy (see page 25). *unless; until.* ■ I am opposed to the imposition of any new taxes *unless and until* major cuts in spending have been implemented. REPLACE WITH *unless* or *until.*

unmitigated gall An inescapable pair (see page 20).

untenable position An inescapable pair (see page 20).

until and (or) unless A wretched redundancy (see page 25). *unless; until.* ■ *Until and unless* these two conditions are met, the second rule does not fire. REPLACE WITH *Unless* or *Until.*

until such time as A wretched redundancy (see page 25). *until.* ■ Lessee shall not be liable for any rent *until such time as* Lessor can deliver possession. REPLACE WITH *until.* ■ The FBI would cooperate but play a subordinate role *until such time as* it became evident that the explosion was caused by a criminal act. REPLACE WITH *until.*

up a blind alley A moribund metaphor (see page 21). 1. *at risk; endangered; hard-pressed; imperiled; in a bind; in a dilemma; in a fix; in a jam; in a predicament; in a quandary; in danger; in difficulty; in jeopardy; in peril; in trouble; jeopardized.* 2. *caught; cornered; enmeshed; ensnared; entangled; entrapped; netted; snared; trapped.*

up a creek A moribund metaphor (see page 21). *at risk; endangered; hard-pressed; imperiled; in a bind; in a dilemma; in a fix; in a jam; in a predicament; in a quandary; in danger; in difficulty; in jeopardy; in peril; in trouble; jeopardized.*

up against the wall A moribund metaphor (see page 21). 1. *at risk; desperate; endangered; frantic; hard-pressed; imperiled; in a bind; in a dilemma; in a fix; in a jam; in a predicament; in a quandary; in danger; in difficulty; in jeopardy; in peril; in trouble; jeopardized.* 2. *caught; cornered; enmeshed; ensnared; entangled; entrapped; netted; snared; trapped.*

(right) up (her) alley A moribund metaphor (see page 21).

up and running A moribund metaphor (see page 21). 1. *at work; functioning; going; in action; in operation; operational; operating; performing; producing; running; working.* 2. *able-bodied; active; fit; healthy; robust; strong; vigorous; well.* ■ We intend to have a smoothly functioning, well-integrated unit *up and running* when we start in February. REPLACE WITH *in operation.* ■ This country needs massive amounts of aid to get these people *up and running.* REPLACE WITH *well.*

> Everyone, even Liam, offered their expertise to get her up and running. — Rebecca Bloom, *Tangled Up in Daydreams*

up a tree A moribund metaphor (see page 21). 1. *at risk; endangered; hard-pressed; imperiled; in a bind; in a fix; in a jam; in a predicament; in danger; in difficulty; in jeopardy; in peril; in trouble; jeopardized.* 2. *caught; cornered; enmeshed; ensnared; entangled; entrapped; netted; snared; trapped.*

up close and personal An infantile phrase (see page 20).

(an) uphill battle (fight) A moribund metaphor (see page 21). 1. *an endeavor; an undertaking; a struggle; a task; drudgery; hard work; labor; moil; toil; travail; work.* 2. *arduous; difficult; hard; laborious; strenuous.* ■ Even though it's been *an uphill battle,* I've learned a lot. REPLACE WITH *difficult.* SEE ALSO *reach epidemic proportions.* ■ Alleging sexual harassment against a supervisor is *an uphill battle.* REPLACE WITH *a struggle.*

up in arms A moribund metaphor (see page 21). 1. *agitated; alarmed; angry; annoyed; aroused; choleric; enraged; fierce; fuming; furious; incensed; indignant; inflamed; infuriated; irate; irked; irritable; mad; maddened; raging; resentful; splenetic; vexatious.* 2. *factious; insubordinate; insurgent; mutinous; rebellious; seditious.* ■ The nurses were *up in arms* because of their work conditions. REPLACE WITH *incensed.*

up in the air A moribund metaphor (see page 21). *confused; dubious; indecisive; in doubt; irresolute; open; questionable; tentative; uncertain; unconcluded; undecided; undetermined; unknown; unresolved; unsettled; unsure.* ■ The issue is still very much *up in the air* despite a series of rulings in the 1980s. REPLACE WITH *unsettled.*

> Or depending on his work schedule, which was now up in the air, he could urinate on them at whatever time he got up. — James Whorton, *Approximately Heaven*

ups and downs A moribund metaphor (see page 21). *alterations; changes; erraticism; fluctuations; fortuitousness; inconstancies; shifts; uncertainties; vacillations; variations; vicissitudes.* ■ A community that can meet many of its needs by using locally available natural, human, and financial resources will be less affected by the *ups and downs* of the national and global economies. REPLACE WITH *vicissitudes.*

upset the apple cart A moribund metaphor (see page 21). *confuse; damage; disorder; disrupt; disturb; jumble; mess up; mix up; muddle; ruin; scramble; spoil; upset.*

up the ante A moribund metaphor (see page 21).

up the creek (without a paddle) A moribund metaphor (see page 21). 1. *at risk; endangered; hard-pressed; imperiled; in a bind; in a dilemma; in a fix; in a jam; in a predicament; in a quandary; in danger; in difficulty; in jeopardy; in peril; in trouble; jeopardized.* 2. *caught; cornered; enmeshed; ensnared; entangled; entrapped; netted; snared; trapped.*

up till (until) A wretched redundancy (see page 25). *till (until).* ■ *Up until* the day he left, they hoped that he would play a major role in the new company as a key senior executive. REPLACE WITH *Until.*

> I'd given him the pipe for Father's Day. Up until then he had never even smoked. — Sue Monk Kidd, *The Mermaid Chair*

up till (until) this point (time) A wretched redundancy (see page 25). *until now.* ■ *Up until this point* we have been working in the dark. REPLACE WITH *Until now.*

(step) up to bat A moribund metaphor (see page 21). 1. *aim for; attempt; endeavor; engage; participate; pursue; seek; strive for; try.* 2. *advance; appear; approach; come forth; come forward; emerge; rise; show; surface; transpire.* 3. *act; perform; speak; talk.* 4. *be accountable; be answerable; be responsible.* ■ In this regard, one campus organization has *stepped up to bat.* REPLACE WITH *emerged.* ■ First *up to bat* is Philip Cercone, director of McGill-Queen's University Press. REPLACE WITH *to speak.*

> So now Lora comes up to bat and tells a story that is basically the same as mine but utterly different.... — David Margolis, *The Stepman*

up to (my) ears A moribund metaphor (see page 21). 1. *bury; deluge; flood; glut; immerse; infest; inundate; overburden; overload; overpower; overrun; overwhelm; sate; swamp.* 2. *altogether; completely; entirely; fully; perfectly; quite; roundly; thoroughly; totally; unreservedly; utterly; wholly.*

up to (my) eyeballs (eyebrows; eyes) A moribund metaphor (see page 21). 1. *bury; deluge; glut; immerse; infest; inundate; overburden; overload; overpower; overrun; overwhelm; sate; swamp.* 2. *altogether; completely; entirely; fully; perfectly; quite; roundly; thoroughly; totally; unreservedly; utterly; wholly.* ■ The campaigns' organizations are all *up to their eyeballs* with delegate-counting. REPLACE WITH *overrun.* ■ We are in this now, *up to our eyebrows* and for the long haul. REPLACE WITH *fully.*

up to par A moribund metaphor (see page 21). 1. *average; common; commonplace; customary; everyday; mediocre; middling; normal; ordinary; quotidian; regular; routine; standard; typical; uneventful; unexceptional; unremarkable; usual.* 2. *acceptable; adequate; fine; good; good enough; healthy; passable; satisfactory; sufficient; suitable; tolerable; well.*

up to scratch A moribund metaphor (see page 21). *acceptable; adequate; fine; good; good enough; healthy; passable; satisfactory; sufficient; suitable; tolerable; well.*

up to snuff A moribund metaphor (see page 21). *acceptable; adequate; fine; good; good enough; healthy; passable; satisfactory; sufficient; suitable; tolerable; well.*

up to speed A moribund metaphor (see page 21). *acceptable; adequate; fine; good; good enough; healthy; passable; satisfactory; sufficient; suitable; tolerable; well.*

use and abuse An inescapable pair (see page 20). ■ We all agree that we have been racially *used and abused.* ■ Lil Franklin said her son had been *used and abused* by two fundamentalist ministers.

utilize A torpid term (see page 24). *apply; employ; make use of; use.* ■ I *utilize* my bike for nearly everything. REPLACE WITH *use.* ■ These are all expository techniques that you will be *utilizing* once you have mastered the basics of writing. REPLACE WITH *using.* SEE ALSO *finalize.*

V

valuable asset An inescapable pair (see page 20). This phrase is, like many inescapable pairs, also redundant, for an *asset* is *valuable.*

variations on a theme A torpid term (see page 24).

> Once she allowed herself to think that, then there was no stopping a flood of other suspicions — primarily variations on the theme of the power and ubiquity of Ray's "friends." — Jane Smiley, *Duplicate Keys*

variety is the spice of life A popular prescription (see page 23).

various and sundry An inescapable pair (see page 20). *assorted; diverse; sundry; varied; various; varying.* ■ I tried *various and sundry* ways to get her to see me. REPLACE WITH *various.* SEE ALSO *all and sundry.*

vehemently oppose An inescapable pair (see page 20). ■ MCA *vehemently opposed* Sony's Betamax and the VCR invasion.

verboten A foreign phrase (see page 19). *banned; disallowed; enjoined; forbidden; prohibited; proscribed.* ■ But once everything was set up, my analog modem worked on a previously *verboten* digital phone. REPLACE WITH *disallowed.*

verily A withered word (see page 24). *actually; indeed; in fact; in faith; in reality; in truth; truly.*

very An overworked word (see page 22). The word *very* is often a needless intensive, but preceding words like *excellent, major*, and *delightful*, it is ludicrous. ■ I think that's a *very* excellent thought. DELETE *very.* ■ It's a *very* major plus for our state and our region. DELETE *very.* ■ You seem *very* delightful. DELETE *very.* ■ She's a biochemist and *very* brilliant. DELETE *very.* ■ If the test cells were to be shut down, it would be *very* detrimental to the operation. DELETE *very.* ■ Moreover, the wind at the peak can be *very* deadly. DELETE *very.* SEE ALSO *really.*

viable alternative An inescapable pair (see page 20).

vicious circle An inescapable pair (see page 20).

vicious rumor An inescapable pair (see page 20).

vim and vigor An inescapable pair (see page 20). *animation; ardor; dash; dynamism; élan; energy; fervor; force; intensity; liveliness; passion; potency; power; spirit; stamina; strength; verve; vigor; vitality; vivacity; zeal.*

virtue is its own reward A popular prescription (see page 23).

vis-à-vis A foreign phrase (see page 19).

viselike grip A moribund metaphor (see page 21).

visible (invisible) to the eye A wretched redundancy (see page 25). *visible (invisible).* SEE ALSO *audible (inaudible) to the ear.*

(a) vision of (loveliness) A moribund metaphor (see page 21).

> After talking for a couple of minutes, I asked Bruce who this vision of ebony beauty was. — E. Lynn Harris, *Invisible Life*

vive la différence A foreign phrase (see page 19).

voice (crying) in the wilderness A moribund metaphor (see page 21).

vote with (their) feet A moribund metaphor (see page 21). ■ People are *voting with their feet*, and politicians know this.

wages of sin A moribund metaphor (see page 21).

(just have to) wait and see (what happens) A torpid term (see page 24). *I don't know; (it's) not (yet) known; (that's) uncertain; (that's) unclear; (it's) unknown.* SEE ALSO *(it) remains to be seen; your guess is as good as mine.*

wait for the ax to fall A moribund metaphor (see page 21).

wait for the other shoe to drop A moribund metaphor (see page 21).

waiting for Godot An infantile phrase (see page 20).

waiting in the wings A moribund metaphor (see page 21).

wake the dead A moribund metaphor (see page 21). *blaring; boisterous; booming; deafening; earsplitting; fulminating; loud; noisy; obstreperous; piercing; plangent; resounding; roaring; shrill; stentorian; strident; thundering; thunderous; tumultuous; vociferous.*

wake up and smell the coffee A moribund metaphor (see page 21). *be alert; be attentive; be awake; be aware; be cognizant; be conscious; be mindful; be perceptive; be sentient; be wakeful.*

wake-up call A moribund metaphor (see page 21). *admonition; caution; warning.* ■ The priest sexual scandal is a *wake-up call* for the church.

walk a fine line A moribund metaphor (see page 21).

walk a tightrope A moribund metaphor (see page 21). *chance; dare; endanger; gamble; hazard; imperil; jeopardize; make bold; peril; risk; venture.*

walk away from A moribund metaphor (see page 21). *abandon; abdicate; avoid; brush aside; deny; desert; disavow; discount; disinherit; disown; disregard; dodge; drop; duck; forgo; forsake; give up; ignore; leave; neglect; omit; pass over; quit; recoil from; reject; relinquish; renounce; shrink from; shun; shy away from; snub; spurn; surrender; turn away from; withdraw from; yield.* ■ The state cannot *walk away from* that obligation. REPLACE WITH *disregard.*

(the) walking dead A moribund metaphor (see page 21).

(a) walking, talking An infantile phrase (see page 20).

walk on air A moribund metaphor (see page 21). *blissful; blithe; buoyant; cheerful; delighted; ecstatic; elated; enraptured; euphoric; exalted; excited; exhilarated; exultant; gay; glad; gleeful; good-humored; happy; intoxicated; jolly; jovial; joyful; joyous; jubilant; merry; mirthful; overjoyed; pleased; rapturous; thrilled.*

walk on eggs (eggshells) A moribund metaphor (see page 21). ■ For years, Robinson *walked on eggshells* as the first black baseball player in the major leagues.

(all) walks of life A moribund metaphor (see page 21).

walk softly and carry a big stick A popular prescription (see page 23).

walk (me) through A moribund metaphor (see page 21). *clarify; clear up; describe; disentangle; elucidate; enlighten; explain; explicate; illume; illuminate; interpret; make clear; make plain; reveal; simplify.* ■ Can you *walk me through* the process of how you wrote it? USE *explain.* ■ Middle-school students will be told the details of the drill in advance, and their teachers will *walk them through* the steps on the day of the event. USE *describe.*

wall of silence A moribund metaphor (see page 21).

(the) walls have ears A moribund metaphor (see page 21).

want to bet? An infantile phrase (see page 20).

war clouds A moribund metaphor (see page 21).

war is hell A quack equation (see page 23).

(as) warm as toast An insipid simile. *heated; lukewarm; mild; temperate; tepid; toasty; warm; warmish.*

warm the cockles of (my) heart A moribund metaphor (see page 21).

warn in advance A wretched redundancy (see page 25). *warn.* ■ Management should be *warned in advance* that fines are no longer the way to satisfy the system for a careless disaster. DELETE *in advance.* SEE ALSO *advance warning; forewarn.*

war of words A moribund metaphor (see page 21). *altercation; argument; bickering; conflict; contention; controversy; disagreement; disputation; dispute; feud; polemics; quarrel; row; spat; squabble; strife; wrangle.* ■ Yesterday's *war of words* seemed like a replay of the bitter 1988 campaign. REPLACE WITH *squabble.*

wash (their) dirty linen in public A moribund metaphor (see page 21).

(all) washed up A moribund metaphor (see page 21). *beaten; condemned; conquered; cowed; cursed; damned; defunct; doomed; fated; finished; gone; lost; ruined; vanquished.*

wash (her) hands of (it) A moribund metaphor (see page 21). *abandon; abdicate; avoid; brush aside; deny; desert; disavow; discount; disinherit; disown; disregard; dodge; drop; duck; forgo; forsake; give up; ignore; leave; neglect; omit; pass over; quit; recoil from; reject; relinquish; renounce; shrink from; shun; shy away from; snub; surrender; turn away from; withdraw from; yield.*

> The gambler apparently had washed his hands of me, but he didn't seem to hold any stubbornness against me. — Dashiell Hammett, *Red Harvest*

waste not, want not A popular prescription (see page 23).

(a) watched pot never boils A popular prescription (see page 23).

(like) watching grass grow An insipid simile. *banal; barren; bland; boring; deadly; dreary; dry; dull; everyday; flat; humdrum; inanimate; insipid; jejune; lifeless; lusterless; mediocre; monotonous; prosaic; routine; spiritless; stale; tedious; tiresome; unexciting; uninteresting; vapid; wearisome.*

watch (him) like a hawk An insipid simile. *be alert; be attentive; be awake; be aware; be eagle-eyed; be heedful; be informed; be keen; be observant; be vigilant; be wakeful; be watchful.*

water over the dam A moribund metaphor (see page 21). 1. *completed; concluded; done; ended; finished; over;*

passed; through. 2. *history; the past; yesterday.*

water (runs) under the bridge A moribund metaphor (see page 21). 1. *completed; concluded; done; ended; finished; over; passed; through.* 2. *history; the past; yesterday.*

> A lot of water runs under the bridge, a lot of it dirty. — Thomas Savage, *The Sheep Queen*

(the) wave of the future A moribund metaphor (see page 21).

(like) waving a red flag (rag) in front of a bull An insipid simile.

wax and wane An inescapable pair (see page 20).

ways and means An inescapable pair (see page 20). *approaches; means; mechanisms; methods; techniques; ways.*

(the) way to a man's heart is through his stomach A popular prescription (see page 23).

(as) weak as a baby An insipid simile. *dainty; debilitated; delicate; enervated; feeble; fragile; frail; infirm; nonmuscular; puny; sickly; unhealthy; unwell; valetudinarian; weak; weakly.*

(as) weak as a kitten An insipid simile. *dainty; debilitated; delicate; enervated; feeble; fragile; frail; infirm; nonmuscular; puny; sickly; unhealthy; unwell; valetudinarian; weak; weakly.*

weak in the knees A moribund metaphor (see page 21). *dizzy; faint; giddy; lightheaded; weak.*

wears (her) heart on (her) sleeve A moribund metaphor (see page 21). *demonstrative; emotional; emotive; sensitive; sentimental.*

(the) weak link (in the chain) A moribund metaphor (see page 21).

wear the pants A moribund metaphor (see page 21). *administer; boss; command; control; dictate; direct; dominate; govern; in charge; in command; in control; manage; manipulate; master; order; overpower; oversee; predominate; prevail; reign over; rule; superintend.*

weather the storm (of) A moribund metaphor (see page 21). ■ A tremendous thank you goes out to each of you who has helped our family *weather this storm.* SEE ALSO *reach epidemic proportions.*

weighs a ton An insipid simile. *bulky; heavy; hefty; weighty.*

weight in proportion (proportionate) to height A torpid term (see page 24). Men should eschew women (and women, men) whom they've not yet met and who describe their physiques as *weight in proportion (proportionate) to height.*

Let us men prefer an *athletic; brawny; firm; fit; medium-build; mesomorphic; muscular; robust; sinewy; toned; well-built* woman or a *bony; ectomorphic; lanky; lean; petite; rail-thin; scraggy; scrawny; skeletal; skinny; slender; slight; slim; small; spare; spindly; svelte; sylphid; thin; tiny; trim; wispy* woman or a *big-boned, big-breasted, big-bellied,* or *big-bottomed; bulbous; bulky; busty; buxom; chubby; chunky; corpulent; curvaceous; curvy; dumpy; endomorphic; enormous;*

fat; flabby; fleshy; full-figured; globular; heavy; heavyset; hefty; huge; large; obese; plump; portly; pudgy; rotund; round; squat; steatopygic; stocky; stout; voluptuous; zaftig woman — if not for her *womanliness* then at least for her *words*.

weird An overworked word (see page 22). *aberrant; abnormal; anomalistic; anomalous; atypical; bizarre; curious; deviant; different; distinct; distinctive; eccentric; exceptional; extraordinary; fantastic; foreign; grotesque; idiosyncratic; independent; individual; individualistic; irregular; novel; odd; offbeat; original; peculiar; puzzling; quaint; queer; rare; remarkable; separate; singular; strange; uncommon; unconventional; unexampled; unique; unnatural; unorthodox; unparalleled; unprecedented; unusual.* SEE ALSO *strange*.

(all) well and good A wretched redundancy (see page 25). *adequate; all right; excellent; fine; good; O.K.; satisfactory; well.* ■ That's *all well and good* for the hobbyist running a bulletin board or the IT worker who does side programming jobs in his off-hours at home. REPLACE WITH *good.* ■ Well, this is *all well and good,* but who's going to pay for it — not my insurance company! REPLACE WITH *fine.* ■ This is *all well and good,* but what do experts say? REPLACE WITH *good.* ■ That's *all well and good,* but what about my son? REPLACE WITH *fine.* SEE ALSO *fine and dandy; still and all.*

well-nigh A withered word (see page 24). *almost; nearly.*

wet behind the ears A moribund metaphor (see page 21). *artless; awkward; callow; green; guileless; immature; inexperienced; inexpert; ingenuous; innocent; naive; raw; simple; undeveloped; unfledged; unskilled; unskillful; unsophisticated; untaught; untrained; unworldly.*

wet (my) whistle A moribund metaphor (see page 21). *drink; guzzle; imbibe; quaff.*

we've all got to go sometime A popular prescription (see page 23).

we've got to stop meeting like this An infantile phrase (see page 20).

what a difference a day makes A torpid term (see page 24).

what are you going to do A plebeian sentiment (see page 23). This is still another expression of resignation. Though phrased as a question, it is rarely spoken interrogatively, so resigned, so hopeless are those who use it. SEE ALSO *such is life; that's how (the way) it goes; that's how (the way) the ball bounces; that's how (the way) the cookie crumbles; that's life; that's life in the big city; that's show biz; what can you do.*

what can I say? An infantile phrase (see page 20).

what can I tell you? An infantile phrase (see page 20).

what can you do A plebeian sentiment (see page 23). SEE ALSO *such is life; that's how (the way) it goes; that's how (the way) the ball bounces; that's how (the way) the cookie crumbles; that's life; that's life in the big city; that's show biz; what are you going to do.*

what (he) doesn't know won't hurt (him) A popular prescription (see page 23).

whatever An infantile phrase (see page 20). As a one-word response to another's comment or question, *whatever* is as dismissive as it is ill-mannered. SEE ALSO *excuse me.*

whatever happens happens An infantile phrase (see page 20). SEE ALSO *it just happened; what(ever) must (will) be, must (will) be.*

what goes around, comes around A popular prescription (see page 23). This is the secular equivalent of "as you sow, so shall you reap." As such, it is nonetheless a moralistic prescription — intoned by those who think in circles — that too easily explains the way of the world.

what goes up must come down A popular prescription (see page 23).

what happened (is) An ineffectual phrase (see page 19). ■ *What happened was* I woke up one morning and just decided to leave. DELETE *What happened was.* ■ *What happened was* we applied for welfare. DELETE *What happened was.* ■ *What happened was* when I said that to him he got upset and left in a huff. DELETE *What happened was.* ■ *What has happened is,* my identity has gotten lost in this ordeal. DELETE *What has happened is.* SEE ALSO *what is.*

what ... is An ineffectual phrase (see page 19). ■ *What* you want *is* someone who will stand by his work once it is completed. DELETE *What is.* ■ *What* we are finding *is* that they want to measure up to our standards of integrity. DELETE *What is.* ■ *What* this course is about *is* empowerment. DELETE *What is.* ■ *What* we have *is* a program that asks some important questions. DELETE *What is.* SEE ALSO *what happened (is).*

what is the world coming to? A plebeian sentiment (see page 23).

what's done is done A quack equation (see page 23). ■ *What's done is done,* but rethinking the choice now will help you make a better choice next time.

what's good for (the goose) is good for (the gander) A popular prescription (see page 23).

what will they think of next? A plebeian sentiment (see page 23).

what you don't know can't (won't) hurt you A popular prescription (see page 23).

what you see is not always what you get A quack equation (see page 23).

what you see is what you get A quack equation (see page 23).

wheel and deal An inescapable pair (see page 20). *bargain; contrive; deal; do business; negotiate; plan; plot; scheme.*

when and if A wretched redundancy (see page 25). *if; when.* ■ People are asking *when and if* there will be a democratic government. REPLACE WITH *if* or *when.* SEE ALSO *if and when; if, as, and when; when and whether; when, as, and if; whether and when.*

when and whether A wretched redundancy (see page 25). *when; whether.* ■ She will decide *when and whether* and under what circumstances she'll become a mother. REPLACE WITH *when* or *whether.* SEE ALSO *if and when; if, as, and when; when and if; when, as, and if; whether and when.*

when, as, and if A wretched redundancy (see page 25). *if; when.* SEE ALSO *if and when; if, as, and when; when and if; when and whether; whether and when.*

whence A withered word (see page 24). 1. *from where.* 2. *from what source.* 3. *from which.*

when (you) come right down to it A wretched redundancy (see page 25). *all in all; all told; altogether; eventually; finally; in all; in the end; on the whole; overall; ultimately.*

when hell freezes over A moribund metaphor (see page 21). *never; no; not at all; not ever; not in any way; not in the least.*

when in Rome (do as the Romans do) A popular prescription (see page 23). *abide by; accede; accommodate; accord; acquiesce; adapt; adhere to; agree; behave; comply; concur; conform; correspond; follow; harmonize; heed; mind; obey; observe; submit; yield.*

when it comes to A wretched redundancy (see page 25). *about; as for; as to; concerning; for; in; of; on; over; regarding; respecting; to; toward; when; with.* ■ I feel I'm more experienced *when it comes to* looking for a job. REPLACE WITH *in.* ■ I'm an expert *when it comes to* marriage. REPLACE WITH *about.* ■ *When it comes to* middle-age dating, there are four stages. REPLACE WITH *As for.* ■ She is not reasonable *when it comes to* me. REPLACE WITH *with.*

when it rains, it pours A moribund metaphor (see page 21).

when push comes to shove A moribund metaphor (see page 21). ■ *When push comes to shove,* liberalism collapses, society polarizes itself, and the gloves are removed.

when the cat's away, the mice will play A moribund metaphor (see page 21).

when the going gets tough, the tough get going A popular prescription (see page 23).

where angels fear to tread A moribund metaphor (see page 21).

whereat A withered word (see page 24). *at which point.*

wherefore A withered word (see page 24). 1. *why.* 2. *for which.* 3. *therefore.*

wherein A withered word (see page 24). *how; in what way.*

where ... is concerned A wretched redundancy (see page 25). *about; as for; as to; concerning; for; in; of; on; over; regarding; respecting; to; toward; with.* ■ Our gangs are just getting off the ground *where* violence *is concerned.* REPLACE WITH *concerning.* ■ Obviously, time doesn't heal all wounds, especially *where* the Red Sox *are concerned.* REPLACE WITH *regarding.* SEE ALSO *as far as ... (goes; is concerned).*

whereon A withered word (see page 24). *on what; on which.*

where's the beef? An infantile phrase (see page 20).

where there's a will, there's a way A popular prescription (see page 23).

where there's smoke there's fire A popular prescription (see page 23).

where the rubber hits the road A moribund metaphor (see page 21). ■ That, for Christians, is *where the rubber hits the road* — where we intersect with people who are poor or marginalized.

wherethrough A withered word (see page 24). *through which.*

whereto A withered word (see page 24). *to what; to which.*

whereunto A withered word (see page 24). *to what; to which.*

wherewith A withered word (see page 24). *with what; with which.*

whet (my) appetite A moribund metaphor (see page 21).

whether and when A wretched redundancy (see page 25). *when; whether.* ■ Lee will be the one to determine *whether and when* he isn't up to the job. REPLACE WITH *when* or *whether.* SEE ALSO *if and when; if, as, and when; when and if; when and whether; when, as, and if.*

which way the wind blows A moribund metaphor (see page 21).

while at the same time A wretched redundancy (see page 25). *at the same time; while.* ■ It provides us with an opportunity to honor his memory *while at the same time* assisting future students. REPLACE WITH *at the same time* or *while.* SEE ALSO *simultaneously at the same time; while simultaneously.*

> Once in the elevator, it was important to stand in silence beside the bags, to erase oneself behind the dignity of the uniform, while at the same time not seeming cold or indifferent and indeed remaining alert to any sign of helplessness in the traveler. — Steven Millhauser, *Martin Dressler*

while simultaneously A wretched redundancy (see page 25). *simultaneously; while.* ■ So you can work on applications *while simultaneously* watching TV in a resizable window. DELETE *simultaneously.* SEE ALSO *simultaneously at the same time; while at the same time.*

whilst A withered word (see page 24). *while.* ■ *Whilst* it delivers the required protection, most users will probably feel strangely unsatisfied after some hard use. REPLACE WITH *While.* ■ Some imply a functional relationship between variables *whilst* others are of a more exploratory nature. REPLACE WITH *while.*

whip into a frenzy A moribund metaphor (see page 21). *acerbate; anger; annoy; bother; bristle; chafe; enrage; incense; inflame; infuriate; irk; irritate; madden; miff; provoke; rile; roil; vex.*

whip into shape A moribund metaphor (see page 21).

whistle in the dark A moribund metaphor (see page 21).

whistling Dixie A moribund metaphor (see page 21).

(as) white as a ghost An insipid simile. 1. *anemic; ashen; blanched; bloodless; cadaverous; colorless; deathlike; doughy; haggard; lusterless; pale; pallid; pasty; peaked; sallow; sickly; wan; whitish.* 2. *achromatic; alabaster-white; albescent; bleached; chalky; colorless; ivory; milk-white; milky; niveous; pearly; pearly-white; snow-white; snowy; uncolored; whitish.*

> He tells me that the Dictator was receiving all this in silence, but that he was as white as a ghost. — Thornton Wilder, *The Ides of March*

(as) white as a sheet An insipid simile. 1. *anemic; ashen; blanched; bloodless; cadaverous; colorless; deathlike; doughy; haggard; lusterless; pale; pallid; pasty; peaked; sallow; sickly; wan; whitish.* 2. *achromatic; alabaster-white; albescent; bleached; chalky; colorless; ivory; milk-white; milky; niveous; pearly; pearly-white; snow-white; snowy; uncolored; whitish.*

(as) white as snow An insipid simile. 1. *achromatic; alabaster-white; albescent; bleached; chalky; colorless; ivory; milk-white; milky; niveous; pearly; pearly-white; snow-white; snowy; uncolored; whitish.* 2. *anemic; ashen; blanched; bloodless; cadaverous; colorless; deathlike; doughy; haggard; lusterless; pale; pallid; pasty; peaked; sallow; sickly; wan; whitish.*

(like) white on rice An insipid simile. 1. *congenital; fundamental; genetic; hereditary; inborn; inbred; ingrained; inherent; inherited; innate; intrinsic; native; natural.* 2. *all over; everywhere; omnipresent; ubiquitous.*

whither A withered word (see page 24). 1. *where.* 2. *wherever.*

(the) whole ball of wax A moribund metaphor (see page 21). *aggregate; all; all things; entirety; everything; gross; lot; sum; total; totality; whole.*

(my) whole, entire (life) An infantile phrase (see page 20). ■ People like you laughed at me *my whole, entire life.* ■ With this on, you will attract more women than you have in *your whole, entire lives.*

(the) whole is greater than the sum of its parts A popular prescription (see page 23).

(the) whole nine yards A moribund metaphor (see page 21). *aggregate; all; all things; entirety; everything; gross; lot; sum; total; totality; whole.* ■ You've won the Sony TV, the VCR, the stereo system, the camcorder, *the whole nine yards.* REPLACE WITH *everything.*

(the) whole shebang A moribund metaphor (see page 21). *aggregate; all; all things; entirety; everything; gross; lot; sum; total; totality; whole.*

(the) whole shooting match A moribund metaphor (see page 21). *aggregate; all; all things; entirety; everything; gross; lot; sum; total; totality; whole.*

who let the cat out of the bag? A moribund metaphor (see page 21).

whoop it up A moribund metaphor (see page 21). 1. *be merry; carouse; carry on; celebrate; debauch; disport; frolic; party; play; revel; riot; roister; rollick; romp; skylark.* 2. *bay; bawl; bellow; blare;*

caterwaul; cheer; clamor; cry; holler; hoot; howl; roar; screak; scream; screech; shout; shriek; shrill; squawk; squeal; vociferate; wail; whoop; yell; yelp; yowl.

who's minding the store? A moribund metaphor (see page 21).

who would have (ever) thought A plebeian sentiment (see page 23).

why didn't (I) think of that? A plebeian sentiment (see page 23).

why me? A plebeian sentiment (see page 23).

(the) why and (the) wherefore A wretched redundancy (see page 25). *aim; cause; design; end; goal; intent; intention; motive; object; objective; purpose; reason.*

wide of the mark A moribund metaphor (see page 21). *erroneous; false; incorrect; inexact; mistaken; untrue; wrong.*

wild and crazy An inescapable pair (see page 20).

> However wild and crazy they may be, they stand by their friends. — Matthew Reilly, *Scarecrow*

wild and woolly An inescapable pair (see page 20).

wild blue yonder A moribund metaphor (see page 21). *air; atmosphere; biosphere; empyrean; ether; firmament; heaven; heavens; outer space; sky; space; stratosphere.*

wild goose chase A moribund metaphor (see page 21).

> Copulatory leads to copulation, the union of the sexes in the art of generation and I don't know what that means and I'm too weary going from one word to another in this heavy dictionary which leads me on a wild goose chase from this word to that word and all because the people who wrote the dictionary don't want the likes of me to know anything. — Frank McCourt, *Angela's Ashes*

wild horses couldn't (keep me away) A moribund metaphor (see page 21).

wild horses couldn't drag it from (me) A moribund metaphor (see page 21).

window dressing A moribund metaphor (see page 21).

window of opportunity A moribund metaphor (see page 21). *chance; occasion; opening; opportunity; possibility; prospect.* Only able writers know that *window of opportunity* is unable to influence or involve us. *Window of opportunity* is a language that lulls and then deadens.

■ I think we have a terrific *window of opportunity* to make progress this year. REPLACE WITH *chance.* ■ There may be *a window of opportunity* between 12 and 1 for us to talk. REPLACE WITH *time.* ■ One redesign of an ASIC can cause the system vendor to completely miss the *window of opportunity* for a particular product. REPLACE WITH *opportunity.* ■ On the conflict in Darfur, the High Commissioner said he saw a *window of opportunity* to reach a political settlement for the strife-torn region. REPLACE WITH *chance*. SEE ALSO *a barrage of.*

window on the (world) A moribund metaphor (see page 21).

winds of change A moribund metaphor (see page 21).

wine and dine An inescapable pair (see page 20).

win hands down A moribund metaphor (see page 21). *beat; conquer; crush; defeat; outclass; outdo; overcome; overpower; overwhelm; prevail; quell; rout; succeed; triumph; trounce; vanquish; win.*

win, lose, or draw A moribund metaphor (see page 21). *regardless.*

win (his) spurs A moribund metaphor (see page 21).

wipe the slate clean A moribund metaphor (see page 21). *begin anew; start afresh; start over.*

-wise A grammatical gimmick (see page 19). We fasten the suffix *-wise* to words when we have not sufficiently thought about what we want to say or, even more so, how we want to say it. With *-wise,* though there may be some substance to our thought, there is scant style.

■ I've been very successful *businesswise*. REPLACE WITH *in business*. ■ *Burialwise*, I don't feel they're responsible enough to take care of *my wishes*. REPLACE WITH *my burial wishes*. ■ I do have a photo of a model *who resembles me bodywise*. REPLACE WITH *whose body resembles my own*. ■ And *academicwise*, he's made the honor role every year. REPLACE WITH *academically.* ■ She is attractive and much smaller *sizewise* than me. DELETE *sizewise.* ■ I'll let you know *what I get from them informationwise*. REPLACE WITH *what information I get from them*. ■ By spending our development time, future ads will be very *reasonable pricewise*. REPLACE WITH *reasonably priced.*

> The cream of the East and Middle West, engineering-wise and managerwise, was met in the amphitheater of the Meadows. — Kurt Vonnegut, Jr., *Player Piano*

(as) wise as Solomon An insipid simile. *astute; bright; brilliant; clever; discerning; enlightened; insightful; intelligent; judicious; keen; knowledgeable; learned; logical; luminous; penetrating; perceptive; perspicacious; rational; reasonable; sagacious; sage; sapient; sensible; sharp; shrewd; smart; sound; understanding; wise.*

wit and wisdom An inescapable pair (see page 20).

with a big (capital) (A) An infantile phrase (see page 20). ■ It's crisp, *with a capital C*. DELETE *with a capital C*. ■ He loves conversation — *with a big C*. DELETE *with a big C*. ■ These establishments offer *dining with a capital D*. REPLACE WITH *elegant dining*.

> So he knew a little bit about Beauty too. Beauty with a capital B: not just a pretty face or a picturesque landscape, ... — Robert Hellenga, *Philosophy Made Simple*

(go over) with a fine-toothed comb A moribund metaphor (see page 21). *analyze; canvass; comb; examine; explore; filter; forage; hunt; inspect; investigate; look for; probe; quest; ransack; rummage; scour; scrutinize; search; seek; sieve; sift; winnow.*

with a heavy hand A moribund metaphor (see page 21). *coercively; draconianly; harshly; oppressively; severely.*

with all (my) heart A moribund metaphor (see page 21). *earnestly; fervently; genuinely; heartily; honestly; sincerely; unreservedly; wholeheartedly.*

with an open hand A moribund metaphor (see page 21). *altruistically; beneficently; bountifully; charitably; generously; liberally; munificently; unselfishly; unstintingly.*

with a vengeance A moribund metaphor (see page 21). *actively; aggressively; dynamically; emphatically; energetically; fast; furiously; fervently; fiercely; forcefully; frantically; frenziedly; furiously; hard; intensely; intently; mightily; passionately; powerfully; robustly; savagely; spiritedly; strenuously; strongly; vehemently; viciously; vigorously; violently; wildly; with vigor.*

with a wink and a nod A moribund metaphor (see page 21). *clandestinely; confidentially; covertly; furtively; mysteriously; in private; in secret; privately; quietly; secludedly; secretly; slyly; stealthily; surreptitiously; undercover.* ■ Boston's most infamous criminal partnership began *with a wink and a nod.* REPLACE WITH *furtively.*

with bated breath A moribund metaphor (see page 21). *agitatedly; anxiously; apprehensively; excitedly; fearfully; nervously; suspensefully; timidly; timorously; tremulously; worriedly.*

with bells on A moribund metaphor (see page 21). *animatedly; eagerly; ebulliently; effervescently; effusively; enthusiastically; excitedly; lively; spiritedly; sprightly; vivaciously.*

with (their) eyes wide open A moribund metaphor (see page 21). *by design; consciously; deliberately; intentionally; knowingly; on purpose; purposely; willfully; with intent.* ■ They did this *with their eyes wide open.* REPLACE WITH *deliberately.*

with flying colors A moribund metaphor (see page 21). *beautifully; brilliantly; dazzlingly; excellently; grandly; impressively; magnificently; marvelously; outstandingly; splendidly; sublimely; successfully; superbly; triumphally; triumphantly; victoriously; wonderfully.*

with (her) heart in (her) mouth A moribund metaphor (see page 21). *anxiously; apprehensively; fearfully; pavidly; timidly; timorously; tremblingly; tremulously.*

within a hair's breadth of A moribund metaphor (see page 21). *(very) close (to); (very) near (to).* ■ Some visionaries are *within a hair's breadth of* achieving unattended computer center operation. REPLACE WITH *close to.*

(beaten) within an inch of (his) life A moribund metaphor (see page 21). *brutally; cruelly; ferociously; fiercely; harshly; mercilessly; ruthlessly; severely; viciously; violently.*

> Alderman Schlumbohm, heckled to within an inch of his life, followed to the council door by three hundred of his fellow-citizens, was there left with the admonition that they would be waiting for him when he should make his exit.
> — Theodore Dreiser, *The Titan*

within a whisker of A moribund metaphor (see page 21). *(very) close (to); (very) near (to).*

(handle; treat) with kid gloves A moribund metaphor (see page 21). *carefully; cautiously; delicately; gently; gingerly; mildly; sensitively; tactfully; with care.*

with machinelike precision An insipid simile. *accurately; easily; exactly; excellently; faultlessly; flawlessly; flowingly; impeccably; indefectibly; methodically; perfectly; precisely; regularly; smoothly; systematically; well.*

with might and main A moribund metaphor (see page 21). *actively; aggressively; dynamically; emphatically; energetically; ferociously; fervently; fiercely; forcefully; frantically; frenziedly; furiously; hard; intensely; intently; mightily; passionately; powerfully; robustly; savagely; spiritedly; strenuously; strongly; vehemently; viciously; vigorously; violently; wildly; with vigor.*

with (her) nose in the air A moribund metaphor (see page 21). *arrogant; cavalier; condescending; contemptuous; despotic; dictatorial; disdainful; dogmatic; domineering; haughty; imperious; insolent; lofty; overbearing; overweening; patronizing; pompous; pretentious; scornful; self-important; supercilious; superior; vainglorious.*

(welcome) with open arms A moribund metaphor (see page 21). *affectionately; cheerfully; eagerly; enthusiastically; gladly; happily; joyously; readily; unreservedly; warmly.* ■ We have welcomed them *with open arms.* REPLACE WITH *cheerfully.* ■ I hope I am welcomed back *with open arms.* REPLACE WITH *unreservedly.*

(went off) without a hitch A moribund metaphor (see page 21). *accurately; easily; exactly; excellently; faultlessly; flawlessly; flowingly; impeccably; indefectibly; methodically; perfectly; precisely; regularly; smoothly; systematically; well.*

without cost or obligation A wretched redundancy (see page 25). *free.*

without further ado An infantile phrase (see page 20). *at once; directly; forthwith; immediately; instantly; promptly; right away; straightaway; summarily; unfalteringly; unhesitatingly; without delay.*

Of course, any speaker who drones *without further ado* at the end of his prefatory remarks probably ought never himself to be introduced.

without missing a beat A moribund metaphor (see page 21). *accurately; easily; exactly; excellently; faultlessly; flawlessly; flowingly; impeccably; indefectibly; methodically; perfectly; precisely; regularly; smoothly; systematically; well.*

without rhyme or reason A moribund metaphor (see page 21). *decerebrate; foolish; idiotic; illogical; incomprehensible; meaningless; nonsensical; senseless; stupid; unintelligent; unintelligible.*

with (my) tail between (my) legs A moribund metaphor (see page 21). *abjectly; ashamedly; humbly; ignobly; ignominiously; ingloriously; in humility; in shame; meekly; shamefully; submissively.* ■ But she was not happy at the school and left before graduation *with her tail between her legs.* REPLACE WITH *ingloriously.*

> Anne came home with her tail between her legs and slumped into her father's smoking chair. — Elle Eggels, *The House of the Seven Sisters*

with the exception of A wretched redundancy (see page 25). *apart from; aside from; barring; besides; but for; except; except for; excepting; excluding; other than; outside of.* ■ We found that our first 50 patients were wide awake and alert the next day *with the exception of* one patient. REPLACE WITH *except for.*

woefully inadequate An inescapable pair (see page 20). Little is *inadequate* that isn't *woefully* so.

(the) wolf at the door A moribund metaphor (see page 21).

wolf in sheep's clothing A moribund metaphor (see page 21). *apostate; charlatan; deceiver; dissembler; fake; fraud; hypocrite; impostor; knave; mountebank; pharisee; phony; pretender; quack; rascal; recreant; renegade; scoundrel; swindler; tergiversator; traitor.*

(a) woman's place is in the home A popular prescription (see page 23).

(a) woman's work is never done A popular prescription (see page 23).

(the) wonderful world of A moribund metaphor (see page 21).

(he) won't bite A moribund metaphor (see page 21).

won't budge (an inch) A moribund metaphor (see page 21). *adamant; close-minded; contumacious; firm; immovable; immutable; inflexible; intransigent; invariable; obstinate; resolute; resolved; rigid; steadfast; stubborn; unalterable; unbending; unchangeable; unchanging; unwavering; unyielding.*

won the battle but lost the war A moribund metaphor (see page 21).

won't take no for an answer An infantile phrase (see page 20). *insist.*

(the) (F)-word An infantile phrase (see page 20). ■ Many men have trouble with *the C-word.* REPLACE WITH *commitment.* ■ During the holidays, many people write and ask about *the D-word,* depression. DELETE *the D-word.* ■ Nearly everyone involved with the contract was using *the H-word,* "historic," to describe it. DELETE *the H-word.* ■ Journalists agonized over asking about the *"A" word.* REPLACE WITH *affair.* ■ For most middle-aged women, *the M-word* is not a laughing matter. REPLACE WITH *menopause.* ■ The see-through Clinton has three schemes in his playbook to divert us all from *the "M" word.* REPLACE WITH *Monica.*

words cannot describe (express) A plebeian sentiment (see page 23). ■ *Words cannot express* the terrible emptiness we feel or how much we miss her. SEE ALSO *there are no words to describe (express).*

work (my) butt (tail) off A moribund metaphor (see page 21). *drudge; grind; grub; labor; moil; slave; strain; strive; struggle; sweat; toil; travail; work hard.*

work (his) fingers to the bone A moribund metaphor (see page 21). *drudge; grind; grub; labor; moil; slave; strain; strive; struggle; sweat; toil; travail; work hard.*

(a) work in progress A torpid term (see page 24). *A work in progress* is often periphrastic for something or someone undone, unfinished, incomplete. ■ Islamicizing liberal democracy is still *a work in progress.* ■ Georgia State is *a work in progress.* ■ She's *a work in progress* and a person to whom we can all relate.

working stiff A moribund metaphor (see page 21). *aide; apparatchik; assistant; cog; dependent; drudge; flunky; helper; hireling; inferior; junior; minion; secondary; servant; slave; subaltern; subordinate; underling; vassal.*

work like a dog An insipid simile. *drudge; grind; grub; labor; moil; slave; strain; strive; struggle; sweat; toil; travail; work hard.*

(the) world is (his) oyster A moribund metaphor (see page 21).

> Suburbs are the best of both worlds, all you need is a car and the world is your oyster, your Edsel, your Chrysler, your Ford. — Ann-Marie MacDonald, *The Way The Crow Flies*

(a) (whole new) world of A moribund metaphor (see page 21). ■ Mail merge can make your word processor more useful and can open up *a whole new world of power.* SEE ALSO *a barrage of.*

(and) (the) world will beat a path to (your) door A moribund metaphor (see page 21).

worlds apart A moribund metaphor (see page 21).

worn threadbare A moribund metaphor (see page 21). 1. *banal; bromidic; common; commonplace; hackneyed; overused; overworked; pedestrian; platitudinous; prosaic; stale; trite.* 2. *damaged; decayed; decrepit; deteriorated; dilapidated; ragged; shabby; shopworn; tattered; worn.*

worried to death A moribund metaphor (see page 21). *agitated; anxious; apprehensive; distraught; distressed; fearful; nervous; panicky; stressed; stressful; tense; tormented; troubled; uneasy; worried.* SEE ALSO *to death.*

(looks) (the) worse for wear A moribund metaphor (see page 21). 1. *broken-down; crumbly; damaged; decayed; decrepit; depleted; deteriorated; dilapidated; dingy; dirty; exhausted; filthy; flimsy; foul; frayed; grimy; grubby; grungy; ragged; ramshackle; rickety; seedy; shabby; shaky; soiled; sordid; sullied; squalid; tattered; tired; tottering; unclean; unsound; used up; washed-out; worn; worn-out.* 2. *aged; aging; elderly; hoary; old; seasoned.*

> The conferees had, by that time, acquainted themselves with the accommodation provided in one of the University's halls of residence, a building hastily erected in 1969, at the height of the boom in

> higher education, and now, only ten years later, looking much the worse for wear. — David Lodge, *Small World: An Academic Romance*

(he) worships the ground (I) walk on A moribund metaphor (see page 21). *adore; cherish; esteem; eulogize; exalt; extol; glorify; honor; idealize; idolize; laud; love; panegyrize; prize; revere; treasure; venerate; worship.*

worst-case scenario An overworked word (see page 22). ■ The *worst-case scenario* would be for Question 3 to pass and for Question 5 to fail. ■ The indictment of a top executive on child-porn charges represents a *worst-case scenario* for any company and its IT managers. ■ He could ultimately be a progressive's *worst-case scenario.*

> Sometimes the worst-case scenario comes true. But, of course, it wasn't the worst-case scenario at all: she could have died; she could have been paralyzed from the neck down rather than the waist; she could have been disfigured as well. — Daniel Stolar, *The Middle of the Night*

(every parent's) worst nightmare A moribund metaphor (see page 21). ■ It's *every mother's worst nightmare.* ■ This defendant is *every person's worst nightmare.* ■ Being a stepparent is *my worst nightmare.* ■ Perhaps the cliché is true about its being a woman's greatest fantasy and *a man's worst nightmare.* SEE ALSO *it was a nightmare.*

> Mariah awakens to her worst nightmare: Ian Fletcher has disappeared with Faith. — Jodi Picoult, *Keeping Faith*

(the) worst of all (possible) worlds A moribund metaphor (see page 21).

worth (her) salt A moribund metaphor (see page 21). *advantageous; beneficial; cost-effective; effective; effectual; efficacious; gainful; lucrative; productive; profitable; serviceable; useful; valuable; worthwhile.*

worth (its) weight in gold A moribund metaphor (see page 21). 1. *costly; dear; expensive; inestimable; invaluable; precious; priceless; prized; valuable.* 2. *advantageous; beneficial; effective; effectual; efficacious; essential; helpful; indispensable; profitable; serviceable; useful; valuable; vital; worthwhile.*

would appear (hope; imagine; seem; submit; suggest; suspect; think) A wretched redundancy (see page 25). *appear (hope; imagine; seem; submit; suggest; suspect; think).* ■ I *would think* so. DELETE *would.* ■ I *would hope* a decision would be reached before the term of office expires. DELETE *would.* ■ It *would appear* that the state wants to jeopardize the project. REPLACE WITH *appears.*

Not only is the *would* in *would appear* (*hope; imagine; seem; submit; suggest; suspect; think*) superfluous, it calls into question the accuracy and knowledge of whoever uses the phrase. Only the intellectually timorous, the dimwitted, need to so qualify their words.

wouldn't be caught (seen) dead A torpid term (see page 24). 1. *abhor; abom-*

inate; detest; hate; loathe. 2. *averse; disinclined; loath; opposed; reluctant; unwilling.*

> Jason wouldn't take her on dates, wouldn't be caught dead holding hands with her in public or stepping onto a dance floor. — Tom Perrotta, *Little Children*

wouldn't hurt a flee (fly) A moribund metaphor (see page 21). 1. *affable; agreeable; amiable; amicable; compassionate; friendly; gentle; good-hearted; good-natured; humane; kind; kind-hearted; personable; pleasant; tender; tolerant.* 2. *dovish; irenic; nonviolent; pacific; pacifist; pacifistic; peaceable; peaceful; peace-loving; unbelligerent; uncontentious.*

(I) wouldn't touch it with a ten-foot pole A moribund metaphor (see page 21).

wrapped up in (herself) A moribund metaphor (see page 21). *egocentric; egoistic; egotistic; egotistical; narcissistic; self-absorbed; selfish; solipsistic.*

wreak havoc An inescapable pair (see page 20). *demolish; destroy; devastate; injure; obliterate; rack; ravage; ruin; shatter; smash; undo; wrack; wreck.* ■ A handful of companies is *wreaking havoc on* the rest of the industry. REPLACE WITH *ravaging.*

wreathed in smiles A moribund metaphor (see page 21). *beaming; glowing; smiling.*

(it's) written all over (you) A moribund metaphor (see page 21).

wrong end of the stick A moribund metaphor (see page 21).

(what's) wrong is wrong A quack equation (see page 23).

(the) wrong side of the tracks A moribund metaphor (see page 21).

(he) wrote the book (on) A moribund metaphor (see page 21).

X, Y, Z

x marks the spot A moribund metaphor (see page 21).

year in (and) year out A moribund metaphor (see page 21). *always; ceaselessly; constantly; continually; continuously; endlessly; eternally; everlastingly; evermore; forever; forevermore; immortally; indefinitely; interminably; permanently; perpetually; persistently; unceasingly; unremittingly.*

(62) years young An infantile phrase (see page 20). ■ I'm 43 *years young.* DELETE *years young.*

yell and scream An inescapable pair (see page 20). *bay; bawl; bellow; blare; caterwaul; clamor; cry; holler; hoot; howl; roar; screak; scream; screech; shout; shriek; shrill; squawk; squeal; vociferate; wail; whoop; yell; yelp; yowl.* ■ Two months later, he'd lost all his hair, and his wife started *yelling and screaming* about my not making him continue. REPLACE WITH *scream* or *yell.* SEE ALSO *yell and scream.*

yell (her) head off A moribund metaphor (see page 21). *bay; bawl; bellow; blare; caterwaul; clamor; cry; holler; hoot; howl; roar; screak; scream; screech; shout; shriek; shrill; squawk; squeal; vociferate; wail; whoop; yell; yelp; yowl.*

yes, Virginia, (there is) An infantile phrase (see page 20).

(the) yin and the yang A moribund metaphor (see page 21).

you are what you eat A popular prescription (see page 23).

you can catch more flies with honey than with vinegar A popular prescription (see page 23).

you can fool some of the people some of the time, but you can't fool all of the people all of the time A popular prescription (see page 23).

you can lead a horse to water, but you can't make (him) drink A popular prescription (see page 23).

you can make a difference A popular prescription (see page 23).

you can say that again An infantile phrase (see page 20).

you can't be all things to all people A popular prescription (see page 23).

you can't buy love A popular prescription (see page 23).

you can't change the world in a day A popular prescription (see page 23).

you can't fight city hall A popular prescription (see page 23).

you can't fit a square peg in a round hole A popular prescription (see page 23).

you can't get blood from (out of) a stone A popular prescription (see page 23).

you can't get there from here An infantile phrase (see page 20).

you can't go home again A popular prescription (see page 23).

you can't have everything A popular prescription (see page 23).

you can't have it both ways A popular prescription (see page 23).

you can't have something for nothing A popular prescription (see page 23).

you can't have your cake and eat it too A popular prescription (see page 23).

you can't judge a book by its cover A popular prescription (see page 23).

you can't live on love alone A popular prescription (see page 23).

you can't live with (them) and you can't live without (them) A popular prescription (see page 23).

you can't lose what you never had A popular prescription (see page 23).

you can't make a silk purse out of a sow's ear A popular prescription (see page 23).

you can't please everyone A popular prescription (see page 23).

you can't put new wine in old bottles A popular prescription (see page 23).

you can't serve God and mammon A popular prescription (see page 23).

you can't take it with you A popular prescription (see page 23).

you can't teach an old dog new tricks A popular prescription (see page 23).

you can't win them all A popular prescription (see page 23).

(so quiet) you could hear a pin drop A moribund metaphor (see page 21). 1. *dumb; hushed; motionless; mum; mute; noiseless; quiet; reticent; silent; soundless; speechless; stationary; still; stock-still; subdued; taciturn; unmoving; voiceless; wordless.* 2. *becalmed; calm; halcyon; irenic; pacific; peaceable; peaceful; placid; quiescent; reposeful; serene; tranquil.*

you don't miss what you never had A popular prescription (see page 23).

you do the best you can A suspect superlative (see page 24). Dwelling on our failures is no better than dismissing them, but *you do the best you can,* still another expression of resignation, may too easily excuse us for our missteps and mistakes, our failures and inadequacies. Here, *the best* is surely suspect.

you (have to) do what you have to (do) A popular prescription (see page 23).

you get what you pay for A popular prescription (see page 23).

you had to be there A grammatical gimmick (see page 19). This is merely an admission of having badly told a tale.

you have everything to gain and nothing to lose A popular prescription (see page 23).

you have nothing to lose A popular prescription (see page 23).

you have to give to get A popular prescription (see page 23).

you have (got) to start somewhere A popular prescription (see page 23).

you have to understand (that) An ineffectual phrase (see page 19). ■ First of all, *you have to understand that* many black men are in prison. DELETE *you have to understand that.* SEE ALSO *it is important to understand (that).*

(do) you know? An ineffectual phrase (see page 19). ■ I felt like I was enlightened, *you know?* DELETE *you know?* ■ You never know what's going to happen, *you know?* DELETE *you know?* ■ The translation sounded too straightforward, *you know?* DELETE *you know?* ■ To an extent, I think everybody is racist. *You know?* DELETE *You know?* SEE ALSO *(you) hear what I'm saying? (you) know what I mean? (you) know what I'm saying? (you) know what I'm telling you?*

you learn something new every day A plebeian sentiment (see page 23). It's the event of having learned something — something taught, not thought — that gives rise to the remark.

you made your bed, now lay in it A popular prescription (see page 23).

you name it A grammatical gimmick (see page 19). *and others; and so forth; and so on; and the like; etc.* ■ Today, in our state, those who do the public's work — teachers, cops, public-health nurses, social workers, highway builders, prison guards, *you name it* — are held up to ridicule.

you never know A plebeian sentiment (see page 23).

you never know till you try A popular prescription (see page 23).

young and foolish An inescapable pair (see page 20).

you owe it to yourself A popular prescription (see page 23). ■ Believe me, *you owe it to yourself* to take advantage of this exciting opportunity.

you're (only) as old as you feel A popular prescription (see page 23).

you're either part of the solution or part of the problem A popular prescription (see page 23).

you're either with (me) or against (me) A popular prescription (see page 23).

you're kidding An infantile phrase (see page 20). This expression is among the most banal we utter. We say it uncontrollably — less in stupefaction than in stupidity — and without a moment's reflection.

The more commonplace the words you use, the more commonplace the person you are. SEE ALSO *really? you've got to be kidding.*

you're not alone A plebeian sentiment (see page 23). ■ Feeling depressed, lonely, restless, bored, upset? *You're not alone.*

you're not the only one An infantile phrase (see page 20). *as I do; I do too; neither do I; no more do I; nor do I; so do I.*

you're only young once A popular prescription (see page 23).

your guess is as good as mine An infantile phrase (see page 20). *I don't know; (it's) not (yet) known; (that's) uncertain; (that's) unclear; (it's) unknown.* SEE ALSO *(it) remains to be seen; (just have to) wait and see.*

yours truly An infantile phrase (see page 20). *I; me.* ■ And you can bet that *yours truly* will do something crazy. REPLACE WITH *I.*

you scratch my back, I'll scratch yours A popular prescription (see page 23). ■ It's an approach that resonates equally with businessmen steeped in the win-win jargon of negotiations and politicians deep in the pragmatic *you-scratch-my-back-I'll-scratch-yours* conversations that make Washington run.

you think too much A plebeian sentiment (see page 23). *You think too much* is, of course, commentary that only those who rarely think could ever offer. These are the people who cower from consciousness. SEE ALSO *I (just) don't think about it.*

you've come a long way (baby) An infantile phrase (see page 20).

you've got to be kidding An infantile phrase (see page 20). SEE ALSO *really? you're kidding.*

you win a few (some), you lose a few (some) A popular prescription (see page 23).

zigs and zags An inescapable pair (see page 20).

(a) zillion(s) (of) An infantile phrase (see page 20). Doubly infantile are the phrases *ba-zillion* and *ga-zillion.* ■ I'll bet their mothers spent *a zillion* hours trying to get their sons to clean up after themselves. REPLACE WITH *countless.* ■ I made *a zillion* mistakes. REPLACE WITH *innumerable.* ■ There may be grating aspects to 20- and 30-somethings earning *kazillion*-dollar bonuses, but at least wealth gives them the self-confidence to ask for a date. REPLACE WITH *million.*

The Vocabula Review

If you've enjoyed The Dimwit's Dictionary, you may want to subscribe to The Vocabula Review (www.vocabula.com). Twelve monthly issues of The Vocabula Review cost only $15.00.

Mail this page with your check or money order — made payable to The Vocabula Review — to:

The Vocabula Review
5A Holbrook Court
Rockport, MA 01996
United States

Name: ______________________________

Email address: ______________________________
(please print clearly)

Once we've received your payment, we will email you a password so that you can read The Vocabula Review's pages.

The Vocabula Review
www.vocabula.com